SOCIAL THEORY
AND EDUCATION

SUNY Series, Teacher Empowerment and School Reform
Henry A. Giroux and Peter L. McLaren, Editors

SOCIAL THEORY AND EDUCATION

A Critique of Theories of Social and Cultural Reproduction

by

RAYMOND ALLEN MORROW
and
CARLOS ALBERTO TORRES

State University
of New York
Press

Published by
State University of New York Press, Albany

Production by Susan Geraghty
Marketing by Dana Yanulavich

Printed in the United States of America

For information, address State University of New York Press, State University
Plaza, Albany, N.Y., 12246

Library of Congress Cataloging-in-Publication data

Social theory and education : a critique of theories of social and
    cultural reproduction / Raymond Allen Morrow and Carlos
    Alberto Torres.
        p.   cm. — (SUNY series, teacher empowerment and school
    reform)
        Includes bibliographical references (p.   ) and index.
        ISBN 0-7914-2251-8 (alk. paper). — ISBN 0-7914-2252-6 (pbk. :
    alk. paper)
        1. Educational sociology. 2. Education—Philosophy. 3. Critical
    theory. 4. Critical pedagogy. I. Morrow, Raymond Allen.
    II. Torres, Carlos Alberto. III. Series: Teacher empowerment and
    school reform.
    LC191.S6575   1995
370.19—dc20   94-3956
                                                                    CIP

10 9 8 7 6 5 4 3 2

CONTENTS

Preface   *ix*
Acknowledgments   *xiii*

PART 1   SOCIAL THEORY AND EDUCATION   1

Chapter 1   Introduction   3

Chapter 2   Metatheoretical Foundations   19

PART 2   STRUCTURAL FUNCTIONALISM AND
SYSTEMS THEORIES   39

Chapter 3   The Functionalist Tradition: Parsons and
Education   41

Chapter 4   Neofunctionalism and Education   79

PART 3   STRUCTURALISM: NEO-MARXIST AND
CONFLICT THEORIES   115

Chapter 5   Structuralism and the Logic of
Reproduction   117

Chapter 6   Structuralist Marxism: Correspondence
Theories   141

v

Chapter 7   Structural Conflict Theories: Culture, Class, and Domination   175

PART 4   THE CONVERGENCE OF NEO-GRAMSCIAN AND CRITICAL THEORY   215

Chapter 8   Critical Theory and Education: From the Frankfurt School to Poststructuralism   217

Chapter 9   The Two Gramscis and Education: Technical Competence versus Political Consciousness   249

PART 5   AGENCY AND STRUCTURE: RESISTANCE AND REPRODUCTION   283

Chapter 10   The Recovery of Agency: From the British New Sociology of Education to Cultural Studies   285

Chapter 11   Critical Pedagogy in the United States: Michael Apple and Henry Giroux   309

PART 6   EDUCATION, THE STATE, AND THE LOGIC OF REPRODUCTION   339

Chapter 12   The Capitalist State and Educational Policy Formation   341

Chapter 13   Education, Race, and Gender: Towards a Critical Modernist Perspective   371

Chapter 14   Education, the Fragmentation of Domination, and Postmodernism   407

Chapter 15   The Logic of Reproduction: Summary and
Conclusions   435

Notes   447
References   467
Index   501

PREFACE

By Peter L. McLaren and Henry A. Giroux

Over the last three decades the social sciences have witnessed a number of exciting theoretical developments. Regrettably, the sociology of education has not always reflected these new developments, preferring instead to restrict its reading of social life to a truncated theoretical framework and epistemological parochialism. *Social Theory and Education* stands as an important exception to such sociological inertia. It is a book that is meant to be read *against* rather than *within* the dominant grain of the sociology of education.

Written by Raymond Morrow and Carlos Alberto Torres, two internationally acclaimed critical social theorists, this wide-ranging and ambitious book does more than simply outline the conventional contours of the sociology of education as a distinct genre within the broader terrain of sociological research. The authors have undertaken an analysis and synthesis of no less than the most important work published in or about the sociology of education over the last three decades in English, French, German, Spanish, and Portuguese.

Stressing the need for a metatheory, this challenging book reasserts the centrality of ideology as a means of understanding numerous perspectives within the social sciences in general and the sociology of education in particular. Morrow and Torres tease out in a nuanced and erudite manner the systems of intelligibility and argumentation informing sociological discourses rather than asserting that such discourses possess an immanent logic of their own. Morrow and Torres invite educators and cultural workers to confront the ideological dimensions of the production of knowledge surrounding a wide range of theoretical issues as well as to interrogate the institutional arrangements of knowledge in response to the social relations of production and the globalization of capital. To this end, *Social Theory and Education* investigates the enabling condition of sociology's discursive and material relations in an attempt to unsettle those relations which further oppression and to facilitate those which promote social justice. Developing the notion of a *political* sociology of education, and with a focus on the relationship among education, power, knowledge, and the state, this book offers a conceptual analysis and criticism of social reproduction in education while advancing new directions for theoretical and empirical research. The concluding chapters in the volume construct an agenda for a research strategy based on the concept of "critical modernism" developed by the authors. This includes discussions of the interactions among class, race, and gender and social reproduction within the context of a postmodernist critique.

The book advances neo-Marxian critical theory of education in a number of important ways, not least of which can be attributed to its rigorous engagement with postmodernist and feminist analysis. What is unique about this volume is that in analyzing the paradigms developed within the sociology of education, such as the sociology of knowledge, theories of resistance, and the state, the authors do so from the perspective of expanding the locations from which such paradigms are produced. The meta-analysis that facilitates such a move engages a wide range of discourses including those associated with feminist theory, poststructuralism, pragmatism, and postmodernism.

What anchors the book firmly in the critical tradition is its approach to the language of sociology itself. Since the authors recognize that the practice of sociology is implicated in the production, maintenance, and transformation of particular subjectivities and forms of social agency, the language of sociology itself must inhere in a social praxis and therefore must be considered more than simply an abstract system of differences. Pedagogically and politically, Morrow and Torres work against reproducing the discipline of sociology as a means of producing passive agents; rather, the sociology of education is reconfigured dialectically as a means of enabling cultural workers to become more aware of their discursive and material situatedness in relation to larger social, cultural, and institutional contexts outside of the academy. Students of the social sciences will welcome this transdisciplinary approach to understanding schooling; policy analysts will gain much from the carefully crafted argumentation and its many urgent implications for social and educational transformation, and students working within the foundations of education and curriculum studies will be challenged by conceptual and ethical positions that cannot be ignored. Educators working from postmodernist perspectives will also be challenged to examine the question of agency as they "look back on the end of the world."

Morrow and Torres have written a splendid book that, in the final analysis, is linked to a much broader context than sociology and education, a context refracted through the prism of social justice and a more intelligent and compassionate democracy.

ACKNOWLEDGMENTS

This book grew out of friendship and mutual intellectual stimulus. Both started in 1985, when Raymond Morrow had just joined the University of Alberta as a faculty member in the Department of Sociology, and Carlos Alberto Torres visited the Department of Educational Foundations, at the University of Alberta, as a Distinguished Visiting Professor. This dialogue, friendship, and collaboration continued during the remaining of the decade, with both authors holding regular teaching appointments at the University of Alberta, until Carlos Alberto Torres move to UCLA in 1990.

Undoubtedly, a number of colleagues and students at that fine Canadian institution of higher learning contributed to our understanding of this issue. Raj Pannu, professor with joint appointments in the Departments of Educational Foundations and Sociology, has always been a patient listener and indeed a most enlightening discussant of some of our ideas. Daniel Schugurensky, a creative and inquisitive mind as a graduate student in the Department of Educational Foundations, many times put to test some of the assumptions, hypotheses, and the consistency of the narrative thread of this book. The countless number of our students who over the years engaged in dialogue with us about social reproduction theories in our seminars in sociology of education and social theory helped to shape this book in many ways. We are also thankful to the contribution of four anonymous reviewers from SUNY Press, and particularly our editor Priscilla C. Ross.

A previous version of the framework for analysis was presented at the Western Association of Sociology and Anthropology Meeting (WASA) held at the University of Alberta, February 1987. An expanded version of the section on Ivan Illich in chapter 8 has been published in *New Education* (1990), and a preliminary version of chapter 12 was previously published by Carlos Alberto Torres in an article entitled "The Capitalist State and Public Policy Formation: A Framework for a Political Sociology of Educational Policy-

Making," in *The British Journal of Sociology of Education* (1989). We are thankful for permission granted for reproducing them, in part, in this book.

There have been a number of opportunities for the authors to discuss some of the premises of this book at international settings. Carlos Alberto Torres taught social theory and a seminar on education from 1984 to 1986 at the Facultad Latinoamericana de Ciencias Sociales (FLACSO) in Mexico City, and conducted a seminar on social reproduction theory at the Universidad Autónoma Metropolitana (UAM-Xochimilco) in 1986 that helped to clarify some theoretical issues. A number of lectures conducted by Carlos Alberto Torres at the research institute IRISE, in Rosario, Santa Fé, Argentina, during 1988; at the Facultad Latinoamericana de Ciencias Sociales (FLACSO) in Buenos Aires, Argentina; and at the National University of Entre Rios, in Paraná, Entre Rios, Argentina during 1993, helped refining the premises on functionalism, feminism, and some Latin American topics. Finally, Raymond Morrow and Carlos Torres presented a paper entitled "Theories of Hegemony and Legitimation: Implications for Political Sociology and Education in the Work of Apple and Giroux" at the Twelfth World Congress of Sociology, Sociology of Education Section, Madrid, Spain, 9–13 July 1990. This paper is the basis for chapter 11.

The first effort to put an end to the ever-growing drafts of the many chapters of this book was made in November 1990 when Raymond Morrow, on sabbatical leave, was invited as a visiting speaker to the Division of Social Sciences and Comparative Education, at the Graduate School of Education, University of California-Los Angeles. The final revision of the entire manuscript took place in Alberta, when Carlos Alberto Torres taught as a visiting professor at the University of Lethbridge, in July 1993.

Raymond Morrow wishes to thank Ioan Davies (sociology, York University, Toronto) for having introduced him to the "new sociology of education" long before he realized educational theory would become a research focus; undergraduates who tolerated the eccentric use of Paulo Freire in courses on interpersonal communications at the University of Manitoba from 1978 to 1981; Max Van Manen for having encouraged presentation of a paper on "Critical Theory and Critical Sociology: The Case of Education" at the Fourth International Human Science Conference, Faculty of

Education, University of Alberta in 1985; Barb Marshall (now at Trent University), whose Alberta sociology dissertation used repro-duction theory for analyzing feminist issues and the state (now revised and forthcoming as a book with Polity Press); and the small stream of outstanding graduate students in Educational Founda-tions (and Secondary Education) with whom he has had the plea-sure to work at the University of Alberta.

A survey of this magnitude and scope, and of a topic as broad and complex as the one tackled in this book, cannot be made without the intellectual support, affection, and friendship of a number of persons, too many to be named here. However, for Carlos Torres, the love of Maria Cristina, Carlos Alberto, Pablo Sebastian, and Laura Silvina deserve to be recognized here. And Raymond Morrow would like to thank his parents (Ray, Jr., and Jane Morrow) for having unconsciously taught him the basic prin-ciples of dialogical learning *avant la lettre*, and Marlene Laslo for existential support under sometimes difficult circumstances.

From the outset, the joys of Macintosh computing facilitated our collaboration through the several drafts of the manuscript, and periodical communication via e-mail helped to smooth out the process. Although no extensive secretarial or specific financial help was involved in the preparation of the book, the general support of the Department of Educational Foundations, the Department of Sociology at the University of Alberta, and the Department of Education at the Graduate School of Education, University of California–Los Angeles, is recognized.

This has been truly a collaborative effort, with no clear or stable division of labor. As Paulo Freire has said many times, the struggle for learning and the process of knowledge acquisition are painful experiences, but also can be fun. Certainly, as we engaged in endless hours of conversations, arguing back and forth, and then trying to sum up our conclusions in front of a computer, we en-joyed writing this book. We hope the reader agrees with us and can share our experience despite its inevitable shortcomings.

We dedicate this book to our mothers: Jane B. Morrow and Maria Laura Novoa de Torres.

PART 1

Social Theory and Education

CHAPTER 1

Introduction

THE PROBLEMATIC

Rationales

The timing is right for asking, Whatever happened to theories of social and cultural reproduction in education? Ironically, though such theories initially flourished in the sociology of education, they have now been taken up in other domains and social theory generally. A recent British anthology seeks to "revivify" the notion of "cultural reproduction" as a "particularly fertile area for social theory" despite it *not* being currently "a fashionable concept" (Jenks, 1993: 1). The present study reflects our longstanding effort to rehabilitate theories of cultural reproduction for the sociology of education.[1] Two obstacles to this process have been (1) the widespread impression that reproduction models had been largely discredited and abandoned—a process reinforced by *postmodernist* attacks on metanarratives and general theory; and (2) a lack of awareness of more recent developments, which often employ somewhat different theoretical terminology and thus disguise the continuity of issues.

Despite the various criticisms and qualifications of the original "correspondence principle" for economically reductionist models, the problematic of social and cultural reproduction continues to be central to critical pedagogy and critical sociologies of schooling. As part of a continuously revised research program, theories of cultural reproduction have incorporated concepts of agency and resistance and expanded the understanding of domination to include nonclass forms of exclusion (race, gender, etc.). More fundamentally, the metatheoretical justification of such theorizing is no longer based on the totalizing, class-based metanarrative as in the case of structuralist Marxism. In this respect, the analysis of cultural reproduction has assumed *poststructuralist* forms[2]

But the term *reproduction* is still tied closely to earlier debates.

3

Does it make sense to preserve the term at all? One rationale for preserving the term is that the concept was "seemingly high-jacked" (at least in Britain) by "the orthodoxy of studies in the theory of ideology and neo-Marxisms (Jenks, 1993: 2.). As a consequence, attention was directed away from the more dynamic and flexible forms of analysis evident in other versions of the theory. From this perspective, it becomes plausible to "attempt to liberate the concept back into the wider arena of sociological debate," a possibility reinforced by the ever-increasing visibility of the work of Pierre Bourdieu in general social theory (Jenks, 1993: 6).

These circumstances have contributed to a couple of theoretical and practical tensions that have accompanied the writing of this study. First, by speaking of social and cultural reproduction, most readers acquainted with contemporary sociological jargon would think most immediately of "Marxist" theories of education. Though there is an element of truth here, part of our objective will be to show the limitations of such a narrow conception of the concept and related problematics which have become central to much of contemporary social theory.

A second tension is reflected in our effort to present a study which is relatively accessible—hence, serviceable as an advanced undergraduate or graduate college or university text—and yet to provide a contribution which synthesizes and/or advances aspects of theoretical debate in the sociology of education and thus is also of interest to researchers. An aspect of dealing with this problem is reflected in attempting to provide an introduction to contemporary social theory *in the context of* educational debates.

The present study builds, of course, on a series of related synthetic critical efforts over the past decade or so. On the one hand, there are pioneering anthologies which introduced the reproduction debates to larger audiences in the English- (Karabel and Halsey, 1977) and Spanish-speaking worlds (Torres and González-Rivera, 1994). On the other hand, there are a number of individual monographs, largely of British origin and now somewhat dated, which have attempted to review and assess the debates at various stages from diverse perspectives and with different audiences in mind.[3]

There are also a number of other more specialized studies (both theoretical and empirical) which often provide excellent reviews of major issues, but are more concerned with developing a plea for specific positions within debates in American (or British, etc.) education.[4] Surprisingly, however, most of this work remains almost completely separated (and this holds in the British context as well) from comparative issues and Third World questions, despite the important collection of papers in Altbach and Kelly (1986) and the contributions of Martin Carnoy and Henry Levin (1985), Joel Samoff (1990) and their collaborators.

As well, there is an extensive literature criticizing theories of social reproduction, most often as associated with structuralist Marxism (e.g., Apple, 1982b; Connell, 1983; Wexler, 1987; Liston, 1988). Generally, however, these studies give a rather hasty critique of reproduction theories, focus on their weakest versions (i.e. structuralist Marxism), ignore functionalist and systems theories in this context, and plunge off in new—however important— directions.

Though we are generally sympathetic with these new directions and their critical stance toward *conventional* reproduction theories (aside from a more adequate understanding of Bourdieu), our objective here is to engage in a more sustained stocktaking of the strengths and weaknesses of reproduction theories viewed from the broader perspective of any effort at developing of the relationship between theories of society and education. The objectives and distinctiveness of our approach can thus be defined in relation to a number of aspects of our treatment:

First, through the unifying concept of reproduction theory, we attempt to provide a more in-depth comparative analysis of structural functionalist and structuralist theories; though these parallels are often mentioned, they are given rather superficial treatment in the literature.

Second, as a necessary aspect of the previous concern, we introduce the metatheoretical and epistemological issues required for an adequate comparison and evaluation of the theoretical perspectives under examination. In particular, the functionalist and structuralist logic underlying reproduction theory discussions is given more thorough attention in this book.

Third, in our discussions of various theoretical perspectives, we attempt to provide a balanced and representative discussion, even as we direct our criticisms toward the development of our own position, which could be broadly characterized as a *practice-oriented, parallelist model of cultural reproduction and change*

(Morrow and Torres, 1994), where *practice-oriented* refers to the poststructuralist recognition of the agency-structure dialectic and the historical specificity of analysis, and *parallelist* refers to the recognition of the autonomous interplay of race, class, and gender. Further, by focusing on the culture, structure, and social agency problematic, we attempt to link macro-sociological issues with social-psychological ones in an attempt to bypass the often arbitrary oppositions between approaches found in most discussions.

Fourth, in linking our discussion of education with recent debates on theories of the state, we introduce a dimension that is lacking, or at best cursorily treated, in most of the research developed by people exclusively concerned with either education or theories of the state.

Finally, given our *comparative historical* orientation, we base our discussion on developments in both advanced societies (North America and the English Commonwealth, continental Europe) and peripheral ones (especially Latin America) with social formations closer to the model of European capitalism. In contrast, most of the existing studies focus on a single national context, or remain within an advanced or underdeveloped context.

Social Theory and Education

The whole history of educational thought has developed in the context of a dialogue with the social theory of its time. Social theory encompasses metatheory, on the one hand, and the range of substantive questions entailed in the construction of the theories of society within which sociologies of education are elaborated. In the context of the sociology of education as a "normal science," to be sure, such models of society can be directly appropriated from sociologists and applied within minor modifications to the study of education. In period of crisis and change—within both social life and sociological theory—however, educational sociology must become more self-reflexive and reconsider its foundational point of departure: the theory of society within which it attempts to analyze the world of educational activities.

We will be focusing on the concept of reproduction in our investigations of educational systems because it provides a convenient synthetic reference point for comparing the full range of conceptions of the relation between society and education. Whatever a sociology of education does, it must make sense of the contribution of educational activity to the processes of socialization as a source of social continuity and potential discontinuity, or reproduction of the given and production of the new.

In part, the focus on education reflects our interest in contributing to the specific series of debates which have developed in this context. Accordingly, part of our task is to bring to the community of educational theory and the sociology of education some as yet inadequately explored and appreciated contributions *outside of* education (e.g., philosophy of social science, sociology, critical theory, political sociology, etc.)—what can broadly be referred to as "social theory". In this sense we seek to broaden and enrich the discussion *within* education. One of the functions of our study would thus be to provide an introduction to many of the leading issues of contemporary social theory—especially contemporary macrosociological theory's concern with the agency/structure problematic—in the context of education.

At the same time, we also direct our discussion toward those *outside of education* proper in order to convey the broader significance of recent work in educational theory and its strategic importance for issues of cultural sociology, theories of the state, and theories of social change and political practice. All too often, discussions in these domains fail to adequately take into account the implications of the research in education. One of our objectives, therefore, would be to make accessible to other students of social theory and cultural studies the rich literature generated by the debates within education, specifically the sociology of education.

THEORIES OF SOCIAL REPRODUCTION IN EDUCATION

The Concept of Social Reproduction

How then do these distinctions help us to understand theories of social reproduction and education? First, we must consider what is meant by the notion of a social reproduction theory and then consider its implications in the context of education. Though associated in recent discussions with its origins in Marxist theory, the concept of reproduction actually has roots in several disciplines. From the interdisciplinary perspective of general systems theory, for example, societies are classified as a particular type of living systems: "Social systems are thus defined as *reproducible social structures*" (Barel, 1974: 93). Yet such reproduction does not imply identical replication in either social or biological systems; rather the opposite is suggested: "reproduction implies differentiation, growth, change (continuous or discontinuous)" (Barel, 1974: 93).

To constitute reproduction, however, some fundamental features must be preserved as the basis of the identity of the system, and the concepts of reproduction theory thus "try to describe certain aspects of this capacity for temporary self-persistence of living systems: self-adaptation, self-organization, self-regulation, homeostasis, finality, ultra-stability, etc." (Barel, 1974: 93). Of particular importance in social reproduction is the effort to determine the elements and relations which are crucial for the transition from one social formation to another. Given that the process of reproduction involves both the dying off of and emergence of social forms, "perhaps what best describes social reproduction is the fact that this reproduction is a unity of *contraries:* unity of social contradictions, unity of change and stability, unity of continuity and discontinuity" (Barel, 1974: 94).

Given the central role of organic, biological models in structural functionalism and systems theories, there has been a reluctance within the Marxist tradition to explore the continuities between reproduction in biological and social systems. But as Giddens—one of the most astute critics of functionalist reasoning in the social sciences—points out, the issue is not the continuity between the natural and social sciences, but the specific form it might take. As he concludes, the continuity is not to be found in the functional analogies about system "needs" which have dominated traditional functionalism, "but rather concern recursive or *self-reproducing* systems"(1979: 75). Of importance here is not so much the theory of automata, which is rather distant from social reality, as "recent conceptions of cellular self-reproduction (autopoiesis) . . . The chief point of connection is undoubtedly recursiveness, taken to characterize autopoietic organization" (1979: 75). Unlike the earlier biological models, autopoiesis includes the possibility of a theory of system contradiction.

Further, Giddens makes a distinction between two levels of reproduction processes in system integration: the homeostatic model of self-regulation found in traditional functionalism (which is redefined as homeostatic causal loops), and the type of reflexive self-regulation where "occur processes of selective 'information filtering' whereby strategically placed actors seek reflexively to regulate the overall conditions of system reproduction either to keep things as they are or to change them" (1984: 27–28). A key aspect of both these forms of reproduction is thus the possibility of "system contradiction."

Social Reproduction and Education

Despite many important differences, models of reproduction applied to educational systems share many specific common analytical features which allow them to be treated together as we have in the present study.

Most fundamentally, they (a) presuppose theories of society as a complex totality, though may restrict (e.g., Weber and neo-Weberians) investigation to empirically observable group relations; (b) take as their object of inquiry relatively complex societies within which formal and specialized educational institutions play a significant role; (c) argue that these educational institutions constitute strategic sites for the stability and further development of these societies; (d) study the relations of mutual interaction between these institutions and the larger society which provide the basis for sociologies of education; (e) suggest that policy formulation within the educational sphere constitutes a crucial context of negotiation and struggle which may have decisive effects on the capacity of society to maintain or transform itself; and (f) consider, paradoxically, that education is either a powerful (and unique) tool for socialization into a given social order or should challenge and resist a hegemonic culture and resulting social practices. In short, educational institutions in theories of social reproduction are linked with power, knowledge, and the moral bases of cultural production and acquisition.

In other words, theories of social reproduction in education point to the interplay between theories of society and education, and hence the larger context which all other forms of the sociology of education (e.g., the study of the school, classroom, curriculum, etc.) must presuppose.

THE CLASSICAL SOCIOLOGICAL TRADITION AND EDUCATION

Contemporary discussions of social theory and education presuppose a set of issues and debates which can be traced back to classical sociological theory, especially the work of Marx and Engels in the mid through later nineteenth century, and of Max Weber in Germany and Emile Durkheim in France in the later nineteenth and early twentieth century (Giddens, 1971). Despite their many and often crucial differences, all of these classical sociologists began with the basic—if somewhat reductionist—proposition enunciated by Durkheim: "educational transformations are always the result and symptom of the social transformations in terms of which they are to be explained" (1977: 166). But they differ in fundamental ways which anticipate the debates and basic positions that emerge by the mid twentieth century: education as a site of ideological reproduction of the interests of the dominant class (Marx and Engels); as integrative institutions essential for social order (Durkheim); and the source of a new principle of control as instrumental rationality or bureaucratic domination (Weber).

Marx and Engels

In the case of education as a site for social and cultural reproduction, for example, the historical materialism of Marx and Engels gives us no explicit answers, despite a number of pathbreaking clues and insights that would be elaborated by later theorists. The central proposition of Marx's theory of capitalist society is that it should be viewed as a specific mode of production with a peculiar combination of forces of production (technology in the broadest sense) and relations of production (ways of organization and exploiting surplus value or profit from labor). Translated into a theory of society, this argument becomes what is generally referred to as the base-superstructure model, where the economic infrastructure (or base) is held to be the primary determinant of the cultural superstructure, that is, the state, the family, and various specialized cultural institutions (e.g., ideology, law, mass media, religion, etc.), which is required for the stable functioning of such a mode of production as a system of class domination.

Matters have been complicated, however, by the fact that Marx's base-superstructure model lends itself to two different interpretations. Traditionally, this relationship was seen in mechanical, causal terms as a form of direct economic determination: the nature of the cultural superstructure thus becomes an immediate reflection of the economic base and the interests of the dominant capitalist class that controls it. Later commentators have argued, however, that this model should be understood in more metaphorical terms, and that the relation between base and superstructure should be seen as reciprocal, giving considerable autonomy to cultural institutions.

A further complication is that the theory of superstructures is not explicitly directed to educational systems, partly because only at higher stages of differentiation of capitalist society has the full significance of educational institutions become evident. Similarly, the theory of ideology has ambiguous implications, especially in the context of the analysis of the cultural presuppositions of educational systems. Marx made allusions to ruling ideologies as those of dominant classes, and his early work is filled with venom regarding the "German ideologists"—typical products of the bourgeois universities of his time. Yet as a general historical thesis, the simple assumption that those who control the means of production necessarily control those of mental production is dubious (e.g., the case of the Middle Ages where education was controlled by the clergy, or even in the case of the advanced welfare states). Such formulations refer to the instrumentalist logic of the base-superstructure model rather than the more complex processes implied by notions such as relative autonomy or cultural reproduction.

More generally, of course, there is a pedagogical motif running throughout Marx's writings, especially the early ones where the notion of "educating the educators" and the problem of transforming alienated working class consciousness is paramount. And free public education is advanced as one of the goals of "revolution" as envisioned in 1848 in the *Communist Manifesto*. And in *Capital* there is a glimpse of the possibility that capitalism would come to require a more flexible form of labor power linked to the introduction of public elementary education and technical schools:

> Modern industry, indeed, compels society under penalty of death to replace the detail-work of today, crippled by life-long repetition of one and the same trivial operation, and thus reduced to a mere fragment of a man, by the fully developed individual, fit for a variety of labours, ready to face any change in production and to whom the different social functions he performs are but so many modes of giving fresh scope to his own natural and acquired powers. (*Capital*, vol. 1: 487–88)

On the basis of fragmentary statements such as this, it was possible for Marxist parties and eventually the Soviet Union to develop a conception of "polytechnic education" which sought to combine general individual development and the acquisition of technical skills (Castles and Wüstenberg, 1979). As the Soviet example reminds us, Marx and Engels were concerned with very different kinds of questions. Marx and Engels' reference to education is not coupled with an explicit analysis of public and private educational systems; and given the isolation of revolutionary theory from the educational institutions of the nineteenth century, there is no basis for concern with such sites as locales for working-class struggle. Inevitably, the gradual introduction of mass, public education toward the end of the nineteenth century put education on the agenda of working-class movements as both a right to be demanded and a resource to be controlled (as in the case of Gramsci; see Manacorda, 1977; Labriola, 1977). Yet, on the whole, mass education was introduced selectively in a manner which prevented it from becoming of strategic importance for the formation of revolutionary working-class consciousness; on the contrary, it was the primary context of resocialization and incorporation within an increasingly "mass" if not classless society. Within historical materialism, therefore, education as a focus of inquiry is very much a twentieth-century phenomenon, and as a part of a theory of social reproduction, the product of the past three decades.

Durkheim

In contrast to the belated emergence of educational themes in the Marxist tradition, the strategic significance of mass, public education was recognized at the very beginning of modern functionalist sociology in the work of its founder Emile Durkheim, whose first university appointment was in a faculty of education in France at the turn of the century. For Durkheim, the modern educational system has come to replace the church as the central integrative institution of society and a crucial aspect of the maintenance of social order through its socialization functions. And even Durkheim's educational concerns can be traced back to a consistent principle of bourgeois social theory: to the liberal technocratic vision of French sociology found in Comte, Saint-Simon, and even the French Enlightenment.

Though this educational theme slipped out of sight in the work of functionalist anthropologists, it reemerges in the work of Talcott Parsons, the leading postwar functionalist theorist, whose vision of advanced industrial society is crowned with the "knowledge complex" and the professions as the carriers of technical rationality. Later students built Third World theories of modernization around similar concepts. In a more abstract manner, the same could also be said for information and cybernetic theories where the concept of "information" is given a strategic role in processes of self-regulation and change. Perhaps, therefore, it is appropriate that on the terrain of educational systems, the affinities and differences between (and within) the historical-materialist and systems-functionalist paradigms and their implications for the problematic of social and cultural reproduction be explored in depth. Only the closely related field of communications and the supposed "information revolution" rival education in this respect.

Weber

Much as in the case of Marx, the explicit influence of the sociology of Max Weber on education has been a belated one. Indirectly, of course, his theory of bureaucracy has been significant in the history of complex organization theory and has some influence within educational administration research. Only by the late 1960s did a specifically neo-Weberian perspective on education emerge. Several distinctive aspects of the Weberian approach are of particular importance to the contrasting examples of Marx and Durkheim.

First, Weber rejects a systems perspective (and hence reproduction theory in the strict sense) at the level of society as a whole in favor of a conception of social integration as social interaction based on the conflicting strategies of concrete groups. Whereas his sense of the prevalence of conflict converges with Marx, he rejects the presupposition that there is a systemic contradiction between labor and capital which inevitably leads to social breakdown. Significantly, however, he does operate with an implicit model of reproduction with respect to his theory of bureaucracy which is the key to his contribution to the sociology of education. Second, Weber also seeks to re-assert the voluntaristic foundations of social action, and hence rejects any purely structuralist or functionalist view of the relationship between structure and agency, a point which follows from the preceding one.

Third, though the state is prominent in Weber's theory, his emphasis is upon its role as an agent of overall societal rationalization and mediator of group conflict, rather than the expression of the interests of a dominant class.

Finally, his approach is developed within the perspective of a strict conception of the distinction between empirical and normative issues which has contributed, at least in his followers, to a "value free" conception of research that has blocked many important directions of inquiry and social criticism.

With respect to education, Weber characteristically shifts attention away from the Marxian focus on the link between education and production to its contribution to the more general process of rationalization. According to Weber, the development of modern educational systems is intimately tied up with three key processes: how expert knowledge is legitimated as the basis of legal bureaucratic domination; how the state constructs the national citizen as a way of undermining traditional communal relations; and how the school becomes the framework for transforming the contractual relations of labor markets into those of a bureaucratic status order based on credentials (Lenhardt, 1984, 1985).

CONCLUSION

A Poststructuralist, Critical-Theory Perspective

Even though we have attempted to provide a balanced treatment of the various approaches surveyed, our overall assessments are grounded in a particular stance toward a critical sociology of education which can be described in relation to (if not as completely identifying with) terms such as *poststructuralist, postmodernist, post-Marxist,* and *post-liberal.*

Our approach is *poststructuralist* in the more limited sense of acknowledging the flaws of classic structuralist theories and methodologies, especially their determinism and lack of a theory of agency; but it is not *postmodernist* in the sense of rejecting all forms of general theorizing understood in nontotalizing, historical terms.

Our approach is also weakly *post-Marxist* in two senses. Along with contemporary critical theories generally, we acknowledge that the types of theoretical revisions required to understand contemporary realities imply a fundamental break with the Marxist orthodox tradition. Take, for instance, two of the central (and essential) propositions of a specifically "Marxist" theory of schooling: the correspondence principle itself (i.e., that the social relations of capitalist production are present in the form of the social relations of education) and the primacy of class determinants. Though we find both of these fruitful hypotheses which have generated important empirical findings and theoretical debate, particularly in the political economy of education, we do not think either of these can be sustained as universal laws or propositions in the manner essential to Marxist theory as conceived in the past. But our position is *not* post-Marxist if that is taken to imply that class or political economy has somehow become irrelevant.

Further, our approach is post-Marxist in the political sense that it is acknowledged that the Soviet model of revolutionary change was fundamentally flawed from the outset and that any transformative political project must begin with democratic assumptions that necessarily have a certain continuity with the *liberal democratic* tradition.

Yet this position is also *postliberal* in the sense that liberalism, whether in its neoconservative or progressive (social democratic) forms, cannot be entertained as adequate responses to the current crisis. As critical theory has made abundantly clear, the constraints upon the democratic public sphere call into question the universalistic claims of contemporary democratic systems (Bowles and Gintis, 1986). A postliberal tradition necessarily acknowledges, however, that any socialist project worthy of the name must incorporate principles of democratic participation of a type that are historically without precedent.

Comparative Historical Method

Consistent with the classical sociological tradition, our orientation toward a comparative historical perspective is designed to offset two of the weaknesses of much contemporary educational research, especially in the tradition of reproduction theories. In part, two tendencies have created difficulties: the use of reproduction as a general theory without due concern with the specificities of education as an institutional context; and a tendency for researchers to work within and generalize upon the basis of a single (or limited type of) national experiences. Much research, whether in the structural functionalist or neo-Marxist tradition, has simply "demonstrated" again and again that specific structures fulfill the designated functions assumed by the theory. A lack of comparative perspective in the case of works in the Marxist tradition stems primarily from obstacles to research funding, a certain reluctance to employ and incorporate into the overall theoretical-methodological perspective techniques of data collection (such as survey research) or statistical data analysis perhaps seen as too closely related to structural-functionalism and empiricist methodologies, and a preoccupation with specific national strategic issues.

Contexts of Educational Research

To study education as a side of social reproduction thus requires consideration of the historical variations in educational systems. On the one hand, it is clear we are concerned with more highly differentiated societies where specialized educational institutions become of increasing importance. On the other hand, even within this delimited context the range of variation among societies is remarkable. To what extent could any theory of social and cultural reproduction claim to deal with such a wide range of cases? One of the practical difficulties in surveying theories of educational reproduction is the variable and often unspecified scope and type of explanation claimed. The systems-functionalist tradition is most weak in this regard, operating within the assumptions of a general theory without adequate criteria of historical specification.

To be sure, the historical materialist tradition gives lip-service to historical specificity, but in practice the structuralist theory of modes of production has tended to serve as a rationale for heavily functionalist and evolutionary analyses which skirt problems of causal evidence and comparative historical method. The historical variations in the relationship between educational systems and different types of societies renders any general theory precarious (cf. Archer, 1984). Yet as we shall see on the basis of the discussion of contemporary research, historical materialism provides a powerful initial thesis with the notion of educational systems existing in a relationship of both correspondence and contradiction with the existing society. The thesis can only provide, however, a general framework for concrete historical investigations.

Though the present study attempts to provide a fairly comprehensive analysis of theories of educational reproduction, it cannot claim to provide a comparable range of reference to empirical cases. In practice, our interrogation of such theories will tend to move back and forth between two basic types of capitalist social formation, that is, those in which such models have been most actively produced, imported and exported, and applied: the advanced liberal democratic societies characteristic of Western Europe, North America, and the English Commonwealth, on the one hand, and the dependent developed societies of Latin America—characterized by unstable regimes, variable democratic pretensions, large agrarian (peasant) sectors, and serious fiscal and external debt crises—on the other.[5]

Limitations and Objectives

Regrettably, the limited focus of the present study does not allow us to address directly the range of issues concerning a *general* theory of cultural reproduction which would require a consideration of the interrelationship between the different sites of cultural activity, though this question does appear in relation to chapter 12 on the state, as well as in various points along the way.

Further, it has not been our objective to amass and assess systematically *all* of the empirical research pertinent to the assessment of the theories discussed. At times we will address or allude to such research where it has had a strategic impact upon theoretical debate, but our focus of attention lies elsewhere: the origins and theoretical structure and presuppositions of the theories in question, as well as their comparison and general evaluation from a broader historical and comparative perspective.

Outline of the Study

This book is organized into five parts. Part 1, on "Social Theory and Education," includes this introduction and requires outlining the metatheoretical foundations for such a task, which becomes the basis for a typology of the paradigms of reproduction theory that have influenced debates in education (chapter 2).

Part 2, on "Structural Functionalism and Systems Theories," considers these as a type of reproduction theory, and then examines in detail the previously dominant functionalist tradition influenced by Talcott Parsons in the United States (chapter 3) and the more recent move to neofunctionalist approaches (chapter 4).

Part 3 is concerned with the variety of conflict-oriented models of educational reproduction associated with the notion of "structuralism" in the European sense, hence the title "Structuralism: Neo-Marxist, and Conflict Theories." First, the structuralist logic presupposed in different ways by many conflict approaches is taken up (chapter 5). This is followed by a detailed discussion of the French structuralist Marxist tradition (Althusser, Poulantzas) and its theory of correspondence (chapter 6). A second important form of non-Marxist yet still relatively closed reproduction theory, with strong roots in the Durkheimian tradition as well as Marx and Weber, is also reviewed and criticized in the structuralist conflict theories of symbolic capital associated with Pierre Bourdieu and his associates in France; in the related sociolinguistic model of reproduction developed by Basil Bernstein in Britain; and in relation to more recent developments of social-closure theory (chapter 7).

Part 4 is concerned with the reconciliation of agency and structure in social theory—a problematic bequeathed by structuralism and broadly identified with the notion of poststructuralism—and the implications of this reconciliation for theories of educational reproduction. It is titled "The Convergence of Neo-Gramscian and Critical Theories" because it is within these two traditions that a broadly poststructuralist discourse emerges which allows the reconceptualization of the social psychological dynamics of resistance and its relation to transformative social movements. Chapter 8 traces the development of Frankfurt critical theory in relation to education, and chapter 9 is devoted to the Gramscian tradition and its relation to educational theory and research. Chapter 10 then considers the appropriation of European tendencies first within the new sociology of education, and later within British (often neo-Gramscian) cultural studies generally. Further, in chapter 11 parallel developments in the United States are considered in the context of the convergence of critical and neo-Gramscian theory. This is explored in the context of the work of Michael Apple and Henry Giroux and their relation to a tradition of radical democratic populism.

Part 5 shifts to thematic issues: education and the state (chapter 12); race, class, and gender (chapter 13); and postmodernism (chapter 14). Chapter 15, in conclusion, offers a synthesis of the main agendas of social and cultural reproduction, and some of their key dilemmas and paradoxes.

CHAPTER 2

Metatheoretical Foundations

WHY METATHEORY?

In the broadest sense, metatheory is concerned with all of that which goes beyond—or, more precisely, is presupposed by—theory as a substantive or concrete analysis of some aspect of social reality. As theory about theory, metatheory takes up issues associated with the philosophy of social sciences (i.e., epistemology, ontology, ethics, etc.) and methodology (strategies of providing evidence for theoretical propositions). In short, from our perspective metatheory encompasses a set of assumptions about the nature of things (the social world, the nature of science), including the possibility of knowing them, and the normative assumptions required for assessing or evaluating different forms of reality (as a construct), experience (everyday life), and thought (the rational reconstruction of reality, experience, and the history of thought). Metatheory, thus, takes as a necessary and legitimate activity the construction of a metalanguage as distinct from substantive theoretical discourse and/or empirical analysis (whether explanatory or interpretive).

Yet one of the most striking features of debates within and between theoretical paradigms or perspectives is that empirical evidence rarely is sufficient as the basis for choosing between substantive theoretical perspectives. The reason for this is based upon what philosophers refer to now as the *theory-laden* character of facts. In other words, facts are not just brute data lying innocently out there in the social world; rather, they are constructed by and sought after only on the basis of different theoretical perspectives which provide a rationale for the significance of, or the potential existence of, certain types of facts. One of the consequences is that theories are rarely chosen exclusively or even primarily on the basis of their superiority in relation to the facts (though this may eliminate the most outlandish of theories), but on the basis of a whole

19

series of criteria which only metatheory can reveal and open up for critical assessment.

In this chapter a metatheoretical framework for the study of social reproduction in education is presented. A theory of educational reproduction presupposes both a specific theory of society and a paradigm of sociological theory. Further, these are necessarily macrosociological theories: theories about how the institutions of society are shaped by large-scale structural forces. In contrast, microsociological theories focus on individual interaction, and by their very nature could not be the basis of a theory of educational reproduction and change. Some macrosociological theories do, however, include a significant microsociological or social psychological dimension to their structural analysis.

In contemporary sociological theory it is customary to differentiate a number of theoretical paradigms among which the following will be central to our discussion of the problematic of cultural and educational reproduction: functionalist systems theories, analytical conflict theories, neo-Marxist theories, and post-structuralist critical theories. At this point we do not need to concern ourselves with the often important variants within each type, but to capture the central theme of each approach.

Functionalist systems theories have been historically the most influential within sociology and are based on an organic analogy: societies function like biological systems in that they have differentiated parts that function together to ensure the smooth operation and survival of the organism as a whole. Such an approach is especially concerned with the conditions that maintain social order and stability, and was pioneered by the classical sociologist Emile Durkheim. The most famous version of this approach is the structural-functional theory of Talcott Parsons in the United States.

Neo-Marxist theories represent the most well-known type of conflict theory, one for which the contradictions in the capitalist mode of production, especially those between labor and capital, are taken to be decisive. Further, it is argued that as contradictions, such deep conflicts cannot be resolved within the framework of capitalism, which is consequently inevitably unstable because of various forms of crisis. Neo-Marxist theory differs from that of Marx and Engels primarily because it has attempted to take into account subsequent changes in capitalism, especially the increased importance of massive cultural institutions (such as education and the mass media), as well as the strategic role of the liberal democratic state. For this reason, some neo-Marxists refer to their approach as an analysis of state monopoly capitalism (Torres, 1985).

Conflict theories assume many different forms. Analytical conflict theories are characterized by an openness to all types of structural conflict, and the struggles related to class are central but not the only ones. Analytical conflict theories have been strongly influenced by the example of Max Weber and can be broadly labeled as neo-Weberian in this sense. From this perspective, group struggle is an inherent feature of social life, though the specific forms of conflict vary in different types of society.

Finally, critical theories represent a new type of theorizing that has been influenced by both neo-Marxist and conflict theory traditions. They are distinguished from the neo-Marxist tradition in rejecting the theory of the dictatorship of the proletariat, and the primacy of class and economic determinants in the last instance, and in stressing the multidimensionality of power relations and the role of agency and social movements in social change. Further, the principle of emancipation is extended from that of class—which still retains is strategic place in social struggle—to other sources of potential domination and/or exploitation, including gender, race, and religion, as well as the complex of issues relating to self-sustaining economic development and peace (as expressed in the ecology and peace movements).

All these sociological frameworks seem to share a basic understanding of reproduction processes in capitalist societies. However, they have striking differences among themselves regarding both their elaboration of the notion of reproduction as well as their analytical logic-in-use in producing research findings in education.

Accordingly, we argue that there is *no single general reproduction theory as such*, but that reproduction processes constitute a fundamental problematic which has been tackled in contemporary sociological theory in many different ways. This problematic includes social, cultural, economic, and ideological dimensions of reproduction which may involve simple reproduction, complex reproduction, and, potentially, social transformation.

It is in the context of these multiple sociological, political, and educational debates that the concept of social reproduction is widely used and ought to be studied. Our initial task is thus to define theories of social reproduction and outline the relationships between metatheoretical perspectives, sociological paradigms, and theories of social reproduction in education.

METATHEORETICAL PERSPECTIVES

The reader well-versed in social theory and the philosophy of social sciences may be tempted to skip this introductory chapter. Others may feel trepidation in being forced to enter the difficult, abstract terrain of metatheory—a topic which has often been marginal to the pragmatic focus of the social sciences. But our introduction is addressed to both types of readers; it thus attempts to be more than simply a review of background considerations in that it provides an essential foundation for the arguments developed in the individual chapters—however much they may stand on their own. The issues of theory comparison and assessment cannot be assumed to be common knowledge of the part of readers; nor is there any clear consensus on the part of experts in these areas. Accordingly, we are obliged to develop an approach which will ground our study of theories of social reproduction in education.

Our introduction to metatheory will be guided by the specific problems of analyzing theories of social and cultural reproduction. First, it is important to sketch the grounds for differentiating critical (e.g., structuralist-Marxist or critical theories) from noncritical (e.g., structural functionalism) accounts of societal reproduction. The specific metatheoretical program of Jürgen Habermas's critical theory will be introduced as the foundation of our approach.

Second, we need criteria for differentiating "closed" and "open" models of social and cultural reproduction. For this purpose the polarization between subjectivist and objectivist approaches provides a useful framework for conceptualizing this distinction.

Knowledge Interests and Critical Theory

To those trained in the positivist and empiricist conceptions of social science, epistemology and methodology merge, and theory comparison consists primarily in comparing theories with the "facts" as defined by empirical research. Further, a sharp distinction is made between empirical analysis and normative assessments—the fact-value distinction.[1] Without denying the significance of empirical findings, and bearing in mind the different logical properties of empirical and normative arguments, it is still important and necessary to challenge such a positivist conception of theory at the outset if we are going to make any sense of theories of social reproduction. In so doing, we begin with a brief digression on epistemological (or metatheoretical) issues—questions concerned with the criteria by which different forms of knowledge are assessed and validated—in which we introduce the metatheoretical assumptions that guide our particular approach.

Two major issues will be taken up: first, the pursuit of knowledge in the human sciences will be viewed as guided by three fundamental knowledge-guiding interests, rather than a single (deterministic, causal) explanatory one; and second, these interests will be shown to combine in typical ways to create relatively distinct approaches to, or *paradigms* of, social research. From this perspective, it will be possible to then analyze the specific characteristics of theories of social reproduction.

The positivist or logical empiricist approach to the human sciences is based on the assumption that "theory" and "science" can be defined in a unitary manner based on the model of the natural sciences. In other words, the practical interest which motivates and guides our concern with scientific activity is seen as universal (embracing equally the natural and social sciences in a unified science) and undivided (following a single logical method). Such a universal and unified method is associated with notions such as deductive explanation, reduction of phenomena to their causal determinants, and a resulting capacity for predicting future events.

Such an approach, however, cannot deal adequately with the specific features of social explanation. As the West German social theorist Jürgen Habermas (1971) has pointed out, the human interest in knowledge is a plural one. In the case of the human sciences three knowledge-guiding interests can be identified which correspond to the epistemological foundations of the human sciences.[2] By the notion of *knowledge-guiding interest*, Habermas seeks to show that, both in practice and with respect to the logical conditions of the possibility of science in general, the diversity of the human interest in knowing must be recognized.

In short, scientific knowledge cannot be reduced to a single natural scientific model (e.g., physics) or a single logical model (deductive explanation) because we have multiple needs for knowledge of different types. Though this approach renders the problem of demarcating science from non-science more difficult, it has the advantage of trying to rigorously evaluate knowledge claims that otherwise would be relegated to the nonrational or non-science, and thus would become subject to the irrational battle between warring dogmas.

According to Habermas, there is first an interest in empirical-analytical knowledge oriented toward potential technical control; this form of knowledge is logically comparable to the explanatory (causal, predictive) knowledge associated with the natural sciences. Second, the human sciences are also characterized by a historical-hermeneutic interest which qualitatively sets them apart from the natural sciences. The objects of social inquiry can only be apprehended through a process of interpretation that has only a relatively trivial parallel in natural science because the understanding of cultural differences and patterns is one of the building blocks of social cognition (i.e., the basis of access to meaning) and, in a sense, its ultimate particularistic (ideographic) objective of research.

Third, there is a human interest in critical-emancipatory knowledge. Though this may be considered simply a special case of the hermeneutic interest, it can be distinguished because its objective is not simply comprehension, but a "hermeneutic of suspicion" (Ricoeur, 1986) which calls into question existing cultural traditions as concealing relations of domination to be overcome through the transformation of consciousness. In short, knowledge in the human sciences is based upon a desire potentially to control through the analysis of objective determinants, to understand through the interpretation of meanings, and to transform reality through the demystification of falsifying forms of consciousness.

Theories, Models and Theory Programs

Practical knowledge interests combine, therefore, in different ways to produce theoretical constructs. When then are the type of such constructs of concern in the present study? The conventions of social scientific language force us to use the term *theory* loosely in a variety of different contexts. But it should be emphasized that the object of our inquiry is not the reconstructed formal theories of interest to traditional philosophers of science. Instead, in analyzing theories of social reproduction in education, we will be studying what could be best described as *paradigms of research* and hence *research programs*, a combination of metatheoretical, theoretical, and methodological assumptions about how to develop a cumulative tradition of research.

Originally inspired by the historian of science Thomas Kuhn (1970) and his subsequent followers in many disciplines, the concept of *paradigm* is also associated with a historical community of researchers, specific exemplars of such research, and the normalization or institutionalization of research strategies following "revolutionary" breakthroughs. Further, within these paradigms or theory programs there are specific models which guide research. The concept of model has been defined in a variety of ways, but the following terse definition is appropriate for our purposes: "a *heuristic model* is a figurative representation of a perceived object used to guide one in pursuit of its knowledge. Its functions are two fold: it provides a notional ensemble, a perspective that permits an ordered perception of the empirical world; it is a directing scheme for theory construction and further investigations" (Wacquant, 1985: 19).

In this stricter sense, a model is therefore a point of departure for diverse theoretical possibilities, that is, a single model (e.g., reproduction) may give rise to competing theories. Similarly, different theoretical paradigms may use the same model in different ways. As a consequence, a model in this heuristic sense "can be neither 'true' nor 'false,' only serviceable and adequate to varying degrees, for its *raison d'être* is cognitive productivity" (Wacquant, 1985: 19). In fact, it is the model of reproduction which unites the approaches considered, even if the actual research strategies pursued vary widely. In the course of our study, we will identify and focus upon three distinct theoretical programs which have been developed within the reproduction paradigm: systemic-functionalist theories, structuralist-Marxist approaches, and post-structuralist conflict theories. In order to illustrate the unity underlying the reproduction paradigm, and the bases of divergence between different theoretical programs based on it, let us turn first to the logic of possibilities with respect to sociological paradigms.

SOCIOLOGICAL PARADIGMS

One of the most important consequences of the pluralistic structure of the human interest in knowledge is that the human sciences can construct their objects of inquiry in different ways. In princi-

FIGURE 2.1
Four Paradigms for the Analysis of Social Theory

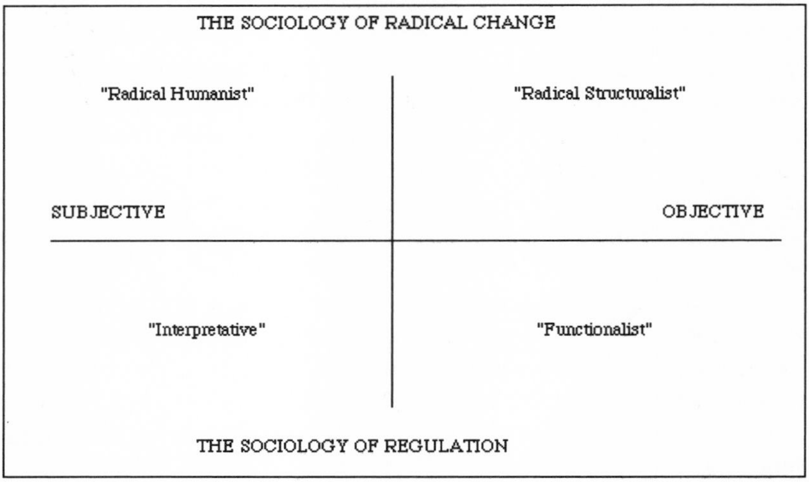

THE SOCIOLOGY OF RADICAL CHANGE	
"Radical Humanist"	"Radical Structuralist"
SUBJECTIVE	OBJECTIVE
"Interpretative"	"Functionalist"
THE SOCIOLOGY OF REGULATION	

ple, each of these has a degree of cognitive and scientific legitimacy. The problem is the question of their interrelationship and relative priority. By classifying different forms of theorizing with respect to their epistemological assumptions, on the one hand, and conception of society, on the other, it is possible to develop a simple typology of possible forms of sociological theory (Burrell and Morgan, 1979).[3] On this basis, we will then be able to provide an analysis of the range of possible types of theories of social reproduction in education. Figure 2.1 shows four possibilities resulting from comparing sociological paradigms in a continuum between objective versus subjective poles, and sociologies of regulation vis-à-vis sociologies of radical change.

The Subjective-Objective Dimension

Throughout the history of the social sciences, theorists have differed with respect to the relative import of the two dimensions of social reality: the subjective and the objective. This duality has been expressed in a number of different ways including idealism versus materialism, humanism versus scientism, and phenomenology versus behaviorism. However, this duality always refers back to an ontological distinction between the two different forms of "being" which constitute social life: consciousness or subjectivity, on the one hand, through which individual and group intentions and beliefs are expressed through symbolic meaning; and, on the other, phenomena (i.e., structures) external to, and outside of consciousness, which, like the material causes in nature, have the effect of causing or determining individual and group behavior in a measurable and predictable way.

Accordingly, social scientists have been divided with respect to whether the subjective or objective should have priority, and whether it is possible to develop a synthetic human science which could incorporate both. For the most part, however, researchers have tended to opt for one or other pole given the methodological problems associated with a more synthetic approach. This dualism is reflected in Habermas's distinction between the empirical-analytic knowledge interest, which would tend to prefer a more objectivist approach, and the historical-hermeneutic interest, which is more consistent with a subjectivist one.

In sum, in the horizontal axis in figure 2.1—that is the subject-object axis of metatheory—theories thus tend to polarize in relation to Habermas's first two knowledge interests: empirical-analytical knowledge, whose ideal is objective and reductionist, as opposed to historical-hermeneutic knowledge, whose ideal is subjective and interpretive. For example, Skinnerian behaviorism is a good example of an extreme version of objectivist knowledge which rules out altogether reference to the cognitive intentions and self-reports of individuals. At the other extreme, one finds forms of phenomenological inquiry which focus exclusively on the "lived-experience" and intentions of agents.

Roughly speaking, this was the basis of the nineteenth-century German debate between the *Naturwissenschaften* (natural sciences) and the *Geisteswissenschaften* (cultural sciences). This polarization can be seen as operating at various presuppositional levels of social inquiry: ontology, epistemology, theory of social action, methodology. It is instructive to think through the polarization at each of these levels and how they interrelate (see figure 2.2).

First, at the level of ontology, one finds a polarization between nominalist and realist orientations. Whereas nominalists stress the distance between concepts and the "reality" to be described (hence an emphasis on the "conventional" and "constructed" character of concepts), realists stress the hard, factual character of external real-

FIGURE 2.2
A Scheme for Analyzing Assumptions About the Nature
of Social Science

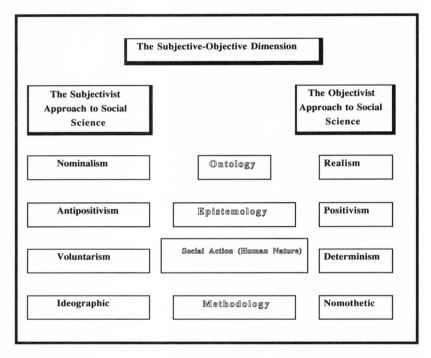

ity and the power of concepts to grasp it directly. Whereas nominalists take a cautious approach to the power of knowledge to
grasp reality, stressing the slippage between concepts and the objective world, ontological realists stress the power of science to
capture a world independent of consciousness.

Second, translated into epistemological positions, this polarization gives rise to the confrontation of positivist versus antipositivist (or humanist) conceptions of social science. Whereas
positivists stress the identity of explanatory principles in natural
and human sciences—hence the priority of identifying causal regularities and predictive explanations—humanist approaches either
reject or downplay causal explanations on the grounds that the
priority of social analysis should be an understanding of actors
intentions and meanings. So if the former are concerned with the

development of a rigorous "behavioral" science, the latter are oriented toward an "interpretive" science along the lines suggested by symbolic interactionism or hermeneutics and phenomenological approaches. Certain sociologists such as Karl Marx and Max Weber have, of course, attempted to reconcile these two strategies.

Third, at the level of social action, there are two contrasting conceptions of the nature of the relationship between the individual and external reality. For humanists, human nature is essentially voluntaristic, and the object of inquiry should be the study of symbolic action; for positivists, in contrast, human nature is essentially deterministic and should be studied in behavioristic terms. Accordingly, this difference can be referred to in terms of two basic approaches to human agency: behavioral theories and action theories.

Finally, at the level of methodology, the contrast is between two conceptions of the goal of analysis: ideographic versus nomothetic explanations. The ideographic approach is particularistic and favours case-study, clinical-type investigations that allow an interpretation of the phenomenon and its description as a unique totality. For a nomothetic orientation, on the other hand, the ultimate objectives of inquiry are generalizations and the reduction of individual cases to general theories.

The Radical Change–Regulation Dimension

A second dimension on which social theories can be classified is their conception of society (see figure 2.1). At issue here are the differences flowing from whether society is viewed as inherently "good" and organized in the interests of the community as a whole or, alternatively, as advancing the interests of some groups at the expense of others and concealing this through cultural legitimations. This polarization was the basis of the earlier division between "order" and "conflict" theories of society, a confrontation that emerged in the mid 1960s with German sociologist Dahrendorf's critique of Talcott Parsons "consensus" theory (Demerath and Peterson, 1967). Whereas a theory of society based on the principle of social order stresses stability, integration, functional coordination, and consensus, one based on conflict emphasizes change, conflict, disintegration, and coercion.[4]

Setting aside for now the relative adequacy of these two approaches or the possibility of their synthesis, it can still be argued that they constitute a fundamental division in social theory and a useful basis for classification. Hence, order or consensus theories are oriented toward a sociology of "regulation" because of the reformist assumption that human needs can best be realized within the given form of society through a process of piecemeal change, that is, regulation within the parameters of the given type of society. In contrast, conflict theories assume that every existing form of society is to a greater or less degree a system of domination and exploitation that constrains and limits human possibilities. From this perspective, therefore, the ultimate goal of social knowledge is to demystify the subjective and structural foundations of existing forms of social life, and to anticipate alternative forms of social organization and society.

One of the peculiarities of this dimension is the difficulty of completely separating normative and empirical issues. Indeed, the question of an orientation toward order as opposed to radical change cannot be a purely empirical or analytical question because taking such a stance cannot be resolved in terms of either empirical-analytical or hermeneutic-historical knowledge. Rather, this order/change distinction also implicates Habermas's third knowledge interest, the critical-emancipatory interest. So, for example, to orient research programs toward a purely regulatory (albeit reformist) relation to society implies, whether this be conscious or not, that human needs and possibilities are best realized—and therefore should be realized—within the given type of society. This normative assumption contrast with that of an orientation toward fundamental change which presupposes the opposite: that the given form of society systematically constrains human possibilities (though some more than others) and that it is objectively possible to imagine and construct a more satisfactory form of a society which more closely approximates a "good society" in the classical sense of political philosophy.

System Integration vs. Social Integration

The preceding general remarks regarding sociological paradigms need to be supplemented by a more refined formulation that locates specific positions within the subjective-objective continuum. One of the distinctive features of theories of reproduction is that they, at least, claim an intention to resolve the split between individual and society, the subjective and objective dimensions of society. To the extent they succeed, they necessarily avoid the extremes of the subjectivist-objectivist continuum even if they ultimately must opt for the priority, in some sense, of one or the other. The outcome is a theory of society that postulates, explicitly or implicitly, a theory of social order or integration, but at the same time links this with a theory of change. What is crucial to note is that conceptions of order vary with respect to how they combine the subjective-objective dimension of social reality.

In this context two distinctions have been of particular importance: on the one hand, the opposition between methodological individualism and methodological collectivism; and on the other hand, that between conceptions of system integration as opposed to social integration. Both oppositions, which are epistemological and analytical, are also closely related. Methodological individualists focus on processes of social integration which are revealed in the concrete empirical actors that produce social order (i.e., social integration), whereas methodological collectivists are concerned with the systemic (structural) properties of societies which transcend group action and constitute a deeper level of social reality (system integration). With reference to theories of social and cultural reproduction, the polarization between these two positions resulted in the standoff between interactionist and phenomenological orientations whose action perspective precluded the structural/systemic level presupposed by such models; the latter, in turn, embraced versions of either structuralist or systems models (Parsonianism vs. Althusserianism) whose determinism effectively undercut the action level.

Though originally developed by Lockwood (1964), the distinction between *social* and *system integration* has been modified in various ways to overcome this problem. Giddens, for example, defines social integration as "reciprocity between actors in contexts of co-presence," and system integration as "reciprocity between actors or collectivities across extended time-space" (1984: 28). For example, at the level of social integration, the question of social change would be analyzed by reference to group actors, whether existing powers or emerging social movements. Such an orientation necessarily has a decisive subjective dimension linked to the intentions of those actors. In contrast, system integration implies a form of analysis which makes no immediate reference to subjective intentions and hence remains purely objectivistic. The

Marxian notion of contradiction between labor and capital, or the notion of forces and relations of production, are concepts of this type, as are functionalist notions of consensus or functional imperatives.

What makes the social/system integration distinction of such critical importance in contemporary theory is that it represents the effort to take into account the duality of social life (reflected in the subjective-objective distinction), without lapsing into either extreme. Indeed, as we will see, this has been one of the central concerns of reproduction theories which are concerned, precisely, with the dialectic of agency and structure.

To understand these distinctions and their implications, let us begin, following Bhaskar (1979) with a simple classification[5] of four basic models of society/person relationships: (1) the voluntaristic Weberian model where the individual creates society; (2) the deterministic Durkheimian model where society determines the individual; (3) the (idealist) dialectical model of Berger and Luckmann (1967), which attempts to reconcile the first two positions by assuming that although society creates the individual, it is individuals in turn who produce society in a continuous dialectic; and (4) a (materialist) transformational model of social activity where individuals do not "create" society, rather "they *reproduce* or *transform* it" (Bhaskar, 1979: 120; see figure 2.3). Unlike model three, it is assumed that society precedes the individual, even though concrete human praxis may either reproduce or transform. Hence, unlike the other models, Bhaskar concludes, the transformation model "can sustain a genuine concept of *change*, and hence of *history*" (ibid., 121).

Another way of interpreting these models is in relation to their implicit conception of the relationship between system integration and social integration. The voluntaristic Weberian model, for example, operates exclusively at the level of social integration because of its methodological individualism. From this perspective, to speak of society as a whole or a totality is a theoretical illusion, a theme going back to its neo-Kantian origins. In contrast, the methodological collectivism of the deterministic (sociologistic) Durkheimian model makes it possible to develop an analysis of system integration, a theme expressed in Durkheim's fundamental distinction between mechanical and organic solidarity. But within this framework, the status of social integration becomes problem-

FIGURE 2.3
Society-Persons Relationships (following Bhaskar, 1979)

MODEL	EXAMPLE	SOCIETY-PERSON RELATIONS
VOLUNTARIST	WEBER	Individual creates society
DETERMINISTIC	DURKHEIM	Society determines individual
IDEALISTIC DIALECTIC	BERGER & LUCKMANN	Individuals create society but are also its product
TRANSFORMATIONAL DIALECTIC	MARX	Individuals reproduce and/or transform society

atic, given Durkheim's fear of psychologism. The third "dialectical" model of Berger and Luckmann attempts to transcend this polarization by looking alternatively at processes of social integration (subjective meaning, group action) and system integration. However, this model lacks any clear way of relating these two levels of analysis. In this respect, their effort is similar to the effort of Parsonian structural functionalism, which also attempts to reconcile Durkheim and Weber in a theory of social systems, a theme that will be explored in a moment. Finally, the transformational model attempts to go beyond a formal analysis to historically analyze the intersection of systemic crisis and group-based mobilization and counter-mobilization, thus effectively coupling the analysis of social and system integration. One of the most sophisticated recent examples of this type has been Giddens' (1979; 1984) structuration theory, though its origins are in Marx. In effect, reproduction theories have ranged from Durkheimian determinist to transformational variants.

Accordingly, it is possible to classify such educational theories in terms of the possible theories of society they presuppose. For that purpose, we need to refer back to the schema for classifying theories: (1) the axis of metatheory (i.e., the objective-subjective continuum); (2) analytical and/or normative orientations toward order theories of regulation versus radical change, a theme that will be illuminated by Habermas's theory of knowledge interests; (3) and analysis at the level of systems or social integration or both.

Let us first consider the axis of metatheory: the nominalist-realist continuum ranging from subjectivistic and individualist theories to objectivistic and collectivist ones. From the perspective of theories of society these can be contrasted as relatively "open" versus relatively "closed" models.[6] Applied to educational systems, for example, relatively closed models tend to be objectivistic and stress the tight fit between educational systems and the social order as a whole. A more or less realistic ontology is presupposed along with a goal of positive "structural" explanation which is deterministic and generalizing. As a consequence, the focus of analysis is upon system integration rather than social integration, that is, the voluntaristic capacity of agents to reshape the existing forms of society. What is most important, then, is a general theory of educational reproduction rather than an understanding of specific cases or variations between societies.

Relatively open models, on the other hand, tend to be more dynamic than static, and more oriented toward the potential bases of the transformation of educational/societal relations rather than their stability. The ontological point of departure tends to be more nominalistic in that concepts are not viewed as literally grasping reality. Epistemologically, the subjective meanings of individuals and groups—human agency—are viewed as more important than determining structures, and human nature is viewed as creating the possibilities for resistance to, and potential transcendence of, those constraining objective relations. As a consequence, particular attention is given to processes of social integration, and how the shifting constellations of group action, and the emergence of social movements, may transform existing realities.

Finally, this results in a methodological orientation that is more particularistic and interpretive, hence oriented toward historical and case studies. Broadly speaking, neo-Marxist structuralist theories, along with sociological functionalist ones, assume relatively closed models of reproduction and self-regulation, which tends to give them a static and deterministic emphasis, and an orientation towards system integration processes. In contrast, the types of research associated with the "new sociology of education," theories of "resistance," critical theory, and neo-Weberian theories of society tend to assume relatively open models concerned with the interrelationship between system and social integration. Later we will consider the relative strengths and limitations of these two types of strategies with respect to both research and policy implications.

Models of educational reproduction can also be classified with respect to the second axis: orientations toward order as opposed to radical change. This issue is complicated because it can be dealt with at both empirical and normative levels. All neo-Marxist, radical, and critical theories normatively share an orientation toward radical change, to that extent they all assume that educational systems on the whole are (a) biased toward the reproduction of existing power relations (involving class, gender, racial and other social positions) and modes of consciousness that legitimate those relations; and (b) that normatively the task of social research and militant political action is to facilitate challenging these simple and/or complex reproductive tendencies. Of course, there are considerable divergences with respect to whether a relatively open or closed model is employed in the empirical analysis of existing forms of social order. In other words, there is a basic metatheoretical polarization dividing change-oriented theories of educational reproduction: relatively static, closed structuralist models, as opposed to more open ones stressing the dialectic of agency and structure.

The dominant macrosociological theories of education obviously fall into the category of an orientation toward order and consensus, even if there are again significant divergences. Functionalist and systems models, for example, have tended to be relatively closed and objectivistic; the result is a more or less technocratic stance that seeks to develop reformist control strategies for improving the fit between educational systems and the given societal imperatives for stabilization.[7] Relatively open models, on the other hand, tend to stress the way in which the structure of educational systems reflects the outcome of pluralistic group struggles, rather than the imperatives of societal functioning or even the capacity of a dominant class to shape education in the interest of preserving the given mode of production. This strategy also runs into a kind of relativism, however, because it becomes increasingly difficult to evaluate the divergent claims of competing groups.

Finally, it should be stressed that this framework allows us to make a sharp distinction between radical theories of social reproduction and technocratic ones. Indeed, the importance of the differences between these two types points to the question of why functionalist and systems theories should be considered at all under the rubric of "reproduction" theories, which are normally associated exclusively with radical critiques of education. The reason for this inclusion is three-fold. First, the logical and substantive similarities between these two types of theories have been generally ignored.[8] So one of our major concerns is to draw out these similarities that involve methodological functionalism. Second, a discussion of functionalist and systems theories is also necessary to set the stage for understanding the origins and specific themes of the various radical critiques of education. What follows is an application of these metatheoretical concerns in classifying educational paradigms.

PARADIGMS OF EDUCATIONAL REPRODUCTION: AN OVERVIEW INTRODUCTION

Five basic paradigms of education reproduction are discussed in the rest of this study. At this point we will focus on the generic features of each type, giving only occasional attention to variant forms. The task here is rather to present a description of each strategy of reproductive analysis in order to have an overall sense of the logic of each approach. Nevertheless, it should be recalled— as our later discussion shows—that there are examples of models within each of these paradigms that, in the course of developing "ad hoc" revisions, end up transcending in important respects their paradigm of origin. These paradigms can be differentiated with respect to their assumptions at three levels: metatheory, substantive theoretical analysis of the relations between society and education, and their policy and ideological implications.

Systems and Functionalist Theories

Classic functionalist models of reproduction combine methodological and substantive functionalism; hence, the strategy of analysis involves an objectivist search for the positive functions of educational institutions for society as a whole. The consequence for policy is a liberal reformist strategy concerned with adjusting the fit between education and what are assumed to be societal needs. Chapter 3 develops a detailed analysis of the paradigmatic work of Talcott Parsons in applying functionalist theory to education. Chapter 4 surveys the increasingly diverse terrain of neofunctionalist theory, giving particular attention to the differentiation model of Jeffrey Alexander and his collaborators, and Margaret Archer's distinctive morphogenic systems theory.

Economic-Reproductive Theories

Economic-reproductive models, closely associated with structualist neo-Marxist theories, are also objectivistic and methodologically functionalist. However, they argue that in capitalist societies, rather than serving the interests of society as a whole, educational institutions are in correspondence with the needs of the production system and the interests of capitalists and managers (the owners and administrators of capital). Accordingly, it is argued that education can be fundamentally changed only by abolishing the capitalist mode of production: a revolutionary socialist position. The structuralist metatheory of such approaches is introduced in chapter 5, and the variants of structuralist Marxism discussed in chapter 6.

Class-Cultural Reproductive Theories

Class-cultural reproductive theories are objectivistic, but also claim that attention should be given to the meanings and strategies of individuals, as well as social (especially class) structures. From this perspective, the educational system is primarily shaped by the struggle of different social classes using it to improve their own status within the system of social stratification. An important consequence is that educational credentials and qualifications have no necessary technical and economic functions and may simply reflect the ability of certain groups to exclude those without such credentials or status characteristics. Presentation, appraisal, and discussion of these types of conflict models are develop in chapter 7.

Class-Bureaucratic Theories

Class-bureaucratic theories largely agree with class-reproductive theories, but add an important qualification: there is an overall logic to status competition, that is, the imperatives stemming from bureaucratization and technical rationalization. It is argued, however, that obsession with the expansion of science, technology, and bureaucracy has no necessary relation to the fulfillment of human needs, even if it does contribute to capital accumulation and political legitimation. These approaches are discussed in chapter 8 (the Frankfurt tradition; Ivan Illich).

Integrative-Reproductive Models

Finally, integrative-reproductive models conclude that there is an inevitable subjective-objective split in social theory—which, in a way, reflects the reality of everyday life—that cannot ultimately be resolved theoretically. Consequently, it is argued that educational reproduction and change can only be understood through the use of two complementary research strategies: *state-hegemonic theories* that focus on the state as the mediating point through which various economic, class, and technical factors are regulated to create social order; and *transformative-resistance theories* that are concerned with the conditions under which individual and collective subjects become mobilized as part of counter-hegemonic resistance against existing educational institutions and related forms of domination. A crucial feature of such state-hegemoniac theories is that they are *parallist* (as opposed to class reductionist) in recognizing the autonomous interplay armory class, gender, race, and other bases of domination. On the otherhand, the transformative-resistance theories are *practice-based* in that their knowledge-guiding interest is political rather than strictly explanatory. These themes have been most consistently and influentially developed in relation to the more recent reception of the work of Antonio Gramsci (chapter 9). Such neo-Gramscian theory, coupled with diffuse influence from more recent Frankfurt-type critical theory, has been especially evident in the integral, poststructuralist approaches that have emerged in Britain in the wake of the "new sociology of education" and cultural studies (chapter 10), in the work of Michael Apple or Henry Giroux in the United States (chapter 11), in critical theories of the state (chapter 12), in efforts to incoporate gender and race into models of cultural reproduction (chapter 13), and in responses to the challenge of postmodernism (chapter 14).

CONCLUSION

In summary, the next chapter will begin our journey through the various paradigms, research agendas and theory programs. Parts 2 and 3 (chapters 3–7) conform fairly closely to the paradigmatic orientations just described: functionalist, economic-reproductive, and class-reproductive. Parts 4, 5, and 6 (chapters 8–14) address the class-bureaucratic and integrative-reproductive models.

PART 2

Structural Functionalism and Systems Theories

CHAPTER 3

The Functionalist Tradition: Parsons and Education

INTRODUCTION: THE FUNCTIONALIST TRADITION

In order to understand the continuity between the general concept of reproduction and its specific form in the functionalist and systems theory tradition, it it first necessary to consider the concepts of equilibrium and self-regulation as implying an implicit model of reproduction. Within sociology, the dominant form of this approach has been structural functionalism, but it is important to note the influence upon and criticism of sociological functionalism by more recent cybernetic and systems theories. All of these approaches share, however, a specific mode of reasoning about society in terms of part-whole relations which can be characterized as the logic of functional analysis. Though the pioneering work on a functionalist analysis of education was that of Durkheim, his work has been subject to divergent interpretations. The most influential has been that of Parsons, as part of a complex general theory of evolution and social systems. Neofunctionalism, as represented in the work of Jeffrey Alexander and Niklas Luhmann has continued the Parsonian tradition with important modifications and will be taken up in the next chapter. Finally, the morphogenic systems model of Margaret Archer—which was developed specifically to deal with the history of educational systems—represents the most theoretically innovative and empirically rich effort to draws systems theory away from its static bias and neglect of social conflict.

REPRODUCTION AND FUNCTIONAL ANALYSIS

Equilibrium and Self-Regulation

Outside of the Marxian tradition, the problem of a theory of society as a whole or totality, and the closely related question of a

41

theory of social and cultural reproduction, has had a rather different history. The approach characteristic of "bourgeois" sociological theories has been indebted primarily to biological theory. Though Marx was fond of biological metaphors, the primary source of his theory of totality was Hegel and the production/reproduction concepts of English political economy. In contrast, the sociological tradition, beginning with Auguste Comte and further elaborated by Spencer, Durkheim, Malinowski, Radcliffe-Brown, and Parsons, has consistently been preoccupied with organic metaphors to understand society as an integrated social "system." There is an element of overlap, however, in that functionalist sociologists have been extensively concerned with the problem of "equilibrium"—a theme whose understanding has been strongly influenced by the economist (and sociologist) Vilfredo Pareto. As Boudon and Bourricaud (1982: 466) note, *"in fact, the concept of reproduction is merely a double in the vocabulary of the Marxist tradition for the concept of equilibrium."*[1]

The key difference, of course, remains the type of system within which such self-regulating processes are said to operate, and how they are to be analyzed normatively and empirically: the Hegelian or structuralist Marxist conceptions of totality are at first sight a long way from the "social system" of Talcott Parsons; and yet the formal parallels point to important similarities.

For those trained in the orthodoxy of American sociology in the late 1960s and early 1970s, when the fundamental division within sociological theory was characterized by the confrontation of so-called conflict and consensus approaches (e.g., Demerath and Peterson, 1967; Friedrichs, 1969), to speak of such affinities may appear to be surprising. In this earlier context, consensus theory was associated generally with functionalism and above all the work of Talcott Parsons, whereas conflict theory was associated with C. Wright Mills and Ralf Dahrendorf. Yet at this stage conflict theory remained a hybrid category. For the most part the dominant forms in sociology were Mannheimian and neo-Weberian in inspiration because neo-Marxism had not yet regained a respectable place within the academic social sciences, and Frankfurt Critical Theory was not available in translation. Most importantly, Marxism and functionalism were seen as polar opposites, largely because of a lingering "instrumentalist" and "economistic" interpretation of Marx, along with the political context of the Cold War which profoundly shaped American academic life (cf. Buxton, 1985). As a consequence, most comparisons focused on the economic determinism of Marx, as opposed to the cultural-ism and consensus orientation of Parsonian functionalism. Nevertheless, Merton had already pointed out the logical affinities between Marxian theory and functional analysis, a theme expanded upon in Alvin Gouldner's (1971) critique of Parsons. The task of the present discussion is to outline the origins and development of the basic concepts of functionalist and systems theories which have affinities with theories of social and cultural reproduction.

The social theory debates of the late 1960s and the 1970s tended to suggest a complete polarization between between theories of order (functionalism and systems theories) and radical change (conflict theories). In the 1980s, however, the problematic aspects of this polarization became apparent by those critics who pointed to the functionalist methodological assumptions of certain conflict theories (e.g., structuralist Marxism) and the centrality of conflict in some functionalist models (e.g., Gouldner's early work, influenced by Merton). For such reasons a number of authors have more recently echoed Yves Barel's (1974) ambitious proposal some years ago, that the concept of "social reproduction," drawing upon both the traditions of historical materialism and aspects of systems-functional theory, is the most appropriate basis for a general theory of society and social change (e.g., Archer, 1982; Giddens, 1979, 1984). A similar strategy is echoed in the work of Offe (1985) and Habermas (1975), which selectively (and critically) draws upon concepts from functionalist and systems theory in the context of a reconstructed materialism. To this extent, even critics of functionalist and systems theory need to be aware of its basic concepts.

Structural Functionalism

The origins of modern functionalism can be traced to English anthropology's rather selective appropriation of Durkheim's sociology after the turn of the century. Intellectually, this reception was rooted in a reaction against the dominant diffusionist, historicist, and evolutionist models of society in anthropology. In particular, the evolutionist models proved unsatisfactory for anthropologists because they required forcing primitive societies into arbitrary developmental stages, thus reducing research to classification, given the general absence of historical records. Developing a limited aspect of Durkheimian theory, anthropological functionalism (as developed by Radcliffe-Brown, Malinowski, and others) provided a way of looking at the social system at a given moment in time—a synchronic as opposed to the more conventional diachronic approach. Parsons, in turn, further systematized this strategy, drawing it into the mainstream of Anglo-American sociological theory and eventually incorporating evolutionary themes to deal with the problem of social change (cf.Turner and Maryanski, 1979).

As Gouldner pointed out long ago, "From a sociologist's standpoint, the two most important aspects of a 'system' are the 'interdependence' of a number of 'parts' and the tendency of these to maintain 'equilibrium' in their relationships" (in Demerath and Peterson, 1967: 142). What is particularly distinctive about the form of functionalism identified with the work of Talcott Parsons is its emphasis upon the problem of equilibrium, a theme that has a long history in American social thought (Russett, 1966). Yet the logic of functional analysis, as described for example by Merton (1968), does not by itself preclude that equal attention be given to processes of disequilibrium or dysfunction. Nor, in principle, does functional analysis completely ignore social change; in fact, in his later work Parsons was very much preoccupied with a theory of social evolution.

The crucial aspects of Parsons' approach that define it as a theory of societal reproduction is the concept of an equilibrium based on the *homeostatic model* of a self-regulating process. By eventually incorporating evolutionary stage concepts within this model, a notion of transformation is introduced that points to the possibility of a transition from one type of system to another. More precisely, his theory might be characterized as a type of "cultural" reproduction theory, inasmuch as his overall evolutionary model postulates the primacy of the development of cultural systems, rather than economic ones, as in the classic materialist formulation. Another feature of Parsons' theoretical program, which has increasingly become recognized as anticipating aspects of structuralist thinking, is the underlying logic of his categorical schemas. Though Parsons himself attempted to understand the meta-theoretical foundations of his work in traditional epistemological (empiricist) terms, in his later work he increasingly drew upon developments in cybernetics and systems theories. Some have even attempted to justify aspects of Parsons' approach in structuralist terms drawn from Piaget (e.g., Lidz, 1982; Gould, 1985).

THE LOGIC OF FUNCTIONAL ANALYSIS

The Varieties of Functionalism

Functionalist theorizing has taken rather different forms, which are important to distinguish. The most well known, to be sure, is that of Talcott Parsons, which is based on a system-maintenance conception of reproduction and is cast within a general evolutionary model. Yet there are a number of other examples of less ambitious and more cautious functional approaches (such as the middle range theory of Merton), which also have been influential. A number of writers in education have only been indirectly influenced by these theoretical debates, given their focus on more restricted empirical phenomena.

In order to clarify these differences and their implications, it is necessary to begin with the logic of functional analysis, especially as formulated by Merton.[2] From this metatheoretical perspective it will then be possible to characterize Durkheim as the founder of functional analysis in sociology and outline the basic argument of Parsons' theory of social systems.

In his classic article on "Manifest and Latent Functions," Robert Merton long ago outlined a codification of the basic principles of functional analysis as a method—as opposed to structural functionalism, a specific application of that method—whose detailed argument needs to be reviewed for the purposes of our discussion. He begins by rejecting three interrelated postulates which, especially in anthropology, have been considered necessary to the orientation: "first, that standardized social activities or cultural items are functional for the entire social or cultural system; second, that all such social and cultural items fulfill sociological functions; and third, that these items are consequently indispensable" (1968: 79). Further, from the perspective of his analysis of a generic functional method, he can reject that it is inherently conservative by demonstrating the use of functional analysis in the work of Marx and Engels. Finally, he outlines a "paradigm" for functional analysis in sociology that identifies a series of assumptions of such a general functional approach. A brief review of these assumptions will show an aspect that has been typically neglected or inadequately dealt with in structural functionalist theories of education.

First, Merton is concerned with the the item(s) to which functions are imputed, suggesting that, in the case of education for instance, nonformal types of instruction should in principle be objects of investigation because they too constitute "patterned and repetitive" forms of activity. Second, a focus of the analysis is the concept of subjective dispositions (e.g., motives, purposes). Thus, Merton distinguishes between "subjective dispositions" and "objective consequences" (1968: 105), and in principle, therefore, concepts of ideology and falsifying consciousness—forms of "objective consequences"—are not precluded in the study of the motivation of agents in educational institutions. A third aspect, the concept of objective consequences, is based on the distinction between functions and dysfunctions of the system (1968: 105); further, it is necessary to distinguish between "manifest" (intended) and "latent" (unintended) consequences of structures. Accordingly, nothing precludes that a given educational structure might have net dysfunctional consequences, or that the latent functions may contradict the official, manifest ones. There is no a priori reason to assume that educational structures necessarily or inevitably contribute to social order. Fourth, Merton is concerned with concepts of the unit subserved by the function, thus it is imperative to consider the "range of units for which the item has designated consequences" (1968: 106). This distinction opens the way to the possibility of interpreting educational institutions in relation to the interests of a dominant class as opposed to subordinate classes (or regions, ethnic groups, etc.). A basic suggestion of Merton is to consider the notion of functional requirements (e.g., needs, prerequisites). This poses the problem of what different kinds of functional requirements exists (universal vs. specific), as a consequence, there is a crucial problem of validating such requirements. Obviously, this remains one of the most fundamental difficulties of all reproduction theories that are based on some version of the thesis that the given form of the educational system is a functional requirement for the reproduction of the given social order.

Another suggestion of Merton is to focus on the mechanisms through which functions are fulfilled, not one of psychological mechanisms but of a sociological account of the mechanisms that allow functions to be fulfilled. Thus, another assumption is that of functional alternatives (e.g., functional equivalents or substitutes), which opens up the option of a "range of possible variation" with respect to the potential types of structures that could fulfill a given function. Merton contends that a basic assumption of functionalist theories is to focus on concepts of structural context (or structural constraint). The basic point is that there are limits on the range of variation of structures: "This consideration is recognized by both Marxist social scientists (e.g., Karl Marx) and by non-Marxists (e.g., Malinowski)" (1968: 107). Further, the concept of "constraint" here points to the importance of a structuralist type of analysis that cannot be reduced to the variable analysis of cause and effect.

A key suggestion from Merton is the emphasis on concepts of dynamics and change. He argues that the focus of conventional functional analysis on social equilibrium rather than social disequilibrium is partly circumstantial and contributes to a focus on statics as opposed to dynamics (1968: 108). In principle, therefore, some version of the concept of contradiction is compatible with a generic functional method. Educational systems may play a variable role in such conjunctures. Finally, Merton is concerned with problems of validation. Considering the logic of experimentation, Merton argues that even if "functional analysis has no intrinsic commitment to an ideological position," it does not preclude that "particular functional analyses and particular hypotheses advanced by functionalists may have an identifiable ideological role" (1968: 108). This caution applies equally to educational research influenced by American functionalism and various neo-Marxist analogues.

From Merton's perspective, therefore, it is necessary to approach the structural functionalist tradition in education in relation to the types of functional explanations employed, rather than lump all such analyses together in relation to some abstract notion of "functionalist." Since all reproduction analyses presuppose functional arguments, this problem will be of comparable importance for discussing variants stemming from historical materialism and conflict theories. As more recent discussions in the Marxist tradition have acknowledged, functional explanations are also a central and often problematic aspect of radical theories of education (Liston, 1988). We will return to this question in the context of structuralist Marxism and structuralist conflict theories. Here the central point is to reaffirm the usefulness of our generic conception of theories of reproduction.

THE DOMINANT TRADITION: PARSONIAN THEORY

Durkheimian Influences

The legacy of Emile Durkheim has exerted a powerful effect on the history of the sociology of education, but what is not usually recognized is that there are two contrasting lines of influence. The first and most well known is that of the Durkheim of American sociology: the Durkheim for whom *Suicide* (and the corresponding methodological sections of the *Rules of Sociological Method*) were, along with the basic principles of functionalism as appropriated by Talcott Parsons, the most important contributions. In this version, particular emphasis is given to order, consensus, and value integration at the expense of the various contexts where Durkheim recognizes conflict and change.

There is a second Durkheim, however, one characteristic of the French tradition and a few individuals elsewhere (e.g., Basil Bernstein in Britain, Alvin Gouldner in the United States), where his most important contributions are to be found in his religious writings and methodological principles, which became the basis of structuralist anthropology. Needless to say, this tradition is highly critical of Durkheim on many points, but still does not hesitate to borrow and build upon his pioneering examples and intuitions. It is this version of Durkheim that influenced the "Annales School" of historical research and the structuralist tradition from Lévi-Strauss to Bourdieu, and has had a profound effect upon conflict-oriented reproduction theories of education. What this stream of discussion highlights is the way aspects of his theory "indicate the convergence of his sociology with a syndicalist (but nonrevolutionary) socialism" (Gouldner, 1980: 368). Durkheim was aware that "class differences made it impossible for 'just' contracts to be negotiated and led to an unequal exchange of goods and services, being thus conducive to a sense of injustice which had socially unstabilizing effects" (Gouldner, 1980: 368). The approaches discussed in this chapter, however, were influenced primarily by the first stream, which stressed his orientation toward order and consensus.

Three aspects of Durkheim's sociology were of direct significance and decisive for the subsequent development of functionalist sociologies of education. First, he advanced the historical thesis that changes in educational systems were the causal consequence of external social and economic changes in society as a whole. So, for example, in his *Evolution of Educational Thought* (1977) he attributes the sixteenth-century Renaissance transformation of the university to the economic effects of the discovery of the New World, the expansion of trade, the expansion of a bourgeoisie intent on emulating the this-worldly orientation of the aristocracy, and the demand for freer inquiry and national autonomy arising from the collapse of a church-based European community:

> Peoples modify their mental outlook to such an enormous extent only when very fundamental features of social life have themselves been modified. We can therefore be certain in advance the the Renaissance derives not, I repeat, from the fortuitous fact that certain classical works were exhumed at this time, but rather from profound changes in the organization of European societies. (1977: 169)

Second, he asserted that the specific characteristics of educational structures and their cultural contents had a strong functional relationship with the needs of society—as defined by the groups concerned—for cultural integration and a specialized division of labor. This theme is the basis of the conventional functional theory of socialization. As he puts it in *Education and Sociology*, this means that education must

> arouse in the child: (1) a certain number of physical and mental states that the society to which he belongs considers should not be lacking in any of its members; and (2) certain physical and mental states which the particular group (caste, class, family, profession) considers, equally, ought to be found among all those who make it up. (1956: 70)

Third, he asserted that, as a consequence of the transition from mechanical to organic solidarity (i.e., from traditional to complex, highly differentiated societies), greater individuation was necessary and that this was expressed in shifts in pedagogy and school organization. On the one hand, this necessitated a turn from a religious to a rational, secular conception of morality consistent with an individualism, a shift that would necessarily induce "a greater thirst for justice" (1973: 12). On the other hand, a reform of pedagogy was also implied:

> It is not enough to exclude harmful punishment; we must seek out and prefer those punishments that are useful to him who is punished. In a general way, the penal discipline of the adult tends increasingly to be informed with humanitarian feelings; it becomes increasingly a kind of educational rehabilitation. Nor can education, properly speaking, fail to concern itself with similar problems. (1973: 197)

Each of these themes are, taken generally, crucial assumptions for any sociology of education. What was distinctive about the functionalist tradition of research is the manner in which each of these arguments was advanced: how the external social and economic changes are analyzed, the way in which the functional relationship between schools and society is conceptualized, and the implications that follow from the transformations in schooling that have accompanied those in the division of labor. Functionalist sociology—under the influence of Parsons—remained generally faithful to the conservative side of Durkheim, in that there was an almost complete neglect of the contradictory aspects of the division of labor (i.e., class conflict), conflictual dimensions of the school-society relationship, and the very truncated conception of individuation implied by his theory of socialization. To use Merton's terminology, stress was placed upon the manifest and a limited number of latent functions of education, positive functions were analyzed to the exclusion of negative or dysfunctions, and there was uncritical acceptance of assumptions such as the high level of systemic integration of society and the methodological principle that the "whole" served by the "part" (i.e., education) was indeed society as a whole rather than some powerful class within society. From Merton's position, therefore, this could be viewed as a selective and unrigorous application of the principles of functional analysis and in part inconsistent with Durkheim's overall approach. As we will see in the next chapters, people such as Pierre Bourdieu and Basil Bernstein extend principles of functional analysis that push Durkheim in rather different directions that link up with aspects of Marx and Weber.

The Functionalist Tradition

Defined in metatheoretical and methodological terms, as in the case of Merton, the concept of functional analysis becomes a generic concept: one useful to speaking of theories of reproduction in general, but not designed to encompass any single one. For this latter purpose, other specifying assumptions are required, such as the brief account of Durkheim functionalist theory of education. But to narrow the conceptual terrain of an approach to single author is misleading within any living and developing "tradition" of research.

Parsons' Theory of Social Systems

Talcott Parsons' enormous corpus of work spans a period of more than fifty years and remains the most important single point of reference within the contemporary functionalist tradition. Not surprisingly, his conception of society went through significant changes, and three basic phases can be identified. The first culminated in the late 1930s in a voluntaristic theory of action which owes as much to Weber as Durkheim. The second, from the 1940s to the 1960s, is the most important, in the sense that during this period he developed the form of structural functionalism for which he is best known. It is in this phase that the concepts of equilibrium, differentiation, and system emerge as central, and the Weberian influence wanes in favor of a particular version of Durkheim, which Parsons tries to bolster with findings from the biological theory of homeostasis. The third phase, from the 1960s through his death in 1979, was marked by a shift from the statics to the dynamics of social systems and included the development of a general evolutionary schema and recourse to cybernetic concepts. It is in these latter two phases that the question of education becomes central.

Before turning to the tradition of structural-functionalist educational research, and the specific contributions of Parsons, it is necessary to outline some of the basic themes of his theoretical program for those who are not already familiar.[3] To do so is also important because certain key themes of his third phase have never been integrated into the more popular critiques, which focus on the second and most vulnerable phase. The following themes will be touched upon in this context: (1) the concept of general theory; (2) the AGIL (adaption, goal-attainment, integration, latency) schema of universal functions and the concept of integrated social systems; (3) the theory of pattern variables; (4) the cybernetic foundations of the evolutionary model; and (5) the concept of value-generalization.

Parsons' theoretical program is based on the possibility and necessity of a fully general, categorical schema capable of encompassing all past and possible forms of society. In contrast, Merton proposed a focus on "middle range" theory on the assumption that the possibility of a more general theory required a longer process of accumulating social-scientific knowledge. Others, such as C. Wright Mills, have defended a version of the Weberian assumption that meaningful theory should retain a degree of historical particularity.

Parsons is joined by structuralist Marxism in the search for a general theory, though in the latter case it is based upon the concept of modes of production. Instead, Parsons proposes a fourfold schema of functions, customarily referred to as the AGIL schema:

Adaptation: the problem of gaining and distributing resources from the external environment (economic processes)

Goal-Attainment: aspects of the action system oriented toward the realization of goals (political processes)

Integration: problems of coherence, control, and coordination (societal community)

Latency: the storage and distribution of motivational energy by dealing with the problem of pattern maintenance (i.e., the symbolic basis of the cultural system) and tension management (i.e., resolving strains and tensions between actors)

These abstract, universal functions are mobilized to understand concrete societies and social change with the theory of social differentiation, which is, in effect, a model of complex reproduction. Differentiation, however, can only be understood in relation to other related key concepts: the pattern variables, the cybernetic hierarchy of controls, value generalization, and others. The five pattern variables are an ideal type schema that allow one to grasp the logic underlying the shift from traditional to modern societies at the level of the personality, social, and cultural systems: affectivity versus affective neutrality; diffuseness versus specificity; particularism versus universalism; ascription versus achievement; collectivity versus self. Thus the pattern variables underlie the process of differentiation by creating the possibility of more flexible actors and institutions. The result is a directional, evolutionary account of the development of human societies based on the assumption that at higher levels of social differentiation societies have greater adaptive capacity (i.e., are more productive, powerful, and capable of adaptive upgrading in the face new environmental challenges). It is important to note that, as part of a general theory of social systems, these arguments apply equally to all industrial societies, including bureaucratic collectivist ones.

Though we will discuss the underlying features of the change model suggested here in the next chapter in the context of educational systems, it is useful to note some of the key assumptions of this differentiation model. First, it is held that there is a process of increasing differentiation of the four functional complexes *from each other*; for example, political, economic, and other institutions become separated out as specialized institutions, rather than being embedded in kinship systems as they are in traditional societies. Second, this is coupled with increased internal differentiation *within* each subsystem. Third, crises emerge around the strains created by differentiation processes and are only resolved at the point of successful reintegration at the higher level of complexity; and four, such a successful transition implies that adaptive upgrading has taken place, again rendering the system stable. Finally, the cultural system plays the decisive role in this upgrading process, an assumption ground in the cybernetic priority of information over energy as control processes.

PARSONS AND EDUCATION

In the previous section we have developed the premises of structural and functionalist analysis, and its relationships with system theories. In the following sections, the structural functionalist tradition's contribution to educational research will be presented and critically assessed. Taken in its most generic form, the functional analysis of education obviously touches upon many of the important aspects of the relationship between modern societies and education. In the first two sections we briefly review these rather obvious but not insignificant contexts of functional analysis. Then, in the third section, we turn to the case of Parsons' effort to analyze education within the framework of a much more elaborate general theoretical and evolutionary schema. The actual relationship between educational research and functionalism has been much more complex than simply the influence of Parsons, and the fourth section touches upon some of the key contexts of debate about education in advanced societies. The fifth section, on the other hand, takes up the question of the implications of functionalism for relatively underdeveloped societies, that is, the theory of "modernization." In the sixth section, various criticisms of Parson's account of education, and sociological functionalism more generally, are developed.

Education and Industrial Society

At the outset, it is important to recognize that the structural-functionalist approach to education did not develop in isolation, but rather as part of a series of theoretical developments related to the ongoing adaptation of the modern state to the crises of capitalist development. This point is most explicit in Durkheim's status within the French educational system and as an exponent of reforms of the type eventually associated with the welfare state.

In the context of subsequent developments in political philosophy and ideology formation, the emergence of social-liberal and social-democratic options in the post–World War II period opened the way for a "third way"—a vision of equality of opportunity and educational reform as the basis for an alternative to the revolutionary Marxist scenario of a grim choice between Fascism and Bolshevism. Within economics, parallel and complementary doctrines emerged in the form of Keynesian economic theory, which paved the way for a mixed economy balanced by central fiscal and monetary policies (indicative planning), as well as the theory of human capital, which justified educational expenditures as part of a long-term strategy of economic growth. Though having origins quite different than either of these two developments, functionalist sociology provided the most well articulated general theoretical position in the social sciences for legitimating both social-liberal/ social-democratic ideological options, as well as a conception of the interventionist welfare state as the necessary basis for controlling the self-destructive tendencies of capitalist growth.

Consensual Middle-Range Perspectives: The Four Functions of Education

Despite many differences of detail and emphasis, functionalist approaches to education share a number of key analytical arguments which, as noted above, converge with and reinforce the more general consensual assumptions that have been characteristic of postwar welfare states. The characteristic stress is upon the *manifest* and selective *latent* functions of education and their overall *positive* influence upon social development, despite the residual need for ongoing reforms and adjustments. Instructive here is the distinction between what has been described as the four primary functions of education: the academic, distributive, economic, and political socialization functions (Muñoz Izquierdo et al., 1979). The academic function corresponds to its responsibility for inculcating those universal cognitive skills held essential to society's capacity to provide for its members. The distributive function relates to education's role in preparing individuals for their roles in the division of labor, and providing an efficient distribution of talent through competive selection. The economic function (conceived similarly in human capital theory) is related to the link between education and higher levels of productivity on the part of individuals once in the workforce. In the context of the political socialization function the importance of education is acknowledged as indispensable to social integration and social control. Moreover, these four broad functions coincide with a general societal consensus with respect to the tasks of education in society. These functions are explicitly addressed in the work of Parsons on education.

The World of Talcott Parsons and Education

The selection of Talcott Parsons for a more intensive discussion of structural-functional theory and its relation to education is justifiable for a number of fairly obvious reasons related to his capacity to provide a legitimation for the dominant understanding of the functions of education just noted. First, his decisive role in the emergence of this perspective is undeniable, as is the fact that he was the most well known and influential sociologist in the United

States from the 1940s through the 1960s. For this reason, as well, traces of his work can be found in the most famous sociologists and political scientists of American social science, whether in the context of defending or polemicizing against him, including Shils, Lipset, Gouldner, Selznik, Tumin, Merton, Bendix, Moore, Blau, Kingsley Davis, Smelser, W. Goode, Inkeles, Janowitz, and even C. Wright Mills. Second, Parsons sought to provide a systematic and metatheoretically grounded approach to structural-functional analysis; in contrast, most students of education have largely taken the functionalist perspective for granted and not attempted to question or refine its basic assumptions. As a consequence, from the perspective of Parsons' work it is possible to more readily link up with the general theme of theories of cultural and social reproduction in education as a general theme in contemporary social theory. Third, the topic of education was of central concern to Parsons, especially in his later work. Even if most of those who worked within the functionalist tradition of educational research were not Parsonians in the strict sense of discipleship or attempting to explicitly develop his particular approach, his influence is generally acknowledged, and it contributed in important ways to the overall legitimation of functionalist approaches to educational research. Further, the more explicit theoretical approach of Parsons has the advantage of revealing many of the more implicit assumptions of functionalist educational research generally. Finally, though Parsons' work was highly criticized in the late 1960s and 1970s, contributing to the eclipse of his influence, the 1980s has witnessed a partial rehabilitation of his work and the emergence of neofunctionalist approaches (e.g., Alexander, 1985b), which have to an extent influenced certain critical theories of society (e.g., the work of Offe and Habermas). Let us now turn to Parsons' specific work on education.

In an article published in 1959—and now considered a classic functionalist analysis applied to education—Parsons analyzed the relationships between the structure of the school class and its functions in socialization and in the granting of social roles in the structure of status roles in American society (Parsons, 1961: 434–55). Parsons' argument is as follows: individuals are born with ascriptive statuses (the socioeconomic status of the family and, beyond this, gender and birth order); subsequently, due primarily to education, begins a process of differentiation by acquired roles.

In this manner children enter the primary school relatively homogeneous in terms of socioeconomic status and age. The schools constitutes in practice a "contest" or competition where the contestants initially find themselves in conditions of equal opportunity (1961: 437–38).[4]

The teacher is the representative of adult society and, having diffuse expectations with respect to the academic future of pupils, contributes to this equality of opportunity. The cognitive components of instruction cannot be separated from the moral ones, and gradual differentiation will result from the axis of academic performance and its success. This general process, through differential performances, confers a new acquired status by means of grades and qualifications and constitutes a fundamental criterion for the assignment of future status in society (Parsons, 1961: 439–41). The fact that there is a preponderance of female teachers in primary education implies that the teacher will combine the female role of the mother with that of teacher, thus complementing the emotional aspects of education with the cognitive. Nevertheless, she will privilege the cognitive aspect, given that her role is to legitimate the differentiation of pupils on the basic of their academic success. The size of the school class prevents her from treating pupils in a particularistic manner, thus forcing the adoption of universal norms of treatment and evaluation. The rotation of teachers each year contributes to eliminating a tendency toward intimacy or particularism (from the child toward the teacher or the teacher toward certain children). With the changing of teachers every year, the child learns to distinguish between the role of the teacher and the personality of the teacher, all of which contributes to adopting models of universality in behavior. As a consequence, the child becomes oriented to achieved roles, displacing an initial predisposition toward ascriptive roles. This process is sanctioned through academic success and the fulfillment of educational obligations (Parsons, 1961: 443–45).

The resulting sense of shared communal values, of community and solidarity, serve to integrate the system when differentiation between the status of members develops. A fundamental principle of these values is that the assignment of differential rewards for differential success appears rational and just, under the condition that there is equality of opportunity for all of the competitors. Still, it can be inferred that it is legitimate to consider that this structure of rewards enhances subsequent opportunities (Parsons, 1961: 445–48). For Parsons intellectual abilities do not coincide with socioeconomic status, even if there are strong correlations between the two. As a consequence, "There can then be a genuine selective process within a set of 'rules of the game'" (Parsons, 1970: 145). The secondary school formalizes differentiation on the basis of educational achievement by means of channeling the student, whether in a terminal stream or one leading on to university studies. Further, these provide differentiation corresponding to distinct types of success, directing them toward cognitive technical roles or toward moral or humanistic ones (Parsons, 1970: 148–54).

The education of girls, in this perspective, permits them to contribute functionally to extrafamilial and community activities, even if their adult status will be above all with the relation to marriage and the family. The educated mother has important functions as a wife and mother, particularly in influencing her children, supporting them in school, and making them aware of the importance of education.

Despite this universe of order, there are conflicts and tensions. The typical case for Parsons are children of high intellectual ability and low socioeconomic status who are subject to cross-cutting pressures deriving from the family and school. They would have to minimize their good educational results in order to continue maintaining good relations with their family and friends (who in general do not get such results and lack the education level that these students would gradually realize). This would lead in the end to either indifference to or rebellion against school discipline.

Nevertheless, the general rise of the intellectual level of the population increases the pressure for improving individual school achievement. Students who have difficulty in adapting themselves to these rising educational expectations (because of their lack of intellectual ability) will tend to advance protests against adults, develop anti-intellectual ideologies, cheat in school, and be inclined toward specific types of juvenile delinquency. In short, educational improvement, and the rising role of the educational system as the principle agency of selection and socialization, would result in the structural differentiation of American society.

In sum, in this study Parsons puts into motion all of the central categories of his structural functional schema: the notions of system, needs, functions, integration, diffusion, consensus on common values, and pattern variables, especially ascriptive versus achieved roles and particularism versus universalism. Parsons has also discussed issues of postsecondary education. In one of his later works, Parsons turns to the questions of the functions of the university (Parsons and Platt, 1973).[5]

Parsons and Platt defined the university as a cognitive complex linking knowledge, rationality, learning, competence, and intelligence. This cognitive complex represents "the most critical single features of the developing structure of modern societies" (1973: vi), and "the central institution in the society" (1973: 103). This follows from the authors' assumption that modern society has its origins in the seventeenth century in "three processes of revolutionary structural change: the Industrial Revolution, the Democratic Revolution, and the Educational Revolution" (1973: 1).

It would be the institutions of higher education that preserve, organize, and create the cognitive culture that is the basis of mastering intelligence and competence in the modern world. At the same time, endogenously, the university institutionalizes this cognitive complex, administering the structures of evaluation that sustain it. The authors note how the central aspect of these institutions, upon which all of the other functions of the university depends, is the *preservation and development of the academic profession,* that is, postgraduate teaching and scientific and humanistic research. Yet the university has, according to the authors, a multifunctional character, which is expressed not only in the academic profession but in the fact that it educates and socializes the young (undergraduate or bachelor degree students), supports professional schools that are interested with the development of applied knowledge, and provides intellectual definitions of critical problems for the culture and society.

For Parsons and Platt, this multifunctional character is the source of conflict. The crisis has its clearest source and manifestation in the formation of undergraduate students, who are "in their tension-laden socialization situations and more sensitive to injustices in society than those in more secure social positions" (Parsons and Platt, 1973: 218–19). This process implies that while students are learning to cut their ties with their groups of origin (based especially in ascriptive statuses), the tensions of the process of socialization impede and obstruct the development of a compromise with broader groups of reference (based in achieved statuses). In conclusion, it would be the tensions rising from the process of university socialization, especially for the youngest and least established socially, that would constitute the motive force of student discontent and protest: "The crisis itself we shall interpret as centering in the undergraduate sector of the institutions of high academic quality" (1973: 27).

The cognitive complex is based on the notion of cognitive rationality, which is defined in the following terms: "The term 'cognitive' has a cultural reference whereas that of the term 'rational' is primarily social. Cognitive rationality is a value-pattern linking the cultural and the social levels which are not reducible to one another" (1973: 47). As they also note, "the autonomy of the university with respect to cognitive rationality is paralleled by the autonomy of the economy with respect to economic rationality." What then are the effects of this cognitive rationality? The authors suggest that "cognitive rationality also fosters institutionalized conditions for autonomous behavior. Students who do not go beyond high school are *more* likely than the college-educated to be more responsive to hierarchical authority and readier to base evaluations on ascribed positions. They are *less* likely to have developed the tools of rational criticism with which to direct their own lives. Respect for authority and the capacity to challenge it is class related" (1973: 215).

Many criticisms have been levelled at this approach. In Parsons (1949, 1951, 1959), the structure of social roles appear as given, and the school constitutes a mechanism of selection and assignment of persons' preexisting statuses; however, the consequences of a structure do not explain its causes: Parsons explains neither the origins of this function of selection attributed to the school in modern capitalism nor its social determinants, nor does Parsons consider other possible functions of the school and how the fiction of the unity of the pluralistic primary school conceals its role in reinforcing preexisting class-based differences.[6] Parsons, curiously, is not completely unaware of the limits of the assumption of a unified school (culminating in the American system of comprehensive high schools) when he recognizes the presence of a certain double system of scholarization, whether it be the case of parochial schools or the type of student with low academic performance but high socio-economic status who has "cushioning mechanisms" that protect him or her from the consequences of not "making the grade." Further, though citing data (dating from 1953) that imply the inequality of opportunity (e.g., that for the top quintile in ability "the range in college intentions ranges from 29% for sons of laborers to 89% for sons of major white collar persons," he still concludes that, "the main process of differentiation (which from another point of view is selection) that occurs during elementary school takes place on a single main axis of *achievement*" (1959: 133). Nevertheless, his metatheory of social integration, and in general the horizon of vision of his theoretical discourse, do not allow him to draw out the implications of these observations, which remain marginal to his discourse.

On the other hand, what is it that makes the values of the roles of the social structure and those of the school identical or very similar, as Parsons assumes? This is a fundamental presupposition of structural functional analysis, but is not sufficiently explicated. Parsons does not ask how consensus is constituted, around which predominant values it forms, and to which groups, individuals, or classes or fractions of class the given consensus serves. This would imply in the Parsonian schema that the school does not serve as a power factor for processing or constructing an established consensus, an assumption that is polemic. Another debatable aspect of Parsons is the assumption of the virtual equality of all the contestants at the beginning of school. The evidence shows, against Parsons' argument, that there is a very strong association between desires to continue formal education, socio-economic status, and cognitive ability (Carnoy, 1977). The second assumption of Parsons regarding the similarity (equality) of student neighborhoods can be questioned even more strongly. On the one hand, even if were possible to assume some degree of homogeneity of public schools located in a neighborhood (e.g., the characteristics shared by a middle-class and a working-class area), upon leaving the primary school children will be confronted with the powerful inter-neighborhood heterogeneity of secondary schools; and it is there precisely that is consolidated the competence for moving on to the higher levels of the educational system. On the other hand, the homogeneity of each neighborhood appears completely formal, even in the United States. At the level of material resources, characteristics of teachers, and related criteria, homogeneity would in face be qualified by its magnitude and quality: whether (as would be the case in Latin America) the level of such resources in neighborhoods in suburban and rural areas, would be below the level in middle- and upper-class neighborhoods. Even if the contrast is more marked in Latin American that in an advanced industrial society like the United States, it is still certain that such contrasts clearly existed when Parsons wrote at the beginning of the 1960s, as the War on Poverty revealed a little later.

These problems are important because Parsons appears to ignore that there is a displacement in the justification of social inequality. That is to say, ascriptive statuses are legitimated through academic achievement by converting them into acquired statuses in such a manner that the transmission and legitimation of inequality can be consider a (latent) function of the school.

Even more interesting results follow from the assumption that the assignment of future roles are given in terms of individual achievement based on ability and the initial equality of competitors. The individual is socialized in the belief that this success in achievement is based completely on ability or individual capacities and not in structural, political, or social factors—all of which implies in the final analysis that the student is responsible for his or her academic failure.

Another important point is the critique of the hypothesis that the size of the class and universal norms constitute restrictions upon teachers to keep them from applying particularistic criteria in the assigning of educational roles, evaluation, and the process of school socialization generally. Diverse studies, including some from a functionalist perspective, show that the presumptions of teachers regarding the intelligence and abilities of pupils, their physical appearance, their verbal ability, their conduct, their race, or their gender, constitute variables that influence fundamentally the practice of teachers and rebound on the educational output of pupils (Rosenthal and Jacobsen, 1968; Wexler, 1982; Kelly and Nihlen, 1982).

A final critical aspect in elementary and secondary education can be found in the question of students who do not adapt to educational change, especially due to lack of intellectual ability, which, according to Parsons, can result in delinquency and other forms of social anomie. It is clear that for Parsons the only type of social change acceptable is that which contributes to the social differentiation of society. Yet this ignores a whole series of contradictory phenomena. For example, considering once again the experience of Latin America, working-class protest does not always arise from those who are least paid and most impoverished, but at time from those who have higher wages and may even constitute a type of labor aristocracy (Torre, 1968; Gerchunoff and Llach, 1975). Further, student protest does not necessarily arise from mediocre students (i.e., low achievers), but at times surges from elite schools and includes many of the best students. The latter may become severe critics of the system despite having shown (for example, by their high academic achievements) their adaptation to the mechanisms of learning, motivation, or socialization. This academic or political activation does not necessarily convert them *ipso factum* into delinquents or anomic subjects, but simply as nonconformist critics, participants in protest movements or populist programs of social transformation (Lipset and Solari, 1971; Solari, 1968; Labarca, 1976; Portantiero, 1978; Landinelli, 1983).

The criticism of the Parsonian approach to postsecondary education poses somewhat different—even if closely related—problems, which can be elaborated with respect to a number of themes: the empirical basis of its arguments; its ahistorical character and reliance upon the supposed universality of the American case; the problematic application of general theoretical concepts to university-level education; and the one-dimensionality of the evolutionist functional analysis of the university.

What is the empirical basis of Parsons and Platt's work on the university? For the most part, the evidence that is presented has its origins in the personal experience of the authors, as university professors, and as the result of an exercise in the application of structural-functional analysis, rather than any systematic empirical investigation. Affirmations regarding the differential value of education for students with high school or less and for university students appear completely gratuitous in the context of the work; they never refer to prior research to ground such assertions, nor point to specific data from which could be inferred this link equating higher education with the high rationality of the work force. The centrality of the cognitive complex is simultaneously viewed as necessary and as a justification for increasing social investment in universities (Gusfield, 1974).

In characterizing the American university at the end of the

1960s as a cognitive complex, the historical character of the argument appears in an expressive manner. It sets aside the importance of social protest in the United States originating in the Vietnam War, and the role of students in this protest. It equally ignores the tensions generated in universities by the movement for civil rights led by MartinLutherKing which had extensive impact on university intellectual life. In the same manner, it does not analyze the contradictions generated within universities by racial and ethnic minorities questioning the "establishment" and the lack of educational opportunities. In sum, the most general context of the university crisis is ignored, centering exclusively upon the processes of socialization and tensions that emerge within the university as completely cognitive, entirely separated (or perhaps immune, in the opinion of the authors) from the complex process of social, political and economic determination.

All of which leads us to question the possible applicability of concepts allotted to the university for understanding higher education. Certainly, it would be difficult to imagine a university in dependent capitalism that is separated from the networks and processes of national political struggle, differentiated sharply from the alternative political and economic projects fighting within civil society and in the state, and thus constituting itself as a center for the production of "cognitive rationality" that illumines the total socioeconomic formation.

But even within the context of advanced capitalism studied by Parsons and Platt, the university system is so complex that it would difficult to apply their analysis to the situation of all universities. Further, it would be difficult to apply it to the elite universities, which are those the authors have in mind in offering their analysis and conclusions. Also must be considered the junior colleges, the confessional universities, universities closely linked to business interests, or technical or vocational institutions, which could only with difficulty be considered as "cognitive complexes" *strictu sensu*. The diversification, fragmentation and hierarchical differentiation of the system of higher education in the United States requires a theoretically more sophisticated approach than that provided by the authors.

Despite affirming the multifunctionality of the university, the authors' analysis can be considered "one-dimensional" in the way it privileges academic functioning and socialization. Given the complex of processes and structures that interact, it is difficult to justify that the effects (or functions) of universities could be simply grouped in the functions listed by the authors. Along with the development of the academic profession, the education and social-ization of students, and the contribution to the critical elaboration of cultural problems, the universities are linked intimately with industry, and on occasion constitute virtual factories for the pro-duction of science and technology with applied goals. The typical case is the linkage of centers of research and development among some universities, the war industry, and the American federal gov-ernment (Sutton, 1984; Machlup, 1962). Universities also contrib-ute directly to production, mediating the expansion of capital and the transformation of labor by capital (as in the cybernetic and computing industry); in addition, they make important contribu-tions to the process of investment through the funds that are direct-ly administered as property of the private universities in the United States.

In addition to the above, universities constitute a very signifi-cant labor market for certain segments of the labor force to the degree that they maintain a large contingent of the economically active population outside the labor market. Since otherwise this population would be pounding on the doors of employers, the university has, according to some analysts, a "parking effect" by removing people from the employment lines (Dore, 1976).

The "cognitive complexes" have a definite role in the constitu-tion of the "habitus of class" and in the political culture of contem-porary capitalist societies (Harker, 1984; Gordon, 1984). From the perspective of the sociology of professions, the universities pro-duce and administer the forms of knowledge socially accepted and associated with the practices of certain professions. Such produc-tion and administration of professional practices is more specified given the close association, in some cases, between university con-texts, stage agencies charged with sanctioning the norms for pro-fessional practice, and the advice of professionals, especially in the paradigmatic cases of medicine and law (Dingwall and Lewis, 1983).

Given the differentiation and segmentation of the university structure in practically every country, the elite institutions shape the limits of functioning of the complex of university institutions by defining models at the level of administration, organization, university politics, and even the production and appropriation of knowledge. In the case of universities in advanced capitalism, some authors have noted that they contributed to the transnationalization of knowledge and to the development of transnational capitalism (Fuenzalida, 1983; Sunkel and Fuenzalida, 1979).

In conclusion, to reduce the multiplicity of the aspects of university life to the cognitive complex is to propose a tour de force, because the empirical reality is adapted to the model of analysis instead of the model of analysis being used as a heuristic instrument for the comprehension of social and educational processes.

THE STRUCTURAL FUNCTIONALIST RESEARCH AGENDA I: ADVANCED SOCIETIES

The Postwar Social-Liberal/Social-Democratic Consensus

Though inadequate to the extent that it implied the disappearance of ideologies as such, the "end-of-ideology thesis" did express an important feature of post–World War II liberal-democratic societies: the combined threats of fascism and Soviet communism brought about a degree of class compromise and cooperation necessary for the construct of the modern welfare state. To this extent liberal (e.g., Daniel Bell, 1962) and radical (e.g., Herbert Marcuse, 1958) interpretations shared certain fundamental perceptions. However historically unique and fragile, this unprecedented form of relative consensus led a certain credibility to the notion of consensus underlying Parsons' theory of society. The dominance of discussions in the United States regarding these issues, a fact arising from the rapid expansion of the social sciences and their relative backwardness and/or devastation by war and economic depression, should not obscure the wider comparative context of advanced societies.

In particular, it is important to stress the way in which functionalist sociology contributed to the reformulation of social democratic party policies in education and other areas. The United States was rather unique in that functionalism was associated with debates within a social-liberal tradition; elsewhere—Canada, Australia, New Zealand, Britain, Scandinavia, the continental democracies—the more strategic debate was the crisis of socialist theory confronted with the failure of revolutionary Marxism.

What is of particular interest is the way in which social democratic policy makers were initially seduced by functionalist educational theory and attempted to use it as a resource for legitimating what were, in the specific contexts in question, relatively radical proposals for educational reform. Before we turn to this context of appropriation of functionalist educational theory, however, it is useful to present the basic tendencies within the more visible and well-known discussions in the United States.

Modernization, Rationalization, and Education: Social Differentiation

In most general terms, advanced societies were approached from a comparative theory of development whose essential outlines are captured in Parsons' theory of pattern variables. Endless subsequent studies (e.g., Parsons and Platt, 1973; Inkeles and Smith, 1974; Fagerlind and Saha, 1983) sought to illustrate this thesis (though most of these studies saw themselves replicating or verifying it), showing how education contributes to the transition of individuals from less developed pattern variables (such as particularism and ascription) to modern ones (such as universalism and an achievement orientation).

As an illustration of another form of this type of research, Herriott and Hodgkins' (1973) elaborate study of formal education as an "open social system" is most instructive. Their study as based on the empirical testing of the general hypothesis that "the degree of modernity of an educational system varies as a function of the degree of modernity of its socio-cultural environment." Needless to say, the result is a rather simplistic model of complex reproduction that suggests that school systems are open systems constantly adapting to changes in the external environment. Here we find combined all of the major themes of the research following the path of Parsons and systems theory: an aspiration for formalization and empirical verification, the notion of the United States as a lead society, the evolutionist theory of rationalization as modernization applied to a static empirical analysis, the attempt to complement Parsonian theory with systems theoretical terminology, and chronic problems of dealing with social change and related issues of inequality and bureaucratization.[7]

Despite the practical tendency to apply functionalist theory in static case studies that merely illustrate the operation of a given set of structures at a moment time, functionalist theory also attempted to develop a larger explanatory model of the development of education systems based on the the model of social differentiation. Though the concept of the "educational revolution" stands at the center of Parsons' evolutionary model, along with the democratic and industrial revolution, he never makes an attempt to systematically elaborate its social history. As he admits, "The three revolutions have developed with different sequential patterns in different societies . . . the three revolutions have tended to unfold in different patterns of complex causal interdependence" (Parsons and Platt, 1973: 398). Yet Parsons' openness on this point verges on an indeterminate formulation and calls into question his reliance on the unique characteristics of developments in the United States as the basis for his general theory.

Dysfunctions: Liberalism and the Problem of Equal Opportunity

Despite the subordinate role of dysfunctional phenomena in Parsons' theory generally and in education in particular, the actual history of post-Parsonian educational research in the United States has been characterized by a preoccupation with the dysfunctional aspects of the operation of schools, especially their relation—along with other social factors—to the reproduction of social and educational inequalities, especially for ethnic and racial minorities, women, and the working class. The origins of these concerns, however, was either more immediately political or generated by empirical status-attainment research, rather than guided by functionalist theory, for which unequal opportunity and racism were residues of the past that actually conflicted with the overall process of instrumental rationalization.

Though structural functionalism has been conventionally characterized by its opponents as "conservative," this term is misleading to the extent it refers either to classical European (Burkean) conservatism or contemporary neoconservatism of laissez-faire (neoliberal) inspiration. Rather, its most immediate roots in political philosophy are the social liberalism that has animated the left wing of the Democratic Party in the twentieth century. This position is thus conservative only in relation to a radical democratic socialist or revolutionary Marxist perspective; as well shall see in a moment, the relation to social-democratic theory is ambivalent.

Here it is necessary to consider the famous Coleman Report (Coleman et al., 1966) which provided one of the first systematic efforts of evaluating (sponsored by the federal Department of Education) the effects of educational subsidies on the equality of opportunity. This report was very important because it provided one of the first great databases for studying phenomena such as the quality of education, learning, and educational mobility at a national level in the United States, and because it appeared at a moment when increases in the federal subsidy to education were the order of the day, due above all, to the War on Poverty promoted by Lyndon B. Johnson in 1964 through the Economic Opportunity Act.

As Jencks and his associates point out, the programs of the War on Poverty are based on assumptions like the following: (a) the elimination of poverty in the United States requires simply helping children born in poor families to escape from their situation (under the presupposition that there is no falling back into poverty); (b) the principle reason why children do not escape poverty is that they do not acquire the basic cognitive competences for succeeding in the world; (c) the best and most efficient mechanism for breaking the vicious cycle of poverty are educational reforms based on compensatory programs for families and neighborhoods to keep them above a minimal acceptable threshold (Jencks et al., 1972: 7–8).

Other critics questioned the manner in which the data on the links between educational resources, the socioeconomic level of families, and educational outcomes were analyzed (Bowles and Levin, 1968: 3–24; Jencks et al, 1972), or how the effects of the environment were accumulative, affecting educational results over time (Stinchcombe, 1969: 511–12).

Another area of research that was sometimes developed from a functionalist perspective was the question of genetic inheritance, the intelligence quotient. and its effects on educational success. In this context the social psychologist Arthur Jensen pointed out that racial differences had to be interpreted in relation to the differences in educational attainment and evidence of IQ differences between Whites and Blacks. Jensen argued that between half and three quarters of the average IQ differences between Black and White Americans could be attributed to genetic factors and the rest to environmental factors and their interaction with genetic ones (Jensen, 1969: 1–123; 1973).

Jensen noted that approximately 80 percent of the variations in the results in IQ tests could be explained by genetic factors over which educational reformers had no control whatever. To be sure, this type of research and its conclusions unleashed a violent wave of criticisms and refutations, whether with respect to the statistical analysis and inferences or considering tests of this type immune to cultural differences and bias given that they represent the dominant (Anglo-Saxon) culture (Jencks et al., 1972; Bowles, Gintis, and Meyer, 1975; Selowsky, 1980).

A final area of research developed by structural functionalism constituted in practice a negation of assumptions regarding the links between education and possibilities of using it for reducing social inequalities. This new area explored the relative independence of different dimensions of social inequality, concluding that educational reforms of the liberal-egualitarian type had little effect in promoting a more egalitarian society. The works of Jencks et al. (1972) and Boudon (1974) provide clear examples. Structuralist reproduction theories developed out of the reaction against the failure of liberal- and social-democratic—to which we now turn—strategies of educational reform.

Dysfunctions and Planning: Social Democracy and Education

Despite its characterization as a "conservative" sociological perspective in the late 1960s, sociological functionalism was considered by most of its proponents as having progressive political implications: it did not conflict with neo-Keynesian economic policies or a mixed economy, was compatible with extensive state planning, and located the advance of personal and civil rights, as well as a movement toward equality of opportunity and economic redistribution, within a broader evolutionary context. Though certain elements of sexism lingered—as evident in Parsons' discussion of primary education—Marxism and the Left generally were not immune from criticism in this regard. In the United States, as we have seen, functionalism was directly engaged in confronting the issues of unequal status attainment and the effects of race in education. Though the functionalist theory of stratification provided a rationale for a certain hierarchy of rewards—hence a rejection of absolute equality—it also required on grounds of efficiency and civil rights, equality of opportunity. The *failure of functionalist educational theory stemmed therefore from an inability to fully explain, let alone suggest a plausible strategy for dealing with, problems of unequal opportunity and the role of the educational process within this.*[8] The general disillusionment with American "liberalism" led leading social theorists either back toward a more pessimistic neoconservative liberalism or to an emergent, if marginal and divided, democratic-socialist Left.

In other advanced, liberal-democratic societies—all of whom were characterized by the existence of a significant social-democratic party with roots in labor, and in some cases a significant Communist Party as well—the reception and appropriation of functionalist theories of education was rather different. In Europe generally, the existence of a conservative tradition in education and politics allowed the American combination of progressive education, comprehensive secondary schools open to all, and tertiary system with relatively open admission standards (contest mobility) to be associated with radical reform. Hence, we find the irony of labor parties supporting policies rationalized—partly because of their effectiveness against the claims of defenders of traditional elitist education—by American functional theory and empirical mobility and status-attainment research.

Most significant here was the case of Britain, where the sociology of education had its roots in the work of Karl Mannheim, who had ended up in exile in England. As Karabel and Halsey (1977) note, in Britain in the 1950s a theory of "technological society" provided the context for educational research, even if there was greater attention given to conflict and the obstacles to change. Yet T. H. Marshall's (1965) influential analysis of the welfare state and the principle of citizenship gave hope for reconciliation of liberty and equality in a democratic society, a theme that had been complemented in Mannheim's work on social planning. Though the existence of a powerful labor movement made equality of opportunity a central theme, the problem of efficiency and the wastage of human resources was also central (Karabel and Halsey, 1977: 10). As Bernstein remarks regarding the institutionalization of the sociology of education at the London School of Economics in the 1950s, there was a complementarity between LSE's ongoing interests in stratification, mobility, and industrial society and the manner in which the sociology of education "could be fitted into a *weak* structural-functionalist approach in the context of social policy and educational planning. This approach did not call for any major rethinking of classical and contemporary sociology in terms of its potential application to a sociology of education" (Bernstein, 1977: 162). This entailed a "weak" version of structural functionalism because in the English context the reality of dysfunctions (an archaic, elitist system) and challenges to consensus could not be denied; as Floud and Halsey noted in their influential review essay in 1958 with respect to the notion of "social integration based on shared values": "This is a difficult notion to apply to developed industrialized societies, even if the notion is interpreted dynamically. They are dominated by social change, and 'consensus' and 'integration' can be only loosely conceived in regard to them" (cited in Bernstein, 1977: 165).

Despite a great number of reforms of English education from 1944 onward, however, the result of Labour Party reforms and their sociological mentors was fundamentally different from the experience of America liberals and the Democratic Party. As more recent critics have put it, the peculiar (and contradictory) fusion of social-democratic politics, technocratic functionalism, and empirical research could not take into account either the relationship between school outcomes and society as a whole, or the cultural processes involving education:

> The main paradox hinged upon the persuasiveness of this record of inequalities as, on the one hand, indicating the goals of policy and, on the other, the inadequacies of the forms of explanation that were adopted to account for these recurring phenomena. In so far as sociology influenced policy, this paradox progressively deepened. Research continued to show that policies, informed by sociological understandings, did not in fact remove inequalities. On the contrary, they seemed to produce, with monotonous regularity, the same or similar educational outcomes. There was a dynamic of self—destruction or, at least, of self-critique at the very heart of the tradition. (Baron et al., 1981: 130)

In Scandinavia, similar paradoxes emerged, but the greater success of the welfare state and less-rigid class differences contributed to less-radical responses. After a long career of research and contributions to educational reform, Husén (1986) is led to conclude with resignation: "We have begun to discover that education is not the Great Equalizer that some nineteenth century liberals hoped it would be" (1986: 256). West Germany initiated, under the impetus of the labor party and sociological research demonstrating the unequal recruitment to universities, a process of "modernization" in the late 1960s, which eventually ground to a halt. The work of Bourdieu was a response to calls for similar reformist policies in France in the 1960s. Even in Canada, the educational research of Porter (1965), otherwise identified as the author of the first major postwar study of social stratification and associated with the social democratic New Democratic Party, advanced reformist suggestions along lines similarly influenced by a British-influenced (he had been a graduate student at LSE) fusion of Fabian politics, functionalist sociology, and empirical stratification research.

In short, the alleged "conservatism" of functionalist educational theory was a limited one, having few affinities with either classic European religious conservatism or that of the laissez-faire New Right. Further, even this "social-liberal" conservatism was not due exclusively to the theoretical model employed, but to the manner of its employment and the general assumptions of the time about education, which were shared, to a great extent, by both the liberal center and the social-democratic left. Such assumptions only became challenged in the late 1960s in the form of the reproduction theories. These "progressive" views were also exported to the Third World, where they were confronted by a situation analogous to the European context where, by comparison to the conservatism of the entrenched oligarchies, structuralist functionalist theories of education were initially radically reformist, progressive, and anti-traditional in their implications.

THE STRUCTURAL FUNCTIONALIST RESEARCH AGENDA II: MODERNIZATION THEORY

As noted in the discussion of the distributive functions of education, it was generally held that educational and economic development were closely correlated, a theme most rigorously developed in human capital theory. In the context of underdeveloped and Third World societies, analogous arguments were applied in the broader context of the theory of "modernization" based on the American and Western European experience. One of its central theses was the assumption that the introduction of the techniques of educational planning and the massification and diversification of the educational system were prerequisites for planned social change, modernization of the social structures, and a high level of sustained development and economic growth. This argument was also closely associated with a complementary conception of the strategic role of communications in development (e.g., Deutsch, 1963; Fagen, 1969). Let us explore the implications of functionalist theory and its linkages with modernity theory in Latin America.

This theory of development, in conjunction with functionalist theories in sociology, dominated the social sciences for most of the 1950s and 1960s. During this period the development and expansion of educational systems acquired unprecedented importance. Between 1960 and 1970, for example, higher education and secondary education registered rates of growth of 247.9 percent and 258.3 percent respectively. For UNESCO, the expansion of education in Latin America represented in the 1970s the highest educational growth rate in the world (UNESCO, 1974; Torres, 1990: 33–45).

In Latin America the most articulate expression of the theory of modernization is found in the work of Germani (1964), who postulated, following the general theory of Parsons (1951), that the transition from a traditional to a modern society was linked to distinct changes in specific social factors. In the first place, it was linked to a change in the types of social action pursued by individuals (Parsons, 1951). This implied that through a process of generalized rationalization a society would move from prescriptive to elective social action (Weber, 1944; Germani, 1964; Parsons, 1951).

In the second place, there would have to be a change in the attitudes of individuals with respect to the process of change itself. This implied a modification of traditions toward a process of institutionalized social change. This entailed a shift from the primacy of primary group structures (with the predominance of affectivity, particularism, diffuse orientations, ascriptive roles, and inner-directed values) toward the primacy of secondary group structures, which possessed values antagonistic to the primary ones: affective neutrality, universality, specificity, a success orientation, achievement values, and other-directed goal direction (Parsons, 1951; Hoselitz, 1960; Germani, 1964).

More generally, education also contributed to the political socialization function, especially to the emergence and consolidation of a stable democratic tradition in developing societies.[9] As a consequence, education not only would prepare strategic social elites for the carrying out of their roles in social modernization, but also would enhance the capacity of all members of society such that the capacity of the entire polis would be maximized (Coleman, 1965). In brief, for the functionalist perspective, modern education contributes to the strengthening of liberal democracy.

Finally, development required a change in the basic social personality of individuals, a change that suggested moving from an inner-directed personality toward an externally directed personality (Germani, 1968). Education was thus considered a variable with unique properties for promoting all (or the grand majority) of these changes in the social structure and the social psychology of individuals (Herbert, 1957). Particularly influential was the concept of "achievement motives," which provided social psychological foundation for the thesis that the primary obstacle to modernization was the inculcation of "modern" attitudes and the changing of political cultures (Torres, 1990: 131–33; Hoselitz, 1960: 23–51).

METATHEORETICAL, METHODOLOGICAL, AND CONCEPTUAL ISSUES: CONCLUSION

As the criticisms of Parsons suggest, many of the problems of his theory are idiosyncratic and ethnocentric, that is, they reflect his personal interpretations and over-reliance upon the model of the United States. Other problems stem from analytical assumptions about the nature of social systems, which have been explored in greater depth in the technical social theory literature. To a great extent, Gouldner's (1971) criticisms remain most telling, and anticipate most subsequent developments. Not surprisingly, Parsons' approach only gets lip-service within the more recent educational literature, even though the dominant ideological assumptions remain very close to the Parsonian position. His delegitimation within sociology, however, has reduced his usefulness for researchers in education. But the functionalist approach is so close to common sense and the consensual center of liberal-democratic political systems that such sophisticated, all-encompassing theoretical legitimation is not necessary. In countries such as Thatcher's Britain or Reagan's United States, crass ideological justifications will do.

Curiously, more recent discussions rarely defend Parsons' educational theory as a whole, or his functionalism. More typical is the use of a kind of generic "systems" framework that allows a comprehensive classification of factors to be accounted for in the sociology of education, without directly offering any explicit hypotheses. Specific issues are discussed in an ad hoc fashion, comparing different theoretical approaches. Typical here is Ballantine's text (1983), which briefly reviews the "theoretical approaches" to the sociology of education under the headings of functionalist theory, conflict theory, and interaction theory. As she notes, "Most research studies focus on parts of the whole system, and most theoretical approaches have biases or limitations. An open systems approach is not a panacea for all the problems we face when trying to get the total picture, but it can help us to conceptualize a whole system and understand how the small pieces fit together into a working unity" (1983: 16). This pluralistic eclecticism is fully revealed in the approach of open systems theory to change: "The open systems approach is based on the assumption that change, whether evolutionary or revolutionary, is inevitable and ever-present in systems" (1983: 365). At least Parsonian functionalism had the courage to advance a specific, provocative conception of the processes of change and stability affecting the transformations of the twentieth century. More generally, however, open systems theory as applied to educational administration has an exclusively reformist and evolutionary orientation (e.g., Hoy and Miskel, 1982; Bates, 1985; Burrell and Morgan, 1979), and hence remains squarely within the functionalist framework.

As the example of Boudon's work demonstrates (1974), work within a systems-functional framework need not have conservative implications; nor need it retreat into the cliches of an open systems theory that tries to be everything for everyone. Indeed, one of the paradoxes of Boudon's research on educational mobility is that it provides an explicit example of a theory of complex reproduction based on multivariate analysis *and* systems model building. Likewise, Smelser's more recent acknowledgement of the importance of competing value systems and interest groups in determining the conditions under which differentiation occurs and is assessed marks an important step toward bases for future convergence between structural-functionalist and conflict-based theories of social and cultural reproduction.

The similarities between the Marxian and mainstream structural-functionalist uses of functional analysis are largely formal, but there are important signs of convergence in some of the more recent literature. The fundamental substantive differences stem from the differing definitions of the internal and external functions of education. Of pivotal importance here is that the structural-functionalist tradition has almost exclusively identified the "functions" of given educational systems, as well as their specific structural form, with the needs of society (defined as instrumental rationality) as a whole. Even where structural functionalists are aware of conflict and disequilibrium, discussion still tends to accept this assumption. Efforts at verification and replication suffered from an inability to find convincing cross-cultural examples of the relationship between educational and societal development (e.g., the modernization literature). More careful and rigorous comparative research, such as that carried out by neo-Weberian conflict theorists (e.g., Collins, 1979), shows quite dramatically the fallaciousness of the assumption of any consistent relationship between the size and type of educational system and rates of growth and development. Education certainly has functions, and certainly "system maintenance" is crucial, but the structural functionalist tradition failed to provide adequate analysis of what those functions are, how they interrelate, the groups and interests they serve, and under what conditions they might be transformed.

Not surprisingly, the revitalization of theoretical research on education has occurred elsewhere than the older functionalist tradition: in theories of social reproduction, studies of the ideological content of the curriculum and resistance to the educational system, and theories of the state. What is at stake is not simply "system maintenance" but sustaining a given system of domination, a concept that has been extensively dealt with by reproduction theories in the strict sense, that is, those theories which point to the intimate *functional* relationship between education and social reproduction (i.e., education and the reproduction of a given set of power, race, gender, class, and economic relations). However, reproduction theories from nonfunctionalist perspectives failed to supersede structural functionalism, and many of them become embroiled with the same type of explanation that functionalism has attempted (Liston, 1988), although couched in the terms of an opposite political and analytical tradition. The next chapter will discuss in detail the contributions of neofunctionalism and morphogenic systems theories.

CHAPTER 4

Neofunctionalism and Education

Rumors of my death are greatly exaggerated.
(Mark Twain, after hearing about the publication of his obituary)

INTRODUCTION: VARIETIES OF NEOFUNCTIONALISM

Though the ostensible decline—if not death—of the functionalist tradition was often noted in the late 1960s and 1970s, its revival in the 1980s suggests the prematurity of such prognoses. In this chapter the notion of *neofunctionalism* used will be somewhat broader than that identified with the self-designation of Alexander and his colleagues (Alexander, 1985b), which might be better described as neo-Parsonian functionalism or *differentiation theory* (Alexander and Colomy, 1990). In addition, two other basic types of neofunctionalism with implications for education will be identified: *positivist neofunctionalism* (e.g., *ecological and adaptation theories*) and *morphogenic systems theory*.

The most visible spokesperson for this revival has been Jeffrey Alexander: "The Parsonian legacy—if not Parson's original theory—has begun to be reconstructed. We are witnessing today the emergence of neo-functionalism, not functionalism exactly, but a family relation" (Alexander, 1985a: 8). He has suggested six key features of this tradition, which link its past achievements and future potential:

1. A general (nonexplanatory) model of society that is open-ended and pluralistic as opposed to monocausal

2. A concern with action as well as structure, and with expressive activity and goals as well as practicality and means

3. Equilibrium—understood in many different ways, both static and dynamic—is a focus for systemic analysis where integration "as a possibility" is analyzed in relation to deviance and social control processes

4. Processes of change and control are studied in the context of the interpenetration of personality, society, and relatively autonomous culture, making socialization a central concern

5. Differentiation is taken to be the central mode of change and a source of individuation and strain

6. Theorizing is preserved as a distinct level of social analysis (Alexander, 1985a: 9–10)

Alexander's characterization of neofunctionalism is misleading, however, to the extent that it neglects a rather different tendency with stronger roots in neopositivist forms of systems theory and ecological models of adaptive competition. Before we turn to the more influential contributions of differentiation theory—and the distinctive variant of morphogenic systems theory—to the sociology of education, it is instructive to briefly consider these positivist varieties of neofunctionalism.

POSITIVIST NEOFUNCTIONALISM

Social Entropy Theory

Despite being colleagues in the department of sociology at UCLA, the neofunctionalisms of Jeffrey Alexander and Kenneth D. Bailey are theoretically worlds apart. The foundation of that difference is the postempiricist metatheory of the former and the preoccupation of the latter with general systems and information theory. Whereas Alexander completely ignores the social entropy approach, Bailey holds out the possibility that "although the model advocated here is essentially a concrete, living system model . . . I can see no way that its use precludes abstracted systems analysis . . . as advocated by Parsons" (1990: 44). On the other hand, Bailey's aversion to non-statistically-based systems theory (implicitly Alexander) becomes apparent at moments: "Some social scientists see themselves as 'theorists' and eschew numerical analysis, while others see themselves primarily as 'statisticians' and pay little attention to verbal analysis. Yet scientists of either persuasion will routinely utilize an interplay of numerical and verbal symbols in their every day life . . . For example, when the verbal theorist, who displays disdain for numerical analysis, goes on a simple trip to the supermarket, this shopping venture will . . . generally entail use of *both* numbers and verbal symbols" (1990: 211). Quite problematic, however, is Bailey's general claim that the occasional use of statistical procedures in everyday life somehow validates grounding a theory of society in terms of a statistical theory of social entropy.

Bailey begins with a question that clearly echoes an implicit dismissal of Alexander's neofunctionalism: "Does the death of functionalism spell the doom of all systems analysis in sociology, or is there a viable nonfunctional approach?" (1990: 15). General systems theory, as pioneered by Bertalanffy and others, is advocated as the way forward, presuming its abstractness and lack of content can be overcome with some of the "social content" provided by functionalism. The result is "an isomorphic concrete systems model." Its specific task as a theory of social entropy is one of rethinking the concept of social equilibrium: "The concept of entropy is efficaciously used as a continuous measure of system state . . . it is much superior to the concept of equilibrium in this regard and actually subsumes equilibrium . . . Further, entropy has a relatively precise statistical formulation, so that it can be successfully operationalized to a degree never attained (nor attempted) by the functionalists in their concept of equilibrium" (1990: 51). Whereas "the concept of entropy lay slumbering in the shadows of sociology for decades . . . its sibling concept of equilibrium was widely applied in functionalism" despite the critiques directed against it (1990: 73). "The thesis of this book is that the sociological entropy literature, both statistical and verbal, is sufficiently large and mature to support substantial theoretical and applied advances" (1990: 74). Perhaps so, but the results appear rather meager for a theory of society.[1]

The value of this approach, according to Bailey, is that it avoids the fallacy of Parsons and Shils, who link *equilibrium* and *order*:

> Thus, Parsons defines *equilibrium as the self-maintenance of order . . . this is simply not correct.* Equilibrium (as opposed to homeostasis or a steady-state) is defined only for an isolated system and only for maximum entropy . . . This means that *true equilibrium is not the maintenance of order but the maintenance of randomization (maximum entropy), which is the most stable and statistically probable state of the system.* Again, all that is needed is to broaden the analysis. Instead of depending upon a dichotomous measure (equilibrium-disequilibrium) that measures constancy but not order, it is obviously necessary to switch

to a broader, continuous, direct measure of the degree of order (defined as departure from randomness). This measure is entropy. (1990: 265)

The outcome is a generic model of society based on six global variables: population size, total information content, total technology possessed, total number of organizational positions, total level of living. Accordingly, "from the standpoint of social entropy theory, it is the *conjunction* or interrelationship of these six globals that is most important, and that constitutes the key to our understanding of complex society . . . These variables can be represented by a system of simultaneous differential equations—this mathematical work remains to be done" (1990: 266).

As the discussion of the epistemological foundations of this approach makes clear, the goal here is a full-blown systems-theoretical version of the positivist project. The central concept here is that of the formal identity or *isomorphism* between model and reality:

> a system model can be made isomorphic with the social system if it has a component to correspond to each of society's components . . . The value of true isomorphism should be evident. If we can construct a model—whether verbal, mathematical, or a combination of both—that truly represents all societal components and their interrelationships, then in effect by understanding the model we should be able to understand the society that it represents. (1990: 20–21)

What differentiates Bailey's approach to systems modeling is his focus on "concrete" rather than "abstracted" systems (as in the case of Parsons). This distinction draws upon a pervasive dichotomy in the social sciences related to the distinction between conceptual and empirical reality: "Among the terms that have been used to signify the conceptual level are *conceptual, abstract, ideal, heuristic, theoretical, definitional,* and *construct.* Among the terms applied to the other level are *empirical, concrete, operational, data, and 'real world'.*" (1990: 22) This two-level model of research is rejected in favor of a three-level model which introduces an "indicator level" between the conceptual and empirical ones. From this epistemological and methodological perspective the project of a concrete systems theory becomes possible. As Bailey concludes:

it seems to be somewhat ironic that an action theorist such as Parsons would advocate the utilization of pattern (abstracted) systems rather than acting (concrete) systems. I believe that Parsons is correct in emphasizing the study of the symbolic elements of society . . . However, we must not be too quick to label all models that are empirically grounded and subject to operationalization as overly empiricist and incapable of properly serving the aims of interpretive and subjective sociology. (1990: 46)

Whatever value Bailey's exercise in model building may have for illustrating the possibilities of entropy statistical analysis for certain other purposes, it does not appear to avoid its "empiricist" shortcomings as a theory of society, and therefore we find little that allows it to serve "the aims of interpretive and subjective sociology" concerned with the relationship between society, education, and social change. As Bailey at one point admits, his approach amounts virtually to a kind of reduction of sociology to "econometrics": "Sociology is better served by utilizing methods that effectively analyze categorical data, and entropy . . . is optimal for this. Indeed, probabilistic analysis of categorical data is clearly the statistical frontier in social science, and entropy is a major generic component of this class of measures . . . Theil calls such methods (including entropy) the *frontier of econometrics* . . . and this is equally true for sociology" (1990: 253). This may indeed be *one* frontier of theory and methodology, but it offers little prospect of the discovery of the El Dorado of social theory.

Dynamic Functionalism and Adaptation Theory

Much closer to the problematic of conventional functionalism is the "dynamic functionalism" proposed by Michael Faia (1986). Here the lure of general systems theory is resisted and there is no attempt to translate equilibrium analysis into statistically based social entropy analysis. But these two approaches share affinities as a form of *positivist* neofunctionalism in their aspiration to formalize equilibrium-type systemic processes with quantitative methodologies.

Two aspects of Faia's approach are suggestive of its positivist underpinnings. First, though acknowledging that functionalist methods can be situated in relation to Merton's manifest-latent function distinction, Faia suggests that the specificity of functionalism lies in its effort to reduce social explanations to latent functions rather than intentions of actors. For this reason "exercises in the sociology of knowledge are not an essential task of functional analysis, because functional analysis is concerned primarily with the consequences of social structures for the survivorship of larger social entities or interests" (1986: 10). In this respect, he rejects the action-structure problematic so central to neo-Parsonian theory. The alternative is a *social selection* (or *ecological*) model of change in place of notion of functional requisites. A focus on social selection process "would force us to define prerequisites more carefully, perhaps even to abandon the notion of prerequisites altogether in favor of the reasonable conviction that certain quantifiable conditions have a measurable impact on quantifiable aspects of social survivorship. Such a perspective would necessarily lead us to adopt the 'variation-and-selective-retention' model." (1986: 26).

The second aspect of Faia's approach is that social selection is viewed in cybernetic terms: "this sort of social selection is a form of negative feedback involving circular causation and 'cybernetic' control" (1986: 24). Ironically, this has not been characteristic of most research labeled "functionalist": "If feedback and circular causation are essential elements of functional analysis, and if, as I believe, these concepts are rarely used in social theory, then it follows that functional analysis has been rarely undertaken" (1986: 5). The reason for this is that functional analysis has been falsely linked to virtually any kind of investigation that attempts to explain social structures in terms of the consequences without adequately referring to feedback and self-regulating processes.

The potential value of this focus on social selection and survivorship is illustrated by organizational analysis and the need for a metric for studying change. "If such a metric were to take the form of life-table analysis, as advocated herein, we would quickly realized the advantages of studying large cohorts of small organizations rather than small cohorts of large organizations. The latter tend to get us caught up in idiographic explanations, when we should be seeking nomothetic levels of explanation" (1986: 29).

More generally, "the major goal of any functionalist inquiry is to clarify the nature, determinants, and consequences of a given time-series process" (1986: 56). Examples of such "process theories" are growth models, diffusion models, ecological models, and cybernetic control processes. From this perspective the kind of catastrophic systems model proposed by the Club of Rome is viewed as analogous to Marxist catastrophe theory: both are engaged in the impossible task of predicting catastrophic transformations: "Social scientists (functionalists and otherwise) do not focus on social stability because they deem it more important than social change; they do so because stability is easier to predict and explain. And even Marxists, with their promising premise that the basic contours of a given social system are always implicit in preceding systems, have achieved little success in predicting fundamental social changes . . . The 'bottom line,' however, is that there is almost nothing in Marxian theory that cannot be incorporated into dynamic functionalism" (1986: 66).

For Faia, one of the most important types of functional theorizing is what he calls "adaptation theories": "Malinowski's theory of magic belongs to a large class of theories that I propose to call *adaptation theories*; that is, it is a theory showing how changes in one sector of a social organization, herein to be called adaptations, help to resolve problems in another sector. Problems (departures from homeostasis) tend to *increase* adaptive efforts, whereas adaptations (when they are effective) tend to *reduce problems*" (1986: 69). Many such theories are reviewed and held to share the assumption of a homeostatic variable—a condition to be maintained —which is followed by an adaptation. As he concludes, following Stinchcombe's account of the logic of functional explanation, such adaptation theories involve "a nearly inescapable commitment to the use of time-series data. Because only those time-series variables that actually vary substantially over time are likely to play an important role in social research, we conclude that *functional analysis is inherently dynamic* in the sense of focusing on social variables that change (i.e., have temporal instability). According to the typical adaptation theory, a social problem (i.e., a disruption of a homeostatic variable) produces adaptive responses; the latter, in turn, diminish the initial problem or disruption"(1986: 87).

The Postwar Expansion of Mass Education: Ecological World Systems Theory

Though Faia does not note any examples drawn from theories of educational systems, it is possible to locate a form of adaptation theory in some theories of educational expansion. This research is grounded in a positivist, methodologically driven problematic: multivariate comparative research on development, as found, for example, in Meyer and Hannan's *National Development and the World System* (1979b). In this respect much, if not all, of the resulting work is very different from the case-study and comparative case-study analysis typical of neo-Parsonian and differentiation theories, even if—as we shall see—it can be identified as a species of neofunctionalism.

On the other hand, the somewhat eclectic theoretical underpinnings of this body of work can be broadly associated with the kind of modernization theory associated with theories of social differentiation. Three kinds of theoretical frameworks intermingle here: reference to ecological models derived from neo-Darwinian theories of organizational competition; institutional analyses that stress the interplay among nation building, the state, and education; and allusions to the importance of the world system context for explaining the post–World War II expansion of educational systems. What all three of these aspects point attention to is the interplay of factors that contribute to environmentally induced (or exogenous) determinants of differentiation and expansion. In contrast, neo-Parsonian differentiation theory focused, as we will see, on endogenous—especially political—factors in differentiation.

We have taken the liberty to loosely identify tendencies as constituting a kind of "ecological world systems theory" for several reasons. First, even though not all of the authors directly identify with Hannan's population ecology model, their accounts rely on it in crucial ways because competition is viewed as the driving force of social selection in the broad similarity of patterns of educational expansion. From Faia's perspective, as noted above, such adaptation or social selection models lie at the core of functionalist theorizing.

In the case of Nielsen and Hannan (1979), a formalized competition model is made explicit with respect to an analysis of educational organizations. In the case of the others, even those who ostensibly work within an institutional perspective, the state's role is closely identified with its adaptive need to compete within the world system (a concept largely used in ways distinct from that of Wallerstein's school). To be sure, such research views itself as a rejection of functionalist modernization theory in finding that "the expansion of educational enrollments was found not to be related to most measures of societal modernization or differentiation" (Ramirez and Rubinson, 1979: 77). Similarly, they reject status-competition or class-conflict models of this process because those models fail to explain two sets of things: the uniformities of educational expansion, and the processes that determine national incorporation of education. They propose instead (following Bendix's a "creating-members model") that "this alternative emphasizes the expansion of state authority and the role of education as a contemporary initiation ceremony and conceptualizes its incorporation and expansion as the national construction of citizenship and its extension through the population" (Ramirez and Rubinson, 1979: 78; see also Ramirez and Boli, 1987).

But the claim to originality here is dubious in suggesting that viewing education's role in national identity formation is an aspect largely overlooked in functional and conflict theories of education. In fact, such an interpretation—though evaluated differently—is broadly in keeping with versions of either functional or conflict theories, even as it provides minor qualifications. For functionalists the role of education in creating the consensus for assimilating ethnic differences in a plural society has always been a central claim. And for conflict theories, the role of education in incorporating the working class through mass education has been a central theme of theories of hegemony, as well as a source of opposition to nationalism as a betrayal of class interests.

The ambitious attempt of Meyer et al. to explain the postwar "educational revolution" through aggregate comparative analysis fails to turn up any significant results: "For our major finding is that national educational systems have expanded from 1955 to 1970 primarily as a function of the population and organizational characteristics of the educational system itself, and not as a function of the political, social, and economic characteristics of countries" (Meyer, et al. 1979: 49). At this point, another explanation is proposed and disconfirmed: that the presence of an independent state might affect educational expansion. But they find no evidence that colonial states have lower educational growth rates and "there are no discernible spurts in the rates of educational growth following the time of political independence" (Meyer, Ramirez and Robinson, 1979: 50).

Though questions could be raised with respect to multivariate methods used, more important for our purposes is the alternative explanatory framework proposed: the world system as a context of social selection. The central theme is that the crucial processes are linked to characteristics of a single world system. Four aspects are noted. First, despite differences in level of development and performance, the universality of national economic goals and their support by international agencies, and the need for a capacity for technical expertise, is acknowledged by all societies. Second, state authority is linked to expanding citizenship, which in turn is linked to educational expansion. Third, a general commitment to "progress" also requires more education. And fourth, we find the linchpin argument that holds the others together:

> all of this occurs in a capitalist world economy in which development occurs from success in economic competition. Elites that do not pursue economic and political development as ends, and education as a means to those ends, are likely to fall from power. They are replaced by more aggressive elites who better conform to the demands of the world market and actively champion its goals and methods. (Meyer et al., 1979: 52)

Or again:

> The world cultural system authorizes states to control national societies and to implement modern institutional forms . . . But the functional need for states to mobilize their populations does not really explain how it happens that they can do so. Here the state system plays an important role, especially in peripheral areas. (Meyer and Hannan, 1979a: 303)

In keeping with other neofunctionalist tendencies, the authors argue that there is nothing inevitable about the capacities of states to fulfill these needs given the multiplicity of technical, material, and demographic factors causing instability. As well, they acknowledge that these processes "may create 'contradictions' that undermine structures" (Meyer and Hannan, 1979a: 304). The authors, however, are less inclined than Faia might like (partly given their aggregating, multivariate methodology) to identity the specific feedback mechanisms and circular processes of causation sustaining educational expansion.

NEO-PARSONIAN DIFFERENTIATION THEORY:
OLD WINE IN NEW BOTTLES?

Introduction: Basic Themes

Whereas the preceding two forms of neofunctionalism are closely linked to variants of positivist presuppositions, the final two are clearly indebted to a postpositivist, postempiricist conception of social theory. This is most explicit in the form of neofunctionalism advocated by Alexander and his associates under the heading of *differentiation theory*, and is part of a broader rethinking of Parsons' contributions (Robertson and Turner, 1991). As Alexander puts it: "Simultaneously a theory of social change and a theory of modernity, differentiation theory, like its intellectual cousin functionalism, is currently experiencing a significant resurgence" (1990a: xiii). But whereas the older Parsonian differentiation theory stressed the role of differentiation as a master trend linked with the specialization of institutions, the new version supplements this with "the description and analysis of several distinct patterns of change, particularly backlash movements against differentiation" (1990a: xiii). Second, it suggests "replacing a problem-solving and societal need approach with a more political model that emphasizes group conflict, power, and contingency." Third, "the benign assessment of the consequences of differentiation, which stresses adaptive upgrading and greater efficiency, is balanced by the recognition that differentiation often generates discontents" (1990a: xiii). And finally, "the liberal optimism that infused Parsons' treatment of differentiation is replaced with a 'critical modernism,' which provides a standard for evaluating and criticizing existing societal arrangements" (1990a: xiv). Alexander himself poses the question we would like to pursue further here in a preliminary way: "The movement to reappropriate Parsons in a neofunctionalist way is gaining momentum. Whether it is simply old wine in new bottles, or a new brew, is something history will decide" (1985a: 16).

This revival can be traced to the ability of a younger generation to question Parsons' authority (e.g., Alexander, 1983); a neoconservative political climate that makes his reformist liberalism less ideologically suspect; important European contributions to renewed debate, especially in Germany; and the sophistication of the original Parsonian schema (Alexander, 1985: 10–11). The resulting "neo"-functionalism, "less a theory than a broad intellectual tendency," is held to parallel neo-Marxism because it similarly involves a critique of the original theory; incorporates aspects of apparently opposing theoretical traditions; and assumes a multiplicity of often competing forms (1985: 11).

This involves a response to the ideological and epistemological critiques. In place of Parsons' idealism, neofunctionalists assume some version of epistemological multidimensionality. Given that "virtually every contributor pushes functionalism to the left," neofunctionalism also suggests a move toward "ideological critique" in "warning against Parsons' optimism about modernization," strongly demanding a democratic public life, and in certain forms (which will not be taken up here) effecting versions of "functionalist-Marxist" integration. Nevertheless, Alexander has been charged by an otherwise sympathetic critic with not having adequately dealt with the fact-value question and the moral bases of theorizing, and "more importantly, we have yet to see how neofunctionalism will deal with postmodernism, deconstructive strategies and antifoundationalist epistemology" (Turner, 1991: 246).

Substantively, revival has been associated with responding to the challenges of conflict and interactionist approaches. One result is that Alexander can claim that his contributors all engage in "a 'conflict theory' of one sort or another"; and "these references to conflict, moreover, are often accompanied by an emphasis on contingency and interactional creativity" (1985: 15). Thus, Alexander can conclude with the claim that this tradition represents a "coordinated revision" exemplifying the possibilities of "scientific accumulation":

> The idea of a system with interrelated and relatively autonomous parts, the tension between ends and means, the reference to equilibrium, the distinction between personality, culture, and society, the sensitivity to differentiation as a master trend, and a commitment to independent theorizing—all of these basic fundamentals of 'functional' thinking permeate the chapters . . . Ideological critique, materialist reference, conflict orientation, and interactional thrust can in this way emerge as relatively coherent variations on a theme. (1985a: 15)

Given the limited contributions of this tradition to the sociology of education at this point, it is useful to consider some of the implications of related domains, for example, ethnic inclusion, the mass media, and the democratic state. Further, our discussion will focus on the specifically American contributors directly influenced by Alexander's example. Some contributions rely heavily on arguments that draw strongly on neo-Marxist and critical-theory arguments, and do not clearly fall into the neofunctionalist fold (Gould, 1985). Further, the German contributions are characterized by more general theoretical ambitions (Luhmann, 1990) which do not appear to have directly influenced the American contributions at this point. The most visible international figure in this context has been the work of the West German sociologist Niklas Luhmann (1982), who has drawn upon the concept of "complexity reduction" as part of a far-reaching critique of Parsons and a further development of some of his key themes.[2]

Ethnicity

Though Alexander (in contrast to Parsons) stresses the uneven and historically variable nature of processes of ethnic inclusion (i.e. the importance of "group interest, differential power, uneven development, and social conflict" (1990a: 288), his argument remains squarely within the progressive evolutionary framework of Parsonian theory. And though his analysis provides some valuable insights into a comparative analysis of some sources of variations in this process, his "multidimensional" stress on the autonomy of ethnic phenomena does not really overcome the problems he associates with Marxist class reductionism and theories of internal colonialism. In the process of stressing the autonomy of ethnicity, he effectively suppresses such factors in the name of multidimensionality. As a contribution to current debates about race relations in the United States or elsewhere, this approach does not entail anything more than qualifications and extensions of Parsonian theory.

Mass Media

Even more revealing is Alexander's account of the mass media, which is polemically directed against three other approaches: the tendency of mass society and critical theory to stress the strong impact of the media on individuals, thus discounting the normative reality of secondary institutional life; the "weak media" model of classical media studies based on the two-step flow model concerned with the effects of specific media events; and the orthodox Marxist ruling-class model, which sees the media as an instrument of the dominant class, thus overlooking the strategic importance of voluntary action in the media system (Alexander, 1990c: 335–36). Instead, Alexander develops the paradoxical argument that the highly differentiated media system is in fact open and responsive, but confronted with an inadequately differentiated political system. In this respect, the media system reflects the society around it:

> Because of its very flexibility and integrative power a differentiated news medium cannot be an explicit "organizer" of norms in the way that institutions in other dimension often are: it cannot formulate goals, which is a political responsibility, or basic values, which is a cultural one. In my view, the lack of sharp political focus and perspective in American political news is not a dire commentary on the impact of differentiation on the news media but rather a reflection of the inadequate autonomy achieved by the American political system . . . and particularly the inability of political parties to articulate and maintain distinctive political positions. (1990c: 357)

As a consequence, "the pervasive public criticism of what are mistakenly regarded as instances of inflation of the media's political role can result in the deflation of what is, in itself, a relatively 'healthy' social institution" (1990c: 359).

The Public Sphere and Democracy

Some of the ideological implications of neofunctionalist differentiation theory become even more apparent in Mayhew's analysis of the "differentiation of the solidary public," which is directed against Habermas' conception of the democratic public sphere. For Mayhew, the differentiated public sphere is necessarily linked with the system of stratification but is sufficiently open to provide for gradual change:

> The public, as I have conceptually defined it using Parsons' approach to influence, is inherently a stratified entity. It exists because persons exercise influence based upon their status. . . Systems of influence imply influential people.

The alternative—a completely egalitarian system of communication—implies an impossible burden of dialogue. It is always more efficient to take a certain amount for granted. (1990: 317)

As Mayhew admits, beyond the question of "efficiency," of crucial importance here is the value given to the various issues at stake in dialogue or its absence:

The "importance" of the various demands depend on the perspective and values of the observer . . . It is not difficult to understand why radical critique would be unsympathetic to a conception that takes the public to be an influence system structured by the prestige of leaders within an established social structure.

It is more difficult to accept the radical presumption that social change through the mobilization of public sentiment requires egalitarian communication. The entire history of the differentiation of the public as a political instrument argues against such a supposition . . . The vanguard institution of full differentiation—the strongest egalitarian force—within an emerging differentiated public is the rise of the specialized leadership role. In this context a "specialized" leader is one whose livelihood and career is solely dependent on appeals to the influence market and not on the sponsorship of elite patrons or on his or her own status in a system of stratification . . . The fully differentiated public would be led by free-lance careerists—for better or for worse. Empirical studies of the public could well focus on the careers of such persons as Ralph Nader, Martin Luther King, John Gardner, and Barry Commoner, with special attention to their relative independence, their success in creating constituencies, and the extent of their effectiveness in producing social change . . . Hence the public is not entirely differentiated but reproduces the stratification of the larger society in its own structure. (1990: 318–20)

This emphasis on single issues and individual leadership continues the older functionalist habit of overgeneralizing particular American phenomena. In the process, the broader significance of the new social movements is lost and instead we find apologetics for the close link between inequality and differential political influence—all in the name of efficiency and evolutionary imperatives. At least Alexander's apologetics for the American mass-media system was coupled with an acknowledgment of weakness in the political system. The degree to which neofunctionalist differentiation theory engages in a "critical modernism" is thus quite variable and limited.

DIFFERENTIATION AND EDUCATION

Primary Education

Smelser, one of Parsons' early and most creative students, has reviewed the model of structural differentiation underlying his and Parsons' work and sought to revise it in the context of an analysis of a comparison of nineteenth-century primary educational systems in Britain and the United States (Smelser, 1985, 1990). Education is taken to be a good case for reassessing the theory of social differentiation because of the way in which formal education involves a clear case "of structural differentiation from other social-structural and organizational forms" (1985: 114). A comparison of the origins of primary education in the United States and Britain suggests itself precisely because the differences in the educational systems and the resulting difficulties posed for the conventional differentiation model (including his own early research on the industrial revolution).

On the basis of this educational comparative case study, Smelser found it necessary to "extend" the structural differentiation model in significant ways. The original conception was based on an assumption fully explicated only in Parsons' later work: the notion of society as a problem-solving entity oriented toward instrumental rationality. As a consequence, sequences of differentiation were associated with crises affecting productive requirements. Smelser finds several important problems in his earlier application of this model. First, he calls into question the notion of a consensus (the "dominant value-system of the time") for not taking into account change over time and the fact of competing value systems. Further, he notes that he did not adequately specify the "elements of the population" that expressed dissatisfaction, and now he describes them as primordial (religious, ethnic, etc.,) and functional (class, status, etc.) groups. Third, public authorities were seen to be neutrally reacting to protest, rather than actively engaged in and divided by the issues at stake. And finally, it was automatically assumed that the new, more differentiated institutional arrangements were more effective, but "given what has been said about competing systems of legitimation and competing primordial and functional groups, it follows that the creation of new educational structures is *also* a political victory, compromise, or defeat (or all three) worked out in the context of group conflict" (1985: 122). As he concludes, a new model of change is necessary:

> The ultimate "fate" of the emerging structural arrange-
> ments, therefore, depends only in part on the relative "effective-
> ness"; it depends on the kinds and levels of resources that contin-
> ue to be made available to it and on the relative position and
> strength of the contending political groupings whose interests are
> accommodated (and those whose interests are not) by the new
> structural arrangements. Thus a principle of differentiation along
> "interest" lines is invoked in addition to a principle of differen-
> tiation along "performance" lines. This principle promises to
> yield a more comprehensive and detailed account of the shape of
> emerging educational arrangements. (1985: 124)

A more recent study reaffirms this basic strategy. Though accepting the notion that modern societies are characterized by similar types of school systems and the functionalist explanation given
for that, Smelser goes on to argue "that neither tells us very much
about the social and political *process* by which schooling becomes
established" (1990: 166). In other words, there is a significant
discrepancy between the intentions of the agents who created the
system and the outcome. In his case study, for example, Smelser
considers the delay in the differentiation of primary education at
the working-class level in nineteenth-century Britain, a process he
attributes to the specific circumstances of the working-class family.
As he concludes, the history of primary schooling in this case "can
be regarded more accurately as a process emerging in a complicated three-way tug-of-war among profound social forces puling in
opposite direction than as a series of functional adaptation as we
usually understand them" (1990: 184). Economic forces inhibited
the process; reformist political forces facilitated it; and though
religious groups were supportive, their internal differences slowed
the process of state intervention. Little that is specifically functionalist remains in this kind of argument.

Political Competition in Higher Education

Rhoades' comparative study of differentiation in four university
systems (United States, France, Sweden, England) from 1960 to
1980 is instructive, in part because it largely concludes (though
this it not fully admitted) that differentiation theory does little to
explain the different patterns (Rhoades, 1990). Because differentia-

tion theory has traditionally focused on the *effects* of differentiation (largely viewed in terms of system needs, and the resulting
increases in efficiency or adaptive capacity), little attention has
been paid to its *causes*. Consequently, "for the most part sociologists have treated the process as if it were guided by an 'invisible
hand' than by the state's and social group's quite visible hands.
General societal trends are adduced to explain differentiation;
agency is relatively ignored" (1990: 187). Differentiation is thus
explained in terms that bypass the political realm: "If it is not
treated as a process of biological growth and/or of natural adaptation resolving 'strain,' then competition is invoked as the driving
engine" (1990: 188). Instead, Rhoades draws on recent work—
along the lines suggested by Smelser—to suggest that "agency
must be incorporated into explanations of differentiation if we are
to understand particular cases of that process. The proximal cause
of differentiation in higher education systems at least, lies in state
and group political actions" (1990: 189). His conclusion, in fact,
conflicts with differentiation theory: "Contrary to differentiation
theory's underlying logic, this paper suggests that differentiation in
higher education is largely the product of political competition and
state sponsorship, and that the 'natural' trend is toward dedifferentiation" (1990: 188).

The results of Rhoades' comparative analysis are mixed: "The
predisposing climate did not yield the expected harvest. Differentiation proceeded in the four higher education systems at different
rates and in different directions than might have been expected
given the general trends they had experienced" (1990: 211). Accordingly, this paper "suggests that in higher education if general
trends have a broad predisposing influence their effects depend on
how they are perceived and acted upon by human agencies. Differentiation is activated and actuated through political competition
between academics and lay groups. And an undertow drags the
system toward dedifferentiation" (1990: 211). In this case, not
only is there little left of the differentiation model: aspects have in
fact been refuted.

Differentiation vs. Social Reproduction

A recent collection of work on the rise of the modern European
educational system illustrates some of the important points of affinities and difference between neofunctionalist differentiation the-

ory and (largely) non-Marxist conflict models of social reproduction (Müller, Ringer and Simon, 1987). Ringer and Müller and most of their other contributors start from the assumption that "the economic functionalist approach to educational change is seriously flawed in several respects," for example, problems of linking particular curricula with particular technical or business interests; and the relatively low status given to scientific and technical education, especially on the part of the dominant classes. Accordingly, the editors are forced toward what we will later call a class-reproductive model: looking at the transformations in later nineteenth- and early twentieth-century educational systems "primarily in terms of their *social effects,* rather than primarily in terms of their *economic causes.* The educational systems that emerged from the structural changes of that crucial period, it seems to us, ended by perpetuating and reinforcing the hierarchical organisation of their societies, and we really want to ask just how this came about" (Ringer, 1987: 3). For this purpose they refer to Pierre Bourdieu's theory of social reproduction and cultural capital, which shifts attention away from individual mobility toward "the re-creation of hierarchical social relationships over time, or from parental to filial generations . . . Indeed, what is reproduced, according to Bourdieu, is always a set of *relative* advantages and disadvantages, positions in a set of class *relationships,* not absolute quantities of economic, social or cultural capital" (Ringer, 1987: 4). But Bourdieu's model (which will we will consider in a subsequent chapter) is criticized for its unhistorical character, and it is suggested that—rather than timelessly fulfill its reproductive function—the relationships between education and various forms of capital have operated differently at different times and places. The resulting historical case studies trace some of these variations in Germany, France, England, and elsewhere.

What is interesting in the present context is the attempt by Schriewer and Harney (1987) to reconcile this conflict model of class reproduction with a systems theoretical differentiation theory. Again, we see the claim on the part of neofunctionalists to have incorporated conflict into their theory of change, but from the perspective of a more general theory of differentiation.

Several grounds for such a translation make it plausible. First, the neofunctionalist emphasis on conflict, political processes, group interests, and the uneven character of differentiation opens the way to recognizing phenomena of the type identified by Bourdieu's approach. Second, the unifying thesis of reproduction is an issue which in somewhat different terms has indeed been central to systems theories, as we have seen. Third, as historians of education the authors tend to develop their analyses primarily "as an account of determinants specific to a unique historical context," despite the apparent unifying theoretical notion of social reproduction:

> If the reproduction thesis is actually to structure a comparative study, a kind of systematic translation must relate the general level of theory to that of middle-range constructs, which in turn will make it possible to identify functionally equivalent indicators in various historical contexts by a methodical procedure open to review. For if the findings of the comparative social history of education are not to be limited to the repetition of general similarities, this field of study should be able to explain precisely why, for example, secondary education in Germany was shaped into a hierarchy of clearly differentiated institutions with differentiated curricula, while the English pattern was characterized by institutional and curricular adaptation to a single standard model. (Schriewer and Harney, 1987: 205)

From this perspective, such historical approaches tend to focus on "exogenous" explanations: those, for example, related to issues of stratification and social reproduction at the expense of being "integrated into an embracing sociological theory" of the type proposed by Niklas Luhmann:

> Problems of *comparative methodology* are avoided by recourse to theoretically defined concepts that are not context-bound and are hence suitable for comparisons. Problems of *systematic conceptualisation* are avoided by acknowledging in a non-reductive way the "systemic" nature of educational systems. Problems of *interpretive theory* are avoided by extending the range of explanatory references and taking into account both the autonomy of systems and their dependence on the outer environment. (Schriewer and Harney, 1987: 206)

Such systems theory thus links up conceptions of sociocultural evolution with those of the increasing capacity of societies to deal with environmental complexes through internal differentiation, which does not allow giving only one function primacy as in Bourdieu's model. From the differentiation perspective, the crucial process is that of "inclusion" in the shift from stratification to functional differentiation:

> In place of a structured hierarchy of unequal subsystems based on social classes, the primary scheme of societal organisation is not in principle the equal access of everybody *to* every *subsystem* . . . Therefore "inclusion" and the "selective focusing of interactive and communicative processes on special societal functions" are the decisive features necessary for theoretically defining "educational system" and "system formation," *not* the historically context-bound features of administrative standardisation or organisational co-ordination. (Schriewer and Harney, 1987: 208)

Again, differentiation theory does not appear to take us much beyond Parsonian functionalism with its stress upon the evolutionary uniqueness of knowledge societies and its apologetic implications for high levels of inequality and social stratification.

Morphogenic Systems Theory: Culture and Agency

The work of Margaret Archer has a unique position within sociological theory and the sociology of education in particular. Though known originally primarily as a sociologist of education, she has emerged recently as an important social theorist (Archer, 1988), as perhaps reflected in her election to the presidency of the International Sociological Association. On the other hand, her research has not enjoyed the prominence one would expect in the sociology of education, even though that has been the primary focus of her empirical research (Archer, 1984). For example, her contributions are not referenced by those working within the framework of neofunctionalism (Alexander, 1985b), largely because she has pursued the morphogenic strain of systems theorizing represented by Buckley and Etzioni, rather than that of Parsonian structural functionalism. Even more surprisingly the differentiation theorists writing on education—despite their focus on the state—do not refer to Archer (Smelser, 1990; Rhoades, 1990). Nor is her work mentioned in most reviews of the sociology of education (e.g., Hurn, 1985) or by radical critics of functional analysis in education (Liston, 1988). Even more surprising is the complete omission of her work by those working within the tradition of comparative historical European research on educational systems (e.g., Müller, Ringer, and Simon, 1987)[3]—the primary focus of her own empirical work (comparative research on Britain, France, Russia, and Denmark).

In order to grasp the significance of her approach, we will first situate it within the distinctive tradition of morphogenic systems theory, which attempts to deal with problems of change and transformation neglected in more traditional systems models. Second, we will discuss the ambitious application of her approach to the social origins of European educational systems. And finally, we will touch upon some of the problems of morphogenic theories in general, and her most original approach to the problematic of culture and agency.

Basic Concepts

Though in his later work Parsons drew selectively upon concepts drawn from cybernetics (the study of self-regulating systems, including purely physical ones) and systems theories, he saw these as merely confirming and complementing the basic insights to be derived from the study of homeostatic biological systems. Yet some social scientists have followed Walter Buckley in contending that the Parsonian emphasis on equilibrium represents a rather simplistic use of systems concepts, one which does not fully incorporate the insights of general systems theory and cybernetics. From the perspective of the more general theory of self-regulation inspired by cybernetics, for example, equilibrium processes are characteristic primarily (like homeostasis) of lower-level organic phenomena, not the more open, complex adaptive systems of social life. On this basis Buckley argued that equilibrium models are most applicable to stable systems that tolerate limited variations of disturbance, representing what can be called simple reproduction. Yet this type of homeostatic model is insufficient to comprehend more complex systems, which require a "complex adaptive system model" that allows the understanding of why such organizations have the capacity to elaborate new structures and in fact "thrive on" highly disturbing environments (Buckley, 1967: 40).

Of particular importance to students of complex adaptive systems is the distinction between *morphostatic* processes (which correspond to the lower level controls associated with equilibrium, homeostasis and negative feedback) and *morphogenic* processes, which "tend to elaborate or change a system's given form, structure, or state . . . biological evolution, learning, and societal development are examples of 'morphogenesis'" (Buckley, 1967: 58–59). Clearly the concept of morphogenesis relates to the problem of complex reproduction and even transformation, and provides an important alternative to the older mechanical functionalist equilibrium models and a challenge to structuralist-type approaches, as Archer (1982) has argued.

Several distinctive features of Archer's theoretical approach suggest that it falls outside any simple notion of neofunctionalism as a unitary tendency. We have located it here primarily because of its explicit reliance on aspects of systems theory. Yet these distinctive features need to be stressed.

First, central to her approach is the problem of agency and structure in a manner that is paralleled by Alexander's neofunctionalism and opposed to the positivist variants discussed earlier: "The problem of structure and agency has rightly come to be seen as the basic issue in modern social theory" (Archer, 1988: ix). Hence, the association with systems theory should not obscure the crucial actional component of this approach as a theory of "structural elaboration."

Second, this strategy of analysis has a strongly historical aspect that cautions against classifying it as a form of positivist neofunctionalism (despite the influence of systems theory). As opposed to the kind of abstracted general theory dominant in the Parsonian tradition or even in neofunctionalist differentiation theory, her approach as applied to education has a crucial historically specific dimension: it applies only to highly differentiated institutional orders with relatively autonomous and differentiated interest groups (1984: 12–3). Of those associated with neofunctionalist differentiation theory, her approach is probably closest in spirit to that of S. N. Eisenstadt.

Third, her approach is associated with a broader, morphogenic theory of culture and cultural elaboration designed to unify structural and cultural analysis. However, aspects of her approach were developed subsequent to her comparative educational research. The central theme here is the relation between agency and culture, thus extending discussion beyond the more familiar agency-versus-structure question. As she notes: "The conceptualization of culture is extraordinary in two respects. It has displayed the weakest analytical development of any key concept in sociology and it has played the most wildly vacillating role within sociological theory" (1988: 1).

More specifically, she proposes to apply her morphogenic model of change to culture, and to extend Lockwood's distinction between the levels of "social integration" and "system integration" to the cultural sphere:

> Hence the morphogenic perspective is not only dualistic but sequential, dealing in endless three part cycles of Structural Conditioning–Social interaction–Structural Elaboration. The suggestion is that this framework be transferred to the cultural field, using equivalent analytical phases (i.e., Cultural Conditioning–Socio-Cultural Interaction–Cultural Elaboration), in order to unravel the dialectical interplay of culture and agency over time. (1988: xxii)

The key to this strategy is the assumption of analytical dualism in the context of culture, following Lockwood:

> Lockwood insisted on the possibility and profitability of distinguishing the orderly or conflictual relations pertaining between groups of actors (the degree of social integration) from the orderly or contradictory relations prevailing between parts of the social structure (the degree of system integration). The point of the exercise was to theorize about the *interplay* between them, for he rightly argued that neither element alone provided the sufficient conditions of structural change. (1988: xiv)

On this foundation she proposes to deal with the chicken-and-egg question left unresolved by arguments about the relative autonomy of structure and culture (the Fallacy of Conflation), which establishes their relative importance at any given time:

> Analyzing both structure and culture from the morphogenic perspective allows one to get to grips with these problems. By utilizing this common framework it becomes easier to see *how* structure and culture intersect in the middle element of their respective morphogenetic cycles: through structural-interest groups endorsing some corpus of ideas in order to advance their material concerns but then becoming enmeshed in the situational logic of that part of the cultural domain; and through ideal-interest groups seeking powerful sponsors to promote their ideas but then immediately embroiling cultural discourse in power-play within the structural domain . . . The final step, then, is to argue that the question "when does structure exert more influ-

ence over culture and vice versa?" is one which now becomes amenable to solution. (1988: xxvi)

This dualistic methodological position leads to a critique of the two dominant forms of conflation: upward (where either imposed by dominant groups or spontaneously arising as an expression of unconstrained agency) and downward (from a central values system or code). Both are based on the "myth of cultural integration" stemming from the conflation of the distinction between system and social integration at the level of culture.

The third possibility is "central conflations" (e.g., Giddens, Bauman), where elision takes place in the "middle":

> Instead what happens is that autonomy is withheld from both "parts" and "people" and this has precisely the same effect of precluding any examination of their interplay. Here the properties of cultural systems and the properties of cultural interaction are conflated because they are presented as being so tightly constitutive of one another . . . Once again the net effect of conflation is that the possibility of gaining explanatory leverage on cultural dynamics from the interplay between "parts" and "people" is relinquished from the outset. (Archer, 1988: xiii–xiv)

The approach to cultural analysis . . . can thus be summarized in the following propositions:

> (i) There are logical relationships between components of the Cultural System (CS).
> (ii) There are causal influences exerted by the CS on the Socio-Cultural (S-C) level.
> (iii) There are causal relationships between groups and individuals at the S-C level.
> (iv) There is elaboration of the CS due to the S-C level modifying current logical relationships and introducing new ones.
> Taken together they sketch in a morphogenetic cycle of Cultural Conditions–Cultural Interaction–Cultural Elaboration. Cycles are continuous: the end-product of (iv) then constitutes the new (i) and begins another cycle of cultural change. Separating out the propositions in this way is prompted by the adoption of analytical dualism: its profitability must be judged by the explanation of cultural dynamics which results from it. (1988: 105–6)

The Social and Cultural Origins of Educational Systems

Archer begins her study of the social origins of state educational system in Europe with two "deceptively" simple responses to the two basic macroscopic questions that guide her approach to the question of why educational systems have "the particular structure, relations to society, and internal properties" at a given point in time, on the one hand, and "why do these characteristics change," on the other: (1) "education has the characteristics it does have because of the goals pursued by those who control it"; and (2) "change occurs because new goals are pursued by those who have the power to modify education's previous structural form, definition of instruction, and relationship to society" (1984: 1). The most obvious implications of these responses is a neo-Weberian critique of methodological functionalism of various types, which "embodies implicit beliefs in hidden hands, evolutionary mechanisms, infrastructural determinism, and spontaneous adjustments to social change". From this deterministic perspective, all education is held to be adaptive to social requirements that "metaphysically" respond to the demand of society rather than individuals. Yet her alternative is not a pure voluntarism: "our theories will be *about* the educational activities of people, even though they will not explain educational development strictly in terms of people alone" (1984: 2).

The neo-Weberian aspect of this general perspective (a tendency also evident in some forms of neofunctionalist differentiation theory) is evident in the stress upon the thesis that educational forms are "political products of power struggles": "Thus to understand the nature of education at any time we need to know not only who won the struggle for control, but also how: not merely who lost, but also how badly they lost out" (1984: 2). To be sure, this struggle is shaped by certain logical constraints (e.g., the existing state of knowledge, skills, and resources) and the historically specific cultural and structural factors that constitute its environment.

This approach differs from certain interpretations of Weber in that it is developed from the perspective of a subtle conception of "methodological collectivism" (shared in different ways by "neo-Marxists, general functionalists, systems theorists, and proponents of exchange theory") as opposed to "methodological individualism"—one of the reasons it can be classified as an open functionalist model (1984: 4–5). The key aspect here is the treatment of the relationship between structural conditions (the level of systems integration) and social interaction (the level of social interaction), or (broadly) the relation between structure and agency. Whereas methodological individualists hold that change can be explained adequately at the level of social interaction, collectivists insist in different ways about the priority of structure as the context of interaction.

The most original aspect of Archer's approach, however, is her effort to avoid the functionalist determinism of either orthodox structural-functionalist or structuralist-Marxist approaches. Her alternative is based on viewing change in terms of a three-part morphogenic cycle (composed of structural conditioning, social interaction, and structural elaboration) in which *time* is viewed as a crucial dimension:

> Time is incorporated as a theoretical variable rather than simply as a medium in which events, like the progressive structuring of an educational system, necessitates our theorizing about the temporal relations between structure and action. What is crucial is that the macro-sociological perspective maintains that structure and action operate over different time periods—an assertion which is based on two simple propositions: that structure logically predates the action(s) which transform it; and that structural elaboration logically post-dates those actions. (1984: 8)

It is beyond our concerns here to trace in detail the historical application of this model to a comparative analysis of the social origins of educational systems in Europe (especially Britain, France, Germany, Denmark, and Russia). Yet is appropriate to acknowledge that it provides a powerful framework for understanding the specific mechanisms and processes of educational change, giving particular insight into the emergence and characteristics of decentralized as opposed to centralized educational systems and how the interplay between structural conditions and social interaction produces structural elaboration. In short, no comprehensive historical sociology of education can ignore either the usefulness of her open-ended and flexible morphogenic model or the specific results of her examination of the origins of European educational systems. In contrast to the neofunctionalist differentiation theorists of education, her emphasis on political factors does not erode altogether any relation to functionalism given her morphogenic perspective on social (and more recently, cultural) change. But this is not a familiar form of neofunctionalism given its explicit neo-Weberian presupposition of a theory of domination.

Of particular interest from the perspective of a critical sociology of education is her account of the dynamics that ensure domination, as well of the conditions of "assertion" at the level of social interaction. Given its partial origin in Weberian conflict theory, the resulting analysis broadly converges with social-closure conflict theory, which will be examined later. As she points out (in a manner that deviates from her normal value-neutral stance), only through understanding the necessary conditions of assertion can domination be overcome "to evade its constraints, to reject its ideology, and to damage its monopoly" (1984: 47). Though she avoids the loaded language of "counter-hegemony," her analytical categories often converge with both social-closure theory and neo-Gramscian theory:

> Ideology is a central factor in challenging domination, since the legitimation of educational control must be negated by unmasking the interests served, thus reducing support for the prevailing definition of instruction. Secondly, it is crucial in legitimating assertion itself and is thus related to the consolidation of bargaining power. Finally, it is vital for the specification of an alternative definition of instruction, the blueprint which will be implemented in schools if the assertive group is successful. (1984: 51)

The basis of the superiority of her approach over that of Parsonian structural functionalism and neofunctionalism generally is thus to synthesize action and structural theories by retaining their core premises in such as way as to preserve a capacity for understanding social change, an understanding otherwise lacking in the functionalist tradition: "Action theory is held to be incomplete because it has to take the social context of action for granted, and structural theories are considered equally inadequate if they make no reference to social interaction, but instead perpetuate an empty form of determinism" (1984: 4). What is of particular interest here is that in general terms Archer's formulation captures the essential principle of an adequate historical sociology of education, one that is in principle compatible with a critical sociology of education even if she defines it in relation to a neo-Weberian and morphogenic systems perspective: "In other words, it is argued that an adequate sociology of education must incorporate statements about the structural conditioning of educational interaction and about the influence of independent action on educational change. Weber's analysis, which gives equal emphasis to the limitations that social structures impose on interaction and to the opportunity for innovatory action presented by the instability of such structures, is the prototype of this theoretical approach" (1984: 4).

At this point, Archer has not fully reconnected her more recent analysis of *cultural* elaboration with that of *social* elaboration stressed in her earlier work. Nevertheless, the many examples drawn from education to illustrate cultural elaboration are suggestive of some of the implications. As she notes, there is a fundamental difference between structural and cultural elaboration, despite the applicability of both to the three phases of the morphogenetic cycle. Structural elaboration, whether of society as a whole (the feudalism to capitalism transition) or to a part (the origins of a state educational system from private ownership of education), has the advantage of being "once and for all":

> Thus, until a corpus of work exists which, having forged its own concepts appropriate to cultural entities, events, and changes, then provides equivalent substantive studies of cultural configurations, we are confined to generalities, to discussion of a generic sequence, and to the elucidation of general similarities characterizing both Structural and Cultural Elaboration when suggesting the possibility of theoretical unification between them. (1988: 280)

Commentary

Why, it might be asked at this point, have we insisted upon locating Archer's approach here, under the heading of a sophisticated form of "neofunctionalism," given its overtly neo-Weberian tendencies and Weber's well-known rejection of functionalist explanation and action orientation?

The answer is fourfold: (1) the use of morphogenic models (derived from systems theory) to understand innovation as "structural" and "cultural elaboration"; (2) the suppression of any critical emancipatory interest that guides the selection of research questions or definition of crucial terms (e.g. domination); (3) as a consequence of the above, an empirical analysis of the class dynamics of the formation of state systems that obliquely obscures aspects of the hegemonic character of the modern capitalist state and crucially deflates its "democratic" pretensions; and (4) the research questions and policy implications of analysis are thus restricted at the outset by these metatheoretical and substantive decisions.

(1) As noted previously, morphogenic systems models have a decisive advantage over the homeostatic models of traditional functionalism and systems theory. But it may be questioned whether appeal to morphogenesis as a way of understanding structural elaboration in education has anything more than metaphorical significance, at least until it is more clearly connected with her more recent account of *cultural elaboration*. In other words, since structural elaboration is viewed by Archer as a completely historically contingent process resulting from the struggles shaped by structural conditions and social interaction, the concept of morphogenesis tends to obscure the ideological content and implications of educational change. In dropping all of the evolutionary baggage implicit in biologically based structural differentiation and complex adaptive models, she backs into an indeterminism and a form of radical historicism that undermines her capacity to grasp precisely the cultural implications of the *reproductive* effects of educational systems addressed in structural-functionalist and structural-Marxist models. The change processes highlighted by the emphasis upon structural elaboration are unconsciously disconnected from the static processes (the dynamic equilibrium or complex reproduction) that are the basis of the "evolutionary" continuity of capitalist educational systems. In short, her version of cultural reproduction is so open that it risks undermining the original insights of reproduction models, that is, that apparent social change is constrained by systemic imperatives that limit voluntary action in ways that have a profound ideological and political significance. But it is plausible to argue that her more recent theory of culture and agency opens the way to dealing with this and related questions.

This metaphorical use of the morphogenetic concepts derives from inherent difficulties in applying the complex adaptive model to society. The problem is that all systems models presuppose a formal ideal that does not correspond to actual societies. As Buckley admits, "A simple, cybernetic model of explicit group goal-seeking does not fit most societies past and present because of a lack . . . of informed, centralized direction . . . Extensive, conscious attempts to direct a complex society in a viable, adaptive manner have only begun in modern history" (1967: 207). Not surprisingly, the most ambitious attempt to apply such a morphogenic approach has had little impact on research and culminates in a contradictory, elitist conception of an "active society" (Etzioni, 1968) that virtually ignores the structural obstacles—above all relations of class domination—to such utopian planning proposals. Yet such approaches have had considerable influence in planning and policy research where systems thinking constitutes the dominant paradigm.

To be sure, in rejecting the evolutionism of functionalism, Archer backs off from a strong, teleological formulation of morphogenic theory, but at the price of a kind of neo-Darwinian stress upon particularistic (if not random as in the biological case) processes of competition, which results in a form of relativistic historicism that can only be dealt with through applying her morphogenic theory of culture to a rethinking of her earlier analysis of the origins of educational systems.

(2) By suppressing any critical emancipatory interest under the pretext of a value-neutral comparative historical sociology, Archer is also not in a position to be self-reflexive about her use of theoretical concepts (whether drawn from systems theory, Weberian conflict theory or whatever), however much she may liberate them from determinism. Her lack of reference to metatheoretical issues, in short, makes it difficult to situate her approach clearly with reference to contemporary theoretical debates.

For example, an obvious implication of morphogenic systems approaches is that despite their focus on change and environmental disturbances (e.g., the contingency theory of organizations), they do not adequately address the ideological implications of the concept of their implicit ideal of complex reproduction. What is proposed and studied is change "in" systems rather than fundamental changes "of" systems; as a consequence, there is no possible conceptualization of "transformation" in the sense of a revolutionary transformation. To this extent, even morphogenic systems models remain within the purview of sociologies of "regulation" even though they do introduce a more dynamic conception of the requirements of adaptive change—an implicit model of complex reproduction. Structural elaboration is only conceivable within the limits of capitalist reform.

Similarly, value-laden empirical concepts are defined in value-neutral Weberian terms; for example, the "educationally dominant group" is described as "a neutral concept to designate the educational powers once enjoyed by a particular social group," and domination is characterized as "the opportunity to have a command concerning education obeyed by a given group of persons" (Archer, 1984: 39–40).

(3) This lack of reflexivity also has consequences for substantive theorizing. The value-neutral and general character of such concepts are justified by the cross-cultural imperative of avoiding the automatic association of educational control with any particular group since it may or "may not be the ruling class, the political elite, or the most wealthy groups in society" (1984: 40). This point granted, however, it should be added that it glosses over the fact that such a vocabulary also tends to obscure the simple historical truth that such control has most typically been held precisely by ruling classes, political elites, and wealthy groups.

The consequence for her theorizing is a peculiar combination of generic conflict theory and a Eurocentrism that results in an account of the "social origins of educational systems" in which the specificity of *capitalist* societies and capitalist *states* is often lost. What we see instead is a subtle account of the differential patterns of development (e.g., centralized versus decentralized based on respective interactional strategies of restriction and substitution) operating within the logic of a process of capitalist transformation that itself is not theorized. To be sure, her general model has the advantage of being cast at a level of theoretical generality which would allow it, for example, to be applied to a wide range of social formations with state-controlled educational systems (e.g., state socialism). Yet her model does not allow adequate specification of the particularities of the capitalist state *as such*. Nor do her particular empirical findings lend themselves readily to generalization beyond the European context. She is nevertheless careful (unlike most traditional functionalists) to note that her focus is upon "the autonomous emergence of . . . macroscopic change . . . in countries where it cannot be attributed to external intervention, via conquest, colonization, or territorial redistribution" (1984: 14).

(Of course, neo-Marxist theories of capitalist social reproduction suffer from precisely the opposite dilemma: an inability to speak of reproduction in noncapitalist social formations).

(4) The cumulative effect of these metatheoretical and theoretical decisions is to truncate, if not altogether undermine, the strategic political, ideological, and policy implications of her approach and historical analyses. To this extent she does not altogether escape the tendency in substantive functionalism and systems theory in general to be open to appropriation into the ideology of new scientific and technical elites (e.g., Lilienfeld, 1978).

How can we account for the relative neglect of Archer's work within the sociology of education, despite its apparent advantages as *the most innovative neofunctionalist theoretical framework for an historical sociology of education*? First, her work does not have quite the same apologetic ideological implications more generally associated with functionalist and neofunctionalist systems theories and their tendency to identify processes of differentiation and complexity reduction with "progress." As she notes, structural elaboration as an analytic concept does not presuppose that the changes described result in educational systems that "are more adaptive, efficient, or legitimate than their antecedents" (1984: 209 n. 1) Her more open-ended model allows for more divergent outcomes and is not constrained by a rigid evolutionary model. Accordingly, her approach cannot be immediately and directly adapted to the interests of dominant groups and the given educational order.

Similarly, her approach so mutes its political and ideological implications that it does not readily lend itself to appropriation by leftist critics of education who, in any case, have had various structuralist and conflict theories of educational reproduction at their disposal. Nevertheless, as we have implied, such critics might learn a great deal from Archer's approach.

Another reason for the limited reception and use of Archer's approach may be that her macrosociological perspective does not fall neatly into any of the existing schools and tendencies, and she does not consistently attempt to locate her work in relation to social theory and theories of the sociology of education. Though aware of French research on education and the work of Bourdieu, she does not explicitly acknowledge the influence of his work. Though a political sociology of the state is central to her approach, she does not explicitly take a position with respect to the contemporary debates about theories of the state. Though working explicitly with a morphogenic systems model, her work falls outside the Parsonian and neofunctionalist framework. And though her work could in part be interpreted as a form of neo-Weberian social-closure theory, her inclusion of a macrosociological analysis of systems integration and use of morphogenic systems concepts clearly departs from the methodological individualism of most neo-Weberian theory, which explicitly rejects the systemic level of analysis that is the cornerstone of her theoretical approach. We are forced, however, to include her under the heading of functionalist and systems theories, because her macrosociological categories are derived from systems theory rather than structuralism, as in the case of Bourdieu. But it should be stressed that the result is a form of historicist conflict functionalism oriented toward the analysis of change in educational systems.

Consequently, there is a certain arbitrariness in locating her in the context of the functionalist tradition when she could have been equally as well classified under the heading of conflict theory. We place her approach here in part because its anomalies provide an instructive introduction to the choices that must be made in macrosociological theories of education, as well as an illustration of the consequences of the shift from more closed to open systemic models.

CONCLUSION

The diversity of approaches that can be classified under the heading of *neofunctionalist* is striking. Whereas social entropy theory and the formalism of general systems theories appears to offer little for educational research, dynamic functionalism and ecological systems models have some capacity of analyzing selected macrosociological processes related to education, even if they fall short as general approaches to the sociology of education. Neo-Parsonian revisions of differentiation models through recognition of the strategic effects of conflict and politics have made possible forms of historical investigation that go beyond the early deterministic evolutionism of structural functionalism. But this comes at the price of undercutting the specifically *functionalist* aspects of the approach; moreover, though more sensitive to group and class conflicts, such research still largely evades the questions posed by theories of cultural and social reproduction. Morphogenic systems theory, on the other hand, appears to provide the most rewarding appropriation of systems-theoretical concepts and converges in important ways with research influenced by critical theory and related forms of historically contingent reproduction theory.

PART 3

Structuralism: Neo-Marxist and Conflict Theories

CHAPTER 5

Structuralism and the Logic of Reproduction

This chapter, and the two that follow, are concerned with "structuralist" theories of education as opposed to the "functionalist" ones discussed in the preceding chapter. As the second chapter indicated, however, the simplistic opposition between functionalist and structuralist theories tends to obscure some of the underlying affinities between structural-functionalist and—for lack of a better term—"functionalist-structuralist" approaches. Both are based upon a conception of totality or system, both are concerned with processes of system integration and disintegration, and both posit relatively closed reproductive processes which result in complex reproduction. The focus of the next three chapters, however, will be on the differences between these two strategies for studying education/society relationships. In the next chapter the basic assumptions of structuralist Marxism are outlined in relationship to education. Following that, applications of this approach, based upon some version of the principle of correspondence, are reviewed in the context of France, the United States, and Latin America. Chapter 7 will discuss issues of class, culture, and domination in structuralist-conflict theories. A key point is to identify the conceptual framework of structuralism as relatively distinct from functionalism. We turn now to that endeavor.

WHAT IS STRUCTURALISM? THE STRUCTURALIST MOVEMENT

Since the concept of structuralism has come to mean different things to different people, several important distinctions must be noted at the outset to establish in what sense theories of social reproduction are based upon structuralist methodological foundations. First, European structuralist tendencies should not be confused with the "empirical structuralism" associated with a wide

117

variety of approaches to social structure employed in mainstream sociology (e.g., Coser, 1975, versus Rossi, 1982) or even network theory which claims some affiliation with European structuralism.

Second, the form of structuralism that has most strongly influenced discussions of social and cultural reproduction (and hence education) must be distinguished from the forms of symbolic structuralism associated with semiotics, linguistics, and the structuralist anthropology of Claude Lévi-Strauss.

THE LINGUISTIC ANALOGY

To be sure, these latter forms of symbolic structuralism based on linguistic models have been of strategic methodological importance for understanding the logic of structuralist analysis; and they have provided examples of cultural analysis (e.g., discourse theories) of considerable significance for social research and theories of education. But the object of inquiry of what might be termed macrosociological structuralism in the historical materialist tradition is a theory of society, not simply of symbolic structures. Thus, for example, it is possible to say there is an abstract methodological sense in which both Lévi-Strauss and Althusser are "structuralists"; but the latter is not concerned in the least with the specific procedures of decoding mythological systems found in the former. But Althusser does share key basic aspects of the general structuralist perspective: "These include a predilection for the notion of structure itself, a stringently critical attitude towards 'humanism,' and a certain conception of the social whole" (Giddens, 1979: 159–60).

What then is epistemologically and methodologically distinctive about structuralist approaches, especially as opposed to empiricist ones? The epistemological point of departure is the assumption that social phenomena can become the objects of inquiry, can be constructed as social "objects," at different levels of reality. Further, these different levels of analysis relate as phenomenal appearances (which are empirically accessible to relatively naive observation) and more essential realities which can only be indirectly apprehended through appropriate theoretical categories. Perhaps the easiest way of expressing this methodological (and ultimately ontological) distinction can be found in the linguistic notion of a "surface" as opposed to a "depth" structure, or in the classic distinction of the Swiss linguist de Saussure, between the study of *paroles* (speech acts) as opposed to *la langue* (underlying linguistic system). Those working in the tradition of Hegel and Marx tend to give this type of distinction an ontological significance by referring to it as a contrast between "appearances" and "essences," where a focus on the former entails a falsification of consciousness (e.g., Kosik, 1966). Those Marxists closer to the neo-Kantian tradition (e.g., Della Volpe, 1969), while making a similar distinction between transcendental categories and empirical events, are less willing to formulate the surface-depth structure distinction in such evaluative terms. An important source of this reluctance is considerably less confidence about the methodological bases for securing epistemologically the knowledge of deep structures, which they claim can only be known via appearances, hence indirectly. But in both traditions, the "empirical" is associated with surface phenomena, where the structural level lies behind these immediate appearances as the generative conditions of their very possibility. In short, though the linguistic model has extended and refined the theory of structural analysis, its origins lie in the Kantian-Hegelian tradition as transformed into social theory by Marx.

The origins of structuralist thinking is therefore usually traced back to Marx and Freud (Godelier, 1972). But the extraordinary success and further development of structuralist metatheory is closely linked to early twentieth-century developments in linguistics (de Saussure, Roland Jakobson) and then generalized to anthropological study of folk myths by Lévi-Strauss. Subsequently, efforts have been made to reread Freud in linguistic structuralist terms (Lacan), as well as rereading Marx in explicitly structuralist ways. Yet many of these efforts have made virtually no explicit self-reference to the structuralist tradition of metatheory (e.g., Althusser) and the understanding of structuralism has diverged widely. Consequently, though it is possible to broadly contrast "structuralist" with "instrumentalist" or "economistic" readings of Marx, the variety of structuralist readings precludes assuming that there is a single structuralist version. Hence, while it is useful to contrast a general split between the historicist and would be "scientific" approaches noted above as two paradigms of Western Marxism (Gouldner, 1983), it is misleading to define this as a contrast between a structuralist and a nonstructuralist (i.e., historicist/humanist) in the manner of Althusser. Despite significant differences, however, both share the essential features of the general concept of structuralism developed by Piaget in his wide-ranging survey of the human sciences: "the notion of structure is comprised of three key ideas: the ideal of wholeness, the idea of transformation, and the idea of self-regulation" (Piaget, 1970: 5).

CLASSICAL HISTORICAL MATERIALISM AND STRUCTURALISM

There is an important sense in which Marx does not provide the basis for a theory of education at all. As one recent critic has charged, there are a number of social phenomena (e.g. family life, education, social mobility, leisure activities, the distribution of mental and physical health, etc.) "that do not fit into the traditional Marxist categories, such as base or superstructure" (Elster, 1985: 34–35). Though contemporary Marxist sociologists have considered such phenomena, Elster suggests that they have been forced to fall back upon "functional explanations" that are inadequate. Setting aside for now the validity of Elster's charge, it is evident that it is necessary to consider the basic categories of Marx which might relate, even if indirectly, to the question of education. The central concepts that need to be considered from this perspective include: the concept of social reproduction, the theory of ideology, the base/superstructure metaphor, and of course the theory of class (see chapter 7) and the state (see chapter 12). Since Marx's own discussions are often fragmentary and inconsistent, and given that our ultimate goal is the analysis of theories of social and cultural reproduction as developed in twentieth-century Western Marxism, our brief discussion will be oriented toward understanding these contemporary debates.

The Concept of Social Reproduction

The concept of "social reproduction," has become central only in the past two decades and it was not directly implicated in the classic Marxian discussions of ideology, base and superstructure, and the state. Indeed, it was the absence of attention to this concept that facilitated interpretations based on reductionistic analyses of ideology, the centrality of the dubious base/superstructure metaphor, and instrumentalist theories of the state. One potentially constructive aspect of these late nineteenth- and early twentieth-century developments, however, was that it also forced a shift from a very restrictive and negative conception of ideology to a more general and neutral one: only in this way was it possible to legitimate how Marxian and proletarian thought could be part of the very totality to be transformed and still be the carrier of historical "truth." But this shift in the meaning of ideology was achieved at a price: the dilemma of relativism versus dogmatism. It became increasingly difficult to sustain the claim of the truth of proletarian as opposed to other forms of socially determined consciousness. This aporia found its classical expression in Mannheim's "relationism"—an heroic but ultimately inadequate effort to reconcile an undogmatic but critical conception of ideology with a utopian vision that could also make some claim to relative truth.[1]

Marx introduced the concepts of production and reproduction in the context of the analysis of capitalist production in chapter 23 of the first volume of *Capital*:

> Whatever the form of the process of production in a society, it must be a continuous process, must continue to go periodically through the same phases. A society can no more cease to produce than it can cease to consume. When viewed, therefore, as a connected whole, and as flowing on with incessant renewal, every social process of production is, at the same time, a process of reproduction. (Marx, 1971, vol. 1: 531)

For Marx, the process of simple reproduction constitutes the mere continuity of the process of production by perpetuating the separation between the product of labor from labor itself, between the objective conditions of labor and subjective labor power (535). Thus, "The reproduction of the working class carries with it the accumulation of skill, that is handed down from one generation to another" (538). In this way Marx notes that:

> Capitalist production, therefore, of itself reproduces the separation between labor power and the means of labor. It thereby reproduces and perpetuates the condition for exploiting the laborer. It incessantly forces him to sell his labor power in order to live, and enables the capitalist to purchase labor power in order that he may enrich himself . . . Capitalist production, therefore, under its aspect of a continuous connect process, of a process of

reproduction, provides not only commodities, not only surplus value, but it also produces and reproduces the capitalist relation; on the one side the capitalist, on the other the wage laborer. (541–42)

As used in sociology, the concept of reproduction thus had its origins here. In its "simple" form it suggests that even though individuals may be replaced, the system retains its essential identity because of a constant level of production and the stability of the relations of production. Further, Marx speaks of "expanded reproduction" to refer to conditions where production may increase but the basic relations of production (hence class relations) remain constant. What is less widely recognized is that these general distinctions have been transposed to other domains by non-Marxist scholars, especially in demographic and social mobility research (e.g., Boudon, 1979; Boudon and Bourricaud, 1982). Two other distinctions can also be derived from Marx's discussions of reproduction: "complex reproduction" and "transformation." In the case of complex reproduction the overall stability of society is preserved but at the price of, or despite fundamental modifications of, the relations of production, which do not thereby alter the identity of the system as such. The emergence of the welfare state could be taken as an example of such complex reproduction.[2] In other cases, changing individual behavior may have overall similar consequences (e.g., the constancy of mobility rates). Transformation, of course, entails processes leading to a qualitatively different type of system. In this respect its represents a very abstract formulation of what might more concretely be referred to as a revolutionary change. Marx's theory of economic crisis was based, of course, on the knowledge that processes of expanded reproduction are inherently unstable, leading to eventual limits and contradictions. The possibilities of complex reproduction, on the other hand, did not get comparable treatment in Marx, even though retrospectively it is clear that the relative stability of capitalism in this century has been achieved in this manner.

These circumstances have given the phenomenon of social reproduction a strategic significance for understanding the overall process of the complex reproduction of capitalism as a whole. Whereas for Marx the social (and cultural) reproduction of labor power is relatively unproblematic, it has become the center of attention in post–World War I Western Marxism in the wake of the continued failure of working-class mobilization along the lines anticipated by Marx. And post–World War II discussions have stressed the cooptation of the working class in developed societies (e.g., Gorz, 1967; Bowles and Gintis, 1986) as opposed to the growing dissatisfaction of the intelligentsia (Marcuse, 1964; Gorz, 1967). As a consequence, the theory of reproduction is linked with posing the question of the social subject that could initiate fundamental social change.

It should also be noted, however, that extending the concept of reproduction beyond the more regular phenomena of economic and demographic processes (which are readily quantifiable and determinate) poses difficulties and becomes increasingly metaphorical. Further, the theory of reproduction does not, by itself, provide clear specifications of whether—or under what conditions—simple, expanded, or complex reproduction will occur as opposed to transformation. Though the overall thesis of contradictions between labor and capital, along with that between the forces and relations of production, posit the necessity of transformation, this assumes the form of a tendential law, not a prediction.

In the context of the mid nineteenth-century, Marx was primarily concerned with dynamics rather than statics, given the prospect of revolutionary transformation. Accordingly, the theory of social reproduction remained in the background and virtually undeveloped. Marx in his later days was preoccupied with economic phenomena, not only because of their strategic place as the objective basis of crisis—one that would break the cycle of economic reproduction—but also because they lent themselves to more rigorous, scientific treatment. As he points out: "In considering such transformations a distinction should always be made between the material transformation of the economic conditions of production, which can be determined with the precision of natural science, and the legal, political, religious, aesthetic, or philosophical—in short, ideological forms in which men become conscious of this conflict and fight it out" (in Tucker, 1978: 5). And let us add—educational forms.

It is not the place here to trace the subsequent development of the preceding issues in the history of the Marxist tradition as a whole, given our focus on the problematic of social reproduction as a question specific to Western Marxism. This is not to say, however, that important issues relating to reproduction and education have not been touched upon in the work of people such as Lenin, Trotsky, and Mao in particular. But the historical contexts of their contributions—Czarist Russia and twentieth-century China—do not lend themselves to generalization to Western Europe or North America. The case of parts of Latin America is more ambiguous, where the existence of large agrarian populations produces resemblances to the Russian and Chinese cases, but it is clear that the major impetus for theories of social reproduction in education have come from Western Marxist contributions.[3]

Despite having its origins in economic theory, the Marxian concept of reproduction has become prominent in the past two decades primarily in the context of the analysis of superstructural phenomena. Initially, such efforts built upon the notion of social reproduction just cited in relation to Marx's account of the reproduction of labor power. But beyond this narrower focus, the term has also been extended with reference to the notion of "cultural reproduction" more generally. As critics in various fields have charged, theories of social reproduction tended to neglect "a theory of consciousness and culture" and hence "the mediating role of culture in reproducing class societies" (Giroux, 1983: 87; Apple, 1982a: 1). The focus of traditional social reproduction theories is rather upon the sources and consequences of inequality and the more immediate economic determinants of reproduction.

Such disputes point to the tenuous nature of the link between the original political economic concept of reproduction and current uses. There is no self-evident way in which the purely economic concept of reproduction can be extended to the sociocultural realm. Beyond loose distinctions between types of reproduction (e.g., simple, expanded, complex), the use of the concept for social and cultural phenomena has been largely elaborated independently. The import of the concept has therefore been primarily methodological rather than substantive in that it symbolized (a) a way of understanding the logic of Marx's theoretical categories in structural rather than instrumental terms, hence based on the analogy of economic equilibrium and the distinction between phenomenal appearances and deeper essential realities; and (b) the thesis that superstructural phenomena, along with the institutions of civil society, play a strategic role in the process of overall societal reproduction. The result is a very general argument, therefore, which has been characterized by its critics as a "dominant ideology thesis": the claim that "especially in late capitalism, the coherence of industrial society is to be explained primarily by the ideological incorporation of the labor force" (Abercrombie, Hill, and Turner, 1980: 1).

STRUCTURALISM AND THE TWO PARADIGMS OF WESTERN MARXISM

The internal divisions within twentieth-century Western Marxism mirror those in mainstream sociology in that there is a similar split along the axis of theory construction previously described as the subjective-objective polarization. This basic split has been described by Alvin Gouldner (1983) as the "two Marxisms": the critical, humanist, and historicist wing associated with a critique of positivism and a concern with problems of agency and the human subject, as opposed to a positivist wing concerned with reaffirming the scientific credentials of Marxism as an explanatory political economic theory. In their extreme forms, these two approaches have characteristic tendencies. Critical Marxism becomes increasingly voluntaristic and idealist, losing interest in the analysis of structural determination. Scientific Marxism becomes increasingly deterministic and structuralist, reducing the role of the subject to an epiphenomenal status. As a consequence, structuralist Marxism tends to operate almost exclusively at the level of system integration to the exclusion of social integration; critical, humanist approaches are, in contrast, also very much concerned with agency and the theory of social integration. Accordingly, structuralist Marxism develops a relatively closed model of reproduction in contrast to the more open one of the historicist tradition. A similar polarization can be observed in historical materialist approaches to cultural studies (Hall, 1983) and the problematic of social reproduction generally.

But it should be emphasized that both of these contemporary paradigms of historical materialism are "structuralist" in two important senses. First, both follow Marx in viewing social formations as structured totalities that constrain human agency; and both are broadly structuralist, in the methodological sense of a critique of social-scientific empiricism.[4] This first aspect separates various forms of critical theory (e.g., the Frankfurt tradition) along with various forms of critical neo-Marxism (e.g., Lefebvre, Kosik) from versions of existentialism and phenomenology that can be charged with subjectivism and an illusory form of humanist voluntarism that effectively denies the realities of domination and political economy. More complicated and controversial is the second assumption: that critical theories and historicist versions of neo-Marxism share a structuralist method. Structuralist Marxists such as Althusser, for example, have developed their position on the basis of a critique of historicist theories which are characterized as having an "expressive" as opposed to a "structural" theory of causation.

We will contend, however, that there are two other important sources of reproduction theory within modern social theory: the Hegelian concept of totality (the Frankfurt School; Gramsci), and the Durkheimian conception of social structure. The theory of totality has been developed primarily within the historicist versions of Western Marxism associated with Karl Korsch, George Lukacs, Lucien Goldmann, the Frankfurt School, and Gramsci. One of the essential features of this tradition of so-called Hegelian Marxism, has been a critique of economistic and instrumental interpretations of Marx, and an insistence upon understanding the relationship between society and its elements in structural terms, giving particular importance to the processes of symbolic reproduction and change. Henri Lefebvre, for example, who is also a long-time critic of "structuralist Marxism" in the more restrictive and extreme senses associated respectively with Claude Lévi-Strauss and Althusser (Lefebvre, 1971), has developed an analysis of the "reproduction of the relations of production" (Lefebvre, 1976). And outside an explicitly Marxist framework, Pierre Bourdieu has also developed a general theory of cultural reproduction that draws extensively upon the inspiration of Durkheim, as well as upon Marx and others. The influence of Durkheim can also be seen indirectly in the French tradition as a whole (e.g. Althusser, Godelier).

Existential Marxism

It may appear contradictory to consider the existential-phenomenological concern with the human subject as an important influence upon materialist reproduction theories, given that the phenomenological tradition was singled out by structuralist Marxists as the primary obstacle to a correct understanding of Marx. But it is important to distinguish the origins of such philosophical concepts (idealist philosophy) and the way in which they have been subsequently transformed within a larger historical-materialist framework. This strategy was, of course, anticipated in the early works of Marx and his theory of alienation, and finds its most sophisticated expression today in various forms of so-called phenomenological Marxism (cf. Pike, 1986; Kosik, 1976; Paci, 1972) and in the work of Paulo Freire (Torres, 1978b, 1980, 1993), as well as in Giddens' theory of structuration.

Hegelian Marxism

Though the concept of social reproduction theory in education is most closely associated with structuralist Marxism, it would be misleading to suggest that the latter had somehow completely invented the idea, as opposed to providing a distinctive account of its operation as a state ideological apparatus. The understanding of society as a contradictory totality found in what is often termed the tradition of "Hegelian Marxism" has given rise to a very similar type of analysis. To be sure, however, it involves an analysis that its structuralist Marxist critics characterized as suffering from a faulty "expressive" theory of causality, that is, where the part of society (e.g., educational institutions) come to manifest or express essential properties whose origins are to be found in the production process. Nevertheless, it is clear that Hegelian Marxism in its various forms, ranging from Georg Lukacs, Antonio Gramsci, the early Frankfurt School, and Henry Lefebvre, contains a version of a correspondence theory of social and cultural reproduction, even though it does not go under that name and was applied only obliquely (except in the case of Gramsci) to educational institutions.

For our present purposes the purportedly crucial distinction between expressive and structural causality is of marginal importance. As has been noted in relation to Althusser's conception of structural causality, "this conception is by no means as distant from Hegelian or Hegel-influenced versions of the totality as he seems to believe" (Giddens: 1979: 159).

Althusserian Structuralism

Though the concept of reproduction is associated most strongly with the structuralist Marxism of Louis Althusser, Nicos Poulantzas and (in a significantly different form) Maurice Godelier in France, one of our central themes will be that the concept has been central, sometimes explicitly and sometimes implicitly, for a number of theoretical schools. To this extent, further, the concept of "structuralist" approaches is a rather diffuse one, which should not be exclusively identified with this French tradition. Nevertheless, the latter must be credited with having provided the catalyst for a more self-consciously "structuralist" rereading of Marx and recognizing the problematic character of a Marxism divided by economistic approaches, on the one hand, and excessively voluntaristic existential and phenomenological tendencies, on the other. In the next chapter, Althusser's structuralist Marxism is discussed in detail.

Ideology and Superstructures

A useful way to compare the implications of historicist and structuralist variants of historical materialism is to consider their respective approaches to the problem of ideology and the related question of the superstructures in Marx's theory. The most influential form has been that of existential and Hegelian-influenced versions, which posit the possibility of the subject in some sense transcending or overcoming ideology. From this perspective, there is a fluid relationship between science and ideology, a position which tends toward relativism. In contrast, those who stress a more objectivistic, scientific version of Marx's theory, as in the case of certain forms of structuralism, posit a sharp distinction between ideology and science, as well as the capacity of intellectuals in the appropriate vanguard position to distinguish between the two. Here dogmatism tends to be substituted for relativism as an extreme expression of this position. As we will see in subsequent chapters, this is a central issue in the conflict and dialogue between the two traditions of Western Marxism: the humanist and the scientific.

It is clear that, at least in Latin America and in some European countries, the most influential and persuasive interpretation of the notion of ideology from a Marxist perspective has been the scientific and structuralist one proposed by Althusser. The French philosopher proposed the interpretation of ideology as a system of deforming representations given the necessarily opaque character of the social structure (Althusser, 1971). This deformation is systematic, oriented, and determined (De Ipola, 1982: 2). In the perspective of Althusser, the social function of ideology consists in guaranteeing the linkages that relate individuals to their "tasks." That is to say, (a) every ideology "interpellates" or "hails," and thus constitutes the individuals in subjects; (b) every ideology will guarantee that every individual will be related to a central Subject; (c) also, it will guarantee that each subject will reciprocally recognize the position of the other subjects in the social structure; (d) finally, it will guarantee that if every subject recognizes what they are and behaves accordingly, everything will be run smoothly. However, on this issue, it should be said that indeed, the notion of ideology as false consciousness in Althusser is subordinated to the notion of an suprafunctional activity of the ideology as a process that subordinates people and keeps them in line. Second, it should be stressed that the role of ideologies in constituting subjectivities (at the individual and social-class level) is decisive in Althusser's perspective and in most of the Marxist perspectives of ideology. Third, ideology is not only a set of concepts somewhat articulated in a program, strategy, philosophy, or the like. It could be thought of as a program, but this formalization of ideology goes beyond and above the basic functions attributed to the ideological realm of society in Althusser's perspective.

A word of caution is in order here. It should be clarified that at least two different interpretations of the notion of ideology are sometimes simultaneously used in contemporary Marxisms. On one hand, ideology will express the fact that there is always an ideological dimension in every social action. That is to say, the "ideological" factor should be recognized in analyzing every social and technical process. On the other hand, ideology could be understood as [the] "forms of social existence and exercise of social struggles in the domain of the social processes of production of meanings" (De Ipola, 1982: 73). The complexity of ideology as producer of meanings and input and outcome of conflicts and contradictions is that social struggle is not only related to class struggle but to a number of social conflicts that are meaningful in capitalist societies (e.g., ethnic oppression, gender oppression, regional imbalances in development, cultural issues, etc).

The Base-Superstructure Model and the Correspondence Principle

The specific contribution of Marxist theory to education is closely linked to the structuralist notion of "correspondence" as a way of understanding the determination involved in the base-superstructure model. Traditional Marxist accounts based on an instrumental analysis of the base-superstructure relationship stressed the over ideological functions of education as evident in its overt content. Correspondence theories marked an advance because the nature of determination was interpreted in structuralist terms through the distinction between the manifest context of education and its latent structural properties as expressed in its form. From this point of view, it became possible to analyze the link between the social relations of capitalist production and those of education in terms of, for example, the kind of authoritarian social relations characteristic of both, despite the surface "democratization" of the school system. Though structuralist Marxism stressed the relative autonomy of the school, it still adhered to the structuralist principle that the latent function of that autonomy was still to secure the ideological reproduction of the given social order; again an assumption based on the ostensible relations between production relations and social relations in education.

Interestingly, whether that correspondence is understood in terms of a more traditional conception of the base-superstructure model (whether in economistic or Hegelian-Marxist terms) or a structuralist analysis of state ideological apparatuses, this does not fundamentally affect the essential principle of correspondence. What both of these share is a relatively closed model of reproduction within which the functions of education are held to be grounded in the imperative of the economic production process. Whether that correspondence be understood in specifically formalist structuralist terms or the older concept of structure involved in the Hegelian Marxian essence versus appearance distinction only changes the details and methodological assumptions, not the substance of the argument.

Durkheimian Conflict Structuralism and Correspondence Theory

Though methodological structuralism in sociology is usually associated with either structuralist Marxism or Lévi-Straussian symbolic anthropology, it is also important to distinguish a version of conflict structuralism (e.g., Bourdieu and Bernstein), which in certain respects is the analogue of conflict functionalism. This approach is easiest to distinguish by its opposition, in the first place, to certain neo-Marxist assumptions (e.g., the theory of revolution and proletariat, as well as the dialectic of societal contradiction and related philosophy of history). To this extent it converges with neo-Weberian critiques of historical materialism. On the other hand, such conflict structuralism remains faithful to Durkheim (and Marx) in retaining a systemic perspective that rejects methodological individualism in the Weberian sense. Unlike Durkheim, however, conflict figures centrally in the analysis of systemic relations (e.g., process of societal integration), without necessarily the Marxian assumptions of the logic of contradiction and transformation. Further, conflict structuralism does not adhere to other aspects of Weberian methodology, that is, the rejection of functional analysis and the advocacy of a value-free stance. To this extent, structuralist conflict theory remains a non-Marxist but radical form of functional analysis, which incorporates many important concepts from historical materialism, and thus power and ideology remain central concepts that distinguish it from structural functionalism. Further, it is based on a variant of the correspondence principle, but the locus shifts from the relations of production to class relations more generally as the locus of correspondence: educational outcomes thus come to correspond to the strategies of different social classes and class fractions. This will be discussed in greater detail in chapter 6.

STRUCTURALISM AND NEO-WEBERIAN CONFLICT THEORIES

As in the case of Marx, interpretations of Weber have been polarized between more or less voluntarist and structuralist interpretations. But whereas Marx has been traditionally considered a determinist (hence, structuralism only refines such accounts), Weber has more typically been considered a voluntaristic social theorist. As a consequence, more structuralist interpretations of his work provide a rather new version of Weber, one that pushes his analysis toward that of Marx, in often surprising ways, ways that become most apparent in theories of cultural capital and social closure, as we shall see. *From such a neo-Weberian perspective, however, it becomes impossible to speak of correspondence any longer* because social outcomes in education are not held to be determined by any external set of systemic social relations to which they must "correspond" in some fashion. Instead, education is viewed as part of a more general process of societal rationalization that structures the struggles within which educational institutions are formed. What is reproduced then is legal bureaucratic domination or perhaps the interests of specific classes, rather than capitalist productive relations per se. What is ambiguous in the structuralist neo-Weberian account is the precise relationship between economic and class factors, on the one hand, and legal bureaucratic domination on the other—a theme which eventually becomes central to the appropriation of Weber in critical theories of society and social closure theory. But it is important to stress that neo-Weberian theory provides some of the crucial assumptions for rejecting and or moving beyond traditional correspondence theory and has had a significant impact on many of those who earlier identified with it. This will be discussed in detail in chapter 7.

POSTSTRUCTURALISM: POWER AND CRITICISM

Within social theory, the term *poststructuralism* refers most directly to the dissatisfaction with extreme forms of structuralism that in various ways proclaimed the "death of the subject." Though sensitive to the difficulties of the naive voluntarism of much existentialism and phenomenology, poststructuralist theorists (see Foucault, 1980; Wexler, 1987) have sought to reconnect agency and structure in ways that were impossible in the context of the French polarization between existentialism and structuralism. As we will argue in part 4, this reconciliation has been achieved primarily in the context of neo-Gramscian and critical theories over the past decade.

There are a number of directions of poststructuralist critique, particularly in curriculum theory. Cleo Cherryholmes' poststructural investigation in education is built upon the notion that power and criticism are intimately linked. Cherryholmes refers to power as "relations among individuals or groups based on social, political, and material asymmetries by which some people are indulged and rewarded and others negatively sanctioned and deprived . . . For my purposes, the effects of power are as important as the exercise of power itself" (Cherryholmes, 1988: 5). Armed with this relational definition of power, mostly based on the work of Foucault and the implications of Derrida's literacy criticism, Cherryholmes defines his investigations in education as poststructuralist, thus linked to postmodernism, postpositivism, and post-analytical thought.

Structuralism is linked to modern and analytical thought and seeks "rationality, linearity, progress, and control by discovering, developing, and inventing metanarratives, metadiscourses, and metacritiques that define rationality, linearity, progress, and control"; while "postmodern, postanalytic, and poststructural thought are skeptical and incredulous about the possibility of such metanarratives" (Cherryholmes, 1988: 11). What is underscoring this skepticism? Essentially, the fact that the nature of meanings, statements, and discourses cannot be validated through either metadiscourses or metanarratives themselves, that is, by rules of validity developed a priori of the scientific discourse itself—partly because "narratives about narratives can express different kinds of claims and evaluations about discourse and practice" (Cherryholmes, 1988: 11), and partly because "a narrative in one setting can operate as a metanarrative in another and vice versa" (Cherryholmes, 1988: 13).

But what are the sources of poststructuralist criticism's dissatisfaction? Cherryholmes focuses his dissatisfaction on the assumptions of the dominant paradigm (logical positivism) regarding the epistemological conditions for knowledge to be true, valid, and eventually useful. That is to say, Cherryholmes will criticize a set of assumptions well-entrenched in the tradition of logical positivism and empiricism including the distinction between fact and value, the distinction between analytic and synthetic statements, and the distinction between theory and/or models and observation or empirical phenomena. From Cherryholmes' perspective, these premises are false, and obscure the real fact that substantiates validity claims: "Construct validity focuses attention on the juncture of words and things, concepts and objects, theory and practice, where social theory and research and theoretical constructs and research operations converge and diverge" (Cherryholmes, 1988: 99–100).

Using construct validity to justify the measurement and testing as true reflections of students performance or knowledge is problematic for Cherryholmes insofar as "construct-validity and research discourses are shaped, as are other discourses, by beliefs and commitments, explicit ideologies, tacit worldviews, linguistic and cultural systems, politics and economics, and power arrangements" (Cherryholmes, 1988: 106).

Cherryholmes argues that the most articulated representatives of mainstreams—methodology-based, for the most part on quantitative assessment—are aware of these complexities but have chosen not to explore them, since any exploration would thwart the explanatory ability of their measurement and analytical techniques. Essentially, construct validity and scientific discourses are entangled with power relationships, to the point, argues Cherryholmes in a fierce criticism of conventional methodology and social sciences, that

Construct validity and validation is what those in authority choose to call it. If they choose to exclude phenomenological investigation, so be it. If they choose to exclude ideological criticism and discussions of power, so be it. If they choose to stipulate meanings for constructs and enforce them, so be it. But embracing what is in place does not free authorities from the strictures of inherited discourses. They simply are indulged for being in a privileged position. (Cherryholmes, 1988: 129)

Recognizing the validity of phenomenology and interpretative research, critical theory, interpretative analytics, and deconstruction, Cherryholmes proposes a scientific approach that he calls "critical pragmatism." The logical consequences of Cherryholmes' criticism to conventional methodology is not a libertarian-relativist approach—e.g., if power is so intimately linked to (and eventually guiding) scientific explorations, then "everything goes," and science, like everything else, to put it in a Hegelian terminology, is a fight for pure prestige. Thus, those who accumulate more authority—that is to say, who hold the upper hand in power relationships—will produce the more persuasive or most forceful explanations, or at least these will be accepted as such. Cherryholmes' critical pragmatism will distance itself from such a vulgar relativism and libertarianism.

Critical pragmatism is in direct opposition to logical positivism and empiricism. Social and educational discourses result from the exercise of power, and the security of establishing a sound, normative, and foundational ground for scientific analysis may be illusory at this point of human history:

We are confronted with historical events, trends, and objects whose meaning is subject to continual reinterpretation. It is arguable that the apparent autonomy of our efforts to produce knowledge and control is oftentimes fictive and illusory. Our social and educational discourses-practices result, in substantial ways, from effects of power and its exercise. Furthermore, the meanings we ascribe to our lives, texts, and discourses-practices are continually dispersed and deferred. Our texts and discourses-practices continuously require interpretation and reconstruction. We choose and act, furthermore, without the benefit of positivist victories. Our choices and actions, in their totality, are pragmatic responses to the situations in which we and those around us find ourselves. They are based upon visions of what is beautiful, good, and true instead of fixed, structured, moral, or objective certainties. Poststructural analysis contributes criticism, which is sometimes radical, to our pragmatic choices. (Cherryholmes, 1988: 151)

The implications of critical pragmatism for the scientific discourse are many. Critical pragmatism will be antifoundational, antiessentialist, and will reject the attempt to create the mark of a fallible science. In addition, critical pragmatism opposes logical positivism inasmuch as it is built almost exclusively on Habermas's empirical-analytical knowledge oriented toward potential technical control—a form of knowledge, as we explained in chapter 2, that is logically comparable to the explanatory (causal, predictive) knowledge associated with the natural sciences. On the contrary, critical pragmatism will incorporate within scientific discourse a historical-hermeneutic interest and a human interest in critical-emancipatory knowledge.

Critical pragmatism involves making continually epistemological, ethical, and aesthetic choices (Cherryholmes, 1988: 179). Insofar as knowledge is grounded, critical pragmatist set out a problem assuming that they can solve it. Critical pragmatists nurture a critical community rather than a set of scientific rules to be followed universally. They look at the consequences, starting from a situational framework that marks the scientific experiment, and from the traditions of criticism that helps evaluation:

Poststructural analysis and criticism contribute interpretation, criticism, and evaluation to a pragmatism that possesses a sense of crisis. We are as much a product of time and place as are the texts and discourses-practices around us. We make decisions about beliefs and actions against this background. A vulgar and naive pragmatism, functionally reproducing things for good or ill, plays itself out if we remain uncritical and unreflective and attend only to what is "practical." Critical pragmatism is realistic because it begins with what is in place. Critical pragmatism is relativistic because it is relative to what is in place. (Cherryholmes, 1988: 186)

This is a puzzling appraisal of the thin line between relativism and realism, particularly when at the conclusion of his book Cherryholmes endorses a legacy of scientific thought and social action: "if we can be critically pragmatic in the construction, deconstruction, construction . . . of how we live and together build communities using our best visions of what is beautiful, good, and true, then the unreflective reproduction of what we find around us, including some of its injustices, might be tamed and changed a bit" (Cherryholmes, 1988: 186).

Cherryholmes' book is a fascinating attempt to recover in the context of positivist America the pragmatist philosophical tradition that dominated the United States from 1870 until 1920, and eventually culminated, although not excepted from contradictions, with the pedagogical philosophy of John Dewey. In spite of Cherryholmes' sharp arguments, there are a number of loose ends, particularly when compared against the background of reproduction theories discussed in this book.

First, there is no exploration in Cherryholmes' book about the demise of American pragmatism, and its implications in education. After all, if educational and philosophical discourses are intimately linked to power, any attempt to reconstitute an approach that has fallen away from academic (and eventually political) grace should imply an explanation of why did it happen, and what are the reasons why logical positivism become so prominent. This at the risk of being poisoned by critical pragmatism's fundamental premise that it is relative to its place, and begins to act with what is in place—namely positivism.

Cherryholmes' deconstruction of the positivist foundations of social science is persuasive, but his attempt to propose critical pragmatism as the only alternative to logical positivism is not. After all, it was Weber who suggested in sociology that there is a logical difference between natural sciences and social sciences, thus undermining the basic tenet of logical positivism in historical sciences. For Weber, this logical difference derives from the fact that social sciences cannot have experimental control in a laboratory to reproduce the phenomena studied, but have to rely on a control that is purely rational or conceptual. Thus, inasmuch as conceptual elaboration cannot be experimentally verified, concepts are not independent of values. That is, the conceptual configuration reflecting how an observer makes sense of the historical world is dependent upon a sensorial appropriation of the social world deeply marked by the system of meanings of the observer-scientist; and then even data, as a social construct, is subject to axiological premises.[5] This conclusion, which challenges the basic tenet of positivism, was reached by Weber independently from pragmatist thinkers and is virtually ignored by Cherryholmes in his ambitious attempt to build a decentered and poststructural social science.

A second problem arises with the antifoundational attempt of critical pragmatists that may overlook the fact that the complexities of educational practices may need a theory of knowledge rather than simply an epistemology of scientific practices. It is eventually this reluctance to discuss the normative grounds for scientific activity that probably led Cherryholmes' analysis to dismiss Freire's theory of knowledge and Freire's notion of the politicity of education. This omission or exclusion is a serious shortcoming of Cherryholmes' attempt to link knowledge and power in education,[6] particularly when Freire's analysis cannot be restricted any longer to experiences of developing societies, assuming that—as Cherryholmes does—industrially advanced societies are the most apropriate locus for poststructural investigations in education.

A third problem is the restriction of almost all manifestations of power as relational in nature. Taken in its most extreme form, Foucault's criticism of power relationships is antiorganizational, failing to recognize that the microscenarios of power are built into macroscenarios, with structural power regularities. Why renounce developing a political economy of education, even from positivist epistemologies, if the treatment of empirical data could be applied to different political ends than vulgar positivism and conservative empiricism? Perhaps even Marx's moderate functionalism, so aptly defended by the analytical Marxists (for instance, G. A. Cohen, Erik Olin Wright, and Adam Przeworski), could throw light into the structure of domination and exploitation of industrially advanced societies. After all, discourses of power (in education and elsewhere) are produced in the context of political (symbolic and material) struggles and not in the somewhat controlled environment of philosophers of science discursive rationales. Discourses of power should be contested not exclusively in terms of construct-validity claims but also in political-economic terms, making the debate on structuralism and poststructuralism more "messy" than an exchange of astute interpretations of validity claims.

Notwithstanding these objections, and perhaps others, Cherryholmes' poststructural investigation of education is compelling, particularly because in linking Foucault and Derrida's continental philosophies to American pragmatism, Cherryholmes has sought a synthesis that is more intelligible to American teachers and policymakers. There is no doubt that deconstructivist, postanalytical philosophies, and poststructuralist concepts are somewhat difficult to grasp, to understand, but above all to implement in concrete analysis of concrete situations. However, naming the world is a way of interpreting (and eventually changing) it. The power of logical positivism does not reside in the fact that its concepts are easy to grasp or that they can be easily translated into mathematical sentences—although the logical argumentation and mathematical support make the arguments more readily translatable for different domains in social science and policy. The power of positivism resides in its ability to convince us of the validity of the dichotomies underlying its foundations (e.g., fact/value distinction, etc.) and its overwhelming although growingly contested presence in most academic and policy domains. Its conceptual apparatus becomes prevalent not because it is more logical, or clear, or easy to grasp than poststructuralist concepts of discourse, practice, speech acts, text, or discourses-text, but because the positivist conceptual apparatus has prevailed as a normal science and guiding knowledge interest for policymaking, socializing scholars and policymakers in understanding its "lingua." The self-imposed task of poststructuralism is to persuade scholars and policymakers of the validity of its claims, debunking logical positivism without constructing a new metanarrative. The task at hand, then, is immense.

CONCLUSION

In the next chapter we will take up the forms of correspondence theory initially inspired by structuralist Marxism. At this point we have merely sought to establish three basic points as the foundation for later discussion. First, that concerns with structuralist conceptions of social and cultural reproduction have been developed within both the traditions of Western Marxism. Second, that these have produced two competing paradigms of social and cultural reproduction, which result in models of society that can be contrasted as relatively "open" as opposed to relatively "closed." Finally, that in between these two can be found a form of conflict structuralism (influenced by both neo-Weberian and neo-Durkheimian tendencies), presupposing relatively closed models of reproduction but without Marxist assumption of structural contradiction. Poststructuralism—and variants such as critical pragmatism—can be understood as attempting deal with the problems bequeathed by structuralism in all its varieties.

CHAPTER 6

Structuralist Marxism:
Correspondence Theories

INTRODUCTION: ALTHUSSER, BALIBAR, AND POULANTZAS

The term *structuralist Marxism* will be used in a strict sense, referring to the approach initially inspired by the French philosopher Louis Althusser and carried on most immediately by Etienne Balibar and Nicos Poulantzas and eventually a wide international following. Without exaggeration, it can be said that this current of thinking is responsible for inspiring the renewal of a Marxist theory of education—which had never been really established in any case—and generating the debates surrounding the concept of "reproduction theory" generally, though Bourdieu's rather different approach also popularized the term (as we shall see in chapter 7).

The task of the present discussion is first to contextualize the emergence of structuralist Marxism in the context of French intellectual life and Western Marxism generally; second, to outline the basic presuppositions of this approach that contributed to educational reproduction theory, and closely related to this, to identify the distinctive and original features of this approach and its relation to eduction; third, to locate one of the most important original features of this approach in one of its most problematic contributions: a structuralist reading of Antonio Gramsci; and finally, to consider some of the empirical applications of this approach in diverse national settings.

Intellectual Context

One of the most remarkable features of Althusser's case is his rapid intellectual ascendancy and subsequent dramatic decline. As Erik Olin Wright, one of the leading contemporary American neo-Marxist sociologists, remarks in reviewing a book titled *The Rise and Fall of Structuralist Marxism* (Benton, 1984): "By the late 1960s he was a powerful intellectual force within he French left, and by the early 1970s, as translations of his work and that of his followers became readily available, Althusserian Marxism was one of the leading theoretical tendencies on the left in the English-speaking world. By the mid 1980s that influence—at least explicitly—had almost entirely disappeared" (Wright, 1987: 14). Needless to say, this general rejection of Althusserian Marxism had profound effects upon those educational reproduction theories influenced by his example.

The remarkable success of Althusser's "interventions" is closely related to an effort to rehabilitate Marxist philosophy that stimulated (and some would say seduced) part of an intellectual generation, especially in France, Britain and much of the Spanish-speaking world. Investigating the reasons for this would provide the basis for an interesting study in the sociology of knowledge. Even students who have moved a great distance away from his positions retain this sense of awe: "It is to Althusser more than to any other individual or group that we owe the current renaissance of Marxist philosophy" (Callinicos, 1976: v). Further, there is resistance to the "outrageous" claim that "Althusser's work simply reenacts Stalinism in modern dress" (Benton, 1984: xi). More importantly, by pushing to the limit the argument for Marxism as an autonomous science beyond ideology, and linking that thesis to a radical reformulation of the base-superstructure problematic, Althusser set the stage for both the renaissance of and the emerging crisis of Marxist theory. To that extent, his failures were not merely his own, but revealed latent difficulties in the very tradition for which he was such an incisive, if mannered, spokesman.

For the purposes of the present discussion, four aspects of structuralist Marxism require brief elucidation: (a) a radically structuralist epistemology based upon a rigid science-ideology distinction and a critique of "humanism" and "historicism"; (b) at the level of methodology, a concept of totality and contradiction based upon the logic of "overdetermination" and "structural causality"; (c) a theory of society based upon Marx's later political economic works and the crucial significance of the process of "social reproduction"; and (d) a theory of "ideological apparatuses" that accords the capitalist state a decisive role in the process of social reproduction. Though each of these themes stimulated important discussions, each is characterized by major difficulties, which neither Althusser nor his followers were ever able to adequately resolve, leading to the collapse of this approach as a distinct school of neo-Marxist theory.

Epistemology

As Althusser points out in an introduction to the English edition of *For Marx*, two key "interventions" guide his argument: first, on the terrain of the Marx-Hegel relation, he draws a line of demarcation between scientific Marxist history and philosophy and pre-Marxist idealism and humanism; second, on the terrain of the relationship between Marx's "Early Works" and *Capital*, he unveils an "epistemological break" that points to the difference between the ideological "problematic" of the first and the scientific "problematic" of the latter (Althusser, 1977: 33). One of the most decisive effects of this strategy of reading Marx is that it facilitates a complete break with the contaminations of bourgeois thought and opens the way for Marxist philosophy to catch up with Marxist science as a fully autonomous discipline. Even if, for example, he borrows terms from bourgeois philosophy (e.g., the term *problematic* comes from Jacques Maritain and *epistemological break* from Gaston Bachelard), the reader is assured that they are already "present and active" in Marx's thought (Althusser, 1977: 32). Needless to say, this aspiration for a rigorous science accessible primarily to avant-garde intellectuals had considerable appeal in societies where intellectuals either had a grandiose sense of the their self-importance or were isolated from the dominant bourgeois culture, however much it may have reinforced prejudices regarding the dogmatic character of Marxist theory. In any case, it provided the epistemological platform for trying to elaborate an alternative conception of the logic of Marx's theory, a concern with some more fruitful consequences that relate to the specifically "structuralist" aspects of Marx's method.

Method

The key methodological innovation proposed by Althusser was a reformulation of the base-superstructure thesis in terms that allowed him to overcome the instrumentalism of crude reflection theories, which assumed a mechanical, causal relationship (the linear or "transitive" causality found in Descartes and Galileo) between economic and cultural phenomena. This thesis was directed against both Soviet Marxism (especially Stalinism) and the positivist Marxism of the Second International. At the same time, however, he rejected the "humanist" and "historicist" alternative of resorting to the Hegelian concept of "totality" to deal with this problem. This move facilitated a rather indiscriminate rejection of every form of theory contaminated with the "essentialism" of Hegelianism: Lukacs, the Frankfurt School, existentialism, even this dimension of Gramsci. The source of the problem with Hegelian Marxism was a defective "expressive" conception of causality of the type implied by the essence-appearance distinction (Althusser and Balibar, 1968, vol. 2: 62). From this perspective the various parts of society (e.g., the superstructure) are explained as manifestations or expressions of some essential underlying principle (the totality) . Althusser suggests that a third conception of causality—structural causality—is in reality the basis of Marx's scientific breakthrough and the necessary foundation for understanding the real meaning of the base-superstructure relationship. Structural causality presupposes a very different conception of the unity of phenomena than the spiritual totality of expressive causality.

Althusser had first introduced this theme in *For Marx* in his discussion of "contradiction and overdetermination"; there, the Freudian concept of overdetermination was introduced to provide a way of "dealing with some quite different from the Hegelian contradiction" (1977: 101).

THE THEORY OF STATE IDEOLOGICAL APPARATUSES

The central analytical contribution of Althusser and Balibar in *Reading Capital* was an effort to rigorously to elaborate the implications of a theory of history based on the succession of abstractly conceived "modes of production" determined economically but only in the "last instance." If the first step in this process was to analyze the discontinuities between modes of production, the turn to an empirical specification of the formation and dissolution of modes of production pointed to the need for a complementary abstract concept to understand the transition from one social formation to another: the concept of reproduction (Althusser and Balibar, 1968, vol. 2: 157). In this context the passages on Marx's reference to reproduction are noted and what has become to be known as the principle of "correspondence" is introduced: an analysis of the relationship between between the mode of production and the social relations of production in terms of structural causality. Rather than having any real autonomy of laws unique to themselves, all reproduction processes are ultimately determined by and correspond to the mode of production that "determines the modes of circulation, of distribution and consumption as so many moments of its unity" (1968, vol. 2: 169). These social relations—which include the superstructure—thus constitute the necessary conditions for the process of production. These elements must possess a significant autonomy if they are to adequately fulfill the imperative of reproduction: "in capitalist production the autonomy of the economic instance or juridical forms *correspond* to the forms of commodity exchange, i.e., to a certain form of correspondence between the diverse instances of the social structure" (1968, vol. 2: 173) Following the objectivist principle of structural causation, finally, the production of social relations is a "process without a subject" (1968, vol. 2: 75).

This shift to the problematic of the processes of social reproduction thus opened the way toward an analysis of the more specifically sociological implications of Marx's theory. Even if introduced in the theoretical context of deriving a theory of transition from one mode of production to another, it in fact has served primarily to guide investigations seeking to "explain" capitalism's surprising stability, that is, its capacity for complex reproduction.

As early as 1962, Althusser had alluded to Antonio Gramsci as a pioneer analyst of superstructures and hence social reproduction processes. This incomplete aspect of Marx and Engels' work is described as the challenge of Marxist theory:

> Like the map of Africa before the great explorations, this theory remains a realm sketched in outline, with its great mountain chains and rivers, but often unknown in detail beyond a few well-known regions. Who has *really* attempted to follow up the explorations of Marx and Engels? I can only think of Gramsci. (1977: 114)

Althusser himself would only take up this challenge several years later, in an article that became the founding document of reproduction theory in education as well as other complementary superstructural research. His "Ideology and Ideological State Apparatuses" (1971) was first published in French in 1970 and modestly subtitled "Notes Toward an Investigation." As one ex-Althusserian has noted: "It is precisely here (and especially where Gramsci's work was used) that structural Marxism made real advances over the Marxist classics. Ideas such as 'interpellation,' and the 'relative autonomy' of ideology, as well as the attempt to link psychoanalysis with Marxism . . . did provide means with which 'class-reductionism' and 'economism' could be opposed within Marxism" (Benton, 1984: xiii).

Althusser's point of departure is the theme introduced by Balibar at the end of *Reading Capital*: the question of social reproduction. The reproduction of the conditions of production requires not only the reproduction of productive forces (the means of production), but also the existing relations of production (labor power). The latter entails not simply the inculcation of "skills" but "also the reproduction of its subjection to the ruling ideology or the 'practice' of that ideology" (Althusser, 1971: 133). For Althusser, explaining this process requires completing the base-superstructure metaphor with a theory of the state and ideology. On the one hand, he wants to preserve the thesis of economic determination in the "last instance"; the "floors of the superstructure are not determinant in the last instance. . . they are determined by the effectivity of the base" (1971: 135). To the extent the superstructure is determinant, this is ultimately limited by the base. On the other hand, he also wants to stress the importance of the superstructure opened up by abandoning the instrumental thesis of linear, mechanical determination. For this purpose he draws upon two traditional themes: "(1) there is a 'relative autonomy' of the superstructure with respect to the base; (2) there is a 'reciprocal action' of the superstructure on the base"; within the superstructure, therefore, one can only speak of a " 'derivatory' effectivity" (1971: 135–36).

The traditional Marxist theory of the state as a "repressive apparatus" is the necessary point of departure for a theory of the superstructure. To be sure, this does define the "basic function" of the administrative bureaucracy, police, courts, prisons, and army, but cannot fully explain the process of social reproduction. Second, it is important to distinguish "state power" as an act of controlling it and the "state apparatus," which may operate more or less independently. Third, class struggle focuses on state power and, finally, use of the state apparatus and revolution requires both seizure of state power and destruction of the existing bourgeois apparatus.

To go beyond this descriptive theory, however, requires adding considerations hinted in the practice of classic Marxism, though not in its theory. To go beyond the repressive state apparatus, based predominantly and ultimately on violence, it is necessary to conceptualize the "ideological state apparatus" based predominantly on ideology as manifest in education, the family, legal institutions, the political system, trade-unions, communications, and culture (Althusser, 1971: 143). There are three basic features that distinguish the repressive state apparatus from the ideological: the unity of the repressive apparatus as opposed to the plurality of the ideological; its location in the public domain as opposed to the private; and the primary reliance upon force as opposed to ideology or symbolic domination. (1971: 144–45) As Althusser admits, at first sight the most problematic aspect of this schema is the diversity of the ideological state apparatus and its location in the "private" sphere. The unity of the latter lies in its "functioning" within a framework of a "ruling ideology" and a "ruling class": "To my knowledge, no class can hold State power over a long period without at the same time exercising its hegemony over and in the State Ideological Apparatuses" (1971: 146). Accordingly, the ideological apparatuses are not only a "stake" but also a "site" of class struggle.

Of particular importance in the present context is how Althusser deals with the relative importance or weight of the different ideological state apparatuses. Whereas in the past the Church was generally dominant, "the ideological State apparatus which has been installed in the *dominant* position in mature capitalist social formations as a result of a violent political and ideological class struggle against the old dominant ideological State apparatus, is the *educational ideological apparatus*" (1971: 152). The Church-family couple has been replaced by the school-family nexus. This marks the official point of birth of the Marxist theory of reproduction in education (though Bourdieu can claim a certain priority with respect to reproduction theory as such) :

> one ideological State apparatus certainly has the dominant role, although hardly anyone lend an ear to its music: it is so silent! This is the School. It takes children from every class at infant-school age, and then for years, the years in which the child

is most "vulnerable," squeezed between the family State apparatus and the educational state apparatus, it drums into them,
whether it uses new or old methods, a certain amount of "know-
how" wrapped in the ruling ideology . . . Each mass ejected *en
route* is practically provided with the ideology which suits the
role it has to fulfil in class society: the role of the exploited . . . the role of the agent of exploitation . . . of the agent of
repression . . . or the professional ideologist. (1971: 155–56)

Beyond this, Althusser outlines a theory of ideology to theoretically secure his overall argument. Since his controversial formulations are complex and lead us beyond the main argument of this
chapter, only the highlights need to be noted. In line with his
structuralist method, Althusser begins with a distinction between
ideology "in general," which has no history, as opposed to class
and regional ideologies, which do have a history (which is determined economically in the last instance). His focus of attention is
this general theory, which leads him to reject Marx's early conception of ideology as pure illusion that could somehow be transcen-
ded. As we introduced in the previous chapter, for Althusser ideology is eternal in the same sense that Freud referred to the
unconscious. The resulting account of the structure and functioning of ideology is developed in terms of two theses. First, "ideology
represents the imaginary relationship of individuals to their real
conditions of life" (1971: 62). To be sure, this "imaginary" relation alludes to reality, opening the way for forms of interpretation
that reveal that underlying reality. More problematic, for Althusser, is the origin of this need for imaginary representation. He
rejects both the Enlightenment approach, which blamed priests
and despots, and that of Feuerbach and the early Marx—the alienated conditions of existence. He rejects this latter approach because "it is not their real conditions of existence, their real world,
that 'men' 'represent to themselves' in ideology, but above all it is
their relation to those conditions of existence which is represented
to them there" (1971: 64) In short, it is not an accident of history
that this occurs, because it is built into the very process of representing reality.

The second thesis argues that "ideology has a material existence." Part of a polemic against the humanist habit of viewing
ideology as purely spiritual phenomena, this point seeks to stress
that ideology always operated "in an apparatus, and its practice,

or practices. This existence is material" (1971: 166). One could also say, then, that ideology has a "social existence."

More striking—and problematic—is the conclusion drawn from the materiality of ideology: "(1) there is no practice except by and in an ideology; (2) there is no ideology except by the subject and for subjects" (1971: 170). This "central" thesis can only be understood in relation to the peculiar definition of "subjects" used here, which are contrasted with "concrete individuals." In this terminology, the concept of subject refers to the opposite of what is suggested in phenomenological or existential discussions where the subject is the concrete, free individual. Althusser's reference is rather to the notion of the "subject" as one subjected to power, as the subject of authority. To say, therefore, that "all ideology has the function (which defines it) of 'constituting' concrete individuals as subjects" suggests that all humanistic references to individuality are based on false consciousness. The reason is a process of structural determination through which "all ideology hails or interpellates concrete individuals as concrete subjects." (1971: 173). But this is not a temporal process; it is co-extensive with the very idea of a subject. In this sense, "an individual is always-already a subject, even before he is born . . . appointed as a subject in and by the specific familiar ideological configuration in which it is 'expected' once it has been conceived" (1971: 176). From this perspective, all freedom is illusory, serving rather to tighten the bonds of subjection: "the individual is interpellated as a (free) subject in order that he shall submit freely to the commandments of the Subject, i.e., in order that he shall (freely) accept his subjection." (1971: 182). Though resembling in certain respects the sociological thesis of the "social construction of reality" or the functionalist theory of socialization, the Althusserian formulation, by linking this process to the imaginary representations of ideology, suggests both the illusory character of subjectivity and its functional relationship to the correspondence between the mode of production and the reproduction of the social relations of production—in the last instance.

THE STRUCTURALIST APPROPRIATION OF GRAMSCI

Two features of the Althusserian conception of social reproduction and ideology are especially noteworthy. First, it represents an effort to specify the mediating mechanisms of social reproduction with a theory of the state, thus marking an important advance over interpretations based on strict economic and class determination. Second, the source of inspiration of this strategy of analysis is a problematic reading of Antonio Gramsci, the Italian Marxist whose work had been previously criticized in *Reading Capital* as "humanist" and "historicist." In short, Althusser's objective is to rescue Gramsci's empirical and substantive insights about the state and hegemony by separating them from his overall interpretation of Marxism. As Althusser admits:

> To my knowledge, Gramsci is the only one who went any distance in the road I am taking. He had the "remarkable" idea that the State could not be reduced to the (Repressive) State Apparatus, but included, as he put it, a certain number of institutions from "*civil society*": the Church, the Schools, the trade unions, etc. Unfortunately, Gramsci did not systematize his intuitions, which remained in the state of fragmentary notes. (1971: 142, n. 7)

Without taking anything away from the originality of Gramsci's formulations, it should be noted (to anticipate the later discussion of Gramsci in chapters 8 and 10) that Althusser is mistaken here to the extent that the whole research program of the early Frankfurt School in the Weimar Republic (e.g., research on authority and the family and its impact on the German working classes) is oriented toward the same problematic. More important in the present context is the particular interpretation of Gramsci that results from Althusser's "structuralist" appropriation. This point is of strategic significance to the extent that Althusser's interpretation has been widely influential, especially in France, and is the basis of a common association between Gramsci and reproduction theories of education. As we shall attempt to demonstrate later, there is another tradition of interpretation of Gramscian theory—and one much more consistent with his own intentions—which has resulted in what might be termed a second wave of Gramscian theory, one that goes far beyond and breaks in fundamental respects with the epistemological and methodological basis of structuralist Marxism, as well as with the original theory of state apparatuses and ideology developed by Althusser and the early Poulantzas.

The most important consequence of Althusser's structuralist appropriation is that Gramsci's theory of the state is transformed into a rigidly teleological and functionalistic argument. From this perspective, the theory of the state is rescued from any crude instrumentalism but falls into a hyperstructuralism that introduces other equally fundamental difficulties. Further, the reduction of the "subject" to an epiphenomenal status within a larger schema of structural determination completely eliminates the central concerns about developing forms of counterhegemonic praxis that are crucial for Gramsci's approach. Some of the implications and problems created by this interpretation of Gramsci become fully apparent in the various efforts to apply structural Marxism to the study of different educational systems.

APPLICATIONS OF STRUCTURALIST MARXISM

One of the standard criticisms of Althusserian structuralist Marxism has been the absence of sustained empirical research. Education is actually the primary exception in this regard in that the work of Baudelot and Establet is based directly on Althusser's theory of ideological apparatuses. However, as we shall see, they deviate with respect to other aspects of his approach, such as his lack of an account of resistance. In Vasconi's work, as well, we have an example of the application of structuralist Marxism to Latin America. The third example we will take up is not a direct byproduct of the Althusserian approach, but has its origins rather in forms of political economy that in the work of Bowles and Gintis, include an unstable combination of instrumentalism, functionalism, and voluntarism.

The Capitalist School in France: Baudelot and Establet

In Christian Baudelot and Roger Establet's *L'Ecole capitaliste en France* (1971), we are provided with an application of structuralist-Marxist theory to the case of French education. Originally published in 1971, this book provides a useful point of comparison to Bourdieu's early work (which we will take up in the next section), as well as an example of the kind of empirical analysis to which the theory of state ideological apparatuses might give rise. The continuity with the work of Althusser is clear, as the authors are part of this milieu and explicitly cite Etienne Balibar (who prepared the section in *Reading Capital* on social reproduction).

Yet it would be an exaggeration to say that their work was a completely faithful application of Althusser's approach as a whole. None of his epistemological concerns enter in, even if he is credited with having established the importance of the material existence of ideology in practices, thus opening the way for their own analysis of the "material ritual" of bourgeois ideology. But there is an implicit tension with respect to Althusser's work that derives from the authors own peculiar fusion of Marxist-Leninist orthodoxy and Maoist inspiration. Indeed, they note that "we would have never suspected the vital importance of the educational front in class struggle without the experience of the Chinese cultural revolution" (1971: 316). In this connection, a Chinese document attacking Soviet educational theory is attached. In particular, they are inspired by the belief that "the Chinese are in the process of finding the first organic forms which will permit putting an end (after a long process) of the division between manual and intellectual labor, i.e., the material and ideological basis of the existences of classes" (1971: 319). Obviously, this stress upon a critique of expertise, even in a postcapitalist society, conflicts with the elitism found in Althusser's theory of knowledge and the "Party." A further expression of difference is the attention the authors give to working "resistance" in education, a theme that has a most problematic status within Althusser's theory of the subject.

Baudelot and Establet's point of departure is an attack on the ideology of the school, especially the illusory claims of the unified school and aspirations for its further democratization. All of these reformist approaches ignore the "real basis" of class division (working class and proletariat) on which the school functions; rather than viewing the school's contradictions as a sign of imperfections and survivals, they must be seen "as an ensemble of *necessary* contradictions, which have by themselves an historically determinant meaning and function, and that they can be explained by their *material* conditions of existence within a determinant mode of production" (1971: 18). More specifically, there exists a "capitalist educational apparatus," part of the ideological state apparatus, which divides the school system into two streams—the "secondary-advanced" and the "primary-occupational"—whose primary function is the reproduction of the capitalist relations of production. In short, in the last instance, class antagonism explains "not only the existence of these two streams, but also. . . the *mechanisms* of their functioning, their causes and their effects" (1971: 42).

The argument is developed in four steps. First, an effort is made to statistically demonstrate the existence of two streams throughout the educational system and their class basis, despite the official existence of a third "technical" stream. Second, these two streams are shown to be characterized by two types of pedagogy; though the same dominant ideology is imposed, it is done so in a manner appropriate to the working class as opposed to the bourgeoisie. Third, this basic division is traced back to the primary school, where the most crucial initial bases of class emerge. And finally, all of the key features of this educational system are linked to their contribution to the reproduction of capitalist social relations (i.e., the correspondence thesis).

Several comments are necessary to preface any overall evaluation of their resulting study. On one level, the data they cite with respect to status attainment (defined primarily by level of education obtained) and class background simply repeats similar findings in all advanced capitalist societies. Similarly the contention that class division can be traced back to primary school is a general finding, though the rigidities of the French system have particularly strong effects. And the general argument that education socializes all members of society into an ideology of democratic consensus is fairly obvious, even if it bears repeating to offset the mystifications of official ideology. In general terms, therefore, these aspects of their argument converge broadly with a number of different conflict-based sociologies of education, such as those of Bourdieu and Bernstein (see chapter 7).

What is more problematic and central to their specific thesis is the two-fold structure of division and its relationship of correspondence with the system of production. In particular, it is possible to view their overall argument as a mirror image of a somewhat simplistic version of a functionalist argument (especially popular in business circles) that school should prepare people for the job market; from this perspective, the difference between manual and intellectual do in fact require different types of training.

The use of more recent data (theirs is derived mostly from the early 1960s) would render much more difficult their claim of a simple dual structure in education. Their schema allows no place for the middle strata and for the divergence of interests between these and the grand bourgeoisie of capital. At best, their model provides the basis for a very high level of generality regarding the way in which an educational system is interdependent with the economic system. But on the basis of their evidence (and lack of a comparative perspective), they have no clear grounds for arguing why the French educational system has taken the form it in fact has. Nor can they demonstrate that the parallels between the educational system and the labor markets and production process constitute "correspondence" in any rigorous sense. Again, a comparative perspective suggests there are a wide range of looser or tighter "fits" between educational and occupational systems. These issues can be defined even more clearly in the case of Bowles and Gintis's more empirically elaborate research.

As mentioned at the outset, a crucial aspect of Baudelot and Establet's approach conflicts with a central theme of structuralist Marxism, namely, their attempt to demonstrate resistance in the educational system. In contrast to the pessimism generally associated with structuralist reproduction theories, their Maoist euphoria leads them to a certain revolutionary optimism. The basis of this argument is the contention that there is an "instinct of class" that produces spontaneous forms of resistance to exploitation and its effects (1971: 174). But "proletarian ideology is not constituted by ideas or opinions. It exists first in the practices in which it comes into being" (1971: 178). Bourgeois sociology makes the mistake of identifying ideology with an explicit discourse and then concludes it does not exist. In contrast, Baudelot and Establet cite a number of examples of type of resistance to the process of schooling (ranging from violence to passive resistance) and attempt to establish the proletarian basis of specific forms within the primary-occupational (working-class) stream. Yet they admit these forms of specifically proletarian resistance tend to be deflected by the dominant bourgeois ideology toward "petit-bourgeois anarchistic" forms (1971: 183). Proletarian ideology here is given a very explicit meaning as the "ensemble of ideas and practices" that allows the proletariat to lead a struggle to constitute itself as the dominant class (1971: 187). However, their own work was not backed up by any systematic ethnographic research, and subsequent developments lend little credibility to the optimistic assumption of specifically proletarian revolutionary resistance of this type as a significant force in advanced capitalism. But Baudelot and Establet should be credited with having introduced the question and pointed toward the kind of research that might evaluate such possibilities. Their own work, however, remains content to impose a theoretical apparatus upon rather limited and recalcitrant data. Nor do they confront the theoretical problems of how the formation of proletarian subjectivity can be reconciled with Althusser's structuralist theory of the "hailed" and hence determined subject.

Marxism and Education in Latin America (1960–1973): Tomás A. Vasconi

A second application of structuralist Marxism in the Latin American context is also instructive. Not unlike the case of Bowles and Gintis, Vasconi eventually became dissatisfied with the correspondence theory of educational reproduction.

Dependency studies reacted against modernization theories in sociology of development. Likewise, Tomás A. Vasconi and some colleagues working in Argentina first and in Chile[1] later, developed a Marxist-structuralist approach to education, inspired but not totally tied to the Althusserian framework.

In a sort of division of labor, Vasconi argued that he assumed, from the perspective of dependency, the study of the superstructural phenomena (1981: 306). The Marxist perspective of Vasconi and associates (Labarca, et al. 1977) has been compiled in a book suggestively entitled *Bourgeois Education* (1977). Indeed, in the early seventies, they represented a critical reaction against Durkheimian, Weberian, and functionalist tendencies in Latin American sociology, and attempted to build a Marxist sociology of education.[2]

The work of Althusser, Bourdieu, and Passeron, but above all Baudelot and Establet, were landmarks for that endeavor. The theme that informs all their work is the attempt to explain from a Marxist perspective the relationships between education and development, with a special reference to the situation in the Southern Cone countries (Argentina, Chile, Uruguay, and Brazil), and with a special focus on the impact of modernization processes in higher education (Vasconi and Recca, 1977: 17–68; Labarca, 1977: 239–61).

This structuralist programme of research used concepts such as schooling as the ideological apparatus of the State, hegemony, ideology as the diffusion and imposition of the dominant class's worldview, pedagogical violence, and the like. Similarly, a strong attack against the illusory claim of the unity of the school reflected the influence of the two streams system à la Baudelot and Establet (Vasconi, 1977a: 176ff.).

In spite of this attempt to rewrite the contemporary history of education in Latin America in the 1970s through such a repertoire of Marxist concepts, Vasconi's more systematic study of education and development in Latin America (1977: 173–236) utilizes aggregate empirical data and indicators such as rates of schooling, enrollment rates, and rates of growth to support his claim of the educational system as an ideological apparatus of the state and the contradictions of educational expansion (Vasconi, 1977a: 236).

The influence of the New Left, particularly Rosanna Roxanda's "theses sur l' enseignement" and Mao Tse Tung's perspective on the student movement, is also evident in their analysis. Vasconi's work—which become the landmark of this Marxist attempt—was originally entitled "Against the School" (published in Buenos Aires in 1973) and bore some resemblance to Illich's approach.[3] This essay was republished several times in several countries. One of the best known editions in Venezuela added a subtitle, "Draft for a Marxist Critique of Education," that become virtually a must for whoever wanted to approach the study of education from a Marxist perspective in the region. When this article was collected in the 1977 publication, it had as a new, less ambitious title: "Contribution for a Theory of Education" (Aportes para una teoría de la Educación).

Some of the main theses presented at the end of this essay have a definite Althusserian flavor:

Thesis 1: In the capitalist society, the school is an instrument of domination of the bourgeoisie. The school is an ideological apparatus of the state.

Thesis 2: The fundamental function of the school—as an ideological apparatus of the state—is to contribute to the reproduction of the capitalist society—that is to say, the reproduction of the social relationships of exploitation.

Thesis 3: The capitalist school is not a perfect machine ("una máquina bien aceitada") that works on behalf of the bourgeoisie. It is also the place where multiple contradictions take place. Contradictions that are not other than the localized (and specific) effects of the contradictions between the proletariat and the bourgeoisie.

Thesis 4: In the capitalist school, educators' role—beyond their personal goals and individual consciousness—is to be the ideological agents of the bourgeoisie. However, they live or better yet reproduce subjectively the objective contradictions of the capitalist school.

Thesis 5: The students have a contradictory class location because they express vividly the contradictions of the school system and the overall system.

Thesis 6: It is impossible to reform the capitalist school in order to use it in a socialist society. The period of social transition requires a period of destruction of the school apparatus—as an ideological apparatus of the state—and the transition toward a superior organic form (Vasconi, 1977b: 338).

This last thesis, about the necessity of the destruction of the capitalist school in a period of socialist transition, reflects the dynamics of political conflict in Chile at the time of the Popular Unity regime, so well captured in the historical study of Joseph Farrell on the National Unified School during Allende's Presidency (Farrell, 1986). Farrell argues that the rhetoric of the NUS proposal alienated the middle classes and especially the military because it was seen as conflicting with the basic value structure of the Chileans rather than simply as an educational reform. In this way, it contributed to accelerate the inevitable down fall of Allende's government through a military coup (Farrell, 1986).

In the introduction of the collection of essays republished in Mexico in 1977—*Bourgeois Education*—the authors seem to have second thoughts about emphasizing the perspective of the class struggle they claim to sustain (Vasconi and Recca, 1977: 11). They take exception with the overall theoretical elaboration known as studies of dependency or dependency theory, as well as with the interpretations on the role of superstructures. First, they reject what they called the economic reductionism of the positivist correspondence principle. Second, they reject their previous analysis of the school as eminently an ideological apparatus because this perspective in fact overlooked the role of education in the production of surplus value.[4]

It is also claimed that in Latin America there is an strange "cohabitation" of a "pedagogic anti-imperialism" in politics, Christian existentialism in educational ideology, and modernization (developmentalism) approaches in human resource training. They see that this is possible because all of them reject or deny the class character of education, and the possibility of political struggle within the educational systems (1977: 12).

In reaffirming that education should be at the service of the interests of only the revolutionary class, the proletariat, the authors stress that their work falls within the framework of a "Marxist theory of domination." Freire is severally criticized from this perspective because (a) his pedagogy of the oppressed does not portray class antagonism; (b) hence, exploitation becomes not a scientific category but a moral one; (c) liberation is then a process that takes place between educator-learner and not in the class struggle; and (d) the mediating agent for liberation is the content of education and the attitude of the educator, not the political party (1977: 13).

Vasconi's self-criticism of his earlier positions (Vasconi, 1981: 303–14) refers to his last years in Chile, emphasizing that he adopted the terminology of Althusser but not his entire epistemology. Nonetheless, the historical dynamics of the complex process of social transition in Chile showed them the inadequacy of their structuralist framework to understand what was going on in the streets (1981: 307). After his exile from Chile to Venezuela—and later to Cuba— Vasconi turned to other endeavors. Education stopped being a priority for analysis and political action; instead the role of the Army and the State become a central concern in explaining the deterioration of the fragile Latin American democracies (Vasconi, 1978).

All in all, Vasconi's production is a tributary of the European structuralists, but was never developed as an consistent agenda for research in Latin America. Although highly influential in the mid seventies and early eighties, his work is fragmented, written as research notes more than polished final products, and his attempt to write an antipositivist, antiliberal history of education in Latin America did not go beyond some sketchy and fairly ambiguous analysis.[5]

Structuralism and Socialist Pedagogy

To this point we have focussed on an analysis of the implications of structuralist Marxism as an analysis of the contribution of education to social reproduction in capitalism. But it is also instructive—and decisive—to evaluate all such approaches in relation to the form of social pedagogy that they suggest for "postrevolutionary" societies, given that they all postulate the impossibility of meaningful reform within capitalism, or even as part of a transitional phase. The obvious point of departure here is the example of existing "socialism" as evidenced in the most widely cited Soviet, and sometimes Chinese, models. Though these were not elaborated within explicitly structuralist-Marxist terms, it is nevertheless true that those influenced by this tradition in France and Latin America, for example, have looked upon these examples as models of polytechnical education and (as well shall see later) developed an interpretation of Gramsci consistent with this.

The notion of communist education emerged in the Soviet Union in the context of a very unique revolutionary experience, coupled with the imperatives of primitive accumulation. As a consequence, priority was necessarily given to the pedagogical implications of creating a disciplined industrial working class in a predominantly peasant society. The overall consequence was a selective interpretation of Marx and Engels, particularly the tension between their theory of the dictatorship of the proletariat as a transitional stage towards a more advanced, and hence liberating, mode of production and social arrangements, and their libertarian goals for self-reliant communities of the type that would be more appropriate for advanced industrial democracies.

The basic principles of communist pedagogy were elaborated in the work of Anatoly Vasilyevich Lunacharsky (Fitzpatrick, 1970), first Commissar of Education for the October revolution; Nadezhada Krupskaya (King, 1948), Lenin's long-time companion, and Anton Semyonovitch Makarenko (Lilge, 1958; Makarenko, 1973; Bowen, 1962), with his pedagogy of duty and self-discipline. Most contemporary are the principles of pedagogical communism that were advocated by Polish pedagogue Bogdan Suchodolski (Suchodolski, 1966). There are a number of educational philosophers and pedagogues that have developed this notion of communist pedagogy in a number of postrevolutionary societies. For instance, in Latin America, communist education (and education as help in the class struggle) has been advocated, paradoxically, from a Marxist perspective linked with the basic principles of liberalism by Anibal Ponce (Terán, 1983), or from an Marxist orthodox perspective by Cuban educator Gaspar García Galló (1974).

Communist education was in dialogue with progressive education, but Dewey's principle of starting learning from experience was considered too abstract and translated into learning from work as production, that is, the learner as a worker. As Suchodolski pointed out: "The new education seemed to be an ally since it brought to the fore criticism of the old school, but it was an inadequate ally since its positive program did not correspond to the conditions and objectives that the revolutionary country was struggling to achieve" (Suchodolski and Manaconda, 1975: 22).

A quick glance at the history of education in the Soviet Union will show that in communist education progressive principles are subordinated to the imperatives of revolutionary transition: experience becomes production, democracy becomes democratic centralism, individual personality gets subsumed into the collective, and the notion of education as caring gets transformed into an input in the process of constructing the dictatorship of the proletariat.

In contrast, Lunacharsky, who was himself a Menshevik not a Bolshevik, stood firmly on the side of the contemporary European and American progressive educational movement. He advocated the encouragement of the child's individuality and creativity, the development of his or her social instincts, informal relations between pupils and teachers, activity methods of teaching, broadening the school curriculum to include study of the surrounding environment, physical and aesthetic education, and training in elementary labor and craft skills—all of that which when coupled with a dialectical notion of history and the basic premises of Marxist pedagogy was characterized as the principle of polytechnical education. A strong supporter of higher education, Lunacharsky engaged in a polemic with Preobrazhensky in the early 1920s, defending the need to expand higher education while Preobrazhensky argued that there were too many unemployed intellectuals and instead provided a rationale for the expansion of middle technical and vocational education (Fitzpatrick, 1970: 218–20).

As the first Commissar of Education, jointly with N. K. Krupskaya, Lunacharsky was involved in building the new communist education. Krupskaya's contributions involved, first, the extension of the polytechnic principles through a restructuring of the curriculum oriented toward a conception of the "organization of work" that would ensure the correspondence between the imperatives of the production process and the school. This did not

require simplistic vocationalism so much as a more general application of scientific principles to production, along with bringing
children to the workplace as part of their training. Second,
Krupskaya had a visionary sense of the importance of the "Young
Pioneer Movement" as the affective basis of the formation of the
new Soviet collective individual.

Makarenko, who is perhaps the best known Soviet pedagogue,[6] undertook the task of resocializing the homeless juvenile
delinquents known as "besprizornye," who resulted from the social and family dislocations of drastic, sudden, and, in this case,
bloody revolutionary change (Lilge, 1958: 2). His unifying principle is an anticognitive conception, stressing the moral and affective
foundations of the types of personalities required to build a collective project such as socialism—hence his emphasis on education as
an aesthetic and moral enterprise and his strong biases towards an
education that molds the character of a child, a strategy which has
been followed in other revolutionary experiences, including Cuba
(García Galló, 1974).

In sum, Soviet polytechnical education created the foundations
for a process of cultural reproduction attuned to the specific requirements of a bureaucratic collectivist dictatorship of the proletariat. Whatever rationale this may have had as a transitional stage
of development, it was self-contradictory in that it did not provide
any basis for the transformative self-consciousness required for the
official principle of the "withering away of the state," or more
concretely, a process of democratization that would lead to the
direct appropriation of the production process by the workers
themselves.[7] As a consequence, the transformative principles of a
critical pedagogy had to eventually be imported from outside,
ironically interpreted in highly individualist and liberal terms. The
rigidity of the Soviet system thus failed to effectively produce the
new "Soviet man" and was consequently vulnerable to a severe
legitimation crisis with the underground contact with new definitions of individuality.

The significance of polytechnical education in alternative educational policies pursued by socialist governments is clearly por-
trayed in Joseph P. Farrell's (1986) book on the National Unified
School (NUS) in Chile. The NUE was a project of educational
reform combining productive labor, mental education, bodily exercise, and polytechnic training following the standard Marxist ped-

agogical principles that were supposed to be implemented during Allende's presidency in Chile. For Farrell, the attempt to implement the NUS project was one of the key reasons that precipitated the downfall of the otherwise peaceful transition to socialism attempted by the socialist coalition led by President Salvador Allende.

CORRESPONDENCE THEORY IN THE UNITED STATES: BOWLES AND GINTIS

Introduction: Intellectual Context

Samuel Bowles and Herbert Gintis's *Schooling in Capitalist America* (1976) represents the culmination of correspondence theories of education and the most important and influential empirical application of its general principles. Though their study is based on a more traditional base-superstructure model, it is structuralist in the sense that, on the assumptions of a variant of structuralist Marxism, it postulates a correspondence of form between education and the production processes. Hence, it is not directly inspired by the Althusserian tradition and, in fact, diverges widely from it in certain key methodological and political respects. Indeed, one of the most interesting aspects of Bowles and Gintis's work is that it represents both the high point of correspondence theory and research as well as the point of its precipitous decline. For these reasons, *Schooling in Capitalist America* constitutes a crucial point of departure for subsequent developments in theories of educational reproduction.

Crucial to understanding the work of Bowles and Gintis are its origins within the context of the libertarian North American New Left, more specifically its political-economic wing. This context sharply differentiates their work from either European or Latin American structuralist Marxism, which was associated with models of socialist pedagogy based on the Soviet and Chinese models of polytechnical education. The American New Left has its origins in a critique of liberalism and the Old Left, rather than a critique of existentialism or Stalinism as in the European and Latin American cases. In the American context, moreover, the pressures of academic life precluded any reliance upon intellectual authority—i.e., arguments based on the exegesis of Marx or Althusser—and demanded an empirical strategy compatible with the reigning positivism of American social science. Indeed, this empiricist imperative was the basis of a certain division within the North American Left between its political-economic wing—which sought to apply the methods of traditional social science to a Marxist problematic—and tendencies inspired by Frankfurt and other forms of critical theory, which began with a critique of positivism and sought to elaborate alternative research strategies. The most important and influential early research, however, was inspired by the nascent tradition of political economy (cf. Attewell, 1984) as exemplified in education in the work of Bowles and Gintis.

Among the distinctive features of their approach are the following: (1) An avoidance of epistemological issues and a general acceptance of the canons of empiricist methodologies in economics (where they were initially trained) and sociology; as a consequence, they resisted structuralism as an epistemological position, even as they developed a structuralist correspondence theory. (2) The resulting critical socialist perspective, though defined in largely neo-Marxist terms, was eclectic in relation to the socialist tradition as a whole and was strongly influenced by the free-school movement (closely associated with the New Left) and critiques of orthodox Marxism and its political strategies. (3) Their work attempts to combine theoretical analysis, an empirical case study of the social history of American education, and a programmatic strategy for revolutionary political change in the United States; here we find none of the pessimism and determinism characteristic of European and Latin American structuralist Marxism.

The outcome of this overall strategy was an approach that, from a European structuralist (Althusserian) perspective, suffered from all the sins of empiricism, voluntarism, and humanism. Yet their eclectic approach can be credited with attempting to come to terms with the major difficulties of formalist structuralism and, in so doing, anticipating most of the subsequent developments in theories of educational reproduction.

The significance of the origins of the New Left in a critique of American liberalism lies primarily in its effort to demystify what had been generally regarded to be the most impressive achievement of American democracy: the creation of the most open educational system of any liberal democracy. In that respect, the United States represents a kind of model case of the ostensible autonomy of education and its capacity to foster social mobility and equality.

And it is not accidental that most of those who turned to neo-Marxist theory in the late 1960s did so out of disillusionment with the failure of liberal reform programs.

Bowles and Gintis thus begin with an effort to demonstrate what are taken to be three fatal aspects of liberal reform movements and alternative accounts for their failure: (1) a misunderstanding of the history of educational systems; (2) the inadequacy of any effort to explain the weak link between education and overcoming economic inequality as a result of genetic (racial) difference in intelligence as measured by IQ tests; and (3) the failure to understand the relationship between education and the capitalist economy, a failing most evident in the goals of the free-school movement (1976: 8–9).

The Correspondence Thesis

The point of departure of Bowles and Gintis's alternative perspective is the classic theory of neo-Marxist political economy: "Education in the United States plays a dual role in the social process whereby surplus value, i.e., profit, is created and expropriated" (1976: 11). Hence, education not only increases productivity by imparting skills, it contributes to the reproduction of a given set of class relations by diffusing the potential for class conflict. Five basic arguments are developed on the basis of the model: (1) the forms of economic inequality and personal development are attributed to the "market, property, and power relations which define the capitalist system"; (2) "the educational system does not add to or subtract from the overall degree of inequality and repressive personal development"; (3) this process of reproduction is achieved not primarily through the conscious intentions of the participants, "but through a close correspondence between the social relationships which govern personal interaction in the work place and the social relationships of the educational system"; (4) "though the school system has effectively served the interests of profit and political stability, it has hardly been a finely tuned instrument of manipulating in the hands of socially dominant groups"; and (5) "the organization of education—in particular the correspondence between school structure and job structure—has taken distinct and characteristic forms in different periods of U.S. history" (1976: 11–13).

Even if in general terms these arguments follow from the familiar application of the theory of social reproduction to education, the distinctiveness of Bowles and Gintis's analysis should be stressed: first, the empirical effort to specify and demonstrate the exact forms of correspondence; second, an attempt to avoid any simplistic functionalist reduction of education to the interests of capital accumulation through a sensitive reconstruction of the dynamics of the social history of education; and third, an effort to develop a constructive political program based on this structural analysis of education and the state.

The point of departure for the analysis of the correspondence between job structures and educational structures is a statistical analysis concerned with rejecting the liberal effort to link skill differences to the failure to achieve social justice. Instead, it is argued that the educational system in fact produces surpluses of skill, which not only increases the control of employers over workers but also contributes to the symbolic legitimation of inequality: "The meritocratic orientation of the educational system promotes not its egalitarian function, but rather its integrative role. Education reproduces inequality by justifying privilege and attributing poverty to personal failure" (1976: 114).

The specific implications of the correspondence thesis are developed at three levels of the relationship between work and eduction: authority relations, reward structures, and task organization. As they put it:

> Specifically, the relationships of authority and control between administrators and teachers, teachers and students, student and students, and students and their work replicate the hierarchical division of labor which dominates the work place. Power is organized along vertical lines of authority from administration to faculty to student body; students have a degree of control over their curriculum comparable to that of the worker over the content of his job. The motivational system of the school, involving as it does grades and other external rewards and the threat of failure rather than the intrinsic social benefits of the process of education (learning) or its tangible outcome (knowledge), mirrors closely the role of wages and the specter of unemployment in the motivation of workers. The fragmented nature of jobs is reflected in the institutionalized and rarely constructive competition among students and in the specialization and compartmentalization of academic knowledge. Finally, the

relationships of dominance and subordinancy in education differ by level. (1976: 12)

Various forms of empirical evidence are ingeniously introduced to confirm these claims. Of particular interest in the present context, however, are some of the specific aspects of the logic of the correspondence argument developed. First, it is stressed that the correspondence is primarily one of the form rather than the content: "The heart of the process is so to be found not in the content of the educational encounter—or the process of information transfer—but in the form: the social relations of the educational encounter . . . individuals are induced to accept the degree of powerlessness with which they will be faced as mature workers" (1976: 265).

Second, the correspondence thesis is coupled with a macrosociological (functionalist) assumption regarding the natural state of equilibrium, that is, a close integration between the "needs" of the economic system and the educational system. But the elaboration of the historical analysis provides a nuanced interpretation of this initial functionalist assumption which follows, of course, from the logic of any reproduction thesis. It is held that the economic sphere tends to be more dynamic and that education tends to be subordinate to it. Yet when confronted with the actual history of American education, the authors are forced to recognize that the distinction or contradiction between these two systems is crucial to understanding social change: "the independent internal dynamics of these two systems present the ever-present possibility of a significant mismatch arising between the economy and education . . . Thus, the relatively static educational system periodically falls out of correspondence with the social relations of production and becomes a force antithetical to capitalist development" (1976: 236). At this point, Bowles and Gintis take an important step away from structuralist-Marxist reproduction models, which tend to take for granted the automatic character of the maintenance of the reproduction process.

This introduction of a notion of disequilibrium—of a potential disjunction between the economy and education—is coupled with another innovative theme: a concern with attempting to specify the mechanisms linking economic interests and educational programs. As critics have long pointed out, this question represents the most important methodological flaw of functionalist explanations that rely on teleological assumptions not linked to empirical evidence. Two primary mechanisms are analyzed which are held to link the accommodation of educational system to economic conditions. The first process, the politics of "pluralist accommodation," corresponds fairly closely to the observations of pluralist political science and empirical sociology. Change in educational systems at this level "operates through the relatively uncoordinated pursuit of interests by millions of individuals and groups as mediated by local school boards, the market for private educational services, and other decentralized decision-making arenas" (1976: 236). Such processes not only provide the basis for a "natural" link between the economy and education, they also legitimate the assumption that this is a democratic process outside of elite control. Ironically, however, what is not acknowledged is that that the outcome is largely determined by the imperatives of the economic structure, despite the forms of democratic participation, hence "re-establishing the correspondence between school structure and the social relations of production" (1976: 237).

The second type of mechanism appears only during periods of crisis, which are identified in the social history of American education. In this context a second process of adjustment emerges that leads to the possibility of a class form of political struggle:

> Particularly in periods of serious disjuncture between school system and the economy—the 1840s and the 1850s, the first two decades of the present century, and the 1960s and early 1970s— the school system appears less as a cipher impartially recording and tallying the choices of millions of independent actors and more as an arena for struggle among major social groups. The response of forward-looking capitalists to popular unrest is typically dual: material amelioration and educational expansion or reform . . . In each case, the capitalist class—through its use of the police power of the state in suppressing anticapitalist alternatives, through more generalized political power naturally attending its control over production and investment, and through its extensive control over the financial resources for educational research, innovation, and training—has been able to loosely define a model of educational change, one which has appeared reasonable and necessary in the light of the "economic realities" of the day. (1976: 238)

Revolutionary Transformation?

One of the most distinctive features of Bowles and Gintis's version of correspondence theory is that unlike most European and Latin American versions, it is coupled with a theory of revolutionary change in which education would be a crucial site of conflict and change. This revolutionary optimism is based upon the principles of contradiction: "social revolution is indeed possible in the United States" because of "the ever-widening gulf between human needs—what people want—and the imperatives of further capitalist expansion and production" (1976: 277). As the authors admit, however, "this position may seem to be out of place in a book which has laid such stress on the reproduction of consciousness and skills consistent with capitalist expansion." Though the authors outline a whole series of contradictions between accumulation and reproduction that are held to support this revolutionary optimism, the crucial aspect that separates their analysis from other versions of reproduction theory is the significance they attribute to conjunctures characterized by a lack of correspondence between job structure and education. Ironically, the major conclusion of that absence of correspondence is the basis of forms of educational change which might contribute to the transformation of the economic structure. But this shift from determinism to voluntarism is based on rather tenuous assumptions that point to some problems with respect to the internal coherency of their whole approach. At least European structuralist reproduction theory was consistent in its negative evaluation of education as a site for revolutionary action.

Critique

The problems of Bowles and Gintis's general approach can be traced to a number of sources. First, their avoidance of epistemological issues puts them in the position of uncritically shifting from hard-nosed empiricism to the the invocation of functionalist type models of equilibrium to the revolutionary dialectic of the contradiction between accumulation and reproduction. This contributes to methodological ambiguities and inconsistencies that have left them vulnerable to critics on both the left and the right.

Second, despite the innovative and skillful use of empirical evidence to support their case for correspondence, the results pose several difficulties. The evidence for the three types of correspondence (authority relations, reward structures, task organization) is mixed. Further, downplaying the content side of potential correspondence entails ignoring a vast body of data which may be of particular significance in some historical contexts where the mobilization of protest may center on curriculum content.

Further, the stress on the formal logic of correspondence invites a potentially devastating rejoinder by neo-Weberian critics: how is it possible to separate the formal link between education and the economy from that of schooling as a preparation for work roles in complex, bureaucratic organizations? What is it that is specifically capitalist about these formal correspondences? The authors argue that the goals of revolutionary socialism extend beyond the Soviet and East European model: "These countries have abolished private ownership of the means of production, while replicating the relationships of economic control, dominance, and subordination characteristic of capitalism" (1976: 266). Is there a danger here of confusing the logic of capitalism with that of complex organization?

Third, there is an unresolved tension between the determinist and voluntarist aspects of social action. Though the concluding part of the book introduces a voluntaristic conception of radical educational reform as a crucial aspect of revolutionary movement, this is not fully compatible with the preceding structuralist argument. Though an abstract conception of the contradiction between individual needs and societal structures is introduced, this is not coupled with a specific analysis of the nature of educational resistance or a social-psychological analysis that would make the proposed revolutionary movement plausible.

A fourth set of issues that have been stressed by a number of critics (see, for instance, Carnoy, 1982; Carnoy and Levin, 1985; Apple, 1982b) is linked to the absence of a theory of the state adequate to deal with the strategic analysis proposed, and the texture and dynamics of public education.

Self-Criticisms

Finally, it is useful to consider the authors' subsequent self-criticisms, as well as some of the empirical inadequacies of their proposed correspondence thesis as revealed by other researchers. What is most striking is that, despite certain impressions to the contrary, (i.e., a significant redefinition of their political position that gives primacy to their radical democratic over their socialist project), Bowles and Gintis have revised their correspondence theory but *retain its essentials*. As they have subsequently argued, the correspondence principle makes "four positive contributions to progressive educational strategy":

> First, its explanatory value is great . . . Second . . . the correspondence principle shows a positive alternative . . . Educational reform requires at the same time economic transformation towards democratic socialism. Third, our formulation rectifies an earlier preoccupation by both liberal and Marxian analysis with the overt content of schooling . . . Fourth, our formulation of the correspondence principle contributes to a more positive understanding of the goals of socialist transition . . . not *ownership*, but *control* is central to social inequities. (1988: 18)

They trace the weakness of their approach, however, to an insufficiently developed understanding of the contradictory relations in the educational system: "by standing . . . as the *only* structural link between education and economy, and by its character as an inherently *harmonious* link between the two, the correspondence principle forced us to adopt a narrow and inadequate appreciation of the *contradictions* involved in the articulation of the educational system with the social totality" (1988: 19). In the earlier formulation they focused almost exclusively on a single, inertial, and passive contradiction: the way in which education fell out of harmony with the development of capitalist production relations. To go beyond this, however, requires significant revisions of their earlier base-superstructure model, which viewed a social formation as "an economic 'base' with a series of social levels successively stacked on top" (1988: 21). Instead, society is now treated as "an ensemble of structurally articulated *sites of social practice*": cohesive domains of social life with specified social relations. The dynamics of advanced capitalist social formations are held to revolve around the three sites of the state, family, and capitalist production: "the site of capitalist production is characterized by private property . . . market exchange, wage labor, and capitalist control of production and investment. The state is characterized by the institutions of liberal democracy, and the family site by the structure of power and kinship known as patriarchy" (1988: 21).

These three sites in turn interact so as to articulate a "contradictory totality" within which sites relate in terms of two dynamic principles: "structural delimitation" and "transportation of practices across sites," which can be either "reproductive" or "contradictory" in their effects. For example, the imperative of economic success puts constraints on potential forms of change—a reproductive form of structural delimitation. Similarly, educators oriented toward educational expansion can import capitalist organization principles to restructure education—a reproductive form of transporting political practices (1988: 22–23). Contradictory structural delimitation is evident in the many ways in which schools, in order to work at all, must operate in ways that fail to conform to the demands of capital—as, for example, in the way the school has given women relatively equal opportunities even though the hierarchy in capitalist production is based on female subordination. A pervasive example of contradictory transported political practices is the apparent efforts to import participatory democratic principles from the state sphere to the educational (1988: 23–24). As they conclude: "If our analysis of social struggles is correct . . . an Achilles heel of the capitalist system lies in its characteristic articulation of the state, economy, family totality. The liberal democratic state is at once the citadel of private property and the instrument of incursions upon this venerable institution" (1988: 26). The crucial consequence is that social struggles occur "wholly *within* the liberal discourse of natural rights," which is the inevitable "structure of cultural practices in advanced capitalist social formations" (1988: 26). To be sure, such liberal discourse is limited by its formulation of issues in terms of individual, personal rights, thus neglecting the issues related to cooperation and solidarity as objectives of political practice; articulating these other principles becomes the task of "the actual discourse of socialism," which "is thus an amalgam of liberal discourse and these expressions of bonding normally banished to the hinterlands of the political idiom" (1988: 28).

The central contradiction of the educational system is thus linked to two aspects of its location in the social totality: as a subsystem of the state site, it is linked to the principle of personal rights; and in its relation to economic production, it is linked to rights vested in property. Hence the contradiction: "education reproduces rights vested in property while itself organized in terms of rights vested in person" (1988: 28). The political consequences are thus unambiguous:

> The goals of progressive educational reform must be framed within the structural boundaries of liberal discourse, and can be simply expressed as the full democratization of education. These goals can be divided into two complementary projects: the democratization of the social relations of education, and the reformulation of the issue of democracy in the curriculum. (1988: 30)

As Moore has forcefully argued, three strategies of repairing correspondence theory are proposed by Bowles and Gintis and others: "(a) by *interpreting* the relationship between education and production by addressing the issues of *policy formation, relative autonomy* and *resistance*; (b) by including the dimensions of gender and race: and (c) by shifting from the concept of *ideology* to that of *hegemony* and the analysis of class culture" (1988: 81). Though these ad hoc revisions add to the complexity of the model and open up analysis of contradictions, they do not really develop it in a fundamental way. Most crucially, their untouched continuity derives from a continuing equation of the concept of "social relations of production" with "the system of social relationship in production":

> By failing to distinguish between the *immediate production of commodities* and the *process of capitalist production as a whole* and by identifying the social relations of production with the immediate form of the capital relation as it is structured in direct production, the correspondence principle grounds education in a category which is insufficient to support its thesis. A major consequence of this is an inability to acknowledge the distinctiveness and specificity of education *as a field (or site) in its own right* based in social relations of *knowledge production*. This, in turn, is related to the lack within the current Marxist sociology of education of a materialist (realist) *theory of knowledge*. (1988: 82)

CONCLUSION

Bowles and Gintis's work is an appropriate point at which to close the discussion of correspondence theories, both because of its status as a landmark and the most influential application of a version of correspondence theory to education *and* as a work whose internal inconsistencies anticipate subsequent developments over the past decade. Before turning to these other developments, however, it is instructive to consider an alternative version of correspondence theory that rejects a direct link between economy and education (as in economic-reproductive theories) in favor of a more flexible (and more vague) account of the relationship between class systems and the reproduction of educational systems in the structuralist conflict theories that are the subject of chapter 7. What is distinctive about this structuralist conflict models in the work of Bourdieu, Bernstein, and others is, however, that unlike correspondence theories, they do attempt to take into account the distinctiveness and specificity of education and its relation to knowledge production.

CHAPTER 7

Structural Conflict Theories: Culture, Class, and Domination

The family of theories discussed in this chapter are unified by their shared stress upon the close link between educational reproduction and class reproduction, but they do not analyze this connection from an explicitly Marxist perspective, that is, a theory of modes of production, a conception of the privileged role of the working class, or a strict theory of correspondence between the economic and educational sphere. At the same time, the theories reviewed differ considerably with respect to epistemological and methodological assumptions, ranging from weak forms of systemic structuralism (in the case of Bourdieu and Bernstein) to the focus on conflict groups (in the case of closure and credentialist theory in the work of Randall Collins and others).

These approaches are thus class-reproductive but not economic-reproductive and do not postulate a formal correspondence principle. Thus the most distinctive feature of such structuralist conflict models is that education is viewed as an independent field with its own principles of organization. In the words of Bourdieu and Passeron, the education/society relationship involves the "dual objective truth of a system defined by its capacity to employ the *internal logic* of its functioning in the service of its *external function of social conservation*" (1977: 177). A crucial difference between Bourdieu and Bernstein, however, is whether the content of intellectual fields is held to be essentially "arbitrary" (Bourdieu) or linked to the "speciality of discourse" characteristic of educational production (Bernstein).

CLASS AND CULTURAL REPRODUCTION: BOURDIEU, PASSERON, ET AL.

Introduction: Intellectual Context

The work of both Pierre Bourdieu and his collaborators has had a peculiar reception in the academic world, especially in the sociology of education. Neither their work nor their personalities lends itself to the cultism associated often with structuralist Marxism; nor are they associated with any distinctive political activist movement even if both are associated with broadly leftist and critical tendencies. Their reception has also been shaped by the interdisciplinary and often linguistically challenging character of their writings, a factor amplified by Bourdieu's writing in French. Bourdieu's training was in part in philosophy, and yet his earliest publications are based on fieldwork in Algeria and affected by his sympathies for the Algerian independence movement. Though education emerged as a central interest by the mid 1960s, this work was from the outset associated with a more general theory of cultural sociology and included research on the arts, museums, and photography. Bernstein, on the other hand, has had a very consistent focus of interest on the relationship between language and education, but his eclectic sources of inspiration have been a source of confusion for more conventional linguists, sociologists, and educators.

In the work of Bourdieu and his collaborators (associated with the Center for European Sociology in Paris and the journal *Actes de recherches en sciences sociales*), as well as the closely related research of Basil Bernstein in Britain, one is thus confronted with a difficult process of classification (a theme dear to Bourdieu and part of his relationship to Durkheim). This point is evident in the various conflicting efforts to "label" Bourdieu—as a "critical functionalist" (Murphy, 1979: 30–31), as converging with "critical theory" (Morrow, 1982), as a neo-Marxist and as "liberal theory in disguise" (Sharp, 1980: 69) and that "whatever the nature of the language which Bourdieu employs to articulate his theories, his framework is essentially Weberian" (1980: 75). Bourdieu has understandably protested such labeling, which he compares to the classificatory strategies of racism and suggests is "the principle obstacle to what appears to me to be the appropriate relationship between texts and past authors" (Bourdieu, 1987: 39).

With this caution in mind, it is important to qualify the characterization of Bourdieu as a structuralist class-reproductive theorist of education, a phrase that serves to superficially locate his work in the trajectory of a comparison to structuralist Marxism. Though offering a profound critique of bourgeois educational systems, Bourdieu's conflict theory is not specifically Marxist; he is "Durkheimian" in the sense that he works within a distinctive tradition of French sociology and employs a structuralist model that allows a combination of methodological functionalism and substantive conflict theory. It should be added, as well, that Bourdieu has been strongly influenced by Marx and especially Weber's theory of class and status.

It is not possible here to deal with Bourdieu's immense oeuvre as a whole; rather, it is necessary to restrict discussion to a characterization of his approach to a theory of educational reproduction. In particular, this will require glossing over the detail and richness of his empirical work (which focuses on the case of the French educational system), which is one of its most distinguishing features. Yet it will still be necessary to touch upon the metatheoretical foundations of his theory of education. Failure to do so, especially in the educational literature, has led to fundamental misunderstandings and superficial interpretations, partly because such themes are treated only indirectly in his and Passeron's book on reproduction (1977). Further, as his translator notes, Bourdieu's work read outside the context of its own production easily lends itself to misreading: "Thus nothing guarantees that, for some readers, this work, written *against* the currents at present dominant in France, 'structuralism' or 'structural-Marxism,' will not be merged with the very tendencies it combats" (Nice, 1977). Accordingly, we will take up (a) his general orientation to epistemology and method; (b) the basic elements of his sociological theory as it relates to the theory of intellectual "fields" and cultural capital; and (c) his theory of social and cultural reproduction in education.

Epistemology and Methodology

Unlike Althusser, who seeks to rehabilitate "dialectical materialism" as opposed to the science of historical materialism, Bourdieu does not begin with specifically "philosophical" intentions. Indeed, Bourdieu's intentions are, in a sense, the opposite in that his writings reveal a consistent thread of the French tradition of philosophical dilettantism and the resistance of French philosophy to the social sciences (cf. Bourdieu and Passeron, 1967; Bourdieu,

1968). Consistent with that intention, it is appropriate to treat Bourdieu's epistemological and methodological concerns together. Given that he does not systematically set out to develop an epistemological position, it is difficult to characterize his approach with any ready labels, partly because it borders on eclecticism and is elaborated indirectly in a series of discussions responding to debates within French philosophy and social theory. Relative to the French context, at least, Bourdieu could be characterized as an "empiricist" in the sense that his whole sociological program reflects a response against the theoreticism and philosophical pretensions of French social theory. In examining the structuralist movement in the late 1960s, for example, he suggests that it merely "revives Durkheim's approach, in the language of structural linguistics—much more appealing to the taste of the day than somewhat coarse references to biology" (Bourdieu and Passeron, 1967: 166). As he suggests ironically, "all the social sciences now live in the house of Durkheimianism, unbeknownst to them, as it were, because they walked into it backwards" (1967: 169).

Accordingly, it is possible to refer to Bourdieu as an "eclectic structuralist," where that refers to a broadly based conception of the social sciences that seeks to avoid either the intuitive and naive spontaneism of pure phenomenology on the one hand, and the atomism, mechanism, and empiricism of a positive approach on the other. This position clearly distances him from the various radical philosophical positions advanced in the name of structuralism and the "death of subject theme." As we shall see in a moment, this also entails a rejection of Althusser's structuralist metaphysics and theory of the subject and ideology.

The ecumenism—and perhaps eclecticism—of Bourdieu's position is even more evident in his contention that in an important sense the great classical sociologists all shared a structural method: "scholars such as Marx, Durkheim, and Weber, totally different in their views of social philosophy and ultimate values, were able to agree on the main points of the fundamental principles of the theory of knowledge of the social world" (Bourdieu, 1968: 682). Most surprising here is Bourdieu's contention that Weber's use of the ideal-type method (if not his methodological interpretation of it) can be viewed as a variant of the structural method of constructing models based on analogical reasoning (1968: 697–98).

More concretely, with respect to the use of actual methodologies, he remains eclectic, as is evident in his own work: ethnographic, historical, and survey methods all find a place, though variable analysis tends to be of limited importance. The mechanical application of multivariate analysis is rejected: "When the sociologist fails to see that by means of a synchronic cross-section, multivariate analysis obtains a system of relations defined by conjunctural equilibrium, and that factor analysis eliminates all reference to the genesis of the ensemble of synchronic relations it is dealing with, he is liable to forget that, unlike strictly logical structures, the structures sociology deals with are the product of transformations which, unfolding in time, cannot be considered as reversible except by a logical abstraction, a sociological absurdity, since they express the successive states of a process that is aetiologically irreversible" (1977: 88). In particular, such a mechanical application tends to underestimate the effect of social origin on academic outcomes (1977: 160).

Yet this empiricist tendency is coupled with both a critique of the limits of objectivism in social science and a transformational model of society following the inspiration of the early Marx (along with complementary readings of Weber and Durkheim). Such a transformational model rejects such dualisms as voluntarism versus determinism, finalism versus mechanism, or structure versus practice:

> Methodological objectivism, a necessary moment in all research, by the break with primary experience and the construction of objective relations which it accomplishes, demands its own supersession. In order to escape the *realism of the structure*, which hypostatizes systems of objective relations by converting them into totalities already constituted outside of individual history and group history, it is necessary to pass from the *opus operatum* to the *modus operandi*, statistical regularity or algebraic structure to the principle of the production of this observed order, and to construct the theory of practice, or more precisely, the theory of the mode of generation of practices, which is the precondition for establishing an experimental science of the *dialectic of the internalization of externality and the externalization of internality*, or more simply, of incorporation and objectification. (Bourdieu, 1977: 72)

This formulation clearly indicates Bourdieu's break with formalist structuralism and its denial of the subject (whether in the form of Lévi-Strauss or Althusser) and his recasting of the generative logic of structural analysis within an empirical framework of inquiry. To this extent, he could be termed an "empiricist structuralist" (so long as this is not to be confused with the formalist empiricism of structuralist network theory, which remains within a version of positivist epistemology). As he ironically suggests:

> Although they assert the immanence of the structure of class relations at all levels of social practice, the structuralist readers of Marx, carried away by their objectivist reaction against all idealist forms of the philosophy of action, will acknowledge agents only as "supports" of the structure and are obliged to ignore the question of the mediations between the structure and practice, because they fail to confer on structures any other content than the power—a very mysterious one in the last analysis—of determining or over-determining other structures. (Bourdieu and Passeron, 1977: 217–18)

The foundation Bourdieu's transformational structuralism is a distinction between three basic modes of theoretical knowledge that construct analytic objects in the social world:

1. "The knowledge we shall call *phenomenological* (or, to speak in terms of currently active schools, 'ethnomethodological') sets out to make explicit the truth of primary experience of the social world"
2. "The knowledge we shall term *objectivist* (of which structuralist hermeneutics is a particular case) constructs the objective relations (e.g., economic or linguistic) which structure practice and representations of practice, i.e., in particular, primary knowledge, practical and tacit, of the familiar world"
3. A "third-order knowledge," oriented toward "*praxeological*" knowledge, which grasps the limits of objectivist knowledge, builds upon an analysis of a "dialectic of strategies" which "does not cancel out the gains from objectivist knowledge but conserves and transcends them by integrating the truth of practical experience and of the practical mode of knowledge which this learned knowledge had to be constructed against" (1977: 3–4)

The implications of this third order knowledge becomes clearer if we consider the example Bourdieu uses: Lévi-Strauss's critique of

Marcel Mauss's "phenomenological" approach to gift exchange. For Lévi-Strauss, as a formalist or objectivist structuralist, it is necessary to make a total break with native experience to find the mechanical (structural) laws of reciprocity. But Bourdieu suggests this type of structuralism is not adequate because it does not take into account the mediating principle of time, of intervals, upon which practical life is organized:

> "Phenomenological" analysis and objectivist analysis bring to light two antagonistic principles of gift exchange: the gift as experienced . . . and the gift as seen from outside. To stop at the "objective" truth of the gift, i.e., the model, is to set aside the question of the relationship between so-called objective truth, i.e., that of the observer, and the truth that can scarcely be called subjective, since it represents the official definition of the subjective experience of exchange; it is to ignore the fact that the agents practice as irreversible a sequence of actions that the observer constitutes as reversible . . . The temporal structure of gift exchange, which objectivism ignores, is what makes possible the coexistence of two opposing truths, which defines the full truth of the gift. (1977: 5)

Only in this epistemological context does it become possible to understand the methodological implications of Bourdieu's use of reproduction theory. Only on the basis of reconstructing his analysis of reproduction in education, however, can we return to the more specific assumptions of his application of reproduction concepts as a structural method.

Culture, Education, and Reproduction

In a curious way, Bourdieu's writings betray rather limited theoretical ambitions, despite their rigor and richness. Again, reacting against the French philosophical tendency to speak out on every possible point, he has not set out to establish a complete theoretical "system" and theory of society. Above all, Bourdieu is a theorist in the tradition of the French version of the sociology of knowledge going back to Durkheim, but which seeks to incorporate the insights of Marx, Weber, and others. More typically, however, he is referred to as a sociologist of culture, within which education has been only one of a multiplicity of interests, especially art and science.

As a consequence there are many silences in his work in the sense that he engages in forms of analysis (e.g., the study of reproduction in education) that presuppose or imply other assumptions, which he does not explicate or develop, or even refer to the work of others in deference. As we shall see, the absence of an explicit theory of social classes and of the state, for example, makes it difficult to interpret the full implications of certain of his arguments.

The broader context of Bourdieu's theory of education is a conception of "intellectual fields"—close to what are often academic disciplines, that is, contexts of cultural discourse and activity that are organized as markets of symbolic goods. A central theme is an analysis of the history of intellectual life in Europe in terms of the history of the transformations of the system of production of symbolic goods. The basic element of his theoretical argument can be introduced in the context of his analysis of education, though it should be noted that he has applied them in a number of other cultural contexts as well.

The point of departure is a general theory of "symbolic violence," which is deployed to indicate "the theoretical unity of all actions characterized by the twofold arbitrariness of symbolic imposition; it also signifies the fact that this general theory of actions of symbolic violence (whether exerted by the healer, the sorcerer, the priest, the prophet, the propagandist, the teacher, the psychiatrist, or the psychoanalyst) belongs to a general theory of violence and legitimate violence, as is directly attested by the interchangeability of the different forms of social violence and indirectly by the homology between the school system's monopoly of legitimate symbolic violence and the State's monopoly of the legitimate use of physical violence" (1977: xii). More formally:

> Every power to exert symbolic violence, i.e., every power which manages to impose meanings and to impose them as legitimate by concealing the power relations which are the basis of its forces, adds its own specifically symbolic force to those power relations. (1977: 4)

Following from this all "pedagogic action" involves a twofold arbitrariness in that both the power is arbitrary and the culture imposed. By using the term "arbitrary" here an attempt is made to neutralize and generalize the formulation, to avoid either the value judgment implicit in the terms *ideology* or *culture*. Further, the social condition of the exercise of pedagogic action requires "pedagogic authority" and hence "the relative autonomy of the agency commissioned to exercise it" (1977: 11–12). This relative autonomy of pedagogic authority allows cultural reproduction to contribute most effectively to the overall process of social reproduction, given that pedagogical actions "tend to reproduce the system of cultural arbitraries characteristic of that social formation, thereby contributing to the reproduction of the power relations which put that cultural arbitrary into the dominant position," a point neglected by people like Durkheim (1977: 10). This is realized over time through "pedagogic work"—"a process of inculcation which must last long enough to produce a durable training, i.e., habitus, the product of internalization of the principles of a cultural arbitrary capable of perpetuating itself after PA has ceased and thereby of perpetuating in practices the principles of the internalized arbitrary" (1977: 31). In short, pedagogic work is a substitute for repression and external coercion and works, most fundamentally by masking the underlying realities of power to both the dominant and subordinate groups in society. These basic reproduction relations are illustrated in figure 7.1.

An important feature of this general formulation should be noted before we turn to the school system. For Bourdieu the theory of symbolic violence is not designed to criticize any particular type of pedagogic communication because it is inherent in the essential nature of such communication. Accordingly, he repeatedly refers to the "naive" proposals of "utopian" critics of education who would liberate education from power relations:

> the most radical challenges to a pedagogic power are always inspired by the self-destructive Utopia of a pedagogy without arbitrariness or by the spontaneist Utopia which accords the individual the power to find within himself the principle of his own "fulfillment" . . . The idea of a "culturally free" pedagogic authority, exempt from arbitrariness . . . presupposes a misrecognition of the objective truth of pedagogic authority in which there is still expressed the objective truth of a violence whose specificity lies in the fact that it generates the illusion that it is not violence. (1977: 17)

Institutionalized educational systems have specific structures, which correspond to both their "essential function" of inculcation

FIGURE 7.1
The Cycle of Reproduction

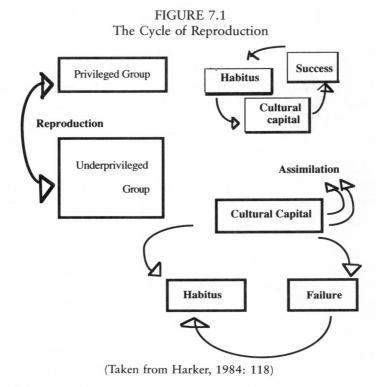

(Taken from Harker, 1984: 118)

and their "external function" with respect to reproducing a cultural arbitrary which it does not produce (cultural reproduction), the reproduction of which contributes to the reproduction of the relations between the groups or classes (social reproduction)" (1977: 54). As shown in the history of Western education, this institutionalization is secured through the convergence between the external and internal functions of educational systems and as a consequence of systematic transformations linked to "sanctioned validation of results" in the form of diplomas (Durkheim) and the emergence of a corps of permanent specialists who bureaucratically monopolize that verification (Weber). By thus delegating authority and conferring autonomy, the dominant educational system is able to operate "without either those who exercise it or those who undergo it ever ceasing to misrecognize its dependence on the power relations making up the social formation in which it is carried on" (1977: 67).

The second part of Bourdieu and Passeron's discussion in *Reproduction* is concerned with an analysis of the French educational system, specifically, the crisis in higher education that emerged in the 1960s. Given the exceptional features of the French university system (at least by comparison to the more advanced and democratic parts of Europe and especially to North America), the details of this case can only be generalized in a highly qualified way. Indeed, to the extent we discuss these particular features, it is to draw out the implications of the reproduction model employed. One of the most simplistic misreadings of Bourdieu is to find that his "generalizations" about the French system do not apply with any consistency to say, the United States, hence concluding the model is inadequate. But that is to misunderstand the type of functional analysis employed, especially the fundamental distinction between the "logic of the system" and the "logic of its transformations," the system model and its application to the study of any specific historical educational system.

History, Reproduction and Change

More recently, Passeron (1986) has given an important clarification of the methodological assumptions of his and Bourdieu's theory of sociocultural reproduction. The key to understanding their work is to grasp the (hypothetical) methodological status given to their reproduction models. As Bourdieu puts it, social scientists have a congenital problem of placing "models, which belong to the order of logic, in the individual or collective consciousness of the individual agents or groups," thus committing the fallacy—attributed by Marx to Hegel—of taking "the things of logic for the logic of things" (1981: 305). Accordingly, "one must beware of taking a model of social reproduction as a comprehensive model for society, as a law or trend which appears to regulate the order of historical evolution" (Passeron, 1986: 629).

Let us consider in more detail some of the implications of this stance. First, it is clear that what Bourdieu and Passeron propose is not a reproduction theory of society or even a reproduction theory of education as a universal law. It is crucial to distinguish between heuristic models and real societies: "no social system of reproduction is so comprehensive as to leave no factors outside it. In other words "society" is not a system" (Passeron, 1986: 629). Accordingly, reproduction models are "applicable only to partial systems" through an idealization procedure that allows capturing its inherent logic and relation to other processes (1986: 626). One important consequence of this strategy of methodological autonomization (i.e., treating the model as if other factors did not intervene) is that conflicts and antagonisms are purposely neglected:

> Constructed on a pattern of extremes, on the hypothesis of what would be the case if they could reach the fullest extent of their systematic perfection, i.e., by temporarily leaving out of account their conflictive relations with other, similarly systematic processes, the reproduction models are therefore based on provisional methodological autonomization. (1986: 629)

In other words, by themselves reproduction models cannot account for social change. In fact, this is identified as the error of Marxist (and related structuralist) theories, which "seek in the internal 'tensions' or 'conflicts' of a social or cultural system the motor and programme of historical change, the key to transform from synchronic equilibrium to diachronic evaluation" (1986: 619). This is not to deny the obvious importance of conflict for change, but to reject the logic of the Hegelian internal contradiction as the basis for understanding reproduction models because of a "confusion between their operating logic and historical necessity." In other words, no suprareproduction model of change and evolution is possible because "change is always the result of a meeting of incompatible reproductive processes. Change cannot follow a model because there is no conceivable model of the 'meeting' between the independent or relatively independent processes that actually occur in every historical situation" (1986: 620).

From this methodological perspective, it is instructive to reinterpret the implications of Bourdieu and Passeron's analysis of French education. What is in fact analyzed are "two distinct reproduction models" even if they are often treated as a single "quasisystem." On the one hand, there is the model of education as a self-reproducing force. On the other hand, there is also a more general model (shared with sociology generally) of intergenerational reproduction of dominant and subordinate classes (1986: 620–21). What their analysis of the French historical case demonstrated was a situation where these two systems (social reproduction and educational reproduction) of reproduction were closely connected:

> The thesis of the work is obviously not that these two models are doomed to remain bonded into a hypermodel, that of sociocultural reproduction, whose transhistorical validity could sup-

posedly provide a description, in every society and in every age, of the functions of social reproduction for which formal schooling is responsible . . . The work merely described the reproductive associations to which a historical meeting between the two models and their reciprocal adjustment has given a stable character since the nineteenth century. (1986: 621)

Indeed, from a comparative historical perspective this convergence between social and educational reproduction is relatively unique. Thus, not only a general correspondence thesis between economic structure and education must be rejected, but also any general theory of education as a primary source of social reproduction. Accordingly, this comparative perspective reminds us that historically "the diffuse education found in archaic societies and illiterate groups of traditional societies" has been the "mainspring of their cultural continuity" (1986: 623). In short, Bourdieu and Passeron's use of reproduction models is a very historical and empirical one whose assumptions surprisingly converge with aspects of Weber's use of ideal types:

> Thus, in using concepts such as "reproduction," "system," and "internal" or "external" function, we are only arriving at conclusions that are justifiable on the basis of the ideal-type status given by Weber to describable social science concepts. The models of social functioning constructed by such concepts are appropriate instruments for use on historical material and not direct apprehensions of the logic governing history.
>
> To be more precise, the description stemming from the model of educational self-reproduction uses no other principle that than of the structuralist and functionalist schemata Weber applied to the analysis of the ecclesiastical "routinization" of an initially prophetic message, that is, to the process that establishes a functional parallel between the constitution and imposition of a body of doctrine on the characteristics of a priestly bureaucracy. (1986: 621–23)

Transformation and Resistance

As a couple of the more sympathetic and astute critics of Bourdieu's educational theory have concluded, "the power of reflexive thought and historical agency are relegated to a minor theoretical detail in Bourdieu's theory of change" (Aronowitz and Giroux, 1985: 84).[1] Though valid as a criticism of omission, it is somewhat misleading to characterize this as a "minor theoretical detail." The effort to incorporate a theory of agency clearly distinguishes the position of Bourdieu and his colleagues from structuralist Marxism and is the basis of a general critique of structuralism. As a consequence, it provides the point of entry for reconciling a theory of reproduction with problems of agency.

There are three crucial aspects of Bourdieu's theory that provide the basis for the opening up of reproduction analysis, without dissolving it into another form of action theory or voluntarism. First, as we have seen, the concept of habitus is designed to deal with the praxiological dimension where objective structure and subjective experience are fused.

Second, though not discussed in any detail, resistance is postulated as a pervasive part of the ordinary functioning of institutions. Indeed, Bourdieu identifies a world without resistance as a limiting case of the type suggested by Goffman's notion of a "totalitarian institution"; in this context the "the ordinary functioning of fields as fields of struggle" are contrasted to the "limiting states, which are perhaps never reached, in which all struggle and all resistance to domination have disappeared" (Bourdieu, 1981: 313).

Third, Bourdieu explicitly denies that objective structure does not absolve agents of responsibility; as he puts it in criticizing structuralist Marxism: "The 'apparatus' theory no doubt owes part of its success to the fact that it can lead to an abstract denunciation of the state or the education system which acquits agents of personal responsibility, so that their occupational practice and their political choices can be treated as separate issues" (1981: 316).

Finally, Bourdieu's model does formally describe—in a typically cryptic formulation—the conditions of possibility of fundamental (revolutionary) transformation:

> The conjuncture capable of transforming practices . . . into *collective action* (e.g., revolutionary action) is constituted in the dialectical relationship between, on the one hand, a *habitus*, understood as a system of lasting, transposable dispositions which, integrating past experiences, functions at every moment as a *matrix of perceptions, appreciations, and action* . . . and, on the other hand, an *objective event* which exerts its action of conditional stimulation calling for or demanding a determinate response . . . the dispositions and the situations which combine synchronically to constitute a determinate conjuncture are never

wholly independent, since they are engendered by the objective structures, that is, in the last analysis, by the economic bases of the social formation in question. (1977: 82–3)

To be sure, Bourdieu's focus is upon the ability of dominant institutions to subvert protest and resistance within the educational system and expose the illusory side of student rebellion in particular. But this is *not* proposed as an *"iron law" of reproduction*; rather, it was developed in the context of an historically specific analysis of the French university system. Retrospectively, it is clear that his account was a salutary one that captured the evanescent character of student protest in the French context (and could be generalized in certain respects to other advanced capitalist societies).

Problems of Assessment

To summarize, it is useful to draw out those features of Bourdieu's reproduction theory that are most distinctive and that, on the whole, make it the most fruitful point of departure for an opening up of reproduction theory:

- Its structuralist presuppositions are grounded in in epistemological and methodological terms by reference to the most sophisticated debates in the postpositivist philosophy of social science.
- There is a selective borrowing from a wide range of classical and contemporary sociological theory while preserving a distinctive theoretical approach that avoids the extremes of either hyperfunctionalism or voluntarism.
- Even if structural conflict remains the central aspect of the underlying theory of society, this is not coupled with any dogmatic assumptions with respect to an objective dialectic of revolutionary contradiction; consequently, the use of reproduction models remains heuristic, partial, and historically specific.
- Agency, resistance, and transformation are given a formal place within the theoretical model, even if these themes are not extensively investigated.
- Theory is united with a broadly based empirical research program that draws upon the range of methodological resources in contemporary social science and is thus open for revision and further development.

At the same time, it is important to acknowledge a series of gaps in Bourdieu's research program that are in part sins of omission (dictated in part by the methodological autonomization required) and emphasis, but at crucial points may be necessary to deal with problems even within his own research problematic:

- Issues of agency, the role of critical consciousness, research and ideology, the potential of resistance, and the role of social movements are all treated in a cursory fashion and require further development.
- Though class structure is postulated as the structural context for the formation of the relative autonomy of educational systems, the absence of an explicit theory of class inhibits the ability to provide a theoretical analysis of relationships between types of class systems and types of educational systems; what is provided is rather an account of the interpenetration in the context of French society.
- Similarly, though the state is postulated as a mediating structure for the articulation of the interests of classes, no explicit theory of the state is proposed, a problem that complements and aggravates the preceding one.
- The absence of attention given to the preceding questions gives the overall theoretical model a static quality, despite its explicit dynamic presuppositions and latent concern with the study of change.
- No consideration is given to the conditions under which coercion and material economic force may supplement symbolic violence as a significant or perhaps crucial aspect of the process of reproducing domination (a theme of considerable importance for nondemocratic societies).

LANGUAGE AND EDUCATIONAL REPRODUCTION: BERNSTEIN

Introduction: Intellectual Context

In certain respects Basil Bernstein, whose essays on the sociolinguistics of education go back to the late 1950s, could be credited as the real pioneer of reproduction theory in education. Bourdieu and Passeron (1977: 133) refer in their early work to "the remarkable analyses of Basil Bernstein and his school." If priority is given to Bourdieu in this chapter, it is because he eventually developed his analysis of education within the broader framework of a larger sociological research program. In these circumstances, it is perhaps appropriate to now view Bernstein's work as the in-depth elaboration of certain issues regarding language and educational transmission that is broadly compatible with and has been in fact influenced by the work of Bourdieu and his colleagues. This affinity was initially obscured and not further developed because of Bernstein's lack of facility in French and despite research stays in Paris in the early 1970s (hence prior to the translation of some of the key texts of Bourdieu and his colleagues). As Bernstein himself puts it:

> Although Durkheim is not as central to Bourdieu's thesis as he is perhaps to mine, it was this shared element which provided the relationship. In discussion with the group at the Centre, it became clear that our work was complementary. Whereas they were concerned with the *structure* of reproduction and its *various* realizations, I was essentially concerned with the *process* of transmission. (1977: 15)

Working in the English context where, until more recently, the structuralist roots of his approach were not well understood, Bernstein has been subject to considerable misunderstanding and superficial criticism. His theory of language deficits (based on the elaborate/restricted code distinction) has been widely cited, but "the use of Bernstein as a 'taken-for-granted reference' in textbooks and research reports on child development, educational attainment, sociolinguistics, and the like fostered an uncritical reception of some versions of the work, and critical—but equally poorly informed—rebuttals" (Atkinson, 1985: 10). Similarly, his complementary relationship with Bourdieu, based on a narrower focus on processes of transmission but within a largely implicit structuralist conflict macrosociology, has been obscured by surveys that misleading pigeonhole Bourdieu as a "Marxist" and Bernstein a "Durkheimian" who has "adapted the worst aspects of Durkheim and neglected the best" (Blackledge and Hunt, 1985: 60)

Sensitized by postwar work in social work and teaching, as well as Labour Party affiliations, Bernstein's approach to educational sociology was concerned at the outset with questions of language, even if it has gone through several shifts of direction. The first phase focused on moral order and ritualization in schools, a second phase toward the late 1960s began to focus on the curriculum framing and pedagogy, and the most recent phase has been concerned with codes, pedagogic discourse, and cultural reproduction.

Not without significance is that Bernstein inherited the Karl Mannheim chair at the University of London, given that "Bernstein's career-long preoccupation with the social distribution of orders of meaning and control is in direct line of descent from the spirit of Mannheim's work, if not the letter" (Atkinson, 1985: 78). Ironically, Mannheim's own contributions to education did not stress the application of the sociology of knowledge to curriculum analysis; further, one of the criticisms that has been advanced against his otherwise insightful treatment of ideology is that he lacked an adequate sociolingusitic basis for his work. But the more immediate source of inspiration for Bernstein was a variety of philosophical and anthropological authors concerned with cognition and linguistic categories, most of them continental (Whorf, Cassierer, Vygotsky, Luria), combined with Durkheimian sociology as the foundation for a "neo-Kantian concern with the cultural and linguistic frameworks that shape and regulate our experience of the world, and the transmission of such experience through symbolic forms" (Atkinson, 1985: 14). As the British sociologist Macrae noted in the preface to the first volume of Bernstein's collected papers, "its concerns, but not its procedures, are Durkheimian"; and as Bernstein himself later admitted, "I have yet to find *any* social theorist whose ideas are such a source (at least to me) of understanding of what the term *social* entails" (cited in Atkinson, 1985: 21). But not more than in the case of Bourdieu can this Durkheimian influence be used reductively to understand the broader reach of Bernstein's educational sociology.

Structuralism and the Theory of Schooling

The most important source of confusion with respect to Bernstein's work has been the tendency of textbooks to label his work almost exclusively in the context of a "deficit theory" theory of learning based on dialect differences that has been, in part, refuted by the "difference" hypothesis established by the linguist Labov in his research on American Black dialects. As Atkinson has extensively detailed, this is misleading on a number of crucial points. First, it ignores that Bernstein's concerns are not those of conventional linguistics and that his object of inquiry is not "dialect" differences but with the sociological consequences of different types of speech forms (Atkinson, 1985: 104). As a consequence, Bernstein is not an advocate of the crude versions of deficit theory because his argument is not based on a normative denunciation of restricted codes or a deterministic conception of the impact of codes upon social life. The assumption of determinism springs from a failure to comprehend the methodology underlying Bernstein's argument. And as Atkinson demonstrates, Labov's own data actually confirms the central themes of Bernstein's work in this context (Atkinson, 1985: 104–113).

From the outset, Bernstein's work points toward "an embryonic anthropology of schools as agencies of reproduction" (Atkinson, 1985: 21). His problematic is Durkheimian, beyond his structuralist method, and his primary concern is with working out the implications of the theory of social differentiation based on the transition from mechanical to organic solidarity. (But as we shall see, his affinities with Marx and Weber allow him to put relations of class and power at the center of this problematic.) In short, Bernstein uses the institutional microcosm of the school to understand the transformation of modes of social control. As he put it as early as 1966:

> This analysis . . . points to the critical importance of both the organizational structure of the school *and* the principles of transmission. In other words, *how* the expressive order is transmitted, *how* the instrumental order is transmitted, *what* is transmitted by both, what the official and unofficial goals are, of both orders, will structure the roles positions of teachers and pupils, affect the nature of teacher and pupil relationships and their respective friendship and pressure groups, and affect the pupil's relationship to his family and community. (cited in Atkinson, 1985: 35)

Bernstein's project has been to elaborate the structural homologies evident in education in the transition to a new mode of social control (i.e. educational reproduction) at various levels of analysis; these can be schematically seen in figure 7.2.

It is in this context that the elaborated/restricted code distinction must be understood. In its earlier version the problem was formulated with reference to a distinction between the "formal" and "public" use of language, where "formal" is analogous to "elaborated" and "public" to "restricted." What is significant in

FIGURE 7.2
Bernstein's Sociology: Themes and Variations

SOCIAL INTEGRATION	mechanical	organic
DIVISION OF LABOR	segmental/ stratified	complex/ differentiated
BOUNDARY MAINTENANCE	strong	weak
SOCIAL ROLES	ascribed	achieved
RITUAL EXPRESSIVE ORDER	strong	weak
CULTURAL CATEGORIES	pure	mixed
SOCIAL CONTROL	collective values/ punishment, 'guilt'	individualized/ therapeutic 'shame'
MESSAGE TYPES	condensed, implicit in ritualized collective forms	explicated individual motives

(Taken from Atkinson, 1985:36)

this earlier formulation is that it clear that the distinction does not refer exclusively or even primarily to dialectics of sociolects (i.e., specific patterns characteristic of subgroups), "but orientations to means, ends and objects, relationships between objects, the creation and re-creation of identities, and modes of social control" (Atkinson, 1985: 40). More specifically, the primary objective of the distinction was to contrast authority and role relationships in the context of family socialization. Whereas "public" language sustains control without verbal elaboration and establishes authority on the basis of ascribed positions, "formal" language has the capacity to construct complex logical relations that can articulate personal motives and sensibilities. Accordingly, public language is defined by its use of contextual, community-based stocks of idiomatic expressions, which have the effect of restricting dialogue. "It is important to note that this argument does not, of itself, propose a strict linguistic determinism" (Atkinson, 1985: 44).

Several other features of this formulation are noteworthy. First, females are given a central role in the class-based formation of socialization. Second, the distinction avoids some of the problems of the distinction between authoritarian and democratic patterns of family socialization in that the latter is also recognized as a form of social control. In short, it is necessary to understand the "deficit" implications of restricted codes not in the context of pluralist subcultural theory, but in structuralist terms as part of differential effects of class-based socialization processes and authority relations. From this perspective, neither remedial strategy of "compensatory" education nor a pejorative characterization of restricted code speech are justifiable conclusions in the sense usually attributed.

Language, Codes, and Knowledge Classification

The elaborated/restricted code distinction emphasizes that the ritualistic basis of restricted code speech contributes to fluency and predictability; elaborated code speech, in contrast, contributes to the communication of novelty and individualized meaning. In short: "codes are principles of structuration which underpin linguistic and social forms, their variation and their reproduction" (Atkinson,1985: 66). In the terms of structuralist linguistics, codes are thus "descriptive terms for regulative principles which are realized through different possibilities for selection and combination" (1985: 68)—in Saussure's terms, the paradigmatic and syntagmatic axes of communication.

Applied to curriculum research, Bernstein's approach provides a basis for analyzing the transformation of the social organization of knowledge in the movement from mechanical to organic solidarity. In this context the distinction between "collection" and "integrated" curricula is analogous to restricted and elaborated codes. In this connection the curriculum is viewed in semiotic terms as message systems: "Curriculum defines what counts as valid knowledge, pedagogy defines what counts as a valid transmission of knowledge, and evaluation defines what counts as a valid realization of this knowledge on the part of the taught" (cited in Atkinson, 1985: 136). A collection-type curricular code is characterized by its strong classification of knowledge within strict boundaries. At the level of the pedagogical encounter a strong "framing" occurs ("visible" pedagogy) with respect to what is or is not permitted to be communicated. This corresponds to the ritualistic aspect of restricted code communication. An integrated curriculum structure, in contrast, is defined by weak classification and porous boundaries, where selection and combination can take place more freely. Accordingly, framing is weaker (resulting in an "invisible" pedagogy) and the pedagogic relationship more fluid. At the level of evaluation occurs a parallel difference between visible pedagogies in collective curricula and the invisible ones in integrated ones: explicit, rigidly defined criteria as opposed to implicit, diffuse, and diverse criteria of assessment.

Power, Reproduction and Pedagogic Discourse

In many respects, Bernstein's analysis of the transition from mechanical to organic solidarity (and transformations within the latter) could be viewed as merely a structuralist and sociolinguistic rereading of Durkheim that converges broadly with the Parsonian conception of pattern variables, the shift from ascribed to achieved roles, and the more general process of rationalization and democratization. On this basis, it might be assumed he is following in the footsteps of Durkheim and Parsons in describing the innocent transformations of the division of labor and modernization. Yet this type of characterization misses most of the distinctive features of his approach and its convergence with Bourdieu. Attention to Bernstein's concerns with power and social control reveal clearly the importance of locating his sociology of education in the context of a structuralist conflict theory.

This point has been obscured or ignored by many commentators and critics, in part because of the structuralist conception of power informing Bernstein's approach. Yet at various points he is quite explicit:

> "Class relations" will be taken to refer to inequalities in the distribution of power and in principles of control between social groups, which are realized in the creation, distribution, reproduction, and legitimation of physical and symbolic values that have their source in the social division of labour (cited in Atkinson, 1985: 99).

Some might object, to be sure, that this is not a classic Marxist definition of class in terms of a specific relationship to the economic infrastructure; it also clearly includes ethnic and gender relations. Yet it clearly converges with Bourdieu's version of class analysis, and more generally the diffuse conception of power found in the work of Foucault and others. On this basis, Bernstein stresses how power is expressed in boundaries and positions, between the "thinkable" and the "unthinkable," and how "at its most general 'power' is to silence as 'control' is to communication" (cited in Atkinson, 1985: 99).

If we return to the context of the school and curriculum, it can be seen that Bernstein's work revolves around the structural relations uniting school, family, and work, that is, the "systemic relations between *fields of production and fields of reproduction*" (Atkinson, 1985: 156). But as we will see in a moment, what is at stake here is *not* a version of correspondence theory. Otherwise the shift from visible to invisible pedagogies would neither be possible nor necessary. What are, then, the implications of the movement from explicit hierarchy and rules to implicit? In part, it reflects the interests and cultural presuppositions of the new middle class: "Whereas the old middle class is concerned primarily with the manipulation and control of the means of production, the new middle class has a more indirect relationship to such material means, while being directly committed to means and relations of symbolic or cultural reproduction" (Atkinson, 1985: 160). As a consequence, the manipulative side of invisible pedagogy is exposed and revealed as a potentially even more effective form of control, precisely because of its implicit and personal character, one apparent at all three levels of the socialization process: family, work, school.

But this position rules out a correspondence interpretation of the relationship between work and the family/school couple because of inherent discrepancies. The relative autonomy of the school, in fact, is derived from the degree of "classification" separating the two, even they do not operate completely independently.

The consequences of these discrepancies between domains of pedagogic communication (i.e., the boundaries and classifications) have been explored most recently by Bernstein by analyzing the processes of "decontextualization" and "recontextualization," which are required in movement between, or communication between, bounded domains of knowledge (Atkinson, 1985: 170–71). One of the ironic forms of this has been evident in the textbook packaging of Bernstein's work in the context of deficit theory and Labov's supposed refutation. The first step in this double process is a decontextualization of an item from its original context (deficit theory), and then a recontextualization within an another framework that communicates to a target audience. In this way potentially threatening forms of knowledge can be integrated into the curriculum in ways that do not threaten. This process is further revealed by the distinction between "instructional discourse," which determines how skills and competencies are to be communicated, and "regulative discourse," which shapes social identities, social relations, and social order (Atkinson, 1985: 173). In short, Bernstein's interest in the coding of power radically transforms the problematic of Durkheim and liberal interpretations of modernization as democratization.

International Applications and Criticisms

As noted previously, Bernstein's work is known in educational circles primarily on the context of the narrower concept of the "deficit hypothesis," with which he is somewhat carelessly associated. Further, it is suggested that the deficit hypothesis has been refuted in favor of Labov's conception of linguistic variability (1966). Now, to the extent that Bernstein's theory is not concerned with dialectic variants but class-based differences in skills valued by the school, it is more a question of talking about different issues. More significant, however, is the difficulty of empirical researchers in establishing significant class differences based on restricted-elaborated code use where intelligence is held constant (even assuming that lower-class intelligence is not systematically underestimated).

As Dittmar (1976: 78) concludes on the basis of a thorough review of the international literature through the early 1970s, "no investigation was able to prove conclusively that lower-class children have an intellectual or linguistic deficit. Such a conclusion is dubious not only because of the types of tests and the way they were carried out but also because the methods used to analyze linguistic and cognitive differences were shown to be largely inadequate." A further corroboration of these results is evident in the failure (aside from occasional short-term results that disappeared over time) of the compensatory education programs originally legitimated by the deficit hypothesis. For Dittmar, both the rise of sociolinguistics and the strategy of compensatory education were linked to a "deeper-lying factor which must be regarded as giving impetus to these investigations: the increasingly urgent necessity in Western society to mobilize educational reserves in order to maintain the prevailing levels of production" (1976: 29). Dittmar's interpretation remains overly reductionist, yet, leads him to deal with a number of important issues. Most obviously, he assumes a dubious version of the educational capital argument and neglects altogether the way in which educational reforms directed to enhancing equalities of opportunity represent real struggles to which the democratic states have attempted to respond, not primarily for reasons of accumulation but rather legitimation.

More important in the present context is the bearing of the limited evidence for the deficit hypothesis and the failure of compensatory education upon Bernstein's overall theoretical approach. First, it should be recalled that though he supported compensatory education for experimental purposes, he had great reservations about the potential efficacy of such programs. In response to these problems he also moved toward a more consistent conception of cultural reproduction in which education was only one component of a larger process of socialization. Second, Dittmar's characterization of Bernstein's position as a normatively biased middle-class deficit thesis is a caricature of his position (Atkinson, 1985: 112– 13). Above all, Bernstein does not attempt to attribute the "cause" of low educational achievement of working-class students to a lack of mastery of elaborated codes, so much as analyze it as a mediating factor expressing a whole class-based life situation. Third, the limited findings of difference in relatively progressive comprehensive schools in advanced societies is not that surprising. More significant are the cumulative effects of small differences: that elaborated code skills are acquired in ways that are experienced as more aversive thus undermining motivation to compete beyond a certain point, and then atrophy in later work settings that do not require or encourage them. In societies with high levels of illiteracy, weak public mass-educational systems, and more rigid class distinctions, the effects of differential competencies are considerably more dramatic. In short, the restricted-elaborated code distinctions makes sense and is justifiable with a broader theory of domination and socialization. Needless to say, however, there is much to be done to develop empirical strategies which can complement and refine the rich implications of Bernstein's more recent work.

There are other difficulties with which Bernstein has attempted to come to terms in more recent work. For instance, at the outset there was a tendency to assume that elaborated code discourse dominated school life whereas "the majority of studies of classroom interaction, based on observation and recording of everyday practice, suggest that processes of teaching and control approximate to 'restricted' code" (Atkinson, 1985: 79). Bernstein's more recent work on pedagogical discourse attempts to deal with this problem by distinguishing between the elaborated character of the knowledge to be transmitted and the restricted mode of actual classroom encounters, leading to a discrepancy between the imperative of communicating knowledge and sustaining control. In any case this argument converges with Bourdieu's contention that pedagogical strategies provide implicit resources for control, but that advantaged students are more capable of decoding the knowledge performances ultimately required (Atkinson, 1985: 81).

Bernstein's structuralism has not been complemented by any systematic concern with problems of agency and the subject. Even though the early proponents of the "New Sociology of Education" included Bernstein within their fold, it is clear that their concerns drew a primary inspiration from theories of action and phenomenology. Unlike Bourdieu, who explicitly incorporates a "praxiological" dimension into his theory, Bernstein remains silent, a fact which renders it difficult to translate his work into proposals for either radical curricular reform or its potential relation to related social movements. Applications of Bernstein's approach in other contexts, such as Scandinavia, West Germany, Iceland, and Latin America promise to provide valuable qualifications and amendments to his general approach.

Beyond Correspondence: Education and Production

In sum, Bernstein illustrates most clearly the implications of a "dual systems" model of the relationship between education and reproduction, one that stresses the historical specificity of those relations and the dynamic of the internal and external relations of educational systems. In particular, his theory of educational classification gives rise to an general account of the bases of educational autonomy in the ability of the middle classes to insulate education from the direct demands of the production process:

We shall argue that, where there is a strong classification between education and production, this creates the condition for the relative autonomy of education, and thus a division of labour between those who are located in production and those who are located in cultural reproduction (education): that is, between power and control. We shall argued that a fraction of the middle class has become the producers and disseminators of theories of social control which are institutionalized in agencies of cultural reproduction and which are incorporated at different historical periods into the social relationships of production. We shall be concerned to examine the relationship between the relative autonomy of education and the formation and reproduction of the consciousness of the middle class. (Bernstein, 1977: 175)

SOCIAL-CLOSURE THEORY: GENERALIZING STATUS COMPETITION AND CREDENTIALIST THEORIES

Credentialism: Collins

In using the term *credentialist educational theory* we are referring primarily to the broadly convergent formulations of Pierre Bourdieu and Randall Collins, despite important differences in their overall sociological approaches. What they share, however, is analysis of status competition in education based on a critique of the technocratic assumption that given structures of education and professional training correspond to some rational economic and technical logic, as opposed to being shaped by the competition between groups to use educational qualification as a means of legitimating class positions. Further, unlike economic correspondence theories, they do not tie credentialization to the immediate economic imperatives of capital, as opposed to the competition between and among class actors. In short, credentialist theory challenges the uncritical functionalist (Parsonian) assumption that the evolution of the "knowledge complex" represents the progressive unfolding of instrumental reason (Parsons and Platt, 1973).

In the case of Collins, of course, his approach is explicitly defined as neo-Weberian. It is useful to begin with his work (even though Bourdieu's dates back earlier and influenced Collins at certain points) because it represents a relatively pure version of status competition theory. Collins begins with a critique of the limitations of Bourdieu's theory of cultural capital: "The specifics of Bourdieu's reproduction argument are quite plausible. But the model does not actually disprove a technocratic interpretation of education-based work skills or even a biological hereditary explanation of class advantages" (1979: 9). Further, "the larger mechanism explaining the macro pattern of educational stratification and its historical development is obscure in Bourdieu's model" and implies a functionalist argument, even if a critical one (1979: 10).

Instead, Collins proposes an historical analysis that effectively demonstrates that "the enormous expansion of education since the mid-nineteenth century *has had no effects at all* for increasing social mobility" (1979: 182); that beyond the transition to mass literacy, the contribution of education to economic productivity is limited and that the educational system is vastly overexpanded for other reasons (1979: 1–21); that the resulting "income revolution" has had quite diverse consequences, but none that can be reduced a white-collar/blue-collar opposition or that has produced a widespread increase in the equality of opportunity (1979: 183–90); and that the United States entered an era of "sinecure politics" resulting from the ongoing crisis of the credentialist system with continuing credential inflation (1979: 191–204). This last aspect creates a particular problem for school reformers, even radical ones:

> None of them came to grips with the underlying issue: the fact that education is part of a system of cultural stratification and that the reason most students are in school is that they (or their parents on their behalf) want a decent job. This means that the reasons for going to school are extraneous to whatever goes on in the classroom. (1979: 192)

Cultural Capital: Bourdieu

The sociology of education of Pierre Bourdieu (and his collaborators) is generally regarded, not without justification (as we have seen), as a species of cultural reproduction theory. What is distinctive about his approach, however, is that unlike economic correspondence reproduction theories (Althusser; early Bowles and Gintis), the focus of analysis is upon the reproductive consequences of educational systems for the strategies of class actors, not the economic system as such. What is also missed, in stressing the structuralist (and functionalist) side of this argument, is that Bourdieu is primarily indebted to Weber for his theory of "cultural capital."[2] The result is that in Bourdieu's work an account of status competition is embedded in a more general theory of cultural reproduction that gives particular attention to the rising and declining elements of the middle strata.

Whereas Collins' argument, given its objective of disconfirming technocratic and human capital theories, focused on the size of the American education to demonstrate its irrelevance to work requirements, Bourdieu begins with the assumption that schooling is indeed relevant for job placement, but for the "habitus" or status qualities it inculcates rather than the technical skills acquired.

Critical Commentary

The respective advantages and problems of Collins' and Bourdieu's work is thus evident. Collins effectively provides empirical support for a critique of the functionalist and technocratic proposition that the expansion and particular structure of the American educational system can be explained in terms of objective, rational criteria. But his effort to translate this into a more general account of social stratification suffers from an inadequate, exaggerated account of the role of credentialed groups with the notion of a "credential society". As well, his reductive and cynical treatment of credentialed knowledge leaves little scope for constructive critique and policy alternatives.

Bourdieu, on the other hand, provides an analysis which, though biased by the peculiarities of French education and culture, illustrates in great empirical detail the various mechanisms and processes of cultural competition and their relation to class reproduction. In this respect, his analysis usefully complements Collins' historical analysis. As well, he provides considerable insight into the various strategies of components of what he calls the petite bourgeoisie, thus going beyond Collins in acknowledging the continuing relation of such groups to the structures of labor and capital as axes of power and inequality, that is, part of a process of social and cultural reproduction. But his analysis does not adequately address or take into account current debates in stratification theory, largely ignores the contradictory aspects of reproductive processes (i.e., resistance), and does not go much beyond Collins with respect to a constructive critique of professional knowledge.

The Origins of Social-Closure Theory

Social-closure theory provides—we would like to argue, following Murphy (1988)—a more general framework for revising credentialist and status competition theories by developing a general theory of domination and resistance, as well as (potentially) more explicitly linking the theory of cultural reproduction with an analysis of the empirical mechanisms through which reproduction is maintained and/or transformed.[3] In particular, it helps deal with the latent functionalism and ahistorical character of much of Bourdieu's theorizing, as well as the absence of attention by Collins to noncredentialist bases of power and stratification in capitalist forms of society. Moreover, it is more explicitly open to the insights developed by critical theories of professional domination and related redefinitions of the class form of the middle strata and the class structure of advanced capitalism generally.

Though rooted in certain Weberian insights, contemporary social-closure theory has its origins in Frank Parkin's (1979) biting and acerbic critique of Marxist class theory in the name of a "bourgeois critique."[4] Parkin's theory begins with a distinction between two reciprocal modes of closure (exclusion and usurpation), which represent distinct strategies for gaining rewards and resources. Exclusionary closure involves the downward exercise of power by a dominant group able to close off opportunities to subordinate groups; usurpationary closure is characterized instead by an upward exercise of power (usurpation practices) that is oriented to gaining advantages from the dominant group.

MURPHY'S EXTENSION OF SOCIAL-CLOSURE THEORY

Basic Concepts

The approach of Parkin (and the related notions of "sinecures" and credentialization in Collins [1979]) is criticized by Murphy, nevertheless, for not considering the "deep structure" of closure (Bourdieu is more successful here), as opposed to its surface aspects. Hence Parkin's voluntaristic and subjectivist theory of class is charged (as is that of E. P. Thompson) with overreacting to structuralist Marxism. Instead, a rich set of concepts based on social closure theory are developed for recovering the distinction between "structural class situation and conscious collective action in order to refocus class analysis upon the dialectical interaction of the two" (Murphy, 1988: 128). In the process, Murphy develops what could be called a *structuralist* reading of Weber, which converges with that of critical theory and avoids voluntarism and methodological individualism of much neo-Weberian theory. Collins' more limited theory of credentialism is also criticized for its narrow stress upon a "particular set of exclusion rules" (such as credentials), thus ignoring the "deep structure of closure." If Collins had done so, Murphy argues, it would have required him to have written not *The Credential Society*, but *Credentials in Capitalist Society*, thus taking into account the derivative and secondary nature of exclusion through educational qualification, as opposed to the principal types stemming from property ownership.

Murphy's revision of social-closure theory, however, provides conceptual resources for reintegrating the theory of professional domination and that of the class character of credentialed groups into a more general theory of credentialization and power that can be used to deal with some of the limitations of existing models of cultural reproduction.

Murphy's critique of existing closure theory is based on his effort to elaborate "the relationships between rules of closure and their structure" (1988: 65). The strategic importance of this is demonstrated by the way Parkin (along with Collins) fails to account for "the vastly different power and advantages accruing to credentials and to property and the unequal importance of the two as rules of exclusion under capitalism" (Murphy, 1988: 66–67). To deal with this problem Murphy presents a threefold distinction between "principal", "derivative," and "contingent" forms of exclusion. Principal rules of exclusion are ultimately backed by the apparatus of the state (legal and ultimately coercive sanctions) and are rooted in the primary determinants of "access to, or exclusion from, power, resources, and opportunities in society" (1988: 70). Title to private property has served as the primary form of exclusion in capitalist societies, as has the communist party in state socialist societies.

Derivative rules of exclusion are derived from, but not the same as, the primary ones. Typical here are the more traditional collectivistic forms of derivative rules, such as racial, ethnic, religious, or gender criteria, as well as the individualistic forms more typical of credentialism. Derivative forms may be legally sanctioned, but more often and increasingly operate on an informal basis. The other forms of exclusion are contingent in that though not based on the principal form, their mode of use cannot be understood except in relation to the overall structure determined by it. Typical examples of this form are professional credentialization and elements of gender exclusion that precede capitalism or the party apparatus. In reality, of course, derivative and contingent rules normally overlap: "A particular set of *rules* of exclusion can have both derivative and contingent *forms*" (1988: 72). Credentials thus may be characterized by a derivative aspect deriving from their origin as a type of private property, along with a contingent dimension originating in rules related to training requirements.

This framework is in turn applied to a classification of three types of overall societal structures of exclusion: a more typical tandem model where derivative and contingent rules are tied to a principal one (e.g., Western capitalism, East-Bloc state socialism); a dual or paired structure characterized by two complementary principal systems (e.g., property and race in South Africa; property and citizenship in the case of the poor of the Third World who are excluded from migration); and two opposed sets of principal exclusion rules (e.g., the opposition between capitalist and state socialist societies at the world system level).

As Murphy argues, the creation of codes of credential exclusion is not arbitrary. Nor it adequate to focus on either status-cultural requirements (e.g., Collins) or technical-functional ones (e.g., Parkin) in isolation from each other or from the larger structures of power:

> The success of any credentialled group in carving out a monopoly depends on its success in propagating the claim that its credentials certify the presence of some skill (and that their absence indicates lack of that skill) and that the skill itself is necessary and of value. Such success is not a matter of intellectual rigor, bur rather of ideological struggle, itself founded on the structure of power in society. *It is not just a question of the power of that particular credentialled group, but of the structure of power in society within which the group can carve out its own position of power.* Whether particular skills are judged necessary, valuable, or even present, and hence the exchange value of the credentials . . . depends on the nature of the overall societal context and its power structure. (1988: 182; emphasis added)

In developing this line of thinking, Murphy suggests several types of analysis: (a) the types of skills claimed; (b) the organization of credentialed groups; (c) their relationship to the principal form of societal exclusion; and (d) the role of credentials as individualist codes of exclusion:

(a) It is proposed that skills can be differentiated into three basic types: *cultural skills*, related to the development and diffusion of knowledge and the manipulation of symbols (e.g., artists, pure scientists, intellectuals, teachers, etc.); *technical skills*, which allow the application of knowledge in the sense of manipulating things (e.g., engineers); and *political skills*, linked to management or the exercise of control over people (i.e., "the capacity to act to one's advantage in a field of power relationships" [1988: 184]). A credentialed group, to be sure, is typically based on all three, with one dominating. Medicine, for example, is defined by a core of technical skills, but is coupled with political and cultural ones as well. Where Murphy stops short, nevertheless, is linking these skills as types of knowledge to the existing literatures on professional domination, a point also evident in his analysis of the "rationalization" of closure (as we shall see in a minute).

(b) Further, credentialed groups vary along an atomist-corporatist dimension with respect to their organization. The holders of university degrees are atomized because they are not directly represented by an association promoting their interests; in contrast, medical doctors are at the corporatist end of the continuum, given their legal monopoly over medical services and the evaluation of medical competence. Such corporations differ significantly from unions because the primary stress is upon credential exclusion.

(c) In capitalist societies the key aspect of the relationship to the primary form of exclusion is whether credentialed groups are located in the private sector (hence, willingness and ability of clients to pay) or public sector (based on needs as defined by the state). Nevertheless, both share an interest in avoiding competition which requires different strategies in these two context.

(d) Finally, there has been a profound historical shift from collectivist to individualist codes of exclusion, resulting in what Murphy refers to as the "rationalization of exclusion, monopolization, and closure" (1988: 190). Earlier forms of exclusion were, to put it in terms of pattern variables, ascriptive (e.g., class, religion, ethnicity, etc.), whereas now they are increasingly based on individual achievement criteria. Weber's theory of rationalization is outlined in terms of his stress upon the following key elements of this process: formal versus substantive rationality; intellectualization; depersonalization; and control (1988: 196–201). The key rationalized institutions are held to be bureaucratic organizations, the formal legal system, the capitalist market economy, and an "inner orientation" of personality structures (1988: 202–8). As Murphy concludes, "there is an implicit end in this process of formal rationalization: that of control (over nature, economic competitors, ideological adversaries, political opponents, and military enemies)" (1988: 218). But the resulting form of change is hardly revolutionary, i.e. "a change towards the elimination of domination and closure, rather it consists of controlled change-modification of domination and closure in order to strengthen mastery and render it deeper, more comprehensive, more subtle, and more legitimate" (1988: 218–19). The individualization of closure criteria result in a "formal equality" but does not lead to substantive equality:

> The rationalization of closure involves the monopolization of the means, not only of production, but also of destruction, administration, and of knowledge, and the exclusion (or "separation" to use Weber's term) of those who directly use those means and of the population generally from their control. It involves centralized, hierarchical, bureaucratic control over those means, whether by private enterprise and the bourgeoisie under capitalism, or by the Communist Party and its dominant class under state socialism. Structurally both are systems of closure and domination. (1988: 231)

These processes, to be sure, are not without contradictory aspects, especially the tension between formal and substantive rationality. With failure of performance and the inability to define and realize substantive ends, existing primary structures of domination can be surprisingly vulnerable (witness the East Bloc in Europe). This is linked to the usurpatory potential of the dominated: "The great untapped resources of human capital and intelligence in the remaining members of excluded groups generates a contradiction based on the logic of rationalization itself, on unequal resources in a contest where all are supposed to compete on an equal footing. This is a potential basis of usurpation using the logic of rationalization itself" (1988: 226).

Critical Commentary

The potential empirical applications of social-closure theory in virtually all areas of social research is immense and would complement and enrich many existing theories constructed at a less general level of analysis. It is particularly useful for comparative and cross-cultural research, given that its categories are not limited to Western European or capitalist social formations. As Murphy's many examples based on the peculiar place of women in exclusionary processes suggest, social-closure theory should be thoroughly exploited by feminist theorists (and any other of the less transparent victims of exclusion) frustrated by the traditional gender versus class debates. Needless to say, some of these more specialized investigations may reveal theoretical and empirical problems in Murphy's specific formulations, but are unlikely to undermine his general argument.

As for some constructive suggestions, there are several obvious areas where social-closure theory could be expanded and reconciled with related approaches. First of all, though the whole book is predicated upon a Marx-Weber synthesis in the spirit of a critical theory of society, almost no reference is made to the existing traditions of critical theory (e.g., Held, 1980; Fay, 1987; Kellner, 1989) that have attempted to provide the epistemological, analytical, and normative groundings of such a project, aside from an allusion to Gouldner's conception of a "reflexive sociology," and occasional references to his own approach as contributing to a critical theory of domination. This must interpreted as a sin of omission on Murphy's part, but it has important consequences for the overall defense of his project, as well as for shoring up some of its weaknesses. Indeed, all of the following constructive comments flow from this omission.

Second, as Murphy himself suggests in his brief commentary on Bourdieu and Passeron's theory of educational reproduction, closure theory has the capacity to empirically specify in precise ways "how the school system can be autonomous and yet at the same time contribute to the reproduction and legitimation of the existing social class structure of society" (1988: 150). Implicitly, the resulting reconceptualization of the concept of relative autono-

my could be extended to all other areas of cultural life, thus rescu-
ing now languishing theories of cultural reproduction from the
well-known limitations of functionalist reasoning (see Connell,
1983: 140–161; Liston, 1988). In this context, the crucial shift
from collectivistic to individualistic codes of exclusion, which are
also referred to as involving "class protection" *rather than* "class
reproduction" (Murphy, 1988: 166), is potentially misleading in
that, as Murphy himself argues, the result is merely an opening up,
not an abolition of, class reproduction. Within this general framework, however, it becomes possible to more adequately historicize
the concept of reproduction.

A number of other problems remain with Murphy's analysis.
Social-closure theory needs to be reconciled with critical theories
of the state and hegemony. In addition, although Murphy's three-
fold typology of power (as command, constraint, and capacity to
profit from) is useful for his specific analyses of education and
credentialization, it is not clear that it operates at the same level of
generality as his other categories. Although social-closure theory
in Murphy's reconstructed version is organized around the dialectic of structure and agency, his approach is not adequately
grounded in a social psychology of domination and emancipation.
Finally, the implications of social-closure theory for critical theory
generally, for example the work Jürgen Habermas, would certainly
provide a rich area of investigation, but Murphy stops short of
exploring these implications. In particular, critical theory has long
been criticized by neo-Marxists for having abandoned the theory
of surplus value for an insufficiently "scientific" general theory of
domination. Social-closure theory appears to provide a rigorous
alternative to the Marxist theory of exploitation, one which—as a
more general theory—complements and clarifies the traditional
focus of critical theory on the forms of domination specific to
advanced capitalism, as well as its general postulate that all hither-
to known forms of society have been based on relations of domination and subordination. On the other hand, the normative foundations of the resulting critique of domination remain dangerously
relativistic in concluding that whether exclusion should be resisted
cannot be resolved by the judgment of the sociologist: "it is the
belief of the subordinate class itself that this or that particular
exclusion practice is exploitative and merits usurpation" (1988:
100). Such a conception of the relation of theory and practice is

clearly unsatisfactory because it opens the way for the justification of all types of irrational and regressive actions on the part of subordinate groups and undermines altogether any notion of falsifying consciousness. In this connection, Habermas's effort to ground critical theory in a conception of communicative action offers a more promising alternative.

CONCLUSION

On several points, Bourdieu's approach to social and cultural reproduction (and indirectly Bernstein's) converges with Althusser's structuralist Marxism. First, education is viewed as the decisive institutional complex for symbolic reproduction, whereas the state has the monopoly on physical violence. Second, symbolic violence—or "ideology," in Althusser's vocabulary—is viewed as an anthropological invariant, an inherent feature of all conceivable forms of socialization; both would reject as utopian the aspiration to abolish or transcend symbolic violence (or ideology) *as such*, though they clearly refrain from drawing relativistic or cynical conclusions. Third, both wish to link the relatively autonomous educational system with the process of social reproduction (though Althusser does not clearly distinguish between cultural and social reproduction) and class struggle. But the residual differences have fundamental implications:

Bourdieu's preference for the more neutral term *cultural arbitrary* over *ideology* speaks of a different and less dogmatic approach to processes of mystification; this difference is rooted in a rejection of a purely objectivist position of the type assumed by structuralism, that is, Bourdieu is also concerned with the practical reasoning of agents.

Methodologically, Bourdieu is concerned not simply with the abstract functional logic of the system, but with the consequences of its transformation within history, specifically the shift in France from a traditional mode of educational domination to a more democratic one.

In Bourdieu's work, the link between the educational system and social reproduction is analyzed from the perspective of a structural homology rather than correspondence, a procedure that lends itself to a considerably more nuanced and differentiated form of empirical analysis (than found, e.g., in Baudelot and Establet, Bowles and Gintis, and Vasconi).

Though the political—and policy—implications of Bourdieu's argument are ambiguous, it is not rooted in an objectivistic revolutionary dialectic in which the contradiction between dominant and subordinate classes has a logically necessary outcome. Despite certain difficulties of application and interpretation, Bourdieu's model in principle lends itself to application in a wide variety of historical and cross-cultural contexts, whereas Althusser's theory of Ideological State Apparatuses leads at best to a problematic reassertion of the correspondence principle.

Bernstein's effort to deepen the analysis of pedagogical discourse (a theme implicit in Bourdieu's research program) opens up possibilities for a critical sociology of the curriculum that need not fall back upon the dogmatic assumptions of the type of discourse theory associated with Althusserians such as Pecheux and others..

To point to the advantages of Bourdieu's reproduction theory (as complemented by Bernstein's) over Althusser's is not to say, however, that it is not without its difficulties. As we have noted, both Bourdieu and Bernstein leave open (even if they do not in principle exclude) consideration of a whole range of questions, especially about resistance and contradiction, as well as the theory of class and state presupposed by a model of educational reproduction. Althusser at least addresses those questions, even if his response (and that of those following in his footsteps) may be questionable. Most importantly, Bourdieu and Bernstein and their respective colleagues and followers have opened up a vast terrain of theoretical and empirical exploration that is now only beginning to be adequately understood and subjected to the more precise and sympathetic criticism, as well as complementary research, which it deserves. Still, their work needs to be criticized and expanded along the lines suggested by social-closure theory, which offer the basis of a fully general theory of domination and exploitation.

To summarize, the great contribution of structuralism, whether in the form of Althusser's hyperfunctionalism or Bourdieu's relatively open model, has been to situate the sociology of education in relation to a critical use of functional type analysis that points to the paradoxical features of the continuities of class stratification and the more or less subtle participation of educational systems in that process. The rapid rise and fall of Althusserian structuralism is suggestive, however, of the deficiencies of his overall approach and its inability to develop the necessary refinements and adjustments for a cumulative strategy of research.

Bourdieu, in contrast, has established a broad program of research that has redefined the sociology of education in France. If his example has not produced the quantity of research one might have expected elsewhere, this is to be regretted and related to a a number of problems of interpretation and appropriation, which we have touched upon at various points. Most importantly, if one can get beyond the peculiarities of the French case, his approach clearly is applicable to the full range of educational systems. Needless to say, the theoretical demands and range of empirical skills required are a practical obstacle; it is important to remember that Bourdieu himself has benefited from the assistance of a number of gifted collaborators and a series of well-funded research projects. But all of this points to the difficulties of "replication" elsewhere; this clearly remains the most persuasive model of reconstruction of social histories of education from the perspective of a model of cultural and social reproduction. Even if it abandons the simplicity and purity of a strict correspondence principle, his approach points to the crucial empirical issue of historically specifying the structural relations between education and society in any given case. As we have seen, these contributions are further extended with Murphy's social-closure theory, in spite of the limitations and omissions already noted.

It is fair to say that dissatisfactions with the lack of historicist and dialectical analysis in structuralism (perhaps due to structuralism's reliance on concepts that may be, in the end, too abstract and, on occasion, difficult to apply empirically) and the need to perceive with more clarity the political implications of social struggles' cultural dimensions, has led a number of critics of structuralism to embrace a convergence between neo-Gramscian and critical theory. We turn in the next chapter to discuss this convergence.

PART 4

The Convergence of Neo-Gramscian and Critical Theory

CHAPTER 8

Critical Theory and Education: From the Frankfurt School to Poststructuralism

As Part 3 illustrated, the interplay between structuralism, Marxism, and analytical conflict theories has provided some of the most important influences upon theory in educational sociology, both in the contexts of research and conceptions of educational practice. The failure and decline of structuralist Marxism, however, undermined the most ambitious program for the unification of a practice-oriented revolutionary theory with an empirical analysis of ideological apparatuses. Structuralist conflict theories, on the other hand, were more successful in refining analysis of various aspects of cultural reproduction in education, but eschewed any systematic effort at developing a theory of practice, or even an explicit policy analysis.

The roots of these failures were simultaneously epistemological and theoretical. Structuralism was implicated in a new form of positivism that blocked theoretical development on three fronts: a self-reflexive theory of knowledge capable of addressing a critique of technological rationalization and bureaucratization; an interpretation of the subject and social movements adequate for thinking of educational and social transformation; and a complementary theory of the state capable of conceptualizing the obscure concept of relative autonomy in nondogmatic (functionalist) terms. Our general thesis will be that the most fruitful responses to these issues can be grouped under the heading of striking convergence between neo-Gramscian and critical theories, both under the broad influence of poststructuralism.

The rest of this study attempts to trace the responses to the crisis of structuralism through an exploration of the convoluted debates in each of these three domains. We will do so by means of a

217

somewhat arbitrary strategy of separating out four closely interrelated and mutually-influencing sets of discussions. The Frankfurt School tradition (this chapter) and Gramscian theory (chapter 9) provide the transitional critiques of historical materialism that set the stage for contemporary debates as developed, respectively, in Britain (chapter 10) and the United States (chapter 11).

The influence of critical theory in the Frankfurt School tradition upon educational theory in the English-speaking world is largely a product of the late 1970s and especially the 1980s. Though its impact has been limited, German critical theory has been a significant force within the critical pedagogy movement, especially with the waning of structuralist Marxism, the criticism of the cruder political economic correspondence theories, and the awareness of the need for greater attention to problems of resistance and subjectivity. The Anglo-American reception has been geographically dispersed and has differentially influenced different areas of educational theory, practice, and research. Though British discussions have been largely untouched by critical theory, it has been central to radical educational theory in the United States (e.g., Giroux, Wexler, Aronowitz), Canada (e.g., Misgeld, 1985) and Australia (e.g., Bates, 1985).

One of the surprising features of this reception, other than that it followed a little more slowly than in other areas (such as political sociology and mass communications), is that it has been piecemeal and largely undebated. In other words, whereas some of the applications themselves in a given national context may have been controversial, little attention has been given to whether or in what respect it was consistent with, or drew from a particular tendency within, the Frankfurt School tradition or West German educational research. Matters have been further complicated by the difficulty, at times, of separating out the specific influence of Frankfurt Critical Theory, as opposed to a number of other closely related tendencies in radical and neo-Marxist social theory.

The task of the present chapter is to pose the question of the Anglo-American reception of the educational theory in the Frankfurt School tradition. The result is a twofold set of concerns: the first and overriding objective will be to sketch the unfolding of the problematic of education in relation to the changes within the Frankfurt tradition from the Weimar Republic to the present; the second will be to draw upon this historical sketch in order to raise a number of issues about the appropriation and critique of Frankfurt educational theory in contemporary Anglo-American educational research.

EARLY CRITICAL THEORY

Critical Theory and Education in the Weimar Republic

Curiously, the topic of education as such never emerged as a domain of systematic research or commentary in the early Frankfurt School, whether in the Weimar Period or the publication of the *Zeitschrift für Sozialforschung* in exile. This fact is anomalous for several reasons. The investigation of pedagogical and educational issues was clearly legitimated by Horkheimer's earliest programmatic statements about the general goals of an interdisciplinary research institute, as well as its more specific early projects. As Horkheimer described the tasks of the institute in 1930:

> Not only within social philosophy in the narrower sense, but likewise in sociological circles as well as those of general philosophy, discussions about society have gradually and ever more clearly crystallized around a question which is not only presently important, but is at the same time the topical version of the oldest and most important philosophical problems: namely, the question of the connection between the economic life of society, the psychic development of individuals, and changes in the cultural domains in the narrower sense. To these belong not only the so-called spiritual contents of science, art, and religion, but also law, custom, fashion, public opinion, sports, leisure pastimes, life style, etc. (Horkheimer, 1972: 43; our translation)

Clearly the absence of education in this listing is as incidental as the absence of reference to the family (which became the focus of one of the institute's first major projects) in relation to "the psychic development of individuals." As Horkheimer wrote in his notebooks in the late 1920s—not published until 1934—

> In society as presently constituted, the following law applies to individual development: the more elevated the social position, the more easily intelligence and every other kind of talent will grow. On the higher social levels, the objective conditions for the development of socially necessary qualities are more favorable

than on the lower ones. This is obvious as regards education in family and school. (1978: 47)

Not only does the educational system serve to reinforce class advantage, it distorts the process of learning in the interests of a form of social control based on "bourgeois morality." For Horkheimer, therefore, Protestant education in particular makes a mockery of the principle of "education to truthfulness":

> Bourgeois morality is like a schoolmaster who not only thrashes bad boys when they misbehave but also demands that they raise their hand when the mere thought that they might shoots through their heads. Education to truthfulness indeed! The thoughts that are locked up in the heads are themselves a forbidden pleasure the good child denies himself. They may also mature in those heads and break out at a moment when the schoolmaster would find it difficult to control them with his cane. (1974: 69)

Further, the resistance to the very existence of the institute within the German university system, as well as the fact that academic careers were closed for most of its members for political reasons, suggested an immediate context that might have made the university system a topic of investigation. Similarly, the focus of early research on the consciousness of the German working class and the family as a source of authoritarian dispositions, might well have been complemented by the consideration of the class-specific character and effects of educational systems. That this did not occur most likely reflects the effects of setting priorities with rather limited resources and the absence within this network of a productive individual whose areas of expertise were related to education.

Nevertheless, as we should expect, the *Zeitschrift* routinely (if very briefly) reviewed books on education under the heading of "spezielle Soziologie," and then under "Political and Social Science" with the transition to English. Though such titles were infrequent relative, for example, to those on the family, they drew from both German and international sources and dealt with issues such as the family and education, proletarian education, and the effects of the Nazi transformation of German social institutions. Representative of the commentary, ironically, was the sympathetic response to the relatively progressive educational debates and research in the United States.

Yet in a generalized sense, pedagogical questions were at the very center of the research agenda of the institute in that its central projects were a study of the family and authority and of working-class consciousness, namely, a theory of class-specific socialization. These interests were extended in exile in research on prejudice and mass communications.

In sum, the topic of education was peripheral to the immediate agenda of research in the Weimar Republic, and the conditions of exile did not create circumstances for changing this (unlike the case of communications research). Further, the relative lack of autonomy of the German educational system, and its resulting conservatism, was largely consistent with the assumptions of the institute members' understanding of historical materialism. Indeed, it was so much so that it did not elicit any obvious explanatory problems under the given circumstances. Yet it did potentially pose the question of the role of the capitalist state, especially since it represented institutional structures largely developed outside the marketplace.

Authority, Education, and the Family

Though rarely discussed in the context of educational theory, the series of historical investigations on "authority and the family" directed by Horkheimer in the mid 1930s provide important insights to the pedagogical principles underlying critical theory (Friesenhahn, 1985: 78). The central theme of this research was a social-psychological account of authority from the perspective of a materialist analysis of society, though the focus of this analysis was a differentiation between authority as a source of domination as opposed to its playing a constructive role in the learning process.

The larger theoretical framework of these investigations was based on the thesis that there had been a functional change in the role of the family in the socialization process. As a consequence, the family had increasingly lost its capacity to serve as a source of resistance against the reification and functionalization flowing from the production process. This transformation of the family, associated with the loss of the authority of the father, contributed to the increasing influence of the state, school, and modern mass media and resulted in the formation of new kinds of irrational authority structures within the family. The central assumption of studying these phenomena was that though "authority is a central historical category," it cannot be defined as such and its significance can only be understood in specific social contexts (Horkheimer, cited in Friesenhahn, 1985: 79).

Central to Horkheimer's analysis is a distinction between rational and irrational forms of authority, a distinction that was later challenged by the West German student movements' anarchist attack on authority as such. In its constructive sense—"as voluntary dependence" (*als bejahte Abhängigkeit*)—subordination to the other lies in one's own interest, as illustrated by the case of the child's subordination to a "good education" as a condition of developing its human capacities. Crucial is the assumption that the goal of education is the cultivation of human capacities (*Bildung*), a process which is oriented toward the realization of individual rational autonomy (*Mündigkeit*), and that, further, this rational autonomy is not given, but dependent on the process of *Bildung* itself: "Bildung is the prerequisite for rational autonomy, and in the process of Bildung authority is indispensable" (Friesenhahn, 1985: 82—our translation). From this perspective, pedagogical leadership is not an end in itself but a means to enlightenment; hence, authoritarian deformations of authority are inconsistent with its inner logic. Further, this point is closely linked to the way in which pedagogical leadership as a form of authority is oriented toward its own self-abolition with the maturation of the learner. The task of a critical theory of education thus becomes a question of investigating those forms of irrational authority that contribute to the role of education in reproducing domination as opposed to its original emancipatory intentions. More broadly, the educational theory of critical theory is the counterpoint to the opposite of, the theory of the authoritarian personality.

State Capitalism and Halbbildung

By the late 1930s the most influential core members of the institute—Horkheimer, Adorno, Marcuse, Pollock—abandoned any hope for the mobilization of the working class against Hitler. The outcome was a break in their thinking and a retreat from certain fundamental assumptions of historical materialism, especially the historically privileged status of the revolutionary proletariat. For Horkheimer and Adorno, in particular, this shift culminated in a disillusioned, pessimistic philosophy of history in which instru-

mental reason had undermined objective reason. More constructively, however, this shift was also accompanied by an effort to
understand the emerging social formation of the type represented
by the United States. Despite an initial hesitation between a more
orthodox conception of the state as an instrumental of capital, they
opted for a theory of "state capitalism," which recognized the
importance of the emergent form of state autonomy and its role in
stabilizing a new form of capitalism. A corollary to this was the
theory of culture industries, which postulated that mass communications had played a crucial role in undermining class cultures and
created a mass culture that effectively integrated the working class
into a (pseudo) liberal (pseudo) democratic society. By the late
1940s critical theory had in effect outlined the framework for a
version of a rather deterministic theory of cultural reproduction
distinguished by the crucial epistemological role given to modern
science and technology as part of the legitimation of such state-
capitalist forms of society.

Again, education did not play a central role in this analysis,
partly because attention had shifted away from the family toward
the mass media as the site of a decisive change in the socialization
process. Further, in exile in the United States, the choice of research
opportunities were largely determined by the host, hence the focus
on prejudice and communications. Upon their return to Germany
in the early 1950s, however, Horkheimer and Adorno took an
active part in attempting to revive the institute in Frankfurt and
eventually some of their students did take up the question of the
relationship between the German educational system and democracy in the late 1950s (a topic to be taken up in the context of
Habermas's early work and the emergence of the student movement).

Yet Adorno and Horkheimer, in particular, did on a number of
occasions make remarks or address issues that were suggestive
with respect to how their conception of critical theory could be
applied to pedagogy and the sociology of education. Most of their
remarks derived from assumptions following from the conception
of the "dialectic of enlightenment" and the consequences of the
"total administration" of society characteristic of state capitalism.
From this perspective, debate about culture was caught between a
traditionalist defense of state-supported and upper-class—based
"affirmative culture" and a technocratic rationalization that "de-

mocratized" culture by turning it over to the culture industries in the marketplace. Their comments on education tended to be directed at both representatives of retreating traditional culture and prophets of the new mass culture and the role of educational institutions, the postwar university in particular, in passively reproducing this transition. Adorno's notion of *"Halbbildung"* or "half-education" conveys the sense of disillusionment with postwar educational systems, which had made certain ostensible gains in the direction of democratization but remained constrained within a new, more sophisticated system of domination known as "total administration." The most widely known variant of this argument was developed by Herbert Marcuse in the context of his theory of "one-dimensional" society.

The result for Adorno and Horkheimer paralleled their ambivalent stance toward cultural changes generally: a general plea for democratization coupled with a qualified defense of university autonomy against the inroads of market-oriented demands, even if at times that meant siding with certain conservative interests within the university system. Their ambivalent opposition to the German student movement in the 1960s was a consistent expression of this stance. The plea for "relevance" was, for them, as fraught with dangers as the isolation and indifference of the traditional German university to social problems. As Horkheimer put it in his notebooks in 1956:

> Educational Reform: In *my* platonic academy, the lowest grades would be taught the critique of political economy, and would have to draw all the consequences that follow from it. They would be brought up to be active dialecticians, and introduced to practice. In the upper grades, they would have to understand Mallarmé, but without forgetting the other. (1978: 130)

But the anachronistic reference to Plato reveals a general disillusionment with the revolutionary project, despite an insistence that it not be coupled with a simple replacement of bourgeois culture by proletarian. As he noted several years later, "freedom is not an end but a transitory means" of adaptation, and the purpose of man's education "is probably nothing but reproduction under conditions of minimal resistance. All systems are false, that of Marx no less than Aristotle's—however much truth both may have seen" (1974: 198).

ILLICH AND FRANKFURT CRITICAL THEORY

The Context of Illich's Thesis

We would like to take up next the case of Ivan Illich's critique of education, even though it would not ordinarily be closely associated with the Frankfurt School tradition of critical theory. As we have argued in more detail elsewhere, however, his overall approach to modern societies and underdevelopment is incomprehensible outside this context (Morrow and Torres, 1990). As well, it also represents one of the few applications to Third World educational issues of theoretical concepts related to the Frankfurt tradition.

Our first objective in this section is to argue that Ivan Illich's critique of industrialization represents the most influential extension of a version of the Frankfurt's School's critique of technical rationalization to education and many other human endeavors, particularly those related to social welfare policies. This is an appropriate time and place to attempt an assessment, twenty years after the thesis of deschooling was advanced.

Illich's approach to education is based on a unique fusion of the Frankfurt School critique of instrumental rationality with various strands of argument from the progressive, free-school, and libertarian anarchist traditions. First published in 1971, Illich's *Deschooling Society* had a catalytic effect by pushing to its logical conclusion the radical critiques of modern education found in the works of people like Paul Goodman, Edgar Friedenberg, and Neil Postman.[1] Beyond that, his approach incorporated a less widely recognized general theme (at least in educational circles): a critique of science, technology, and professionalization rooted in the critical theory of the Frankfurt School tradition.

Illich's argument suggests a rather different model of reproduction from those discussed thus far: structural-functionalist models (Parsons), economic-reproductive theories (Althusser), and cultural-reproductive models (Bourdieu and Passeron, 1977).[2] Rather, his approach could be called a "*class-bureaucratic reproductive model*," where that suggests compulsive universal tendencies of systems of formal rationalization to reproduce themselves at higher and higher levels (hence his reference to an "industrial mode of production"), though this process is also shaped and reinforced by social-class antagonisms generated with a wide variety of social formations (capitalist, bureaucratic socialist, etc.).[3]

Yet Illich's approach is consistent with the general logic of reproduction theory within the neo-Marxist tradition in its demystification of the ideology of schooling and the futility of liberal reform measures. Not only does education invariably reproduce existing class structures, "it also grades the nations of the world according to an international caste system" (1971: 13). Whereas for most materialist reproduction theorists this leads to some combination of resignation, pessimism, and vague appeals to an inevitable revolution, Illich quickly couples his analysis with a instant, provocative solution: "deschooling." However, the concept of deschooling and its rhetorical richness has been lost upon many unsympathetic critics who simply point to the fact that deinstitutionalization of any major area of social life would lead to chaos—anarchy.

But this kind of response misses the point in several ways. First, by deschooling, Illich does not mean so a complete deinstitutionalization as a transformation of institutions; hence he speaks of "postindustrial bureaucracies" as "convivial" institutions (1973a) and refers explicitly to the need for "new formal educational institutions" (1971: 108). In a subsequent article, he even details some of "the dangers of a rash, uncritical disestablishment" of schools, which "could lead to a free-for-all in the production and consumption of more vulgar learning, acquired for immediate utility or eventual prestige" (1973b: 15). In a broader sense, Illich admits, the process of deschooling cannot be separated from the transformation of other institutions of society. Whether or under what conditions schools might take a lead role in that process is, obviously, one of the areas where Illich is most vulnerable. Yet his essential point remains of enduring significance: "The radical functional inversion of our major institutions constitutes a revolution much more profound than the shifts of ownership or power usually proposed"(1973a: 51), a theme foreshadowed in the notion of "cultural revolution" introduced in *Celebration of Awareness*:

> Let me call this alternative program either institutional or
> cultural revolution, because its aim is the transformation of both
> public and personal reality . . . The cultural revolutionary must
> not only be distinguished from the political magician but also

from both the neo-Luddite and the promoter of intermediary technology. (1970: 172–3)

Illich and Critical Theory

Though capable of formidable erudition, compiling empirical evidence, and skillful theoretical discussion, Illich has not been prone to contextualizing his work's origins or situating his own theoretical trajectory. What his work does in fact represent is the first sustained effort—other than that of Erich Fromm—to popularize Frankfurt critical theory as part of an practical agenda for revolutionary change.[4] This connection, however, is only implicit in *Deschooling Society* (1971) and becomes fully evident, if peripherally, only in *Tools for Conviviality* (1973a) a couple of years later. The educational debates about Illich took place largely without reference to the latter or subsequent works.

What *Tools for Conviviality* reveals is that Illich's whole theory is grounded in Marcuse's *One Dimensional Man* (1964) and represents an original and ingenious effort to specify and popularize Marcuse's thesis, as well as offer an optimistic alternative to the option of a "grand refusal." This is not to belittle Illich's accomplishments or to characterize his work as derivative, but it does point to the basis for an immanent critique and reevaluation. This connection is generally not made because of the seeming distance between the rarefied abstractions of *One Dimensional Man* and its focus on capitalism as opposed to Illich's detailed dissection of the "industrial mode of production." Yet if we recall that Marcuse also wrote an indictment of Soviet Marxism (Marcuse, 1958) and its relation to alienation and instrumental rationalization, it is easy to see how Illich could easily formulate his indictment more broadly.

A crucial aspect of Illich's strategy is thus a concept of "tools," which is synonymous with the more cumbersome (at least for a popular writer) notion of *instrumental rationalization* introduced by Max Weber and incorporated within a Marxian problematic by the Frankfurt theorists in the 1940s (Horkheimer and Adorno, 1972):

> I use the term "tool" broadly enough to include not only simple hardware . . . and not just large machines . . . I also include among tools productive institutions such as factories that produce tangible commodities . . . and productive systems for intangible commodities such as those which produce "educa-

tion," "health," "knowledge," or "decisions." I use this term because it allows me to subsume into one category all rationally designed devices, be they artifacts or rules, codes or operators, and to distinguish all these planned and engineered instrumentalities from other things such as basic food or implements, which in a given culture are not deemed to be subject to rationalization. (Illich, 1973a: 22)

Beyond that, the notions of "convivial tools" (as opposed to "manipulatory tools") and "natural scales" that if ignored lead to ecological and social crisis can be seen as grounded in Marcuse's more deeply philosophical discussions of reconciliation with nature and conception of a "new science" that escaped the logic of positivistic technical control (Marcuse, 1964; Leiss, 1974). Yet Illich's position on technology (calls, for example, for "counterfoil" research) appears to lie between Marcuse's more utopian notion of a "new science" and Horkheimer and Adorno's more insistent claim that reason was inherently contaminated by destructive tendencies. The outcome is a selective interpretation of critical theory that implicitly draws it in the direction of anarchism. Not surprisingly, this led the authors of a study on organizational theory to describe the critical theory tradition as a species of "anti-organization" theory, citing the example of Illich (Burrell and Morgan, 1979). Another author has sought to characterize the outcome as a form of conservative Christian anarchism:

> Ivan Illich's call for institutional transformation is the demand of a true cultural revolutionary. It is *revolutionary* because it demands nothing less than the total revision of society; it is *cultural* because it argues that the revolution must begin with the transformation of individual consciousness. In a way, Illich fits perfectly Henry Adams' description of himself as a "conservative Christian anarchist": *conservative* because it is the humanistic image of man which he is trying to conserve; *Christian* because he posits a natural order to show limits man must not trespass; and *anarchist* because he insists that the individual become the master of his own life. (Levine, 1975: 75)

Not surprisingly, though educators have largely abandoned Illich, he is more widely appreciated in recent discussions as an important contributor to a critical theory of ecology (Luke, 1987; Jones, 1987). Unlike the earlier Frankfurt generation, however, Illich gives primacy to the educational system as the crucial aspect of the reproduction of technical reason. In contrast, the original dialectic of Enlightenment thesis was developed in the context of a analysis of the emergence of mass cultural industries: the modern mass media and instrumental rationalization (Horkheimer and Adorno, 1972). Despite a more general pedagogical conception embodied in a critical appropriation of the classical notion of "Bildung" or intellectual formation, the educational system as such emerges as a central target of critique only slowly in the 1960s in the later West German postwar context (Habermas, 1969; Friesenhahn, 1985; Lenhardt, 1984). Surprisingly, Illich actually carries even further than the original Frankfurt theorists the dialectic of Enlightenment thesis by his sustained attack on all professionalized knowledge and education: "The industrial mode of production was first fully rationalized in the manufacture of a new invisible commodity, called 'education'" (1973a: 20). In the process, he often forgets a point made by one of his early commentators that "the most potent teachers of our day are not in the schoolrooms. They are the masters of the mass media, the major professions, government, those who design our cities, organize our work, make our music and movies" (Gross, 1973a: 157). Though he makes amends for this focus on education in his attack on the service professions in general in *Tools for Conviviality*, he does not really address the mass media and the role of the state. Yet they remain even more important as part of the three major obstacles to change, identified as "the idolatry of science, the corruption of ordinary language, and the loss of respect for the formal process by which social decisions are made" (1973a: 92).

Finally, Illich's project presupposes in an important way the categorical distinction between "labor" and "interaction" developed by Habermas (1971: 81ff.) but considered unnecessary by Marcuse given his broad understanding of the Marxian notion of praxis.[5] But in Illich's hands, communicative interaction is characterized ontologically as having an inherently antagonist relation with instrumental rationality. In Illich's words:

> I choose the term "conviviality" to designate the opposite of industrial productivity. I intended it to mean autonomous and creative intercourse among persons, and the intercourse of persons with their environment; and this in contrast with the conditioned response of persons to the demands made upon them by others, and by a man-made environment. I consider conviviality

to be individual freedom realized in personal interdependence and, as such, an intrinsic ethical value. I believe that, in any society, as conviviality is reduced below a certain level, no amount of industrial productivity can effectively satisfy the needs it creates among society's members. (1973a: 11)

At the same time, however, Illich's position was subject to the same criticisms that Habermas has directed against the older generation of Frankfurt theorists and their insufficiently critical appropriation of Weber's theory of rationalization and Lukacs's theory of reification. For Illich, reconciliation with technology in a convivial society remains coupled with a very pessimistic interpretation of the apparently inexorable consequence of instrumental rationalization.

To grasp the thrust of that early critique, however, it is useful to consider Illich's argument as a specific form of social and cultural reproduction theory, what we have termed a "class-bureaucratic reproduction model."[6] Essentially, he is suggesting that educational institutions are self-reproducing, on the one hand, and contribute to the reproduction of a certain type of society on the other: "We cannot go beyond the consumer society unless we first understand the obligatory public schools inevitably reproduce such a society, no matter what is taught in them" (1972: 55). Like other reproduction theories (Bourdieu and Passeron, 1977; Bowles and Gintis, 1977), the stress here is upon the form of education rather than the content. Similar to Althusser (and Durkheim), Illich speaks of education as the sequel to the church as the primary source of social integration (1971: 54).

From this perspective the primary function of the hidden curriculum is that it "teaches all children that economically valuable knowledge is the result of professional teaching and that social entitlements depend on the rank achieved in a bureaucratic process" (1973b: 8–9). The resulting commodification of knowledge certificates is in turn explicitly linked to the "exercise of privilege and power" and the aspirations of the lower middle classes to gain entry to the professions (1973b: 10). This general approach to reproduction is close to that of Bourdieu in that the autonomy and re-reproducing capabilities of the school are linked to class strategies and legitimation of the system of stratification in general. Though his focus is on the reproduction of capitalist "consumer" societies, his thesis is generalized to all "schooled" societies, "be

they fascist, democratic or socialist, big or small, rich or poor":
"This identity of the school system forces us to recognize the profound world-wide identity of myth, mode of production, and
method of social control, despite the great variety of mythologies
in which the myth finds expression" (1971: 106).

The general direction of the political economic response is
obvious: the source of social decay is not in the manipulative behavior of state and corporate bureaucracies, but in "the normal
operation of the basic economic institutions of capitalism which
consistently sacrificed the healthy development of work, education, and social equality to the accumulation of capital and the
requisites of the hierarchical division of labor" (Bowles and Gintis,
1977: 260). In general, of course, Illich's argument is not incompatible with this correspondence principle, though he would generalize it in two directions. First, all the other major institutions also
"correspond" in this way (i.e., in their manipulative form). And
second, all industrial modes of production (e.g., the Soviet Union)
have corresponding manipulative educational systems. Further,
Bowles and Gintis charge, Illich's formulation of the consumer
consciousness found in the socialization process forgets that these
are grounded in the production process and that any strategy of
change (e.g., the construction of nonaddictive, convivial institutions) that does not alter those economic structures is doomed to
failure (Bowles and Gintis, 1977: 260–611). Obviously these are
important criticisms, which even Illich tacitly admits in noting that
his proposals are designed for a society that does not exist. His
optimism stems from a peculiar notion of contradiction grounded
in the assumption that imbalances in "natural scales" of tool use
will generate a crisis leading to the transition from an industrial to
a postindustrial mode of production (Illich, 1973a: ix–xi).

Curiously, however, Bowles and Gintis in their early work do
not take into account the reductionist implications of their own
argument, namely, that all the significant manipulative aspects of
institutions are rooted in the capitalist mode of production. In
short, they appear unwilling to concede the possibility of the autonomous capacity of bureaucracies and technology to develop
manipulative strategies of control. This failure then leads them to
some anomalous—if not contradictory—references to noncapitalist educational experiments. On the one hand, they dismiss Illich's
criticisms of China and Cuba on the grounds that "these countries

are following new and historically unprecedented directions in social development" (Bowles and Gintis, 1977: 261). And yet, on the
other hand, they admit that the Soviet Union and Eastern Europe
"have abolished private ownership of the means of production,
while replicating the relationships of economic control, dominance, and subordination characteristic of capitalism" (1977:
266). But this is precisely Illich's point, which they gloss over: all
schooled societies link social control and learning and suffer from
"pedagogical hubris," that is, the "belief that man can do what
God cannot, namely, manipulate others for their own salvation"
(Illich, 1971: 73). Nor, by the way, do Bowles and Gintis deal with
the broader implications of Illich's critique for developing societies: "Transferring a modern institution to the developing nations
provides the acid test of its quality" (1971: 84). Moreover, a non-
technocratic conception of the notion of "alternative technologies"
has both immediate practical applications and long-term implications for countering global limits to growth (Dickson, 1974). In
short, Bowles and Gintis had not, at this stage (i.e., before formu-
lating a theory of democracy), grasped the full implications of
Illich's central theme which has profound implications for the
transformation of reproduction theories into strategies for political
and social practice: "fundamental social change must begin with a
change of consciousness about institutions and to explain why the
dimension of a viable future turns on the rejuvenation of institutional style" (Illich, 1971: 88).

Conclusion

Curiously, Illich has virtually disappeared from discussions in the
context of more recent critical theories of education.[7] What is the
significance of this continuing silence in educational circles? Have
his more enduring insights been forgotten, or have they become so
commonplace that they have simply become pervasive features of
contemporary progressive educational theory? The situation appears to be more complex than either of these possibilities.

Only by the early 1980s, especially in the work of Giroux and
Aronowitz, was a new application of critical theory to education
possible outside the specific deschooling framework proposed by
Illich. What distinguishes their work, however, is locating educational theory in the context of a state-hegemonic theory of social
and cultural reproduction, rather than a class-bureaucratic theory

of reproduction deriving from the dialectic of Enlightenment thesis largely shorn of the critical theory of the welfare state with which it is otherwise associated.[8] From this perspective, the illusory aspects of the deschooling strategy as a whole, if not specific innovative strategies suggested by the term, become apparent. On other hand, it also allows a more appreciative and constructive critique of Illich than was possible either for earlier conservative, liberal, or political-economy critiques, as this chapter has attempted to demonstrate. Further, Illich anticipates in important ways the kinds of issues that emerged in the 1980s under the heading of "postmodernist" critiques of Enlightenment theories of education and modernization.

CONTEMPORARY WEST GERMAN DEBATES

The Student Movement and Educational Reform: Early Habermas

Though it is rarely noted, Habermas's first published book, *Student und Politik* (1961), was a collaborative study based on a survey of the political consciousness of West German students. The authoritarian character of the German educational system facilitated education emerging as a topic of radical reformist debate (into which liberals such as Dahrendorf contributed) and made West Germany the source of origin of the international student movement of the European type.

The Rise and Crisis of Critical Pedagogy

By about 1970 a broadly based critical education movement had emerged in West Germany on the basis of an appropriation of the antiauthoritarian principles of Frankfurt Critical Theory and its theory of society, especially as formulated in Habermas's early work. Seen retrospectively, three features of this phenomenon are striking.

First, this West German critical-pedagogy literature had virtually no impact upon the Anglo-American educational literature, either then or even to this day. The influences of the past decade have stemmed from a direct appropriation of leading critical theorists and applying that to education in specific contexts, rather than referring to the West German literature that attempted to do so. Though it is possible to argue that the uniqueness of educational systems made this necessary, it is more likely the absence of translations and personal contacts that were of decisive importance.

Second, the West German educational reform movement ground to a halt by the mid 1970s, at least at the level of reforming secondary and postsecondary institutions. Nevertheless, the critical-pedagogy literature sustained a certain continuity and continues to have a significant place in and influence upon aspects of teacher education that is, relative to North America at least, relatively elitist and academically demanding.

Third, the diversity and range of this critical educational literature is paralleled only by that found in Holland (and strongly influenced by the West German example; see, for instance, Miedema, 1985). Representative of this diverse and early development is the three-volume collection of texts (Klafki et al., 1970) which have their origin in a pioneering, experimental effort, organized by Wolfgang Klafki, to use radio as the basis for a type of "open university." Remarkably, the team from Marburg University were able to organize their project around the goal of contributing to the development of "a critical pedagogical consciousness" in presenting "educational science as critical theory" (1970, vol. 3: 262). Citing the slightly earlier work of educational theorists such as Klaus Mollenhauer and Herwig Blankertz, they note that "critical" is understood in a sense similar to that of "the so-called Frankfurt sociological or social-philosophical school, which can be described above all by reference to the names of Theodor W. Adorno, Max Horkheimer, and Jürgen Habermas" (1970, vol. 3: 263–64). Needless to say, this specific *educational appropriation* of critical theory has rarely been noted in the English-speaking world, despite the subsequent general reception of critical theory.

The State and the Critical Sociology of Education:

The German debate centers on the works of Joachim Hirsch and Claus Offe. They have views different from those of Nicos Poulantzas regarding the relevant key variables in an analysis of the role of the state. They differ also in the characterization of education's role in an advanced capitalist society.

Both Offe and Hirsch retain the basic notion of the state as the point of articulation of the social relations of domination and production in capitalist society. The analyses of Hirsch and Offe constitute an attempt to advance beyond the "instrumentalist-structuralist debate," which is exemplified in the Miliband-Poulantzas controversy (Blackburn, 1973). The core of Hirsch's argument is that the law of capitalist surplus value, and not the class struggle, has determined the form of the state; thus, the investigation of the state's public policies must begin with an analysis of the capital-accumulation process (Hirsch, 1978). Hence, this approach attempts to derive the fundamental characteristics of the state from a single basic category: the capital relation, whose contradictory nature necessarily leads to the separation of political and economic spheres. Neither of these spheres can be explained adequately if they are seen as independent "regions" functioning according to their own "autonomous" laws of operation. Hirsch's theory has been named state-derivation theory (Holloway and Picciotto, 1979: 122).

Hirsch emphasizes that to understand the state's educational policy, it is necessary to understand the current role of the state in the laws of motion of capital accumulation. Thus, the state will design its policies according to the logic of capital, becoming increasingly involved in providing infrastructure services in terms of providing skills to (or even deskilling) the labor force. Education, therefore, has a concrete economic function that surpasses the ideological or political function stressed by other Marxist theories (Gerstenberger, 1976). In short, Hirsch's theory of the state cumulates in a new variant of an economic-reproductive model, though one whose political economic assumptions differ significantly from those found in either Bowles and Gintis or Althusser.

For Offe, on the other hand, the state comprises the institutional apparatuses, bureaucratic organizations, and formal and informal codes that constitute and regulate the public and private spheres of society. Though he retains a strong emphasis on the political-economic constraints upon the state, especially as manifest in the accumulation demands linked to the fiscal crisis of the state, he avoids a reductionist form of political economy and develops a flexible model of the state that avoids the simplifications of correspondence theories.

His starting point is the problem of the class character of the state. He tries to clarify that the state, although not itself capitalist, nevertheless must be understood as a capitalist state—and not, for example, merely as a state in capitalist society. He conceptualizes state-organized governance as a selective, event-generating system of rules, as a "sorting process" (Offe, 1974: 37). This means that the state is able to integrate the empirical plurality of isolated interests into a class interest, but it also needs a complementary selectiveness that consists in protecting collective capital against anticapitalist interests and conflicts. These selection mechanisms anchored in such institutions can be analytically identified in the political system on at least four levels—structure, ideology, process, and repression—which represent a system of filters. As the materialization of relations of domination, the state's apparatuses consist of a set of complex differentiated organizational structures united by their joint claim to legitimate authority and their monopoly of coercion. Offe's analysis emphasizes the relative autonomy of the state to the point that bureaucracy becomes the independent mediator of the class struggle inherent in the capitalist accumulation process.

With respect to the role of education in an advanced capitalist society, Offe claims that the state has an abstract systemic interest in counteracting those constant tendencies of a capitalist economy that paralyze the employability of the labor force. He envisages the existence of some reformist policies commanded by the government that try to change the mismatch between educational outcomes and the workplace rather than emphasizing the ideological inculcation or compulsive socialization of the labor force through educational activities. Similarly, the relative autonomy of the bureaucracy enables diverse policies without concrete reference to a specific process of economic correspondence or political legitimation. Therefore, some educational levels might institute certain innovations and changes that correspond more closely to the needs of their own self-reproduction as a bureaucracy (the law of motion of bureaucracy) than to the needs of the overall social reproduction of the entire system. In short, Offe's theory of the state applied to education retains reference to economic and political functions, but these cannot be reduced to anything like a correspondence principle. Moreover, the complexity of the role of the state-education relation can be understood only in relation to the overall dynamics of crisis tendencies in advanced capitalism, a theme that can best be taken up in the context of Habermas's legitimation crisis theory in a moment.

EDUCATION AND THE THEORY OF COMMUNICATIVE ACTION

There is a fundamental continuity in the impact of Habermas on educational theory, which stems initially from his practical interventions in the German student movement debates but was consolidated theoretically in his treatise on *Knowledge and Human Interests* (1971a), first published in 1968 but going back to his lecture on assuming a professorship at Frankfurt in June 1965, which was published in article form shortly thereafter. But the concept guiding this project goes all the way back to his first major statement on education in 1957 (now Habermas, 1981: 13–40). As he notes in a 1981 introduction to that essay on "The Chronic Suffering of Post Secondary Educational Reform," it was written in close association with Adorno and develops the thesis that such reform requires a materialist critique of science.

Science and Technology as Ideology: The Critique of Functionalism and Technocracy

In Habermas's work we see a fundamental shift with reference to the problematic of education, though it is continuous with themes apparent at the outset in the Frankfurt tradition. On the one hand, it is basically taken for granted that education has reproductive effects in relation to both the sphere of economic production and class relations. But these effects are not the focus of analysis because it is argued that what is decisive about the educational complex cannot be reduced to these factors, even if their empirical consequences—directly through the state and indirectly through larger social processes—cannot be ignored. Instead, Habermas implicitly turns back to the question of the content of education, a theme that has largely slipped out of sight in view of the correspondence thesis, which linked the hidden curriculum and formal properties of education to the production process. Further, his argument is based on the observation that some of the most important forms of resistance in education have taken place in unexpected (according to a traditional Marxist perspective) places: among the most privileged and well-educated students.

In certain respects, Habermas's point of departure is a mirror image of that of Parsons, especially the latter's understanding of the "knowledge complex" that crowns the university system. Whereas for Parsons this represented an evolutionary breakthrough, for Habermas it is more suggestive of a new stage of ideological reproduction, one in which science and technology themselves have come to function ideologically by masking political decisions as purely technical ones. From this perspective, the most decisive reproductive consequence of educational systems derives from the complicity in the perpetuation of a positivistic scientific worldview that systematically blocs the formation of critical consciousness, even as it legitimates itself in liberal democratic and pluralist terms. In short, this requires a critique of epistemology, ideology, and social theory that could carry through in more concrete terms an analysis of the distortions within education described earlier by Adorno as "Halbbildung" and more generally by Marcus as a "one-dimensional society.

Education and Legitimation Crisis

Habermas's relation to educational issues cannot be separated from his overall theory of advanced capitalist crisis, which should be understood not so much as a "predictive" model but as a set of considerations required for understanding crisis dynamics. In other words, legitimation crisis theory should not be understood as having predicted a legitimation crisis in the early 1970s and thus as having been refuted in the interim by Thatcherism and Reaganism.

Based on a generalization of Marx's crisis theory, as well as drawing upon selected concepts from systems theory, Habermas's theory develops a multilevel analysis of crisis potentials emerging in three different spheres: the economy, the state, and the sociocultural system. Economic crisis occurs at the systemic level of contradictions in the production system; political crisis can occur at both the systemic level as a rationality crisis and at the level of social integration and interaction as a crisis of legitimation. Crisis in the sociocultural system can develop only at the level of social interaction as a crisis of motivation. For Habermas, therefore, the specific crisis potentials of "late" capitalism can only be understood in relation to the articulation of these three forms of crisis and their respective levels of operation.

The outcome of this analysis is not so much a specific theory of education in advanced capitalism as a general framework for understanding the various factors impinging on education as a site of struggle related to the general displacement of crisis responses from the economic sphere to legitimation in the political one. Of critical importance for the possibility of the emergence of a severe legitimation crisis is a potential discrepancy between the demands placed upon the political system and the motives expressed in the sociocultural system. In this early formulation Habermas gave particular importance to the relationship of the motivational orientation toward the performance principle as symbolized by professional success based on formal education. Given the inequality of educational access and related factors, however, the expansion of the educational system—and the failure of liberal reforms that have accompanied this process—has been characterized by an increasing tension between expectations and outcomes. As he put it writing in the early 1970s:

> While educational justice, in terms of opportunities for admission and standards of evaluation, may have increased in all advanced capitalist countries since World War II, a countertendency can be observed in the other two dimensions. The expansion of the educational system is increasingly independent of changes in the occupational system. Consequently, the connection between formal schooling and occupational success may become looser in the long run. At the same time, there are more and more areas in which production structures and labor processes make evaluation according to individually accountable achievement increasingly improbable; instead the extrafunctional elements of professional roles are becoming more and more important for conferring occupational status. (1975: 81–82)

But subsequent events—especially the emergence of the New Right—have not led to the forms of resistance (as part of a broader motivational crisis) against educationally based inequities anticipated by the model. As was the case with various neo-Marxist and neo-Gramscian theorists, Habermas has had to come to terms with the emergence of the New Right, a process that few on the left anticipated at the outset of the 1970s (Habermas, 1989a). In particular, he has stressed the theme of modernity as an incomplete project and drawn out the conservative implications of many "postmodernist" tendencies. More concretely, the suppression of potential resistance is traced to the processes related to the colonization of the lifeworld by bureaucratic power and commodification, which undermine the capacity for ideology formation: "Everyday consciousness is robbed of its power to synthesize; it becomes fragmented" (Habermas, 1987). Given the process of rationalization that differentiates science, morality, and art into autonomous domains controlled by specialists, and given the isolation of the these from everyday life, the forms of synthesis required for critique are undercut:

Everyday consciousness sees itself thrown back on traditions whose claims to validity have already been suspended; where is does not escape the spell of traditionalism, it is hopelessly splintered. In place of "false consciousness" we today have a "fragmented consciousness" that blocks enlightenment by the mechanism of reification. It is only with this that the conditions for a colonization of the lifeworld are met. (1987: 355)

In the context of education, such colonization is closely associated with processes of juridification promoted by the welfare state's interventionist policies. Undercutting the autonomy of the school and its relation to the lifeworld thus endangers the pedagogical relationship between teacher and learner:

The protection of pupils' and parents' rights against educational measures . . . or from acts of the school . . . is gained at the cost of a judicialization and bureaucratization that penetrates deep into the teaching and learning process . . . This has to endanger the pedagogical freedom and initiative of the teacher. The compulsion toward litigation-proof certainty of grades and the overall regulation of the curriculum lead to such phenomena as depersonalization, inhibition of innovation, breakdown of responsibility, immobility, and so forth. (1987: 371)

Education, the Ideal Speech Situation, and the Public Sphere

As against the thorough pessimism of his Frankfurt mentors such as Marcuse and Adorno, Habermas's revision of critical theory has consistently sought to translate the critique of enlightenment into a politically relevant strategy of theory and praxis closely associated with the closely linked concepts of the "ideal speech situation" and the "democratic public sphere."

As an historical concept, the notion of a democratic public sphere refers to the emancipatory potential embodied in the Enlightenment concept of democratic participation as a process of public debate. Closely related to this liberal conception was the role of universal schooling as an institution for ensuring the acquisition of general levels of competence of the type required for the formation of an enlightened public opinion. As Habermas's historical survey suggests, various constraints emerged in the course of the development of Western democracies that have thwarted the realization of those emancipatory possibilities, especially the rise of the culture industries and the scientization of politics (Habermas, 1989). Nevertheless, such a conception is held to contain the basis of a normative critique of the failures of liberal democracy, and to point to the institutional alternatives that might unleash previously suppressed potential for participation. Within this context, the school serves as a site of strategic importance, despite the suppression of its possibilities in the hands of technocratic specialists and functionalist theories. Postsecondary institutions also have a crucial importance as the potential source of critical social science.

The concept of an ideal speech situation, on the other hand, is in the first instance epistemological, given that it does not refer to any actual empirical situation so much as a regulative ideal. Implicit in the notion of a democratic public sphere is a conception of knowledge as something realized through processes of argumentation, through which truth is impersonally arrived at. A crucial aspect of this model, however, is that such a process of dialogue has certain presuppositions, especially that its members possess sufficient "communicative competence" to ensure that various cultural and power differences do not distort communication. As Misgeld puts it: "The relevance of Habermas's theory of communicative competence for a social theory of education is this: he provides the idea of a norm in terms of which we can state and assess the role of power and privilege in interactional contexts . . . Constraints on communication can then be explored in terms of (1) conditions of economic scarcity, (2) conditions of social and political inequality . . . , and (3) psychologically operative repressions such as the censoring of need interpretations, dependent on variations of the first two points" (1975: 34–35).

FOUNDATIONS OF A CRITICAL THEORY OF EDUCATION: ACTION THEORY

Early Developments

Setting aside the complex West German and now pan-German situation, the single most important influence of critical theory in the Frankfurt tradition on education has been in the context of so-called action research or participatory action research in the domain of curriculum research (Kemmis & McTaggart, 1988). In the original German-language context, the theoretical presuppositions of such approaches were initially most well developed in the writings of the Swiss educational theorist Heinz Moser (1975) and the projects associated with the (then) West German researcher Wolfgang Klafki (Klafki et al., 1970, 1988b).

Moser's approach essentially involves an effort to draw out the practical, pedagogical implications of Habermas's theory of knowledge interests in terms of three basic issues: the relation between theory and practice; the relation between subject and object; and the criterion of emancipation. As a relation between theory of practice, this suggests a politicizing rather than technocratic conception knowledge construction; as a relation between subject and object, it implies that understanding the nature of power requires breaking down the divisions between researchers/educators and actors; and as a criterion of emancipation, it is entailed in the notion of dialogical conception of truth realized through discourse situations (Moser, 1975). For Klafki, on the other hand, educational action research projects are characterized by three strategies: *educational practice* (practice within education) is the *starting point* for the theory . . . ; educational action research takes place in *cooperation with the educational practice* that the research seeks to serve . . . ; and educational action research rejects the division between researchers/scientists and educational practitioners (Klafki, et al., 1970).

Action Research In Latin America

Some of the implications of this can be seen in the cases of efforts at revolutionary educational reform in Nicaragua (Arnove, 1986; Carnoy and Torres, 1990; Arrien and Matus, 1989) and Chile (Farrell, 1986). In these contexts, one finds the kind of polarization between "bourgeois" and "Marxist" perspectives frequent in British discussions. The primary exceptions here have been the examples of Illich, with his work of alternative education in CIDOC, Cuernava, Mexico, until it was closed in 1976, and Paulo Freire's political philosophy of education, which have had a greater impact in educational experiments than actual research, but have contributed to nonformal and informal educational activities of increasing importance (Torres, 1978a, 1980, 1982).

Perhaps, one of the most important discussions regarding knowledge and power in practice and research relates to the emerging paradigm of participatory action research that became central in the Symposium of Cartagena in April of 1977 (Molano et al. 1978), and particularly the contribution of Colombian sociologist Orlando Falls Borda (Fals Borda, 1978). The notion of action research emerged out of criticisms of scientistic and positivist paradigms and call for an alternative scientific practice in Latin America in the late sixties. It was considered by Swiss researcher Moser as a new paradigm in social sciences (Moser, 1978).

Informed by diverse but related conceptions of a critical sociology (mostly based in new accounts of Marxist theory, and the various linkages of theories of revolution with concrete revolutionary experiences in Latin America), the paradigm of action research set out originally to link, and then reconcile, epistemology and politics. This is well reflected in a telling statement made by Peruvian sociologist Anibal Quijano in the Symposium of Cartagena, in Colombia, that captured the spirit of the age—paraphrasing John Stuart Mill's collection of essays. Quijano distinguished between left-wing and right-wing epistemologies, along lines similar to left-wing and right-wing political ideologies (Quijano, cited in Molano, 1978, xxx).

To solve this schizophrenia, the remnants of positivist theories and methodologies (mostly structural functionalism) in social research should be eliminated. New theories linking epistemology, theory, and praxis should be created, thus placing the origins and use of knowledge at center stage. New methods based in a new ethic of social solidarity rather than one of individualism (or institutional planning) should be designed, and a call for action, that is, how to investigate reality in order to transform it, was issued. The notion of *research for praxis* was central to Colombian sociologist Orlando Fals Borda's contribution to the Cartagena's meeting.

The central component of this research paradigm—*action research*, or *participatory action research*,[9] as it was later identified—starts as an attempt to understand the historical and social situation of workers, peasants, and indigenous people as the more exploited and backward sectors of Latin American capitalist societies. The "object" of research is then defined and shaped by the "subjects" of research. The relationship between abstract thought and practical activity is essential: praxis comes before reflection, and praxis reflects the objective truth. This, of course, will question the notion of causality: criteria for validation of knowledge can result only from the criteria for social praxis—knowledge is validated by praxis and not vice versa (Fals Borda, 1978: 215).

Science then becomes subordinated to politics in this model. In the dramatic circumstances of social life in Latin America, there is no place for experimental observation as a purely scientific exercise. This observation has two important implications: Researchers should have political commitments, and scientific knowledge should be articulated with popular knowledge (commonsense knowledge). Critical social science is interdisciplinary in itself—as science for the people, not only exclusively for specialists (Fals Borda, 1978: 221). The central notion of this new paradigm of participatory action research was thus "the possibility of creating and having scientific knowledge in the very same action of the workers" (1978: 223). Eventually, the ultimate goal is the creation of a science of the proletariat, not a proletarian science (1978: 240). A crucial premise of participatory action research, then, is that the dualism between subject-object of knowledge can be overcome.

Action Theory in Advanced Societies

Working independently of these earlier German discussions, researchers in Canada and Australia have more recently drawn upon Habermas for very similar purposes (Carr and Kemmis, 1986). In this context the strong affinities between Habermas and the work of Paulo Freire have been used to deepen the conception of the issues of action research (Misgeld, 1975; Grundy, 1987). But this work has criticized the utopian and abstract character of German critical pedagogy, a fact that has contributed to its disarray and marginalization.

The most important and sustained *extension* of Habermas's theory for the specific purposes of a critical theory of education has been undertaken in Australia by Robert E. Young (1989; 1992). Young is particularly concerned with rejecting some of the earlier tendencies in (West) German critical pedagogy, even where it spoke in the name of Habermas. Central to this critique of idealism and utopianism is resisting the temptation to use the concept of the ideal speech situation to create norms than are manipulatively imposed on those to be "emancipated". Further, an unwarranted systematic rejection of empirical research is held to have contributed to the lack of concreteness and the resulting abstract and unsituated character of educational alternatives. As Young stresses in his argument for "responsible critique," these tendencies cannot be justified by reference to a close reading of Habermas, especially in light of his later writings on language and communicative action

(1989: 68–69). As a consequence, he rejects the confrontational style associated with some forms of critical pedagogy:

> The general theory of the life-world can only be a *guide* for actual critique through reflection, neither construction nor specific critique can grasp the life-world in its totality. Nor can either reject it in its totality. We must remember that critique is always limited, fragmentary, and unsure. Anything else is utopian fantasy . . . There is methodological justification for neither the criticism of a whole form of life nor for rejection of large segments of it. Critical teachers have fostered free-floating fear and an amorphous guilt, especially in white males, a fear and guilt which, unresolved, has now turned on its creators. (Young, 1989: 70)

Instead, Young links up Habermas's approach with Dewey's conception of problem solving and develops a critique of the classic question and answer format of pedagogy as a form of indoctrination, despite overly "progressive" intentions. The theory of distorted communication, on the other hand, provides suggestive alternative strategies consistent with Dewey's claims about the capacity of children (in the right situation) to enter into rational discourse at an early age as part of a longer-term process of developing communicative competence (Young, 1989: 114). These basic arguments are then extended with respect to their implications for the organization of critical practice, the analysis of context for research, and action at both the level of the school and of other social institutions. More recently, this argument has been extended more concretely in the application of critical theory to "classroom talk" (Young, 1992).

CONCLUSION: EDUCATION AND THE LEGACY OF FRANKFURT CRITICAL THEORY

A Class-Bureaucratic Reproduction Model

Gero Lenhardt (1985), who has worked with Claus Offe analyzing educational policies (Offe, 1975), has developed a similar analysis of educational expansion that draws somewhat different conclusions from the failures of educational reform, drawing considerably more pessimistic conclusions with respect to potentials for crisis. His argument is based on an interpretation of the theories of capitalism of Marx and Weber that are for his purposes largely identical, but diverge sharply from existing Marxist theories of schooling, thus resembling in important respects social-closure theories. He unites the two through a structural analysis in which Marx's concept of alienation is linked to the Weberian theory of bureaucratization and rationalization: for both, the central theme is the alienation of individuals from control over their life conditions.

Lenhardt's central thesis is thus: "The theoretical perspective from which educational expansion is to be understood is that the development of society sharpens the contradiction between the individual and social structure" (1985: 8). This interpretation contrasts with that of those on the left and right who respectively fear and hope that schools resolve the individual/society contradiction by anchoring the structures of capitalism in the need structures and competencies of individuals. Actually, individuals widely resist this process and seek to retain their individuality. But they simply cannot escape the larger structural relations in which they must live because the formalization of professional qualifications in the school system in effect robs them of the cultural, social, and material resources for any other form of self-realization. Thus, it is the logic of technical rationalization, the shift from work as an open market contract to a professional status, not false consciousness, that undermines individual autonomy. What is decisive is not what acting subjects want or aim for, but rather the consequences of the objective structure on contexts of action.

From this perspective, the decisive aspect of the modern school system is thus its relation to the state's need for modern citizens. Weber's concept of the "expert" as the ideology of postbourgeois capitalism is held to be complemented by Adorno's concept of "Halbbildung" and Bourdieu's theory of cultural capital—all of which point to the reified individuals that are institutionalized by school systems. At the same time, however, efforts to overcome these relations in the general interest become defined as particular interests, hence are self-destructive. In this sense, motivational crisis may occur but remain ungeneralizable as the basis for effective oppositional movements.

A Complex Legacy

As the preceding review suggests, it would be misleading to attribute to the Frankfurt tradition a unified theory of education, a problem evident in the complex and uneven process of its reception in educational circles. What we see instead is a complex set of contributions to educational questions that have their origins in broader theoretical and political issues. Nevertheless, a number of consistent themes can be identified:

There is a critique of domination and authority that preserves a place for rational authority as a necessary means to the end of individual self-realization and rational autonomy. This theme has extraordinary relevance for modern schooling, teacher training, and the role and functions of education, especially in the context of action research and curriculum theory.

In addition, critical theory postulates an awareness of the reproductive economic and political functions of education in capitalism. However, this reproductive process may be offset by a stress on (a) the latent ideological effects of education as part of the emergence of science and technology as the basis of a new form of ideology and domination, and (b) education's primary role in facilitating the expansion of the powers of the modern state.

A very important insight from critical theory is the analysis of education as part of a state-organized process of bureaucratization and rationalization that more or less effectively attempts to deal with crisis tendencies displaced from the economic sphere. The issue of education as compensatory legitimation has been developed by a number of scholars paying tribute to the critical theory tradition (e.g., Weiler, 1983, Torres, 1990).

An important, although somewhat inconsistent, account of the decline of the individual subject has been incorporated in the tradition of critical theory. It stresses, on the one hand, the internalization of these new forms of scientific-technical ideology, and on the other, points to a residual capacity for resistance (reflected in potential motivational crisis) that is blocked by the structural features of this process of educational bureaucratization in a world in which work qualifications become the basis of individual survival. Most importantly, however, a consistent application of Habermas's approach (as in the work of Robert E. Young, Burbules and Rice [1991]; Burbules, [1993]) points to concrete and situated forms of critical pedagogy that are relatively immune from most of the criticisms voiced in quite different ways by conservative, feminist, and postmodernist critics.

CHAPTER 9

The Two Gramscis and Education: Technical Competence versus Political Consciousness

HISTORICAL CONTEXT

The writings of Antonio Gramsci (1891–1937), who founded the Italian Communist Party and who died in 1937 after eleven years of captivity in a Fascist prison, are increasingly acknowledged to be—along with the contemporaneous work of the early Frankfurt School—among the most theoretically important contributions to Marxist and critical theory since Marx and Engels. What both Gramsci and Frankfurt critical theory share was above all a rereading of Marx reflecting a sense of the Hegelian origins of many of Marx's concepts and an effort to reinterpret his theory in light of twentieth-century developments, especially the strategic importance of cultural institutions and the subjective bases of revolutionary mobilization. Gramsci's work differs, in part, because the early writings were written in the heat of revolutionary praxis: his rise to the leadership of the Italian Communist Party until his imprisonment by Mussolini in 1937. His final writings in prison, in contrast, were written in the shadow of the failure of working class revolution and the rise of fascism, and under the stresses of poor health, the hassles of censors, and limited access to reading materials.

The distinctiveness of Gramsci's contributions is closely linked, first of all, to a reading of Marx that reasserts the subject-object dialectic underlying his theory of praxis. Though Gramsci's choice of the term "philosophy of praxis" for Marxism is related to avoiding the censor's eye, it also has a theoretical rationale. Given his earlier training in the Italian tradition of Hegelianism inspired by Benedetto Croce, Gramsci was sensitized to the subjective dimen-

249

sion of social action implied by Marx's theoretical categories and, therefore, was not tempted to reduce his analysis of capitalism to political economy alone.

A second distinctive aspect of Gramsci's approach was based on the effort to understand the nature of social order as cultural hegemony, that is, a system of power based not only on coercion but also on the voluntary consent of dominated, subaltern classes. From this perspective it became possible to ask some new, fundamental questions about the nature of both social order and the conditions of possibility of its transformation. If individuals have come to hold beliefs that reinforce the very social order than oppresses them, then these will not automatically disappear when the objective conditions for revolutionary change (i.e., economic crisis) occur. From this perspective, therefore, a crucial aspect of a revolutionary strategy had to be cultural (and in the broadest sense, educational) struggle prior to the emergence of a revolutionary crisis. Revolution, in other words, was not only a question of capturing the state because the institutions of civil society provided the context within which social subjects are formed and transformed.

In relation to education, Gramsci's writings thus develop around three major themes: (1) the role of education as part of the process of the formation of cultural hegemony in bourgeois capitalist societies; (2) the possibilities of formal and nonformal educations as sites for the formation of revolutionary, counterhegemonic consciousness prior to any revolutionary transition; and (3) the principles that should underlie the socialist pedagogy of a postrevolutionary society. Before turning to the specific implications of Gramscian theory for education, it is necessary to reintroduce briefly, drawing upon the growing specialized scholarship on this matter, some of the basic concepts of his social theory.

BASIC CONCEPTS

The originality of Gramsci's approach in relation to the Marxist tradition lies in his creative reworking of the base-superstructure model, theory of social classes and state, and analysis of the conditions of possibility of revolutionary transformation. To be sure, Gramsci always considered his views to be consistent with those of Marx, even though Gramsci went beyond Marx in important respects. As well, Gramsci considered his approach essentially Leninist, though adapted to the specific conditions of Italy (Torres, 1978a). Nevertheless, it is retrospectively clear that Gramsci's conception of leadership and the role of the Communist Party in a revolutionary transition cannot be subsumed within the Leninist conception of the vanguard party, let alone the epistemological foundations of Lenin's version of historical materialism.

Three key concepts are central to Gramsci's position: hegemony, civil society, and historical blocs. Though used earlier by Lenin in a different sense, referring to the strategic role of leadership in proletarian revolution, the term *hegemony* literally means domination and in Gramsci's usage serves as a general theory category for understanding processes of what today would be called cultural reproduction. For Gramsci, the power of one class over another was sustained through two forms of control: that of politically based force (or "coercion"), and that of "consent" (*direzione*) (which is to say, leadership by means of consent). In broader terms, this also suggests that the relationship between a dominant and subordinate class always has a pedagogical or educational dimension of variable importance. Whereas political force is concentrated in the state, ideological domination is more closely associated with the institutions of "civil society." Though the concept of civil society was still associated with economy as well as other nonstate institutions, for Gramsci it becomes most closely linked with ideological superstructures generally: education, religion, mass communications, the family, and so forth.

The major strategic consequence of this position is that "direct action" by the working class could not, by itself, bring about the new conditions required for establishing a new working-class form of hegemony. Rather than simply a "war of movement," a revolutionary transition required a "war of position" in which class struggle could be carried on in domains that prepared the way for eventual proletarian hegemony:

> Every revolution has been preceded by an intense labor of criticism, by the diffusion of culture and the spread of ideas amongst masses of men who are at first resistant, and think only of solving their own immediate economic and political problems for themselves, who have no ties of solidarity with others in the same condition. (Gramsci, 1977: 12)

Further, such a war of position could not be won in isolation, but only as part of a "historical bloc" or coalition or alliances of classes and class fractions. Nor was this just another version of the "popular front" strategy designed out of expediency as part of the struggle against fascism. Central to Gramsci's conception is the importance of the differentiations within the working class and the complex relation of the latter to other class(es) and regional and ethnic groupings. Within the process of forming alliances, intellectuals play a strategic role, given their skills at reconstructing ideas and bridging the gap from the particular to the universal. As well, "every social group, coming into existence . . . creates together with itself, organically, one or more traits of intellectuals which give it homogeneity and an awareness of its own function, not only in the economic but also in the social and political fields" (Gramsci, 1971: 5). Yet the activity of intellectuals is only a specialized and well-developed version of competences that are inherent in all people: "All men are intellectuals, one could therefore say: but not all men in society have the function of intellectuals" (1971: 9). Accordingly, the educational role of intellectuals in providing leadership was essential to his conception of the preparatory work required in civil society prior to social transformation. Let us then look at the specific implications of this orientation for education.

The State, Education and Hegemony

Studies on the relationship between the state and education acquired new vigor at the beginning of the 1970s when they became associated with new developments in Marxist political theories of the state. In spite of the fragmented nature of his reflections, it is clear that Gramsci's notes on hegemony and the state altered the direction, scope, and weight of Marxist political theory. However, Gramsci's contribution is "antinomical," as Anderson (1977) has claimed. These antinomies are due in part to Gramsci's endeavor to formulate new theoretical concepts that were not at all common in political theory. Therefore, Gramsci's cryptic writings on education, which are dispersed throughout his works and not directly unconnected with his main theoretical concepts, must be deciphered. Although highly stimulating for theory building and even empirical research, his works are in need of critical systematization and analysis. Fortunately, the critical Italian edition of his *Prison Notebooks* (Gramsci, 1975) has now been published and translated into several languages, and solid studies, albeit from contradictory standpoints, are beginning to appear (see, for instance,

Manacorda, 1977 [1970]; Entwistle, 1979; Adamson, 1980; Tavares de Jesús, 1989; Díaz-Salazda, 1991).

This discussion of Gramsci's contribution to education can be summarized in five main hypotheses:[1]

1. Insofar as hegemony is founded on coercion and consensus, it is an educative relationship.
2. Despite the fact that hegemony is exerted by the ruling class, it is organized in capitalist society by a particular social category: the intellectuals.
3. Education is the process of formation of "social conformism."
4. The state, as an "ethical state" or, indeed, as an educator, assumes the function of building a new "type" or "level" of civilization; thus, it constitutes an instrument of rationalization.
5. The establishment of a classless society and the building of a collective will must be achieved through an intellectual and moral reform (Gramsci, 1975a).

Gramsci's notion of hegemony in civil society is a central theme within his analysis of the functioning of the capitalist social formation. The notion of hegemony refers to the relationships between groups, especially social classes, given that a social class can be thought of as exercising hegemony over other "subaltern" classes. Basically, it means the ideological predominance of bourgeois values and norms over the subordinate social classes. In Gramsci's formulation, hegemonic direction is by moral and intellectual persuasion rather than control by the military, the police, or the coercive power of the law: "rule by intellectual and moral hegemony is the form of power which gives stability and . . . wide-ranging consent and acquiescence, every relationship of hegemony is necessarily a pedagogical relationship" (Gramsci, 1975a, vol. 2: 1321). For Gramsci, a social group can and must already exercise "leadership" before winning governmental power (indeed, this is one of the principal conditions for winning such power).

Gramsci's notes on hegemony proceeded by establishing a crucial analytical distinction by which the state (as a political society) seems to be the realm of organized coercion while civil society is the realm of "spontaneous" consent to the general leadership imposed on social life by the dominant classes—sometimes expressed at the level of saturation of the citizen's consciousness. The role of the intellectuals is to be experts in legitimation (Karabel, 1976: 146–56), acting as intermediaries between the masses and the party leadership in the organization of the dominant-class hegemony. Gramsci asserts that the bourgeoisie was the first class in history that needs, in order to be the dominant class, a body of organic intellectuals. Meanwhile, through the acceptance of the worldview produced by these organic intellectuals of the dominant classes, the subordinate classes have internalized this hegemony.

Therefore, the schooling system is a privileged instrument of socialization for the hegemonic culture. As Gramsci insists:

> The hegemony of a directive centre over the intellectuals asserts itself by two principal routes: (a) a general concept of life, a philosophy, which offers to its adherents an intellectual "dignity" providing a principle of differentiation from the old ideologies which dominated by coercion, and an element of struggle against them; (b) a scholastic program, an educative principle, and original pedagogy which interest that fraction of the intellectuals which is the most homogeneous and the most numerous (the teachers, from the primary teachers to the university professors), and gives them an activity of their own in the technical field. (Gramsci, 1971: 103–4)

Gramsci emphasizes that the school and the church are the major cultural organizations in every country, not only in terms of the number of people they employ and the ideological material they manipulate but, above all, because they are filling the gap between the popular masses and the organic intellectuals from dominated classes. It is so because "however much of the ruling class may affirm to the contrary, the state, as such, does not have a unitary, coherent, and homogeneous conception, with the result that intellectual groups are scattered between one stratum and the next, or even within a single stratum" (Gramsci, 1971: 342). Thus, there are the priests and school teachers who are relating hegemonically one stratum with another, thus symbolically coopting the subordinate classes by integrating them with the dominant hegemonic culture. In this sense, control of consciousness is as much or more an area of political struggle as control of the forces of production (Carnoy, 1984; Gadotti, 1990: 60–75).

In this regard, Gramsci's characterization of the capitalist state is highly relevant. This is a state that embodies a broad set of institutions (including the bourgeois law or "private institutions" such as the church), and which has a set of ideological-juridical state apparatuses that contribute to the diffusion and reinforcement of this ideological and political hegemony. Only when the dominant-class hegemony enters a crisis, Gramsci argues, are the repressive forces (the repressive state apparatus) brought into play by the bourgeoisie. In either case, the power expressed is that of the coercion-consensus exerted by the state and ruling classes. As he put its: "If every state tends to create and maintain a certain type of civilization and of citizen . . . and to eliminate certain customs and attitudes and to disseminate others, then the law will be its instrument for this purpose (together with the school system, and other institutions and activities)" (Gramsci 1971: 246). In reality, concludes Gramsci, the state must be conceived as an "educator" inasmuch as it tends precisely to create a new type or level of civilization.

The "Americanized" and "Fordist" system of industrial production of commodities, a modern expression—at that time—of the process of accelerated industrialization and rationalization that took place in America, led Gramsci to consider the state not only as a superstructural factor that develops spontaneously, but also as a manipulator of essentially economic forces, reorganizing and developing the structure of economic production or even creating new structures: "The state, in this field, too, is an instrument of rationalization, of acceleration, and of Taylorization" (Gramsci 1971: 247, 301–8).

In summary, even though they are antinomical; these relationships between state, civil society, and hegemony are crucial to an understanding of the process of exploitation and political domination in society. The state through its apparatus contributes a great deal to the process of reproduction of the capitalist relations of production, acting as a system of enforcement and threat, but also struggling to control people's consciousness. In this regard, the creation of a social "conformism"starting with the intellectuals and, in particular, in the schooling system, is a complex task undertaken by the capitalist state. In Gramsci's words:

> Every state is ethical inasmuch as one of its most important functions is to raise the great mass of the population to a particular cultural and moral level, a level (or type) which corresponds to the needs of the productive forces for development and hence

to the interest of the ruling classes. The school as a positive educative function and the courts as a repressive and negative educative function are the most important state activities in this sense; but in reality, a multitude of other so-called private initiatives and activities tend to the same end—initiatives and activities which form the apparatus of the political and cultural hegemony of the ruling classes. (Gramsci, 1971: 258)

This overall political project can only be achieved through a profound moral and intellectual reform, challenging and eventually changing the prevailing common sense, thus emerging as resistance, as worker-organized practices (Tavares de Jesús, 1989).

RESISTANCE AND COUNTERHEGEMONY

If people are subsumed under relationships of hegemony, how and why should they challenge that situation, developing actions and principles of resistance and eventually counterhegemony? For Gramsci, people's common sense does not constitute an intellectual order; it cannot be reduced to unity or coherence, either at the level of individual or collective consciousness (Gramsci, 1971: 326). However, Gramsci would argue, there are practical distinctions between the philosophy elaborated by intellectuals and the practical philosophies underlying the thought and action of common men and women (Torres, 1992). This is so because there is a point at which highbrow culture and people's common sense as a philosophical understanding can be related; in fact, the philosophical activity of intellectuals impinges upon the construction of individual and collective understandings of the world by "common sense" people: "In philosophy the features of individual elaboration of thought are the most salient: in common sense on the other hand it is the diffuse, uncoordinated features of a generic form of thought to a particular period and a particular popular environment" (1971: 330).

The historical bloc is constituted precisely by the combination of a given dominant worldview that underlies the construction of common sense in the society, and the basic premises of the material bases of a given society: "the conception of historical bloc in which precisely material forces are the content and ideologies are the form, though this distinction between form and content has purely didactic value, since the material forces would be inconceivable historically without form, and the ideologies would be individual fancies without the material forces" (Gramsci, 1971: 377).

Is this universe of domination perfect? Are the people-nation so immersed in a given common sense cementing the hegemonic unity of the historical bloc that there is no point in resisting or searching for an alternative principle of order? In this context, Gramsci's theoretical reconstruction reaches out to Marx when he emphasized the "solidity of popular beliefs" as an essential element of specific situations (Gramsci, 1971: 377). Gramsci argues then that: "Another proposition of Marx is that a popular conviction often has the same energy as a material force or something of the kind, which is extremely significant" (1971: 377). Ideology is also a source of change, and Gramsci assumes a dialectical relationship between base-superstructure without a preconceived communist ordering principle.[2]

It is this notion of "common sense"—defined originally in Gramsci as a worldview (1971: 197)—that has been borrowed by, or imposed upon, the people-nation inasmuch as "for reasons of submission and intellectual subordination, [the people, subaltern classes] adopted a conception which is not its own but is borrowed from another group; and it affirms this conception verbally and believes itself to be following it, because this is the conception which it follows in 'normal times'—that is when its conduct is not independent and autonomous, but submissive and subordinate" (1971: 327).

Common sense defined in these terms is analogous to the classic Marxist notion of alienation; however, there is an important twist in Gramsci's argument that should be emphasized. In classical Marxism, individuals became alienated because the separation of the direct producer from the products of his/her work; because of the repressive action of the state (either through law or physical repression); and because of the surplus value that is taken in the relationships between labor and capital. However, there is a significant change in Gramsci's view: in common sense, as a set of behavior norms and styles of thought, there is a "good sense" at the heart of all "common sense." This "good sense" is basically rational, but given the structures of oppression that the people-nation continually face in everyday life, it cannot be objectively externalized, and reflexively used as an alternative to "common sense" (i.e., building a counterhegemonic movement). However, this "good sense", in Gramsci's perception, "deserves to be made more unitary and coherent" (1971: 328). And it is in this context that one should understand Gramsci's cryptic formulation derived from Hegel: "the 'rational' is actively and actually real" (1971: 366). For a political activist and intellectual such as Gramsci, this is the principle of order that calls for a new "organic" intellectual linked to dominated classes, and a new set of values and behavior (i.e., the philosophy of praxis in Gramsci's reconstruction) that can challenge, resist, and eventually reorient society. It is in this sense that Gramsci would argue that: "The active man-in-the-mass has a practical activity, but has no clear theoretical consciousness of his practical activity, which nonetheless involves understanding the world in so far as it transforms it. His theoretical consciousness can indeed be historically in opposition to his activity" (1971: 333).

If a people-nation's theoretical consciousness can be, historically, in opposition to their practical activity—ruled by hegemonic cultural principles—then this, in itself, would justify the introduction of a new, political-pedagogical principle to organize resistance and counterhegemonical practices (Torres, 1992; Morrow, 1991).

Only the diffusion of a new worldview can change the economic-corporative phase of common sense into an ethical-political phase—a prerequisite for Gramsci's counterhegemonic politics. Is this political-pedagogical principle to be found in Gramsci's pedagogy? We turn now to address this subject.

SOCIALIST PEGAGOGY

According to Manacorda (1977), by 1929 Gramsci started to define sharply the two central themes of his pedagogical analysis. First, the methodological option between spontaneism and authority; and second, the option between classical humanities and modern technical training. The first dilemma of Gramsci is to either opt for Rousseau's voluntarism or to exert a principle of authority and impose discipline:

> I continue debating between two conceptions of the world and education: either to be Rousseauean and allow nature to take its course since it never errs and is fundamentally good, or to be a voluntarist and force nature into evolution? the expert hand of man and the principle of authority. Until now this uncertainty

has not dissipated and my head contains both ideologies. (Cited in Manacorda, 1977: 75—our translation)

The second major conflict in Gramsci was the debate between classical education and modern technological education, despite his suspicions about the culture of positivism:

> In general, I believe that a modern culture (American type) whose expression is the "erector set." It makes man a little dry, machine-like, bureaucratic, and engenders an abstract mentality in a different sense than abstract was understood in the last century. There was an abstraction determined by metaphysical intoxication, and there exists an abstraction determined by mathematical intoxication. (Cited in Manacorda, 1977: 72—our translation)

For Manacorda, Gramsci solved both dilemmas in 1929–1930. In a letter to his wife regarding the education of his children, Delio and Guliano, and discussing the relationships between spontaneity and coercion, he—in disagreement with his wife and his wife's family, whom he considered too close to a Rousseauean philosophy—took a position against spontaneism, and in favor of intellectual discipline and rigor: "I believe that man is completely constituted historically, obtained by means of coercion (understood not only in the brutal sense and extreme violence) and I only believe this; otherwise we will fall into forms of transcendence or immanence" (cited in Manacorda, 1977: 81—our translation).

The second doubt, whether to promote a classical or a technological education was addressed in favour of the latter. In his reflections on Fordism, Taylorism, and the American industrial mode of production, Gramsci considered technical education a form of rationalization of higher civilizational value. Comparing Americans with Europeans, he concluded that:

> We Europeans are still too bohemian, we believe we can do any kind of work and live according to our whims, like bohemians; for this reason, as it is natural, mechanization grinds us down, and I understand mechanization in its general sense, as scientific organization, including the work of the concept. We are too romantic, in an absurd way, and because we do not want to be petty bourgeois we fall into the most typical form of the petty bourgeois spirit, which is precisely bohemian. (Cited in Manacorda, 1977: 94—our translation)

In his classic study of Gramsci's pedagogy, Manacorda concludes that it is the nexus between two themes, conformism and Americanism, that constitutes the most original and authentic feature of Gramscian pedagogy. Conformism as adaptation to the rule of authority, in a dynamic way, as opposed to conformism as accepting the state of nature in a folkloric way:

> The freedom to remain immersed in nature and folklore, in localist and individualist barbarism, without reaching the more advanced level of contemporary society, would be the worst of conformisms—a mechanical conformism, very different than the dynamic conformism that not only adapt the individuals to their environment, but also educates them so they can dominate their environments. Thanks to this conformism, automatism becomes freedom, and freedom becomes responsibility and personality. (Manacorda, 1977: 307–8—our translation)

For Manacorda, then, Gramsci, in dealing with the tensions between freedom and necessity, chooses to overcome necessity, even if that implies a limitation of freedom—otherwise understood as a bohemian attitude, or anarchism. However, for Manacorda, given the conditions of Gramsci's writings under censorship, he was using "Americanism" as a way to show that conformism means sociability, and Americanism (or industrialism) does not necessarily mean American-mindedness, but could eventually imply sociability as socialism, and industrialism as Sovietism (or the Soviet industrial mode of production), which was considered as the humane way to overcome this tension between freedom and necessity (Manacorda, 1977: 309).

This issue of vocational versus classical education is part of an important debate that perhaps can be exemplified in opposing contributions of Entwistle (1979) and Adamson (1980). Entwistle's position is that Gramsci advocates a traditional school curriculum as the avenue for the working class to develop proletarian hegemony, providing that members of the working class have full access to it. So it seems that in this version of Gramsci, equality and access to education and the acquisition of the universal cultural baggage was the task of the school. This was so because Gramsci would have considered working-class culture as incomplete and contained elements of folklore and superstition (hence mystification). At this point Entwhistle believed that Gramsci's view is that the school should transmit the systematic worldview of specialized scholars. The principle of authority was derived not from social but intellectual criteria (1979: 36). If that is the case, knowledge is cumulative and constitutes the treasure of human civilization, and the school is the institution for knowledge distribution and cultural transmission.

It is in this context that Gramsci's suggestion that people should read Greek and Latin for no practical reasons makes sense: "To know firsthand the civilization of Greece and Rome—a civilization that was a necessary precondition of our modern civilization . . . they learned to be themselves and know themselves consciously" (1971: 37). Learning a dead language ("bringing a dead corpse to life," as he described it) served the purpose of inculcating precision, diligence, poise, physical conditioning, and the ability to concentrate on specific subjects (1971: 37). As Gramsci would ask: "Could a scholar at the age of forty be able to sit for sixteen hours on end at his work table if he had not, as a child, compulsorily, through mechanical coercion, acquired the appropriate psycho-physical habits?" (1971: 37). So, in his study comparing Gramsci's and Freire's experience and thought, Mayo concludes, following Entwistle's views, that Gramsci believed in the validity of the liberal arts for the education of the working class, and that essentially for Gramsci "the problem regarding a humanities education is not so much the content as accessibility" (Mayo, 1989: 96).

Thus, Entwistle's reading of Gramsci argues that conservative schooling is a prerequisite for revolutionary politics.[3] Undoubtedly, this apolitical portrayal of Gramsci's conception of school knowledge brings out a possible reading. Adamson (1980), on the other hand, challenges this interpretation. For him the development of workers' political consciousness was one of the key principles of Gramsci's understanding of political education. The technical skills embedded in the process of instruction loses its prominence in Adamson's analysis, while the political objectives and analysis become the central question.

It is curious to note Gramsci's casual comments on the teaching of Latin and Greek, because they suggest an issue not well addressed by Entwhistle but central to Adamson: education for what purpose and in what historical context? If education relates to hegemony, then the building of counterhegemonical principles (worldviews), personality structures and practices becomes the goal. In a prerevolutionary context, that goal can be achieved through many means, but to have access to universal knowledge or schooling per se is for the working class a necessary but not sufficient condition. It could be part of constructing working-class hegemony, it could be one of the sites in which organic intellectuals develop part of their own practice, but the overall fate of the project would hinge upon the construction of a new historical bloc and the accumulation of power by popular movements.

In a postrevolutionary situation, on the other hand, the new hegemony still has to be constructed, since hegemony is always a contested process. However, it is safe to assume that in the aftermath of a revolution, "the dominant ideas" are not those of the dominant class, as Marx postulated, and that the ethical-moral principles of the new state could be more attuned to with values underlying a new working-class common sense. We also have to remember that Gramsci was resisting a tendency in the later-nineteenth-century Marxist tradition which argued that there was an irreconcilable gulf between "bourgeois" and "proletarian" knowledge and culture. This position implied that smashing the bourgeois state also required the destruction of bourgeois culture as a whole. Gramsci, in contrast, as a classicist could not accept this abrupt break in cultural history because it implied that the working class could not share in the gains of universal history. It is in this context, then, that the teaching of discipline in schools (eventually the teaching of moribund languages) as an exercise could make a lot of sense in a postrevolutionary situation. But in the postrevolutionary context of an underdeveloped country such as Nicaragua—with an economy under siege, external and internal aggressive threats, and the obvious lack of qualified workers—and in spite of Gramsci's credentials, it would have been very difficult to convince the Sandinista leadership to implement Gramsci's suggestions in the short run.[4]

CRITICAL COMMENTS: THE RECEPTIONS OF GRAMSCI

Though we briefly discussed Gramsci in chapter 6 in the context of Althusser's structuralist Marxism reception of Gramsci, that gave little indication of the pervasive Gramscian influence in contemporary debates about cultural reproduction. First, in order to grasp the source of considerable confusion and debate, it is necessary to examine more closely the polarization between readings of Gramsci on education: whether he opts for a skill-oriented conception or one stressing the formation of political consciousness (understood in highly culturalist terms). Second, it is necessary to consider one of the earliest and most influential receptions of Gramscian theory: Latin American debates about politics, cultural studies, and the nature of popular education. Finally, the more general and diffuse reception in advanced capitalism can best be understood with respect three conflicting interpretations: (1) the structuralist Marxist appropriation previously discussed; (2) the neo-Gramscian cultural Marxism of those who have sought to draw out the multidimensionality of his theories of hegemony and resistance; and (3) poststructuralist interpretations that have challenged the essentialism of his theory of class and revolutionary transformation.

An obvious question arises from these multiple readings: why is it that his writings have been interpreted in such diverse ways? A number of reasons can be cited. First, the fragmentary character of his work, as well as certain tensions between the earlier political and later prison writings, opens the way for divergent readings. Further, censorship forced the use of a number of terminological circumlocutions, such as the substitution of the term "philosophy of praxis" for "Marxism," a fact that sometimes leads to questions about the meaning intended by certain concepts. Third, the canonization of Gramsci by the Italian Communist Party, along with fratricidal conflicts within Western Marxism, contributed to his work being used as part of intraparty struggles. Fourth, and perhaps most fundamentally, the theory of knowledge underlying his own concept of theorizing was historicist in the sense of insisting on the historical contextualization of theories. In other words, his own theory suggests that later interpreters exercise their judgment in reapplying his work to new historical situations rather than dogmatically applying his interpretation of the Italian crisis of the 1920s and 1930s.

For these kinds of reasons Gramsci's influence in contemporary social theory has been complex and multifaceted. Most importantly, his influence can only be understood in the context of several strategies of reception, as well as his broader relationship to other tendencies in neo-Marxist and critical theory. Let us start by discussing two divergent appropriations and readings of Gramsci's Marxist social theory.

The Two Gramscis

As we have seen, the comparison of Entwistle's (1979) and Adamson's (1980) books on Gramsci's education theory point to two apparent logical alternatives in Gramsci's work: either to use education to promote workers' acquisition of universal cultural baggage (cognitive and practical skills) or the development of political consciousness (thus incorporating, for instance, the experiences the working-class education—as in the case of adult education programs—developed for Liverpool dockworkers (Yarnit, 1980a: 174–91), the Italian working-class adult education Yarnit (1980b: 192–218), or adult education for socialism (Youngman, 1986).

Entwistle's argument is built on Gramsci's paradox: "the pursuit of a radical political education through a traditional curriculum and pedagogy. If schools are a major hegemonic instrument of existing class rule, how can counter-hegemonic change occur except through radical reform and a liberal pedagogy?" (Entwistle, 1979: 16). Entwistle proceeds to distinguish Gramsci's analysis of compulsory schooling for children and youths and his prescriptions for adult education. School curriculum, school assessment and examinations, teachers and teaching, the structure and organization of schooling, the relationships between education and work, the relationships between instruction and education, the notion of authority, the critical incorporation of the cultural past, Gramsci's view of the proposal for educational reform under Fascist rule, the applicability of sociology of knowledge to curricular knowledge—in short, the relationships between politics and schooling—are all treated by Entwistle, in exploring Gramsci's *Notebook* writings. For Entwistle, Gramsci concluded that "to emphasize discipline, intellectual order, and the authoritative transmission of the 'thought of the past' is to inoculate the learner against political authoritarianism, as well as to transmit the skills and knowledge necessary for the pursuit of radical social change" (Entwistle, 1979: 86).

Entwistle's itinerary is marked by the question that has occupied radical researchers for more than two decades: correspondence and contradiction models of school (1979: 87–110). Entwistle's hypothesis is that "the impetus towards a person's political orientation of one kind or another owes little to the ideology of schooling" (1979: 89). For Entwistle, school knowledge is neutral and empowering—thus the need for disinterested school—and it is up to the individuals to put their knowledge or skills to the service of status quo or its change (1979: 91). The crucial elements are the imperatives of the extraschool environment. Gramsci's standpoint for Entwistle is that "first, that the schooling of children should not be vocational in the sense of providing technical or professional training: a 'unity' school should transmit a common humanistic culture to every child without premature vocational specialization. But, second, the humanistic culture of the school should enshrine the traditional academic values of objectivity, pluralism . . . and, rationality—the disinterested pursuit of knowledge" (Entwistle, 1979: 92). School then maintains hegemony not because of its hidden curriculum, nor because of the content of what is taught at school but because "its denies a traditional humanistic education to children of the subaltern classes" (1979: 93).

Middle and high school, however, should be provided—according to Entwistle's interpretation of Gramsci—only to those who have demonstrated themselves to be sufficiently intelligent and capable. This is yet another paradox discovered by Entwistle in Gramsci's writings: that he simultaneously advocated a call for equality of all children and youth before culture, but that only those that search for excellence—and have the conditions to achieve it—should be rewarded with further schooling at the secondary level. Dogmatic pedagogy, discipline, and austerity in the lower levels of schooling may lead—for those who have succeeded—to the more liberal stage of higher education. In short, early discipline and late freedom (Entwistle, 1979: 109). Thus, "a conservative theory of schooling is not supportive of the existing hegemony but, on the contrary, is a necessary preparation for the education of working-class intellectuals, for the creation of a new humanism and, hence, is a precondition for the exercise of working class hegemony" (1979: 110).

The second main preoccupation of Gramsci's pedagogical thought, that of the political education of adult workers, emerges in Entwistle's agenda: "Resolution of the paradox of Gramsci's pedagogical conservatism in pursuit of aims which were politically revolutionary is found in the fact that although his explicitly educational writings refer to the schooling of children, the key to his theory of political education lies in the education of adults, especially as workers within an occupational context" (1979: 111).

This is fundamental for Gramsci's distinction, outlined above, between career intellectuals (many of them traditional intellectuals, in Gramsci's classification) and working-class, or organic, intellectuals, who may be able to communicate with workers; further, according to Entwistle, Gramsci's views on political education were linked to technical and vocational education, given that work is intrinsic to learning itself. For Gramsci, then, specialized vocational preparation—"in both its technical and cultural aspects—is a function of adult education, [and it] was based upon social rather than pedagogical assumptions" (Entwistle, 1979: 148). Entwistle concludes his work by arguing that

> I have tried to show that a proper inference to be drawn from the work of Gramsci is that it is unrealistic to look to schools for a radical, counter-hegemonic education: the burden of such an enterprise lies squarely in institutions for adult education, especially in those political associations dedicated to social change and in economic associations where workers are involved in productive relationships which have their own educational imperatives. (1979: 176)

Claiming that Gramsci was able to theorize the first version of a Western Marxist alternative from a Hegelian-Marxist perspective, Walter Adamson's study of the ironies of Gramsci offers important insights into Gramsci's proposal for political education. First, Gramsci's political education approach is entirely embedded in his approach to the development of a philosophy of praxis. Political education in Gramsci was always connected with the notion of developing class consciousness, and this, in turn, with overcoming of common sense. For Gramsci, "consciousness could only develop in a setting where the self-construction of the world through labor was organically combined with political self-governance and agitation against the existing state. In the Notebooks these insights became parts of a larger theory of political education grounded by a pragmatological dialectic and incorporating both individual and collective perspectives" (Adamson, 1980: 139–41).

In Gramsci, the first task of political education is to supplant traditional intellectuals with organic intellectuals. The second task is to ensure that this "process of maturation proceeds smoothly. It depends on the active self-dedication of a class to its own self-education. For the proletariat, this means the mastery of techniques whereby 'unskilled workers become skilled,' and more broadly, a self-transformation which allows 'every citizen to govern' or at the very least, places him or her 'in a general condition to achieve this capacity' " (Adamson, 1980: 144). Can this be achieved, at the school level, through Entwistle's libertarian although authoritarian pluralism? In Adamson's perspective, this view of political education demands the constitution of a new historical, intellectual/moral bloc (1980: 145).

For Gramsci, the philosophy of praxis attempts to overcome the primitive philosophy of common sense, leading the masses to a higher conception of life, into a process of enlightenment undertaken by self-conscious participants. This should place under scrutiny every social, psychological, cultural, and political element of a given ethical/moral bloc, including school knowledge and curricula. For Gramsci,

> individuals are born into a world already shaped by class struggle. Out of that struggle some class or alliance of classes has emerged in a dominant and very often a "hegemonic" position; such a class will always attempt to secure a hegemonic position, i.e., to gain political legitimacy by weaving its own cultural outlook deeply into the social fabric. For this purpose it will place its own organic intellectuals at strategic points within the cultural and ideological apparatus and will make alliances with the most influential traditional intellectuals. Over the long run, this world view articulated by its philosophers in the realm of high culture will trickle down and solidify into common sense. (Adamson, 1980: 149)

It is for this reason that school curriculum will be suspected of having been subject to this process of struggle over a definition, not only of what should be the the prevailing hegemonic common sense in school (including content, hidden curriculum, and school practices), but also what knowledge—and perhaps more importantly, whose knowledge—should be taught.

Adamson thus contends that,

> While Gramsci defined political education functionally within society as a whole, he always conceived of its operation within concrete institutional settings. He did not analyze operations in details for each one that he considered relevant, however, since his list would have included at least schools, churches, the press,

political parties, trade unions, the courts, medical centers, and the army. (1980: 155)

Gramsci's harsh criticisms of Fascist educational reform were directed towards what he considered a central component, spontaneism: "The only students who might be educated in such a system were those who, like the Emile of Rousseau's romance, were exposed to an environment so rich that it was itself almost a dialectical counterpart. Gramsci sensed that this exclusiveness was quite intentional" (Adamson, 1980: 156). This idealist model of education, in Gramsci's view, hid the fact that "When the teacher pays no heed to 'the contrast between the type of culture and society which he represents and the type of culture and society represented by his pupils,' his work becomes nothing more than the dissemination of rhetoric . . . the Italian idealists had constructed merely 'rhetorical' schools in the service of a corrupt political order" (Adamson, 1980: 156–57). Hence Gramsci's adamant opposition to Gentile's version of progressivism.

Undoubtedly, Gramsci was well aware that the implementation of progressive philosophies in the context of democratic politics and freedom of speech that may allow critical and free examination of issues by teachers, students, parents, and concerned citizens might produce very different results from the implementation of progressivism under a Fascist disciplinary regime.

Gramsci, for Adamson, did not argue for classical schooling for children and vocational school for adults, as Entwistle suggests, but "first, he argued that there ought to be one common school for everyone which would combine 'classical' and 'vocational' approaches in an attempt to 'strike the right balance' between the capacities fostered in each . . . Secondly, Gramsci aimed at a synthesis of 'instruction' and 'education' . . . The common school must be 'instructive' he thought, at least in the sense that its curriculum is 'rich in concrete facts' . . . Finally, Gramsci sought a synthesis between school and life" (Adamson, 1980: 157–58).

Adamson concludes that

> One may suspect, of course, that Gramsci intended these prescriptions mostly as suggestive anticipations of education in a socialist society. To the extent that current policy could be pushed in these directions, the conditions for an intellectual-mass dialectic would naturally be enhanced, but Gramsci did not

attempt to portray the political education transitions in this particular setting. Rather, he thought of them only in the more general terms of collective political action. (1980: 159)

In the context of collective political action, the question of what kind of knowledge should be taught cannot be easily answered. It is usually understood as the transmission of knowledge, generation by generation. However the question is, What kind of knowledge and political skills come into play here? The problem is the nature of the relationship between knowledge and its contamination by the arbitrariness of cultural capital. What is most important is how that cultural capital is appropriated. That assumes a practical-political consciousness and control of the educational system by popular movements, that is, the capacity for an active appropriation of "banking" knowledge (Freire, 1970).

So, first of all, the strategy of educational reform must deal with the kind of knowledge to be appropriated and the effects of the hidden curriculum of the schools—a question that cannot be answered except in historically specific terms. Does it make sense, for example, to expose children to universal knowledge which is transmitted—and on occasion mutilated—by poorly paid and badly trained teachers who will exert authoritarian attitudes in the classroom? Two issues are related here. One is the fact that especially in the Third World, the relationship between teachers and knowledge could parallel that between philosophers and sophists. Unfortunately, by and large teachers are taught as sophists (i.e., reproduction of someone else's knowledge in a fragmented and limited way) rather than philosophers (i.e., possessing the ability to systematize and criticize knowledge and eventually to produce new knowledge).

The other issue is that given the authoritarian attitudes of teachers, the inherent difficulty of learning, and the limited cultural capital of the popular sectors, which may not match that of the schools, this attempt at knowledge appropriation by the working class may result in simply an exposure to authoritarian banking education of low quality that is rarely completed. By and large, it is known that more than half of elementary pupils in Latin American—and in some areas up to three quarters—drop out before completion of elementary schooling, and that the gulf continues to widen between the ethnic composition of the high school graduating class in the United States and that of the eligibility pool of applicants to universities. These dropouts, or less-than-qualified applicants, would have been exposed to the "right" knowledge and wrong authoritarian hidden curriculum (a Third World version of Bowles and Gintis's correspondence theory in Latin America).

In criticizing "reproductivism," Reicher Madeina and Nàmo de Mello (1985), Rama (1985), Tedesco (1985), and other staunch Latin American liberal defenders of democratic school expansion, though taking into account the necessary moment of banking education (justifiable on Entwistle's reading of Gramsci), simply fail to acknowledge the force of the more sophisticated political economy arguments. Moreover, despite superficial resemblances, their position is at odds with that of the Frankfurt tradition, which also defended high culture as part of the curriculum. After all, Horkheimer wanted to teach the lower grades political economy, and then move on the higher reaches of a humanities education (e.g., French poetry). Without, in short, sufficient prior development of political consciousness, popular groups have no defense against the hidden curriculum, let alone the basis for an active, critical response to the cultural capital handed down by the school.

This debate on Gramsci's pedagogical theory is far from over. Eventually his pedagogical antinomies—well expressed in Entwistle's title *Conservative Schooling for Radical Politics*—will continue to hunt socialist-minded pedagogues in their attempts to understand, education, cultural studies and in their specific contributions to social change.

Popular Education in Latin America

It is little known that Gramsci's writing were translated in Spanish and published in Argentina and Brazil perhaps earlier than any other place outside Italy.[5] What Marxists in Latin America found captivating was the national character of Gramsci's thought (Aricó, 1988: 54): that is to say, the fact that Gramsci's Marxism was elaborated as a serious and profound reflection on the specific conditions of the Italian social formation, rather than as a tedious repetition of the Communist slogans of the Third International. Francisco Aricó's comments, as a privileged witness to and one of the leading figures in the discovery, reception, and diffusion of Gramsci in Latin America, are valuable:

> What captivated us in Gramsci was precisely this, the national character of his thinking: the fact that for the first time we could

dialogue with a form of thought that was closely linked with the history of a country as close to us as was Italy; the fact that his reflections on the problems of intellectuals, or the formulation of concepts such as the historical bloc and hegemony, or the distinction between an economic-corporative and an ethical political moment, or the war of movement as opposed to a war of position, that is, the overall analytical categories were the result of a profound reflection on the cultural and political formation of the Italian nation. (Aricó, 1988: 54–55—our translation)

These parallels (whether historical, formal, or otherwise) between the Italian social formation and the Argentinean and Brazilian situation, given respectively the experience of Peronism and Varguism,[6] the important cultural connections between the Italian cultural life and that of South American societies, and the growing dissatisfaction with the standard Communist analysis (of Soviet Marxist-Leninist orientation) decisively underscored the early translation of Gramsci's works into Spanish.

The interest of Gramsci's thought for political analyses can perhaps be explained in the above-noted historical parallels, but the interest of Gramsci's thought in education is related to an original aspect of educaton of Latin America—the role of popular education.[7] The paradigm of popular education has been defined as the education of the working class or as public education. It was originally used in Latin America to define the mood of public education conceived by liberal governments in 19th century. Contemporary popular education was also associated to political actions from Christian and Socialist groups originated in the early contributions of Paulo Freire in Brazil in the early sixties (Rodrigues Brandão, 1982; La Belle, 1986), but there are other decisive influences in its constitution since then, including the contributions of other important intellectuals in Latin American such as the Brazilians Jõao Bosco Pinto (1969), Carlos Rodrigues Brandão (1980, 1982), Moacir Gadotti (1990); Colombian sociologist Orlando Fals Borda (1978); Dutch methodologist Anton de Shutter (1980)—who worked in Chile until 1973, and later in Pátzcuaro, Michoacán, Mexico, until his untimely death in 1984—Chilean sociologist Marcela Gajardo (1985), one of the earlier and most talented collaborators of Paulo Freire during Freire's exile in Chile (1964–1969), and philosopher Juan Eduardo García Huidobro (1985: 231–72).

Besides the political parallels above noted, there are epistemological and theoretical parallels in the workings of Paulo Freire—even in his original work in Brazil and Chile—and the conceptual framework provided by Gramsci.[8] Peter Mayo (1989) has shown historical and biographical affinities between Gramsci and Freire. For instance, while Freire comes from one of the most underdeveloped areas of Northeast Brazil, Gramsci comes from a comparably underdeveloped area of Italy (Sardinia). Further, Freire's original work with literacy is linked to the magnitude of the problem in the Northeast. Illiteracy in Sardinia (50–70 percent) was extremely high compared to Piedmont (around 11 percent). Third, both Freire and Gramsci worked in a context of highly politicized situations. For Freire, the Cuban example magnified the implications of rural unrest much the same way the Soviet revolution inspired the Turin factory councils in which Gramsci participated. Both processes of political mobilization were followed by authoritarian restorations of order: the 1964 military coup in Brazil exiled Freire, while Mussolini's rise to power culminated in Gramsci's imprisonment. Fascism, however, is an historical category. Obviously the historical parallels here could be deceiving. For instance, while the rise of fascism in Italy and Germany is associated with the defeat of the industrial working class (Boron, 1977), the Brazilian military coup challenged a populist reorganization of Brazilian society. One of the most obvious differences is that Gramsci was a revolutionary militant, whereas Freire was affiliated with a socialist party only in 1979 upon his return to Brazil.

This is not the place for a systematic comparison of Freire and Gramsci's work, however. Freire's fundamental principle of linking education and politics, his recurrent theme of learning to read the word and the world (Freire and Macedo, 1987), and the very definition of popular education that Freire has proposed most recently will show the connections to an analysis based on people's common sense (and "good sense"), practical activity as the basis of popular knowledge, and education as a counterhegemonic practice. Freire's recent definition of popular education deserves to be considered here: "Popular education postulates, then, as the effort of mobilizing and organizing the popular classes with the goal of creating a popular power" (cited in R. M. Torres, 1988: 59).

There is no doubt that the paradigm of popular education has had a significant impact in Latin America, both in the domains of nonformal (adult) education and public schooling (Arnove, 1986; La Belle, 1986; Torres, 1990). The basic principles of popular education in its original nonformal education version can be summarized as follows:

1. It has an explicitly political and social intentionality (rationale), which is to work in favor of the poor and socially dominated classes of Latin America societies.

2. It attempts to combine educational research with educational processes and processes of popular participation, thus attempting to incorporate in the same political-pedagogical process both educators as learners and learners as educators (i.e., the Freirean dictum of teachers as students and students as teachers; Mayo, 1989; Gajardo, 1985).

3. It understands knowledge both as popular (or common-sense) knowledge and as elitist knowledge, and as an instrument of social transformation, thus criticizing any attempt to separate theory and practice or to dichotomize knowledge as popular wisdom and educated (scientific) thought. What is sought in this approach is a dialectical (that is, mutually beneficial) interaction between these two types of human knowledge resulting from initially diametrically opposed social and cultural experiences, or in Bourdieu's terms, from different habitat/habitus experiences.

4. It assumes the need to have, at the outset of any educational practice, a vision of the concrete totality, therefore questioning both the degree of specialisms that foreclose an integrated understanding of social and symbolic practices and the attempt to impart instruction basically to improve the workings of a given social system without questioning the epistemological, social, and political economic foundations of such a system—for example, the hermeneutics of suspicion as suggested by Ricoeur (1986).

5. As a result, popular educational practices attempt to develop not only critical consciousness of the population involved (e.g., conscientization "à la Freire) but also concrete alternatives for the organization (political, social, and even economic) and mobilization (participation) of the poor in overcoming the conditions of their own poverty and powerlessness (Muñoz Izquierdo, 1979).

6. Finally, popular education has been developing in relation to the educational practices of social movements in Latin America,

which struggle to link education to health care, demands for affordable housing, land tenure, and the like in the peripheries of the cities or in the rural areas of Latin America. A sociological feature of popular education, however, as Marcela Gajardo has convincingly argued, is that the emphasis of popular education and participatory action research projects has shifted over the years from working with peasants and poor people in the rural areas to developing projects in the urban areas, particularly in the peripheries of the great urban areas (shantytowns) where the levels of poverty, due to rampant unemployment and the growing immigration of rural inhabitants to the cities, are the greatest (Gajardo, 1982).

This definition of popular education is closely linked with the concept of popular movements, which have been described as follows:

> By popular movement we understand all of the forms of the mobilization of all people from popular classes directly linked to the production process, either in the cities or countryside. Popular movements include neighborhood (barrio) associations in the periphery, clubs of mothers, shantytown (favela) associations, groups of illegal land settlements, (Christian) base communities, groups organized around the the struggle for land and other forms of struggle, and popular organizations. Due to their very nature, these movements have a definite class character given the occupational categories of their members. (Documento de São Bernardo, cited in Rodrigues Brandão, 1984: 115—our translation).

In the context of the popular education movement, as Gadotti forcefully argues (1990: 68–75)—and as is reflected in a number of other excellent contemporary Brazilian works on Gramsci and education (Junqueira Paoli, 1981; Tavares de Jesús, 1989)—the reception of Gramsci's arguments could not have created greater expectations. Gramsci's theses on the role of organic intellectuals (e.g., as political militants) working with social movements, his notion of hegemony as an explanation of why the poor people may not rebel against their own miserable conditions, his principle of a unitary school system, his notion of education as a totality of reflection and action, and his criticism of the notion of spontaneism have all been incorporated in the tradition of popular education striving to expand democracy in capitalist Latin America.[9]

Moacir Gadotti, in his comprehensive study on education in Brazil, argues that: "The itinerary suggested by Gramsci is very current not only in terms of educational content, but also in the theme of struggle for democracy (democratization), the only way possible to achieve overcoming what Gramsci calls 'groups or castes' of privileged people" (Gadotti, 1990: 69—OT). Indeed, Gadotti concludes by arguing that since he highlighted the importance of nuclei of popular culture, "Gramsci has attributed to these nuclei the function of undermining capitalist structures in society, and strengthening the organization of popular movements" (71).

With the collapse of the Somoza regime and the emergence of a Sandinista revolutionary government in Nicaragua (1979–1989), the paradigm of popular education was used not only to guide educational reform at the level of nonformal education, but also to inspire the overall principles of the "new education" proposed by the revolutionary state (Arnove, 1986; La Belle, 1986; Carnoy and Torres, 1990; Torres, 1991). It has been argued elsewhere that in Nicaragua, the "Sandinista education" has been defined as popular education:

> First, this notion means that education is a right for all Nicaraguan people, particularly the lower classes, which were excluded from the benefits of the educational system in the past. Second, "popular education" means that this education cannot be constructed without the active and conscious political participation and support of mass organizations. Third, popular education is considered a powerful ideological weapon in the process of ideological class struggle during the process of transition to socialism. Fourth, it means that the revolution is, in and of itself, an immense and continuous "political workshop" where revolutionary politics become a sort of pedagogy of the masses and the leadership. Finally, "popular education" means, following Sandino's pedagogical principles, that a learning process can be carried out only through praxis and fighting, thus combining manual with intellectual labor, theory with praxis, productive skills with political consciousness raising. (Torres, 1990: 111)

Finally, the reception of Gramsci in popular education includes not only experiences of nonformal education (governmental or originated in nongovernmental organizations or popular movements; for adults, youth, or children) but also impinges upon the debate of public schooling in Latin America.[10] The debate on Gramsci is not present only in the context of Brazilian education, but it permeates many of the educational debates in Latin America.[11]

In short, the polarized reception of Gramsci in popular education is reflected in two conflicting positions: a dialectical perspective represented in Brazil in the work of of Paulo Freire and Moacir Gadotti, and a perspective that emphasizes the critical and social appropriation of universal knowledge on behalf of the popular sectors—by improving the popular sector's access and control of public schooling—represented in Brazil in the writings of educator and politician Giomar Namo de Mello, philosopher Dermeval Saviani, and others.

The arguments can be simply summarized in the following terms. The critical-and-social-appropriation-of-knowledge position will argue, with Namo de Mello, that "I know how much the idea of an universal knowledge has been questioned, but I cannot stop asking myself if a solid general formation, based on the existent dominant knowledge, is not the best that the school can offer to the popular classes. In fact, they can criticize that knowledge and improve it. How can it be improved without passing through it?" (1985: 58—our translation).

Thus, in trying to establish the specificity of education, Dervermal Saviani has inspired an interpretation of Gramsci that has been criticized by McLaren and Da Silva (1993) as a conservative reading of Gramsci à la Entwhistle that argues that the key role of the school is the socialization of the people in systematized knowledge, in connecting people to cultural capital (Saviani, 1983: 3).

In Saviani's reasoning, which takes the form of what da Silva and McLaren (1993) consider syllogistic thinking, educators should identify the specificity of education in the transformation of the social activity. Education and politics should be clearly separated, and education becomes, at best, a preparation for politics. The two, education and politics, have different objectives. Saviani argues that education is a relationship between nonantagonists, and educators act in favor of learners. In politics, the inverse is true, and the relationship is fundamentally between antagonistic parties. While in education the objective is to persuade by argumentative strategies based on an interpretation (or recognition) of the power of truth, in politics the objective is to win, not to convince, and what counts is the truth of power (Saviani, 1983, 87—92).

In short, Saviani, Namo de Mello, and others defend the

school as the principal (if not exclusive) environment to guarantee the education of the people, an education that allows the popular sectors, the subaltern sectors, a more competent participation in the world of work, culture, and politics (Namo de Mello, 1985: 255). A similar view is held by Brazilian sociologist Vanilda Paiva (1981).

The alternative view of popular public schooling is well expressed in Gadotti's perspective, when he argues that, "To the contrary of the techno-bureaucratic tendency that sees the extension of technical rationality, the popular tendency sees essentially the political education of the working classes for the exercise of hegemony. It privileges politics (of contents) over the technical (reform), insisting on an education that emerges with a popular organization, with the educational projects that the people-nation have. This tendency is sustained by our political analysis, whose central point is the relationships between capital and work, the central contradiction of our society, the reason for violence, of misery and poverty" (Gadotti, 1990: 161—our translation).

In short, a depoliticizing view of educational reform (as the critical-social-appropriation-of-knowledge approach pretends, i.e., to create the citizen through enlightenment), as opposed to a political view (i.e., popular public schooling) proposes using education and schooling as a tool in the struggle for hegemony. Is it the case that there are two Gramscis?

In concluding this point, Tamarit's criticism of the critical-social-appropriation-of-knowledge perspective is telling:

the [thesis of the] appropriation of cultural capital [argues that] it strengthens the dominated classes and weakens the power of the dominant classes. This, expressed in the framework of hegemony, makes no sense given that what happens is exactly the opposite. The more that hegemonic discourse penetrates the common sense of subjects (members of the dominated classes), the more it saturates their world-view, their moral and lifeworld, and the more it will increase the power of dominant classes, which in that way will consolidate themselves also as hegemonic classes. (Tamarit, 1990: 37—our translation)

This analysis is compatible with the view of one of the leading proponents of public popular schooling in Brazil, Moacir Gadotti, when he claims that technical competence is based on class premises and practices—a theme that reconciles Gramsci with Ivan

Illich. From a political education perspective, technical competence (or a *pedagogia critico-social dos conteudos* (social critical pedagogy based on contents), is necessary but not sufficient:

> The training (formação) of a competent teacher is not sufficient. It is needed that this technical competence be sustained on political commitment. Competence depends on the particular point of view of a class. We are not competent "in general," but we are competent for a given class while we are not competent for another class. (Gadotti, 1990: 14—our translation)

Advanced Capitalism[12]

As we have seen, the structuralist-Marxist reception of Gramsci (Althusser) reinterprets the theory of hegemony as a theory of state apparatuses. On the one hand, this approach does have the advantage of acknowledging the changed role of the state in welfare state capitalism, especially its more directive position in ensuring that the institutions of civil society do in fact contribute to social order. On the other hand, this historical updating was achieved as the price of undermining some of the most crucial and original features of Gramsci's argument. Above all, the closed functionalist identification of the state and civil society denies the tensions between the two, made evident in various forms of resistance to state power and the hegemonic institutions of capitalist society. Essential to Gramsci's argument is the assumption that hegemony is never fully secured, remains precarious, and must be continually renegotiated. Indeed, the whole theory of the role of revolutionary organic intellectuals—the possibility of forming a new historical bloc capable of redefining the cultural bases of an alternative system of hegemony—assumes an openness to the process of cultural reproduction that is denied by structuralist Marxism in general and the theory of correspondence between the economy and education in particular.

By the end of the 1970s, the limitations of the structuralist-Marxist interpretation of Gramsci led a number of cultural and educational theorists back to the original texts, especially in Britain (a theme that will be developed in chapter 10 on the British cultural studies tradition). The key aspect of this shift was a rejection of abstract functionalist formulations about state apparatuses and a turn to rethinking the nature of popular culture as a site of both resistance, as well as cultural reproduction. As Hall put it,

"Gramsci's work became recognized as a 'veritable Copernican revolution in Marxist approaches to the state' because of both its acknowledgement of the productive, positive aspects of state power (not simply its negative, repressive functions) and its stress on the strategic significance of popular culture" (1986: 23)—a theme that will be discussed in more detail in chapter 10 on British cultural studies and education, as well as in chapter 11 on the parallel reception of Gramsci in the United States.

What is involved in a poststructuralist reception of Gramsci? The term *poststructuralism* refers to a diffuse complex of theoretical tendencies associated with the decline of extreme forms of structuralism, whether as structuralist Marxism or the formalist semiotics found in literature and anthropology. These reactions against structuralism tended to share, however, a critique of structuralism's formalism as well as its inability to adequately deal with subjectivity, the linguistic or discursive nature of social experience, the decentered nature of power, and the pernicious effects of essentializing theoretical concepts. Poststructuralist theorists have argued that a rereading of Gramsci is required, one that acknowledges that he was still caught up a class essentialism that blinded him to the full implications of the theory of hegemony:

> Our principle conclusion is that behind the concept of "hegemony" lies hidden something more than a type of political relation *complementary* to the basic categories of Marxist theory. In fact, it introduces a *logic of the social* which is incompatible with those categories . . . As we shall argue . . . the expansion and determination of the social logic implicit in the concept of "hegemony"—in a direction that goes far beyond Gramsci—will provide us with an *anchorage* from which contemporary social struggles are *thinkable* in their specificity, as well as permitting us to outline a new politics for the Left based upon the project of radical democracy. (Laclau and Mouffe, 1985: 3)

CONCLUSION: GRAMSCI, NEO-MARXISM, AND CRITICAL THEORY

We have argued that though those who stress Gramsci's opting for technical education over political and discipline over spontaneity draw out an important dimension of his approach, their reading remains insufficiently contextual and hence historicist. In a traditional culture such as that of Fascist Italy, the conjunctural circumstances allowed a peculiar combination of class schooling (vocational versus technical) and idealism to serve as powerful sources of educational reproduction: Gramsci's specific practical conclusion must thus be viewed in terms of this discursive context. In the context of democratic modernization strategies in Latin American, or efforts at preparing advanced societies for global competition through new forms of rationalization, the strategic terrain has shifted dramatically.

Second, we have concluded that the limits of Gramsci's thinking in these domains should also be underscored: a conception of hegemony still under the sway of class reductionism (a theme introduced by poststructuralist critics); the residual traces of Leninism in his conception of authority; an implicit but undeveloped theory of individual development; and a relatively uncritical understanding of instrumental rationalization.

The latter three limitations become apparent by contrast with the contemporaneous reflections of Adorno and Horkheimer. First, though the early critical theorists have been justifiably lacking an adequate theory of working-class practice for confronting Fascism (the strength of Gramsci's position), they did touch upon some of the fundamental problems of Gramsci's position. First, the Frankfurt critical theorists build their pedagogical arguments around a critique of authority and substantial rationality, even if preserving a place for rational authority, especially at the earlier stages of education. Second, their arguments are developed within a developmental model (originally influenced by Freud) that suggests that the relationship between spontaneity and coercion should change over the life cycle as part of the overall formation of an autonomous individual. Third, their conception of revolutionary transformation is built around the notion of a transformation of the social relations of production in a manner that would in principle abolish the division of labor and alienation, rather than merely intensify them along the lines of a Soviet version of Fordism.

By contrast, Gramsci is forced to work with rigid categories that lead him to opt for discipline, coercion, and an uncritical embracing of the industrialization of work. Though there is an important sense in which he serves as a valuable antidote to Illich in stressing the interplay between popular and expert culture, it is not formulated in a manner adequate to the issues of a critique of technical rationalization and the forms of domination characteristic of more advanced societies. At this point, we wonder whether Gramsci's pedagogical reflections—inspired both by his own unique early experience of overcoming handicap, deprivation, and adverse health conditions, and by the need to offer at a distance advice and guidance to his own children and nephews—can be truly be understood as a general educational principle, or as an individual principle that was hammered down to sort out a critical family situation. In other words, can we infer an universal pedagogic principle from an argument elaborated in fairly idiosyncratic and less-than-universal conditions of intellectual production? This question is even more important given Gramsci's isolation from the main theoretical debates within the left, especially his lack of access to Marx's Economic and Philosophical Manuscripts, published for the first time in German in the late 1920s and incorporated, eventually, into the Marxist tradition through Frankfurt school, most notably in Herbert Marcuse's essays on Hegel (e.g., 1960) and his early essay on alienated labour (Marcuse, 1969).

As we shall see in chapters 10 and 11, the most incisive contemporary debates in critical pedagogy are characterized by a complex interplay of themes and concepts drawn simultaneously from critical theory and Gramscian theory (in both its neo-Gramscian and poststructuralist forms). What is particularly significant about the Anglo-American debates in education in this context is that we find the most explicitly developed version of the emerging convergence between critical and neo-Gramscian theory in the area of cultural studies (Morrow, 1991). Not surprisingly, therefore, all of the remaining chapters reflect this cross-fertilization and debate.

PART 5

Agency and Structure: Resistance and Reproduction

CHAPTER 10

The Recovery of Agency: From the British New Sociology of Education to Cultural Studies

Part 5 will focus on a set of issues that are outlined suggestively in an abstract way in the more recent work of the Frankfurt tradition, but insufficiently integrated into related debates or the problematic of resistance and transformation: the relation of culture, agency, and structure in social transformation. We have argued that Gramsci's theory of education and transformation had not adequately incorporated a theory of instrumental rationalization and was open to appropriation in a wide variety of ways. The theme underlying this chapter is that the recovery of a theory of agency within the British tradition of educational research (with asides to related developments elsewhere) can best be followed through the emergence of neo-Gramscian tendencies that culminate in a theory of resistance within agency and structure and are united in a type of integral reproduction theory, a tendency broadly associated with cultural studies. Chapter 11, on the other hand, is concerned with related North American developments which are distinguished in part by a rather different political and educational context, as well as the much stronger mutual interaction between neo-Gramscian and critical theory; indeed, it is in this latter context that one can more readily see the convergence between neo-Gramscian and critical theory that is largely implicit in the British debates.

As a consequence, it is more fruitful to offer a logical presentation than a chronological one, because of the large national variations and shifts within individual intellectual careers. Even if there is a general pattern of movement over the past twenty years from voluntarist to structuralist approaches, and then to perspectives that attempt to unite the subjective and objective moments of social and cultural reproduction, it is not possible to use this as a schema for reconstructing the resulting chronological history from a comparative perspective. More fruitful is to begin with the formal models of reproduction and then turn, as we do now, to the origins of the resulting criticism and the alternatives proposed. Paradoxically, the most significant and constructive criticisms of reproduction theories have important links with phenomenological, existential, and interpretive forms of sociology.

The present chapter focuses on largely British developments, which can be broadly characterized as the shift from the "new sociology of education" to a "cultural studies" approach that effectively restores—through a more adequate appropriation of Gramsci than found in French structuralist Marxism—the macrosociological dimension lacking in the new sociology of education. The first section is concerned with the origins of modern radical educational theory in the contexts of voluntaristic theories of social action. Accordingly, attention is given to the various voluntaristic perspectives that have their roots in the radical liberal, libertarian, existential, and anarchist traditions which predated formalist reproduction theory, were harshly criticized by it, and yet served often as an indispensable resource for postreproduction theories.

The "new" British sociology of education is viewed as influenced by this voluntaristic tradition, on the one hand, and yet challenged by the rise of neo-Marxist and reproduction theories. In response, the "new sociology of education" split in different directions, but the most fruitful empirically was evident in critical curriculum research, which was in turn divided between objectivistic studies of ideology and a search for strategies of curricular reform. The confusions and uncertainties within curriculum research reflected those in social theory throughout the 1970s with the proliferation of intellectual positions, productive and destructive polemics, self-criticisms, and the haphazard translation of continental research.

Toward the end of the 1970s, however, two broadly based responses to structuralist Marxism emerged (or at least became more widely known and accessible), which facilitated the reconciliation of conceptions of culture, structure, and agency in ways that made possible a revision and deepening of cultural reproduction theory: what has become known as the "cultural studies" approach (which is of largely cultural Marxist or Gramscian

Marxist inspiration) in Britain, on the one hand; and various forms of critical theory related to the Frankfurt School (the subject of chapter 8) on the other. In chapter 11, we will turn to the reception of these two traditions in the United States in the work of two leading exponents of a radical pedagogy that reflects more strongly the influence respectively of the British cultural studies tradition (Apple) and critical pedagogy (Giroux) as mediated by the work of Paulo Freire.

THE VOLUNTARISTIC TRADITION: LIBERTARIAN EDUCATIONAL THEORY

Structuralist theories are very vague with respect to transformative change, even where they posit revolutionary contradictions (e.g., Althusser). Though Bourdieu's approach gives a formal place to praxis, it ends with a very pessimistic conception of the rigidity of society. Further, a new form of society would entail new forms of constraint, with relationship to which educational institutions would have to adapt. Normatively, education would have to reflect and cultivate the form of personhood that justified change in the first place. Clearly reproduction theories have not dealt adequately with these issues. Not surprisingly, therefore, the rise of reproduction theories did not have the effect of completely undercutting voluntaristic analyses of education, even if it may have forced a rethinking of many of their presuppositions. Such issues have, however, long been part of libertarian and anarchist critiques of the Marxist tradition.

Libertarianism and Anarchism

Theories of education and educational reform have long been at the centre of utopian thought in the West; indeed, the entire tradition of utopian socialism from the late eighteenth century onward has been closely linked to proposals for transforming the socialization process with the goal of creating a new version of man and woman (Manuel and Manuel, 1971). To this extent the confrontation between materialist reproduction theories and humanistic radicalism replays the original division between what Marx and Engels referred to pejoratively as "utopian" socialism as opposed to "scientific" socialism.

Ironically, though Marx may have raised his daughters more in the spirit of a middle-class utopian socialist (leaving them unfit for the realities of sexist Victorian England), his scientific "realism," as expressed in the 1866 "Geneva Resolution" of the General Council of the International Workingmen's Association, leads in very different directions. For instance, considering the objective necessity of child labor, it is argued that:

> We consider the tendency of modern industry to make children and juvenile persons of both sexes co-operate in the great work of social production, as a progressive, sound and legitimate tendency, although under capital it was distorted into an abomination. In a rational state of society every child whatever, from the age of 9 years, ought to become a productive labourer in the same way that no able-bodied adult person ought to be exempted from the general law of nature, viz.: to work in order to be able to eat, and work not only with the brain but with the hands too. (Cited in Castles and Wüstenberg, 1979: 38)

Optimistically, it is concluded that "the combination of paid productive labour, mental education, bodily exercise and polytechnic training, will raise the working class far above the level of the higher and middle classes" (cited in Castles and Wüstenberg, 1979: 39). To compound the problems of interpreting this working-class educational program, its inspiration can be traced back to Robert Owen:

> As Robert Owen has shown us in detail, the germ of the education of the future is present in the factory system; this education will, in the case of every child over a given age, combine productive labour with instruction and gymnastics, not only as one of the methods of adding to the efficiency of production, but as the only method of producing fully developed human beings. (Cited in Castles and Wüstenberg, 1979: 36; Marx, 1971, vol. 1: 614)

The paradoxical side of these formulations is that they refer to only one side of the utopian-socialist tradition—its most "productivist" version, one with little relation to the vision of transcending and overcoming the capitalist division of labor and alienation found in Marx's early writings and associated with the anti-authoritarianism of the anarchist tradition. A similar shift of emphasis can be found in Engel's remarks "on authority" in 1872 where he concludes that organization cannot exist without authority:

> The automatic machinery of a big factory is much more despotic than the small capitalists who employ workers ever have been . . . If man, by dint of his knowledge and inventive genius, has subdued the forces of nature, the latter avenge themselves upon him by subjecting him, in so far as he employed them, to a veritable despotism independent of all social organization. Wanting to abolish authority in large-scale industry is tantamount to wanting to abolish industry itself, to destroy the power loom in order to return to the spinning wheel. (Cited in Tucker, 1978: 731)

To be sure, this must be seen in the context of a polemical response to antiauthoritarian (anarchist) tendencies within the late-nineteenth-century social movements:

> Why do not anti-authoritarians not confine themselves to crying out against political authority, the state? All Socialists are agreed that the political state, and with it political authority, will disappear as a result of the coming social revolution, that is, that public functions will lose their political character and be transformed into the simple administrative functions of watching over the true interests of society. But the anti-authoritarians demand that the authoritarian political state be abolished at one stroke, even before the social conditions that gave birth to it have been destroyed. They demand that the first act of the social revolution shall be the abolition of authority. Have these gentlemen ever seen a revolution. A revolution is certainly the most authoritarian thing there is. (Cited in Tucker, 1978: 733)

The Progressive Movement(s)

Needless to say, the most extreme anarchist conceptions of education never have had a profound influence on educational policymaking and research. More indirectly, however, the spirit of such critiques of conventional education's emphasis on authority, discipline, and memorization did have a diffuse effect. The most visible and effective route whereby libertarian principles were adapted and combined with others to challenge traditional education is associated with the notion of "progressive education." Though linked most commonly with developments in the United States, and especially with the name of John Dewey, it reflects a tendency found throughout capitalist societies toward the beginning of this century.

It is important to bear in mind, however, that even in the American context, progressive education was not a unified phenomenon and reflected three fairly distinct reformist tendencies (Kliebard, 1986): first, the child-study movement led by G. Stanley Hall who combined a search for a child-oriented developmental curriculum with an experimental research orientation and a somewhat romantic conception of the potential of children; second, the social efficiency experts who attempted to apply scientific management principles to the curriculum to preserve social order and economic progress; third, the social meliorists anticipated by Lester Frank Ward and culminating in Dewey. As Kliebard concludes, "according to the social meliorists the new social conditions did not demand an obsessional fixation on the child and on child psychology; nor did the solution lie in simply ironing out the inefficiencies in the existing social order. The answer lay in the power of the schools to create a new social vision" (1986: 29).

To be sure, the form of social liberalism and planning advocated by Dewey and his followers in the 1930s suffered from its inability to incorporate some of the important insights of the Marxist tradition because of the stunted version that was available in this period. Yet the political failure of this independent liberalism (Lawson, 1971) should not obscure its important contributions and insights into problematic aspects of the Marxist tradition, which would resurface only with the rise of the New Left in North America. Accordingly, it could be argued that in many respects this tradition of radical liberalism developed insights in advance of, or at least complementary to, what became postwar European social democracy. Reductionist neo-Marxist interpretations that conclude that Dewey "was at all times proposing an educational enterprise whose ideological content was consonant with the determining economic structure and the social and political relationships inherent in that structure" (Gonzalez, 1982: 104) avoid any kind of meaningful confrontation and critique. Though Dewey could be accused of a certain optimism and wishful thinking, his debts to Veblen are evident in his more somber moments, which give hints of an implicit theory of hegemony underlying his understanding of American society:

The reactionaries are in possession of force, in not only the army and police, but in the press and schools. The only reason they do not advocate the use of force is the fact that they are already in possession of it, so their policy is to cover up its existence with idealistic phrases—of which their present use of individual initiative and liberty is a striking example. (Cited in Lawson, 1971: 128)

Significantly, "progressive" educational tendencies have had much less effect and tended to develop much more slowly in Britain (and Commonwealth countries influenced by its example), despite the existence of fairly strong, labor-based social democratic parties. In general terms, to be sure, Britain followed a familiar pattern: "at once the challenger of many features of the school, and a means by which the school adapted itself, the better to survive" (Jones, 1983: 32). The British adaptation of Deweyean themes took on a particular deradicalized form in stressing "practical activity" and "anti-bookishness": "in the context of an unchallenged segregated system, which kept mental and manual labour firmly separated, a stress on practical activity in the elementary school amounted to endorsing the ineluctable destiny of most of the students" (Jones, 1983: 31). The case of one of the more radical and well known of these progressives is A. S. Neill, who interpreted the "Labour teacher's task" as one concerned with "the spiritual life, not the political and economic . . . To abolish the East End of London is a psychological rather than an economic problem." Or in a more realist moment: "If I tried to reform society by action, society would kill me as a public danger . . . Hating compromise as I do, I have to compromise here, realizing that my primary job is not the reformation of society, but the bringing of happiness to some few children" (cited in Jones, 1983: 23–25).

The progressive activists, largely of middle-class origin, had some sympathy from the Labour Party, but this "was not accompanied by any sustained or critical dialogue" (Jones, 1983: 34). Nor was there any connection with any of those elements on the fringe of the Labour Party who called for a politically independent working-class education (Simon, 1965). Unable to develop a constructive response to either the progressives or those seeking to develop an autonomous revolutionary culture, the Labour Party remained tied to the essential assumptions—shared by liberal functionalist theories of education—of modernization and the comprehensive school as a means for the equalization of opportunity. Only with the attack of the "new sociologists" was this called into question within the sociology of education. From this perspective—challenging the myth of the school as a vehicle of equality of opportunity, calling into question the neutrality of school knowledge, and pointing to the school as a potential vehicle of radical change—the new sociology of education in Britain made a *decisive* contribution to the revitalization of critical thought on the Left.

The Free-School Movement

In certain respects the "free school" movement became a point of departure for similar challenges in the context of North America; and indeed, the British new sociology was influenced by its example. The free-school movement can be described as a generalized phenomenon found throughout advanced societies in the late 1960s and peaking in the early 1970s, though more successful and popular in particular locales. Its significance lies in several areas. It had certain continuities with the waves of romantic and utopian enthusiasm that have arisen at specific points since the Enlightenment: the 1830s, the turn of the century, and the late 1960s. Based on the celebration of alternative or "countercultures" as the basis for radical change, such movements also had a decisive (and, some would say, pernicious) impact on the New Left, even if various tensions persisted. In particular, countercultural romanticism contributed to a shrill anti-intellectualism, which infected much of the New Left in the United States in particular, and contributed to the subversion of its leadership through mass-media agenda setting.

As a spin-off from these broader developments, the free-school movement also represented an acknowledgement that "progressive" education, especially in the form represented by Dewey, had either never really been implemented or, if so, in a very distorted form. Moreover, it entailed a further radicalization of the Deweyan problematic; Dewey's concern with an active adaptation—as democratic citizens—to the process of industrialization was abandoned in favor of more specifically antiauthoritarian anarchist themes, along with goals for gender and sexual liberation. And for many participants, it was justified as forms of concrete practice that would contribute to the transition to a new form of society.

The free-school movement—also associated with the somewhat less radical notion of "open schools"—flowered in the late 1960s and withered in the early 1970s. Though on most accounts the free-school movement has been interpreted as a failure and as based on naive, anarchist assumptions about human nature, learning, and the relationship between education and society, its impact upon debates about educational reproduction—whether by reaction or identification—should not be discounted. Not only did the free-school movement set the stage for many of the problems posed by the "new sociology of education," its failure served—not always with full justification—as a confirmation of the theses of more determinist theories of educational reproduction.

As a consequence, the free-school movement remains an important point of reference as a set of experiments that put on the agenda of educational theory three fundamental issues that called into question assumptions that had dominated the Old Left as well as mainstream educational theory. First, it called into question the "authority" of the school, the teacher, and the curriculum by advocating mobilization of pupil and student participation as an integral part of the learning process as well as any struggle against inequality. Even while running the risk of a romantic conception of the child and adolescent, such concerns pointed to the crucial issues of the absolutism of school knowledge and authority as a problem within both contemporary societies and any vision of alternative ones.

Second, the free-school movement provided an instructive laboratory for experiments with "organization without authority" (Swidler, 1979). Even sympathetic critics have had a tendency to view the theoretical tradition complementing such experiments as a form of "anti-organization theory" (Burrell and Morgan, 1979: 310–25) in search of alternative cultural forms. Such a formulation, however, has a tendency to lump together rather too hastily various forms of critical theory (Marcuse, Habermas) and the most extreme forms of antiauthoritarianism by obscuring the distinction between a search for alternative forms of authority and organization, as opposed to its abstract dissolution. In this regard, the free-school movement tended to suffer from an inadequate conception of how to establish alternative forms of social control, that is, ways of regulating social activity without formal authority, especially within an unchanged society.

Finally, for all of its failures, the free-school movement pointed to the necessary spontaneous, popular cultural bases of any aspirations for fundamental social transformation. As Swidler summarizes in her response to the study of the free-school movement in Berkeley:

> Watching teachers and students in free schools, I became convinced that culture, in the sense of symbols, ideologies, and a legitimate language for discussing individual and group obligations, provides the crucial substrate on which new organizational forms can be erected. The ability to make altered patterns of social control effective depends on the development of new cultural resources . . . Organization innovation and cultural change are continually intertwined, since it is culture that creates the new images of human nature and new symbols with which people can move one another. (1979: viii)

THE "NEW" BRITISH SOCIOLOGY OF EDUCATION

With these historical and conjunctural circumstances in mind, it becomes possible to comprehend the peculiar character of—and response to—that controversial set of tendencies associated with the British "New Sociology of Education." From the perspective of the sociology of knowledge, the initial impetus behind a break within the research tradition in the sociology of education was an actual set of challenges and crises within public educational systems. Historical events—student protests, educational critics, continuing unequal educational attainment, free schools, and even Illich's orientation toward a popular rather than exclusively academic or professional public—had called into question curricular knowledge. The new sociologists of education began with the problematic of opening up, as a theoretical and research question, the nature of school knowledge and whether this could be linked with a movement for transforming curricula.

Contradictory New Directions

Though the term *new sociology of education* gained a certain currency as a label in the early 1970s, it never designated a precisely defined set of tendencies. The first reason is evident in the apparently contradictory character of the articles assembled in the anthology edited by Michael F. D. Young, *Knowledge and Control:*

New Directions for the Sociology of Education (1971), which is generally referred to as the founding document of this tendency. Though the concept of "new directions" is associated with the incorporation of *phenomenology* and the *sociology of knowledge* into curriculum research, it is important to recall that articles by Bourdieu and Bernstein are included as well. In other words, Young and his associates were convinced that *reproduction theory* in the form represented by Bourdieu and Bernstein was in fact complementary to the concerns of those attempting to develop an analysis of the more subjective pole of educational knowledge. As Young concludes his review of the implications of the Marxist, Weberian, and Durkheimian traditions of sociology:

> consideration of the assumptions underlying the selection and organization of knowledge by those in positions of power may be a fruitful perspective for raising sociological questions about curricula. We can make this more explicit by starting with the assumptions that those in positions of power will attempt to define what is to be taken as knowledge, how accessible to different groups any knowledge is, and what are the accepted relationships between different knowledge areas and between those who have access to them and make them available. (Young, 1971: 31–32)

Though concerned about the social context of curricula, Young abstained from advancing any specific conception of educational reproduction: "we do not know how relations between the economy and the educational system produce different degrees and kinds of stratification of knowledge" (Young, 1971: 40). Though those advocating a stricter neo-Marxist position tended to label this approach inherently contradictory, it is clear retrospectively that the general objective of confronting reproduction theory with its subjective moment was an enduring issue that anticipated developments in the 1980's.

A second reason why the "new sociology of education" concept remained diffuse was that its practitioners were in a constant state of intellectual development. In a fair, if perhaps overly self-confident neo-Marxist critique, Sharp (1980) usefully charts three stages in Young's development. The first (1967–71) introduces the concept of a sociology of the curriculum drawing rather eclectically upon Marxist, Weberian, and Durkheimian concepts.

Though the question of curricular knowledge is coupled with an awareness of its relationship to social stratification, power, and dominant values, this is not articulated in relation to a a coherent theory of society and ideology (Sharp, 1980: 77–81).

The second stage (1971–76) sets aside these macrosociological issues in the interest of exploring the various ramifications of the "social construction of reality" as understood in the works of George Hebert Mead the American pragmatist and Alfred Schutz the social phenomenologist as reinterpreted by Berger and Luckmann (1967). This phase entailed a relativization of curriculum knowledge, which led to some of the most vituperative attacks on Young and his associates. Further, it was held to lead to a naive conception of social reproduction as the fault of teachers, who in turn could be the basis of a romantic vision transforming these subjective meanings and hence society (Sharp, 1980: 81–83).

The third stage (1976 to the present) involved an admission of the naive aspects of the previous analysis of subjective possibilities and the need for a better understanding of the constraints on action. At the same time, continued opposition to fatalistic theories of social reproduction is maintained. As Sharp concludes, Young's good intentions with respect to political practice have not been followed up by an adequate account of ideology, class, and the state: "a political practice which does not locate the state as the crucial moment of class power and *the* significant object of a radical, socialist, political practice" is "doomed to failure" (Sharp, 1980: 86). As we shall see in a moment, Whitty's (1985) more recent work points to the continuing development of the new sociology of education in such directions.

The Lure of Subjectivism: The Phenomenological Turn

Neo-Marxist critics, especially in Britain, have tended to argue— and Sharp's is simply the most articulate and fair expression of this—that the phenomenological turn of the new sociology was inherently misguided and hence a waste of time at best and an ideological diversion at worst. From this point of view, the Marxist theory of ideology, class, and the state—properly understood— was perfectly adequate to the task of correcting the excesses and limitation of the form of hyperfunctionalist reproduction theory found in the work of Althusser. As we shall see in part 6, a more fully developed theory of the state is a crucial aspect of filling out the macrosociological and policy aspects neglected (if not denied in principle) by the new sociology of education. Yet there is considerable evidence (which is ignored by Sharp and like-minded critics) that the phenomenological turn of the new sociology introduced a number of important issues regarding the subjective dimensions of reality construction, which need to be taken into account in an adequate theory of ideology. Further, it is significant that Young, Whitty, and others drew upon Mead, Schutz, Berger, and Luckmann in ways that were, by no means, uncritical and sharply differentiated from the typical uses of interactionist theory in the United States.

OLD LEFT AND NEW LEFT: THE GREAT DIVIDE

Tranforming Marxism

Responses to the new sociology of education cannot be separated from the specific ideological context of different national educational systems. But the general line of cleavage on the left was clear: the "Old Left" (whether of neo-Marxist or social democratic inspiration) and the "New Left" (in its various guises and transmutations). In countries with a strong, entrenched Old Left, such as Britain, the response to the new sociology of education was vituperative and at points hysterical. Some adherents of a "classical Marxist socialist" position thus concluded that the "new sociology" culminated in a "fascistic . . . dictatorship of the anti-intellectual and uneducated":

> The paradigm of the 1960s was broadly functionalist in theoretical orientation and in its prescription basically Fabian in implication. The "new wave" sociology of education of the 1970s has been informed, by contrast, by the interpretive approach of both phenomenologists and the ethnomethodologists. In its methodology, this sociology of education is unscientific and lacking in rigour. In its analytic mode, it is either naively Idealist or in emphasis excessively Materialist. In its prescriptions, it is in our view profoundly unsocialist, increasingly flirting with the disestablishment of the school system, the tolerance of the eccentricities of bourgeois individualism and the acceptance of a wide variety of "cultures" as adequate and worthy of study . . . Whilst proponents of the new radicalism promote a fascistic society characterized by the dictatorship of the anti-intellectual and the

uneducated, the prescriptions implicit in our socialist sociology of education promote the contrasting idea of a society controlled and developed by the democracy of universally, compulsorily and excellently educated. (Reynolds and Sullivan, 1980: 190–91)

From a social democratic perspective, Demaine is no more charitable. The "new directions" are castigated as "*mis*-directions" because Young's borrowing from Schutz and phenomenology lead to extreme relativism, subjectivism, and "speculation on meanings." (Demaine, 1981: 63) Further, "Young's conception of knowledge is combined with conceptions and politics and radicalism adopted from the work of Freire and Illich," which commits him to "an object of inquiry which is a fundamentally idealist and teleological conception of man" where "politics is the mere epiphenomenon of man, and it is an epiphenomenon whose characteristics inhabit a realm of ultimate personal commitment" (Demaine, 1981: 64). The result is a completely "indeterminate" conception of politics. Similarly, Bernbaum sees the new sociologists of education as influenced by fads in sociology "in a discrete and eclectic fashion" and as "fail[ing] to recognize the full significance of their claims" (1977: 68). In the process they undermined the progress of knowledge: "Both the old and the new sociologies of education are not immune to ideological influence, but within the old there was contained the notion that it was possible to be wrong" (Bernbaum, 1977: 67).

Needless to say, these dismissive judgments portray an enemy that generally bears little resemblance to the leading figures associated with the new sociology of education, even if they may touch upon the excesses of certain fellow-travellers at moments. What is clear, however, is that the new sociology of education touched upon a vulnerable strain of dogmatic positivism found in both the social democratic and neo-Marxist Left.

Though more even-handed, Sharp extends her criticisms to the structuralist wing of the new sociology of education, namely, the reproduction theories of Bourdieu and Bernstein. The basis of her argument is a "sharp" distinction between bourgeois social science and Marxism. As opposed to "New Left" deviations of Young, Whitty, and others, the sociological reproduction theorists are chided for their ultimately bourgeois theories. Despite Bernstein's "use of Marxist categories, he has never engaged in a confrontation with Marxism" and "his problematic remains firmly within the terrain of bourgeois social science" (Sharp, 1980: 46). And as noted previously, Bourdieu's approach is labeled as "liberal theory in disguise" because "like Bernstein, he is operating within a problematic largely defined by bourgeois sociology" (Sharp, 1980: 69). Not only is Bourdieu's analysis of educational selection "little more than a theory of cultural deprivation," he also does not provide an adequate account of the "context" of schooling. Though Bourdieu refers to asymmetrical power relationships, "his apprehension of the class structure is through class categories firmly embedded within bourgeois ideology"—that is, they are conceived in terms of occupational hierarchies rather than the social relationships of production (Sharp, 1980: 69–70). Though Sharp is introducing some important issues here, her simplistic distinctions based upon the validating criterion of what is or is not really Marxist begs the question. Such issues will be considered in more detail in the the following chapters.

To summarize this British debate, which has its parallels in all advanced societies where one finds a sharp Old-New Left polarization, it is important to stress the way in which the New Left in its various manifestations challenged the epistemological, normative, and practical presuppositions of orthodox neo-Marxist, as well as social democratic, educational theory. This challenge also had, potentially, important substantive and empirical implications regarding actual and alternative forms of curricula and school organization. Above all, the taken-for-granted assumption of the totalizing priority of class in the reproduction process was called into question. Issues of gender, race, and ethnicity moved to the fore, along with fundamental normative issues with respect to form of society and institutions that might legitimate an alternative to existing forms of "socialism" as well as to capitalism.

Those neo-Marxists influenced by structuralist Marxism were in a particularly difficult position to respond to these challenges to the extent that the structural imperatives of revolutionary transition and party organization defined normative issues as residues of a "humanist" conception of man. Even where some effort was made to take up these issues against the structuralist current, as in the case of Lucien Sève's (1974) theory of personality, the results leave much to be desired. Sève's case is especially noteworthy because his position is developed in explicit opposition to Althusser's antihumanism. Arguing that human history is a history of social formations, Sève suggests that it is "at the same time the history of the formation of men" and, as opposed to any speculative humanism, "Marxism founds *theoretically a scientific humanism, or theory of the historical conditions of the universal development (épanouissement) of individuals*" (Sève, 1974: 569—our translation). The more controversial question, of course, is what that might mean in practice, a consideration that points immediately to the question of education. Surprisingly, Sève only mentions education in passing with reference to the Soviet pedagogue Makarenko, "who remains almost completely unused by us from the perspective of the fundamental theory of personality" (Sève, 1974: 371)—a point whose implications will be taken up in a moment.

What is striking about Sève's line of argument, however, is its largely definitional resolution of fundamental issues. The point of departure is to ground the theory of personality in the social relations of production, a step which is held not to imply "the reduction of all the richness of social life solely to an economic basis" (Sève, 1974: 215). But the problem of universal development is linked to the fulfillment of needs, which are in turn also linked to the social relations of production. As a consequence, the communist goal of "from each" according to "ability" and "to each" according to "need" does not imply the artificial needs induced by the capitalist relations of production. Rather under communism, "work becomes the first need" in a novel sense that "the needs which communism satisfies are the needs of the man *of communism*" (Sève, 1974: 406). Given that by definition the relations of production have become nonantagonistic, the formation of individual needs by work becomes identical with human self-realization. Little wonder the harsh judgment of the West German critical theorists Honneth and Joas:

> Because he neglects the normative moments of human sociality, Sève is not only no longer able to ground the necessity of human beings' emancipation. His ideal of full personal development is the attainment of polytechnical skills and knowledge, but not in addition political socialization for the purpose of self determined action in democratic decision-making processes. His concept of the forms of individuality remains vulgarly functionalistic, insofar as that concept contains only the determination of individuals by social requirements, but not the individual's self-definition and practical contributions. (Honneth and Joas, 1988: 36)

The reference to A.S. Makarenko (1888–1939) is significant given his official definition as the greatest Soviet educator (who, not surprisingly, rose to prominence at the beginning of Stalin's consolidation of power). What is obscured by this definition, however, is the contradictory beginnings of Soviet education and his role in organizing a form of education which approaches Sève's model of creating a world in which individual needs are those defined by the work process: "Makarenko had a clear idea of the sort of 'communist personality' he wanted to achieve: the well-trained, disciplined, skilled worker, accustomed to accepting and exercising authority, loyal to the party and state" (Castles and Wüstenberg, 1979: 77). It is instructive to consider the long-suppressed alternative model for education in the new Soviet society: that of S. T. Schatzky, whose work preceded the revolution but enjoyed the support of Lenin's wife Krupskaya, herself a teacher. Though there are formal similarities between Schatzky and Makarenko in that both are concerned with a new form of society, collective education, and the integration of work and learning, they had rather different things in mind.

What is most striking about Schatzky's experimental schools is that they combined elements of principles found in both the free school and deschooling concepts. The experimental school was actually a colony within which both learning and work took place; though adults were present, the community was democratically run by children "without being dictated to by adults" (Castles and Wüstenberg, 1979: 71). Teaching was based on the principle of the "complex method," which replaced the formal teaching of subjects with participation and studying in nearby communities. Schatzky was attacked, however, for such things as not preparing children for the class struggle, the agricultural rather than industrial basis of his experiments, and the "complex method" he employed, which was forbidden by 1931. Despite certain efforts to accommodate to Stalinist policies, he was dismissed from his experimental station in 1932 and passed into oblivion. The underlying principle of his conception of collective education was the sense of the possibility that the perception and expression of authentic collective interests *presupposed* an open learning environment not dictated by adult and bureaucratic imperatives:

> Indeed Schatzky was strongly opposed to forms of education which prepare children for a predetermined future and for involvements in a particular political party. He argued that adults

did not really understand the world of the children. By allowing children to develop freely and to organize their own work life and work, Schatsky thought they would develop in an all-sided and creative way. Play was the children's form of work, through which they took possession of the material and social world and came to understand their own needs and interests. Schatzky regarded the free and autonomous development of the children's community as the best preparation for future class struggle. People brought up in this way would be able to recognize their own interests and fight for them collectively. (Castles and Wüstenberg, 1979: 72)

In underdeveloped countries, on the other hand, the new sociology of education has had relatively little impact, for three key reasons: first, the problem of the relativity of knowledge was not addressed (on the part of those who would simply import models from advanced capitalist societies); second, it was considered unproblematic because of a taken-for-granted revolutionary agenda based on a Marxist-Leninist conception of polytechnical education; and third, expert knowledge came to be challenged on different grounds than in the new sociology: the experiences of participatory action research.[1]

Rethinking Theoretical Foundations

Significantly, Whitty's most recent book (1985) has received a somewhat hostile reception in Britain. Apple even felt compelled to respond to Whitty's English critics and argues that "there is no volume currently available that does a better job of reviewing the growth, and the conceptual, political, and ideological lacunae, of the new sociology of education and of critical work on the curriculum" (Apple, 1986: 319). In particular, he takes to task the possible implication that Whitty's reformist stance entails the necessity of embracing a neo-Weberian position or is rendered illusory by Rachel Sharp's conception of the state as inevitably an instrument of capital. Though Whitty's revisionist survey does not focus on the theme of a revitalized understanding of cultural reproduction per se, it does reflect the pervasive impact of Gramscian Marxism as an alternative to structuralist Marxism given that an historicist reading of Gramsci opened the door to the kinds of questions opened up by a phenomenological sociology of knowledge.

CULTURAL STUDIES AND EDUCATION:
REREADING GRAMSCI

In the British context, the term *cultural Marxism* refers to a set of debates that gave shape to a distinctive tradition of cultural studies within which theories of educational reproduction have played a central role. Unlike the situation in the United States, where the rise of right-wing politics[2] has been associated with a revitalization of leftist theory and research, in Britain such politics has directly undercut the autonomy of university research. This situation may account in part for the dominance in the 1970s of structuralist approaches wedded to a more conventional conception of neo-Marxist revolutionary politics, as well as the weakness and isolation of the currents represented by Whitty's effort to move beyond the new sociology of education. The evident failure of the Labour Party and the Left generally gave even less room for the kind of visionary perspective of American authors. Nevertheless, Whitty's programmatic contributions give some sign of the ongoing efforts to preserve a conception of educational reproduction and transformation compatible with what is sometimes pejoratively referred to as the "culturalist perspective" of Raymond Williams, E. P. Thompson, and others.

As an account of the interactions among reproduction theory, the new sociology of education, and curriculum research in the 1970s, the previous section illustrated the effects of the dependence of educational researchers upon broader debates in social and political theory. Confronted by having to get on with their research on educational institutions, educational theorists often find themselves dependent upon, and caught off guard by, changing trends and positions within sociology and philosophy. What is missing in this literature, however, is an adequate synthetic sense of the basic shifts in social theory in the 1970s and the resulting convergence, from often surprising different directions and traditions, upon a series of shared questions, though often disparate answers.

The task of this section is to argue that this past decade in Britain was the occasion of three crucial and often overlapping developments of profound significance for the further development of reproduction theories in education: (1) the retrieval of a non-structuralist version of Gramsci's theory of hegemony; (2) the emergence of a form of cultural materialism in Britain that moved beyond the excesses of structuralist Marxism and provided the framework for a reconciliation between the "culturalist" and "structuralist" wings of cultural studies and the development of a theory of resistance; and (3) a poststructuralist reinterpreation of Gramsci that sought to rethink resistance in terms that went beyond Gramsci's residualism, class reductionism, and essentialism. All three of these developments are linked to a rethinking of the relationship between culture, structure, and agency in ways that move substantially beyond the kind of polarization found, for example, in the initial confrontation between the new sociology of education and its various neo-Marxist critics.

The Theory of Hegemony

Antonio Gramsci, as we demonstrated in chapter 9, occupies a unique place in the history of social and political thought. On the one hand, as the leader of Italy's Communist Party until Mussolini's rise to power, Gramsci's fragmentary writings have largely been a concern of, interpreted by, and adapted to the line of various neo-Marxist factions. As a consequence, his work scarcely came to the attention of those working within the traditions of academic social science until the past decade or so. On the other hand, the way in which his open-ended work could serve the interests of different factions has made it difficult to incorporate it into the larger context of social theoretical debate.

The major theoretical consequences of the structuralist-Marxist interpretation of Gramsci were the charges that his approach suffered from the effects of the humanism and historicism that underlie his theory of hegemony and revolution. On this assumption, it was necessary and appropriate to reincorporate his remarkable analytical insights into the framework of a structuralist-Marxist epistemology and political agenda, namely, the specific crisis of the Communist Party of France and the efforts of Althusser and Poulantzas to find a theoretical basis for forward movement.

In the British context, the structuralist interpretation of Gramsci was closely related to the development of a polarization between two paradigms of cultural studies: the culturalist wing, associated with the work of Raymond Williams and E. P. Thompson; and the structuralists, associated with the film journal *Screen* and for a time with Stuart Hall. Not only did these represent "home grown" versus continental versions of cultural studies, they presented quite strikingly different versions of cultural analysis: "In the perspective of structuralism, popular culture was often regarded as an 'ideological' machine which dictated the thoughts of the people . . . with law-like regularity . . . Culturalism, by contrast, was often uncritically romantic in its celebration of popular culture as expressing the authentic interests and values of subordinate social groups and classes" (Bennett, 1986: xii). Structuralism was more influential in areas such as film, television and popular writing where culturalism dominated in the study of sport and subcultures with the consequence that "it was almost as if the cultural sphere were divided into two hermetically separate regions, each exhibiting a different logic" (Bennett, 1986: xii). The rediscovery of Gramsci, however, points the way out of this polarization: "the only way out of this impasse, therefore, seemed to be to shift the debate on to a new terrain which could displace the structuralist-culturalist opposition, a project which inclined many working in the field at the time to draw increasingly on the writings of Antonio Gramsci, particularly those on the subject of hegemony" (1986: xii).

In most respects, Gramsci's formulations stand at the crossroads of theories of educational reproduction in education. Without providing any definitive solutions, he points to the four key themes of contemporary debate: the issue of the relative autonomy of the state; the conditions of possibility of counterhegemony and resistance in education; whether culture can be reduced to ideological struggle; and the nature of the historical respecification required to apply the theory of hegemony to different types of social formations in diverse historical contexts.

But the outcome in British educational research, especially as revealed by the twists and turns in Open University texts that have pursued the Gramscian turn, have been contradictory and ambiguous. As Harris (1992) has tellingly argued, the effects of "Gramscianism" on British cultural studies in general, and education in particular, has been distorted by the particular crisis of British intellectuals and cultural theorists. On the one hand, Gramsci is invoked inconsistently as the last word on all questions of theory and practice; optimistic readings of popular resistance are advanced in the name of a taken-for-granted populist politics of struggle; and the findings and arguments of other approaches (especially sociology and critical theory) are superfically dismissed if mentioned at all (1992: 15–18).

Resistance Theory

Perhaps the most influential example of British research research influenced by this neo-Gramsian turn is Paul Willis's study *Learning to Labor* (1981), which can be used to illustrate this neo-Gramscian reconciliation of culturalist and structuralist tendencies in educational research associated with the notion of "resistance theory." First, Willis"'s approach illustrates what have been suggested as the key defining traits of resistance theory: a focus on the contradictory relations between home, school, and workplace; a dialectical understanding of domination that includes not only external structural and ideological constraints, but also the subjective dimension involved in self-formation; stress upon the importance of culture and cultural production; and a deeper analysis of the nature of the relative autonomy of education, especially the nonreproductive moments where agency is active (Aronowitz and Giroux, 1985: 97–99). But there is little in this analysis to sustain the "metaphysics of struggle—struggle as a justification of all theory—found in most Gramscian works," even though Willis has joined the optimistic chorus in more recent work (Harris, 1992: 61).

Poststructuralism, Post-Marxism

Most recently, it has been argued from a post-Marxist perspective (Laclau and Mouffe, 1985) that even Gramsci did not go far enough in deconstructing the essentialist categories of classical Marxism and thus remained wedded to the primacy of class:

> Only if we renounce any epistemological prerogative based upon the ontologically privileged position of a "universal class," will it be possible seriously to discuss the present degree of validity of the Marxist categories. At this point we should state quite plainly that we are now situated in a post-Marxist terrain. It is no longer possible to maintain the conception of subjectivity and classes elaborated by Marxism, nor its vision of the historical course of capitalist development, nor, of course, the conception of communism as a transparent society from which antagonisms have disappeared. (Laclau and Mouffe, 1985: 4)

As neo-Marxist critics have charged, this position *undercuts social analysis in favor of a discursive conception of reality that undercuts historical materialism—and a coherent conception of cultural reproduction—altogether.*

CONCLUSION

British debates with respect to theories of social and cultural reproduction in education have followed a distinctive course. The point of departure was the phenomenological and interactionist revolt of the "new sociology of education," which sought to challenge reigning functionalist and social democratic (technocratic) views with a critical sociology of knowledge. The voluntaristic limitations of that approach quickly became apparent, and the focus shifted toward the incorporation of more Marxian strategies of analysis, whether in the name of Althusser or later neo-Gramscian approaches. The outcome—best exemplified in Willis's *Learning to Labor*—was an important focus on agency and structure and an analysis of resistance that idenfied many of the crucial questions necessary for overcoming the limits of structuralist Marxist models of social reproduction. Though this model is suggestive of important aspects of an integral model of cultural reproduction, it does not develop this as a coherent approach that moves beyond a class-cultural model of reproduction that thematizes the possibility of cultural resistance. The issues of class-bureaucratic models of the type suggested by Illich and the Frankfurt tradition are largely ignored and analysis tends to remain parochially British, thus without a comparative frame of reference or applications to Third World contexts. Many of these limitations can be traced back to the peculiar political constellation of British politics (Thatcherism and the collapse of Marxist politics), and the neglect of sociological and critical theory contributions. These factors have limited the development of such work as part of a coherent tradition of educational theory and practice, despite the often provocative uses of Gramscian themes.

CHAPTER 11

Critical Pedagogy in the United States: Michael Apple and Henry Giroux

WHY A FOCUS ON M. APPLE'S AND H. GIROUX'S WORK

What we are concerned with in this chapter is a significant muta-
tion in social theory associated broadly with the confluence of
themes originating from the more recent convergence of debates in
the Frankfurt school tradition of critical theory, neo-Gramscian
cultural Marxism, and related developments associated with the
terms *poststructuralism* and *post-Marxism*.[1] Though our specific
focus will be the form taken by critical pedagogy in U.S. educational theory, our discussion will concentrate on the contributions
of Michael Apple and Henry Giroux and their associates. The
choice of these two scholars not only reflects the quantity and
quality of their work, but also its consistent development in relation to the changing historical and intellectual scenes.

Our discussion will be built around a discussion of Apple's and
Giroux's response to four central challenges to critical pedagogy
and sociology of education over the past decade: (1) elaborating a
theory of cultural reproduction that draws upon the insights of
both the Gramscian theory of hegemony and the Frankfurt theory
of domination and preserves the essential insights of reproduction
theory; (2) coupling this theory of cultural reproduction in education with an analysis of resistance and social movements capable of
grasping the range of potential sources of transformative action;
(3) responding to the challenge of poststructuralist and postmodernist theories with respect to the limits of social theory and the
novel features of the cultural context of advanced capitalism; and
(4) the articulation of a theory of the state and political practice
oriented toward a conception of democratic populism.

HEGEMONY THEORY, DOMINATION THEORY, AND CULTURAL REPRODUCTION

Hegemony Theory

The distinctiveness of the problematic of hegemony is closely linked to Gramsci's reinterpretation of Marx's theory via an anti-economistic, Hegelian reading within which cultural struggle comes to supplement the naked confrontation of economic interests in class conflict. The interpenetration of force and consent thus becomes the frame of reference for social change. Of decisive importance from this perspective are the cultural and intellectual struggles within civil society prior to any objective societal crisis and the necessary formation of a broadly based class alliance or counterhegemonic bloc.This relationship between hegemony, new conformism, intellectuals, and state is central to any cultural studies from a neo-Marxist or critical-theory perspective. As we have seen, the openness of Gramsci's texts, along with the transformations of the Left in advanced capitalism, led to at least three distinctive appropriations of Gramscian themes: the structuralist version influenced by Althusser; the neo-Gramscian theory developed by Stuart Hall and others in British cultural studies; and the post-structuralist interpretation and critique developed by Laclau and Mouffe.

With the waning of the Althusserian influence by the late 1970s, a second reception—initially in the context of British cultural studies—of Gramsci took place that was more sympathetic to his historicism as a necessary aspect of taking into account historical specificity, recognizing that his treatment of the subject was more subtle and complex than that pejorative epithet "humanist" suggests and that the resulting political strategy of forming a counterhegemonic bloc was fundamentally at odds with any Leninist conception of revolutionary change. Of central importance to this neo-Gramscian turn—which was especially influential in cultural studies and education—was the construction of a theory of resistance (as we shall see in a moment) capable of accounting for potential agents of transformation.

Apple: Bowles and Gintis Revisited   The early work of Apple can be placed within the context of correspondence theories of educational reproduction, though this was always qualified by a Gramscian understanding of the dynamics of hegemony. The essays culminating in *Ideology and Curriculum* (1979) work within the framework of correspondence theory, but are quickly followed by those in *Education and Power* (1985), which is a "sequel" and thus "takes up where the latter leaves off, seeking to explore the structures and relationships . . . that both control *and* enable fruitful, more democratic activity to go on" (1985: vi). As he admits, his "analysis has progressed in more recent work, a progress that, again, has been strongly influenced by the exceptional work being currently done within the Marxist literature, and my own involvement in political activity" (1985: 11).

By the time of Giroux's earliest publications, Apple had abandoned correspondence theory sufficiently that Giroux could cite him in the context of his own discussion of "beyond the correspondence theory" (Giroux, 1981: 100). On the other hand, Giroux's critique of correspondence theory was also couched in terms that sought to preserve the economic moment of reproduction: "the importance of the economic realm becomes meaningful only if we see it as 'the ultimate determinant' that is caught in a dialectical relationship with other institutions that both actively structure it and are structured by it. Thus, such an analysis does not deny either the notion of determination or the importance of the economic realism, it simply attempts to make concrete the nonmechanistic relationships that exist between the economic realm and other ideological spheres" (1981: 102).

In a recent evaluation of Bowles and Gintis's contribution in their landmark text *Schooling in Capitalist America*, (1976) heavily influenced by Althusser's appropriation of Gramsci, Apple (1988b) concludes that Bowles and Gintis were giants, crediting them for laying the foundations of the analysis linking the reproduction of social division of labor, people's acceptance of such selection and control, and the relationships between class formation, outright domination, and schooling in America. The growing sophistication of recent neo-Marxist theorists, well reviewed by Apple in this article, has demonstrated a more realistic and complicated dynamic of class formation and capitalist schooling.

The most important development for a neo-Marxist theory of schooling, according to Apple, has been to move away from a bipolar class model (dominant class—working class, as outlined in Bowles and Gintis original contribution) towards looking at conflicts and contradictions within the multilayered, multiclass society, and the state. The diffuseness of power, and the state as a site or arena of class dynamics, expressly recognized in the most recent work of Bowles and Gintis (1986), is seen by Apple as contributions that were made possible by standing on the shoulders of Bowles and Gintis.

Particularly, Apple emphasizes the importance of distinguishing between class structure and class formation; while class structure refers to the organization of social relations into which people enter, and that very often determines their class interests, class formations refers to "organized collectives" found in this structure. Class formation is more dynamic and complex, particularly because many of its mechanisms are relatively autonomous from the state and the economy. Beyond this new understanding of class formation, Apple has argued, a parallelist position has emerged by which class relations do not necessarily dominate over those of gender and race. The strength of the parallelist position (McCarthy and Apple, 1988; Apple and Beyer, 1988) is the growing awareness of the contradictory dynamics between class, race, and gender, each one having its own realm of cultural politics.

Praising Bowles and Gintis for opening up a new avenue for theoretical explorations on the relationships between capitalism and schooling, in spite of the Althusserian influences, Apple argues that a more dynamic approach has been built in understanding how the economic, political, and cultural spheres operate in this society and how power and culture interact with the educational system (Apple, 1988b; 1986: 7–31).

Giroux's relationship to Bowles and Gintis' structuralism is critical to the point of rejecting not only their contribution to curriculum studies and educational theory but also the same notion of social reproduction as outlined in post-Gramscian social theory. In Aronowitz and Giroux's account of the radical debate over schooling (1985), Giroux argues (and on this particular score will find Apple as a fellow traveller) that Althusser's and Bowles and Gintis's account of the relationship between culture and the economy was too simplistic. Radical education as represented in Bowles and Gintis has been tied to the legacy of scientism, functionalism, ahistoricism, and ideological reductionism. It is a language of critique devoid of any language of possibility. Giroux would argue that much of radical educational theorizing tends to celebrate theory as method and verification that the theory must be empirically secure. This antiutopian nature may be particularly due to radical theorists being out of touch with wider social movements (Giroux, 1988).

This early work influenced by Bowles and Gintis's correspondence principle did go beyond their position in recognizing the broader cultural significance of reproduction, as well as arguing "for a notion of the school as a productive, as well as reproductive, apparatus. However, the orientation here still remained at too functional a level" (Apple, 1985: 23).

Apple points to several key influences in reshaping his theoretical perspective and bringing it into harmony with his political experience: Stuart Hall's rereading of Gramsci, Erik Olin Wright's stress on the multidimensional nature of social determination, closer attention to the labor process in the school and industry where contradictions and resistance are more evident than at the level of analyzing the hidden curriculum, the ethnographic research of Paul Willis and others on the active contestation within schools, recognition (again through the influence of Wright) of the centrality of the state as part of the relation of the school to hegemonic processes, and a shift from stress upon the content to an analysis of its interrelationship with the form of the curriculum (Apple, 1985: 23–35).

Theoretically decisive in this shift of emphasis was the rereading of Gramsci (e.g., Apple, 1985: 16–17) inspired by Stuart Hall in England, the latter in the context of loosening his earlier ties with an Althusserian interpretation. As Apple concludes, "Contestation is central to reproduction. Even concepts like reproduction may be inadequate. It is easier for me to say this now, and to begin to understand fully the significance of what his perspective articulated by Hall implies today, than it was even three years ago when I was completing the work on *Ideology and Curriculum*" (1985: 18). Still, the focus on reproduction is held to have been "critically important . . . at that particular historical moment" (1985: 18).

Giroux: From Domination to Hegemony   Under the influence of critical theory—and particularly Paulo Freire—(Giroux, 1992: 177–88), Giroux's point of departure is a more specific engagement with interpretations of Western Marxism and an effort to develop an approach to educational theory. Though he could be accused of an eclectic tendency, this strategy led him to a wide-ranging synthetic effort which he has described as follows:

> The essence of the problematic underlying my own critique is drawn primarily from the tradition of "Western Marxism," which in the most general sense is based upon a rejection of the economistic model of orthodox Marxism, supports the libertarian dimensions of Marx's early work, and strongly adheres to the notion that as a form of radical theory and practice " 'Marxism must be . . . made possible for every generation.'" Included in this tradition is the early work of Lukacs, the thought of Gramsci, the Frankfurt School, the writings of Agnes Heller and the Budapest School, and the more recent work of Karol Kosik, Stanley Aronowitz, Anthony Giddens, and other neo-Marxists, theorists, and educators. (Giroux, 1981: 17)

Having never passed through an "Althusserian" phase, Giroux was in a position from the outset to elaborate aspects of a theory of resistance and its relation to a critical pedagogy. Partly as a consequence, he was able to retain a closer relation to the Frankfurt tradition, despite its "humanist" tendencies rejected by structuralist Marxism. For Apple, the emerging reinterpretation of Gramsci in British cultural studies is the key to working through the limitations of the Althusserian problematic, which lie behind *Ideology and Curriculum*.

LEGITIMATION/DOMINATION THEORY AND CULTURAL REPRODUCTION

Legitimation as Belief

Historically, neo-Marxist theory has viewed theories of legitimation—and related conceptions of consensus, authority, and class consciousness—as rooted in a normative philosophy derived from the "bourgeois revolution" and hence not useful empirical analyses of power and ideology (Therborn, 1980: 100–103). Even if one may dissent from such a dismissive, orthodox conclusion, Therborn is certainly correct in identifying the association of legitimation theory with the liberal problematic of rights, democratic participation, and consensus formation. The question is whether or not there is something to be learned from this tradition, despite

its flawed and biased origins in the work of Max Weber and pluralist political theory.

To a considerable extent, a similar attitude was shared by the
older Frankfurt School tradition (Adorno, Marcuse), which largely
dismissed the discourse of liberal democratic theory as a mystification of the realities of "total administration" in a "one-
dimensional" society. However, by 1959 Adorno had all but sur-
rendered to the pessimistic conclusion that the only basis from
which critical theory could critique modernity was the very instrumental reason at the focus of that critique (Adorno, 1973).[2]

Though not altogether blind to the important differences between authoritarian despotisms and liberal democracies, Adorno
and Marcuse did not hesitate to label aspects of the latter "totalitarian" in substance, if not in form.[3] But is important here to
distinguish two forms of legitimation theory: relativistic liberal
belief approaches, which uncritically identify overt consent with
authentic consensus; and power-based theories of legitimation,
which incorporate a theory of domination (Merquior, 1980).

The work of Max Weber represents the most influential and
sophisticated version of a belief-oriented conception of legitimacy
that is not only subjective but viewed as if from above (i.e., "ruler-
centred"). This approach is based on Weber's well-known typology
of forms of legitimation authority (domination): traditional, charismatic, rational-legal. From this subjectivist perspective, authority
is by definition "legitimate" if consented to by subjects, thus eliminating the possibility of a pseudoconsensus or falsifying forms of
consciousness on the part of the ruled.[4]

Legitimation and Power   What is less widely recognized is that an
alternative conception of legitimacy can be traced in theories of
participatory democracy from Jean-Jacques Rousseau to C. B.
Macpherson. Merquior has referred to this second approach as one
of conceiving legitimacy in terms of "power," that is, where the
"credibility"—the capacity for wielding power—of ruling groups
figures more crucially than the mere "faith" of those who consent.
From this perspective, it is possible to envision a range of power
situations with quite different implications for the authenticity and
role of consent. Such a model is suggested by Merquior by differentiating two aspects of the legitimation of consent: patterns of dependence on the part of subordinates related to access to resources;

and the relative ability of subordinate groups to find "escape routes" from domination. To the extent that legitimacy is secured either under conditions of power inequality or where subordinates have no escape routes, then its validity is suspect.

In the work of Habermas and Offe, on the other hand, we find a self-conscious effort to appropriate legitimation theory without succumbing to the problems of its association with belief-based approaches, namely, elitist and pluralist theories of democracy. As Habermas has explicitly noted, he consciously broke with his mentors with respect to their stance toward liberal democratic institutions: their "under-evaluation of the traditions of democracy and the constitutional state" (Habermas, 1986: 97) represented a fundamental weakness of their approach: "On the level of political theory, the old Frankfurt School never took bourgeois democracy very seriously" (Habermas, 1986: 98).

To be sure, however, Habermas's concern about bourgeois democracy was not an uncritical one; indeed, upon closer examination it is clearly based on a power-oriented conception of legitimation. The thesis of the decline of the "public sphere" documented the erosion of the original potential of democratic institutions (as envisioned by Rousseau) because of fundamental class-based power differences and the emergence of cultural industries in the twentieth century (Giroux and McLaren, 1994; Galhoun, 1992). His argument attempted, however, to use the principle of immanent critique to turn the historical failure of liberal institutions against their original claims and intentions. The political gain of this strategy, of course, was a mode of empirical and normative theorizing that could be heard within the discourse of contemporary political discourse, as opposed to speaking from the outside in the name of an illusory proletarian counterhegemonic revolutionary movement of the type presupposed by Therborn's critique.

In the German tradition, the theory of legitimation was from the very outset in Weber's work associated with the ambiguity of its link to a theory of domination (*Herrschaft*). Parson's translation of this term as "*authority*," or Dahrendorf's notion of "*imperatively coordinated association*," is suggestive of the range of possible meanings in the original German. In the Frankfurt tradition, however, the term *Herrschaft* is clearly used in a way that suggested domination in the sense of hegemony: not as mere coercion, but as having an essential cultural dimension lending it legitimacy. The primary difference between the Gramscian and critical-theory traditions is that the latter also developed a critique of science and technology as a potential source of domination, as well as attempted to understand domination in terms of a depth social psychology. Gramscian theory, on the other hand, had the advantage of a more differentiated analysis of the forms of hegemony and a framework within which resistance could be conceptualized more effectively.

Curiously, the language of hegemony (as well as references to Gramsci) are virtually absent in the writings associated with critical theory. Obviously, this is not a matter of simple ignorance, as debates about Gramsci's work emerged in West Germany by the early 1970s (Morrow, 1975). Nor is there any basis for assuming some kind of polemical hostility to the Gramscian tradition as a competitor. Most likely, writers such as Habermas and Offe did not make use of the concept of hegemony because the whole Frankfurt School tradition, in drawing upon Lukacs's theory of totality and cultural reification, already had the equivalent of a theory of hegemony (qua cultural domination) adequate for its purposes. If anything, Habermas inherited from his mentors a totality-oriented base/superstructure model (the theory of cultural industries and reification) that was rather too functionalist and reductionist (Honneth, 1987: 356). The dominance of the Althusserian interpretation of Gramsci in the 1970s probably led to the impression that Gramsci offered little that was not already available in the older critical theory. In contrast, the theory of legitimation offered a framework within which challenges to dominant ideologies could be understood and facilitated in the context of new social movements. For example, Hearn's *Domination, Legitimation, and Resistance* (1978), a study of the incorporation of the nineteenth-century English working class, is based on the theories of Marcuse and Habermas and makes no mention of either Gramsci or hegemony. Though his study could certainly have been enriched through consideration of the latter, it is clear that there is no fundamental discontinuity between the two approaches, despite the use of the power-based vocabulary of legitimation theory. Within this context, the term *domination* includes references to both the cultural dimensions of state control and their distortion through power relations. Hearn describes his study in terms of a shift in the forms of domination:

I will attempt to explain this transformation by demonstrating that the suppression of the practical interest and the corresponding suppression of culturally meaningful frameworks—by preventing the worker from locating himself in history and society—had the effect of circumscribing the worker's capacity to challenge the legitimacy and authority of prevailing power structures. (1978: 23)

In contrast, in some neo-Marxist discussion the term *domination* is relegated to a purely Weberian problematic or becomes identified exclusively with the coercive aspect of state power and thus as a contrast term to *hegemony*: "The crucial aspect of 'hegemony' in this context is the capacity to define *ideologically* what kinds of social alternatives are possible at a given moment. (Hegemony must be contrasted with "domination," which refers to the capacity to *enforce* a certain range of social alternatives regardless of whether people believe other alternatives are possible or not)" (Wright, 1978: 248).

Education and Power: Michael Apple   Apple's general silence with respect to the Frankfurt tradition (reflected in rare citations), and Habermas in particular, is anomalous. Certainly, a lack of familiarity with this tradition is not the problem. As he noted in an interview, "Much of the work that I engaged in originally was something like politicized phenomenology, Habermas, and critical theory (before these last two were changed into something safe)" (1990: 276; 1993). At a certain point, however, he abandoned this effort to "blend together a non-structuralist Marxist position with phenomenology" for one closer to that of Althusser and Bowles and Gintis. As he notes, "I was taken by Althusser's structuralism, in part because of its emphasis on contradictory moments at a number of levels . . . but clearly what it didn't do was allow any room . . . for human agency, for resistance, for struggle . . . The next books I wrote began to push at that" (1990: 276–77) The theoretical impetus for that was, of course, the reception of Gramsci just reviewed.

To a great extent, therefore, Apple's theoretical itinerary parallels developments within the British cultural studies tradition: an initial flirtation with French existential Marxism and Frankfurt critical theory, an Althusserian phase that led to a rejection of the former and a certain ideological polarization vis-à-vis those who persisted in defending a more humanist position; and a post-

Althusserian phase defined by an engagement with poststructuralism and postmodernism, as well as greater openness to Frankfurt critical theory.

Education and Power: Henry Giroux Those such as Giroux who had never passed through an Althusserian phase (at least in published work), on the other hand, remained within the framework of the Frankfurt tradition, and continued the effort of appropriating its concepts for educational theory (Giroux, 1983: 7–41), though no similar systematic use is made of Habermas, as opposed to the earlier tradition of Horkheimer, Adorno, and Marcuse. What is most distinctive about Giroux, however, was that *he was one of the few who persisted in attempting to reconcile neo-Gramscian and Frankfurt theory*, hence recognizing the affinities between theory of hegemony and the domination/legitimation themes in critical theory.

The Frankfurt influences were, however, selective and mediated by his relation to Freire and Gramsci. Above all, Giroux remained untouched by Adorno's pessimism and drew upon Marcuse in his more optimistic moments. Most generally, Frankfurt critical theory served as the epistemological basis for a critique of instrumental rationalization (1981: 5–35) and the "culture of positivism" in educational research (1981: 37–62); the basis of a critique of "strategy-based" and "content-based" radicalism in educational theory (1981: 63–90); and an interpretation of the dialectic's roots in an emancipatory conception of subject-based praxis (1981: 113–26; 1993: 367–77). The influence of Habermas is especially selective, that is, confined to the use of his knowledge interests, epistemological schema, and related critique of science and technology as ideology, and (following Misgeld) a brief allusion to the use of his theory of distorted communication as a complement to Freire's account of dialogical communication (1981: 138–39). On the other hand, he makes no explicit effort to make use of Habermas and Offe's legitimation crisis theory to ground his own argument for the possibilities for transformation.

PRAXIS AND RESISTANCE THEORY

In part, the term *resistance* has come to substitute for the term *revolutionary* in a historical context where revolutionary mobilization and potentials are virtually absent. As well, it has served as an analytical concept signalling a working through of the critique of structuralist (Althusserian) conceptions of cultural and social reproduction. Though its origins are more specifically in the tradition of hegemony theories, the phenomena represented by the concept apply equally well in the context of power-based legitimation theories where questions of subject mobilization were already central. Indeed, the whole problematic of legitimation theory is built around the potential of crisis tendencies to unleash resistance in the form of new social movements oriented toward societal transformation and the revitalization of what Habermas has termed the "public sphere." In short, in more recent discussions there is evidence of a convergence of these two traditions with the abandonment, on the part of many, of the working class as the privileged agent.

Hegemony Theory: Resistance as a Counterhegemonic Bloc

The theory of resistance within the hegemony tradition is largely a by-product of a critique of Althusser and Poulantzas's appropriation of Gramsci, which was influential in the late 1960s through the 1970s. With the full recovery of a nonstructuralist version of Gramsci, it became apparent that his theory of hegemony offered fundamental insights into the social psychology of mobilization, alliance formation, and collective action that went far beyond the older Frankfurt School, given the latter's pessimistic focus on the social psychology of domination (e.g., authoritarian personality theory) as opposed to transformative action. Though many of Gramsci's specific points have been rendered obsolete by subsequent transformations of European politics, his general conceptualization of the hegemony-resistance relation has inspired much recent discussion.

Though Gramsci's theory requires a theory of the active subject, it remains only fragmentarily developed in his work. Within the neo-Gramscian tradition, however, efforts have been made to develop such a theory through recourse to a theory of resistance. Of strategic importance here is a reconsideration of the concept of "popular" struggle, which is held to be much broader than class struggle in the narrow sense.

With respect to the problematic of resistance (i.e., the conditions of possibility of the formation of the subjective and cultural bases of counterhegemonic mobilization), the hegemony and power-legitimation approaches have respective advantages and disadvantages. The crucial insights of hegemony theory derive from the notion of forming an "historical bloc," a configuration of class and nonclass alliances that goes beyond the tactical formation of a "popular front." As well, hegemony theory provides the basis for important insights into subaltern subjectivity and the importance of the appropriation of popular culture as part of any fundamental societal transformation—a theme alien to the older Frankfurt tradition in particular. The advantages of power-based legitimation theories, on the other hand, are linked to their development of a theory of social movements, an orientation to the emergent forms of subjectivity in advanced capitalist social formations (as opposed to classical working-class or peasant consciousness), and insight into the dilemmas of counterhegemonic mobilization within strongly developed liberal democratic traditions. Hegemony theory, by contrast, originated in efforts to conceptualize political domination in quasi–liberal-democratic or fascist contexts.

Resistance as Social Movements and Revitalization of the Public Sphere

Though the concept of an historical bloc opens the way to a popular front alliance, Gramsci's conception still remains closely linked to a traditional conception of working-class mobilization in a war of attrition against the bourgeois state. Further, the motivational dynamics of resistance remain obscure, though that it required a cultural foundation marked an important advance within the Marxist tradition.

Within the critical theory tradition, the problematic of resistance has revolved around the question of agency as embodied in social movements. The more common terms for such potentials, however, were found in reference to emancipatory potentials. The primary difference, beyond mere terminology, is that the critical theory discussions are grounded in efforts to appropriate social-psychological theories of the subject as active agent and to specify the implications for the type of class structure and cultural industries characteristic of advanced capitalism (Wexler, 1983). The notion of a revitalization of a democratic "public sphere" becomes in this context the equivalent of establishing a counterhegemonic bloc capable of challenging the rule of dominant classes. The framework of argumentation is the acknowledgement of the necessity to work within the context of parliamentary politics, drawing upon the language of legitimation as part of a process of an immanent critique of existing democratic forms (Giroux, 1991a). A further consequence, at least in more recent discussion, is abandonment of the privileged status of the working class and an acknowledgement of the multiple sources of resistance against domination.

Reception: Apple and Giroux

Within the American context, writers such as Apple and Giroux never invoke the language of working-class revolution. Even in his Althusserian analytic phase, Apple never embraced an Althusserian political stance, which was, of course, very specific to French politics and the history of its Communist Party. In order to recouple his theory with practice, therefore, Apple was logically forced to rethink the theory in a way that opened the way for a theory of resistance. Gramsci provided the way.[5]

From Giroux's theoretical perspective, of course, the "agents" of transformation were from the outset multiple and thus outside the classical Marxist problematic. From the beginning, given his debts to legitimation theory, Giroux couched his strategic arguments in the vocabulary of radical democratization in which the Gramscian terminology (e.g., counterhegemony) meshes with critical theory (counterpublic sphere). This approach opened the way as well for a critical reappropriation of Deweyan themes.

For Giroux, teachers as intellectuals, as cultural workers (Giroux, 1992), act as an emancipatory model of authority (Giroux, 1988b). Teachers could then became transformative intellectuals and expand their options in understanding and enhancing the practices of resistance that occurs in schools. Reproductive practices in this early reception of Gramsci, argues Giroux, are seen as teaching knowledge and skills in a fairly instrumental way, rather than improving democratic practices and building a citizenship.

In "Teacher Education as Cultural Politics: Towards a Counterpublic Sphere" (1986b), Giroux and McLaren argue that redefining teacher education requires a strong commitment to counterhegemony, which is superior to the less intentional and political concept of resistance. In this sense, student-teachers are moved from the more simple domain of critique to the more political and theoretical domain of the "counterpublic sphere," which creates a critical understanding of both the existing domination in society and the type of active opposition it should stimulate. Hence, the teacher curriculum must take on the form of cultural politics, making school an "embattled arena brimming with contestation, struggle, and resistance" (1986b: 1–10).

For Giroux—following closely the analysis provided by Freire—the problem with the curriculum and student's resistance is not an academic but a political one, and involves a border pedagogy, rethinking the boundaries of educational discourses (Giroux, 1991a). In one of his most recent formulations, Giroux argues that cultural workers must address notions of representation (e.g., commonsense notions of identity and difference and the different dominant modes of representation that are always rooted (and disputed) in the realm of politics. In this respect, argues Giroux that there are three principles of a pedagogy of representation. First, "cultural workers must identify the historically contingent nature of the form and content of a particular form of representation" (1994: 48); second, "cultural workers must do more than insist on the complicity of representations doing violence to those who are either represented or misrepresented" (1994: 49); and third, "representations are always produced within cultural limits and theoretical borders, and as such are necessarily implicated in particular economies of truth, value, and power" (1994: 49).

From the perspective of cultural studies, and discussing a popular movie that involves a Hollywood view of race relations (*Grand Canyon*), Giroux asks himself: "Whose interests are being served by the representations in question?" Where can we situate such representations ethically and politically with respect to questions of social justice and human freedom? What moral, ethical, and ideological principles structure our reactions to such representations? (1994: 49).

With a language that although borrowing from postmodernism still remains conceptually at the center of critical modernist preocupations, Giroux concludes that "I want to reiterate that if representational pedagogy and a pedagogy of representation are to address the challenge of the new cultural racism, they will have to rework the relationship between identity and difference as part of a broader struggle over institutions and ideologies designed to extend and deepen greater forms of political, economic, and cultural democracy (Giroux, 1994: 52)."

POSTSTRUCTURALIST AND POSTMODERNIST THEMES

Critical Theory

The relations between contemporary critical theory and poststructuralism is complex and not yet fully resolved. From a position originally close to the Frankfurt tradition, Philip Wexler independently underwent a similar self-critique (parallel to Laclau and Mouffe) based on a reading of the poststructuralist literature and applied specifically to the discourse of the new sociologies of education. As he concluded, the more or less realistic discourse of the "new sociology of education" simply did not take into account the transformations of language and subjectivity implied by an information society; the school has largely been displaced as the locus of subject formation by mass-mediated processes in an increasingly "semiotic society":

> When the literary theorists speak or write about "discourse forming the subject," they are not describing a purely theoretical discovery, but a real historic change in the mode of production and education. *The relation between mass discourse and individual formation and motivation is the emergent educational relation* . . . The mass communications/individual relation now already better exemplifies the educational relation than does the school. (Wexler, 1987: 174)

We will see, in chapter 14, that Giroux has also extended his analysis of resistance theory, public spheres, and cultural workers by taking advantage of the new ammunition provided by postmodern thought. For instance, drawing from postmodern feminism, Giroux argues that critical pedagogy should create a new language, new forms of knowledge, and a territory for normative and analytical encounters beyond disciplinary boundaries. Thus critical pedagogy "must be reclaimed as a cultural politics and a form of counter-memory" (Giroux, 1991a: 50).

It is clear, that postmodernism has also impacted Apple's most recent work (Apple, 1993). Yet, postmodern themes are still closely linked within Apple's perspective to the relationships among politics, power, and education, and the broader political economy and democratic politics. After reviewing diverse strategies to deal with critical literacy in the context of growing moral regulation through texts and the demands for substantive democracy, Apple argues that it should be clear that I oppose the idea that there can be one textual authority, one definitive set of "facts" that is divorced from its context of power relations. A "common culture" can never be an extension to everyone of what a minority mean and believe. Rather, and crucially, it requires not the stipulation and incorporation within textbooks of lists and concepts that make us all "culturally literate," but the creation of the conditions necessary for all people to participate in the creation and recreation of meanings and values. (1993: 212)

Neo-Gramscian Theory

In the context of neo-Gramscian theory, the most important confrontation with poststructuralist thought can be found in the work of Laclau and Mouffe (1985), previously discussed. A central theme of that confrontation, as we have seen, is a critique of the essentialism of a purely class-based theory of hegemony and a recognition of the multiple subject positions for social movements. With respect to education, such considerations require rethinking the earlier discussions of educational resistance (e.g., Willis, 1981), which were largely constructed within those assumptions criticized by poststructuralism.

The response to postmodernist discussion has been more oblique. One of the most provocative responses, however, is the rethinking of Gramsci's concept of modernist "Fordism" in the transition to the "flexible accumulation" associated with the compression of space/time relations associated with the postmodern condition, that is, the "volatility and ephemerality of fashions, products, production techniques, labour processes, ideas and ideologies, values and established practices" (Harvey, 1989: 285).

Reception: Apple and Giroux

Both Giroux and especially Apple are cautious and selective in their use of poststructuralist and postmodernist themes. As Apple insists, the materiality of structures remain with us and there is a danger in the endless proliferation of centers of power: "we can multiply forms of domination to such an extent that there are no meaningful organizations left to combat opression. I think that position runs the risk of becoming an embodiment of the postmodern condition itself: that is, it mirrors our inability to see and to recognize what structures exits and how they actually work in relation to large-scale forms of domination and exploitation" (1993: 176).

Undoubtedly, Apple's parallelist and relational position, particularly in his work with McCarthy, is an attempt to reestablish the complexity of power and social reproduction processes in capitalist societies. Thus far, however, Apple has not found it necessary to revise his basic position in light of the poststructuralist and postmodernist debates.

Interestingly, the encounter with poststructuralism has forced Giroux to begin to address the questions of the normative foundations of critical pedagogy under the heading of "the politics of ethics" (1988: 37ff). The surprising previous neglect of this theme—given its centrality in Habermas's theory of communicative action—may be linked to a latent moral self-righteousness in the American Left stemming from the crudity of the moral appeals of the New Right and the crisis of liberalism as both public philosophy and political philosophy, and the ability to fall back on the language of populist democratic theory. As Giroux puts it, "radical theory needs to develop *a moral discourse and theory of ethics*":

> Central to this approach is the need for critical educators to develop a substantive moral rationality that moves beyond both the conservative reliance on an essentialist, prior set of moral principles as well as the free-floating anti-foundationalism so prominent in various forms of liberal post-modern and post-structuralist thought. (1988: 39–40)

Accordingly, Giroux explicitly identifies anti-utopian tendencies with class reductionism and scientism (Don Liston is singled out here) on the one hand, and poststructuralist vanguardism (Philip Wexler) on the other (Giroux, 1988: 205, 207). Postmodernism in conjunction with poststructuralism and related tendencies, on the other hand, is explicitly associated with a "flight from ethics": "Various brands of postmodernism, poststructuralism, and neo-pragmatism have declared war on all the categories of transcendence, certainty, and foundationalism . . . What is most notable about this trend in postmodernist philosophy, in both its liberal and radical strains, is its refusal to link the language of critique to a viable political project. The flight from foundationalism is at the same time often a flight from politics" (Giroux, 1988: 61).

Giroux returns over and over again to these themes in his discussions on border pedagogy, representational pedagogy, and a pedagogy of representation (Giroux, 1992; Giroux and McLaren, 1994). The challenge of postmodernism and the general question of what Wexler calls a "semiotic society" has been met by Giroux and his associates with a shift of attention toward popular culture and its relation to schooling (Giroux and Simon, 1989). As they express their objective:

> to bring together certain elements of the discourse of modernism and postmodernism . . . talk about popular culture, daily life, and reason must be simultaneously about the discourse of an engaged plurality and about critical citizenship . . . The modernist concern with enlightened subjects, coupled with the postmodernist emphasis on the particular, the heterogeneous, and the multiple, points to educating students for a type of citizenship that does not separate abstract rights from the realms of the everyday by stressing a view of lived community that is not at odds with the issues of justice, liberty, and the good life. (Giroux and Simon, 1989: xii)

POPULISM AND DEMOCRATIC SOCIALISM

The Dilemma

The fourth question we wish to consider concerns the convergence of the educational theories of Apple and Giroux around the notion of a social-democratic populism attuned to the specificites of American culture and capitalism. It is essential to grasp the way in which this strategy represents a way of working through the oppositions between the "Old" and "New" Left in a context without a strong tradition of working-class–based parties. With the fall of the Berlin wall, the globalization of capitalism in the world system, and the attempt to roll back the gains of the welfare state, this position has emerged as a fundamental anchor for progressive politics in the United States.

In his much commended work, *Capitalism and Social Democracy*, Adam Przeworski (1985), from the perspective of analytical Marxism, has outlined the three major tasks of every socialist party in seeking power in capitalist societies, tasks that are multidimensional choices rather than prescriptive actions: "These choices have been threefold: (1) whether to seek the advancement of socialism within the existing institutions of the capitalist society or outside of them; (2) whether to seek the agent of socialist transformation exclusively in the working class or to rely on multi- or even non-class support; and (3) whether to seek reforms, partial improvements, or to dedicate all efforts and energies to the complete abolition of capitalism" (Przeworski, 1985: 3).

In fact these choices are political dilemmas, very similar to those presented to scholars attempting to improve social change in education by resorting to hegemony and legitimation theories. Przeworski's conclusion is important. In the process of electoral competition, socialist parties are forced to undermine the organization of workers as a class; in addition, compromises over economic issues between workers and capitalists are possible under capitalism and at times preferred by workers over more radical strategies.

The Convergence of Apple and Giroux

In the late 1960s and early 1970s, radical educational theory was split between the idealist tendencies of the "new sociology of education," which concentrated on the construction of educational knowledge, and the structuralist formalism of correspondence theory, which functionally linked educational systems and economic infrastructures. By the late 1970s, however, criticisms of both these idealist and materialist tendencies opened the way for a reconciliation of agency, structure, and historical specificity in the critical analysis of educational systems. As we have seen, two of the leading representatives of such a critical theory of education in the United States have been Michael Apple and Henry Giroux. Of particular interest here is, on the one hand, their initial divergence, reflected respectively in early their affiliation with the structuralist Gramscian tradition (Apple) and Frankfurt critical theory (Giroux). On the other hand, during the 1980s their positions converged in significant ways, despite continuing differences of terminology and emphasis.

Though we have largely confined our discussion to Apple and Giroux, there are a number of scholars, cultural workers, and activists writing in the area of education (e.g., Popkewitz, 1984, 1987a,b; Connell, 1987; Livingstone et al., 1987; Apple and Weis, 1983) or other fields that suggest a more widely based process of convergence reflecting a reconsolidation of themes apparent in the mid-1960s split between the "Old" and "New" Left, the divergence in the 1970s between political economy and critical theory, and the impact of poststructuralism and postmodernist theory in the 1980s. The 1970s was characterized by a dual appropriation of European theory on the part of a New Left confronted with the failures of student movement, culminating in the Reagan era and the rise of the New Right.

During this period a split in the New Left emerged. On the one hand, those influenced by political economy and structuralist Marxism attempted to incorporate a materialist dimension that had been absent in the more naive formulations of the New Left. On the other, there was a second tendency closely associated with the appropriation of the Frankfurt School, hence critical of neo-Marxism but unwilling to abandon the project of a praxis-oriented critique of advanced capitalism.

In the course of the 1980s, however, a number of those who earlier flirted with neo-Marxism moved in directions that converged with developments in critical theory. Apple is exemplary in this regard. Similarly, certain American proponents of critical theory attempted to sustain their links with the Marxist traditions, albeit in a highly "revisionist" manner (e.g., Kellner, 1989).

As applied to politics, however, this counterhegemonic convergence has been characterized by a stress upon radical democratization and populism as the necessary point of departure for mobilizing the Left in the United States. It is also striking how otherwise convergent discussions virtually ignore education as a site of democratic mobilization (e.g., Bowles and Gintis, 1986; Birnbaum, 1988; Kellner, 1989; Howard, 1988). Ironically, it appears that only those within the field of education give it such a decisive role (e.g., Apple, Popkewitz, McLaren, Shor, Giroux, Carnoy, Levin, etc.).

What Apple (after his flirtation with correspondence theory) shares above all is an effort to combine a nonstructuralist account of Gramsci's theory of hegemony with a radical democratic populist appropriation of the theory of legitimation. The incorporation of the theory of legitimation in Apple and Giroux is strongly rooted in the specific characteristics of the American educational system (i.e., its early conceptualization as a medium of pragmatic, democratic reform in the Deweyean sense), as well as the absence of a significant socialist tradition in postwar American politics.

The first aspect has the tendency of perhaps excessively privileging the school as the site for democratic transformation; the second has the effect of shifting the debate away from the classical

economic themes of socialism toward its democratic presuppositions. The implicit argument of this emergent counterhegemonic
popular tradition is that socialist policy changes will inevitably
follow from preceding radical democratization; as well, it implies
that the content of such policy changes cannot be ideologically
determined in advance, but must itself be the outcome of popular
struggle.

For both Giroux and Apple, the appeal to a radical democratic
populism is assumed to have socialist implications, though this
relation is never sketched out. Following Richard Edwards, for
example, Apple suggests that democratization necessarily implies
"a practice that is based in the control of decisions about production, distribution, and consumption in the hands of the majority of
working people . . . one that is not limited to the political sphere
but to, say economics and, critically, gender relations" (Apple,
1985: 172). More recently, he has favorably cited Laclau and
Mouffe's conception of radical democracy, along with Aronowitz
and Giroux's notion that "the languages of a genuine populism, of
democratic faith, and, within education, of the progressive tradition, can be re-appropriated, reconstructed, and made more politically astute" (Apple, 1988a: 198). Again citing the example of
Laclau and Mouffe, he also acknowledges that "people are constructed by a variety of discourses, in a multitude of institutions
from the paid workplace to the family, the school, the media, and
so forth. In *political terms* none of these has a *necessarily* privileged place. It is the effect of all of these together that matters . . . Our task is to make concrete linkages between our own
actions in the educational arena and those of other arenas. From
this, a shared, yet pluralist, 'discourse' of democracy can grow"
(Apple, 1988a: 197–98)

Similar themes emerge in Giroux's book (*Theory and Resistance in Education*, 1983), where the concept of "citizenship"
emerges as a central theme of democratic transformation. Unlike
Apple, however, Giroux takes more seriously the problem of normatively grounding critical pedagogy and of specifying the utopian
dimensions of the link between populist democratization and progressive change.

It is significant that both Apple and Giroux reject the position
of Therborn with respect to the inherently ideological character of
discussions of "legitimation" and democratization. Indeed, the dis-

tinctiveness of their argument is precisely to synthesize the hegemony and legitimation problematics in a way that can effectively address the conditions of advanced liberal-democratic societies (a context quite different from Gramsci's).

Differences do remain, but appear to stay at the level of minor strategic divergences. Apple is somewhat critical of the focus on theory (without denying its importance) at the expense of "actually applying these tools. Because of this, we have a relatively highly developed body of meta-theory, but a seriously underdeveloped tradition of applied, middle-range work" (1988a: 200). As he puts it, the practical questions are "For whom are we writing?" and "What are the purposes of these analyses?" (1988a: 202–3).

Giroux, on the other hand, is less apologetic about his "theoreticist" tendencies and views such theoretical struggle, and the construction of a new language, as a crucial aspect of counterhegemonic mobilization within the academy. Partly as a consequence, an important theme in his early work is the Frankfurt critique of positivism in social science and the implications for different approaches to curriculum theory. As well, he has been more open about the explicitly "utopian" themes in his work, a point captured in the notion of the "language of possibility." Though Apple has more recently embraced this terminology, he tends to stress the origins of such possibilities in grassroots, commonsense experience rather than the provocations of a theoretical utopian discourse. With Gramsci, of course, one could argue that moral-intellectual leadership implies grounding alternatives at all levels of cultural experience: from common sense to theories of epistemology and ontology.

What is most striking—especially in the case of Apple, given his stronger materialist leanings—is the absence of any sustained effort to describe the kind of structural conditions (i.e., the objective conditions of possibility) that would open the way for the effective emergence of popular democratic forces. In his interview with Morrow and Torres (Apple, 1993: 163–81), Apple points to the fragility of the right-wing hegemony, but he does not try to analyze this as an objective necessity in the classical Marxist fashion. Though he frequently cites the stratification research of his Wisconsin colleague Erik Olin Wright, he does not attempt to deal with the anomaly that Wright's structuralist determinism gives little basic for optimism. Again, in Wright we see the explicit linkage of radical democratization and socialism: "Taken together, this implies that socialism *means* radical democratic control over the physical and organizational resources used in production"(Wright, 1985: 287). But as Wright himself concludes, his own conception of contradictory class locations has somber consequences for the structural imperative of socialist transformation: "This poses a deep dilemma for socialists: socialism is achievable only with the cooperation of segments of the population for whom socialism does not pose clear material advantages" (1985: 288). That forces Wright into grounding transformation in forms of consciousness that are motivated by "a range of interests other than individual consumption" (1985: 289).

Giroux faces this dilemma with an explicitly utopian stance by attacking the anti-utopian positions he finds dominating critical educational theory. He falls back on an appeal to "solidarity" and crossing borders in cultural studies and critical pedagogy.

There is a fundamental convergence between Apple and Giroux. Both argue from a relative autonomy perspective by suggesting that teachers should become transformative intellectuals. This is the manner in which Apple and Giroux have found to politicize curriculum and to educate politics. In many respects, they face the same dilemma than socialist democratic parties have faced in capitalist societies.

CRITICAL OBSERVATIONS

In concluding, we need to link our discussion of Apple and Giroux back to the more general problematic of hegemony, legitimation, and resistance—along with the implications of poststructuralism and postmodernism for these themes—with which we began. Four fundamental questions can be asked to which we can give some tentative answers.

First, is the effort to synthesize the discourses of hegemony and legitimation a viable one? Or, as Therborn would suggest, are these fundamentally incommensurate forms of analysis about politics and transformation in advanced capitalism?

Second, can the synthetic approach defined by Apple and Giroux be generalized? Would fundamental modifications be required to adapt it to other advanced capitalist contexts? Does it have any direct pertinence to the specific conditions of various Third World educational contexts?

Third, is their approach fundamentally called into question by poststructuralist and postmodernist critics? Have Apple and Giroux adequately taken into account the implications of poststructuralist discussions of agency and power, or have they fallen back—despite their intentions—into a subjectivist and humanist discourse of possibilities without material foundations? Have they, in short, developed an eclectic synthesis of theories of hegemony and legitimation that fails to satisfy the theoretical requirements for the effectiveness of either strategy of analysis?

Finally, what are the political implications (and dilemmas) of a radical populist approach to education in the United States?

Eclecticism?

As we have argued, the charge of eclecticism is misleading to the extent that there exist real if previously ignored affinities between a neo-Gramscian theory of hegemony and the power-based legitimation theory associated with the contemporary Frankfurt critique of domination. Indeed, one of the important achievements of Apple, and especially Giroux, has been to forcefully argue for such a synthesis in the context of educational theory, thus moving pedagogy closer to, if not at the center of, cultural studies in the United States. An important consequence of this strategy has been to take advantage of the relative strengths of both approaches and reinterpret their implications for advanced capitalism, at least within the North American context.

Problems of Generalization

But does this origin in educational debates within the United States limit the generalizability of the work of Apple and Giroux? The question poses rather different issues in the context of other advanced capitalist societies, as opposed to the Third World, specifically Latin America.

Symptomatically, though all of the American writers in question do not hesitate to personally adopt either some kind of neo-Marxist, critical theory, or socialist label, their utopian efforts to introduce a "language of possibility" are cast in the vocabulary of a radical democratic populism within which the notion of "socialism" is virtually absent. In contrast, authors writing in a European context—even where going so far as to label themselves as "post-Marxist" (e.g., Laclau and Mouffe, 1985)—continue to speak of a "socialist strategy." Even John Keane, writing from a critical theory perspective, while acknowledging "profound doubts about whether socialism in Europe can be revived as a living discourse," does suggest that "the meaning of socialism can and must be altered radically—into a synonym for the democratization of civil society and the state" (Keane, 1988: xiii).

On the other hand, the stress upon a radical, democratic populism as the point of departure for educational change becomes more problematic in economically and politically unstable societies attempting to make a transition from authoritarian to liberal democratic regimes. Taking Latin America as an example, privileging radical democratization and the formations of an alliance of new social movements over substantive issues of economic redistribution and reorganization becomes problematic. Given lower levels of economic development, along with the extremely marginal character of representatives of the new social movements, the agenda of radical change must necessarily have a more traditional economic focus, and a focus on defending public schooling as the only "choice" for the poor—in this respect, the recent debates on vouchers initiative are exemplary. Many radical educators have largely become advocates of strengthening the resources of public schooling rather than of sponsoring unpredictable social change.

At the same time, however, given that orthodox Marxist strategies failed to take into account the importance of a democratic basis for revolutionary transition, as well as largely ignoring gender and ecological issues, the democratization theme of North American radical educational theory remains an important antidote. But the specific practical implications remain quite distinct and preclude any direct application of the theories of Apple and Giroux. Much the same can be said of the efforts of Giroux, and Ira Shor (Shor 1992; Shor and Freire, 1987) in particular to "adapt" Freirean themes to North American education. While acknowledging the importance of Freire and a politics of liberation (Apple, 1993: 180), Apple has been much more cautious in this regard.

Of decisive importance here is the fundamentally different implications of the notion of "popular culture" in the context of advanced capitalism (e.g., Giroux and Simon, 1989; Pronovost,

1982; Bennett, 1986) as opposed to the notions of "populism" and "popular culture" in Latin America (Torres, 1990; Morrow, 1990; García Canclini, 1982).

Rethinking Culture, Agency and Power

It is instructive to consider the implications of the more recent poststructuralist and postmodernist debates for the critical educational theory of Apple and Giroux. It can be charged that generally speaking they still work within a theoretical framework that conceptualizes power and subjectivity in naive ways that fail to comprehend the specificity of advanced capitalism.[6]

From a poststructuralist perspective (e.g., Laclau and Mouffe, 1985; Wexler, 1987), their acknowledgement of the plurality of subject positions and their complex relation to counterhegemonic mobilization does not go far enough.

The central theme of postmodernist debates, especially in the form initiated by Fredric Jameson (1984), has been that a fundamental shift in the cultural sphere—above all, the emergence of an all-encompassing visual culture—has fundamentally transformed the nature of political discourse. From this perspective, Apple and Giroux remain too firmly rooted in the discourse of writing and literacy to fully take into account the increasingly marginality of the educational sphere alongside of the mass media as agents of socialization and cultural reproduction.

To their credit, however, both Apple and Giroux have begun to grapple with such issues in their more recent work (Apple, 1993; Giroux, 1992; Giroux and McLaren, 1994). If the past is any guide, we can except they will not flinch before the challenges of revising their theories with such questions in mind. Regardless of the outcome of that confrontation, their efforts to synthesize the hegemony and power-based legitimation traditions in the context of education will remain a major contribution to both educational and social theory.

Democratic Populism?

Even considering that socialism is not an explicit part of the agenda presented in Apple and Giroux, at least at this stage of their proposals (see our problems with the generalization of their proposals), they need to articulate a theory of social change that will fit both with the dynamics of schooling (i.e., school-based debates, school daily life) and with the main dynamics of the transformation of the American society. Both dynamics are contradictory (Carnoy and Levin, 1985), and apparently a general theory combining social and educational change is still nowhere in sight.

Secondly, in searching for the teachers as the transformative intellectuals or cultural workers, emphasis is placed on the reproductive and counterhegemonical power of institutions and individuals; perhaps to the expense of bureaucratic routines, larger socioeconomic structures, and the same political economy of the state. The larger society, including students, parents, politicians, and business, is treated analytically mostly as a residual element, while the teacher is placed at center stage in the process of transformation and struggle. In arguing about reforming public education, the dilemma will be whether to build multiclass, multiagency coalitions or to bet mostly on the role of the teacher as a social agent rather than as a state functionary or as a worker.

Thirdly, abolition of capitalism as a system of capital accumulation is out of the question in populist proposals; changing the primacy (logic) of the market to a more collective social democratic arrangement (logic) is the goal. However, the question is that changing social arrangements built on cultural traditions and historical experiences imply changes of magnitude (i.e., revolutionary changes) that are outside any possible unilateral contribution of the educational (or cultural) milieu.

Thus, the problem for a populist proposal lies in the fact that the more down-to-earth the language of the critique becomes to signify a language of possibility, the less likely it is that it will continue to express the power of critical theory. Indeed it may not become at all different from the language portraying "business as usual." However, a somewhat elitist language (as opposed to "commonsense" theoretical impressions) will bring few guarantees for a populist project to succeed. Similarly, at times of financial pressure over public schools, and given the liberal-democratic foundations of the teaching profession, there is no guarantee that if the teacher is singled out as the key social agent, they will opt for a radical populist program of social transformation over a conventional, liberal-democratic (or even a conservative) one.

In fact, when public schooling is linked to economic competition at the level of the world system, the loyalty of the teacher could be directed toward fairly antagonicistic ends. On the one hand, schooling could be oriented to regain economic supremacy in the world system, which may mean to sustain hegemonical policies and asymmetrical power relationships among and between nations and social groups, as well as systematic increases in welfare differences between wage-earners and capital as a way to offset productivity differentials and capital flight. On the other hand, schooling could be directed toward expanding social-democratic traits in the society at the expense of capital accumulation, changing the individualist orientation of mainstream American citizens into a collective orientation. Needless to say, suggesting teachers are capable of unified political action implies the problematic assumption that they are a relatively homogeneous category, despite internal cleavages and contradictions.

These dilemmas are worthy of consideration in light of the structural conditions that sustain the hegemony and legitimation of advanced capitalism. The anti-utopian implications of critical education are not due merely "to the isolation of radical theorists from larger social movements and sources sources of social criticism" (Giroux, 1988a: 206); that separation is itself an expression of a system of hegemonic relations that cannot be moralistically attributed to the moral cowardliness or self-interest of radical intellectuals and their failure to join the evangelical army proclaiming the "language of hope." The agonies of the American Left continue to the beat of new drummers.

PART 6

Education, the State, and the Logic of Reproduction

CHAPTER 12

The Capitalist State and Educational Policy Formation

Though the theories of resistance discussed in part 5 are closely associated with an integral model of educational reproduction, one associated with the interaction between state-hegemonic conceptions of reproduction and resistance, the problematic of the state is generally elaborated in either very general or very specific terms. The task of part 6 is thus first (chapter 12) to look more closely at theories of the state in relation to the analysis of educational policy, with particular reference to the Latin American examples where we can find the closest approximations of critical pedadogy in practice. Finally, chapter 13 will conclude with a reiteration of the models of reproduction with which we began, and point to the implications of an integral model for transformation of possibilites in advanced liberal-democratic and Latin American societies.

In this study we have sought to identify, describe, and criticize a number of models of educational reproduction: economic-reproductive models (correspondence theories—e.g., early Bowles and Gintis, Althusser); class-reproductive (Bourdieu, Bernstein); class-bureaucratic; hegemonic-state reproductive (neo-Gramscian and critical theories of the state); and transformative-resistance theories as a qualification of the latter (Apple; Aronowitz and Giroux).

As we have seen, one of the principal limitations of relatively closed models of educational reproduction—whether structuralist-Marxist, systems-theoretic, or class-bureaucratic in inspiration—is that they tend to conceptualize reproduction in terms of the logic of the reproduction of society as a whole. Though a useful point of departure, such theories suffer from the problems of working at a

---

Parts of this chapter have been adapted from Torres 1988.

very high level of abstraction and the related limitations of teleological explanation. The result is very broad generalizations
about the economic functions of education (correspondence theory), its general societal functions (social integration and differentiation), or its relation to a more general process of bureaucratization
and scientization (instrumental rationalization); in each case there
is a very limited capacity to make sense of the actual historical,
empirical *variations* in educational systems, as opposed to the
modern general shared developments. A cultural class reproduction approach such as that of Bourdieu does not fully escape these
difficulties, even if it provides useful concepts in comparing different class strategies and analyzing the nuances of the cultural dimensions reproduction. The extension of Bourdieu's work in the
direction of a comparative sociology of education is, however, in its
infancy.

Theories of neo-Weberian inspiration (e.g., Collins, Murphy),
which draw explicitly or implicitly on Weber's social-closure theory, offer a basis for more finely grained comparative historical
studies which, complementing and extending some of Bourdieu's
concerns, can pinpoint some of the variations if historical terms, if
not general theoretical ones. Similarly, the morphogenic model
developed by Archer also provides important insights into the
comparative historical formation of educational systems and the
crucial role of the state in that process, but with limitations already
noted.

The implication of these problems is that a general theory of
origins and transformation of educational systems cannot be anchored in either a general theory of society or a general theory of
class conflict focussing on the educational system as a site of social
closure. Both of these approaches provide necessary and important
insights, but neither can give adequate attention to the pivotal
significance of the state.

The important exceptions can be found in the state-hegemonic
theory of neo-Gramscian inspiration (e.g., Apple), state-derivation
theory (Hirsch), critical theories of the state (Offe, Lenhardt, Habermas), and the morphogenic model of the development of state
educational systems (Archer). In this chapter we will argue that in
advanced capitalist societies, and developing ones that successfully
confront the imperatives for sustained development, *the key to a
theory of educational reproduction lies in a theory of public policy*

that can analyze educational policy formation in specific, empirical terms, thus mediating between the abstraction of general societal processes or a microanalysis of conflicts within educational systems (Torres, 1985).

Without attempting to reconstruct the precise borrowings that have influenced the subsequent analysis of the determinants of educational policy formation, the general approach derives from a general neo-Gramscian theory of hegemony and resistance (Apple, Giroux), the theory of legitimation crisis as developed in critical theory (Offe, Habermas), and the structural theory of power concerned with selection rules (Clegg's work, which will be taken up in a moment).

Such an integrative analysis of educational policy should, from the perspective of a critical political sociology of education, have two moments: the objective analysis of the determinants of public policy; and anticipatory analysis of the conditions of possibility of transformative policy changes and probable strategies of implementation.

TOWARD A CRITICAL THEORY OF EDUCATIONAL POLICY FORMATION AND THE STATE

In this chapter, we will argue that a critical theory of power and the state is a necessary starting point to study educational policy making—hence, moving the analysis from the strict realm of individual choice and preference somehow modeled by organizational behavior, to a more historical-structural approach where individuals indeed have choices, but they are prescribed or constrained by historical circumstances, conjunctural processes, and the diverse expressions of power and authority (at the micro and macro levels) through concrete rules of policy formation. Also, we will argue that any study of education as public policy should deal with the issues of the organizational context in which power (as an expression of domination) is exercised. The relationships between power, complex organization, and the state should be understood from a combined perspective of the political economy and a political sociology of educational policy making.

We will argue that policy making should be studied in the context of a theory of politics. Following Clegg (1975, 1989) and critical theories generally, we assume that the concept that political life is is ordered and articulated through forms of domination that have manifold expressions, from economic dominance of one class over others in the material production and reproduction of social life, to patriarchal relations and intersubjective, male-to-female domination in the household (Morrow and Torres, 1988). Similarly, the distinction between surface/deep structure models of rules, borrowed from structural linguistics could be very useful as a starting point in understanding power in decision making (Clegg, 1975: 70). The deep structure is composed of a set of restrictive and enabling rules, "those which operate to modify independently existing forms of behavior and activity, and those which create new forms of behavior and activity" (Shwayder, in Clegg, 1975: 75). At the level of deep structure, a given combination of rules constitute different rationalities—as, for instance, in Weber's three modes of legitimate authority or domination (e.g., traditional, charismatic, and bureaucratic). At the level of surface structure, observable exchanges between individuals and institutions would constitute exchanges of power (which in turn, as Marx pointed out in chapter 23 of volume 1 of *The Capital*, would inhibit or contribute to the simple and complex reproduction of economic exploitation/domination structures in social life). Clegg has graphically described the articulation of these categorical-analytical relationships (table 12.1). In Clegg's terms, "Power is about the outcomes of issues enabled by the rule of a substantive rationality which is temporally and institutionally located. Underlying this rule is a specific form of domination. The progression is from domination, rules, power" (Clegg, 1975: 78).

This approach to rules, power, and domination as applied to policy making needs to be complemented by a discussion of a theory of the state in order to understand what we have called, following Claus Offe, the production rules of public policy. The next section attempts, first, to highlight the importance of a theory of the state for the study of educational policy making, and second, to introduce the notion of state authority in capitalist societies. For the sake of clarity, the theoretical, analytical, and political differences between the theories and authors that are discussed below, and that indirectly or directly inspired our framework (e.g., the state derivationists, Poulantzas, Offe, Therborn, Gramsci, etc.), will not be discussed in great detail. Similarly, illustrations and

TABLE 12.1
Power Structures

Structure	Concept	Objective Processes
Surface structure	Power	Exchanges
Deep structure	Rules	Rationality
Form of life	Domination/exploitation	Economic Activity

Source: adapted from Clegg (1975:78).

examples that may bring to life this theoretical framework will not be extensively used due to space restrictions.

Critique of Conventional Approaches to the State and Policy Analysis

In comparative research in political science and public administration, determinants of public policy have been cataloged from a vast array of contrasting perspectives. Siegel and Weinberg, for instance, have emphasized the following domestic, internal influences in policy making: (a) environmental determinants of public policy (e.g., economic factors, physical environment, and social and demographic factors), and (b) political system determinants of public policy (e.g., political community, political regimes, and the authorities). Among external influences in policy making, they have distinguished the following: (a) international development forces (e.g., military and political developments), and (b) international organizational cooperation, assistance, and pressures (which certainly have proven to be very relevant for some areas of educational policy making in various countries) (Siegel and Weinberg, 1977). An alternative schema has been substantiated by H. Leichter for use in analyzing public policy. He has distinguished between situational factors (divided into six complementary sets of factors, which extend from economic circles to technological change); structural factors (which include the political structure and the economic structure); cultural factors (distinguishing between political culture and general culture); and finally environmental factors (distinguishing between international political environment, policy diffusion, international agreements, and multinational corporations) (Leichter, 1979).

These are merely a few examples of common trends in the empirical analysis of public policy. Unfortunately, there are very few studies that address themselves to an analysis of educational policy formation in capitalist states that at the same time try to overcome the narrow and technical point of view commonly used in studies of policy making and planning.

Policy making, for instance, has been commonly analyzed (1) as the production of interaction between political controllers and professional providers of services (Saran, 1973); (2) through the focus on timing and feasibility as crucial elements in policy making (David, 1977); (3) through research such as that of Wirt and Kirst (1982), which, by assuming that schools are miniature political systems, falls into the contradiction of accepting a pluralist power structure in the United States, but ends up portraying schools as a world of harmony and consensus; (4) through research that deals with local state policy making and the development of educational policies taxonomies, especially basic control mechanisms available to state-level policy makers, in which the independent (explanatory) variable would be the political culture and educational assumptions of policy makers (Peabody Journal of Education, 1985); or (5) through an Eastonian–system-analysis perspective that focuses on education units as parapolitical subsystems that include the processing of demands; the generation of support by authorities, regimes, and the political community; and the feedback response factor (Howell and Brown, 1983). All of these fairly conventional approaches lack an understanding of theory of the state and a critical conceptualization of issues such as domination, power, rules, and political representation in analyzing policy making. But perhaps they are especially faulty in that the methodological individualism of these studies has led to an underestimation of the constraints (or restraints) on policy-makers' actions, and particularly their conspicuously naive worldviews. In short, these types of studies lack the theoretical sophistication needed to understand a very complex and rather sophisticated political process of educational decision making in capitalist societies. As Richard Bates has said, "Underlying this onslaught of criticism was a clear impatience with the value neutrality of classical public administration and its tendency to distance itself from complex and controversial issues while focusing on narrow empiricist studies of administrative processes" (Bates, 1985: 15). They also lack a holistic approach to determinants of policy making, namely, an ability to link what happens in schools and nonformal education settings with what happens in terms of accumulation and legitimation processes in the overall society. Above all, they have a practical-pragmatic bias in which the guiding knowledge interest (borrowing the term from Habermas, 1971) of the research is exclusively empirical-analytical, thus oriented toward potential technical control rather than, or in addition to, an historical-hermeneutic interest or a critical-emancipatory one.

Hence, prevailing methodological individualism in social theory, and pragmatic-empiricist epistemological assumptions in educational administration have defined the study of policy making as a political process where policy-makers make decisions within the framework of existing ideologies.

Theory of the State and Education

A common thread that runs through Marxist and Marxist-influenced educational research is the analysis of education as part of the state-administered reproduction of fundamental societal relations (Broady, 1981: 143). It has been discussed in part 1 that, in general, the notion of social reproduction (a) presupposes theories of society as a complex totality that develops through contradictions; (b) takes relatively complex societies as the object of inquiry within which formal and specialized educational institutions play a significant role; (c) argues that these educational institutions constitute strategic sites for the stability and further development of these societies; (d) studies the relations of mutual interaction between these institutions and the larger society that provide the basis for sociologies of education; (e) suggests that policy formulation within the educational sphere constitutes a crucial context of negotiation and struggle that may have decisive effects on the capacity of society to maintain or transform itself (hence, educational settings are a microscopic representation of the larger macroscopic societal dynamics); and (f) paradoxically considers education to be either a powerful (and somehow unique) tool for socialization into a given social order or a tool with which to challenge and resist a hegemonic culture or social practice. In short, theories of social reproduction in education are linked with power, race, gender, class, knowledge, and the moral bases of cultural production and acquisition (Morrow and Torres, 1988).

Although the relationship between education and the state is at the core of the definition of education's reproduction function in capitalist societies, it has rarely been thoroughly analyzed in contemporary social theory. Research questions concerning the capitalist state and its class-based proceedings, as well as those concerning state impingements on educational structures, practices, codes, and especially educational planning and policy making, still lack sound theoretical understanding and appropriate methodological procedures for their study.

For instance, the influential book *Schooling in Capitalist America* focused on the notion of capital and its intervention in the educational system, particularly in the preparation of students as future workers at the various levels in the hierarchy of capitalist production (Bowles and Gintis, 1976). Bowles and Gintis have suggested a correspondence principle that explains educational development. In brief, there is a perceived correspondence between the social relations of production and the social relations of education (Bowles and Gintis, 1981: 225). Responding to the critics, they have argued that this correspondence principle depicts five main features of capitalist schooling: (a) the surprising lack of importance of the cognitive aspects of schooling in the preparation of good workers and in the intergenerational reproduction of social status; (b) the limits of progressive education that are social rather than biological or technological; (c) the experience of schooling as an arena of structured social interaction and the school curricula as an outcome of these interactive processes; (d) the need for a larger framework to integrate the effects of schooling on individuals (e.g., skills, attitudes, scholastic achievement) into a broader process of structural capitalist transformation and reproduction; and finally (e) Bowles and Gintis claim their analysis shows that, in order to understand the structure of schooling, it is not the ownership but the control of the means of production that matters (Bowles and Gintis, 1981: 226–27).

The emphasis here is on the general, class-based social determination of educational policy and schooling that is expressed in the correspondence principle. In a more recent contribution, Carnoy and Levin (1985) have emphasized that this earlier analysis of education and reproduction lacks a concrete theory of the state. Similarly, although it is important to consider the process of correspondence between education and capital accumulation, it is even more important to focus on the process of state mediation of contradictions. It is argued that the major problem with the type of analyses produced by Bowles and Gintis and Boudelot and Establet is "that it does not account for the contradictory trends towards equality and democracy in education . . . Indeed, Bowles and Gintis argue that the 'laws of motion' of correspondence are so dominant that democratic or egalitarian reforms must necessarily fail or be limited in their impact" (Carnoy and Levin, 1985: 22).

To understand these complex relationships of correspondence and contradiction in education an explicit theory of the state and politics is necessary. We will argue that to study public policy formation, one must identify concretely the institutional apparatus of the state and who directly controls this apparatus. Similarly, it is of fundamental importance to identify the roles of the capitalist state (and education) in regard to the process of capital accumulation and social legitimation (Curtis, 1984).

Before we turn to discuss the notion of the state and policy making, we would like to assume that the capitalist state has a relative autonomy from the social classes, which seem to be recognized by Marxist and non-Marxist scholars alike (Archer and Vaughan, 1971: 56–60; Offe and Ronge, 1975; Bourdieu and Passeron, 1977: 199; Alvater, 1979; Skocpol, 1980: 155–201; Fritzel, 1987: 23–35). Indeed, this relative autonomy is structural and is built into the very foundations of the capitalist mode of production (Boron, 1982: 47). Similarly, we will assume that state intervention in civil society has become one of the state's crucial features, one that takes different forms in different countries and involves such diverse issues as: (a) the articulation and/or independence of the capitalist state and the bloc-in-power, to use the expression developed in Poulantzas' writings (Poulantzas, 1969a: 237–41); (b) the articulation of the state-subordinate class relationships; (c) the degree of direct and indirect state action in the regulation of capital accumulation (i.e., the state's role in the economy); (d) the state-nation relationship in the context of the World System (as a macrocosmic condensation of broader dynamics and strains built into this structural relationship, particularly in the case of peripheral dependent states); and (e) the issue of the crisis of the capitalist states, with its implications in terms of hegemony and legitimation processes.

State Authority and Policy Formation

The concept of the state has become a fashionable term in political science. However, many authors would refer to political authority and policy making as the role of the government or the public sector, and some may even be inclined to use a more comprehensive notion such as the "political system" rather than the state. This is not the place to argue on behalf of the usefulness of the concept. We shall point out that we share the rationale given by Daniel Levy (1986: 12–25) regarding the advantages of using the concept of the state.

We use the notion of the state first of all as a reaction against liberal-pluralist political approaches that, for many decades, worked within a "stateless" theoretical framework; and second in order to highlight particularly the role of the state as an actor in policy making with purposeful and relatively independent action while at the same time becoming a terrain where public policy is negotiated or fought over.

We propose to consider the state, at the highest level of abstraction, as a pact of domination and as a self-regulating administrative system. In analyzing peripheral capitalism, Fernando H. Cardoso has suggested that the state should be considered "the basic pact of domination that exists among social classes or factions of dominant classes and the norms which guarantee their dominance over the subordinate strata" (Cardoso, 1979:38). Similarly, German political scientist Claus Offe (1972a, 1972b, 1973, 1974, 1975a, 1975b, 1984) conceptualizes state-organized governance as a selective, event-generating system of rules, a sorting process (Offe, 1974: 37). Indeed, Cardoso's view is highly complementary to Offe's.

Offe views the state as comprising the institutional apparatuses, bureaucratic organizations, and formal and informal norms and codes that constitute and represent the "public" and "private" spheres of social life. The primary focus, then, is neither the interpersonal relations of various elites nor the decision-making process per se. Therefore, the class character of the state[1] does not reside ultimately in the social origin of the policy-makers, state managers, bureaucracy, or ruling class, but in the internal structure of the state apparatus itself due to its necessary selectivity of public policy, a selectivity that is "built into the system of political institutions" (Offe, 1974: 37).

In a similar vein, Goran Therborn identifies two main sources of determination of policy formation in the capitalist states. On the one hand, those determinations that originate at the level of state power (that is, the specific historical crystallization of relations of forces condensed into a pact of domination that acquires expression in a set of policies concerning the productive process), and, on the other hand, those determinations that originate in the structure of the state apparatus and the class bias of its organizational form (Clegg and Dunkerley, 1980: 433–80; Therborn, 1980: 144–79).

In summary, the emphasis here is on the dual character of the capitalist state and its organizational forms. That is to say, while the state claims to be the official representative of the nation as a whole,[2] it is at the same time the object, product, and determinant of class conflict. Through its policies directed toward the constitution and reproduction of the capitalist system, it is protected from various threats and guides its transformation; by acting as a factor of cohesion, the state's long-term planning synthesizes the goals of economic and social reproduction of capitalism as a system of commodity production, despite the sectoral or factional short-term needs and disputes of individual capitalist or corporative groups (Altvater, 1973; Offe, 1973; Skocpol, 1982: 7–28).

Having outlined in very abstract terms the use of the notion of the state, we turn now to examine a "social-conflict" theory of education before we advance a set of working hypotheses on the production rules of public policy.[3]

A Social-Conflict Theory of the State and Education

Class perspectives on educational policies and social change have been closely associated in recent years with the notion of *social reproduction*. Carnoy and Levin conclude that (a) educational policies and educational development can be better understood in the context of a wider social conflict (and as a result of previous conflicts and contradictions); (b) that knowledge (as a mean and an end) is a substantial and crucial part of such a process of struggle; and (c) that public education and the state are social arenas where the interest of the socially subordinate classes and the ruling elites conflict over the production, appropriation, and use of knowledge.

After carefully reviewing the salient changes in the nature of the process of work, in the patterns of constitution of social, cultural, and political struggles and social movements in industrial advanced societies; and in the process of educational reform—distinguishing between microtechnical and macrotechnical and micropolitical and macropolitical educational reforms—Carnoy and Levin conclude that

> According to our thesis, there are two major forces that mold the agenda of the schools: one presses for an education that will provide opportunity, mobility, equality, democratic participation, and the expansion of rights; the other presses for an education that will provide appropriately trained workers with the required skills, attitudes, and behavior for efficient production and capital accumulation. The struggle between these forces sets the larger framework within which the conventional politics of education is found. The struggle over democratic versus capitalist reforms must always be worked out at a concrete level by the dynamics of political interest groups and social movements. (Carnoy and Levin, 1985: 230)

In assessing Offe's account of the relation between education and the state, Carnoy and Levin conclude that his analysis is unidimensional because it sees education as the principle means of reproducing the capitalist relations of production while ensuring legitimacy through providing labor with better occupational opportunities (1985: 44).

What they see missing in Offe's argument is how to account for the power of capitalists in the media and/or "the power of social movements to alter the ideological conditions under which the state is forced to deal with labor and with capital" (1985: 45). For them the state is central to the definition and expression of capitalist class interests; however, they argue that the state bureaucracy is not only a third force operating with its own rationality (although subject to specific historical conditions), "but also the scene of conflict between both the dominating and the dominated classes and within within the dominating class, whose fractions compete to organize that class and establish its social dominance. The state not only develops its own dynamic, it is is subject to the competing dynamics of both a capitalist class attempting to reproduce capitalist relations of production and of social movements trying to expand their economic power and social and political rights" (1985: 46).

So, in short, they reject the notion of the state as an instrument of the ruling class or as possessing a sort of abstract power (state power) outside the class structure and dynamics. It is both "the place for the dominant class to organize itself strategically in relation to the dominated classes" (1985: 46) and an arena for struggle in which, given the proper political and historical conditions, social movements may prevail.

This notion of social conflict is the reproductive dynamic that shapes state practices in democratic capitalism. In terms of education the capitalist state can produce knowledge that protects the public and extends democratic control over private production. They argue that in this democratic dynamic with the state's use of knowledge for social reproduction,

> the state, including the educational system, is itself the political arena, schools are part of social conflict. Education is at once the result of contradictions and the source of new contradictions. It is an arena of conflict over the production of knowledge, ideology, and employment, a place where social movements try to meet their needs and business attempts to reproduce its hegemony. (Carnoy and Levin, 1985: 50)

In their model of educational change, Carnoy and Levin suggest that in order to understand the dynamic of the American educational system it should be viewed "as part of a much wider social conflict arising in the nature of capitalist production, with its inequalities of income and power. These inequalities lead to struggles by subordinate, relatively powerless groups for greater equality, economic security, and social control" (Carnoy and Levin, 1985: 24). Therefore, in democratic societies, these struggles usually take place in (or are played around) the state, which constitutes the space where social conflicts are located and where the dynamic of democratic transformation of the society find its deepest roots. Hence, the dynamics of American education (and every single democratic advanced capitalism based in parliamentary democracy) is that it is subjected to a tension, represented on one hand by a tradition and practice that creates inequality and, on the other hand, by a tradition and practice that seeks to promote democracy. The schema in figure 12.1 illustrates changing nature of social conflicts and its possible effects upon schooling.

FIGURE 12.1
Carnoy & Levin's model of the changing nature of the social conflict

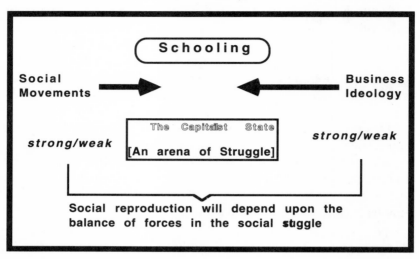

So, "Schooling is shaped by class structures and undemocratic capitalist production, but it is also shaped by the social conflict taking place over that injustice and over the political possibilities in a capitalist democracy of expanding democracy itself. Which of these movements dominates is determined by the larger social conflict and the relative political strength of the groups involved" (Carnoy and Levin, 1985: 25). This basic thesis substantiates a *theory of social conflict in education*, heavily influenced by class analysis but departing from it in many respects. The overall proposal of Carnoy and Levin (1985) is illustrated in figure 12.2.

Valuable as it is, the social-conflict model may present some theoretical and practical difficulties in understanding policy formation. The first one is how to operationalize the notion of the state in the context of the decentralized nature of the state in the United States and Canada. Does the notion of the state refers to the federal governments, the state governments, or the local boards of education, or to all three of these levels with regard to location, autonomy, and mandate?

Second, there is an implicit cyclical theory of history that assumes that neither contesting class can overcome the other, thus resulting in a kind of stand-off. So the problem is how to account for the

FIGURE 12.2
Analytical Model: The Capitalist State Education and the
Labor Process

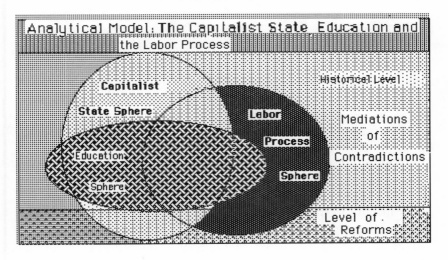

"partial" resolution of sectorial conflict in a point in time (e.g., the overreaching proposals for educational reform after the 1983 report *A Nation at Risk* and its impact in the educational establishment and pedagogical or academic thought on the role and functions of education). This tension is well captured by Michael Apple who, drawing upon the Thatcherite example that precipitated a crisis for British Marxism's faith in popular culture, points to the dangers of assuming an automatic connection between conflict and progressive change:[4]

> Whose knowledge, whose culture, whose common sense is made legitimate in our educational institutions? How does education function in the reproduction and subversion of cultural, political, and economic authority? How do we as educators understand these things? As you would imagine, this connection between knowledge and power is not easy relationship to understand, in part because it shifts as new social conditions later both the connection and our approaches to disclosing it. (Apple, 1990: 291)

Third, Carnoy and Levin work with a largely unexamined theory of polarized class structure, though a passing reference to Erik

Olin Wright suggests the theory they have in mind. At other times, however, they refer more generally to a more diverse complex of groups and interests than can be reduced to a bipolar class model. A strategic consequence is their failure to consider the implications of the middle strata for the process of struggle, a theme so central to social-closure theories such as those of Collins and Murphy.

Fourth, with the end of the sustained boom of the 1960s and early 1970s, economic crisis and the new role of the United States in the world system change the role of education dramatically. An important issue at stake here is how conceptions of state/education relations can be generalized from one advanced society to another (e.g., the United States versus Germany)?

This is related to the question of teacher loyalty. One of the principles is that in education, as an arena of struggle, teacher's groups will be part of these new social movements enhancing democracy. In times of financial retrenchment and conservative ideologies, what is the likelihood that teachers will join the democratic forces as opposed to those of order and restoration? A similar question was put to Michael Apple in these terms: "How can we discuss the creation of a transformative teacher who is part and parcel of a more comprehensive system of domination and control in the context of a metropolitan society in the context of the world system?" (Apple, 1990: 287). Ultimately his answer—in a fairly Gramscian fashion—is that one must "surround the imperial center not just outside the nation but inside it as well with alternate cultural and political forms. Thus our task is also to surround the relations of cultural exploitation at home and also build possibilities here. This, of course, involves concrete work at the level of pedagogy and curriculum to recapture our lost collective memories of successful struggles, and to continue the path that Raymond Williams so cogently called the long revolution" (Apple, 1990: 287).

Fifth, does this involve an implicit evolutionary conception of social movements that always assumes progressive change? Social movements can also by their very nature, (i.e., open democratic practice), bring about unforeseeable and unwanted outcomes (e.g., chaos and/or increased continuous conflict culminating in new forms of oppression to restore order). O'Donnell's *Modernization and Authoritarianism* (1982) argument in the context of dependent-development societies could be applied here. More modernization of the social structure may not enhance democracy but could instead bring about the praetorianization (activation) of the masses and eventually be met by new forms of repression. Another (related) issue is that the gains of social movements can be undermined by the ghettoization and fragmentation of movements when some demands are met in their most moderate form by state institutions, or because the movements own successes are subject to strategic divisions and splits between economic/corporative or ethical/normative grounds among the coalition groups (Apple, 1990: 305).

After these theoretical explorations and with these qualifications in mind, a number of production rules in public policy can be identified and studied. As opposed to the more historically specific analysis of Carnoy and Levin, we propose to focus on the more generic rules underlying policy formation viewed as the outcome of social conflicts of the type they have described (with the problems noted above) for the United States.

PRODUCTION RULES OF PUBLIC POLICY: A THEORETICAL ASSESSMENT AND HYPOTHESIS

Is Public Policy Formation Mainly a Response to or an Anticipation of Social Threats?

At the highest level of generalization, the first hypothesis advanced here will stress that any mode of state intervention is linked to a changing pattern of potential or actual threats, or to structural problems that emerge out of the process of accumulation of capital. Thus, the modes of state activity[5] (which will be identified in the next section) can be seen as responses to these social threats and problems (Offe, 1975b: 137–47; O'Donnell, 1978a, 1978b, 1982; Wright, 1978: 277; Curtis, 1984: 12).

Obviously, this pattern of perceived social threat and state response should not be taken mechanically. As Goran Therborn has so aptly argued in studying the origins of welfare-state policies in Europe and the strengthening of class activism:

> What is being argued is (1) that a threat from the working-class movement, perceived by the political rulers, was a necessary (but not sufficient) condition for welfare-state initiatives; (2) that there is a structural affinity between the first major welfare-state initiatives and the modern labour movement; and (3) that there is a chronological relationship between the emergence of the modern labour movement and the beginning of the welfare state,

which makes it probable that there is a causal link between the two, the nature of which remains to be demonstrated. (Therborn, 1984: 12)

However, after saying that, Therborn claims that there is always a certain tension between the identified historical processes and the analytical categories used for its study. Arguing that public policy is made out of opposing social-policy perspectives, he cautiously emphasizes that

the forms and principles of public social commitments have been politically controversial. These controversies have not been merely conjunctural, and have not only pitted individual politicians or civil servants and political parties and interest groups against each other. They have also developed along class lines, and the various specific issues are to a significant degree intelligible in terms of opposite class perspectives. Classes are not decision-making bodies, which is a fundamental reason why policy making is inherently irreducible to class conflict and class power. Yet a class analysis provides an explanatory framework that can make the study of politics and policy into something more than a modernized *histoire événementielle* of strings and episodes acted out by individual policy-makers. (Therborn, 1984: 25)

The extent to which these changing social patterns of threats alter not only public policy formation but also the very same form of the capitalist state is not our immediate concern here. However, there seem to be certain affinities between the perceived pattern of threat and the pattern of state response/transformation. For example, recent political sociology argues that the emergence of a highly repressive form of political regime (e.g., the bureaucratic-authoritarian state in Latin America), is causally related to the internalization of the production in Latin America and the perceived threats from the subordinate social classes. Guillermo O'Donnell argues that the emergence of such regimes is linked to a particular phase or crisis of capital accumulation encountered in the maturation of dependent, industrializing economies. In short, this is the phase in which "easy" import-substitution possibilities have been exhausted and further expansion seems to depend upon new investments in capital intensive, technologically advanced industries. Included with this "economic framework" of the explanation is an increased activation of the popular sector and working classes that threatens the political stability of the capitalist regime (what political scientist Samuel Huntington has termed the "praetorianiza-tion" of the masses); finally, there is an increased importance of technocratic roles in the State. The evolution of these two major variables, namely, the "deepening of industrialization" and the so-called "background variables," lead the societal situation to an elective affinity between advanced industrialization and bureau-cratic authoritarianism (Collier, 1979: 3–26, 380; O'Donnell, 1982).

Why is this issue of social threats so important, and how are they dealt with by advanced capitalist states? The so-called Ger-man Debate (Holloway and Piccioto, 1979: 19–31; Jessop, 1982; Carnoy, 1984) will give us some clues. A prominent participant in this debate, Eltmar Altvater, pointed out that capital is unable, as a result of its existence as many factionalized and mutually antago-nistic capitalists, to produce the social preconditions of its own existence. State interventionism is derived (deduced) as a particular state form working toward shortening and overcoming those defi-ciencies of private capital by organizing individuals into a viable body (namely, a general capitalist interest).

Altvater derives the nature of state interventionism from the four general functions of the State which he has envisaged:

> There are essentially four areas in which the State is primarily active, namely, (1) the provision of general material conditions of production ("infrastructure"); (2) establishing and guaranteeing general legal relations, through which the relationships of legal subjects in capitalist society are performed; (3) the regulation of the conflict between wage labour and capital and, if necessary, the political repression of the working class, not only by means of law but also by the police and the army; (4) safeguarding the existence and expansion of total national capital on the capitalist world market. (Altvater, 1979: 42)

Claus Offe not only explicitly recognizes his agreement with Altvater (Offe, 1973a: 110) in their mutual criticism of the State Monopoly Capitalism Thesis (STATEMOP Thesis).[6] He also adds to Altvater's formulation that state domination should be under-stood as a regulating system or as a system of filters with the specific selective mechanisms of (a) extracting a general class inter-est from many fractionalized capital units, and (b) oppressing or suppressing any anticapitalist interest that could arise in any cap-italist social formation (Offe, 1975b: 125–44).

Hence, social threats are dealt with by social policies and state institutions as part of this preventive and regulative role of the state. In regard to these state functions, Therborn's comment on the need to look at the state's everyday routines would show a fundamental activity that has not been highlighted so far: the welfare activities that seem to dominate everyday state routine (Therborn, 1984: 32). In support of this, Therborn shows that since education is at the core of welfare policies—and since education and also health systems are labour intensive, they employ a sizable majority of the total public servants—school employees in 1970, at the time of the Vietnam War and for the first time since the United States turned into an imperial world power, became significantly more numerous than military and civilian defense personnel (Therborn, 1984: 35). A similar argument could be developed for a dependent society such as Mexico, where slightly more than half of the total increase in federal employment between 1970 and 1976 was allocated to education (Torres, 1984: 156).

In societies in social transformation, recent research (Carnoy and Torres, 1990: 315–57) has shown that, on the one hand, a new political regime must respond to mass demands for more schooling, better health care, and the redistribution of agricultural land. On the other hand, a fundamental task of these regimes is to accumulate capital in order to expand the national material base. It seems that while, hypothetically, social demands and the accumulation of capital are complementary since healthier, more educated people will have higher productivity and therefore will increase output, to choose one to the relative exclusion of the other may mean, in the worst case, to risk failure of the political project itself. Carnoy, Samoff, and their coworkers (Carnoy and Samoff, 1990) have demonstrated how in all of the case studies (which included Cuba, Nicaragua, China, Tanzania and Mozambique), the expansion of public services such as education and health care also have ideological implications, and that the legitimacy of the State in both low- and high-income countries is therefore affected by its capability to deliver such services to the population at large.

Patterns of State Authority and Modes and Methods of State Intervention

Claus Offe recognizes four main guiding patterns of state action. First, *exclusion*: since the state has no authority to order production or to control it, the state and accumulation are somehow divorced in such a way that production and accumulation cannot be separated. Second, *maintenance*: the state does not have the authority but rather has the mandate to create and sustain conditions of accumulation as well as to avoid, regulate, or repress social threats. Threats may come from other accumulating units (e.g., interfirm, interindustry and international competition), from non-capitalist entities (e.g. the working class, social movements), or from criminal or "deviant" behavior. Third, *dependency*: the power relationship of the capitalist state and its main decision-making powers depend, as do any other relationships in capitalist society, upon the presence and continuity of the accumulation process. Four, *legitimacy*: a last guiding pattern of state activity is the legitimation function of the capitalist state. The state can only function as a capitalist state by appealing to symbols and sources of support which conceal its true nature (Offe, 1975b: 126, 127). In a more crude economic analysis of the advanced capitalist societies, Offe has suggested a structural discrepancy between abstract, surplus-value—related forms and concrete, use-value—related forms used in the implementation of state functions. Thus, this discrepancy can be maintained, if not solved, over time only by a system of legitimacy. Indeed, it is likely that as state power acquires more functions, it also requires an increase in legitimation (Offe, 1973b: 74).

Considering the above-mentioned fundamental parameters of state intervention, what remains to be clarified is the analytical distinction between modes of state intervention and methods of state intervention. The former refers to state action vis-à-vis state-expected functions under the logic of commodity production, while the latter refers to a somehow abstract analytical distinction that embraces those several state alternatives (methods) to choose from in the process of public policy formation.

The principal modes of state intervention can be divided into allocative modes and productive modes. Offe has proposed the following schematic description of these types of activities:

1. *Allocative*: (a) allocation of state-owned resources; (b) response to demands and laws ("politics"); (c) demands that are positive and specific in regard to time, space, group, type, and amount of state resources; and (d) decisions reached by politics.

2. *Productive*: (a) production of inputs of accumulation (organized production process required) in response to perceived threats to accumulation; (b) conflicting or incompletely articulated de-

mands that cannot be eliminated without threatening the overall process of accumulation; (c) decisions reached by policies based on state-generated decision rules (Offe, 1975b: 133).

Using allocative activities, the state creates and maintains the conditions of accumulation by means that simply require the allocation of resources that are already under state control (e.g., taxes, repressive forces, land, mass media). The productive mode represents state action that supplies a variable and a constant capital that the units of private capital are unable to produce. Beyond areas of competence or types of policies considered, what really differentiates these two modes is that the allocative mode is usually controlled and thereby reinterpreted by its inputs, while the productive mode is generally controlled and thereby evaluated by its outputs (Offe, 1972a: 128).

The principal methods of state intervention are the following: (a) state regulation through a set of positive and negative sanctions connected with a certain behavior of social categories (e.g., bureaucracy) or social classes; (b) infrastructure investment either as a partial or supplementary method to private capital activity (e.g., building roads, bridges, airports) or as a total method with which to replace private capital activity (e.g., the case of mass public compulsory education in some countries, law enforcement, or the administration of justice); in these cases, the participation of private initiative is negligible in terms of the amount of investment and the probability of a high and consistent degree of control of systemic outcomes); and (c) participation as the codetermination of policy making and policy operation through consent building in decision-making bodies that incorporate several interest groups or corporative units.

Considering these modes and methods, it is important to propose a second hypothesis regarding the process of policy formation. Thus far, it has been suggested that the state's motivational force is the pursuit of an abstract systemic interest rather than any particular interest; however, it is equally important to distinguish between short-term, conjunctural processes and long-term, historical or organic processes in policy formation. The Gramscian dictum is in this regard very insightful and clear, and deserves to be quoted at length:

A common error in historical-political analysis consists in an inability to find the correct relation between what is organic and what is conjunctural. This leads to presenting causes as immediately operative which in factor only operate indirectly, or to asserting that the immediate causes are the only effective ones. In the first case, there is an excess of "economism," or doctrinary pedantry, in the second an excess of "ideologism." In the first case there is an overestimation of mechanical causes, in the second an exaggeration of the voluntarist and individual element. The distinction between "organic" movements and facts, and "conjunctural" or occasional ones must be applied to those in which a regressive development or an acute crisis takes place, but also to those in which there is a progressive development or one towards prosperity, or which the productive forces are stagnant. The dialectical nexus between the two categories of movement, and therefore research, is hard to establish precisely. (Gramsci, 1971: 178)

Are the "Form" and the "Content" of Policy Making Two Distinct Dimensions?

A third working hypothesis regards the distinction between form and content in the production rules of public policy, which results from the same analytical distinction between deep/surface structure models of rules. For instance, in analyzing welfare-state politics, Therborn has argued that: "One important reason for the intricate complexity of welfare-state history is the fact that public social-policy commitments can take a number of different forms, and questions of form have often aroused more controversy and conflict than the principle of public social responsibility per se" (Therborn, 1984: 16).

First of all, at a lower level of abstraction, it is not to be expected that a situation in which a stated intention of a policy and its actual outcome faithfully coincide could ever be found. Even though at first glance this point seems to be a trivial one, nonetheless it prevents a formal comparison—so common in educational studies—between the state's alleged goals and the practical outcomes, sometimes expressed as the differences between government's rhetoric and real results. In general, such comparisons are too formal and generic to be worthwhile. Therefore, there will always be a gap between what is declared, what is implemented, and what is the actual policy outcome.

Second, at a highest level of abstraction, if the rationality behind a policy decision is treated as an analysis of language-in-use, any conversation will have a basic grammar, but the linguistic rules will not have entire control over the quality, intensity, and meaning of the message. Similarly, "the organization structure can be conceived in terms of the selectivity rules which can be analytically constructed as an explanation of its social action and practice (its surface detail, what it does). The rules collected together, may be conceived of as a mode of rationality" (Clegg, 1979: 122). This mode of rationality, that is, expressing selectivity rules, could be of different origins. Clegg has distinguished four types of rules: technical rules (know-how to carry out a particular administrative task), social regulative rules (any intervention to repair social solidarity in an organization, such as the implementation of human relations), extra-organizational rules (e.g., discriminatory practices based in racism, sexism, etc.), and strategic rules (social contracts, and wages and income policies).

It should be mentioned in passing that an example of a related type of analysis, although applied to education discourses (which influence and inform educational policies), can be found in Giroux when he compares different views of cultural production, pedagogical analysis, and political action in the teacher-student experiences. Giroux distinguishes different pedagogical discourses (or logics-in-use in education), namely the discourse of management and control, the discourse of relevance and integration (progressivism), and the discourse of cultural politics—critical affirmative language; hence, using Giroux's terminology, a discourse that moves from a language of criticism to a language of possibilities (Giroux, 1985: 22–41).

In short, the distinction between form and content of public policy is similar and related to the distinctions between rationality and social action, and between deep/surface structures. In fact, if we take into account all the possible combinations of different selectivity rules (and the fact that all of them may be coexistent at some point, or conversely, given a particular historical and organizational setting, one may predominate over the rest) with inputs (including rationalities), processes of transformation, and outputs (including social action) of policy, a simple distinction of form and content will vanish in front of our eyes; every policy form may or may not have a particular policy content if we take into account selectivity rules.

Is the State a Problem-Solving Agent?

As a result of these theoretical explorations, the fourth hypothesis rejects the notion of the state as simply a problem-solving agent, an approach that in general places too much emphasis on the analysis of policy content and on the predominance of "technical rules" among selectivity rules. The main assumptions of this common approach to policy making are the following: (i) the state seems to be analyzing those processes that occur in the political arena, and through a diagnosis of the chief problems, organizes its political agenda for action; (ii) from this standpoint, it is important for researchers to focus mainly upon which interests are involved in the determination of policy making; and (iii) as soon as this identification has been done, the corollary of the analysis will be to check those interests against the material outcomes and the distribution of tangible benefits that result from policies and implementation (Lindblom, 1968: 12, 13). In general, these shared assumptions are used in the basic approaches to policy planning in education, including such areas as the estimation of social demand, needs analysis, manpower planning, cost-effectiveness analysis, or rate-of-return analysis (Russell, 1980: 1–15; Simmons, 1980: 15– 33; Weiler, 1980).

Is Social Control Built into the Selectivity Rules?

A fifth hypothesis suggests that any organizational structure has controls that are built into the system of political institutions. Following Clegg, an "organization-structure" is a set of sedimented (i.e., historically laid down and superimposed) selection rules: "The organization-structure can be conceptualized as a structure of sedimented selection rules. Those prescribe the limits within which the organization-structure might vary" (Clegg, 1979: 97). Furthermore, those rules of policy formation depend upon the main guiding patterns of state action, the main state resources to carry out its functions, and the principal modes of state intervention.

The central guiding patterns of state activity have been identified as (a) exclusion, (b) maintenance, (c) dependency, and (d) legitimacy. The political puzzle, then, for the capitalist state, is how to reconcile those patterns in the production of public policy; we have maintained, following Offe, that the motivational and structural force underlying policy making is the attempt to reconcile these four elements. To carry on its functions, the state resorts to four principal means: fiscal policies, administrative rationality, law enforcement and repression (which should not be considered only as a special case of administrative rationality), and mass loyalty. In the case of the dependent state,[7] perhaps the most significant feature is that the exercise of coercion and organized repression overlaps (and sometimes will have more prominence than) the other three standard means.

These main resources enable the capitalist state to perform its principal roles of executing preventive crisis management; determining priorities embodied in social needs, social threats, and civil-society problem areas (for example, in Canada, a typical case of a problem area is the native question); and devising a long-term avoidance strategy for further threats and conflicts. In this regard, contradictions can no longer be plausibly interpreted simply as class antagonism. They must, as Offe insists, at least be regarded as necessary by-products of an integral political system of control (Offe, 1975a: 4–5). To this extent, the fiscal crisis of the state,[8] which appears to be the inevitable consequence of the structural gap between state expenditure and revenues, is at the same time a lively testimony and expression of systemic constraints.

Can Functional Interaction and Interdependency Be Differentiated According to Different Political Regimes?

A last hypothesis will stress that the different forms of functional interaction and interdependency within a bureaucratic organization can be analytically differentiated; and similarly, the form that this interaction assumes will vary according to the type of political regime considered.

For instance, Oscar Oszlak, in analyzing political regimes in Latin America, has identified three main types: bureaucratic-authoritarian, democratic-liberal, and patrimonialist. Similarly, Oszlak identifies three main types of bureaucratic interdependency: hierarchical, functional, and material or budgetary (Oszlak, 1980).

It would be necessary to identify and carefully characterize the type of political regime and capitalist state, and which dominant form of bureaucratic interdependency comes into the discussion.

Production Rules of Policy Formation: A Summary

1. The capitalist state has been defined as an arena, a product, and a determinant of class and social conflict. Hence, any mode of state intervention is linked to a changing pattern of threats, potential or actual, or to structural problems that emerge out of the process of capital accumulation and political domination. Particularly in dependent states, but also in industrial advanced social formations, class struggle and the political practice of social movements give shape to the state structure at the same time that an institutionalized set of selectivity rules alter the intensity, degree, and level (character) of class and social conflict. Two implications can be drawn. On the one hand, the form and content of state policies give shape to the forms and content of the class and social struggles, while, conversely, class and social struggles are shaping the form and content of state policies (Sardei-Bierman et al., 1973: 60–69). On the other hand, there is a practical tension between consensus-oriented practices and coercion-oriented practices in the planning and implementation of state policies.

2. There are modes and methods of state intervention that deal with those patterns and threats raised in the class and social struggles; the former (divided into allocative and productive modes) refers to a wide range of probable activities regarding the use of state resources while the latter (distinguishing between state regulations, infrastructure investment, and participation) refers to the range of probable courses of action undertaken by the state. Both methods and modes of state intervention give substance to the process of public policy formation.

3. At the most abstract level, the main determinant of public policy formation is not the pursuit of any particular interest, but of an abstract systemic interest. Nonetheless, two different kinds of historical processes underpin public policy. On the one hand, there are structural determinants, which have a historical-organic origin; on the other hand, there are conjunctural determinants, which do represent, at a particular point in time, the short-term crystallization of a peculiar constellation of forces in class and social struggles.

4. Particularly in liberal-democratic societies, the state will always try to reconcile its contradictory guiding patterns of activity within a concrete corpus of state policies. Then, the process of policy formation will never reach a steady-state situation nor will it be completely coherent; it will always express conflicts, imbalances, contradictions and a fragile stability in policy formation.

5. In this regard, there will always be a gap between the publicly stated goals and targets of state policies and the actual outcomes, as well as a practical and analytical difference between rationalities (as selectivity rules) and social action. Then, to consider the state (and state policies) as only a problem-solving agent would be grossly misleading. However, this seems to be the dominant approach in educational policy planning. This framework of the state as a problem-solving agent (needless to say, an argument usually advanced by technocratically minded and not historically minded scholars and administrators) fails to recognize the internally produced and the externally originated determinants of policies—especially those with the most causal weight in nonstatistical terms. Secondly, this framework omits the display of the basic regularities, what Offe has termed the basic "laws" of public policy formation.

6. By combining the modes and methods of state intervention, three main laws of motion of public policy can be suggested here. These are the law of motion of bureaucracy, the purposive-action law of motion, and the participatory—consensus-building law of motion. In order to study these policy laws of motion, it would be necessary to consider not only a political framework and a theory of the state, but also an organizational approach to policy making. In this regard, any public policy, in its form and content, is bounded by a system of inputs, processes of transformation, and outputs, all of them related to deep/surface structures (rationales) expressing not only social action but domination and power.

7. Looking particularly at the dependent state, a decisive landmark is the state's bureaucratic encapsulation of policy making. In this sense, there are different forms of functional interaction within a bureaucratic organization; those forms of interaction can be analytically differentiated; and the form this interaction assumes will vary according to the type of political regime considered. This point leads us to recognize several common traits in the historical evolution of state apparatuses—for example in Latin America (Os-

zlak, 1981: 3–32)—traits that are of paramount importance in the study of educational policy formation in a corporatist state such as the Mexican state, with the complex interaction among a ruling party in power for more than forty years, the forceful action of corporative trade unions and capitalist associations, and the ideology of efficiency held by the organic bureaucracy of the state (Pescador and Torres, 1985).

8. Since capitalism did develop differentially in each country, the configuration of the state will sharply differ across countries. We have assumed here that it is crucial to characterize the type of state, its historical traits and main features as a mode of political control and political organization, and the balance of power established in the society by the ongoing confrontation between social and political forces, prior to undertaking an empirical analysis of educational policy making. Without such a historical and political background, it would be difficult to understand the particular rationale of resource assignment and the underlying motives for the creation (or elimination) of institutions, services, plans, or policies. By considering a theory of the state and education, it has been possible to assess in detailed fashion the politics of educational policy making, and policy making as politics.

SUMMARY AND CONCLUSIONS

In summary, if the main concern is to study policy formation, a preliminary attempt to do so should offset such distinct analytical dimensions as (1) the state's goals and policy targets (the social history of state apparatus and the ebb and flow of class and social struggle); (2) modes and methods of operation in educational policy formation in dealing with social threats or problems that arise out of capital accumulation problems and/or political legitimation practices, policies, and outputs; (3) the extent and type of bureaucratic organization; (4) the educational bureaucracy's ideologies contained in policy planning (as internal determinants of policy making); (5) material and nonmaterial policy outcomes (perhaps a fundamental issue that ought to be discussed from a post-Marxist perspective is the role of education [and welfare activities in general] in the production and reproduction of productive and unproductive labor, and education's contribution to production and realization of surplus-values); (6) capitalist and noncapitalist units of policy formation (Clegg and Dunkerley, 1980: 486–92), which brings to light the important distinction between use value and exchange value as distinct goals of policy making in education (and other welfare activities and institutions); (7) the role of the educational policy within the overall state public policy, particularly (although not exclusively) at the level of legitimation practices (for instance, Miller [1986: 244] classifies within accumulation expenditures for social investment the levels and modalities of higher education and other nonelementary or secondary school education; elementary and secondary education's expenditures are classified under accumulation expenditures for social consumptions—perhaps adult and nonformal education expenditures, always neglected by the analysts, can also be classified, following O'Connor's original taxonomy as social expenses); and (8) the struggles by groups and social classes to resist the hegemonic practices of the capitalist state. However, if resistance groups have some visible presence and are somehow inserted within the state apparatus, the task will then be to study how they have tried to consolidate or enlarge their position, and to promote specific policies, in the presence of restricting and enabling rules.

CHAPTER 13

Education, Race, and Gender: Towards a Critical Modernist Perspective

THE INTERPLAY OF CLASS, GENDER, AND RACE: CRITIQUES OF CLASS REDUCTIONISM AND THE EMERGENT CRITICAL MODERNIST CONSENSUS

The importance of structuralist Marxism, and the related notion of a correspondence principle between economic and cultural life, was that it facilitated the shift from the base/superstructure model to that of social reproduction as a way of understanding Marx's method and theory of society. To be sure, this theme was already apparent in a somewhat different form in early Frankfurt critical theory and in Gramsci's cultural Marxism. But it was Althusser's structuralist Marxism that provided the catalyst for a fundamental transformation of theories of education (and culture), as we have discussed in our previous chapters. Of more immediate concern here are the poststructuralist theories of educational reproduction that attempt to avoid the hyperfunctionalism and class reductionism still evident in the structuralist correspondence principle and related theories of social class.

The influences that have contributed to the rethinking class and its relation to educational reproduction have been multiple: neo-Weberian theory,[1] contemporary Frankfurt critical theory,[2] the first phase of French poststructuralism,[3] British (neo-Gramscian) cultural studies,[4] and contributions voicing more directly the experiences and perspectives of women,[5] racial minorities, and others whose domination could not be subsumed under traditional class categories (Miles, 1989; Omi and Winant, 1986).

A first consequence of these developments has been that empirical studies based on theories of reproduction increasingly focus on the contingent aspects of state action. Theories of educational reproduction that seek to escape the circularity of functionalist methodology must focus on the state as the context within which social groups actively struggle to reproduce or transform existing relations between society and education (Carnoy, 1984; Torres, 1990).

A second consequence has been a pluralization of the bases of potential domination, namely, *a critique of class reductionism.* On the one hand, this kind of analysis runs the risk of so diluting the analysis of domination as to invoke an infinite plurality of sources of conflict.[6] On the other hand, however, there has been an emerging focus on the interplay of three sources of domination: class, gender, and ethnic group/race. One could add other dimensions of reproduction such as age, urban/rural distinctions, nonracial ethnicity, or minority religious affiliations, but these are not categories that have typically lent themselves to be systematically incorporated in system-threatening social movements oriented toward inclusion of multiple voices, narratives, and experiences, and the redressing of inequities.[7] Nevertheless, in specific historical contexts these other forms of exclusion may move to center stage.

A third consequence of the resulting critiques of early reproduction theory was the emergence of theories of *resistance* that could account for the possibilities of change. This required a theory of social action that endowed subjects with at least the potential for transformative action, a theme closely related to "new social movements" theory. Though enjoying particular prominence in critical pedagogy, this theme was part of a more general rethinking of popular culture, structure, and agency in critical social theory. Within critical social theory the key step has been reconceptualizing society in terms of the distinction between analysis at the level of "systems integration" as opposed to "social integration," a strategy shared by both Habermas and Giddens.[8] Classic social-reproduction theory of the type proposed by Althusser operated exclusively at the level of systemic analysis, hence reducing agents to passive, interpellated "subjects." In contrast, purely interpretive, hermeneutic, and humanistic sociologies have focused on the social action of individuals and groups (social integration) at the expense of an analysis of systemic contradictions. The methodological consequences of linking systemic and social-action analysis in critical theories have been twofold: attention to the agency-structure dialectic in analyzing processes of social and cultural reproduction; and a turn to historically specific (though often explicitly comparative) and ethnographic investigations capable of integrating, generalizing, and case-study analysis—something quite distinct from the neo-Foucauldian opposition of the universal and local, *as if* regional analysis could dispense with generalizing (though not in the sense of ahistorical, invariant laws) social theory.[9]

What is at stake here is the issue of broadening the theory of class as part of a more general *theory of power and domination*. Classic approaches to class and reproduction theory depend upon a utilitarian conception of self-interest based on class structure. For example, Wright puts it as follows:

> If class structure is understood as a terrain of social relations that determine objective material interests of actors and class struggle is understood as the form of social practice which attempts to realize these interests then class consciousness can be understood as the subjective processes that shape intentional choices with respect to those interests and struggles. (1985: 246, cited in Clegg, 1989: 112)

But as Clegg notes, given that these interests are conceived as "objective," how is it that the misrecognition of them occurs routinely? Notions of ideology and hegemony are invoked to explain the process of ideological incorporation into the dominant ideology. But this also begs the question of why it is the working class that is the focus of attention, rather than other interested collectivities. The issue here goes back to the problematic status of objective interests and their diversity.

As we have argued, this issue cannot be resolved theoretically in a deterministic synthesis, but suggests a dialogue between historically specific theoretical formulations and the practices of actors in defining their collective aspirations in a more or less democratic public sphere. To the degree that the latter is absent or partial, theory necessarily makes claims relating to notion of false—or at least falsifying—consciousness, even though this does not justify claims to theoretical absolutism.

The plurality of forms of domination thus poses the question of how to articulate different aspects with respect to a theories of social reproduction. One foundation for this mode of inquiry can be found in neo-Weberian conflict theories, which are not ordinarily included in discussions of reproduction theories, with the partial exception of social-closure theory as found in Bourdieu. As Weber stressed, the original Marxist focus on class at the level of the relations of production could not adequately account for the contribution of various forms of domination evident at the level of market relations and the competition for scarce resources. More recent developments of this insight under the heading of social-closure theory have attempted to reconcile this critique with an awareness of the crucial importance of the link between exclusionary processes and the specific form of production relations (Murphy, 1988; Manza, 1992).

A second impetus for such reformulations derives from post-structuralist critiques of Marxism and other essentializing forms of social analysis, especially the work of Foucault (Poster, 1989). The resulting strategies of interpretation have proved productive in re-reading Frankfurt critical theory and Gramscian theory in particular, calling into question class reductionism from various perspectives under the heading of a "post-Marxist" critique of hegemony theory (Laclau and Mouffe, 1985; Laclau, 1990) or critical theory.[10] But these development were in turn strongly influenced by the spirited interventions of feminist and race theorists against class reductionism. Let us consider these debates in the context of education.

The interplay among class, race, and gender and its contribution to social reproduction has emerged only recently as an *integrated* research endeavor in the sociology of education (as opposed to separate treatments). It is not surprising, therefore, that a special issue of *Sociology of Education* (1989, vol. 62, January) on women, race, and educational experiences included five articles written by assistant professors. One may argue that it may be the result of a specific editorial policy to promote junior scholars, but it is more probable this also reflects a shift of research focus that preoccupies a new generation of scholars. Previously, particularly in the United States, there was a tendency for issues of class, race, and gender to be pursued as more or less *independent* topics without adequate concern over their interrelationships.

As Grant and Sleeter have shown on the basis of a survey of the education literature from 1973–1983 (Grant and Sleeter, 1986; Grant and Sleeter, 1988), these issues were largely treated separately. As they also note, however, the theoretical problems of such research had been pointed out by the early 1980s in British cultural studies, as well as by Aronowitz, Giroux and others in North America. Within educational theory, a similar position was developed by Giroux and Apple (Apple and Weis, 1983; McCarthy and Apple, 1988; Aronowitz and Giroux, 1991). As Giroux aptly notes,

> oppositional behaviors are produced amidst contradictory discourses and values. The logic that informs a given act of resistance may, on the one hand, be linked to interests that are class-, gender- or race-specific. On the other hand, it may express the repressive moments inscribed in such behavior by the dominant culture rather than a message of protest against their existence . . . The failure to include women and racial minorities in such studies has resulted in a rather uncritical theoretical tendency to romanticize modes of resistance even when they contain reactionary racial and gender views. The irony here is that a large amount of neo-Marxist work on resistance, although allegedly committed to emancipatory concerns, ends up contributing to the reproduction of sexist and racist attitudes and practices. (Aronowitz and Giroux, 1985:101–2)[11]

Similarly, responding to the critics of Geoff Whitty's *Sociology and School Knowledge* (1985), Michael Apple situates himself in relation to the neo-Marxist tradition, but does so in a manner that shows his awareness of the difficulties of classical Marxism in the treatment of class, race, and gender.[12] Eventually this position is defined as a "nonsynchronous parallelist"—a position that will be discussed below—one that requires a break with Marxist orthodox class theory (McCarthy and Apple, 1988):

> A paradigm case in point here is the criticism leveled against traditional Marxist interpretations by feminist authors. Many of their arguments have been devastating to orthodox assertions . . . so much so that many people on the left believe that any attempt at understanding our social formation that does not combine *in an unreductive way* analyses of class and gender together is only half a theory at best . . . The same, of course, needs to be said of race as well. *The rejection of major aspects of the received orthodox Marxist tradition and the emerging sensitivity to the truly constitutive nature of gender and race demonstrate not a weakness but the continued growth and vitality of a tradition of critical analysis that is attempting to deal honestly and openly with the complexity of life under present conditions of domination and exploitation.* (Apple, 1986: 320–321, emphasis added)

As McCarthy and Apple point out, this parallelist approach (a notion comparable to but more inclusive than the notion of "dualist" used in feminist theory) is now broadly shared by critical researchers:

> Though subject to debate, it has become one of the more generally accepted positions in the critical community. It holds that at least *three* dynamics are essential in understanding schools and other institutions. These dynamics are race, gender, and class. None are reducible to the others. Class is not necessarily primary. The parallelist position has also led to a reevaluation of economically reductive explanations as well. The economy *is* exceptionally powerful; this *is* capitalism after all. But, rather than economy explaining all, critically oriented researchers have argued that there are three spheres of social life—economic, political, and cultural. These too are in continual interaction. These are, in essence, arenas in which class, race, and gender dynamics operate. Unlike base-superstructure models, it is also assumed that action in one can sometimes have an effect on actions in the another. The result is a theory of *overdetermination,* in which the processes and outcomes of teaching and learning and of school in general are produced by the constant interactions among three dynamics in three spheres. (McCarthy and Apple, 1988: 23)

Apple's reference to British debates is not accidental, given his recognition of the significance of the interrogation of orthodox Marxist assumption in British cultural studies, especially of Stuart Hall with regard to race (Hall, 1986), E.P. Thompson with respect to class consciousness as lived-experience (Kaye and McClelland, 1990), and Angela McRobbie, Michèle Barrett, and others on women's oppression and feminist Marxism (Hamilton and Barrett, 1986).

Without making a strong priority claim, it can be argued that the earlier and broader reception of class-based reproduction theory in Britain led to an earlier debate on the limits of class reductionism, a process that can be broadly associated with the maturation of the cultural studies tradition (Brantlinger, 1990: 108–98). But our particular concern has been with tracing some of the key issues posed by critiques of conventional reproduction theory on the part of socialist feminist theorists and theorists of race. In particular we wished to explore some of the continuing *difficulties* with parallelist models, a question that can be initially approached through issues posed in feminist theory. The central problem of parallelist models is an excessive openness that tends to obscure the internal systematic connections among these three otherwise quite distinct and autonomous modes of domination.

Finally, it is important to remember that despite our focus on state-education relations, educational arenas as sites of reproduction cannot be completely separated from the others with which they are intertwined in the overall process of cultural reproduction, especially such dynamic domains as the mass media and religious movements. Indeed, this is perhaps the greatest challenge that lies ahead for an integral theory of educational reproduction: a theoretical and practical rearticulation of its analyses with the overall dynamic of societal reproduction and potentials for transformation, a theme hinted at in the more recent work of Giroux and his collaborators (Giroux and Simon, 1989) in taking up the question of popular culture. But the theoretical unification of a critical cultural studies with a theory of educational reproduction as a central theme remains on the distant horizon. We turn now to discuss race and gender in social and cultural reproduction.

RACE AND EDUCATIONAL REPRODUCTION

> Unless these questions [related to racism] are raised simultaneously with those of class and sex, the abolition of conditions for the reproduction of capitalist relations of production is beyond realization. (Aronowitz, 1981: 76)

Macrosociological theories of race and ethnic relations have been defined in terms of the "confrontation of Marxism, Weberian forms of class analysis and the theory of the plural society" (Rex and Mason, 1986: ix). A central theme of this chapter will be that, much as in the theory of social stratification generally, the differences between contemporary neo-Marxist approaches and neo-Weberian ones have narrowed significantly in a manner anticipated in other areas by critical social theory. From the perspective of theories of social reproduction, we will characterize this as a shift from closed economic models to multidimensional open ones.

Though our discussion will focus on race, this should not be taken to detract from the potential significance of ethnicity (and

closely related religious aspects of identity) as a form of domination in particular instances. The tragic collapse of Yugoslavia in
ethnically-based civil war provides a sobering reminder of the continuing significance of such issues. There is some justification for a
focus on race, however, given the persistence of racial antagonisms
and the manner in which they are reflected in systems of inequality
and forms of injustice. Though ethnic regional minorities still often
aspire to complete independence, and such ethnic struggles continue to be sites of violence (e.g., Ireland, Basque separatists, etc.),
liberal democracies have proven capable of incorporating ethnic
minorities in a plural society in ways that have significantly narrowed the gap in educational equalities. It is difficult, however, to
point to such relative success stories where race has been a significant factor, most often related to patterns of immigration and
different policies with respect to the citizenship status and educational opportunities available.

The question of race and ethnicity (along with that of gender)
was virtually impossible to deal with in the context of classic
Marxist theories of either base/superstructure or those of structural Marxism. More recently, however, a burgeoning literature on
"Marxism" and "race" has provided various responses that involve fundamental modifications or revisions of classical Marxism
(though this is often denied). The outcome of these debates, as we
shall see, is strikingly similar to the point of departure of critical
social theories, though these have rarely focused on "race" per se
for regrettable circumstantial reasons. The outcome is a shift from
a relatively closed economic model of social reproduction to a fully
open and historically contingent one that loses any clearly "Marxist" self-definition in the classic sense. In the cases of critical theories and so-called post-Marxist theory (Laclau and Mouffe), this
distance is clearly acknowledged; in the case of neo-Marxist approaches of this type, this issue is either ignored or its significance
underplayed.

A very similar approach derived from critiques more closely
associated with the neo-Marxist tradition and theories of social
reproduction is often referred to as a "parallelist" position with
respect to race and gender, or in feminist theory as a "dualist"
position. The advantage of the notion "parallel" is that it encompasses a multiplicity of possibilities, not merely the relations of
gender and class. As often been noted, classical Marxism has had

difficulties in making race (along with gender) a central aspect of political-economic explanations. More recently, however, it has been suggested that some neo-Marxist writers have managed to incorporate these questions with various parallelist type formulations of race: relative autonomy models, autonomy models, and political economic migrant labor models (Rex and Mason, 1986).

One of the themes of this chapter is that understanding the problematic of race and racialism requires reasserting the significance, if in modified form, of the crucial importance of processes of social reproduction understood in open and highly historically specific terms. Our discussion will develop around two strategies for reconceptualizing race and social reproduction. The first formulation by Michael Apple reflects the outcome of critique of class and economic reductionism. Apple and Weis (1983), and later McCarthy and Apple (1988), have argued for a "parallelist" model based on the relative autonomy of class, race, and gender in the economic, political, and cultural spheres.

The second phase of our discussion will be to take up the important effort to respecify race in terms of social and cultural reproduction undertaken by Robert Miles and others (Miles, 1989; Wetherell and Potter, 1992). Though not directed explicitly toward the more general problematic of social reproduction as such, nor to that of educational reproduction in particular, this approach to race sheds light upon more recent debates about American education, particularly where these issues take on a unique form.

Race as a Form of Domination

Race as a Social Category   Race and gender as categories share two fundamental differences from class-based forms of domination: they involve ostensibly biologically grounded or genotypical attributions of an essentially different "human" nature; and they refer to forms of domination that both predate capitalism and are not inevitably required for (and may in fact contradict) capitalist development.

In contrast, class identities have been generally regarded as outcomes of socialization; indeed, the liberal ideology of individual achievement necessarily presumes that class differences can in principle be overcome though the exercise of free will and determination. Exceptions to this are linked primarily to situations where racial differences (which may blend with those of ethnicity, as in the prototypical case of Jews—i.e., ethnic differences are often held to involve "natural" characteristics that are relatively unchanging and ultimately racial in origin) are held to account for the persistent inability of particular fractions of social classes to overcome their class disadvantages, or, in the case of Asians and Jews, their ability to maintain advantages across generations. Further, the modern problematic of class as defined relationships to wage-labor and capital is a peculiarly modern phenomenon tied directly to the origins of capitalism and essential for its continued reproduction and expansion.

Similarly racism is not inherent to capitalism, and the South African case is the best example, where a number of capitalist societies (and fairly strong capitalist regime ideologies, such as Reagan's neoconservatism) have been supporting the abolition of apartheid as a system that has created a welfare state for whites only.[13] Racism goes back to its precapitalist roots, though closely associated with colonial expansion (Wolf, 1982). There is racism in the theological debates in the Middle Ages over whether the "discovered" Indians in the New Indies (America) have a soul or not, and whether black slaves have a soul and deserve to be catechized.[14] Racism is pre-capitalist and is closely related to colonialism. However, we should not overlook that it was the slave trade, and the exploitation of slave work (i.e., nonwage labor) that allows for fortunes to be made and later on be reintroduced in the capitalist circuit. Thus, as a historical process and product, racism, perhaps as much as sexism, originates in the depth psyche as part of the overall process of socialization, reflecting entrenched social customs, prejudices, and common sense (Fanon, 1968).

The targets of domination and exclusion are thus not random. Many targets of domination tend to be easily visible and weak, and so women and people of color were historically located in peripheral regions subject to colonialism, regional or psychological. The same could be said about the handicapped or the mentally disturbed (or minority religions), which could be seen as targets of domination (Foucault, 1965; Bulhan, 1985). As long as the limits of tolerance are invisible it is politically easier to maintain a façade of pluralism and even movement toward greater tolerance and economic freedom.

Race and Modernity   Though racial distinctions and prejudices are a universal feature of human societies, the form of racism that emerged in the nineteenth century is quite distinctive. Only then are the cultural differences associated with race connected to biological theories of heredity and legitimated by reference to Darwinian theory.

Striking evidence of this transformation can be found in the changes in the production of Shakespeare's *Tempest* where Caliban the colonial slave is characterized as part of a "vile race" in limited sense of an individual moral incorrigibility. Only by the end of the nineteenth century and the rise of social Darwinism does the notion of "primitive" peoples become biologized.[15]

Race and Social Reproduction

Progressive, liberal educational researchers acknowledge "the crisis in sorting and selecting" that afflicts the contemporary educational system in the United States (and elsewhere, if in somewhat different forms). On the one hand, in a postindustrial context education has become even more important for later success in a high technology economy, and yet "strong associations persist between social-class background and racial-ethnic status . . . and educational achievement and attainment . . . making it relatively more difficult for many low-status citizens to take advantage of economic opportunity" (Levine and Havinghurst, 1990: 71). On the other hand, the resulting skill deficiencies on the part of low-status groups are also held have a negative impact on international competitiveness.

At least the older functionalist theory of stratification was more candid in its acknowledgment of the need for a fit between the demands of the occupational structure and the output of the educational system. The analytical reason for this was that as a species of social reproduction theory it assumed that the systemic imperatives of the occupational structure functionally required that the educational system adapt. At a particular stage in the expansion of public education, the history of class structure, and industrialization, such a harmony was to an extent realized in the postwar boom of the 1950s. But the subsequent process of "credentialization" gave evidence of the profound discrepancy between liberal ideology and occupational realities.

In any case, Giddens enunciates the basic issues from a critical theory perspective:

> There are three axes of exploitative relationships—observable in societies at widely different times and places—which are not explained, though they may be significantly illuminated, either by the theory of the exploitation of labor in general or by the theory of surplus value in particular. These are: (a) exploitative relations between states, where these are strongly influenced by military domination; (b) exploitative relations between ethnic groups, which may or may not converge with the first; and (c) exploitative relations between the sexes, sexual exploitation. None of these can be reduced exhaustively to class exploitation, nor more particularly can be derived from the theory of surplus value. None of them came into existence with capitalism, though they have taken particular forms with the development of capitalist society, and hence there can be no presumption that they will inevitably disappear if and when capitalism does. These are major "absences" in Marxist theory, and notwithstanding a diversity of efforts to accommodate them to Marxism in a "class-reductive" way they remain among its most obvious limitations. To say this is not, of course, to deny that Marx's analyses, especially his theory of the mechanics of capitalist production, do not illuminate each of these areas. (Giddens, 1981:242)

As Solomos concludes in a manner surprisingly similar to Giddens formulation, a general model following from these debates would necessarily have three essential features:

> (a) there is no problem of "race relations" which can be thought of separately from the structural (economic, political, and ideological) features of capitalist society; (b) there can be no general Marxist theory of racism, since each historical situation needs to be analyzed in its own specificity; and (c) "racial" and "ethic" divisions cannot be reduced to or seen as completely determined by the structural contradictions of capitalist societies. (Solomos, 1986: 104)

While Solomos's suggestion is constructive, it does not necessarily allow for a discussion of curriculum and educational policy. Michael Apple's nonsynchronous paralellist approach points in that direction.

Apple: A Nonsynchronous, Parallelist Approach Critiques of economistic conceptions of educational reproduction have been rejected by Apple and others in favor of theories that describe "social formations as being made up of a *complex totality* of economic, political, and cultural/ideological practices. Unlike base/superstructure models, where 'superstructural' institutions such as schools were seen as being wholly dependent upon and controlled by the economy, these theories held that these three sets of interrelated practices jointly create the conditions of existence for each other" (Apple and Weis, 1983: 20–21). Further, it is argued that in addition to society being constituted by these three spheres, a dynamic understanding of ideology shows that "ideological form is not reducible to class. Processes of gender, age, and race enter directly into the ideological moments. It is actually out of the articulation with, clash among, or contradictions among and within, say, class, race, and sex that ideologies are lived in one's day-to-day life" (Apple and Weis, 1983: 24). In other words each sphere of social life (economic, cultural, political) is the outcome of the dynamics of class, race, and gender: "Each of these dynamics, and each of these spheres, has its own internal history *in relation* to the others. Each dynamic is found in each of the spheres" (Apple and Weis, 1983: 25). In a later elaboration of the general model, it is more explicitly labeled a "parallelist" position. We will come back to this position in our section on gender, feminism, and education.

Miles: Social Reproduction and Exclusionary Practices Though the approach of Miles (and his collaborator Phizacklea) has been labeled by Solomos as a "migrant labor model," this is misleading to the extent this involves an historically specific account of race relations in Britain. More generally, in reacting to the cultural studies approach of Hall and others, Miles and Phizacklea argue that "our object of analysis cannot be 'race in itself,' but the development of racism as an ideology within specific historical and material contexts" (Phizacklea, cited in Solomos, 1986: 98). Though this position has been criticized as reviving an economistic assumption of the primacy of class over race, Miles counters—in a manner convergent with Apple—that "his model is grounded in the notion that internal and external class relations are shaped by a complex totality of economic, political, and ideological processes":

> The "race"/class dichotomy is a false construction. Alternatively, I suggest that the reproduction of class relations involves

the determination of internal and external class boundaries by economic, political, and ideological processes. One of the central political and ideological processes in contemporary capitalist societies is the process of racialization . . . but this cannot, in itself, over-ride the effects of the relations of production. Hence, the totality of "black" people in Britain cannot be adequately analyzed as a "race" outside or in opposition to class relations. Rather, the process by which they are racialized, and react to that racialisation (both of which are political and ideological processes), always occurs in a particular historical and structural context, one in which the social relations of production provide the necessary and initial framework within which racism has its effects. The outcome may be the formation of racialised class fractions. (Cited in Solomos, 1986: 100)

As Miles writes in a more recent formulation,

The argument . . . is not that racism and related exclusionary practices are a minor, even insignificant, determinant of the structural position and experience of racialized populations. Rather, it is that the influence of racism and exclusionary practices is always a component part of a wider structure of class disadvantage and exclusion; the real challenge is to contextualise the impact of racism and related exclusionary practices, partly to highlight the specificity of that impact and partly to demonstrate the simultaneous continuities in the class positions and experiences of (in the case of Britain) people of Asian and Caribbean origin and people of indigenous origin. (Miles, 1989: 9)

In this vein Miles (1989) argues that racism is a necessarily contradictory phenomenon rather than merely functional to capitalism as a mode of production. He has suggested three instances to illustrate this thesis: First, "the reproduction and constitution of non- and precapitalist relations of production is a common dimension of the development of the capitalist mode of production." In particular moments they have been an interpolation of racialization and racism (colonialist state and the ideology of racism). Second, "the historical complimentary between the specific economic forms of the capitalist relations of production . . . and the political form of the nation state has generated an ideology which attempts to make sense of imagined community a basis for political stability." Third, "wherever the number of available persons is an excess of the available positions, some form of exclusionary practice grounded in a process of signification is necessary. Thus, within the capitalist mode of production, the ideology of sexism has justified the exclusion of large numbers of women from the labor market . . . In similar manner, the racialization of a population establishes a hierarchy of suitability and the ideological basis for exclusionary practices" (Miles, 1989: 129–31).

The Social Psychology of Racism: Visible Differences

The paradox of race in social reproduction is that what is reproduced are forms of inequality associated with phenotypical features of individuals. Though this may serve capital and other social groups by providing a convenient mechanism for organizing processes of exclusion and sorting in the social hierarchy, there are many other ways in which allocative processes can and are organized (by gender, region, cohort of birth) and inequalities sustained and justified. Yet race (and in a more mitigated form, ethnicity) is obviously distinctive here, given its persistence and virulence. Similar arguments have, of course, been made with respect to gender differences, which also are linked to ostensible "biological" distinctiveness. But there is a fundamental difference here. Gender is in fact based on biological distinctions relating to sexuality and reproduction that have some real, if socially exaggerated, behavioral consequences. But as in the case of race, efforts to change patterns of gender identification based on early socialization are met with forms of resistance that are depth psychological in character and quite distinct in this respect from changing class relations. Obviously for Freudian-influenced theories the reasons for this are clear enough, given the gender-based notion of psychosexual identity.

In contrast, "race" is not a biological category that can serve as a justifiable scientific tool for representing and comparing human populations. Rather, it is a marker for historically constituted oppressed groups whose domination was perpetuated and reproduced through reference to accidental phenotypical features, those of "visible" minorities. For this reason, the Nazis found it necessary to make the fictitious racial category "Jew" visible through inscribing (tattooing) the Star of David onto the otherwise unidentifiable skin of an ethnic minority.

Despite its fictitious biological basis, however, racial identities are similar to those of gender in the depth-psychological nature of the responses evoked. Though this may parallel strong ethnic differences as well (and in extreme cases have a similar intensity), it operates independently of actual cultural differences. In other words, racist responses may occur strictly on basis of physical traits, even where no significant cultural differences may exist. We have a parallel in sexual responses generally where desire (or repulsion) may be evoked on the basis of socially (and personally) based markers of "beauty" or "sexiness" quite independent of the actual characteristics of the individual. This provides one of the keys to the parallels between racial and gender difference in that both draw upon the human capacity for depth-psychological and libidinal response to somewhat arbitrary objects of desire and repulsion. This also helps explain the oft-noted sexual dimensions of racism, a theme expressed directly in the cultural discourses that constituted the Western forms of racism in the context of colonialism. Purely ethnic differences inevitably have a different status than do racialized ones because the former can always—at least in principle—be washed away through assimilation, conversion, and the like.

Studies of learning and race relations have been a prominent feature of experimental cognitive psychology, and thus we need to discuss the evidence from social cognitive research. Though useful for certain purposes, the standard research on race and prejudice based on experimental cognitive social psychology has been of peripheral interest for theories of social and cultural reproduction. Based on social cognitive and attributional conceptions of prejudice and stereotyping, they focus on analysis of racism as a characteristic of individuals that "reveal typical biases and distortions which can be generally traced back to universally shared shortcomings in human cognition . . . Racism becomes strategically reduced to categorical attitudinal statements and is no longer studied as a problem of broad ideological frameworks in which ethnocentrism and the denigration of minority groups becomes linked to other justificatory doctrines" (Wetherell and Potter, 1993: 36). As another critic of such work has suggested, "in term of the sociohistorical perspective, an attributional account of human behavior is not a neutral description of how the mind operates while processing information, but rather involves social analyses of human behavior that those growing up within a society learn and that play a part in the system of power and privilege with that society" (Sampson, 1991: 100). More valuable is the research tradition of social identity theory, which has also made important contributions to the analysis of intergroup relations.[16]

Race and Education

The poststructuralist (re)discovery of the constructed character of the self and identity has contributed to stress on the arbitrary nature of all forms of identity—sexual, ethnic, racial, national, and so on. This important general thesis tends to obscure the important practical fact that existing populations have already been socialized into identities that they cannot merely shrug off in the process of acknowledging their arbitrary character; and that the specific formation of those identities has been anything but arbitrary because they have arise from highly determinate, if very historically specific, processes rooted in systems of social and cultural reproduction. The upshot of this is that resistance against problematic forms of racial or ethnic attribution must be rooted in the historically specific forms of domination through which they were constructed. Further, potential "solutions" cannot escape the determinacy of those particular settings: the Irish problem, the Yugoslavian crisis, American racism, and the status of the indigenous Indians in Central America resist theoretical unification as racial-ethnic problems for this reason. Paradoxically, racism is everywhere the same and yet everywhere different.

In keeping with our focal historical frame of reference to North and Latin America, the specification of the issues posed by race for theories of social and cultural reproduction requires sketching the general outlines of racial formation in those contexts. Two primary structural features define the origins of racism in the New World. Most fundamentally, it involved the combination of the conquest of indigenous peoples (i.e., Aboriginals, but also the French population of Quebec in a less violent manner) and the importation of a slave population from Africa. Secondarily, but of ongoing significance in many countries, large waves of ethnically and racially diverse immigration created the basis for complex, pluralistic systems of racial and ethnic antagonism.

Nationalism and the imperative of the nation-state have created some of the most important sources of opposition to racism, even though—as critics point out—the state has also been a crucial force in maintaining racism. Unique in this respect have been efforts to valorize "mixed" racial backgrounds as the basis of national identity, as in the case of the "mestizo" ideology of the Mexican revolution and the mulatto in the formation of Brazilian culture. However belatedly, the support of civil rights by the federal government in the

United States represents a similar force for integration, albeit one that could never go so far as to represent racial mixture as the foundation for national identity, despite the misleading image of the "melting pot." Undoubtedly, race matters in the United States (West, 1988). Political debate on the relationship between race and education in the United States is virtually synonymous with the emergence of the civil rights movement in the early 1960s. Backed up by a Supreme Court decision, proponents of educational integration were able to define the segregated school itself as the primary site of the reproduction of racial inequalities. The process of integration was accompanied by various "compensatory" educational schemes designed to facilitate achievement through early interventions.

Despite widespread gains in Afro-American educational achievements from the 1960s through the 1970s, these declined in the 1980s as reflected in college enrollment and completion rates (Levine and Havinghurst, 1992: 363). Though a number of circumstantial factors (i.e., the effects of Reagan-Bush policies) help explain this decline (especially the substitution of loans for grants in federal assistance to students), there are two more fundamental explanations that bear more directly on the link between race and social reproduction. The first refers directly to the effects of the postsegregation school in the form of "second-generation educational discrimination" derived from "academic grouping and tracking":

> Racial biases in special education, ability grouping, curriculum tracking, and discipline have replaced segregation as the single greatest obstacle to equal educational opportunities. Desegregation—the mechanical mixing of race in equal percentages—is not enough; desegregated schools often have little interracial contact and unequal educational opportunities because black students are grouped or tracked into classes different from those for the majority of white students. What is needed is integration—the interaction of students in a multiracial learning environment both in and outside the classroom. Integrated education provides students with equal status and equal opportunities to excel. (Meier, Stewart, and England, 1989: 4)[17]

Second, debate has increasingly centered on the relationship between class and race. One provocative thesis advanced by William Julius Wilson in his *The Declining Significance of Race* argues that whereas substantial gains have been made with respect to overt discrimination, this has not been coupled with changes in the economic obstacles to advancement that become increasingly central to the reproduction of racial inequalities:

> In earlier years the systematic efforts of whites to suppress blacks were obvious to even the most insensitive observer. Blacks were denied access to valued and scarce resources through various ingenious schemes of racial exploitation . . . [But in] the period of modern industrial race relations, it would be difficult indeed to comprehend the plight of inner-city blacks by exclusively focusing on racial discrimination. For in a very real sense, the current problems of lower-class blacks are substantially related to fundamental structural changes in the economy . . .
>
> As a result, for the first time in American history class issues can meaningfully compete with race issues in the way blacks develop or maintain a sense of group position. (Cited in Levine and Havnighurst, 1992: 364)

This discussion on race/ethnicity, race discrimination, and theories of race relations in education, has many parallels *pari pasu* to the discussion on gender and education, from feminist perspectives.

GENDER, FEMINISM, AND EDUCATION

Education and Gender

> Women constitute half of the world's population, perform nearly two-thirds of its work-hours, received one-tenth of the world's income and own less than one hundredth of the world's property. (A United Nations report quoted in Sayer and Walker, 1992: 37).

Despite evident progress in the education of girls and women, women still earn 75 percent of men's wages worldwide (Kelly, 1992: 279). The data presented in Kelly's study show that there is a worldwide trend toward equalizing access to all levels of schooling for both men and women. Yet, greater inequality has resulted given the kind of education that women are receiving compared to the education of men. Kelly has argued that

> In secondary education women have been allocated to general academic studies, to preparation programs for elementary

teachers, and to "female" vocational training for positions as secretaries and clerks. Males, on the other hand, have been channeled into technical, vocational training which articulate more closely with the changing structure of employment. In higher education, women have come to dominate the Arts and Humanities and teachers preparation programs; men, on the other hand, have maintained Engineering, Business Administration, and Computer Science as their preserves. It is little wonder then that women's role in the workforce has eroded in the face of economies increasingly based on extensive use of computer-based technologies. (Kelly, 1992: 280–81)

Clearly enough, schooling is characterized by gender asymmetries—related as well to broader issues of class and race/ethnic social reproduction. There are more illiterate women than illiterate men in the world. In part, this is the result of cultural norms that see women as simply being childbearers. At the same time, it is the result of traditional ideologies (i.e., motherhood and/or religious fundamentalist views) where women are considered primarily in charge of domestic chores and child-rearing and therefore literacy and certainly advanced schooling do not appear as prerequisites for performing those traditional roles. Finally, this is also partly a result of the division of labor.

Gender relations are relations of power, and as suggested by Connell and reiterated in Sayer and Walker's study, the power of men over women involves three basic elements: control over women's labor, control over women's childbearing powers, and control over women's desires and affections—thus sexuality is a constitutive element of gender, and its forms are always socially mediated, whether encouraged, channeled, or repressed" (Sayer and Walker, 1992: 34; 36). Appropriation of women's labor is reflected in unpaid domestic labor, both maintaining the productive and reproductive activities of the household (Sayer and Walker, 1992: 35).

In discussing the role of gender in the division of labor, Sayer and Walker also note that each major structure of oppression (due to class, gender, race, or imperialism) has an intransitive and irreducible nature, and that "gender, division of labor, and class are constructed simultaneously and reciprocally" (Sayer and Walker, 1992: 40). They then suggest to study how patriarchy reinforces capitalist class relations—but at the same time how it is different in nature—and how the integration of class and gender should be discussed without forgetting that class, patriarchy, and division of labor are in constant interplay. This interplay of semiautonomous spheres results not only from the fact that the sexual division of labor has a history of its own beyond patriarchy and capitalism, but because "division of labor imparts much of substance to prevailing notions of masculinity and feminity, and is altered in turn, by those notions in the qualitative dimensions of its play of difference, hierarchy, and exploitation" (Sayer and Walker, 1992: 41). In this sense, the overlap of class with gender can only be understood in the context of a "gendered division of labor" (1992: 49). In short, Sayer and Walker suggest that "the real elements of difference and of oppression in the division of labor need to be recognized and grappled with for what they are, and not forever soldered onto patriarchy and capitalism" (1992: 55).

Likewise, considering the division of labor as a marker in understanding class and gender relations, one may understand how division of labor has a debilitating effect on the solidarity of women and workers (Sayer and Walker, 1992: 54)—for example, the schism and competing loyalties and interests between female wage workers vis-à-vis housewives, or the classical distintion of interests between industrial proletariats and rural workers.

Thus, considering an engendered division of labor, it is no surprise that despite gains in educational development for girls and women, men continue to achieve more years of formal schooling worldwide than women. Likewise, it is no surprise to observe the worldwide trend that a large number of the most educated women, particularly those who have completed higher education, tend to come from wealthy families and/or middle-class families. Finally, as Kelly has argued, it is not surprising to discover that certain fields of study and professions have becoming gendered, particularly nursing and teaching.

This has implications in terms of curriculum content and labor markets, which are not gender-blind. Reviewing the way schools work and the equality of educational opportunity for women, it is concluded that until very recently, "despite a growing body of literature detailing sexist practices in schools, gender is a sorely neglected category in recent reform literature calling for equity and excellence in schooling" (Bennett and LeCompte, 1990: 224).

Bennett and LeCompte conclude their review of curriculum, legislation, and equality of educational opportunity for women, arguing that despite feminist activism, detailed research reporting discriminatory practices in schools, and legislation designed "to insure equality of access and treatment, females [in the United States] do not have equal access to educational and occupational opportunities because of their status as women" (Bennett and LeCompte, 1990: 226), and that schools continue to reproduce a patriarchal society through "subtle (and often not-so-subtle) messages embedded in their organizational structure, curriculum, and social interaction patterns" (1990: 240)

The next section will show how class, gender, and race have been incorporated in a new critical modernist consensus, and how feminist thought has helped to theoretically analyze gender discrimination in society and education.

Feminist Theories and Cultural Reproduction

Our particular concern here, however, is with the question of conceptualizing the gender dimension of theories of social and cultural reproduction in education. Broadly speaking, the version of reproduction theory defended in part 5 is most consistent with socialist feminist theories based on some version of the dual-systems model, coupled with the cautions of "third-wave" feminism. Feminist theories are remarkably heterogeneous, thus constituting a family of schools rather than a single school. Education is necessarily an important topic of investigation given its central role in gender socialization, but different feminist approaches interpret these questions in conflicting ways.

Lengermann and Niebrugge-Brantley (1992), in analyzing contemporary feminist theory, distinguish three main types of feminist theories: theories of difference, theories of inequality, and theories of oppression. Theories of difference include biosocial, institutional, and social-psychological explanations of the differences between men's and women's experiences and situations. Theories of inequality refer to the explanations of why women have fewer privileges and resources in relation to men, as analyzed by liberal and Marxist theories. Theories of oppression imply that women are oppressed by, not merely unequal to or different from, men. Psychoanalytic, socialist, radical, and third-wave feminism have addressed these issues in different ways. With the growing presence of postmodernist discourse and its implications for feminism, third-wave feminist theories are offering one of the most compelling theoretical arguments (e.g., hooks and West, 1991).

Third-wave feminism looks at the notion of "difference" and focuses on women of color in the United States and women in the Third World, assuming that one cannot use the concept of "women" as a generic category in stratification, and focusing instead on the factual and theoretical interpretations of differences among women: "The differences considered are those that result from an unequal distribution of socially produced goods and services on the basis of position in the global system, class, race, ethnicity, and affectional preference as these interact with gender stratification" (Lengermann and Niebrugge-Brantley, 1992: 341; see also Luttrell, 1989).

Historically, limitations of middle-class feminist theorizing was evident in the early emancipation movements in the United States, which failed to recognize the claims of lower-class women and those of color: "the convenient omission of household workers' problems from the programs of 'middle class' feminists past and present has often turned out to be a veiled justification—at least on the part of the affluent women—of their own exploitative treatment of their maids" (A. Y. Davis cited in Grant and Sleeter, 1986: 196). Put more sharply, poet Audre Lorde asked why white feminists do not address differences between women:

> If white American feminist theory need not deal with the differences between us, and the resulting difference in our oppressions, then how do you deal with the fact that the women who clean your houses and tend your children while you attend conferences on feminist theory are, for the most part, poor women and women of Color? What is the theory behind racist feminism? (Lorde, cited in Crosby, 1992: 131)

Feminist theory and particularly third-wave feminism helps us to understand the praxis of new social movements in the Third World and in industrial advanced societies (Jelin, 1990: 185). The specific issues of the *instrinsic* aspects of gender domination must be sought elewhere, most typically sex-role theory (associated with liberal feminism), which is based on traditional socialization theory's analysis of the learning of norms, roles, and behaviors. But this approach cannot comprehend the origins of norms and values in power relations, nor does it adequately conceptualize the heterogeneity of socialization and, above all, the phenomenon of resistance (Connell, 1983: 189–207). Not surprisingly, therefore, radical (and sometimes in more critical ways, socialist) feminist theories have preferred accounts based on some version of categorical theory that makes gender difference a fundamental opposition, resulting in a form of essentialism, offering a metaphysical solidarity (all women . . .) an omnipresent enemy (all men . . .) with a strong (unintended) implication that any struggle in existing relationships is pointless, since the structure and the categories are universal. Connell expresses this point very well: "Since most women do not have the condition in their own lives for substantial withdrawal from relationships with men, the practical result is an unresolvable dilemma with feminism. Tension around themes of purity and guilt has been tangible in the movement for a number of years" (Connell, 1987: 61).

From a Latin American perspective, Elizabeth Jelin argues that although sporadically the presence of "heroic" women has been registered in defining the paths of social movements, "the great majority of women, especially those participating at the grass-root level, remain invisible and silent" (Jelin, 1990: 185). The difference in the context shapes the difference in strategies. María del Carmen Feijoo is quoted to argue that the majority of women do not have control over their bodies, and, like slaves, others make decisions (be they about reproductive rights, areas of health, family, medicine, or social security) about women's needs and fantasies (in Jelin, 1990: 185). Indeed, "Women's subordination and discrimination can be interpreted as the banners of the struggle for justice and equality, seeking to extend to the discriminated or subordinate groups rights already enjoyed by other social categories" (Jelin, 1990: 193).

In the same vein, in a landmark article on feminisms in Latin America, Sternbach and colleagues analyze the five main *encuentros* (meetings) of the feminist movement in Latin America, and they conclude, first, that feminism is a thriving, broad-based social movement that many other feminist movements in the world would aspire to become. Second, that "Black and Indian feminists in Latin America argued that race, like class, is constitutive of gender consciousness and oppression and that their interests as women were not identical to those of white or mestiza Latin American women; that is, that one's *lived* experience of gender encompasses class-and/or race specific dimensions." (Sternbach et al,

1992: 426). Lastly, that the ideological and strategic debates characteristics of contemporary Latin American feminisms have revolved around two central axes: "the relationship between feminism and the revolutionary struggle for justice, and the relationship between what was a predominantly middle-class feminist movement and the growing popular-based *movimientos de mujeres*" (Sternbach et al, 1992: 432).

Lengermann and Niebrugge-Brantley suggest that a prime motif of the feminist critique is to show the multidimensionality of the concept of power. There are many power resources: "Sociologists typically identify five power resources: physical force, the basis for *coercion;* control of necessary material resources, the basis for *domination;* the strength of the better argument, the basis for *influence;* the capacity to deliberately misrepresent, the basis for *manipulation;* and advantageous location within a system of meanings, the basis for *authority*" (Lengermann and Niebrugge-Brantley, 1990: 336). Thus, power cannot be reduced to authority alone, and need to be considered from multiple vantange points. Feminists' critical consideration of power is conmensurate to postmodernist criticism of power relationships—see chapter 14—and anticipates several shifts that can be identified in debates about social reproduction.

Power and Social and Cultural Reproduction

One of the most distinctive features of critical theories of social and cultural reproduction—despite all of their differences—is that they focus on the reproduction of *power* relations. In that, they differ fundamentally from systems and structural-functionalist theorizing, where the concept of equilibrium—analogous to reproduction—refers more affirmatively and generally to the reproduction of order. Originally, of course, it was class that was taken to be the primary mover of power relations, and the notion of social reproduction is often linked primarily with this image. Still, much of what is reproduced in education is in principle (if not in the given context) of universal value.[18] But theories of social and cultural reproduction have been concerned with the way in which seemingly innocent aspects of pedagogy and the curriculum in fact contribute to the reproduction of forms of domination and inequality.

In this chapter, we defend the continuing pertinence and analytical value of a radically revised critical modernist stance.[19] Suitably revised, the concept of totality—including a perspective allowing for an analysis of interactions, interplay, and relationships between class, gender, and race in educational settings—facilitates a reconstructed model of social reproduction. This model is at the same time open-ended, takes modernism as an object of critical inquiry rather than as a premise, takes seriously the postmodernist critique both at the level of epistemology and at the level of culture, and yet considers the political implications of theory, research, and praxis in the context of a project of social, gender, and ethnic/racial emancipation.

Politics is not taken here purely in its instrumental or pragmatical sense, but it is also considered as an horizon that opens up possibilities for human action. Politics, as a contested symbolic, material, and institutional terrain, is intrinsically linked to public policy formation and individual identity and action. We agree with Ginsburg when he states that: "Politics is concerned with the means of producing, reproducing, consuming, and accumulating material and symbolic resources" (Ginsburg, 1993:1). Politics is a difficult concept to grasp considering, as Ginsburg does, that politics and the political cannot be limited to the actions of the government, state, parties, parliament, constitution, or voting, but includes, touches upon, and interacts with all dimensions of human experience. Thus the personal is also political, as feminist theory taught us long ago.

Having shown how the critical deconstruction of the category of class, in a nonreductionist perspective, and the incorporation of the feminist argument help us develop a more complex understanding of cultural, social, and educational reproduction, we turn now to discuss gender and its specific contributions to social (and educational) reproduction. In the remaining of this chapter we will focus on gender and cultural reproduction from feminist perspectives.

Gender and Cultural Reproduction

Feminist theory has provided the context in which the *limits* of class analysis and structuralist theories of social reproduction based on ultimate economic determination have been illustrated in convincing empirical and theoretical ways. In his instructive synthesis, Connell argues that social theory has approached the subject of *extrinsic theories of gender* in three chronological approaches from "class first" to "social reproduction" theory to "dual systems" (Connell, 1987: 47).[20]

Class-first positions argue that capitalism is the root cause of all inequalities, and class struggle is primary. In the social-reproduction model, a more powerful analysis developed—particularly in Britain under the influence of structural Marxism—in which "the family, sexuality, or gender relations at large were the site of *reproduction* of 'relations of production'" (Connell, 1987: 43). Above all, this theory suggests a systemic connection between the subordination of women and economic exploitation of capitalism. The problem with this approach is that it must at the outset postulate an invariant structure, thus denying the historical character of social relations. However, argues Connell, a social structure should be seen as "constantly *constituted* rather than constantly *reproduced*":

> Social reproduction, therefore, is an object of strategy. When it occurs, as it often does, it is an achievement by a particular alliance of social forces over others. It cannot be made a postulate or presupposition of social theory. And the concept cannot take the explanatory weight that reproduction theories of gender place on it. (1987: 44)

Connell's second criticism is that reproduction does not easily makes a connection between the needs of capitalism and what is specific about gender: "It is clear enough that if capitalism is to continue, its dominant groups must succeed with some kind of reproduction strategy. But it is not at all obvious that doing this must produce sexual hierarchy and oppression. Much the same might be argued (and sometimes is) about racial and ethnic hierarchies or about hierarchies of age" (1987: 44)

For example, there is nothing inherent in capitalism to exclude women from the rank-and-file or from the upper levels of management. There are, to be sure, contingent factors that do so—for example, the old boys club as an expression of remnants of premodern patriarchy or the patriarchal organization of early capitalism in relation to family life—but this is not inherent in capitalism as such to thrive as a system. This of course leads to the dual-system notion cautiously defended by Connell. Though the dependent housewife in a bourgeois nuclear family was characteristic of the reproduction of labor in a particular phase of capitalist development, this does not preclude the possibility of quite different forms for organizing such systemic imperatives in the future.

The third approach of dual-systems theory is associated with socialist feminism more generally.[21] Dual-systems theory argues that the basic idea is that capitalism and patriarchy are distinct and equally comprehensive systems of social relations that meet and interact. This is comparable to the debate, on the democratic socialist left, that capitalism and democracy intersect at one point in time, but liberal democracy does not need to be tied to capitalism as a system of production through commodities—that is to say, capitalism needs liberal democracy to thrive, but a multivocal definition of democracy can exist both in the context of a reformed capitalism and outside this mode of production (Bowles and Gintis, 1986; Przeworski, 1985).

Connell notes two difficulties in dual-systems theories that, we would add, are shared by all parallelist-type models (1987: 46). The first difficulty has to do with the ambiguity of the systematic properties of patriarchy, that is, the sense in which it constitutes a system in the same sense as capitalism. It is not clear that both "systems" (patriarchy and capitalism) are the same kind of thing; one may argue that patriarchy refers to a system of domination, perhaps similar to other systems of domination built on exploitation of particular features of groups (e.g., their lack of legal power or recognition), while capitalism is built as a system of exploitation based on differential appropriation of social wealth through ownership of capital and labor power. Thus Marx's theory of labor value comes into play as a different approach from pure domination through force (either physical of mental), through legal or theological norms, or through colonialism.

Second, it is not clear how to conceptualize the nature of the "interaction" between the two, and especially how this relates to either explaining oppression or bringing about change. Dualist and parallelist theories are misleading to the extent that the resulting analytical distinctions imply analogous substantial distinctions. As Nancy Fraser argues in her critique of Habermas, dual systems theory

> is an approach that posits two distinct "systems" of human activity and, correspondingly, two distinct "systems" of oppression: capitalism and male dominance. But this is misleading. These are not, in fact, two distinct systems but, rather, two thoroughly interfused dimensions of a single social formation. In order to understand that social formation, a critical theory requires a single set of categories and concepts that integrate *inter-*

nally both gender and political economy (perhaps also race). (Fraser, 1989: 139)

Further, that internal relationship to capitalism is itself historically variable. As Fraser stresses, "male dominance is intrinsic rather than accidental to classical capitalism, for the institutional structure of this social formation is actualized by means of gendered roles. It follows that the forms of male dominance at issue here are not properly understood as lingering forms of premodern status inequality. They are, rather, intrinsically modern in Habermas's sense, since they are premised on the separation of waged labor and the state from childrearing and the household" (Frazer, 1989: 128).

We would argue that the approaches suggested by both Connell and Fraser are very much within the tradition of what we find useful to term as *practice-oriented, parallelist* models of cultural reproduction grounded in comparative historical explanatory strategies. This point becomes especially clear in Connell's elaboration of a general theory of gender and power. First, it is an approach that is situated in terms of the European structuralist tradition, but one that couples structure with historicity and practice and has been "formalized theoretically" in the "dualist" accounts of Pierre Bourdieu and Anthony Giddens (Connell, 1987: 94). Second, he argues that as applied to gender relations the use of structuralist concepts has suffered from the assumption of some kind of *single* unifying structure: "That there might be some problem here is suggested by the remarkable proliferation of 'ultimate causes' proposed for that single structure" (Connell, 1987: 95). Taking a cue from Juliet Mitchell's early work, he suggests that gender domination be viewed from the perspective of multiple and perhaps even contradictory structures and proposes three fundamental (though interpenetrating) forms: those to do with the division of labor; those linked with power relations generally as authority, control, and coercive systems; and those associated with cathexis, "with the patterning of object-choice, desire and desirability; with the production of heterosexuality and homosexuality and the relationship between them" (Connell, 1987: 97). Third, these processes are held nevertheless to be interrelated in determinate and determinable ways. Yet, as he concludes, this does not take the logical form assumed by classic structuralist reproduction theory:

> In none of this is there an ultimate determinant, a "generative nucleus" to use Henri Lefebvre's terms, from which the rest

of the pattern of general relations springs. There is, however, a
unity in the field, an orderliness, which needs to be understood . . . My argument, briefly, is that this unity is not the unity
of a *system*, as functionalist analysis would imply. Nor is it the
expressive unity that would be provided by the existence of a
generative nucleus. It is a unity—always imperfect and under
construction—of historical composition. I mean "composition"
as in music: a tangible, active, and often difficult process of bringing elements into connection with each other and thrashing out
their relationships . . . The product of the process is not a logical
unity but an empirical unification. It happens on particular terms
in particular circumstances. (Connell, 1987: 116)

Gender and Educational Reproduction: Masculinity and Femininity

There is an empirical literature that basically shows that the school
system tends to reproduce conventional gender orientations that
have their origins in family socialization and workplace expectations. They reflect the turn-of-the-century bourgeois family as the
basic constitutive cell of society. The official ideology works on the
principle of gender equality, but schools, churches, and families
subtly and often inadvertently—but often openly and purpose-
fully—reproduce gender differences. This is probably more obvious at the lower levels of the schools system where emphasis on
discipline or moral education is higher than on cognition or cognitive development.

Central to this debate are conceptions of "masculinity" and
"femininity" that capture the socially constructed nature of gender
without lapsing into biological determinism and essentialism. Useful in this respect is Connell's distinction between "hegemonic
masculinity" and "emphasized femininity," a distinction that stresses the diversity of both and their asymmetrical interrelation:

> "Hegemonic masculinity" is always constructed in relation
> to various subordinated masculinities as well as in relation to
> women. The interplay between different forms of masculinity is
> an important part of how a patriarchal social order works. There
> is no femininity that is hegemonic in the sense that the dominant
> form of masculinity is hegemonic among men . . . At the level of
> mass social relations, however, forms of femininity are defined
> clearly enough. It is the global subordination of women to men
> that provides an essential basis for differentiation. One form is

defined around compliance with this subordination and is oriented to accommodating the interests and desires of men. I will call this "emphasized femininity." Others are defined centrally by strategies of resistance or forms of non-compliance. (Connell, 1987:183)

The relation of these processes to education requires a stronger focus on primary and secondary schooling, even as these in turn build upon early socialization in the family, as has been pointed out in the psychoanalytic literature. Psychoanalytic theories have provided valuable insights into the mechanisms of early socialization that contribute to the exaggeration of original gender differences in ways that set the stage for later extension into the characteristic patterns often mistaken as essential features of "male" and "female." But they do little to explain the profound differences in outcomes that build upon these early tendencies.

Often neglected, as a consequence, are the secondary socialization processes that build upon these initial orientations in ways that conflict with the overtly egalitarian ideology of the democratic school.[22] For example, adolescence is both the stage of the crystallization of gender-based identities linked to sexuality *and* the context within which career-oriented aspirations related to education are linked to concrete decisions and related motivations. For women these two imperatives are essentially contradictory. On the one hand, adolescent courtship patterns tend to reproduce traditional forms of gender difference and give priority of sexuality in terms of adolescent ego development, where males put masculinity as dominant over femininity, and therefore a debate on whether there are two different forms of learning (masculine versus feminine learning) emerges. As Grant and Sleeter conclude: "A final, very important factor was the peer group itself. When students began to think about courtship, they began to shape their behavior and expectations in a way that would complement expectations of the opposite sex. The boys had fewer questions about role and gender-identity, and the girls tended to resolve their own questions by accepting the boys' definition. This facilitated courtship, although it also tended to help reproduce existing gender relations" (1988: 35).

For instance, the learning of mathematics is mostly associated with masculine thinking, while the learning of humanities or careers in education are mostly associated with feminine thinking and caring practices. Nevertheless, these differences are slight and in some studies appear neglible. For example, Richard Kohr and associates (1989) found that though whites scored higher than blacks, achievement differences (although relatively weakly associated) varied directly with socioeconomic status (SES) levels, even though their were no replicable gender differences.

Women who deviate from this pattern not only must overcome influences of early childhood and the weaker gender/differences reinforced in early schooling; they also risk the more immediate rejection from ostensibly desirable males at a crucial stage of their own ego development (as do males who depart from hegemonic masculinity—most obviously in the case of homosexuality—though not usually in a way that carries the same consequences for ultimate career or partner choices).

For women in terms of career aspirations, early adolescence is the crucial transitional period. Women tend to suppress any capabilities or aspirations that will threaten their more immediate desires to please or attract male attention given the priority of eventual family formation. This theme is apparent in one of the original justifications for separate education for women, especially the original "colleges" for women which sought to encourage self-assertion and autonomy in a context outside of male competition and the distractions of competing for male interest.

Similarly, in those subcultures of the secondary school that have some success in breaking down traditional gender differences, it is characteristic that physical gender differences tend to be downplayed by unisex dressing. Interpersonal relations become based on other forms of display, such as a wide range of intellectual and cultural accomplishments, rather than on patriarchal mannerisms, athletic prowess, or standardized perceptions of sexual attractiveness that derive from the norms of hegemonic masculinity and emphasized femininity.

THE MEDIATION OF DIFFERENCE?:
CLASS, GENDER, AND RACE

One of the peculiarities of the Hegelian-Marxist concept of class was its inherent universalism: the working class was destined to be the class to end all classes. Even with the abandonment of that metaphysical assumption in contemporary critical theory, there was little basis for the hardening of class difference into anything more than a recognition of different trajectories of socialization and experience. The decline of the notion of a universal class left open the question of the ultimate meaning of class differences. The partial decline of class concepts in contemporary social theory reflects the loss of any sense of anchorage that would allow some external attribute—say, participation in wage labor or productive versus unproductive labor—to be defined as "essential" categories of humanity. As neo-Marxist critiques point out, however, this undermines the basis for collective strategies of change.

Paradoxically, the emergence of gender and race as central components of the reproduction of domination have suffered a similar but quite distinctive fate. As subjects of suppressed and colonized identities, women and racial minorities clearly have a need to recognize and celebrate their inevitable differences (at least those not contaminated by domination itself). Though a similar process is evident with respect to working-class pride and self-respect in the nineteenth century, there was also a sense of the need to emulate certain qualities that only the privileged had been able to cultivate. Of course, it was easy to mix up the accidental or parochial and universal aspects of "bourgeois" models; this led some to essentialize the "proletarian" as a form of difference that allowed no reconciliation with bourgeois culture. That was plausible because class could be claimed to transcend all other forms of difference as a universal concept, even though it relied on a dubious hierarchy of class that was translated into a notion of moral-ethical superiority.

Considering class, race, and gender as unifying principles with which to understand domination in educational contexts implies a more modest understanding of the relationships between education and social change. First, this suggests a reiteration of the critique of the liberal conception (which, paradoxically, has been appropriated—albeit passively—by neoconservatives) that the school can resolve the problem of inequality through facilitating the social mobility of those who can perform well in the school system.[23]

Second, this approach challenges the liberal view that schools per se can contribute significantly to the solution of the social problems that underlie the difficulties of minorities making use of the opportunities that do exist. This view is also challenged by the neoconservative argument that sees the deterioration of urban inner cities, the overpresence of sexual symbols in youth culture, crack cocaine and drug addiction, and gang proliferation and urban violence, among other things, as a result of lax family values and the erosion of the family as an institution.

Both diagnoses and solutions fail to adequately deal with the growing gap between youth culture and basic tenets of bourgeois modern society, the growing gender gap between male-dominated rationality and women's claims for control of their own bodies and lifeworld (so clearly expressed in the abortion debate in the United States), or the ever-growing disparity between the expectations of lower- and middle-class blacks and Latinos (even if they are not self-contained, homogenous categories), as opposed to whites and other transitional ethnic minorities.[24]

The sociology of school knowledge has identified that schools define success in terms of the subjectivities associated with white, male, affluent codes, with the result that those defined by other forms of subjectivity must undergo massive code switches in order to compete and obtain the higher grades, considered the sure ticket to employment and the best-paid, high-status occupations. These outcomes call into question the assumptions of the notions of equality of opportunity that has guided most research on education in the United States over the past two decades. However, equality should include a more complex matrix of equality of access; then, once within the system, equality of survival (i.e., the probability of children from different social groups to stay and complete different school levels) and equality of output (i.e., the probability that children from different social groups learn the same thing at the same level); and finally, equality of outcome (i.e., that as a result of obtaining similar levels of learning/training, children from different groups would obtain similar or comparable incomes or jobs, and access to positions of political power) (Farrell, 1992: 107–22). Thus, it does not deal with the problems of relative equality of outcomes, and the problem of how to deal with the inevitable exclusions of those who carry out the necessary lower-level occupations, or remain unemployed.

The postmodern condition has changed the logic of tolerance and pluralism as well as the articulation of the components of the great collective social identities of contemporary societies. Facing the challenge of postmodernism, we will attempt to attend to these issues in the next chapter.

CHAPTER 14

Education, the Fragmentation of Domination, and Postmodernism

To this point, our discussion has been couched—rather self-consciously—in the language of critical *modernist* social theory, especially the critiques of structural reproduction theory on the part of critical theory, feminist theory, and theories of race. In many respects, the postmodernist debate calls modernism, and particularly in education notions of social and cultural reproduction, into question. A number of questions can be formulated regarding the educational implications of postmodernity, especially for the critical synthesis of class, race, and gender outlined in the previous discussion.

The language and conceptualizations of postmodernism do not emanate from conventional or mainstream social science. On the contrary, it is the product of a confluence of work in the humanities, particularly literary criticism, psychoanalysis (above all Jacques Lacan), and poststructuralist French philosophy. While we find much in these trends problematic (and a symptom of the times), they also address fundamental issues of social theory and politics that cannot be ignored. With remarkable foresight, C. Wright Mills pinpointed a key aspect of what he called a "post-modern period" as a loss of faith in liberalism, socialism, and reason:

> our major orientations—liberalism and socialism—have virtually collapsed as adequate explanations of the world and of ourselves . . . These two ideologies came out of The Enlightenment . . . In both, increased rationality is held to be the prime condition of increased freedom . . . Now we confront news kinds of social structure . . . The ideological mark of The Fourth Epoch—that which sets it off from The Modern Age—is that the ideas of freedom and of reason have become moot; that increased

rationality may not be assumed to make for increased freedom. (1967 [1959]: 166–67)

This chapter will discuss the methodological challenge of *postmodernist theory* to social theory's ability to represent macrosocial processes, on the one hand; and the related fragmentation of the object of inquiry—domination—in the context of *postmodernist culture,* on the other. First, the close connection between educational theories of development and the problematic aspects of modernization theory is taken up. Second, the postmodernist challenge is identified in terms of in terms of its consequences with respect to the object of inquiry. Third, we will consider some of the issues taken up by efforts to synthesize critical pedagogy and postmodernist theorizing in the context of curriculum and literary theory. Finally, we offer a critical assessment of "educational postmodernity" for theories of cultural reproduction from a four-fold perspective: (i) as epistemology, (ii) as a methodological critique and a theory of the subject, (iii) as a social condition or cultural paradigm, and (iv) as politics of education.

MODERNISM, MODERNIZATION, AND EDUCATION

The terms *modernity, modernism,* and *modernization* have become common currency in contemporary social science and educational research, and are sometimes used as interchangeable terms. But aside from Platonist or conservative nostalgia for stable "organic" societies, and Marxist calls for *different paths* to modernity, this basic civilizational project has rarely been questioned as such.[1] Yet there are other exceptions—from Rousseau to Ivan Illich—that suggest that an unease with "civilization" has long accompanied certain streams of radical educational theory. Indeed, we will argue that the intimate involvement of educational theory with the unquestioned project of progress and Enlightenment is just cause for concern, one that has in part been shared by critical theories of education despite their overall modernist orientation. In this connection we will give particular attention to the modernist impulses of the sociology of development and literacy training. As we will see, education is centrally implicated as the central institution of "modernization," with the contradictions of this project emerging most crucially in the context of development theories.

Modernity as the Project of Enlightenment.

The project of modernity is closely identified with theories of progress. As Habermas points out, however, for Max Weber cultural modernity became problematic because of the "separation of the substantive reason expressed in religion and metaphysics into three autonomous spheres. They are: science, morality, and art" (Habermas, 1990: 347–48). Modernity, in Habermas's view, postulates that "the principle of unlimited self-realization, the demand for authentic self-experience, and the subjectivism of a hyper stimulated sensitivity have come to be dominant" (1990: 345). Thus, the first central element in modernity is the notion of science based on validity (truth, normative rightness, authenticity), and the basic notion of knowledge, justice, morality, and taste that articulate the basic rationality of domination.[2]

Drawing from scientific thought, and the preeminence of reason, modernism is based on specific ideological interpolations, including the prevalence of (a) *Abstract Work* that controls, manipulates, and transforms nature (and also helps to identify a new, specific domain of human action that is culture) and value (as use value and exchange value, the principles of political economy); (b) *Individualization,* which is seen both as a risk of alienation and estrangement of individuals, and as a principle of organization of moral and political rights and obligations, and is considered to provide the basic political philosophical foundation of modern capitalism; (c) *Liberalism* (as the only possible way to link with positive science and political philosophical notions of solidarity, equality and equity); (d) *Futurism,* based on the conviction of the inevitable and relentless future progress of programs based on human reason; and (e) *Secularization,* which, as a basic ethical posture compatible with scientific thought and liberalism, comes in handy to prevent or avoid any relapse to traditional forms of dogmatism based on notions of the sacred, the ineffable, and so forth, all of which lead to faith and religion ruling human affairs.

Scientific discourse, diverse theories of morality and jurisprudence, and the production and criticism of art all become institutionalized in specialized cultural professions that can be used for the rationalization of everyday life, as Habermas argues:

> The project of modernity formulated in the 18th Century by the
> philosophers of the Enlightenment consisted in their efforts to

develop objective science, universal morality and law, and autonomous art according to their inner logic. At the same time, this
project intended to release the cognitive potentials of each of
these domains to set them free from their esoteric forms. The
Enlightenment philosophers wanted to utilize this accumulation
of specialized culture for the enrichment of everyday life, that is
to say, for the rational organization of everyday social life.
(Habermas, 1990: 348)

But the flip side of modernity as a mode of thought was its
implication in an overall social dynamic "staged by industrialization, by capitalism, by urbanization, by the formation of the world
market, by the social and the sexual division of labor, by the great
punctuation of civil and social life into the public and the private;
by the dominance of the nation state, and by the identification
between Westernization and the notion of modernity itself" (Hall,
1991b: 45).

Education and National Development

The *institutionalist approach* to educational expansion take over
this modernist perspective virtually uncritically in its analyses of
compulsory mass schooling and the expansion of education as the
"late stage in the transformation of the West" (Boli and Ramirez,
1992; Meyer and Hannan, 1979; Fuller, 1990). There is no basis
for questioning that this is a "ceremonial induction" resulting
from the emergence and institutionalization of the modern individual, the discovery of the child, and the development of theories of
socialization. In short, compulsory mass schooling is seen "as the
coalescence [in the nineteenth century] of a new model of social
organization based on the enhanced individual and the expanded
state working jointly to pursue national progress" (Boli and Ramirez, 1992: 39).

Underlying these theories of educational modernization are
models based on the advanced Western capitalist societies.[3] However much education may be implicated in the reproduction of
class differences, its overall consequences for the movement of all
social groups toward universalistic values is stressed in these neofunctionalist and neo-Weberian approaches. "Advanced" societies
have become "developed" because "modern" individuals possess
characteristics very different from traditional individuals, including a cultivation of the attitude of achievement, a universalistic

perspective, and a specialized and functional division of labor. In contrast, "underdeveloped" or "traditional" societies struggle under the weight of individuals with an orientation toward ascriptive statuses, a particularistic perspective of the world, and a nonspecialized division of labor. These characteristics in turn provide the basis of a modern economy and democratically organized administrative state. With a fairly linear model of development (some scholars even identified different phases for the developmental take-off for countries to become industrialized, e.g., Rostow, 1960), this approach identified mechanisms and institutions that facilitate the modern condition.

Synthesizing this developmentalist perspective, it has been argued elsewhere that "literacy and basic education count among the privileged mechanisms for increasing contacts with modern societies (and their products), disorganizing traditional cultures (often of oral origin) that are considered an element of backwardness, and permitting development of social heterogeneity in the adoption of innovations" (Torres, 1990: 6). For modernization theorists, literacy and basic education are central inputs in development. It has been argued elsewhere that literacy and basic education contribute to economic development and modernization in diverse forms by

> (a) increasing the productivity of the newly literate; (b) increasing the productivity of those who work with the newly literate; (c) expanding the diffusion of the general knowledge of individuals (training in health and infant nutrition) and generally reducing the cost of transmitting practical information; (d) stimulating the demand for technical training and vocational education; (e) acting as an instrument for selection of the most valuable elements of the population and for enhancing their occupational mobility; (f) strengthening economic incentives (i.e., the tendency of people to respond positively to an increment of the compensation for their efforts) . . . In these terms, literacy is seen as one of the most important elements in the process of modernization and the development of nations undergoing industrialization. (Torres, 1994)

Another fundamental feature of the process of modernization is the relentless continuation (reproduction) of the process of modernization itself—that is to say, the ability of societies to continue their own structural differentiation and social change, to diversify into large numbers of functionally specific organizations, and to break "the importance of kinship and narrow territorial bases of specialized associations on the one hand, and of various 'specialized' associations and broad ascriptive-solidary groups on the other" (Eisenstadt, 1966: 7). This trait, of course, further disorganizes self-sufficient groups which are drawn towards a more common and institutionalized center, the market. Transactions in a enlarged, nonmonopolistic market, in turn, constitute a central element in the process of economic exchanges of commodities and affect the symbolic sphere of society as well.

Such changes are also associated with the progress of social justice and equity. It is argued that increased levels of schooling increase equity in terms of income distribution. In the same vein, it is argued that from a sociological standpoint, there is a close relationship between schooling and upward social mobility. Historical perspectives are invoked to argue that there is a clear link between early rise of literacy and economic take-off of nations. Finally, it is emphasized that, undoubtedly, education plays a role in development, including improvements in health, sanitation, and fertility problems (Psacharopoulos, 1988: 1–7).

When doubts emerge, they stem primarily from fears that education may fail to "keep up" with these dynamic processes. Hence, Levy questions from a pragmatic perspective:

> It has not been proved, or even alleged that school can and will keep up with the rapid changes and additions to the basic knowledge that seems to be a requisite of a modern society. No one knows whether schools can do the job, but no one even dreams that this knowledge can be bestowed on children in family contexts. (Levy, 1972: 51)

POSTMODERN THEMES

Problems of Definition

Andreas Huyssen begins his celebrated essay on "Mapping the Postmodern" by claiming that: "I will not attempt here to define what postmodernism *is*. The term '*postmodernism*' itself shall guard us against such as an approach as it positions the phenomenon as relational" (in Alexander and Seidman, 1990: 355). While sharing Huyssen's caution, it is imperative to clarify some of the basic issues involved in postmodern approaches.

Postmodernist theories criticize eighteenth- and nineteenth-century European thought, particularly reconceptualizations of knowledge, rationality, and historical change. Above all, this is expressed in attacks on universalism, whether as "truth," "science," or "reason"—all of which are linked to *Eurocentric* and *male-centered* views of reality. Most fundamentally, the question post-modern thought poses is whether the situation in the twentieth century in philosophy, arts, sciences, and general culture is so profoundly different that it needs to be seen as part of a deep discontinuity, even a breakdown with the project, promise, thought, and cultural and ethical expressions of modernity—in any of its variants—whether Left or Right, however defined. For the *post-modern condition,* human subjectivity, reason, and knowledge have broken down beyond retrieval. Elements involving certainty, representation of reality, universality, comprehensiveness, and practical imperatives or foundations are challenged. Instead, as Ford describes,

the postmodern human subject is seen as decentered, inseparably involved with the unconscious, the physical and the irrational, and shaped essentially through particular social relations, language, and culture. Indeed, the notion of "a common humanity" is seen as illusory. Postmodern concepts of rationality and knowledge emphasize historical and cultural variability, fallibility, the impossibility of getting beyond language to "reality," the fragmentary and particular nature of all understanding, the pervasive corruption of knowledge by power and domination, the futility of the search for sure foundations, and the need for a pragmatic approach to the whole matter. A specially prominent feature is the "linguistic turn" which says human identity has an interplay of various systems of signs and symbols: we inhabit "texts" of various sorts, their truth is undecidable, they all contain paradoxes and contradictions, and they generate endless interpretations as they are brought into relationship with other texts. There is hostility to theory in favor of more literary or pragmatic forms of discourse, and underlying that is a radical attack on the very notion of truth. The legitimacy of philosophy itself concerned with such notions as truth, being, and goodness, is rejected and replaced by pragmatism (Richard Rorty), "deconstruction" (Jacques Derrida), "paralogy" (Jean-François Lyotard) or "genealogy" (Michel Foucault). As regards history, postmodern approaches are suspicious of some of the main concepts of history-writing, such as causality, linear continuity, narrative unity, origins, and goals. The rejection of "representations of reality" means that the boundary between history and fiction is blurred . . . Those are the particularities that are emphasized by many postmodern thinkers, and the result is a wide variety of contextualized approaches which include irreconcilable contradictions, alternative accounts, discontinuities and ruptures. (Ford, 1989: 291–92)

It is important to distinguish here between postmodernism as a type of social theory from both theories of postmodernity and postmodernity as a cultural epoch. Our discussion in this section is concerned primarily with the implications of postmodernity as a sociocultural context that may have fundamentally transformed the nature of social and cultural reproduction in education. As a cultural paradigm, postmodernity is compatible with and a product of—but not restricted to—postindustrial (or post-Fordist) capitalist economies. Postmodernism is not a condition of, or a type of, society. Postmodernism is instead a cultural condition, compatible with (but not restricted to) the postindustrial capitalist economies (Lash, 1990).

In this regard, postmodernism emphasizes that the breaking of linkages between signifiers, signified, and referent has to do with the growing autonomization of the realm of culture from the material conditions of production (new rationalism), with the development of a mass culture through mass media (new universalization), and with the breaking of the boundaries between culture and the social; as a result, a new mode of transcendence and a new ethics of social action become established. Following Scott Lash (1990), one may argue that the postmodern condition produces a regime or mode of signification addressing the de-differentiation (social, political, ethical, etc.) of modern societies. One of the premises of modernization is that societies become more differentiated through growing specialization in the division of labor. Thus, as a mode or regime of signification, the postmodern condition implies new relations among a signifier, a signified, and a referent, especially the growing autonomization of the realm of culture from the material conditions of culture.

The Consequences of Postmodernism

Let us assume for the sake of the argument, and following some postmodernist tenets, that there is a "new" epoch in society and a new cultural paradigm. Thus the other question is whether such postmodern forms of society, as objects of inquiry, lend themselves to the types of concepts at our disposal given their rootedness in modernity. For our purposes some of the key sociological implications of postmodern society and culture can be summarized in stylized terms as involving various processes of *fragmentation:*

- A decentering and fragmentation of power that calls into question theories of domination and hegemony.
- An uncoupling of material interests and subjective expressions in collective action, resulting in the shift of the demands of social movements from distributional to cultural-ethical issues.
- The emergence of heterogeneity as opposed to the homogenization that has been previously characteristic of the world system.
- A growing distrust and disillusionment with democracy resulting from the fragmentation of political communities and identities.

Let us consider briefly each of these points. Power has become decentered and fragmented in contemporary societies. Thus, to suggest the notion of a ruling elite conducting its business and decisively influencing public policy may hide, in a postmodern view, the multiplicity of powers that interact in society (Bowles and Gintis, 1986). How can one define power that is fragmented, lacking a unifying principle? Does this undermine the nonsynchronous, parallelist conception of the relations of class, gender, and race in cultural reproduction? Does, in short, the fragmentation of power undermine our conceptual frameworks—inspired by obsolete "grand narratives"—of hegemony and domination?

The notion of the decentering of social subjects also implies an uncoupling of the close link between objective social interests and subjective expressions (e.g., class consciousness) assumed by much modernist social theory. The resulting contradictory loyalties of agents increasingly undermines a central organizing principle of struggle. One oft-noted consequence of this relative uncoupling of social position and political action is that the "new" social movements are more concerned with cultural (and ethical-political) demands than distributional ones. Decentered individuals are not supposed to have "class consciousness" in classical terms, yet they strive to achieve "self-actualization" in Giddens' (1991) social-psychological analysis. The dismemberment of the neo-Marxist New Left in Britain is perhaps symptomatic of the postmodern "New Times" (Jacques, 1992).

In addition, nation-states are now being dimmed in the context of a growing interdependent world and in the context of more local struggles. As Immanuel Wallerstein argues, the history of the (capitalist) world system has been a historical trend towards cultural heterogeneity rather than cultural homogenization. Thus, the fragmentation of the nation in the world system is happening at the same time that there is a tendency towards cultural differentiation or cultural complexity (i.e., globalization) (Wallerstein, 1991: 96).

In this increasingly more complexly organized, multicultural, and multilingual world system the bases of traditional forms of political community have been eroded. There is an emerging theory and practice of distrust in democracy. Hence, the previous models of democratic check and balances, separation of powers, and the notion of a democratic accountability no longer work, not even at the level of formal rather than substantive democracy.

POSTMODERNISM, CURRICULUM THEORY, AND SCHOOLING

The Crisis of Knowledge

The more immediate implications of postmodernist debates for curriculum theory and schooling are bound up with the question of the problematic status of "knowledge" in the curriculum and its relation to the neoconservative backlash that has defined the recent defensive agenda of educational politics.

Paradoxically, the educational reform of liberal education in the last decade in England, the United States, and Canada has been undertaken by neoconservatives rather than liberals. It is against this neoconservative agenda in the realism of schooling and culture that postmodernist theorists, joining other progressive scholars, practitioners, and militants of social movements, react. Neoconservative attempts to artificially resurrect traditional "canons" of scholarship involve traditionalist modernism at its worst.

On the other hand, beyond a certain point the central impulses of postmodernist theory do not appear to provide an adequate response to the neoconservative nostalgia for the restoration of intellectual "authority." For strong forms of postmodernism, any appeal to theory is meaningless or potentially totalitarian, any recourse to method is problematic, any resort to empirical proof mere rhetoric, and education and politics become enmeshed as a single, undifferentiated entity. The implications for educational practices and policies of postmodernism are also contradictory. If the egalitarian perceptions cannot be sustained, a call for total individualization may be appropriate and therefore postmodernism may turn into either a progressive or regressive phenomenon.

Following Habermas, Russell Berman has cogently suggested that there are points of intersection between the cultural programs and political economic formations of the neoconservative and neoliberal critiques of the welfare state, as well as attacks on the state bureaucracy by the new social movements—rebellious creatures of postmodernism:

> No matter how postmodernist works may differ from the traditionalist canon advocated by neoconservatives, these same postmodern works in fact reproduce neoconservative values . . . The aesthetic-cultural corollary to the contemporary crisis of welfare-state capitalism can lead, as I have tried to suggest, to the authoritarian cynicism of literary criticism, the culture-industrial duplicity of war films, or the confluence of neoconservativism and postmodernism. Can it lead elsewhere as well? Is there a progressive answer to the question of culture after bureaucratic capitalism? (Berman, 1989: 133–35)

Postmodernism and Critical Pedagogy

Critical pedagogy has evidenced an extensive engagement with postmodernist debates and an attempt to preserve the "critical" implications from the skeptical overall tendencies. As Kanpol has put it, following Giroux, "the major contribution to the current and continuing debate over the functions and roles of schools has now shifted gears to a dialogue concerning critical theory and postmodernism" (Kanpol, 1992). Part of this strategy is to claim that the most important aspects of postmodernist critiques were in fact *prefigured* in critical pedagogy itself.

In their work, Giroux and McLaren (1989) argue that social theorists such as John Childs, Paulo Freire, John Dewey, and Antonio Gramsci provide the foundations for an emancipatory vision of public schooling. For this tradition, instruction is not aseptically removed from politics, education is not considered a neutral undertaking, and schooling becomes linked with daily life, rather than being merely preparatory for life, democracy, and citizenship. As well, it is a framework within which the dimensions of class, gender, race, and other forms of domination can find a voice. The roots of postmodernism in education thus can be traced back to the 1960s, as Stanley Aronowitz and Henry Giroux argue:

> The 1960s witnessed the beginnings of an approach to education that radically diverged from the progressive tradition, even if many of the tenets of this new approach built on progressive ideas, some elements of which we choose to name "postmodern" . . . postmodern educators demanded of theoretical knowledge that it demonstrate its relevance to practice, and insisted on the importance of practice and everyday culture for the constitution of theoretical knowledge . . . postmodern educators believe the curriculum can best inspire learning only when school knowledge builds upon the tacit knowledge derived from the cultural resources that students already possess. (Aronowitz and Giroux, 1991: 15)

It is in this context that Peter McLaren's work on ideology and education situates itself. Taking into account the developments of Marxist and post-Marxist approaches, McLaren proposes a new theory of ideology with a central focus on the body as an ideological site. Drawing from Foucault's "discursive formations," McLaren argues that ideologies are inscribed in signifying practices that constitute various representations of reality. This, of course, does not signify that ideology is merely false consciousness (McLaren, 1989: 174–204). Ideologies are forms of representation that serve to organize experiences and constitute subjectivities. We may even be tempted to argue, taking McLaren's analysis one more step forward, that no subjectivity can be formed without a language, and since every language constitutes subjectivities, therefore, every linguistic practice may combine (even in convoluted form) ideological premises alongside with abstract and practical knowledge. Thus, education and ideology are an inseparable part of the process of forming an individual as interlocutor with a particular language and narrative and a particular perception of the world, a perception that is altogether practical and heuristical and that, under certain conditions, it can be made emancipatory.

Educational practices not only produce individuals, languages, and narratives; they also produce meaning. This meaning can either distort or illuminate reality, and can function both at the level of the subconscious and the conscious, or at the level of consciousness and at the taken-for-granted level of commonsense or daily life experience. Thus, in his anthropological work on rituals, Peter McLaren has argued that ideology appears as ritual performance (McLaren, 1986a). All rituals both pollute and purify, destroy and create subjects. Since a number of rituals take place in the schools—rituals that relate to discipline and behavior, but also to ways of seeing and acting, ways of interpreting and understanding, ways of investigating and resisting social praxis—classrooms do not implacably construct or reproduce subjectivities but become a vehicle for confrontation of ideologies, common sense, scientific knowledge, and (social, political, and ethical) action.

McLaren wants to bring into classrooms (and bodies) a sense of play and work, a sense of creativity and humanity at the same time: "We need to develop within schooling a rhetoric of playful and fictive religiosity, one which will enable us to construe the universe 'as if' it were humanely ordered and meaningful even though we know these constructs are 'not really' true" (1986a: 248).

It would be naive technocratic thinking to argue that a new rationality will do away with the basic rituals surrounding social life. McLaren argues, however, that schooling rituals should not regiment desires (a basic postmodern theme), nor should they domesticate subjectivities. The emphasis on creating emancipated and thoughtfully rigorous yet playful subjectivities in schools has motivated McLaren, and other authors working in the vein of critical pedagogy, to consider the work of Paulo Freire as very important for education, empowerment, and emancipation (McLaren, 1986b: 389–401; Aronowitz and Giroux, 1991; Freire and Macedo, 1987; Shor and Freire, 1987; Shor, 1992).

From a poststructuralist and postmodernist perspective, McLaren argues that "in their attempt to 'deconstruct' the curriculum and to read the 'text' of teacher performance, radical educators have begun to uncover the mutually constitutive process of power/knowledge and how this configuration reproduces itself through particular discourses in school settings" (McLaren, 1986b: 393). Paulo Freire's insight that underlying literacy and learning there is always a political project, and his proposal of "conscientization" as an alternative political project to traditional education, constitutes one of the key breakthroughs in contemporary pedagogy (Torres, 1992, in McLaren and Leonard).

Drawing from Freire (and Derrida, Gadamer, Ricoeur, Lacan, Barthes, Foucault, Deleuze, and Guattari), critical pedagogues, as illustrated in McLaren's work, show that culture built on "multiple discourses" (inhabited by multiple voices) in multicultural, multiracial, or multilingual societies is never depoliticized. Thus it is impossible to set an objective and definitive cultural canon (e.g., a Western Culture canon). On the contrary, since culture is a field of struggle, language, culture, and education should always include the plurality of values, voices, and intentions of subjects; all of whom, by their very nature, engage in dialogical praxis, with all sorts of contradictions, tensions, and conflicts among themselves and with the hegemonic power.

The implications of these considerations for the basic learning process of individuals in late capitalism is paramount. Thus, instead of "classical" literacy, McLaren calls for *cultural literacies* (1988: 213–34) and literacy as cultural politics. Needless to say, the call of Freire, Aronowitz, Giroux, McLaren, Macedo, Shor, and others for a critical pedagogy emphasizing culture rather than canon has lasting implications for curriculum theory and curriculum design (Giroux and McLaren 1986; Freire and Macedo, 1987; Shor and Freire, 1987; Shor, 1987).

Giroux and McLaren's most recent contributions to a post-colonial pedagogy attempt to grasp both the historical implications of colonialism in the constitution of contemporary pedagogical thoughts and the need to liberate the body and desires, in a psychoanalytical fashion, from what they consider "immanentist" pedagogies. In so doing, they invite curriculum theorists to develop a postmodernist, postcolonial pedagogy, rethinking issues of identity, educational praxis, and aesthetics in the cultural realm.

In summary, it is clear so far that postmodernism, as a cultural paradigm, could lead to either a regressive view of emancipatory politics or a critical one. Similarly, it is clear that by confronting educators with a more critical view of the relationships between culture, power, and knowledge (Aronowitz and Giroux, 1991: 234; Popkewitz, 1987a, 1987b), a postmodern discourse of resistance can be accomplished that includes the contributions of multiple feminisms, reconstructed Marxism, and antiracist perspectives. Providing that critical pedagogy moves from theoretical analysis into,

conventionally speaking, empirical research, it can even accommodate, without self-contradiction, political-economy theories that
challenge commodification of lifeworld experiences and growing
class differentiation, social marginality, and poverty in disorganized
capitalism (Offe, 1985). In this context, then, postmodernism artic-
ulates and disarticulates, at the same time, the complex interactions
between class, race, and gender in pedagogical (and sociological)
discourses. A strength of postmodernist discourse is the insights of
its cultural critique. The next section discusses this in some detail.

Gender and Race

Henry Giroux's (1992) most recent attempt to reorient critical
pedagogy through a dialogue with feminist postmodernism is suggestive of *how the gains of critical reproduction theories can be
preserved in the current context,* though this is not his immediate
aim. In this respect, he pursues the strategy, identified by Kanpol,
that "one way to bridge the modern and postmodern debate, *without* seeking closure for ultimate truth, is to theorize about similarity within differences" (Kanpol, 1992: 41). Significant here is
that he draws upon the resistance of race theorists and third-wave
feminist theorists against some of the excesses of postmodernist
attacks on both social inquiry and the indiscriminate emphasis on
difference (e.g., hooks and West, 1991).

If some feminists have been tempted by unselective postmodernist attacks on social theory, few theorists of race and gender
would succumb to throwing out general theories of domination in
the name of a pluralist celebration of difference. A plausible basis
for this is that racial minorities are more familiar with the abuses
to which the denial of the structural bases of inequality and theories of *absolute* difference can be put. At least the subordinate
status of women was accompanied by certain patriarchal protec-
tions and rights otherwise denied "chattel." Further, those historically most denied participation in the universal discourse of civilization are inevitably ambivalent about being told that universalizing discourses are over now—at the very moment that they have
become legitimate members of the academy.

Perhaps this ambivalence is expressed more strongly among
Black male theorists precisely because of their sensitivity to the
potentially disabling effects of the localization and parochializa-
tion of their experience. For example, Paul Gilroy (1992), writing

from a British perspective, is concerned with moving beyond the "local" as evident in some of the forms of "ethnic absolutism" found in very different ways in both Britain and the United States. Instead, he seeks to define the Black experience at least in "intermediate" terms of an "Atlantic" identity, if not global terms. In any case this reflects resistance to the strong postmodernist suggestion that only the "local" can and should be the object of knowledge and identity. On the other side of the Atlantic, Cornel West speaks of postmodernism and "the crisis of Black intellectuals" in complementary terms that resist the reification of difference through recourse to a reconstructed discourse of humanity:

> The idea of taking black people seriously in the life of the mind is a very new notion for white people, so they have to get used to it . . . Now, we could just call that human interaction, but the idea of human interaction across races is a new notion in Western Civilization at some levels, especially at the level of practice, as Ghandi noted quite aptly. So the question is, on the individual level, how do we insure the possibility of this kind of human interaction? I think one way of doing that is by creating very substantive links with colleagues who you are sure are in touch with your humanity and you are in touch with theirs, in the life of the mind. (West, 1992: 704)

But this position is not exclusive to male theorists, despite their complicity in the historical association of masculinity with universalistic modes of thought. As Giroux points out, the central theme of this critical racial appropriation of the discourse of postmodernism among Black women facilitates a politics of difference that does not preclude, but in fact *requires,* one of solidarity that reaches beyond differences:

> But Lorde, like a number of Afro-American writers, is not content either to limit her analysis to the racism inherent in narrowly defined feminist theories of difference or to deconstruct forms of cultural separatism. Lorde is also concerned about developing a politics of solidarity and identity that views difference as a dynamic human force that is "enriching rather than threatening to the defined self when there are shared goals." (Giroux, 1992: 129)

The question is thus not simply one of substituting popular culture for traditional high culture, as neoconservative defenders of universalistic European culture often presuppose (Giroux and Simon, 1989). The question is rather one of widening our understanding of universal issues through the introduction of the understanding of new and different forms of particularity as voicing previously suppressed human concerns. After all, Europe—the cause of Eurocentrism—and its cultural heritage could be seen in the context of human endeavors as a minuscule undertaking compared to the great civilizations of ancient China and India, the pre-Columbian cultures in the Americas, and even the origins of Western civilization in Africa. To the debates of modernity and postmodernity these traditions offer a crucial complement to the inevitable limitations and distortions of Eurocentric interpretations.

RETHINKING CULTURAL REPRODUCTION AND RESISTANCE

Postmodernism has challenged Western thinking in many ways. We shall start this conclusion with a disclaimer. Our critical assessment of postmodernism brings into play our uncertainties as well as our convictions. With respect to the consequences of postmodernism, two fundamental issues are at stake here that define the terrain of the split between what has variously been described as "critical" and "apologetic" postmodernism: the first is metatheoretical and methodological; the second, substantive (McLaren, 1994). On the one hand, are modernist theories of educational reproduction of every stripe destined to fall prey to the critiques of theoretical "grand narratives" and the progressive illusions of modernist theorizing? Is the very aspiration to represent society as a totality condemned at the outset? Here we will be concerned with *the crisis of representation* in social theory associated with postmodernism.

On the other hand, does the social and cultural context of postmodernity fundamentally transform the nature of domination itself, thus further eroding the basis for representing it theoretically? Here we will assess some of the implications of the *fragmentation of domination* identified in postmodernity for theories of educational reproduction.

Postmodernism as Epistemology

A first problem is that usually epistemological critiques conflate or take as the target classical forms of Enlightenment thought associ-

ated, for example, with classic forms of Marxism, Husserlian phenomenology, or positivist empiricism. As a consequence, one may
not avoid a feeling of the construction of a sort of "straw man"
argument that associates all of these with variants of naive realist
theories of representation psychologically derived from a will to
power. European social theory has not stood still, and its modernist excesses were not simply invented by postmodernism, which
necessarily speaks within the same tradition. In this sense, Gayatri
C. Spivak's makes a valuable comment when she refers to leading
French feminist Luce Iragaray as, like Derrida, defining herself as a
critic but within the limits of Western metaphysical thought
(Spivak, 1992: 74). What much postmodernist theory ignores is
that an intense and profound (intertextual and intratextual) critique of historical Reason emerged in the wake of the crisis of post-
Lukacsian Hegelian Marxism (i.e., the Frankfurt tradition as well
as subsequent developments in linguistic philosophy often labeled
"the linguistic turn"). Jameson is right when he argues that the
unity of postmodernism does not reside in itself but in the very
modernism that seeks to displace (Jameson, 1984).

As a consequence, our position will be advanced from the
critical-theory side of the opposition between postmodernist and
critical social theory. On the one hand, this involves siding with
critical theory and the critical realists in assuming that despite
poststructuralist critiques of representation it is still possible to
theorize about social reality, albeit in more self-reflexive and less
totalizing ways (Morrow, 1991, Morrow and Brown, 1994). To
this extent, we reject the all-embracing interpretations of postmodernist theorists such as Lyotard, or readings of authors such as
Baudrillard and Foucault that culminate in relativism and solips-
ism.[4] On the other hand, we also side with the critical theories of
postmodernity that take seriously the need to revise—as good
historicists—our theoretical constructs to take into account emergent and novel features of social and cultural life (Jameson, 1991).

The crucial issue is whether antifoundationalism and deconstructive antiessentialism necessarily culminate in the solipsistic
paradoxes celebrated in some quarters. Judith Butler, from a feminist perspective, qualifies the antifoundationalism of postmodernism by suggesting the possibility of a "new-foundationalism." She
argues that foundations should be placed in the context of a democratic debate: "That foundation would settle nothing, but would of

its own necessity founder on its own authoritarian ruse. This is not to say that there is no foundation, but rather, that wherever there is one, there will also be a foundering, a contestation. That such foundations exist only to be put into question is, as it were, the permanent risk of the process of democratization. To refuse that contest is to sacrifice the radical democratic impetus of feminist politics" (Butler, 1992: 16).

Deconstructionism, as a form of rhetorical analysis, is another pillar of the so-called postmodernist perspective, and yet, it is intimately related to a form of self-reflexivity that has long been considered an essential component of postempiricist epistemologies. Butler is again very perceptive when she argues that a deconstructive critique should imply that "to deconstruct these terms means, rather, to continue to use them, to repeat them, to repeat them subversively, and to displace them from the context in which they have been deployed as instruments of oppressive power" (Butler, 1992: 17). This is exactly the main motif of this book in bringing reproduction in education, culture, and society, as a problematic, back in.

Postmodernism as a Methodological Critique and a Theory of the Subject

The objective of our reconstruction of reproduction theory is effectively captured in Michael Peter Smith's cogent formulation:

> a remaking of social analysis that eschews essentialisms without abandoning the socio-critical power of theoretical discourse. Many of the contemporary writers on social construction, in reacting against the functionalist logic of various structuralisms, have moved so far in a voluntarist direction that they seem to have forgotten that once constructed human inventions act back upon their creators. Socially constructed borders, in their turn impinge upon, and in some degree either enhance or oppress human lives. (Smith, 1992: 524)

Debates in methodology take place in the specific context of historical sociology and ethnography, approaches that reject the positivist search for universal laws or the naive realist attempt to mirror reality. On the other hand, neither historical sociology nor critical ethnography can dispense with various types of intermediate-level generalizations that represent the generative mechanisms always evident in social life despite its inherent singularity.

Therefore, while postmodernism can justifiably criticize Marx's critique of political economy, his masterpiece of historical analysis in the *Eighteen Brumaire* of Napoleon Bonaparte would resist virtually any criticism from a postmodern perspective, and some would even argue that Marx, experimenting with postmodern narratives, anticipated the collapse of enlightened metanarratives. This is hinted at the opening sentence of the *Eighteenth Brumaire:* "Hegel remarks somewhere that all facts and personages of great importance in world history occur, as it were, twice. He forgot to add: the first time as tragedy, the second as farce" (cited in Norris, 1990: 30).

Similar debates have emerged around the question of the implications of postmodernist ethnography. Smith once again captures the key themes when he argues that postmodern ethnography necessarily implies an "oppositional project." First, postmodern ethnography denies that the researcher can work outside of the domain investigated: "Yet paradoxically, it insists that the investigator can intersubjectively experience the lived contradictions of larger social systems as they are 'imploded' into the social relations and everyday lives of the ethnographic subject" (Smith, 1992: 511).

In this respect, postmodernism is a double-edged sword. Postmodernism may help to challenge theoretical reductionism and contribute to clarify the connections between race, class, and gender in educational practice, curriculum, and cultural forms. At the same time, it may also obscure the intricate relationships between culture and production in disorganized capitalism and thus define the concrete political (and everyday) struggles as a chaotic process beyond human comprehension.

The methodological critique of postmodernism cannot be differentiated from attempts to build a theory of the subject, a project smothered by classical structuralism. The postmodernist focus on the process of cultural production of differences seeks to show that because these are historical and constructed categories, something can be done to change them. The subject becomes a *transformative* agent who challenges pseudouniversalities (Popkewitz, 1991).

But this infinite valorization of differences culminates in paradoxes. In other words, postmodernist theory enables reconsideration of the nature of difference from a new standpoint. On the one hand, this *enables* to the extent that it provides a way of overcoming false universality and the vindication of rights to difference. On the other hand, it is potentially *disabling* to the extent that it opens the way to the possibility of the *reification* of difference, or more commonly, to a celebration of difference that either loses sight of or undermines the bases of unity necessary for the formation of political communities. The crucial point is that vast array of groups placed in subaltern positions in societies are themselves unstable and internally differentiated, leading to an infinite fragmentation which makes the constitution of a subject (and of course by implication the notion of agency) both fascinating in its richness and complexity and problematic in terms of its strategic logic and tactics.

From the perspective of hegemonic alliances and power struggles, social protest articulated through new but fragmented social movements may result in growing turbulence but not necessarily in a way that fundamentally challenges public policy in the end. With decentered social subjects and fragmented power the divide-and-rule strategy of the dominant hegemonic bloc may work relatively smoothly while at the same time growing social disturbances can be deemed the reason to return to a romanticized past based on conservative values (Apple, 1990; Scott, 1990). Are such fragmentations of subjectivity the inevitable outcome of the cultural condition of postmodernity?

Postmodernism as a Social Condition or Cultural Paradigm

Jameson, in his path-breaking article (1984), argued that postmodernism is the *cultural logic* of *late capitalism*. This is turn is defined as a stage of capitalist development, compatible with but not restricted to the notion of postindustrial society, characterized by a new cultural logic linked to the predominance of multinationals in a global context. However suggestive and important, this type of analysis clearly falls back on notions of totality that have not fully incorporated methodological critiques of classical Marxism. Yet the notion of a cultural logic refers to alternative interpretations of the so-called postmodern condition (Lyotard, 1984). The contexts of globalization, acceleration of communications, and stylistic transformations evident in fields such as architecture, film, literature, and popular culture, all imply a fundamental transformation of the cultural realm, or, as Lash (1990) puts it, a new cultural paradigm.

Whether one names this "new" condition *late modernism,* as Giddens does (1990), or whether it is indeed a radical departure resulting in a triple phenomena of a *style* (i.e., architecture), *method* (humanities, literary theory), or *epoch* (postFordism, postindustrial society) (Smith, 1992), the question of how to interpret its social foundations—if we can resort to traditional terms—continues to be a problematic one. Moreover, if there is a new type of social reality associated with the postmodern condition, what are the implications for pedagogy?

Representatives of critical pedagogy such as Aronowitz and Giroux argue that there are manifold implications for schooling, including overcoming the "verbal bias" of classical critical theory, which means reinterpreting and expanding the concept of literacy (as critical literacies—McLaren and Lankshear, 1993); breaking the distinction between oral and written sources of cultural training; appraising the importance of mass media and popular culture in the context of open-ended postmodernist texts dealing with key concepts of the politics of the body, desires, graphic representations rather than logical representations of lifeworlds, and so on; and the incorporation of repressed discourses and voices (sexuality, fragmentation of bodies, desire) in the explicit curriculum. This is predicated on the premise that there is no uncontested canon but culture(s) that should be reflected in curriculum and pedagogy.

The impossibility of an uncontested canon results from the impossibility of defining a single, integrated, nonproblematic, and descriptive social and pedagogical identity in the culture of the West. Conversely, there is the need to incorporate social texts and voices suppressed or repressed in the mainstream humanities and sciences, particularly the notion that the classic text, while valuable as *one* experience of humanity, by and large reflects the purview of male, white, heterosexual, and Eurocentric theorists who may have endorsed or condoned the fact that "the culture of enlightenment modernity has also always (though by no means exclusively) been a culture of inner and outer imperialism" (Huyssen, 1990: 374).

Postmodernism as Politics of Culture and Education

Let us begin with the premise that although the process of globalization has taken a planetary dimension, this, in itself, does not guarantee homogeneity, but on the contrary produces a new kind of heterogeneity, and this would be—we claim—differentially reflected in industrial advanced societies and in developing societies.

Industrial Advanced Societies Shifts between levels in cultural understanding of identities become now common and continue to be problematic, not only for individuals but for any attempt to implement a systematic process of learning. For example, Gomez Peña, a Latino writer originally from Mexico City, was asked to characterize his ethnic identity:

> Today, eight years after my departure, I cannot answer with a single word, for my "identity" now possesses multiple repertoires: I am Mexican, but I am also Chicano and Latin American. On the border they call me "Chilango" or "Mexiquillo," in the capital "pocho" or "norteño," and in Spain "sudara" . . . my companion Emily is Anglo-Italian, but she speaks Spanish with an Argentinean accent; and together we walk among the ruins of the Tower of Babel of our American postmodernity. (Cited in Smith, 1992: 523).

The peculiar situation of a multilingual, multiethnic, and multicultural society such as the United States precludes us from generalizing about multiculturalism in education worldwide. It is also clear, however, that differences of perceptions about one's identity would conspire against the creation of a common set of readings in cultural history or language arts that can be uniformly applied, and evaluated, even in the context of say, California or New York, Vermont and Maine, or Nova Scotia public schools.

The notion of cultural politics, then, makes sense, but in such a way that the focus of their original preoccupation (i.e., the fragmentation of everyday life practices) is not misplaced or neglected. That is to say, in the words of Kanpol, progressive educators for instance, predicating the need for teachers as "transformative intellectuals" or the cultural empowerment of minority groups through and within education settings, have yet to come to terms with "the teachers role within the enormously stultifying inner-city school environment that breeds teacher apathy and rampant burnout, or the stereotyping by teachers of certain students as successful (Asian students in the main) or unsuccessful (Hispanics, Black, Puerto Ricans, etc.), or the enormously high drop out rate among non-White students" (Kanpol, 1992: 31).

This notion of education as politics relates, quite naturally, to the approach of deconstruction as implemented by feminism. Butler argues that "to take the construction of the subject as a political problematic is not the same as doing away with the subject . . . To deconstruct is not to negate or to dismiss, but to call into question and, perhaps, more importantly, to open up a term, like the subject, to a reusage or redeployment that previously has not been authorized" (1992: 15).

Of course, Butler needs this preface to address quite an intractable (political) subject in the context of feminist debates: how to assess and describe the constituency to which feminism speaks. Butler is right that, at least in the United States, "lobbying efforts are virtually impossible without recourse to identity politics" (1992: 15), thus the need to define the category of women as a subject. Yet, Butler is also aware of the paradox of building subjects through identity claims: "I would argue that any effort to give universal or specific content to the category of women, presuming that guarantee of solidarity is required *in advance*, will necessarily produce factionalization, and that 'identity' as a point of departure can never hold as the solidifying ground of a feminist political movement" (1992: 15). This is exactly the question in constructing a political subject as human agency. However, this problem is not exclusive to feminism. It cut across a number of categories and movements, including, for instance, the perceptions of contradictions in gender and between race and gender (Popkewitz, 1984).

In the second context, race and gender are caught up in the histories of colonialism. Spivak outlines central tensions in the process of cultural decolonization of cultural spaces, including her concern that "the most urgent political claims in decolonized space are tacitly recognized as coded within the legacy of imperialism: nationhood, constitutionality, citizenship, democracy, socialism, even culturalism. 'Feminism,' the named movement, is also part of this so-called heritage of the European Enlightenment, although within the enclosure of the heritage it is often inscribed in a contestary role" (Spivak, 1992: 57). A central corollary of Spivak's cultural feminism is the question of how the postcolonial feminist negotiates with the metropolitan feminist (Spivak, 1992: 58). In a similar way, Donna Haraway suggests (paradoxically) the possibility of understanding the experience of domination without trying to define a unitary conceptual or experiential matrix: "Gender, race, or class consciousness is an achievement forced on us by the terrible historical experience of the contradictory social realities of patriarchy, colonialism, and capitalism" (Haraway, 1992: 179; cited in Cosby, 1992).

Third World A key discussion is whether postmodernity, as a triple reality of style, method, and epoch, applies to the Third World. Particularly, we question whether the same processes of interplay among race, class, and gender in social and educational reproduction can be predicated in Muslim/non-Muslim, occidental/oriental, industrial/agrarian, developed/developing societies. This is not only an academic discussion, but one that has serious political implications. For instance, some scholars are concerned that by invoking postmodernity, we condone the excesses of spoliatory modernization, colonialism, and imperialism, which are seen not as disappearing under the guise of the postmodern condition, but remain very much alive and well:

> The black hole that is formed by the rejection of modernism is also apt to obliterate the trace of historical Western expansionism that was at least cofunctional, if not instrumental, in producing epistemological hegemonism. Thus a paradox: as postmodernism seeks to remedy the modernist error of Western, male, bourgeois domination, it simultaneously vacates the ground on which alone the contours of modernism can be seen. Furthermore, colonialism and imperialism are ongoing enterprises, and in distinguishing late post-industrial capitalism from earlier liberal capitalism and by tolerating the former while condemning the latter, postmodernism ends up by consenting to the first world economic domination that persist in exploiting the wretched of the earth. (Mioshi and Harootunian, 1988: 388)

In addition to the risk of preserving historical memories and, we would add, the power of anger for social and educational change, a further risk of postmodernism is to obliterate, in analyzing the ills of the modern condition, the fact that high modernity, as for example defined by Giddens (1991), has been fully attained in few places worldwide. Similarly, Habermas (1981, 1987) speaks of the "unfinished" project of modernity, which is compatible with Giddens' effort to consider this question as an empirical, analytical, and normative problem.

Most of the promises of emancipatory or enlightening modernism have not been achieved, not even partially, in the developing world. In places like Canton, Lisbon, the Appalachians, Buenos Aires, Dar-es-Salaam, Rio de Janeiro, Calcutta, South-Central Los

Angeles, Cancun, or Kuala Lumpur, the postmodern condition is coexisting, in uneasy and at times obscene relationships, with incomplete modernity and sometimes premodern cultures. Pockets of postmodern culture and groups (and educational programs) thrive in the midst of disorganized traditional cultures deeply wounded by the introduction, success, and failure of modernization processes, as well as the initiatives of incomplete—and (following Habermas) pathological—modernity and its byproducts of difference, marginalization, and, in some cases, growing structural poverty in the context of psychic as well as cultural disorganization.

The following narrative illustrates our concern. In February 1992, one of the authors spent three weeks in Mozambique as part of an international group of "experts" studying the educational system. This visit invited us to consider seriously García Marquez's premise of magic realism, insofar as the narrative and the reality of educational planning may be blurring the distinctions between the real and the irreal.

Mozambique was considered in 1991 by the World Bank as one the poorest countries in the developing world. The deterioration of the Mozambican economy, the fragmentation of the state's ability to plan and implement a consistent educational policy in the whole country, its extremely low human capital base, and the destruction wrought by the civil war that has been ranging for fifteen years have serious implications in terms of access to and the equity of the educational system, and at the level of efficiency and quality of education.

The research team found school principals with low morale and teachers voicing all sorts of complaints. But we also found (amazingly) in unannounced visits to schools that teachers were teaching, that large number of students were happily attending their lessons, that parents were waiting patiently to receive confirmation that their children had been enrolled in schools, and that school inspectors and government officials, particularly in the provinces and at the school level, were able to immediately produce substantive and written statistical information on request.

In spite of this appalling situation, the following anecdote offers two examples of the vibrancy of the Mozambican primary education system, and, we would add, the importance of the promise of modernity for Mozambicans. When research-team members parked a car near a restaurant for lunch, half a dozen very young children, many of them barefoot and with ragged clothes, approached us telling us their names. They were competing for the designation of car caretaker, with the hope of collecting a tip afterwards. When the team members left the restaurant, the children came to collect their tips. One of the children was asked what he would do with the money—less than 25 U.S. cents. He responded with a smile: "I will buy a 'caneta' (ball-point pen) for school." Obviously, for a group of researchers trying to find clues about the Mozambican primary education system, the answer was both gratifying and puzzling.

Visiting a secondary school in Sinapura, in the province of Zambézia, team members found that the office of the Director, the only one with security bars in the windows and a security lock, housed not only the normal furniture, official wall pictures, and supplies, but also a disarray of typewriters and a mimeograph, all of them sitting on the floor, or resting against arm chairs. The Director apologized for the untidiness, but explained that vandalism and crime in the area forced him to lock up everything of value in his own office. Visiting the school we found that no pupil or teacher had a single desk or chair to sit or work on: all had been stolen from classrooms with broken doors, perhaps to be used as firewood. Despite it all, the motto of the Director, hanging on the wall in the back of his desk, was quite paradoxical:

Não há problem sem solução
Não há solução sem defeitos
Não há defeitos que não possam ser corrigidos

There are no problems without solutions.
There are no solutions without defects.
There are no defects that cannot be corrected.

This seemingly unwarranted modernist optimism amid most unmodern conditions may be part of the driving force that keeps this educational system going. This unwarranted optimism, the driving force toward education in the context of a civil war, is difficult to understand and to explain. However, it is also part of a magic (and yet tragic) realism of educational development in Mozambique.

Taking into account the contradictions of the Third World, a reality which, occasionally, seems to have been taken out of a book of fiction, it is not surprising that many Third World and minority scholars are suspicious of a cultural paradigm that arises in the architectural movements in Vienna, Paris, or Berlin, or that reflects the exquisite kaleidoscope of the "humanities" enjoyed by highbrow cultural groups or, conversely, reflects the new imaginary of mass media and popular culture in advanced industrial societies. After all, the modernity project challenged *from within* by, say, theories of dependency or theology of liberation was also a by-product of a few enlightened intellectuals and scholars living in core countries and metropolitan cities and remains an integral aspect of any comprehensive critical theory (e.g., Leonard, 1990).

The contributions—but also the risks—of postmodernism as a cultural paradigm for education and politics are breath-taking. However, these theoretical risks and practical-political dangers should not thwart the educational imagination of social agents who may agree with the modernist and yet postmodern Gramscian motto of pessimism of the intelligence, optimism of the will. So in concluding, we would argue with Linda Hutcheon[5] that "in both art and theoretical discourse today, there is what Peter Brook has called 'a certain yearning for the return of the referent,' but it can never be a naive and unproblematic return" (1988: 144).

CHAPTER 15

The Logic of Reproduction: Summary and Conclusions

NEW DEPARTURES? POLITICAL ECONOMY AND THEORY OF THE STATE

Our review of theories of the state and how they affect educational policy and planning shows that an analysis of the educational system cannot be separated from some explicit or implicit analysis of the purposes and functioning of the government sector. This is a most promising agenda for research, emerging from the deadlock debate of the seventies and eighties, linking social, cultural, and economic reproduction, and education and power.

During the nineteenth and, especially, the twentieth centuries, education has been increasingly and overwhelmingly a function of the state. Education is sponsored, mandated, organized, and certified by the state (Carnoy and Levin, 1985). Indeed, public education is not only a state function in terms of legal order or financial support: the specific requirements for degrees, teacher requirements and qualifications, mandated textbooks, and required courses for basic curriculum are controlled by state agencies and designed under specific public policies of the state.

Underlying theories of state-society relationships have influenced research designs in educational policy and planning. Theories of state-society relationships, held by any policy-planning group, government coalitions, or social categories within the state (such as intellectuals, bureaucracies, or military corporations) will underpin educational policy formation. In this regard, the basic dividing line between paradigms of state-society relations is crucial: liberal-pluralist theories and class theories of the state hold assumptions that can hardly be reconciled.

As for liberal-pluralism, the state ("political system") is an autonomous political institution "above" the system of production and the class structure. Therefore, the state is basically a passive arena or a neutral referee overseeing the clashes of interest groups, clashes which presumably operate to fashion a general interest of all the citizens. This view suggests that the state is the collective creation of its individual members, providing a set of common social goods—defense, education, a legal system, and the means of enforcing that system—to all or at least to a sizeable majority. In contrast, class theories view the state as intimately involved in the constitution and reproduction of capitalism as a system by protecting it from various threats and guiding its transformation. There is a sharp disagreement, however, as to how the state manages such a complex task. Class theories of the state envisage the capitalist state as an arena of conflict between social classes with different interests, but an arena that the dominant class is able to dominate somehow, based on the domination of society as a whole.

Increasingly, more and more researchers and practitioners have emphasized the role of educational bureaucracies in their evaluation of educational policy and its links and inputs to socioeconomic development, employment, the development of civic culture, and so forth. Research and polemics on the state in the seventies and eighties were centered on the issue of the relative autonomy of the capitalist state. In Poulantzas's thought, such autonomy is indeed constitutive of the capitalist state: it refers to the state's materiality as an apparatus relatively separate from the relations of production and to the specificity of classes and class struggle under capitalism that is implicit in that separation (Poulantzas, 1978: 127). The state is no longer conceived as an administrative and military organization exerting control over territories; it is viewed as differentiated from societies of classes. Instead the relative autonomy of the state, which is not a fixed structural feature of any governmental system, expresses the notion that the formulation of state goals and the core of state capacities to implement their policies are not simply reflective of the demands or interests of social groups, classes, or society. The extreme version of this argument will stress that the state (and particularly state personnel) is autonomous in its contribution to public-policy making (Block, 1977, 1987); that is to say, the rationale of state action is based on very different grounds from societal pressures and interests.

The political economy of education has incorporated within its research agenda much of the discussion about the capitalist state.

The main topics of this research agenda include (a) a critical review of the determinants of education, income, and occupation—in short, the relationships between education and work; (b) the political determination of education, its function in capitalist society, and its contribution to the overall process of social reproduction and capital accumulation; (c) the issue of educational reform and its contribution to economic and political democracy, especially with respect to advanced capitalist social formations; and (d) a recent focusing on the state education relationship as an essential concern regarding educational policy and planning.

The agenda of a political economy of education and a political sociology of education is far from being exhausted. Many critics of the welfare state saw it withering away during the eighties, as a result of neoconservative policies. However, switching the center of public policy from the state to the market may solve neither the fiscal crisis of the state—for instance, in the United States, with a budget deficit acquiring unprecedented dimensions; and in Latin America, a region housing eleven of the seventeen most highly indebted countries in the world,[1] the external debt crisis has comparable dimensions to the United States fiscal crisis—nor ameliorate growing social problems such as unemployment, homelessness, gang crime, or uneducated citizens.

A casualty of the debate between back-to-basics and drive-for-excellence proponents and liberal-progressive–minded people has been a comprehensive understanding of the relationships among education, work, and communicative action. There is a risk that the insights gained by the contributions of many reproduction theories will be lost in the wake of a new political voluntarism (either from liberal or conservative perspectives).

The prospects of educational reform continue to be under siege (Aronowitz and Giroux, 1985). Equality of educational opportunity, equity, quality, and relevance of education continue to be perennial problems in industrially advanced and dependent-development societies. Denying the structural roots of the crisis, or the presence of cultural arbitraries in the hidden and explicit curriculum, or the relationships between educational sites and social relationships and its implications for domination and exploitation will hamper any attempt at an integrated social science of schooling.

Such a strategy will simply reinforce the political opportunism of policymakers and interest groups drawing their conclusions from the deeply entrenched logic of instrumental action in public policy, and will, in the end, fail to address the plight of the poor and the uneducated—the shattered dreams of children and youth who have no choice but to rely on on public education for sociability, knowledge, and skills. From critical and progressive perspectives, dismissing too quickly the problematic of reproduction without having an alternative interpretative framework will have serious political and analytical implications.

The role of the state is critical in social reproduction and public policy. Connell has cogently demostrated that we cannot separate the notion of the state from crucial elements that account for domination of specific groups, particularly gender subordination:

> The state is itself a reorganization of gender relations, particularly the structure of gender power. The sexual division of labor is implicated in the production processes that generate the surplus of goods and services which makes urban population possible. It is important to know to what extent the surplus is appropriated through sexual politics and on gender lines, and to what extent the increased specialization of workers is a gendered one. (Connell, 1987: 152)

This book has attempted a reconstruction of theories of social and cultural reproduction in education from relatively closed structuralist models based on economic and class determination to relatively open-integrative-reproductive-ones based on parallel determinations stemming from class, gender, and race. It is argued that this shift in reproduction theory took place largely within the discursive context of critical modernist social theory, even though more recently in response to postmodernist critiques. A number of residual difficulties in this form of historical reproduction theory are identified and it is concluded that these larger debates in social theory and the critical sociology of education remain central to educational theory and critical pedagogy.

EDUCATION AND THE REPRODUCTION OF CLASS, GENDER AND RACE: RESPONDING TO THE POSTMODERNIST CHALLENGE

As we said at the beginning of this book[2] whatever happened to theories of social and cultural reproduction in educational theory? Some British sociologists have found it necessary to "revivify" the notion of "cultural reproduction" as a theoretical framework (Jenks, 1993). For some time we have similarly argued for revitalizing the concept in the sociology of education. This process of theoretical revitalization has been inhibited by lingering misunderstandings and lack of awareness of more recent developments, as well as "postmodernist" attacks on attempts to generalize about social reality (Morrow and Torres, 1988; 1994).

Certain half-truths about theories of cultural reproduction have become commonplace and have contributed to those theories falling on hard times in educational theorizing. First, given their frequent use of strong forms of functionalist-type explanations, they are rather hastily dismissed as hopelessly "teleological" along with Parsonian structural functionalism. Second, emphasis on the contributions of the "hidden curriculum" to the reproduction of a capitalist social order is taken to imply that education is "nothing but" ideology and thus incapable of contributing to progressive change or communicating things of universal value. Third, reproduction theories are still widely associated with class-based reductionist analyses (i.e., totalizing metanarratives, to use postmodernist terminology) based on the assumption of a strict correspondence between schooling and the functional imperatives defined by the relations of production. Though these are all valid charges against forms of cultural reproduction theories that have been influential at some point in the past (most notably, structuralist Marxism), they fail to hit their mark with respect to the more subtle formulations that have come to inform contemporary critical sociologies of education (Popkewitz, 1988).

Despite the various criticisms and qualifications of the original "correspondence principle" for economically based models, the general notion of social and cultural reproduction has remained—despite appearances—a central assumption of critical pedagogy and critical sociologies of schooling. To be sure, this has required fundamental revisions involving the incorporation of concepts of agency and resistance along with the diversification of the causal nexus of power to include nonclass forms of exclusion and domination. As well, the metatheoretical status of such theorizing has shifted from that of a totalizing (functionalist) structuralism to that of a more fallibilistic, historically specific structural method.[3]

Does it make sense to continue to refer to such approaches with the concept of reproduction at all? As one recent defender of the notion of cultural reproduction has charged, the concept was "seemingly highjacked" (at least in Britain) by "the orthodoxy of studies in the theory of ideology and neo-Marxisms," thus distracting attention from the dynamic and positive dimensions revealed in other sources of this tradition (Jenks,1993: 2). This situation requires "an attempt to liberate the concept back into the wider arena of sociological debate," a process initiated in the work of Pierre Bourdieu (Jenks, 1993: 6). As we have argued, such a rehabilitation has been long under way in both social theory and educational sociology in the guise of what we have termed *practice-based, parallelist models of cultural reproduction.*

Our argument has been built on a systematic criticism of social theory resting on a metatheoretical framework. Three related claims with respect to these theoretical transformations should be considered (Morrow and Torres, 1994). First, though the actual term *reproduction* has often tended to slip out of sight, we suggest that the basic problematic of social and cultural reproduction remains a central preoccupation of critical theories of the relationships between schooling and society. Second, a new model, the parallelist strategies (i.e., social action as the product of parallel determinations stemming from class, gender, and race), while highly sensitive to history, agency, and social practices, still employs structuralist methodological strategies, thus remaining within the realm of theories of social and cultural reproduction. However, the parallelist models have effectively encouraged the exploration of the independent effects of class, gender, race, and other forms of domination in the context of schooling. Third, that despite the analytical progress made by parallelist models of analysis, they have failed to address adequately three fundamental issues: (a) that each of these forms of domination has a significantly different systemic character with crucial consequences for their conceptualization as forms of domination; (b) that the analysis of the interplay of these "variables" has been obscured by the language of "relative autonomy" left over from structuralist Marxism; and (c) that even though the explanatory objectives of parallelist reproduction theory are necessarily more modest and historically contingent than envisioned by classic, structuralist reproduction theories, this still involves avoidance of the postmodernist tendency to endlessly fragment and pluralize conflicts and differences as if there were no systematic links among them.

In this book, we have assumed—and at points, defended—the continuing pertinence and analytical value of a radically revised critical modernist stance in social theory.[4] Whether or not this position is graced with the label "postmodernist" critical theory (in the manner of Aronowitz and Giroux) is less important than the substantive issues at stake. Suitably revised, we argued, the concept of totality—including a perspective allowing for an analysis of interactions, interplay, and relationships among class, gender, and race in educational settings—facilitates a reconstructed model of social and cultural reproduction. This model is at the same time open-ended, takes modernity as an object of critical inquiry rather than as a premise, takes seriously the postmodernist critique both at the level of epistemology and at the level of culture, and yet considers the political implications of theory and research in the context of a project of social, gender, and ethnic (including racial) emancipation. Politics, by the way, is not taken here purely in its instrumental or pragmatic sense, but it is also considered as an horizon that opens up possibility for human action, and as a contested symbolic, material, and factual terrain intrinsically linked to public-policy formation and individual identity and action.[5]

What are some of the consequences that follow from the difficulties of parallelist models? We would like to touch upon three issues here. First, it should be stressed that the analytical approach of seeing gender and race as both abstractly autonomous and yet contingently internal to specific social formations does not yield abstract, determinist conclusions. Nor does it abandon the problem of causal connections to the metaphors of endless plays of difference. Rather, it calls for "local investigations" (which may involve case studies of regional or even national scope) that are formulated with questions posed in terms of comparative historical generalizations about the interplay of race, gender, class, and other forms of domination.

Second, the goal of "solidarity across differences" must be seen as one of variable difficulty. In important respects, it may be that biologically based gender differences (e.g., the capacity for reproduction, the physiology of sexuality, etc.) are more enduring and intractable than those of class (which reflect historically changeable relations of power and opportunity) and those of race (which are based on the added dimension of trivial phenotypical differences). In the case of black women, class, gender, and race combine in the constitution of individual subjectivities and social agents in a manner that has no parallel for white women or black men. It has been argued, for instance, that unlike white women, black working-class women "claim knowledge not only through gender, but through racial identity and relations" (Luttrell, 1989: 33). However Luttrell's explorations of women's ways of knowing suggest that while class-based concepts pit working- and middle-class people against each other and racially based concepts pit whites against blacks, it is "the invisible gender-based concept that pits collectivity against individuality and autonomy against dependence" and becomes the "basis for unequal power relations between working-class men and women" (Luttrell, 1989: 41). A similar claim that students' gender self-definitions are more complex and less shared than those based on race or class has been made by Grant and Sleeter (1988). As they conclude, students in relatively integrated communities saw gender as a more divisive form of human difference than race and class (1988: 40).

Third, the depth-psychological basis of the processes of gender and race (the structure of cathexis, in Connell's terms) makes them more intractable and of a different order than those of class. Whatever the specific problems associated with Lacanian psychoanalysis and its reception, it has provided an impetus to understanding why racial and gender differences (like those of sexual orientation itself) are different from others, especially those of class, which were the particular concern of liberal and socialist enlightenment alike. An important implication is that the nature of cultural criticism and its practical effects requires reexamination (Bracher, 1993).

A final comment regards the interplay of race, class, and gender in education as cultural politics should be taken up. In debates about the problematic of cultural reproduction, it has been argued that schools do not merely produce, distribute, and reproduce knowledge, cognitive and moral skills, and disciplinary molds. In so doing they also constitute places for the formation of subjectivities, identities, and subcultures. Since knowledge and power shape the form and content of curricula through ideological interests coined in class, race, and gender-specific terms, the notion of schools as a battleground is helpful to begin understanding the implication of schools (and nonformal education) practices.

However, with the growing preoccupation with postmodern themes, by reducing the analysis of all educational activities to cultural politics, less attention is paid to structural principles underlying the educational process. The analytical and political implications of these omissions are potentially quite dangerous for political struggle, as every teacher and practitioner trying to make sense of his or her own daily work and struggle, and that of her or his students, will recognize.

Yet the impact of most postmodernist theorizing on educational theory would seem to have rather hastily collapsed these theoretical advances into what is dismissed as the obsolete methodology of "structuralism" and modernist universalizing of a type ostensibly rendered obsolete by poststructuralism. As a consequence, Jennifer Gore can without hesitation claim that her approach is

> consistent with major social theory debates over structural versus poststructural positions (whose which find their grounding prior to the construction of discourses, for example, in the economy or in the category "women," and those which reject such universalized and decontextualized notions and enter debates and critiques in specific contexts). As is consistent with other poststructural critiques, I demonstrate the universalizing, dominating tendencies of critical and feminist pedagogy discourses as regimes of truth. (Gore, 1993: xv)

A central problem of this type of formulation is that it runs the risk, on the one hand, of conflating two rather distinct theoretical discourses *within* critical pedagogy: that of a *model of cultural reproduction,* which is grounded in an explanatory social science; and that of an *emancipatory pedagogical practice,* which is grounded in a normative and practical discourse oriented toward transformative possibilities. To be sure, the original project of critical social theory envisions these two discourses as intertwined and mutually supportive, but their distinct epistemological and methodological status needs to be acknowledged. Indeed, this is the basis of the *internal dialogue* within critical theory, and the basis of the possibility that revisions in the social scientific model may falsify or at least require revisions in the practical-emancipatory discourse, just as the latter may pose new research questions for the former.

For the present discussion, we will accept the plausibility of Gore's focus on the instructional act as the context of a "regime of truth" involving the "micro" functioning of power relations; on the other hand—and this is a second risk of strong poststructuralist formulations—we have implicitly contested the implication that postmodernist critiques of this type adequately address the problem of "universalizing principles" that have indeed at times afflicted formulations of social and cultural reproduction. Even if the "social vision" of critical pedagogies are acknowledged as valuable by Gore, their repressive potential is held to be ultimately rooted in both a lack of self-reflexivity and "in the totalizing discourses of Neo-Marxism and the Critical Theory of the Frankfurt School" (Gore, 1993: 114). But this latter point is misleading, given the explicit *antifoundationalist* intentions of much recent critical social theory associated with critical pedagogy, and the forms practice-oriented models of cultural reproduction discussed here.

Such blanket—dare we say "essentializing"?—postmodernist critiques implicitly draw upon a formalized distinction (a binary opposition) between the "universal" and the "local" that is grounded in the older German debate confronting "nomothetic" and "ideographic" research, rather than the postempiricist realities of both critical social theory and a comparative historical sociology (or ethnography) concerned with the *interdependence* of theoretical generalization and particular case studies.[6] In this respect we agree fully with the recent "materialist" feminist diagnosis of the problematic aspects of the postmodernist privileging of "local" and "regional" analysis:

> I think this rejection of systemic analysis needs to be re-evaluated now, particularly in light of the growing appeal of ludic postmodernism's regional analysis . . . We need to advance a problematic in which the articulations of race, class, gender, and sexuality can be understood in their historical specificity without abandoning analyses that situate them in terms of the social totalities that continue to regulate our lives. A global reading strategy can provide this without re-enacting the totalizing strategies of a master narrative. (Hennessy, 1993: 96)[7]

From this perspective, historically oriented, open models of social and cultural reproduction remain an essential aspect of a critical modernist social science and cannot be readily subsumed under the notion of totalizing master narratives, partly because they originated as critiques of formalist, structural Marxism. As Fraser and Nicholson conclude in their assessment of the implications of these issues for feminist theory:

A first step is to recognize, *contra* Lyotard, that postmodernist critique need not forswear neither large historical narratives nor analyses of societal macrostructures. This point is important for feminists, since sexism has a long history . . . However, if postmodern-feminist critique must remain theoretical, not just any kind of theory will do. Rather, theory here would be explicitly historical, attuned to the cultural specificity of different societies and periods and to that of different groups within societies and periods . . . Moreover, postmodern-feminist theory would be nonuniversalist. When its focus became cross-cultural or transepochal, its mode of attention would be comparativist rather than universalizing, attuned to changes and contrasts instead of to covering laws. (Fraser and Nicholson, 1989: 24)

The preoccupation of this book has been to show the continuing importance of the issues introduced by theories of social and cultural reproduction. In the reconstructed parallelist models entailing class, race, and gender, we find the bases for theoretically driven empirical research that can contribute to political practice and educational policy innovation. We hope it has become clear to the reader that in the background, as a shadow for our theoretical defense of a reconstructed and critical modernist theory, there are ongoing debates with respect to the implications of postmodernism for educational theory and research. We have tried to demonstrate that reconstructed theories of cultural reproduction remain central to the future of educational theory.

An integrated theory of class, race, and gender can only be as insightful as the concrete studies its produces, the ways in which these work back into the theory itself, and their suitability for progressive politics. From this perspective a formalized, systematic theory is impossible, or at best, trivial. But we shall continue stressing the need for historical, comparative, and even quantitative studies at the school level and also in nonformal education. These studies should understand that, while we may not be able to entirely conceptualize the multiple parallel determinations, or the interplays of class, race, and gender in education, at least, the struggle to overcome discrimination, oppression, and the deep structuring of subjectivities with racist, sexist, gender-biased, and classist overtones has had a long history and many anonymous heroes. This is not the time to romanticize the struggle, but neither it is a time to nurture historical amnesia.

NOTES

CHAPTER 1

1. Our initial collaborative exploratory formulation—culminating in the present project—was presented in 1988: Raymond A. Morrow and Carlos Alberto Torres, "Social Theory, Social Reproduction, and Education's Everyday Life: A Framework for Analysis," a paper presented at the Canadian Western Association of Sociology and Anthropology Annual Meetings, University of Alberta, Edmonton, Canada, February 1988; see also, Torres and González Rivera (1994) and Morrow (1985). For an elaboration of the methodological assumptions, see Morrow and Brown, 1994.

2. So, for example, Michael Apple points to the "need to interpret schooling as both a system of production and reproduction," in revising his earlier "correspondence" position in *Education and Power* (1985: 22); and Stanley Aronowitz and Henry Giroux develop a typology of theories of reproduction: economic-reproductive (structuralist Marxism), cultural-reproductive (Bourdieu), and hegemonic-state models (Gramscian) and their relation to theories of resistance in *Education Under Siege* (1985: 74ff). Giroux's more recent flirtation with postmodernism in his *Border Crossings* (1992) does not involve abandoning this theme, though it could be argued that the he fails to articulate adequately the "language of possibility" with the conjunctural constraints of structure.

3. For instance, Murphy (1979) in Canada and Robinson (1981) in Britain attempted to develop well-balanced introductory texts covering the range of debates in the sociology of education and were among the first to consider reproduction theory. But both are now dated, rather elementary, do not explicitly and consistently introduce the social theoretical assumptions of the theories described, and attempt a rather wider focus than is our objective here. Studies such as those of Sarup (1978, 1984) and Sharp (1980) reflect the first stage of the reception of neo-Marxist theory in Britain and Australia and remain rather narrowly fo-

cused on British issues and defend a rather dogmatic (Sharp) and/or eclectic (Sarup) conception of the issues. Demaine's (1981) study covers similar territory in the British context from a more skeptical Leftist position. Most recently, Blackledge and Hunt (1985) provide the most up-to-date and comprehensive survey of theories in the sociology of education, but their neo-Weberian position is advanced rather weakly on the basis of often inadequate and simplistic characterizations and criticisms of rival positions. And again, the North American literature is scarcely touched upon. Gibson (1984) gives prominence to the topic of structuralism but in a rather diffuse and eclectic way that only indirectly deals with the types of issues which are of concern to us. Unfortunately, Gibson's subsequent (1986) study of critical theory and education is highly selective, given lack of access to the nontranslated German literature in education. Price's (1986) survey of Marx and "late capitalism," and similarly Youngman (1986) in the context of adult education and socialist pedagogy, shift the focus of discussion away from education in the stricter sense (whether formal or informal) toward a more general theory of social learning which is held to be more consistent with Marx's own approach.

Now in an updated edition, virtually the only American text to give full coverage of reproduction theory debates (Hurn, 1985) is more oriented toward specialized educational debates (e.g., teacher training, curriculum, etc.), and remains almost exclusively an introductory survey focused on American issues (see also Paulston, 1976). As well, it is based on a pluralist consensus theory that presupposes a simplistic and superficial conception of power that can be challenged from a more refined conflict perspective (see Murphy, 1988: 150–53).

4.   E.g., the critical pedagogy and sociology of schooling associated with the original work of Apple, Aronowitz, Bowles, Gintis, Giroux, Carnoy, Levin, McClaren, Popkewitz, Wexler, etc., which will be discussed later.

5.   Though this range of reference is determined in part by our own experiences, it also has theoretical justifications in that these two types of social formation lend themselves most readily to classical and contemporary European social theory. Asian, Near Eastern, African, and East Bloc societies pose special problems with which we cannot deal. Further, we recognize the wide variations within the two types of social formations that are the focus of our attention. Neither in these advanced or relatively underdeveloped cases does the historical evidence provide the basis for any easy or glib generalizations about the "functions" of education in general, let alone a guideline for progressive educational policies. But we will contend that without the insights derived from the understanding of theories of social reproduction, such strategies will be doomed at the outset.

CHAPTER 2

1. For a succinct critique of this traditional approach to "empirical theory," see Bernstein (1978: 3–54). To be sure, the approach of Karl Popper and his followers does encourage the process of theory proliferation by accepting the difficulty of corroboration and falsification. See, for instance Lakatos and Musgrave (1970).

2. As we shall see, the advantage of Habermas's knowledge-interest schema is that it facilitates seeing how different types of theories of social reproduction combine these interests in distinct ways; further, it provides an epistemological foundation for justifying retention of the agent-structure dialectic as the basis for any adequate theory of reproduction; finally, it points to the importance of justifying the normative aspects of theories of reproduction. On the implications of Habermas for educational theory generally, cf. Misgeld (1985), Weiler (1983), Carr and Kemmis (1986); and Young (1989).

3. Though Burrell and Morgan's schema is applied to classifying theories of complex organization, it serves as a useful heuristic device for classifying sociological theories generally and is based upon presuppositions compatible with Habermas's theory of knowledge interests. We diverge from Burrell and Morgan, however, with respect to various details of the application of their two-axis schema, especially their global characterization of radical humanist (critical) theories as "anti-organization" theories, giving them an essentially (and excessively) anarchist interpretation. Further, it should be noted that comparing theories with a continuum schema produces difficulties for the extremes, which may reveal the logical problems inherent in absolutizing one pole. Also there is a tendency to see the compromise of a middle position as more adequate, despite the methodological problems that result.

4. Pessimistic versions of conflict theory such as that of Max Weber see such domination as essentially inevitable, much as Freud in the case of intrapsychic conflict.

5. Indeed, many would regard this classification as simplistic in that it assumes a distorted version of Weber as a voluntarist and of Durkheim as a determinist. The more important point of this type of ideal typical classification is that it does capture how these theorists have tended to be understood, irrespective of the deeper logic of their respective approach.

6. These terms, borrowed from Burrell and Morgan (and systems theory), should not be taken to have any direct value implications as, for example, in the distinction between "open" and "closed" minds or societies. The distinction is rather analytical, indicating the degree of the integration of society presupposed, at least for methodological purposes, which may be distinct from practical-political ones.

7.   As we will see in the chapter on neofunctionalist theories, however, the differentiation model of Alexander and Archer's morphogenic model move toward more open strategies.

8.   This holds more for educational research than sociological theory generally, where the functionalist assumptions (alleged or imagined) of Marx have become the basis of wide-ranging debate. On the one hand, Althusser and Poulantzas have been attacked as "functionalists" having more in common with Parsons than with Marx (e.g., Cole, 1988); and on the other, G. A. Cohen (1978) has defended in a very influential form the moderate functionalism of Marx's method.

CHAPTER 3

1.   For a discussion of the equilibrium concept in social theory see Russett (1966).

2.   It is not possible here to survey the more recent debates on the role of functional analysis in the social sciences, particularly Giddens' strong antifunctionalist stance. For a rigorous and limited defense of evolutionary and functional explanation, however, see Faia (1986). Merton's discussion has the great merit of clarity and does outline the basic issues.

3.   We have not attempted to document in this brief review the leading themes of the latter two phases of Parsons' work, though they are all touched upon in summary, historical volume edited by Jackson Toby (Parsons, 1977).

4.   Others would provide a more differentiated formulation of this competitive selective process, e.g., Turner's (1960) distinction between "sponsored" and "contest" mobility.

5.   In 1969 the American Academy of Arts and Sciences and Harvard's Assembly on University Goals and Governance commissioned Parsons and Platt to develop a study on the structure of the university and its relation to student protest. The result was a very large volume that applied Parsons' general schema to universities.

6.   This type of criticism is the point of departure of Baudelot and Establet's (1971) analysis of the French system.

7.   This study is atypical in its focus on the environmental determinants of aspects of school system; the primary focus of systems oriented research has been on the school as a social system, drawing upon the standard literature of functionalist organizational analysis (e.g., Hoy and Miskel, 1982).

8.   To his credit, Smelser's long involvement in educational politics has led to a fundamental revision of the differentiation model to deal with this problem, as we have seen (Smelser, 1985).

9. The divergences within the apparent homogeneity of structural functionalism, which is fed by a vigorous progressive liberal political philosophy are vast. An example can be found in an older text of Henry Kissinger who, comparing the advantages of specialization and the strengthening of scientific-technical education confronted with the classical paradigm of expanding the human sciences, shows skepticism regarding the assumption that greater educational development per se would preserve developing societies from authoritarian temptations (Kissinger, 1961).

CHAPTER 4

1. "In its statistical form, entropy (H) is a content-free, continuous measure of system structure—just what we needed to replace equilibrium." (1990: 85–86).

2. The extensive debate between Luhmann and the critical theorist Habermas (Habermas and Luhmann, 1971), as well as Habermas's more recent critique of Parsons (Habermas, 1987), is suggestive of the overlapping aspects of, and residual differences between, neofunctionalism and a reconstructed historical materialism. In any case, neofunctionalism does not appear to deviate in any fundamental way from the more general tendency of substantive functionalism to subsume education within an evolutionary process of progressive social differentiation.

3. Curiously, Maynes (1985)—a social historian—mentions Archer's early work dating from the early 1970s, but not the more recent and theoretical comparative research.

CHAPTER 5

1. The dilemmas of relativism point to the strategic significance of Habermas's (e.g., 1979) efforts to secure the normative grounds of a reconstructed historical materialism on something other than an abstract philosophical anthropology or a dogmatic philosophy of history.

2. The *welfare state* can be defined as a form of the capitalist state that has emerged in the industrial advanced social formations. In its most sharp form, it is represented in the social-democratic Scandinavian States. Some of its features are the following: First, the state promotes a policy of absolute equity among the different social classes but without threatening or affecting the capitalist (private) ownership of the means of production or the capitalist division of labor. That is to say, the state postulates a minimum standard of income, nutrition, health, housing, and education that is guaranteed to each citizen as a political right and not as charity.

Second, there will be a bureaucratic encapsulation of public policy formation, implementation, and evaluation through a decision-making process that is funded in corporative mechanisms of control and cooperation. Third, there will be a self-perception within state high officials and the rest of the corporations that this type of state is a "tertium quid" between the classic democratic capitalist state and the totalitarian communist state. A very articulate liberal representative of the welfare state is Harold L. Wilensky (1975, 1976). For a neo-Marxist analysis of the origins of the welfare state see Theda Skocpol (1980: 155–201).

3. The thesis of the underlying unity of Western Marxism has been most ably defended in Jay's (1984) analysis of the concept of totality. Only from the perspective of this unity, on the other hand, is it then possible to develop a more adequate account of the nevertheless fundamental internal differences.

4. In recent British discussions influenced by the work of Bhaskar (1986), Marx's theory is defended as necessarily implying a realist epistemology that effectively transcends the older forms of positivism without lapsing into an untenable split between explanatory and interpretive methods. From the perspective of Bhaskar's naturalism, therefore, Habermas's account of knowledge interests suffers from an inadequate characterization of the natural sciences (cf., Keat and Urry, 1982).

5. Parsons' introduction of Weber to American social science entailed a fundamental twist of Weber's historicist argument, thus paving the way for a positivist appropriation of Weber's analysis. Parsons' discourse did not accept Weber's "logical" difference in the fact/value distinction but considered it only as a "substantial" difference (Cerroni, 1976; 1992).

6. There is not a single reference in *Power and Criticism* to the work of Paulo Freire in spite of the fact that in many places Cherryholmes recognizes the contribution of Henry Giroux—who cites Freire favourably as a foundation of his own work.

CHAPTER 6

1. Vasconi, an Argentinian philosopher by training, turned to sociology when he was in charge of an Institute of Sociology of Education in Argentina until the dictatorship of General Onganía in 1966 abolished the autonomy of the universities. Then he—and many other intellectuals—went to Chile in repudiation of the loss of autonomy. In Chile they worked from the mid sixties until Allende's fall in 1973. Although initially working for the social institute of the Economic Commission for Latin America (ECLA), Vasconi eventually become a professor of sociology in the Faculty of Economics and in the Center for the Socio-Economic Studies of the

University of Chile, which during the period of the National Unity was controlled by the Mapu, a small but active party in the Popular Unity Alliance. There, Vasconi was influenced by such well-known dependency theorists as Theotonio Dos Santos (1978), and other Marxist scholars such as Ru Mauro Marini (1978) and above all André Gunder Frank. (1969).

2. A testimony of this attempt to build a Marxist sociology of education, and one of the best expressions of the different theoretical perspectives competing for recognition in critical sociology, can be found in a reader organized by Carlos Alberto Torres and Guillermo Gonzalez (1994).

3. For a detailed presentation and criticism of the class-bureaucratic model of reproduction well reflected in Illich's approach, see chapter 8.

4. Guillermo Labarca (1977) developed the structuralist economic concerns in education in this research agenda into a political economy of education from a Marxist perspective. Besides his analysis of planning and education in the 1977 collection, his influential "Political Economy of Education" (brought) to Latin America the first translation of the German Debate of the Derivationists, particularly the issue of the falling rate of profits, productive-unproductive labor, and education. Labarca's short work on capitalist accumulation in Latin America is an attempt to offer an overall framework for a discussion of education and work (1979).

5. In this vein, one of the best studies on the relationships between class, politics, and educational development is Sara Finkel's article on Argentina (1977).

6. Makarenko's book *Pedagogicheskija Poema* (which appeared in English as *The Road to Life*) (1973) has been translated into eighteen languages.

7. Suchodolski, however, has argued that socialist education in the Soviet revolution was organized to lead revolutionary activity, and that the guiding notion of education—socialist humanism—was not far away from the notion of true, participatory democracy (Suchodolski and Manacorda 1975).

CHAPTER 7

1. Aronowitz and Giroux also argue that "[Bourdieu's] theory suggests falsely that working class cultural forms and knowledge are homogeneous and merely a pale reflection of dominant cultural capital" (1985: 84). In contrast, as Bourdieu notes, different segments of the working class approach dominant cultural capital from heterogeneous life (and class) histories: "Differences in dispositions, like differences in position (to which they are often linked), engender real differences in perception

and appreciation" (1981: 315). He goes on to contrast the responses of the privileged industrial working class, the deskilled young, and women and immigrants.

2.   This influence is clearly recognized, however, by Fritz Ringer, who suggests Bourdieu "has given more searching attention to the symbolic contents of educational traditions, and to social categories and meanings more generally, than any other social social theorist since Weber" (1987: 10). This assessment has been reinforced by more recent publications (e.g. Bourdieu, 1990; Bourdieu and Wacquant, 1992)

3.   Though the term *closure theory* is associated with the work of Frank Parkin, as Murphy points out: "The fact that Bourdieu does not use the word 'closure' should not blind us to the theoretical affinity between his analysis and closure theory, just as the absence of the word itself from Collin's writings should not lead us to ignore the fact that his analysis is a form of closure theory" (1988: 40 n.7).

4.   As Abercrombie and Urry charge, "It is not clear that the methods or effects of Parkin's model are greatly different from some of those Marxists he so strongly criticizes . . . In sum, it has become increasingly difficult to decide what theory belongs in which camp . . . Analysis of the middle classes raises this problem particularly acutely. As 'Weberians' have become worried bout the Boundary Problem, and 'Marxists' have recognized the importance of middle classes, the theoretical waters were bound to become muddy" (1983: 91). Nevertheless, as a more highly generalized theory, social-closure analysis avoids the inescapable dogmatism of those still imbued with essentialist conceptions of class and a teleological theory of history as criticized in Cohen (1982) and Laclau and Mouffe (1985).

CHAPTER 8

1.   For a hasty and often ill-advised attack on this tradition of "radical education"—a critique of "free schooling and deschooling"—see Barrow (1978), who takes on Rousseau, A. S. Neill, Goodman, Reimer and Illich, Neil Postman, and Charles Weingartner. Even more than the political economic critiques, Barrow's strategy reveals a fundamental inability to develop a constructive reappropriation of such tendencies; above all, he fails to grasp either the arguments of a critical social-psychology of education, reproduction theories of educational systems, or the specific implications of a critical theory of society. As a consequence, the resulting logic-chopping exercise ends up with "profound" arguments such as the following: "The vulnerability of the radical thesis becomes most apparent on the question of whether the hidden curriculum is necessarily a bad

thing, because one might argue that some of these covert messages embody true and valued beliefs . . . What is wrong with people learning to be punctual? What is wrong with seeing knowledge as divisible provided that the divisions are valid?" (Barrow, 1978: 138).

2.   The latter three models of this typology are developed in Aronowitz and Giroux (1985: 74–95).

3.   Our interpretation differs from most educational discussions in two important ways. First, we take into account his more general theoretical framework as outlined above all in *Tools for Conviviality* (1973) and elaborated in technical and professional contexts out of education in later writings. Second, we situate his work as a form of social-reproduction theory, though it is generally dismissed as completely antithetical to reproduction theories. For an early exception to this, see the French study by Hannoun (1973).

4.   Another exception here was the West German New Left from the mid 1960s through the early 1970s as expressed theoretically in a review like *Kursbuch* founded by Hans Magnus Enzensberger, and sometimes *Zeitschrift für Pädagogik*. This movement and its specific critique of pedagogy largely suffered the same fate as Illich in the English-speaking world. For a more recent evaluation of the West German situation with specific reference to Illich, see Leschinsky (1981). A general introduction to the adaptation of critical theory to different national contexts (with specific reference to Canada) can be found in Morrow (1985).

5.   Illich does not cite Habermas, but it would be hard to believe that he had not either read some of his work (given access to the original German) or at least become familiar with the general argument of *Knowledge and Human Interests* (1971a) or the essays found in *Toward a Rational Society* (1971).

6.   See chapter 15 for further elaboration on different reproduction models.

7.   For example, Illich is not even discussed in any of the following surveys of critical pedagogy: Aronowitz and Giroux (1985), Livingstone, et al. (1987), Giroux (1983), Carr and Kemmis (1986), Apple (1982b). Even Whitty's (1985) more historical account of educational debates only mentions Illich and the concept of deschooling in passing.

8.   It could be argued that Aronowitz and Giroux (1985) in effect incorporate most of the more enduring aspects of a class-bureaucratic model within their state-hegemonic approach, which reflects an ingenious synthesis of neo-Gramscian and Frankfurt themes.

9.   There is a vast bibliography on the subject—see Carr and Kemmis (1986), Freire (1985), Hall and Kassam (1985), Latapí (1988), and Kemmis and McTaggart, 1988.

CHAPTER 9

1. This section draws from previous work; see Torres (1985).

2. In many respects, this is the premise followed by Brazilian educator Moacir Gadotti in his attempt to develop a dialectical approach in pedagogy (Gadotti, 1990).

3. The selection of Gramsci quotations to support this point is indicative. For instance, arguing that history will constitute a central area of study, Entwhistle quotes Gramsci as follows: "If it is true that universal history is a chain made up of the efforts man has exerted to free himself from privilege, prejudice and idolatry, then it is hard to understand why the proletariat, which seeks to add another link to that chain, should not know how and why and by whom it was preceded, or what advantage it might derive from this knowledge" (Entwhistle, 1979: 41).

4. Freire, however, in his *Pedagogy of the Oppressed,* has made an explicit distinction between the role of liberating education in pre- and postrevolutionary situations.

5. Argentinean researcher José Aricó, one of the key representatives of Gramsci's thought in Latin America, argues that " 'The Quaderni dal carcere' were partially published in Buenos Aires, Argentina, between 1958 and 1962; in Brazil they were printed in Portuguese between 1966 and 1968. In those years, both editions were the most numerous and complete produced in any languages other than Italian" (1988: 135—our translation).

6. Peronism is a political movement that originated around the charismatic personality of General Juan Domingo Perón (1895–1974) who ruled Argentina constitutionally, having been elected and reelected between 1946 and 1955, and was overthrown by a "liberal" military coup. Peronism had been considered by the leadership of the Argentinean communist party, since its inception in Argentinean politics in 1945, as a form of Creole Fascism. The historical parallels of the government of Vargas in Brazil with the creation of Estado Novo—a form of corporatism—and Peronism in Argentina to the Fascist experience of Benito Mussolini in Italy that put Gramsci in prison were not to remain unnoticed by a generation of young Marxists in Argentina, as Aricó explicitly acknowledges (1988: 50–62)

7. A more detailed presentation of the paradigm of popular education in Latin America can be found in La Belle (1986), Avalos (1987), Torres (1990), and Gajardo (1985). A detailed analysis of experiences of popular education in societies in revolutionary transition, particularly Cuba, Nicaragua, and Grenada, can be found in Torres (1991), and Carnoy and Torres (1990: 315–57).

8. Freire read Gramsci for the first time circa 1968, in Santiago de Chile, at the suggestion of Marcela Gajardo, who brought to him Gramsci's *Literature and National Life,* suggesting that there were many parallels between Gramsci's analysis and that of Freire (Carlos A. Torres', interview with Paulo Freire, São Paulo, Brazil, October 30, 1990). In Torres' conversations with Freire, Freire mentioned that although he did not read Gramsci before writing either *Education as the Practice of Freedom,* or *Pedagogy of the Oppressed,* he had read Benedetto Croce, and of course Brazilian philosopher Tristan de Ataide who was himself conversant on the thought of Hegel and French Philosopher Bergson. Perhaps, since Gramsci himself was influenced by Croce, and Bergson through Croce, that could explain the parallels between Gramsci and Freire's analysis. A very interesting and informative attempt to compare Freire and Gramsci's views on adult education can be found in Mayo's M.A. thesis (1989).

9. To understand the role of popular education in expanding democracy, the issue of popular participation is crucial. One of the most imaginative engaged researchers, Brazilian anthropologist Carlos Rodrigues Brandão, addresses the issue of participation and popular culture, which is, in turn, related to the notion of popular power. Brandão asks himself: "Why in the world do most of the 'poor and oppressed people,' who abandon themselves (se aboleta) nightly to television soap operas, and entertain themselves with the cheap pleasures of 'consumerism,' resist as much as they can participation in meetings of cultural circles or neighborhood organizations—the dropout rates are at times as large in our 'government' programs as they are in our 'alternative' ones, in the latest 'school-community' experiment or 'community health program'? Why, besides the small groups of concienticized and participating people, does the 'community' resist participating in what in the end could transform its members into 'participants'?

"I will risk an answer. I know there are others. It is because even though television invades the privacy of their homes and their souls, it does not invade the interior life of their popular social order. It does not propose goals, only dreams and illusions. It does not pretend to organize anything, and therefore, does not threaten a popular communal organization that is resisting being changed, particularly when it does not know if it will have the power of controlling the process or even knowing its direction" (Brandão, 1984: 113—our translation).

10. In the preface to Tavares de Jesús's excellent book on the pedagogical thinking of Antonio Gramsci, Paolo Nosella argues that "We can affirm that in the last decade, close to one-third of academic dissertations make reference to this author [Gramsci] who forced the academic and

educational sciences to break the narrow limits of traditional Didactics, defining education as a general process of the struggle for hegemony in society as a whole" (in Tavares de Jesús, 1989: 15—our translation).

11.   A fascinating and documented attempt to compare and contrast critically the "progressive" perspective in Latin America, labeled as a neo-Liberal position in education (whose main representatives are the Argentinean educator Juan Carlos Tedesco; Uruguayan sociologist Germán Rama; and Brazilian educator Guiomar Namo de Mello), and the popular educators (whose main representative is Paulo Freire) can be found in José Tamarit (1990: 7–45).

12.   This section draws on aspects of Morrow (1991).

CHAPTER 10

1.   See the discussion of "action research" in chapter 8.

2.   An excellent discussion of this conservative agenda, as expressed in numerous proposals for educational reforms, can be found in a series of works by Michael Apple, e.g. 1993 and the excellent book by Aronowitz and Giroux (1985). Regarding the impact of reform proposals on teachers education, Thomas Popkewitz (1991) offers an illuminating analysis, linking in a critical manner the notions of agency and structure with a political sociology of education.

CHAPTER 11

1.   Broadly speaking, this could be referred to as the "cultural turn" in social theory that reflects a reaction against both Marxist economism and positivist reductionism—without falling into the problems of Parsonian culturalist evolutionism.

2.   Interesting insights on this matter are found in Donovan T. Plumb's M.A. thesis, "The Significance of Jürgen Habermas for the Pedagogy of Paulo Freire and the Practice of Adult Education" (1989: 27–29).

3.   It is illustrative to note that Habermas develops his discussion of Hegel's Jena period as a way to transcend Marx's viewpoint when he argues that "Liberation from hunger and misery does not necessarily converge with liberation from servitude and degradation, for there is no automatic developmental relation between labour and interaction" (Habermas, 1973: 169).

4.   This raises the interesting question of the parallels and contrasts between Gramsci's theory of hegemony and Weber's theory of domination (*Herrschaft*). Though both stress the consensual as opposed to merely coercive foundations of power, Gramsci's analysis is formulated from

a normative and political perspective, whereas Weber proposes merely a value-neutral description of "authority" relations. In the process, however, the Weberian approach has contributed to the de facto "scientific" justification of existing relations of domination.

5. Bowles and Gintis were confronted with a similar problem. This was already fully apparent in their book on correspondence theory (1976), which concludes with a voluntaristic and optimistic plea for educational transformation at odds with the determinism of their whole argument. They later turn to a radical democratic theory (1986).

6. The complex set of issues involved here go beyond the framework of this chapter, which can only be suggestive. The following brief comments thus do not do justice to the issues involved here.

CHAPTER 12

1. As a pact of domination, as a corporate actor who assumes the representation of popular sovereignty, and as the political authority that enforces the democratic rule, the state becomes also a terrain for struggle of national and sociopolitical (class) projects. These contradictory functions summarize the contradictory unity and inherent complexity of capitalist states. Also, they highlight a crucial problem for Marxist analysis: the class character of the state—a question addressed by the neo-Marxist analysis that tries to overcome the impasse that resulted from the instrumentalist-structuralist debate and was exemplified in the exchanges between Poulantzas and Miliband two decades ago (Poulantzas, 1969a: 237–41, 1969b: 67–78; Miliband, 1970a, 1970b).

2. The foremost penetrating pieces of research on state policies have in one way or another pointed out this essential feature. For instance, Weber views the state as not only instrumental but immanent, that is, the state as the monopoly of force and site for exchange of services and community benefits (Weber, 1944, vol. 1: 210–15).

3. Carnoy and Levin's (1985) self-designation of their approach as a "social-conflict" theory is unfortunate in that its generality gives little indication of its specificity. It differs, however, from traditional class-reproductive models in acknowledging the strategic political importance of its legitimation functions for the mobilization of subordinate groups, thus introducing a dynamic element to class reproduction. We consider it a broad variant of integral state-hegemonic theories, even if it is weak on issues stressed by other state-hegemonic theories (e.g., Apple, Aronowitz and Giroux).

4. See Stuart Hall's collected "New Times" essays (1988).

5. Erik Olin Wright (1978: 15) has suggested a schema of structural causality distinguishing diverse modes of determination and organizing

them into several models of determination. Modes of determination are considered to be distinct relationships of determination among the structural categories of Marxist theory and between these categories and the appearances of empirical investigation. Models of causal determination are schematic representations of the complex interconnections of the various modes of determination involved in a given structural process. Wright has outlined six main modes of causal determination: (a) structural limitation, (b) selection, (c) reproduction/nonreproduction, (d) limits of functional compatibility, (e) transformation, and (f) mediation.

6.   The STATEMOP thesis advocates that Marx's political economy was dealing with competitive capitalism. However, the development of productive forces has progressed and large monopolies have thwarted competition in such a way that the state and "monopoly capital" have become intertwined. This new phase of "monopoly capitalism" is seen to invalidate the general laws advanced by Marx, particularly the lack of commodity exchange, capital accumulation, and the falling rate of profit. Therefore, in this theory the analysis of modern capitalism must build on Lenin's analysis of the state and capitalism rather than on orthodox applications of Marx's methodology. The STATEMOP main thesis and critiques are thoroughly discussed in Holloway and Piccioto (1979).

7.   Since the early formulation of dependency theory, there has been a challenge to the notion that international dependency relies on a set of countries that constitute a central core (industrial advanced countries) and a set of countries that constitute a periphery. Certain countries that have been identified as "Newly Industrialized Countries" (NIC) have assumed new functions in the world division of labour by constituting industrial platforms of development through their labour-cost advantages (e.g., India, Singapore, Korea, Hong Kong, Pakistan, Brazil, and perhaps Mexico). In spite of these changes, the notion of the "dependent state" could be analytically useful if we assume that it refers to states where (i) the majority or a sizeable proportion of the labour force still remains linked with agricultural production; (ii) in many cases, most of the country's exports are essentially nonmanufactured goods; (iii) there is not a political structure resembling the welfare state; (iv) the state is subject to important constraints for future independent economic and political development due to a rising external debt, a continuous outflow of domestic capital and labour, and a huge "underground" of informal, nontaxable, economic exchanges; (v) the role of the Armed Forces is usually prominent in national politics, and it is the ultimate resort for conducting repressive activities; and (vi) the state is further constrained by its operation in a given orbit of geopolitical power and the presence of an imperial ruling country—in spite of the global exchangeability of commodities and the international division of labour due to the World System.

8.   The first premise of James O'Connor's analysis of the fiscal crisis of the state is that the state must try to fulfil two main functions: the accumulation function and the legitimation function. Therefore, at the same time that the State involves itself in the process of capital accumulation, it also tries to win the support of the economically exploited and socially oppressed classes for its programs and policies (O'Connor, 1973b: 64–96). What is initially stressed in O'Connor's claim is that these two functions are mutually contradictory, inasmuch as the growth of the state sector and state spending is increasingly the basis for the growth of the monopoly sector of the economy and the total production. Reciprocally, the growth of state spending and state programs is also the result of the growth of the monopoly industries, and "the greater the growth of the monopoly sector, the greater the State's expenditures on social expenses of production" (O'Connor, 1973b: 13–39, 1973a: 81–82). This, for many years the standard neo-Marxist explanation, is now being critically assessed. As an example of new financial estimates and theoretical developments in radical political economy, see Miller's extension of O'Connors analysis. Miller (1986: 237–60) argues that although it seems clear that the state fulfils an accumulation function and a legitimation function, they should be better formulated to explain the state's ability to promote accumulation in the 1970s and 1980s.

CHAPTER 13

1.   See chapter 7.
2.   See chapter 8.
3.   See chapters 5 and 6.
4.   See chapter 10.
5.   See Luke and Gore (1992) and Lather (1991a, 1991b).
6.   Some have concluded that the result has been at the price of abandoning "true" Marxism (e.g., Woods, 1986; Geras, 1990).
7.   See David Karen (1991) on the success of gender- and race-based mobilization for elite recruitment in colleges, as opposed to class-based. See also, for example, Levy (1987) on the expanding role of fundamentalist education as a uniquely American phenomenon that represents the fastest-growing form of minority education.
8.   See Giddens (1984) and Habermas (1975).
9.   For a formulation of this type of position in social theory, see Calhoun (1992).
10.   We will not take up the contributions of analytical Marxism, which have as yet had little influence in educational theory. See Roemer, 1986.

11. For the original formulation, see also Giroux (1983: 103, 105).

12. See an autobiographical account in Morrow and Torres (1990), reproduced in Apple (1993).

13. For various British perspectives on this issue and its implications for Marxism, see Rex (1986), Wolpe (1986), and Rex and Mason (1986) generally.

14. Enrique Dussel recalls theologian Fernandez de Oviedo's question, five hundred years ago: "Are the Amerindians human beings?" (Dussel, 1985: 3). Frei Bartolome de las Casas, considered by many theologians of liberation as one of their precursors in America, was arguing against medieval Spanish theologians about the qualities of human beings of Blacks and Indians alike, and their spiritual needs.

15. "Race" as an object of social inquiry has suffered from the ideological elements that have afflicted the discourses on race, even those conducted by liberal and radical opponents of racism. This is most apparent in the very concept of "race relations" as a topic of study.

16. Two other frameworks are crucial to understanding the psychodynamics of racism: authoritarian personality theory and what may be described as the racial theory of alienation (e.g., Franz Fanon). Paradoxically, some of the fundamental categories of Marx's theory (e.g., the theory of alienation) lend themselves more readily to theories of racism and colonialism that to those of class.

17. This conclusion is based on careful analysis of data derived from 174 school districts with more than 15,000 students and 1 percent black enrollment.

18. As Lynch (1989: xii) has constructively suggested, theories of educational reproduction "must take cognizance of how the universalistic and particularistic aspects of schooling interface with each other. Comprehending the universalistic-particularistic balances requires, in turn, that one take into account of how unique cultural processes and educational mediators influence the reproduction process."

19. While we agree that "all that is solid melts into air," we are still able to identify key works that inspire critical modernism, including for instance Habermas, Giddens, Bourdieu, and Jameson.

20. As a consequence, early reproduction theories of education were considerably more open to the issues of gender and race, despite the primacy accorded relations of production, as in Bowles and Gintis (1976) and Apple (1979, 1982a).

21. See Heide Hartmann's widely cited essay "The Unhappy Marriage of Marxism and Feminism: Towards a More Progressive Union" (1981).

22. To be sure, this egalitarian ideology has come under attack

from various perspectives based on the assumption that excellence and equality are fully and inevitably incompatible (e.g., Cooper, 1980: 159). This theme is broadly evident in a more vulgar form in the New Right attack on liberal educational policy. For a response from the Left, see Aronowitz and Giroux (1991: 24–86)

23.   See, for example, the policy suggestions in the United States of Meier, Stewart, and England (1989), which focus on the school facilitating opportunity; or, for Britain, Barton and Walker (1983).

24.   White ethnic minorities (and increasingly Asian groups) do manage relatively well within two or three generations to make the transition toward the idealized "American way of life."

CHAPTER 14

1.   A critic of modernity, Daniel Bell, has argued in his book *The End of Ideology* (1962) that the crisis of western developed societies can be traced back to the split between culture and society.

2.   Indeed, the Enlightenment can be understood primarily as a political rather than a scientific enterprise: the ruler should be a rationalist, not someone who has been chosen by God or emerges from tradition or both.

3.   Marion Levy offers the following terse definition: "I will take as the measure of modernization the ratio of inanimate to animate sources of power. The higher the ratio, the higher is the degree of modernization" (1972: 3).

4.   Derrida's critique of representation does not necessarily undermine the concept of social science understood in terms of the post-positivist linguist turn incorporated into the epistemologies of Habermas, Ricoeur, Giddens, and others. This critique of representation calls into question naive realism in the natural and human sciences, but in neither case, does Derrida's work undermines the project of a critical social science, deriving from the post-Kantian notion of Enlightenment. Therefore, we agree with Norris assessment that Derrida cannot be lumped together with Foucault, Lyotard, and Baudrillard, and, to some extent, we share Norris defense of Derrida's work against some of the criticism of Habermas, in his work *The Philosophical Discourse of Modernity*. (1987) In short, while we agree that Derrida's deconstructionism makes the notion of social science more problematic, it does not denies it altogether, and cannot be considered part of a neo-Nietzschean irrationalism. See Christopher Norris (1990)

5.   While Linda Hutcheon is concerned with the realm of literature and literary criticism, given the enormous influence of this field of

humanities in the constitution of contemporary postmodernist theory, her analysis is quite appropriate for a discussion on politics of education. See her work *A Poetics of Postmodernism: History, Theory, Fiction* (1988).

CHAPTER 15

1. See World Bank, World Development Report (1989), and Morales-Gómez and Torres, 1992: 1–20.

2. This final section draws on Morrow and Torres (1994).

3. So, for example, Michael Apple points to the need to revise his earlier position in *Education and Power* (1985); and Stanley Aronowitz and Henry Giroux develop a typology of theories of reproduction: economic-reproductive (structuralist Marxism), cultural-reproductive (Bourdieu), and hegemonic-state models (Gramscian) and their relation to theories of resistance in *Education Under Siege* (1985: 74ff.). Giroux's more recent flirtation with postmodernism in his *Border Crossings* (1992) does not involve abandoning this theme, though it could be argued that the he fails to articulate adequately the "language of possibility" with the conjunctural constraints of structure.

4. We are still able to find persuasive key works that defend a critical modernism, often including a constructive engagement with postmodernist social theory, including otherwise diverse figures as Habermas, Giddens, Bourdieu, and Jameson.

5. We agree with Ginsburg when he states that: "Politics is concerned with the means of producing, reproducing, consuming, and accumulating material and symbolic resources" (Ginsburg, Kamat, Raghu, and Weaver, 1993: 1). Politics is a difficult concept to grasp considering, as Ginsburg does, that politics and the political cannot be limited to the actions of the government, state, parties, parliament, constitution, or voting, but includes, touches upon, and interacts with all dimensions of human experience. Thus the personal is also political, as feminist theory taught us long ago.

6. For an elaboration of the methodological implications of the interpretive-structural character of critical social theory, see Raymond A. Morrow (with D. D. Brown) (1994).

7. But Hennessy's contorted effort to define a global "post-Althusserian social analytic" characterized as an antifoundationalist, "postmodern Marxism" (26–31) remains entangled in the Althusserian conception of mode of production, despite revising its claims in terms of "postmodern marxist arguments for causality that also renounce any objective claims to scientific truth" (31). This attempt to rescue Althusser

is characteristic of those trained in the humanities—cultural studies debates, as opposed to more sociologically grounded social theory where critical modernist forms of antifoundationalism (e.g., Anthony Giddens, Jürgen Habermas) have remained central.

REFERENCES

Abercrombie, Nicholas. 1980. *Class, Structure and Knowledge: Problems in the Sociology of Knowledge*. Oxford: Basil Blackwell.

Abercrombie, Nicholas, Stephen Hill, Bryan S. Turner. 1988. *The Penguin Dictionary of Sociology*, 2nd ed. Harmondsworth, Eng.: Penguin Books.

———. 1980. *The Dominant Ideology Thesis*. London: Allen & Unwin.

Abercrombie, Nicholas, and John Urry. 1983. *Capital, Labour, and the Middle Classes*. London and Boston: Allen & Unwin.

Adamson, Walter L. 1980. *Hegemony and Revolution: A Study of Antonio Gramsci's Political and Cultural Theory*. Berkeley, Los Angeles, and London: University of California Press.

Adorno, Theodor W. 1973. *Negative Dialectics*, trans E. B. Ashton. New York: Seabury.

Alexander, Jeffrey C. 1990a. "Differentiation Theory: Problems and Prospects." Pp. 1–15 in *Differentiation Theory and Social Change*, eds. Jeffrey C. Alexander and Paul Colomy. New York: Columbia University Press.

———. 1990b. "Core Solidarity, Ethnic Out-groups, and Social Differentiation." Pp. 267–293 in *Differentiation Theory and Social Change*, eds. Jeffrey C. Alexander and Paul Colomy. New York: Columbia University Press.

———. 1990c. "The Mass News Media in Systemic, Historical, and Comparative Perspective." Pp. 323–366 in *Differentiation Theory and Social Change*, eds. Jeffrey C. Alexander and Paul Colomy. New York: Columbia University Press.

———. 1985a. "Introduction." Pp. 7–18 in *Neofunctionalism*, ed. Jeffrey C. Alexander. Beverly Hills: Sage.

———, ed. 1985b. *Neofunctionalism*, Beverly Hills: Sage.

———. 1983. *Theoretical Logic in Sociology: The Modern Reconstruction of Classical Thought: Talcott Parsons*, Vol. 4. Berkeley and Los Angeles: University of California Press.

Alexander, Jeffrey C., and Paul Colomy, eds. 1990. *Differentiation Theory and Social Change: Comparative and Historical Perspectives*, New York: Columbia University Press.

Alexander, Jeffrey C., and Steven Seidman, eds. 1990. *Culture and Society: Contemporary Debates,* Cambridge: Cambridge University Press.

Altbach, Philip G., and Gail P. Kelly, eds. 1986. *New Approaches to Comparative Education.* Chicago and London: University of Chicago Press.

Althusser, Louis. 1977. *For Marx,* trans Ben Brewster. London: NLF.

———. 1971. *Lenin and Philosophy and Other Essays,* trans. Ben Brewster. New York and London: Monthly Review Press.

Althusser, Louis, and Étienne Balibar. 1968. *Lire le Capital.* 2 vols. Paris: Maspero.

Altvater, Elmar. 1979. "Some Problems of State Interventionism." *State and Capital: A Marxist Debate,* eds. J. Holloway and S. Piccioto. Austin: University of Texas Press.

———. 1973. "Notes on Some Problems of State Interventionism." *Working Papers on the Kapitalistate* 1 and 2:96–108 and 76–83.

Anderson, Perry. 1984. *In the Tracks of Historical Materialism.* London: Verso.

———. 1978. *Las antinomias de Antonio Gramsci,* trans. Lourdes Bassols and J. R. Fraguas. Barcelona: Editorial Fontamara.

Apple, Michael W. 1993. *Official Knowledge. Democratic Education in a Conservative Age.* New York and London: Routledge.

———. 1990. "Understanding Common Sense: A Personal Preface." *Phenomenology + Pedagogy* 8:291–314.

———. 1988a. "Standing on the Shoulders of Giants: Class Formation and Capitalist Schools." *History of Education Quarterly* 28:231–241.

———. 1988b. *Teachers and Texts: A Political Economy of Class and Gender Relations in Education.* New York and London: Routledge.

———. 1986. "Curriculum, Capitalism, and Democracy: A Response to Whitty's Critics." *British Journal of Sociology of Education* 7:319–326.

———. 1985. *Education and Power.* Boston: Routledge & Kegan Paul.

———. 1982a. "Reproduction and Contradiction in Education: An Introduction." Pp. 1–31 in *Cultural and Economic Reproduction in Education,* ed. Michael Apple. London and Boston: Routledge & Kegan Paul.

———, ed. 1982b. *Cultural and Economic Reproduction in Education: Essays on Class, Ideology and the State,* London, Boston, and Henley: Routledge & Kegan Paul.

———. 1979. *Ideology and Curriculum.* London and Boston: Routledge & Kegan, Paul.

Apple, Michael W., and Lois Weis, eds. 1983. *Ideology and Practice in Schooling,* Philadelphia: Temple University Press.

Archer, Margaret S. 1988. *Culture and Agency: The Place of Culture in Social Theory.* Cambridge: Cambridge University Press.

———. 1984. *Social Origins of Educational Systems.* London: Sage.

———. 1982. "Morphogenesis versus Structuralism: On Combining Structure and Action." *British Journal of Sociology* 33:455–83.

Archer, Margaret, and Michalina Vaughan. 1971. "Domination and Assertion in Educational Systems." *Readings in the Theory of Educational Systems*, ed. E. Hooper. London: Hutchinson.

Aricó, José. 1988. *La cola del diablo. Itinerario de Gramsci en América Latina.* Buenos Aires: Puntosur.

Arnove, Robert. 1986. *Education and Revolution in Nicaragua.* New York: Praeger.

Aronowitz, Stanley. 1981. *The Crisis of Historical Materialism: Class, Politics and Culture in Marxist Theory.* New York: Praeger.

Aronowitz, Stanley, and Henry Giroux. 1991. *Postmodern Education: Politics, Cultre, and Social Criticism.* Minneapolis: University of Minnesota Press.

———. 1985. *Education Under Seige: The Conservative, Liberal and Radical Debate Over Schooling.* South Hadley, MA: Bergin & Garvey.

Arrien, Juan B., and Roger Matus Lazo, eds. 1989. *Nicaragua: Diez años de educación en la revolución.* Mexico: Claves Latinoamericanos.

Atkinson, Paul. 1985. *Language, Structure and Reproduction: An Introduction to the Sociology of Basil Bernstein.* London: Methuen.

Attewell, Paul A. 1984. *Radical Political Economy Since the Sixties: A Sociology of Knowlege Analysis.* New Brunswick, NJ: Rutgers University Press.

Avalos, Beatrice. 1987. "Moving Where? Educational Issues in Latin American Contexts." *International Journal of Education Development* 7:151–172.

Bailey, Kennth D. 1990. *Social Entropy Theory.* Albany: State University of New York Press.

Ballantine, Jeanne H. 1983. *The Sociology of Education: A Systematic Analysis.* Englewood Cliffs, NJ: Prentice-Hall.

Barel, Yves. 1974. "The Idea of Reproduction." *Futures* 6:93–102.

Baron, Steve, et al. 1981. *Unpopular Education: Schooling and Social Democracy in England Since 1944.* London: Hutchinson.

Barton, Len and Stephen Walker, eds. 1983. *Rule, Class and Education.* London, Croom Helm.

Barrow, Robin. 1978. *Radical Education: A Critique of Freeschooling and Deschooling.* New York: John Wiley.

Bates, Richard. 1985. *Public Administration and the Crisis of the State.* Victoria: Deakin University.

Baudelot, Christian, and Roger Establet. 1971. *L'École capitaliste*. Paris: Maspero.

Bell, Daniel. 1962. *The End of Ideology: On the Exhaustion of Political Ideas in the Fifties*. New York: Collier Books.

Bennett, Kathleen P., and Margaret D. LeCompte. 1990. *How Schools Work: A Sociological Analysis of Education*. White Plains, NY: Longman.

Bennett, Tony. 1986. "Introduction: Popular Culture and 'the Turn to Gramsci'." Pp. xi–xix in *Popular Culture and Social Relations*, eds. Tony Bennett, Colin Mercer, and Janet Woollacott. Milton Keynes and Philadelphia: Open University Press.

Benton, Ted. 1984. *The Rise and Fall of Structural Marxism: Althusser and His Influence*. London: Macmillan.

Berger, Peter, and Thomas Luckmann. 1967. *The Social Construction of Reality*. Garden City, NY: Doubleday Anchor.

Berman, Russell A. 1989. *Modern Culture and Critical Theory: Art, Politics, and the Legacy of the Frankfurt School*. Madison: University of Wisconsin Press.

Bernbaum, Gerald. 1977. *Knowledge and Ideology in the Sociology of Education*. London: Macmillan.

Bernstein, Basil. 1977. *Class, Codes and Control*. 2nd. ed. Vol. 3: *Towards a Theory of Educational Transmission*. Boston and London: Routledge & Kegan Paul.

———. 1973. *Class Codes and Control*. vol. 1: *Theoretical Studies Towards a Sociology of Language*. London: Paladin.

Bernstein, Richard J. 1978. *The Restructuring of Social and Political Theory*. Philadelphia: University of Pennsylvania Press.

Beyer, Landon, and Michael Apple, eds. 1988. *The Curriculum: Problems, Politics, and Possibilities*, Albany: State University of New York Press.

Bhaskar, Roy. 1986. *Scientific Realism and Human Emancipation*. London and New York: Verso.

———. 1979. "On the Possibility of Social Scientific Knowledge and the Limits of Naturalism." Pp. 107–139 in *Issues in Marxist Philosophy*, eds. John Mepham and D-H. Ruben. Atlantic Highlands, NJ and Brighton: Humanities/Harvester.

Birnbaum, Norman. 1988. *The Radical Renewal: The Politics of Ideas in Modern America*. New York: Pantheon.

Blackburn, Robin, ed. 1973. *Ideology and Social Science*, London: Fontana/Collins.

Blackledge, David, and Barry Hunt. 1985. *Sociological Interpretations of Education*. London: Croom Helm.

Block, Fred. 1987. *Revising State Theory: Essays in Politics and Post-Industrialism*. Philadelphia: Temple University Press.

————. 1977. "The Ruling Class Does not Rule: Notes on the Marxist Theory of the State." *Socialist Revolution* 7, 3: 6–28.

Boli, John, and Francisco O. Ramirez. 1992. "Compulsory Schooling in the Western Cultural Context." Pp. 25–38 in *Emergent Issues in Education: Comparative Perspectives*, eds. Robert F. Arnove, Philip G. Altbach and Gail P. Kelly. Albany: State University of New York Press.

Boron, Atilio A.. 1982. "The Capitalist State and its Relative Autonomy: Arguments Regarding Limits and dimensions." Mexico, CIDE. Mimeographed.

————. 1977. "El fascismo como categoría histórica: en torno al problema de las dictaduras en América Latina." *Revista Mexicana de Sociología* 39:481–528.

Bosco Pinto, João. 1969. *Metodología de la investigación temática*, Bogotá: IICA-CIDA.

Boudon, Raymond. 1979. *La Logique du social*. Paris: Hachette.

————. 1974. *Education, Opportunity and Social Inequality*. New York: John Wiley & Sons.

Boudon, Raymond, and François Bourricaud. 1982. *Dictionnaire critique de la sociologie*. Paris: Presses Universitaires de France.

Bourdieu, Pierre. 1990. *In Other Words: Essays Towards a Reflexive Sociology*, trans. Matthew Adamson. Stanford, CA: Stanford University Press.

Bourdieu, Pierre. 1987. *Choses dites*. Paris: Minuit.

————. 1981. "Men and Machines." Pp. pp. 304–317 in *Advances in Social Theory and Methodology*, eds. K. Knorr-Cetina and A.V. Cicourel. Boston, London and Henley: Routledge & Kegan Paul.

————. 1977. *Outline of a Theory of Practice*, trans. Richard Nice. Cambridge: Cambridge University Press.

————. 1968. "Structuralism and Theory of Sociological Knowledge." *Social Research* 35:681–706.

Bourdieu, Pierre, and Jean-Claude Passeron. 1977. *Reproduction in Education, Society, and Culture*, trans. Richard Nice. London and Beverly Hills: Sage.

————. 1967. "Sociology and Philosophy in France since 1945: Death and Resurrection of a Philosophy Without a Subject." *Social Research* 34:162–212.

Bourdieu, Pierre, and Loïc J. D. Wacquant. 1992. *An Invitation to Reflexive Sociology*. Chicago and London: University of Chicago Press.

Bowen, James. 1962. *Soviet Education: Anton Makarenko and the Years of Experiment*. Madison: University of Wisconsin.

Bowles, Samuel, and Herbert Gintis. 1986. *Democracy and Capitalism: Property, Community, and the Contradicitions of Modern Thought.* New York: Basic Books.

———. 1981. "Education as a Site of Contradictions in the Reproduction of the Capital-Labor Relationship: Second Thoughts on the 'Correspondence Principle'." *Economic and Industrial Democracy* 2:223–242.

———. 1976. *Schooling in Capitalist America: Educational Reform and the Contradictions of Economic Life.* New York: Basic Books/Harper.

Bowles, Samuel, Herbert Gintis, and P. Meyer. 1975. "The Long Shadow of Work: Education, the Family, and the Reproduction of the Social Division of Labor." *The Insurgent Sociologist* 3–22.

Bowles, Samuel, and H. Levin. 1968. "The Determinants of Scholastic Achievment: An Appraisal of Some Recent Findings." *The Journal of Human Resources* II:3–22.

Brandão, Carlos Rodriques. 1984. *Pensar a prática.* São Paulo: Edições Loyola.

———. 1982. *Lutar com a palavra.* Rio de Janeiro: Graal.

———. 1980. *A questão política da educação popular.* São Paulo: Bra.

Brantlinger, Patrick. 1990. *Crusoe's Footprints: Cultural Studies in Britain and America.* New York and London: Routledge.

Broady, Donald. 1981. "Critique of the Political Economy of Education: The Prokla Approach." *Economic and Industrial Democracy* 2:141–189.

Buckley, Walter. 1967. *Sociology and Modern Systems Theory.* Englewood Cliffs, NJ: Prentice-Hall.

Bulhan, Hussein Abdilahi. 1985. *Frantz Fanon and the Psychology of Oppression.* New York and London: Plenum Press.

Burbules, Nicholas C. 1993. *Dialogue on Teaching: Theory and Practice.* New York and London: Teachers College, Columbia University.

Burbules, Nicholas C., and Suzanne Rice. 1991. "Dialogue Across Differences: Continuing the Conversation." *Harvard Educational Review* 61:393–416.

Burrell, Gibson, and Gareth Morgan. 1979. *Sociological Paradigms and Organizational Analysis.* London: Heinemann.

Burt, Ronald. 1982. *Toward a Structural Theory of Action: Network Models of Social Structure, Perception and Action.* New York: Academic Press.

Butler, Judith. 1992. "Contingent Foundations: Feminism and the Question of 'Postmodernism'." Pp. 3–21 in *Feminists Theorize the Political,* eds. Judith Butler and Joan W. Scott. New York and London: Routledge.

Buxton, William. 1985. *Talcott Parsons and the Capitalist Nation-State: Political Sociology as a Strategic Vocation.* Toronto: University of Toronto Press.

Calhoun, Craig, ed. 1992. *Habermas and the Public Sphere*, Cambridge, MA, and London: MIT Press.

Callinicos, Alex. 1976. *Althurser's Marxism*. London: Pluto Press.

Cardoso, F. H. 1979. "On the Characterization of Authoritarian Regimes in Latin America." Pp. 33–60 in *The New Authoritarianism in Latin America*, ed. D. Collier. Princeton: Princeton University Press.

Carnoy, Martin. 1984. *The State and Political Theory*. Princeton: Princeton University Press.

———. 1977. *Education and Employment: A Critical Appraisal*. Paris: UNESCO, International Institute for Educational Planning.

Carnoy, Martin, and Henry M. Levin. 1985. *Schooling and Work in the Democratic State*. Stanford: Stanford University Press.

Carnoy, Martin, and Carlos Torres. 1990. "Education and Social Transformation in Nicaragua 1979–1989." Pp. 315–360 in *Education and Social Transition in the Third World*, eds. Martin Carnoy and Joel Samoff. Princeton: Princeton University Press.

Carnoy, Martin, and Joel Samoff, eds. 1990. *Education and Social Transition in the Third World*, Princeton: Princeton University Press.

Carr, Wilfred, and Stephen Kemmis. 1986. *Becoming Critical: Education, Knowledge and Action Research*. London and Philadelphia: Falmer Press.

Castles, Stephen, and Wiebke Wüstenberg. 1979. *The Education of the Future: An Introduction to the Theory and Practice of Socialist Education*. London: Pluto.

Cerroni, Umberto. 1992. *Política: Método, teorías, procesos, sujetos, instituciones y categorías*, trans. Alejandro Reza. Mexico: Siglo Veintiuno.

Cherryholmes, Cleo H. 1988. *Power and Criticism: Poststructural Investigations in Education*. New York and London: Teachers College Press.

Clegg, Stewart R. 1989. *Frameworks of Power*. London and Newbury Park: Sage.

———. 1979. *The Theory and Power of Organization*. London: Routledge & Kegan Paul.

———. 1975. *Power, Rule and Domination*. London: Routledge & Kegan Paul.

Clegg, Stewart, and David Dunkerley. 1980. *Organization, Class and Control*. London: Routledge & Kegan Paul.

Cohen, G. A. 1978. *Karl Marx's Theory of History: A Defense*. Princeton: Princeton University Press.

Cohen, Jean. 1982. *Class and Civil Society: The Limits of Marxian Critical Theory*. Amherst: University of Massachusetts Press.

Cole, Mike, ed. 1988. *Bowles and Gintis Revisited: Correspondence and*

Contradiction in Educational Theory. London, New York, and Philadelphia: Falmer Press.

Coleman, James, ed. 1965. *Education and Political Development*, Princeton: Princeton University Press.

Coleman, James, et al. 1966. *Equality of Opportunity*. Washington, D. C.: U. S. Government Printing Office.

Collier, David, ed. 1979.*The New Authoritarianism in Latin America.* Princeton: Princeton University Press.

Collins, Randall. 1979. *The Credential Society: An Historical Sociology of Education and Stratification*. New York: Academic Press.

Connell, R. W. 1987. *Gender and Power: Society, the Person and Sexual Politics*. Stanford, CA: Stanford University Press.

——. 1983. *Which Way is Up? Essays on Sex, Class and Culture.* Sydney, London and Boston: George Allen & Unwin.

Cooper, David E. 1980. *Illusions of Equality*. London: Routledge & Kegan Paul.

Coser, Lewis, ed. 1975. *Structuralist Sociology*. New York: Free Press.

Crosby, Christina. 1992. "Dealing With Differences." Pp. 130–143 in *Feminists Theorize the Political,* eds. Judith Butler and Joan W. Scott. New York and London: Routledge.

Curtis, Bruce. 1913. "Capitalist Development and Educational Reform." *Theory and Society* 41:41–68.

da Silva, Tomaz, and Peter McLaren. 1993. "Knowledge Under Siege: The Brazilian Debate." Pp. 36–46 in *Paulo Freire: A Critical Encounter,* eds. Peter McLaren and Peter Leonard. London and New York: Routledge.

David, M. E. 1977. *Reform, Reaction and Resources, the Three R's of Educational Planning*. Windsor: NFER Publishing Company.

De Ipola, Emilio. 1982. *Ideología y discurso populista*. Mexico: Folios.

De Schutter, Anton. 1980. *La investigación participativa en la educación de adultos y la capacitación rural,* Pátzcuaro, Michoacán: CREFAL.

Della Volpe, Galvano. 1969. *Rousseau y Marx*. Barcelona: Ediciones Martínez Roca, S.A.

Demaine, Jack. 1981. *Contemporary Theories in the Sociology of Education*. London: Macmillan.

Demerath, N. J., and Richard A. Peterson, eds. 1967. *System, Change and Conflict*. New York: Free Press.

Deutsch, Karl. 1963. *The Nerves of Government: Models of Political Communication*. Glencoe, IL, and London: The Free Press.

Díaz-Salazar, Rafael. 1991. *El proyecto de Gramsci*. Madrid: Ediciones HOAC/Anthropos.

Dickson, David. 1974. *Alternative Technology and the Politics of Technical Change*. London: Fontana/Collins.

Dingwall, R., and P. Lewis. 1983. *The Sociology of Professions*. London: Macmillan.

Dittmar, Norbert. 1976. *Sociolinguistics: A Critical Survey of Theory and Application*, trans. Peter Sand, A. M. Seuren, and Kevin Whiteley.

Dore, R. 1976. *The Diploma Disease: Education, Qualification, and Development*. Berkeley and Los Angeles: University of California Press.

Dos Santos, Theotonio. 1978. *Socialismo o fascismo: El nuevo carácter de la dependencia y el dilema latinoamericano*. Mexico: Editorial Edicol.

Durkheim, Emile. 1977. *The Evolution of Educational Thought: Lectures on the Formation and Devleopment of Secondary Education in France*, trans. Peter Collins. London: Routledge & Kegan Paul.

———. 1973. *Moral Education*, trans. Everett K. Wilson and Herman Schnurer. New York: Free Press.

———. 1956. *Education and Sociology*, trans. Sherwood D. Fox. Glencoe, IL: Free Press.

Dussel, Enrique. 1985. *Philosophy of Liberation*, trans. Aquilina Martinez and Christine Morkovsky. Maryknoll, NY: Orbis Books.

Eisenstadt, S. N. 1966. *Modernization: Protest and Change*. Englewood Cliffs, NJ: Prentice-Hall.

Elster, Jon. 1985. *Making Sense of Marx*. Cambridge: Cambridge University Press.

Entwistle, Harold. 1979. *Antonio Gramsci: Conservative Schooling for Radical Politics*. London: Routledge & Kegan Paul.

Etzioni, Amitai. 1968. *The Active Society*. New York: Free Press.

Fagen, Richard. 1969. *The Transformation of Political Culture in Cuba*. Stanford: Stanford University Press.

Fagerlind, I., L. J. Saha. 1983. *Education and National Development: A Comparative Perspective*. Oxford: Pergamon Press.

Faia, Michael A. 1986. *Dynamic Functionalism*. Cambridge: Cambridge University Press.

Fals Borda, Orlando. 1978. "La investigación-acción como nuevo paradigma en las ciencias sociales." Pp. 209–249 in *Crítica y política en ciencias sociales: El debate, teoría y práctica*. Simposio Mundial de Cartagena. Bogotá: Punta de Lanza.

Fanon, Frantz. 1968. *Black Skin, White Masks*, trans. Charles Lam Markmann. New York: Grove Press.

Farrell, Joseph P. 1986. *The National Unified School in Allende's Chile: The Role of Education in the Destruction of a Revolution*. Vancouver: University of British Columbia Press.

Farrell, Joseph P. 1992. "Conceptualizing Education and the Drive for Social Equality." Pp. 107–122 in *Emergent Issues in Education Com-*

parative Perspectives, eds. R. F. Arnove, P. G. Altbach, and Gail P. Kelly. Albany, New York: State University of New York Press.

Fay, Brian. 1987. *Critical Social Science.* Ithaca, NY: Cornell University Press.

Finkel, Sara. 1977. "La clase media como beneficiaria de la expansión del sistema educacional argentino-1880–1930." Pp. 93–136 in *La educación burguesa,* eds. G. Labarca, T. Vasconi, S. Finkel, and I. Recca. Mexico: Editorial Nueva Imagen.

Fitzpatrick, Sheila. 1970. *The Commisariat of Enlightenment: Soviet Organization of Education and the Arts Under Lunacharsky, October 1917–1921.* Cambridge: Cambridge University Press.

Ford, David F. 1989. "Epilogue: Postmodernism and Postscript." Pp. 291–297 in *The Modern Theologians,* vol. 2, ed. David F. Ford. Oxford: Basil Blackwell.

Foucault, Michel. 1980. *Power/Knowledge: Selected Interviews and Other Writings 1972–1977,* ed. Colin Gordon. New York: Pantheon.

———. 1965. *Madness and Civilization,* trans. Richard Howard. Abridged ed. New York: New American Library.

Frank, Andre Gunder. 1969. *Capitalism and Underdevelopment in Latin America: Historical Studies of Chile and Brazil.* Rev. and enlarged ed. New York and London: Monthly Review Press.

Fraser, Nancy. 1989. *Unruly Practices: Power, Discourse and Gender in Contemporary Social Theory.* Minneapolis: University of Minnesota Press.

Fraser, Nancy, and Linda Nicholson. 1989. "Social Criticism and Philosophy: An Encounter Between Feminism and Postmodernism." Pp. 83–104 in *Universal Abandon? The Politics of Postmodernism,* ed. Andrew Ross. Minneapolis: University of Minnesota Press.

Freire, Paulo. 1985. *The Politics of Education: Culture, Power and Liberation,* trans. Donaldo Macedo. South Hadley, MA: Bergin & Garvey.

———. 1970. *Pedagogy of the Oppressed,* trans. Myra Bergman Ramos. New York: Seabury.

Freire, Paulo, and Donald Macedo. 1987. *Literacy: Reading the Word and the World.* South Hadley, MA: Bergin & Garvey.

Friedrichs, Robert W. 1969. *A Sociology of Sociology.* New York: Free Press.

Friesenhahn, Günter J. 1985. *Kritische Theorie und Pädagogik: Horkheimer, Adorno, Fromm, Marcuse.* West Berlin: EXpress Edition.

Fritzell, Christer. 1987. "On the Concept of Relative Autonomy in Educational Theory." *British Journal of Sociology of Education* 8:23–35.

Fuenzalida, Edmundo. 1983. *The Social Reorganization of Knowledge in Latin America, 1950–1980: The Cases of Chile and Venezuela.* Paper presented at the XI International Congress, Latin American Studies Association, Mexico City, September 29–October 1:

Fuller, Bruce. 1991. *Growing Up Modern: The Western State Builds Third-World Schools*. New York and London: Routledge.

Gadotti, Moacir. 1990. *Uma só escola para todos*. Petrópolis: Vozes.

Gajardo, Marcela. 1982. *Evolución, situación actual y perspectivas de las estrategias de investigación participativa en Aaerica Latina*. Santiago de Chile: FLACSO.

———, ed. 1985. *Teoría y práctica de la educación popular*. Pátzcuaro, Michoacán: OEA-CREFAL-IDRC.

García Canclini, Néstor. 1982. *Las culturas populares en el capitalismo*. México, D. F.: Editorial Nueva Imagen.

García Galló, Gaspar. 1974. *La concepción marxista sobre le escuela y la educación*. México: Grijalbo.

García Huidobro, Juan Eduardo. 1985. "En torno del sentido político de la educación popular." Pp. 231–272 in *Educaçao na América Latina*, eds. Felícia Reicher Madeira and Guiomar Namo de Mello. São Paulo: Cortez Editora.

Geras, Norman. 1990. *Discourses of Extremity: Radical Ethics and Post-Marxist Extravagances*. London and New York: Verso.

Gerchunoff, P., and J. J. Llach. 1975. "Capitalismo industrial, desarrollo asociado y distribución del ingreso entre los dos gobiernos peronistas: 1950–1972." *Desarrollo Económico* 57:3–54.

Germani, Gino. 1968. "Secularization, Modernization, and Economic Development." Pp. 343–366 in *The Protestant Ethic and Modernization*, ed. S. M. Eisenstadt. Boston: Little, Brown & Co.

———. 1964. *Política y sociedad en una época en transición*. Buenos Aires: Paidós.

Gerstenberger, H. 1976. "Theory of the State: Special Features of the Discussion in the FRG." *German Political Studies: Theory and Practice in the Two Germany*, ed. K. Von Beyme. Beverly Hills: Sage.

Gibson, Rex. 1986. *Critical Theory and Education*. London: Hodder and Stoughton.

———. 1984. *Structuralism and Education*. London: Hodder and Stoughton.

Giddens, Anthony. 1991. *Modernity and Self-Identity: Self and Society in the Late Modern Age*. Stanford, CA: Stanford University Press.

———. 1990. *The Consequences of Modernity*. Stanford, CA: Stanford University Press.

———. 1984. *The Constitution of Society*. Berkeley and Los Angeles: University of California Press.

———. 1981. *A Contemporary Critique of Historical Materialism*. Vol. I. Berkeley and Los Angeles: University of California Press.

———. 1979. *Central Problems in Social Theory: Action, Structure and Contradiction in Social Analysis.* Berkeley and Los Angeles: University of California Press.

———. 1971. *Capitalism and Modern Social Theory.* Cambridge: Cambridge University Press.

Gilroy, Paul. 1992. "Cultural Studies and Ethnic Absolutism." Pp. 187–198 in *Cultural Studies,* eds. Lawrence Grossberg, Cary Nelson, and Paula Treichler. New York and London: Routledge.

Ginsburg, Mark, Kamat Sangeeta, Rahesware Raghu, and John Weaver. 1993. "Educator and Politics: Interpretations, Involvement, and Implications." University of Pittsburgh. Manuscript.

Giroux, Henry. 1994. "Living Dangerously: Identity Politics and the New Cultural Racism." Pp. 29–55 in *Between Borders: Pedagogy and the Politics of Cultural Studies,* eds. Henry Giroux and Peter McLaren. New York and London: Routledge.

———. 1992. *Border Crossings: Cultural Workers and the Politics of Education.* New York and London: Routledge.

———. 1991a. "Postmodernism as Border Pedagogy: Redefining the Boundaries of Race and Ethnicity." Pp. 217–256 in *Postmodernism, Feminism, and Cultural Politics: Redrawing Educational Boundaries,* ed. Henry A. Giroux. Albany: State University of New York Press.

———. ed. 1991b. *Postmodernism, Feminism, and Cultural Politics: Redrawing Educational Boundaries.* Albany: State University of New York Press.

———. 1988a. *Schooling and the Struggle for Public Life: Critical Pedagogy in the Modern Age.* Minneapolis: University of Minnesota Press.

———. 1988b. *Teachers as Intellectuals: Toward a Pedagogy of Learning.* Granby, MA: Bergin & Garvey.

———. 1985. "Critical Pedagogy, Cultural Politics and the Discourse of Experience." *Boston University Journal of Education* 167:22–41.

———. 1981. *Ideology, Culture, and the Process of Schooling.* Philadelphia: Temple University Press.

———. 1983. *Theory and Resistance in Education: A Pedagogy for the Opposition.* Amherst: Bergin & Garvey.

Giroux, Henry, and Peter McLaren, eds. 1994. *Between Borders: Pedagogy and the Politics of Cultural Studies,* New York and London: Routledge.

———, eds. 1989. *Critical Pedagogy, the State and Cultural Struggle,* Albany: State University of New York Press.

———. 1986. "Teacher Education and the Politics of Engagement: The Case for Democratic Schooling." *Harvard Educational Review* 56:213–238.

Giroux, Henry, and Roger I. Simon, eds. 1989. *Popular Culture: Schooling and Everyday Life*, New York: Bergin & Garvey.

Godelier, Maurice. 1972. "Structure and Contradiction in Capital." Pp. 334–368 in *Ideology in Social Science*, ed. Robin Blackburn. Glasgow: Fontana/Collins.

Gonzalez, Gilbert B. 1982. *Progressive Education: A Marxist Interpretation*. Minneapolis: Marxist Educational Press, University of Minnesota.

Gordon, L. 1984. "Paul Willis—Education, Cultural Production, and Social Reproduction." *British Journal of Sociology of Education* 5:105–117.

Gore, Jennifer M. 1993. *The Struggle for Pedagogies: Critical and Feminist Discourses as Regimes of Truth*. New York and London: Routledge.

Gorz, André. 1967. *Strategy for Labor: A Radical Proposal*, trans. Martin Nicolaus. Boston: Beacon Press.

Gould, Mark. 1985. "Prolegomena to Any Future Theory of Societal Crisis." Pp. 51–72 in *Neofunctionalism*, ed. Jeffrey C. Alexander. Beverly Hills: Sage.

Gouldner, Alvin. 1971. *The Coming Crisis of Western Sociology*. New York: Basic Books.

———. 1983. *The Two Marxisms*. New York: Seabury.

Gramsci, Antonio. 1977. *Pasado y presente*, Gabriel Ojeda Padilla. Mexico: Juan Pablos Editor.

———. 1975a. *Quaderni del carcere* [4 vols], ed. Valentino Gerratana. Turin: Einaudi Editore.

———. 1975b. *Los intellectuales y la organización de la cultura*, Trans. Raúl Sciarreta. Mexico: Juan Pablos Editor.

———. 1971. *Selections from the Prison Notebooks*, ed. and trans. Quintin Hoare and Geoffrey Nowell Smith. New York: International Publishers.

Grant, Carl A., and Christine E. Sleeter. 1988. "Race, Class, and Gender and Abandoned Dreams." *Teachers College Record* 90:19–40.

———. 1986. "Race, Class and Gender in Education Research: An Argument for Integrative Analysis." *Review of Educational Research* 56:195–211.

Gross, Ronald. 1973. "After Deschooling, Free Learning." Pp. 148–160 in *After Deschooling, What?* eds. Alan Gartner, Colin Greer, and Frank Riessman. New York: Harper & Row.

Grundy, Shirely. 1987. *Curriculum: Product or Praxis*. London, New York, and Philadelphia: Falmer Press.

Gusfield, J. 1974. "Review Symposium." *Contemporary Sociology* 3:291–295.

Habermas, Jürgen. 1990. "Modernity versus postmodernity." Pp. 342–354. In *Culture and Society. Contemporary Debates*, ed. Jeffrey C. Alexander and Steven Seidman. Cambridge and New York: Cambridge University Press.

———.1989a. *The New Conservatism*, ed. and trans. Sherry Weber Nicholsen. Cambridge, MA: MIT Press.

———. 1989b. *The Structural Transformation of the Public Sphere: An Inquiry into a Category of Bourgeois Society*, trans. Thomas Burger and Frederick Lawrence. Cambridge, MA: MIT Press.

———. 1987. *The Theory of Communicative Action, Vol. Two: Lifeworld and System: A Critique of Functionalist Reason*, trans. Thomas McCarthy. Boston: Beacon Press.

———. 1986. *Autonomy and Solidarity: Interviews*, ed. and intro. Peter Dews. London: Verso.

———. 1984. *The Theory of Communicative Action*. Vol. 1: Reason and the Rationalization of Society, trans. Thomas McCarthy. Boston: Beacon.

———. 1981. *Philosophisch-politische Profile: Erweiterte Ausgabe*. Frankfurt am Main: Suhrkamp.

———. 1975. *Legitimation Crisis*, trans. Thomas McCarthy. Boston: Beacon.

———. 1971. *Knowledge and Human Interests*, ed.and trans. Jeremy J. Shapiro. Boston: Beacon.

———. 1969. *Protestbewegung und Hochschulreform*. Frankfurt am Main: Suhrkamp.

———. 1961. *Student und Politik*. Frankfurt am Main: Suhrkamp.

Habermas, Jürgen, and Niklas Luhmann. 1971. *Theorie der Gesellschaft oder Sozialtechnologie*. Frankfurt am Main: Suhrkamp.

Hall, B. and Y. Kassam. 1985. "Participatory Research." *International Encyclopedia of Education: Research and Practice* 7:3795–3800.

Hall, Stuart. 1991. "The Local and the Global: Globalization and Ethnicity." Pp. 19–40 in *Culture, Globalization and The World-System*, ed. Anthony D. King. Binghamton: State University of New York at Binghamton.

———. 1986. "Gramsci's Relevance to the Analysis of Racism and Ethnicity." *Communication Inquiry* 10:5–27.

———. 1980. "Cultural Studies: Two Paradigms." *Media, Culture and Society* 2:57–72.

Hamilton, Roberta, and Michèle Barrett, eds. 1986. *The Politics of Diversity: Feminism, Nationalism, Marxism*. Montreal: Book Center Inc.

Hannoun, Hubert. 1973. *Ivan Illich ou l'école sans société*. Paris: Les Éditions ESF.

Haraway, Donna. 1992. "Ecce Homo, Ain't (Ar'n't) I a Woman, and Innappropriate/d Others: The Human in a Post-Humanist Landscape." Pp. 86–100 in *Feminists Theorize the Political,* eds. Judith Butler and Joan W. Scott. New York and London: Routledge.

———. 1984. "A Manifesto for Cyborgs: Science, Technology, and Socialist Feminism in the 1980s." Pp. 130–143 in *Coming to Terms: Feminism, Theory, Politics,* ed. Elizabeth Weed. New York: Routledge.

Harker, R. K. 1984. "On Reproduction, Habitus, and Education." *British Journal of Sociology of Education* 5:117–127.

Harris, David. 1992. *From Class Struggle to the Politics of Pleasure: The Effects of Gramscianism on Cultural Studies.* London and New York: Routledge.

Harvey, David. 1989. *The Condition of Postmodernity.* Oxford: Basil Blackwell.

Hearn, Francis. 1978. *Domination, Legitimation, and Resistance: The Incorporation of the Nineteenth-Century English Working Class.* Westport, CT, and London: Greenwood Press.

Held, David. 1980. *Introduction to Critical Theory: Horkheimer to Habermas.* Berkeley and Los Angeles: University of California Press.

Hennessy, Rosemary. 1993. *Materialist Feminism and the Politics of Discourse.* New York and London: Routledge.

Herbert, M. 1957. "The Social Sciences: Conceptual Framework for Education." *The School Review*

Herriott, Robert E., and Benjamin J. Hodgkins. 1973. *The Environment of Schooling: Formal Education as an Open System.* Englewood Cliffs, NJ: Prentice-Hall.

Hirsch, J. 1978. "The State Apparatus and Social Reproduction: Elements of a Theory of the Bourgeois State." Pp. 57–107 in *State and Capital,* eds. John Holloway and Sol Picciotto. London: Arnold.

Holloway, John, and Sol Picciotto, eds. 1979. *State and Capital,* Austin: University of Texas Press.

Honneth, Axel. 1987. "Critical Theory." Pp. 347–382 in *Social Theory Today,* eds. Anthony Giddens and Jonathan H. Turner. Stanford, CA: Stanford University Press.

Honneth, Axel and Hans Joas. 1988. *Social Action and Human Nature.* trans. Raymond Meyer. Cambridge: Cambridge University Press.

hooks, bell and Cornel West. 1991. *Breaking Bread: Insurgent Black Intellectual Life.* Toronto: Between the Lines.

Horkheimer, Max. 1978. *Dawn and Decline: Notes 1926–1931 and 1950–1969,* trans. Michael Shaw. New York: Seabury Press.

———. 1974. *Eclipse of Reason.* New York: Seabury.

————. 1972. *Critical Theory: Selected Essays,* trans. Matthew J. O'Connell. New York: Herder and Herder.

Horkheimer, Max, and Theodor W. Adorno. 1972. *Dialectic of Enlightenment,* trans. John Cumming. New York: Herder and Herder.

Hoselitz, B. 1960. *Sociological Aspects of Economic Growth.* Glencoe, NY: The Free Press.

Howard, Dick. 1988. *The Politics of Critique.* Minneapolis: University of Minnesota Press.

Howell, D. A., and Roger Brown. 1983. *Educational Policy Making: An Analysis.* London: Heinemann.

Hoy, Wayne K., and Cecil G. Miskel. 1982. *Educational Administration: Theory, Research, and Practice.* 2nd ed. New York: Random House.

Hurn, Christopher J. 1985. *The Limits and Possibilities of Schooling: An Introduction to the Sociology of Education.* 2nd.ed. Newton, MA: Allyn and Bacon.

Husen, Torsten. 1986. *The Learning Society Revisited: Essays.* Oxford: Pergamon Press.

Hutcheon, Linda. 1988. *A Poetics of Postmodernism: History, Theory, Fiction.* New York: Routledge.

Huyssen, Andreas. 1990. "Mapping the Postmodern." Pp. 355–370. In *Culture and Society. Contemporary Debates.,* ed. Jeffrey C. Alexander and Steven Seidman. Cambridge and New York: Cambridge University Press.

Illich, Ivan. 1973a. *Tools for Conviviality.* New York: Harper & Row.

————. 1973b. "After Deschooling, What?" Pp. 1–28 in *After Deschooling, What?* eds. Alan Gartner, Colin Greer and Frank Riessman. New York: Harper & Row.

————. 1971. *Deschooling Society.* New York: Harper & Row.

————. 1970. *Celebration of Awareness: A Call for Institutional Revolution.* Garden City, NY: Doubleday Anchor.

Inkeles, A., and D. H. Smith. 1974. *Becoming Modern.* Cambridge, MA: Harvard University Press.

Jacques, Martin. 1992, May 9. "Why I stopped editing Marxism Today." *Globe and Mail* (Toronto), (D5).

Jameson, Fredric. 1991. *Postmodernism, or, The Cultural Logic of Late Capitalism.* Durham, NC: Duke University Press.

————. 1984. "Postmodernism, or The Cultural Logic of Late Capitalism." *New Left Review* 146:53–92.

Jay, Martin. 1984. *Marxism and Totality: Adventures of a Concept from Lukacs to Habermas.* Berkeley and Los Angeles: University of California Press.

Jelin, Elizabeth. 1990. "Citizenship and Identity: Final Reflections." Pp.

184–207 in *Women and Social Change in Latin America,* ed. Elizabeth Jelin, trans. J. Ann Zammit and Marilyn Thomson. London and New Jersey: Zed Books.

Jencks, Christopher, et al. 1972. *Inequality: A Reassessment of the Effect of Family and Schooling in America.* New York: Harper & Row.

Jenks, Chris, ed. 1993. *Cultural Reproduction.* London and New York: Routledge.

Jensen, A. 1969. "How Much Can We Boost I. Q. and Scholastic Achievement?" *Harvard Educational Review* 39:1–123.

Jessop, Bob. 1982. *The Capitalist State: Marxist Theories and Methods.* Oxford: Martin Robertson.

Jones, Alwyn. 1987. "The Violence of Materialism in Advanced Industrial Society: An Eco-Sociological Approach." *The Sociological Review* 35:19–47.

Jones, Ken. 1983. *Beyond Progressive Education.* London: Macmillan.

Junqueira Paoli, Niuvenius. 1981. *Ideologia e hegemonia. As condições de produção da educação.* São Paulo: Cortez editora-autores associados.

Kanpol, Barry. 1992. *Towards a Theory and Practice of Teacher Cultural Politics: Continuing the Postmodern Debate.* Norwood, NJ: Ablex.

Karabel, Jerome. 1976. "Revolutionary Contradictions: Antonio Gramsci and the Problem of Intellectuals." *Politics and Society* 6:123–172.

Karabel, Jerome, and A. H. Halsey, eds. 1977. *Power and Ideology in Education.* New York: Oxford University Press.

Kaye, Harvey J., and Keith McClelland, eds. 1990. *E. P.Thompson: Critical Perspectives,* Philadelphia: Temple University Press.

Keane, John, ed. 1988. *Civil Society and the State,* London and New York: Verso.

Keat, Russell, and John Urry. 1982. *Social Theory as Science.* 2nd ed. London: Routledge & Kegan Paul.

Kellner, Douglas. 1989. *Critical Theory, Marxism and Modernity.* Baltimore: Johns Hopkins University Press.

Kelly, Gail P. 1992. "Education, Women, and Change." Pp. 267–282 in *Emergent Issues in Education: Comparative Perspectives,* eds. Robert F. Arnove, Philip G. Altbach, and Gail P. Kelly. Albany: State University of New York Press.

Kelly, Gail P., and A. S. Nihlen. 1982. "Schooling and the Reproduction of Patriarchy: Unequal Workloads, Unequal Rewards." Pp. 162–180 in *Cultural and Economic Reproduction in Education,* ed. Michael Apple. London and Boston: Routledge & Kegan Paul.

Kemmis, Stephen and Robin McTaggart, eds. 1988. *The Action Research Reader.* 3rd ed. Victoria, Australia: Deakin University Press.

King, Elizabeth. 1948. *Russia Goes to School: A Guide to Soviet Education.* London: Heinemann.

Kissinger, Henry. 1961. *The Necessity for Choice: Prospects of American Foreign Policy.* New York: Harper.

Klafki, Wolfgang, et al. 1970. *Erziehungswissenschaft.* Frankfurt am Main: Suhrkamp.

Kliebard, Herbert M. 1986. *The Struggle for the American Curriculum 1893–1958.* Boston, London, and Henley: Routledge & Kegan Paul.

Kohr, Richard L., et al. 1989. "The Relationships of Race, Class, and Gender with Mathematics Achievement." *Peabody Journal of Education 66.*

Kosik, Karel. 1976. *Dialectic of the Concrete,* trans. K. Kovanda and J. Schmidt. Boston: Reidel.

Kuhn, Thomas. 1970. *The Structure of Scientific Revolutions.* 2nd ed. Chicago: University of Chicago Press.

La Belle, Thomas J. 1986. *Nonformal Education in Latin America and the Caribbean: Stability, Reform, or Revolution?* New York: Praeger.

Labarca, Guillermo, ed. 1980. *Economía política de la educación,* Mexico: Nueva Imagen.

———. 1979. *Para una teoría de la acumulación capitalista en América Latina.* Mexico: Nueva Imagen.

———. 1976. "Crisis de la universidad, alianzas de clase y pensamiento crítico en América Latina." *Revista del Centro de Estudios Educativos* IV:115–126.

Labarca, G., T. Vasconi, S. Finkel, and I. Recca. 1977. *La educación burguesa.* Mexico: Editorial Nueva Imagen.

Labov, William. 1966. *The Social Stratification of English in New York City.* Washington, D. C.: Center for Applied Linguistics.

Labriola, Antonio. 1977. *Pedagogía, historia y sociedad: Textos escogidos,* trans. Sebastián Alvarez. Salamanca: Ediciones Sigueme.

Laclau, Ernesto. 1990. *New Reflections on The Revolution of Our Time.* London and New York: Verso.

Laclau, Ernest, and Chantal Mouffe. 1985. *Hegemony and Socialist Strategy: Towards a Radical Democratic Politics,* trans. Winston Moore and Paul Cammack. London: Verso.

Lakatos, Imre, and Alan Musgrave, eds. 1970. *Criticism and the Growth of Knowledge,* Cambridge: Cambridge University Press.

Landinelli, J. 1983. *El movimiento estudiantil universitario en el Uruguay. I: De los orígenes a la conquista de la ley orgánica de 1958; II: De la emergencia de la crisis estructural al glope de estado de junio de 1973.* México: FLACSO, Working Papers 7 and 8.

Lankshear, Colin, and Peter McLaren, eds. 1993. *Critical Literacy: Politics, Praxis and the Postmodern,* Albany: State University of New York Press.

Lash, Scott. 1990. *Sociology of Postmodernism*. London and New York: Routledge.

Latapí, Pablo. 1988. "Participatory Research: New Paradigm?" *Alberta Journal of Educational Research* 34:310–319.

Lather, Patti. 1991a. *Getting Smart: Feminist Research and Pedagogy With/In the Postmodern*. New York and London: Routledge.

———. 1991b. "Deconstruction, Deconstructive Inquiry: The Politics of Knowing and Being Known." *Educational Theory* 41:152–171.

Lawson, R. Alan. 1971. *The Failure of Independent Liberalism, 1930–1941*. New York: Capricorn Books.

Lefebvre, Henri. 1976. *The Survival of Capitalism: Reproduction of the Relations of Production*, trans. Frank Bryant. London: Allison & Busby.

———. 1971. *L'Idéologie structuraliste*. Paris: Seuil.

Leichter, Howard M. 1979. *A Comparative Approach to Policy Analysis: Health Care Policies in Four Nations*. Cambridge: Cambridge University Press.

Leiss, William. 1974. *The Domination of Nature*. Boston: Beacon Press.

Lengermann, Patricia Madoo, and Jill Niebrugge-Brantley. 1992. "Contemporary Feminist Theory." Pp. 308–357 in *Contemporary Sociological Theory*, ed. George Ritzer. 3rd ed. New York: McGraw-Hill.

———. 1990. "Feminist Sociological Theory: The Near-Future Prospects." Pp. 316–344 in *Frontiers of Social Theory*, ed. George Ritzer. New York: Columbia University Press.

Lenhardt, Gero. 1985. "From Contact to Status: The Educational System in Weber's Theory of Bureaucratic Rationalization." Jablona/Warsaw, unpublished paper 19, April.

———. 1984. *Schule und bürokratische Rationalität*. Frankfurt am Main: Suhrkamp.

Leonard, Stephen T. 1990. *Critical Theory in Political Practice*. Princeton: Princeton University Press.

Leschinsky, Achim. 1981. "Schulkritik und die Suche nach Alternativen." *Zeitschrift für Pädagogik* 27:519–538.

Levine, Daniel U., and Robert J. Havinghurst. 1992. *Society and Education*. 8th ed. Boston: Allyn and Bacon.

Levine, Paul. 1975. *Divisions*. Toronto: Canadian Broadcasting Corporation.

Levy, Daniel C. 1986. *Higher Education and the State in Latin America: Private Challenges to Public Dominance*. Chicago: University of Chicago Press.

Levy, Marion Jr. 1972. *Modernization: Latecomers and Survivors*. New York and London: Basic Books.

Lidz, Charles W. 1982. "Toward a Deep Structural Analysis of Moral Action." Pp. 229–256 in *Structural Sociology,* ed. Ino Rossi. New York: Columbia University Press.

Lilge, Frederic. 1958. *Anton Semyonovitch Makarenko: An Analysis of His Educational Ideas in the Context of Soviet Society.* Berkeley: University of California Press.

Lilienfeld, Robert. 1978. *The Rise of Systems Theory: An Ideological Analysis.* New York: John Wiley & Sons.

Lindblom, Charles E. 1968. *The Policy-Making Process.* Englewood Cliffs, NJ: Prentice-Hall.

Liston, Daniel P. 1988. *Capitalist Schools: Explanation and Ethics in Radical Studies of Schooling.* New York and London: Routledge.

Livingstone, David, et al. 1987. *Critical Pedagogy and Cultural Power.* Toronto and South Hadley, MA: Garamond Press/Bergin and Garvey.

Lockwood, David. 1964. "Social Integration and System Integration." Pp. 244–257 in eds. G.K. Zollschan and W. Hirsch. London: Routledge & Kegan Paul.

Lorde, Audre. 1984. *Sister Outsider.* Trumansburgh, NY: The Crossing Press.

Luhmann, Niklas. 1990. "The Paradox of System Differentiation and the Evolution of Society." Pp. 409–440 in *Differentiation Theory and Social Change,* eds. Jeffrey C. Alexander and Paul Colomy. New York: Columbia University Press.

———. 1982. *The Differentiation of Society,* trans. Stephen Holmes and Charles Larmore. New York: Columbia University Press.

Luke, Carmen, and Jennifer Gore, eds. 1992. *Feminisms and Critical Pedagogy.* New York and London: Routledge.

Luke, Timothy W. 1987. "Social Ecology as Critical Political Economy." *The Social Science Journal* 24:303–315.

Luttrell, Wendy. 1989. "Working-Class Women's Ways of Knowing: Effects of Gender, Race, and Class." *Sociology of Education* 62:33–46.

Lynch, Kathleen. 1989. *The Hidden Curriculum: Reproduction in Education, A Reappraisal.* London: The Falmer Press.

Lyotard, Jean-François. 1984. *The Postmodern Condition: A Report on Knowledge,* trans. Geoff Bennington and Brian Massumi. Minneapolis: University of Minnesota Press.

Machlup, F. 1962. *The Production and Distribution of Knowledge in the United States.* Princeton: Princeton University Press.

Makarenko, Anton S. 1973. *The Road to Life,* trans. Tatiana Litvinov. New York: Oriole Editions.

Manacorda, Mario Alighiero. 1977. *El principio educativo en Gramsci: Americanismo y conformismo,* trans. Luis Legaz. Salamanca: Ediciones Sígueme.

Manuel, Frank E., and Fritzie P. Manuel, eds. 1971. *French Utopias: An Anthology of Ideal Societies,* New York: Schocken.

Manza, Jeff. 1992. "Classes, Status Groups, and Social Closure: A Critique of Neo-Weberian Social Theory." *Current Perspectives in Social Theory* 12:275–302.

Marcuse, Herbert. 1969. *Negations: Essays in Critical Theory,* trans. Jeremy J. Shapiro. Boston: Beacon.

———. 1964. *One Dimensional Man.* Boston: Beacon.

———. 1960. *Reason and Revolution: Hegel and the Rise of Social Theory.* Boston: Beacon Press.

———. 1958. *Soviet Marxism: A Critical Analysis.* New York: Vintage.

Marini, Ruy Mauro. 1978. "Las razones del neodesarrollismo (o por qué me ufano de mi burguesía)." *Revista Mexicana de Sociología* 40:57–106.

Marshall, T. H. 1965. *Class, Citizenship, and Social Development.* Garden City, NY: Anchor Books.

Marx, Karl. 1971. *Capital.* Moscow: Progress Publishers.

Mayhew, Leon. 1990. "The Differentiation of the Solidary Public." Pp. 294–322 in *Differentiation Theory and Social Change,* eds. Jeffrey C. Alexander and Paul Colomy. New York: Columbia University Press.

Maynes, Mary Jo. 1985. *Schooling in Western Society: A Social History.* Albany: State University of New York.

Mayo, Peter. 1989. "Gramsci, Freire and Adult Education." Doctoral Dissertation. Edmonton, AB: University of Alberta, M.A. thesis, Dept. of Educational Foundations.

McCarthy, Cameron, and Michael W. Apple. 1988. "Race, Class and Gender in American Educational Research: Toward a Nonsynchronous Parallelist Position." Pp. 9–39 in *Class, Race and Gender in American Education,* ed Lois Weis. Albany: State University of New York Press.

McLaren, Peter. 1994. "An Exchange with Eugene E. García, Director of the Office of Bilingual Education and Minority Language Affairs, U. S. Department of Education." *International Journal of Educational Reform* 3:74–80.

———. 1989. "On Ideology and Education: Critical Pedagogy and the Cultural Politics of Resistance." *Critical Pedagogy, the State and Cultural Struggle,* eds. Henry A. Giroux and Peter McLaren. Albany: State University of New York Press.

——— 1988. "Culture or Canon: Critical Pedagogy and the Politics of Literacy." *Harvard Educational Review* 58:213–234.

McLaren, Peter L., and Colin Lankshear, eds. 1994. *Politics of Liberation: Paths from Freire.* London and New York: Routledge.

McLaren, Peter, and Peter Leonard, eds. 1993. *Paulo Freire: A Critical Encounter.* London and New York: Routledge.

McLellan, David, ed. 1977. *Karl Marx: Selected Writings*. Oxford: Oxford University Press.

Meier, Kenneth J., Joseph Stewart Jr., and Robert E. England. 1989. *Race, Class and Education: The Politics of Second-Generation Discrimination*. Madison: University of Wisconsin Press.

Merquior, J. G. 1980. *Rousseau and Weber: Two Studies in the Theory of Legitimacy*. London, Boston and Henley: Routledge & Kegan Paul.

Merton, Robert. 1968. *Social Theory and Social Structure*. New York: Free Press.

Meyer, John W., and Michael T. Hannan. 1979a. "Issues for Further Comparative Research." Pp. 297–308 in *National Development and the World System: Educational, Economic, and Political Change, 1950–1970*, eds. John W. Meyer and Michael T. Hannan. Chicago and London: University of Chicago Press.

————, eds. 1979b. *National Development and the World System: Educational, Economic, and Political Change, 1950–1970*. Chicago and London: University of Chicago Press.

Meyer, John W., Francisco O. Ramirez, Richard Rubinson, and John Boli-Bennett. 1979. "The World Educational Revolution, 1950–70." Pp. 37–55 in *National Development and the World System: Educational, Economic, and Political Change, 1950–1970*, eds. John W. Meyer and Michael T. Hannan. Chicago and London: University of Chicago Press.

Miedema, Siebren. 1985. "Theory and Practice of Critical Pedagogy." *4th Annual Human Science Conference*, University of Alberta, Edmonton (May).

Miles, Robert. 1989. *Racism*. London: Routledge.

Miliband, Ralph. 1973. *The State in Capitalist Society: The Analysis of the Western System of Power*. London: Quartet Books.

Miller, John A. 1986. "The Fiscal Crisis of the State Reconsidered: Two Views of the State and the Accumulation of Capital in the Postwar Economy." *Review of Radical Political Economics* 18:236–260.

Mills, C. Wright. 1967. *The Sociological Imagination*. London, Oxford, and New York: Oxford University Press.

Mioshi, Masao, and H. D. Hartootunian. 1988. "Introduction (Special Issue on Postmodernism and Japan)." *South Atlantic Quaterly* 87.

Misgeld, Dieter. 1985. "Education and Cultural Invasion: Critical Social Theory, Education as Instruction, and the 'Pedagogy of the Oppressed'." Pp. 77–118 in *Critical Theory and Public Life*, ed. John Forester. Cambridge, MA: MIT Press.

————. 1975. "Emancipation, Enlightenment, and Liberation: An Approach Toward Foundational Inquiry into Education." *Interchange* 6:23–37.

Molano, Alfredo. 1978. "Introducción." Pp. xi–lvi in *Crítica y política en ciencias sociales: El debate teoría y práctica,* Simposio Mundial de Cartagena. Bogotá: Punta de Lanza.

Moore, Robert. 1988. "The Correspondence Principle of the Marxist Sociology of Education." Pp. 51–85 in *Bowles and Gintis Revisited: Correspondence and Contradiction in Educational Theory,* ed. Mike Cole. London, New York, and Philadelphia: Falmer Press.

Morales-Gómez, Daniel, and Carlos Alberto Torres, eds. 1992. *Education, Policy, and Social Change,* Westport, CT, and London: Praeger.

Morrow, Raymond A. 1991. "Critical Theory, Gramsci and Cultural Studies: From Structuralism to Poststructuralism." Pp. 27–70 in *Critical Theory Now,* ed. Philip Wexler. London, New York, and Philadelphia: Falmer Press.

———. 1990. "Post-Marxism, Postmodernism and Popular Education in Latin America." *New Education* 12:47–57.

———. 1985. "Critical Theory and Critical Sociology." *Canadian Review of Sociology and Anthropology* 22:710–747.

———. 1982. "Théorie critique et matérialisme historique: Jürgen Habermas." *Sociologie et Sociétés* 14:97–111.

———. 1975. "Gramsci in Germany." *Telos* 32:193–116.

Morrow, Raymond A., and Carlos Alberto Torres. 1994. "Education and the Reproduction of Class, Gender and Race: Responding to the Postmodern Challenge." *Educational Theory* 44:43–61.

———. 1990. "Ivan Illich and the De-Schooling Thesis Twenty Years After." *New Education* 12:3–17.

———. 1988, February. "Social Theory, Social Reproduction, and Education's Everday Life: A Framework for Analysis." *Paper presented at the Canadian Western Association of Sociology and Anthropology Annual Meetings,* University of Alberta, Edmonton, Canada.

Morrow, Raymond A., with David D. Brown. 1994. *Critical Theory and Methodology.* Newbury Park and London: Sage.

Moser, Heinz. 1978. "La investigación-acción como nuevo paradigma en las ciencias sociales." Pp. 117–140 in *Crítica y política en ciencias sociales: El debate teoría y prática.* Simposio Mundial de Cartgena. Bogotá: Punta de Lanza.

———. 1975. *Aktionsforschung als kritische Theorie der Sozialwissenschaften.* Munich: Koesel Verlag.

Müller, Detlef K., Fritz Ringer and Brian Simon, eds. 1987. *The Rise of the Modern Educational System: Structural Change and Social Reproduction 1870–1920,* Cambridge: Cambridge University Press.

Muñoz Izquierdo, Carlos. 1979. *El problema de la educación de México: ¿Laberinto sin salida?* Mexico: Centro de Estudios Educativos, CEE.

Murphy, Raymond. 1988. *Social Closure: The Theory of Monopolization and Exclusion.* Oxford: Clarendon Press.

———. 1979. *Sociological Theories of Education.* Toronto: McGraw-Hill Ryerson.

Namo de Melo, Giomar. 1985. "Las clases populares y la institución escolar: una interacción contradictoria." *Educación y clases sociales en América Latina,* Mexico: DIE.

Nielsen, François and Michael T. Hannan. 1979. "Expansion of National Educational Systems: Test of a Population Ecology Model." Pp. 56–71 in *National Development and the World System: Educational, Economic, and Political Change, 1950–1970,* eds. John W. Meyer and Michael T. Hannan. Chicago and London: University of Chicago Press.

Norris, Christopher. 1990. *What's Wrong with Postmodernism: Critical Theory and the Ends of Philosophy.* Baltimore: Johns Hopkins University Press.

O'Connor, James. 1973a. *The Fiscal Crisis of the State.* New York: St. Martins Press.

———. 1973b. "Summary of the Theory of the Fiscal Crisis." *Working Papers on the Kapitalistate* 1:79–83.

O'Donnell, Guillermo. 1982. *El Estado burocrático-autoritario: Argentina 1966–1973.* Buenos Aires: Editorial de Belgrano.

———. 1978a. "Apuntes para une teoría del estado." *Revista Mexicana de Sociología* 40:1157–1199.

———. 1978b. "Reflections on the Patterns of Chage in the Bureaucratic-Authoritarian State." *Latin American Research Review* 12:3–38.

Offe, Claus. 1985. *Disorganized Capitalism,* ed. John Keane. Cambridge, MA: MIT Press.

———. 1984. *Contradictions of the Welfare State,* ed. John Keane. London: Hutchinson.

———. 1976. "Structural Problems of the Capitalist state: Class Rule and the Political System." *German Political Studies: Theory and Practice in the Two Germanies,* ed K. Von Beyme. Beverly Hills: Sage.

———. 1975a. "Notes on the Laws of Motion of Reformist State Policies." Mimeographed.

———. 1975b. "The Theory of the Capitalist State and the Problem of Policy Formation." *Stress and Contradiction in Modern Capitalism,* eds. et al Lindberg. Toronto: Lexington Books.

———. 1974. "Structural Problems of the Capitalist State: Class Rule and the Political System. On the Selectiveness of Political Institutions." *German Political Studies,* ed. Von Beyme. Beverly Hills: Sage.

———. 1973a. "the Abolition of Market Control and the Problem of Legitimacy." *Working Papers on the Kapitalistate* 1:109–116.

————. 1973b. "the Abolition of Market Control and the Problem of Legitimacy." *Working Papers on the Kapitalistate* 2:73–5.

————. 1972 a. "Advanced Capitalism and the Welfare State." *Politics and Society* 2:497–488.

————. 1972 b. "Political Authority and Class Structures—An Analysis of Late Capitalist Societies." *International Journal of Sociology* 2:73–108.

Offe, Claus, and V. Ronge. 1975. "Theses on the Theory of the State." *New German Critique* (Fall):137–147.

Omi, Michael, and Howard Winant. 1986. *Racial Formation in the United States: From the 1960s to the 1980s.* New York and London: Routledge.

Oslak, Oscar. 1980. *Políticas y regimenes políticos: Reflexiones a partir de algunas experiencias latinoamericanas.* Buenos Aires: Estudios-CEDES.

Paci, Enzo. 1972. *The Function of the Sciences and the Meaning of Man,* trans. P. Piccone and J. Hansen. Evanston: Northwestern University Press.

Paiva, Vanilda P. 1981. *Paulo Freire y nacionalismo desarrollista,* trans. Manuel Arbolí Gazcón. Mexico, D.F.: Editorial Extemporáneos.

Parkin, Frank. 1979. *Marxism and Class Theory: A Bourgeoisie Critique.* London: Tavistock.

Parsons, Talcott. 1961. "The School as a Social System: Some of its Functions in American Society." Pp. 434–55 in *Education, Economy and Societey: A Reader in the Sociology of Education,* ed A. H. Halsey. New York: Free Press.

————. 1959. "A Short Account of My Intellectual Development." *The Alpha Kappa Delta* 39.

————. 1951. *The Social system.* Glencoe, NY: Free Press.

————. 1949. *The Structure of Social Action.* Glencoe, NY: Free Press.

Parsons, Talcott, R. Bales, and E. Shils. 1970. *Apuntes sobre la teoría de la acción,* Buenos Aires: Amorrortu.

Parsons, Talcott, and Gerald M. Platt. 1973. *The American University.* Cambridge,MA: Harvard University Press.

Passeron, Jean-Claude. 1986. "Theories of Socio-cultural Reproduction." *International Social Science Journal* 38:619–629.

Paulston, Rolland G. 1976. *Conflicting Theories of Social and Educational Change: A Typological Review.* Pittsburgh: University Center for International Studies, University of Pittsburgh.

Pescador, J. A., and C. A. Torres. 1985. *Poder político y educación en Mexico.* Mexico: UTHEA.

Piaget, Jean. 1970. *Structuralism,* trans. Chaninah Maschler. New York: Harper Torchbooks.

Pike, Shirley. 1986. *Marxism and Phenomenology.* London and Sydney: Croom Helm.

Plumb, Donovan. 1989. "The Significance of Jürgen Habermas for the Pedagogy of Paulo Freire and the Practice of Adult Education." Saskatoon: University of Saskatchewan, M. A. thesis.

Popkewitz, Thomas. 1991. *A Political Sociology of Educational Reform: Power-Knowledge in Teaching, Teacher Education, and Research.* New York and London: Teachers College Press.

Popkewitz, Thomas. 1988. *"Educational Theory."* "Educational Reform: Rhetoric, Ritual, and Social Interest" 38,1: 77–93.

———, ed. 1987a. *Critical Studies in Teacher Education: Its Folklore, Theory and Practice,* London, New York, and Philadelphia: Falmer Press.

———., ed. 1987b. *The Formation of School Subjects: The Struggle for Creating an American Institution,* New York, Philadelphia, and London: The Falmer Press.

———. 1984. *Paradigm and Ideology in Educational Research: The Social Functions of the Intellectual.* London and New York: Falmer Press.

Portantiero, J. C. 1978. *Estudiantes y política en América Latina. El proceso de la reforma universitaria (1918–1938).* México: mimeographed.

Porter, John. 1965. *The Vertical Mosaic: An Analysis of Social Class and Power in Canada* Toronto: University of Toronto Press.

Poulantzas, Nicos. 1978. *Classes in Contemporary Capitalism,* trans. David Fernbach. London: Verso.

———. 1969a. *Poder político y clases sociales in el estado capitalista.* Mexico: Siglo XXI Editores.

———. 1969b. "The Problem of the Capitalist State." *New Left Review* 58: 237–241.

Price, R. F. 1986. *Marx and Education in Late Capitalism.* London and Sydney: Croom Helm.

Pronovost, Gilles, ed. 1982. *Culture populaires et sociétés contemporaines,* Montréal: Presses de l'Université de Québec.

Przeworski, Adam. 1985. *Capitalism and Social Democracy.* Cambridge: Cambridge University Press.

Psacharopoulos, George. 1988. "Critical Issues in Education and Development: A World Agenda." *International Journal of Educational Development* 8:1–7.

Rama, Germán. 1985. "Transición cultural y la aspiración de la juventud." Pp. 61–80 in *Educação na América Latina,* eds. Felícia Reicher Madeira and Guiomar Namo de Mello. São Paulo: Cortez Editora-Autores Associados.

Ramirez, Francisco O. and John Boli. 1987. "The Political Construction of Mass Schooling: European and Worldwide Institutionalization." *Sociology of Education* 60:2–17.

Ramirez, Francisco O., and Richard Rubinson. 1979. "Creating Members: The Political Incorporation and Expansion of Public Education." Pp. 72–84 in *National Development and the World System: Educational, Economic, and Political Change, 1950–1970,* eds. John W. Meyer and Michael T. Hannan. Chicago and London: University of Chicago Press.

Recca, Tomás. 1977. "La educación: un sistema de dominación." Pp. 17–68 in *La educación burguesa,* eds. G. Labarca, T. Vasconi, S. Finkel, and I. Recca. Mexico: Editorial Nueva Imagen.

Reicher Madeira, Felícia, and Guiomar Namo de Mello. 1985. "Apresentação." Pp. 7–32 in *Educação na Aaerica Latina,* São Paulo: Cortez Editora-Autores Associados.

Rex, John. 1986. "The Role of Class Analysis in the Study of Race Relations—A Weberian Perspective." Pp. 64–83 in *Theories of Race and Ethnic Relations,* eds. John Rex and David Mason. Cambridge: Cambridge University Press.

Rex, John, and David Mason, eds. 1986. *Theories of Race and Ethnic Relations,* Cambridge: Cambridge University Press.

Reynolds, David, and Mike Sullivan. 1980. "Towards a New Socialist Sociology of Education." Pp. 169–195 in *Schooling, Ideology and Curriculum,* eds. Roland Meighan, Stephen Walker, and Len Barton. Sussex: Falmer Press.

Rhoades, Gary. 1990. "Political Competition and Differentiation in Higher Education." Pp. 197–221 in *Differentiation Theory and Social Change,* eds. Jeffrey C. Alexander and Paul Colomy. New York: Columbia University Press.

Ricoeur, Paul. 1986. *Lectures on Ideology and Utopia,* ed. George H. Taylor. New York: Columbia University Press.

Ringer, Fritz. 1987. "Introduction." Pp. 1–14 in *The Rise of the Modern Educational System,* eds. Detlef Müller, Fritz Ringer, and Brian Simon. Cambridge: Cambridge University Press.

Robertson, Roland, and Bryan S. Turner, eds. 1991. *Talcott Parsons: Theorist of Modernity,* London: Sage.

Robinson, Philip. 1981. *Perspectives on the Sociology of Education.* London, Boston, and Henley: Routledge & Kegan Paul.

Roemer, John (editor). 1986. *Analytical Marxism.* Cambridge, GB and New York: Cambridge University Press.

Rosenthal, Robert, and Lenore Jacobson. 1968. *Pygmalion in the Classroom.* New York: Holt, Rinehart and Winston.

Rossi, Ino, ed. 1982. *Structural Sociology*. New York: Columbia University Press.

Rostow, W. W. 1960. *The Stages of Economic Growth, a Non-Communist Manifesto*. Cambridge: Cambridge University Press.

Russell, David G. 1980. *Planning Education for Development*. Cambridge: Harvard University Press—CRED.

Russett, Cynthia Eagle. 1966. *The Concept of Equilibrium in American Social Thought*. New Haven and London: Yale University Press.

Samoff, Joel. 1982. "Class, Class Conflict, and the State in Africa." *Political Science Quarterly* 97:105–127.

Sampson, Edward E. 1991. *Social Worlds, Personal Lives: An Introduction to Social Psychology*. New York: Harcourt Brace Jovanovich.

Saran, R. 1973. *Policy Making in Secondary Education*. Oxford: Oxford University Press.

Sardei-Bierman, Jens Christiansen, and Knuth Dohse. 1973. "Class Domination and the Political System." *Working Papers on the Kapitalistate 2*.

Sarup, Madan. 1984. *Marxism, Structuralism, Education: Theoretical Developments in the Sociology of Education*. London and New York: Falmer Press.

———. 1978. *Marxism and Education*. London: Routeldge & Kegan Paul.

Saviani, Dermeval. 1983. "Escola e democracía." São Paulo: Cortez e Autores Associados.

Sayer, R. Andrew, and Richard Walker. 1992. *The New Social Economy*. Cambridge: Blackwell.

Schriewer, Jürgen, and Klaus Harney. 1987. "On 'Systems" of Education and their Comparability: Methodological Comments and Theoretical Alternatives." Pp. 197–209 in *The Rise of the Modern Educational System: Structural Change and Social Reproduction 1870–1920*, eds. Detlef K. Müller, Fritz Ringer and Brian Simon. Cambridge: Cambridge University Press.

Scott, Alan. 1990. *Ideology and the New Social Movements*. London: Unwin Hyman.

Scott, Joan W. 1992. " 'Experience'." Pp. 22–40 in *Feminists Theorize the Political*, eds. Judith Butler and Joan W. Scott. New York and London: Routledge.

Seidman, Steven, ed. 1989. *Jürgen Habermas on Society and Politics: A Reader*, Boston: Beacon Press.

Seidman, Steven and David G. Wagner. 1992. "Introduction." Pp. 1–16 in *Postmodernism and Social Theory*, eds. Steven Seidman and David G. Wager. Cambridge, MA, and Oxford: Basil Blackwell.

Selowsky, M. 1980. "Preschool Age Investment in Human Capital."

Pp. 97–111 in *The Educational Dilemma*, ed. J. Simmons. London: Pergamon Press.

Sève, Lucien. 1974. *Marxisme et théorie de la personalité*. Paris: Éditions Sociales.

Sharp, Rachel. 1980. *Knowledge, Ideology and the Politics of Schooling: Towards a Marxist Analysis of Education*. London: Routledge & Kegan Paul.

Shor, Ira. 1992. *Empowering Education: Critical Teaching for Social Change*. Chicago and London: University of Chicago Press.

———, ed. 1987. *Freire for the Classroom: A Sourcebook for Liberatory Teaching*. Portsmouth, NH: Boynton/Cook Publishers (Heinemann).

Shor, Ira, and Paulo Freire. 1987. *A Pedagogy for Liberation: Dialogues on Transforming Education*. South Hadley, MA: Bergin and Garvey.

Siegel, R., and Leonard B. Weinberg. 1977. *Comparing Public Policies: United States, Soviet Union and Europe*. Homewood, IL: Dorsey Press.

Simmons, John. 1980. *The Educational Dilemma*. Oxford: Pergamon Press.

Simon, Brian. 1965. *Education and the Labour Movement: 1870–1920*. London: Lawrence & Wishart.

Skocpol, Theda. 1982. "Bringing the State Back in: False Leads and Promising Starts in Current Theories and Research." Working Paper. Seven Springs Conference Center, Mount Kisco, New York, 25–27 February.

———. 1980. "Political Response to Capitalist Crisis: Neo-Marxist Theories of the State and the Case of the New Deal." *Politics and Society* 10:155–201.

Smelser, Neil. 1990. "The Contest Between Family and Schooling in Nineteenth-Century Britain." Pp. 165–186 in *Differentiation Theory and Social Change*, eds. Jeffrey C. Alexander and Paul Colomy. New York: Columbia University Press.

———. 1985. "Evaluating the Model of Structural Differentiation in Relation to Educational Change in the Nineteenth Century." Pp. 113–130 in *Neofunctionalism*, ed. Jeffrey C. Alexander. Beverly Hills: Sage.

Smith, Michael Peter. 1992. "Postmodernism, Urban Ethnography, and the New Social Space of Ethnic Identity." *Theory and Society* 21:493–531.

Solari, A. 1968. *Estudiantes y política en América Latina*. Caracas: Monte Avila.

Solari, A., and S. M. Lipset, eds. 1968. *Elites y desarrollo en América Latina*, Buenos Aires: Paidós.

Solomos, John. 1986. "Varieties of Marxist Conceptions of 'Race', Class and the State: A Critical Analysis." Pp. 84–109 in *Theories of Race and Ethnic Relations,* eds. John Rex and David Mason. Cambridge: Cambridge University Press.

Spivak, Gayatri C. 1992. "French Feminism Revisited: Ethics and Politics." Pp. 54–85 in *Feminists Theorize the Political,* eds. Judith Butler and Joan W. Scott. New York and London: Routledge.

Sternbach, Nancy S., Marysa Navarro-Aranguren, Patricia Chuchryk, and Sonia E. Alvarez. 1992. "Feminisms in Latin America: From Bogotá to San Bernardo." *Signs* 17:393–343.

Stinchcombe, A. 1969. "Environment: The Cumulation of Effects is Yet to Be Understood." *Harvard Educational Review* 39:511–22.

Suchodolski, B. and Mario Manacorda. 1975. *La crisis de la educación.* México: Ediciones de Cultura Popular.

Suchodolski, Bogdan. 1966. *Teoría marxista de la educación.* Mexico: Grijalbo.

Sunkel, O. and E. Fuenzalida. 1979. "Transnational Capitalism and National Development." Pp. 67–93 in *Transnational Capitalism and National Development.* New Jersey: Humanities Press.

Sutton, J. R. 1984. "Organizational Autonomy and Professional Norms in Science. A Case Study of the Lawrence Livermore Laboratory." *Social Studies of Science* 14:197–224.

Swidler, Ann. 1979. *Organization Without Authority: Dilemmas of Social Control in Free Schools.* Cambridge, MA: Harvard University Press.

Tamarit, José. 1990. "El dilema de la educación popular: entre la utopía y la resignación." *Revista Argentina de Educación* 8:7–45.

Tavares de Jesus, Antonio. 1989. *Educação e hegemonía no pensamento de Antonio Gramsci.* São Paulo: Editora Unicamp-Cortez.

Tedesco, Juan Carlos. 1985. "Reproductivismo educativo y sectores populares en América Latina." Pp. 33–60 in *Educação na América Latina,* eds. Felícia Reicher Madeira and Guiomar Namo de Mello. São Paulo: Cortez Editora-Autores Associados.

Terán, Oscar. 1983. *Anibal Ponce.El Marxismo sin nación.* Mexico: Pasado y Presente.

Therborn, Goran. 1984. "Classes and State. Welfare State Developments, 1881–1981." *Studies in Political Economy* 7–41.

———. 1980. *The Ideology of Power and the Power of Ideology.* London: Verso.

———. 1979. *What Does the Ruling Class Do When it Rules?* London: Verso.

Torre, J. C. 1968. "Sindicatos y clase obrera en la Argentina post-Peronista." *Revista Latinoamericana de Sociologiaa* IV:108–114.

Torres, Carlos Alberto. 1994. "Adult Education for National Development." *The International Encyclopedia of Education,* eds. Torsten Husén and T. Neville Postlethwaite. 2nd ed. Oxford: Pergamon Press.

———. 1993. "From the Pedagogy of the Oppressed to a *Luta continua*:. The Political Pedagogy of Paulo Freire." Pp. 119–145 in *Paulo Freire: A Critical Encounter*, eds. Peter McLaren and Peter Leonard. London and New York: Routledge.

———. 1992. *The Church, Society, and Hegemony: A Critical Sociology of Religion in Latin America*, trans. Robert A. Young. Westport, CT, and London: Praeger.

———. 1991. "The State, Nonformal Education and Socialism in Cuba, Nicaragua and Grenada." *Comparative Education Revew* 35:110–130.

———. 1990. *The Politics of Nonformal Education in Latin America*. New York: Praeger.

———. 1985. "The State and Education: Marxist Theories." Pp. 4793–4798 in *International Encyclopedia of Educational Research and Studies*, eds. Torsten Husén and T. N. Postlethwaite. Vol. 8. Oxford: Pergamon Press.

———, ed. 1982. *Ensayos sobre la educación de los adultos en América Latina*. México, D. F.: Centro de Estudios Educativos, A. C.

———. 1980. *Leitura critica de Paulo Freire*. São Paulo: Loyola Ediçoes.

———. 1978a. "Filosofía política y sujeto histórico-político del cambio social: Notas sobre Lenin y Gramsci." *Estudios Filosóficos* 27:1–12.

———. 1978b. *Entrevistas con Paulo Freire*. Mexico, D.F.: Ediciones Gernika.

Torres, Carlos Alberto, and Guillermo González Rivera, eds. 1994. *Sociología de la educación: Corrientes contemporáneas*. 3rd ed. Buenos Aires: Miño y Davila editores.

Torres, Rosa María. 1988. *Educación popular. Un encuentro con Paulo Freire*. Buenos Aires: Centro de Estudios de América Latina.

Tucker, Robert C., ed. 1978. *The Marx-Engels Reader*. 2nd ed. New York: W.W. Norton.

Turner, Bryan S. 1991. "Neofunctionalism and the 'New Theoretical Movement': The Post-Parsonian Rapproachement between Germany and America." Pp. 234–249 in *Talcott Parsons: Theorist of Modernity*, eds. Roland Robertson and Bryan S. Turner. London: Sage.

Turner, Jonathan, and Alexandra Maryanski. 1979. *Functionalism*. Menlo Park, CA/Reading, MA: Benjamin Cummings.

Turner, Ralph H. 1960. "Sponsored and Contest Mobility and the School System." *American Sociological Review* 25:855–867.

UNESCO. 1974. *Evolución de la educación en América Latina*. 2 vols. Santiago de Chile: UNESCO. mimeographed.

Vasconi, Tomás A. 1994. "Etapas de un pensamiento." Pp. 283–295 in *Sociología de la educación: Corrientes contemporáneas*, eds. Carlos Alberto Torres and Guillermo González Rivera. Buenos Aires: Miño y Davila.

———. 1978. *Gran capital y militarización en América Latina*. México: Ediciones ERA.

———. 1977a. "Ideología, lucha de clases y aparatos educativos en el desarrollo de América Latina." Pp. 173–236 in *La educación burguesa*, eds. G. Labarca, T. Vasconi, S. Finkel, and I. Recca. Mexico: Editorial Nueva Imagen.

———. 1977b. "Aportes para una teoría de la educación." Pp. 301–339 in *La educación burguesa*, eds. G. Labarca, T. Vasconi, S. Finkel, and I. Recca. Mexico: Editorial Nueva Imagen.

Vasconi, Tomás, and Inés Recca. 1977. "La educación: un sistema de dominación." Pp. 17–68 in *La educación burguesa*, eds. G. Labarca, T. Vasconi, S. Finkel, and I. Recca. Mexico: Editorial Nueva Imagen.

Wacquant, Loïc J. D. 1985. "Heuristic Models in Marxian Theory." *Social Forces* 64:17–45.

Wallerstein, Immanuel. 1991. "The National and the Universal: Can There be Such a Thing as World Culture?" Pp. 91–106 in *Culture, Globalization and the World System*, ed. Anthony D. King. Binghamton: State University of New York at Binghamton.

Weber, Max. 1944. *Economía et sociedad*, trans. José et al Medina Echavarría. Vol. 1. Mexico: Fondo de Cultura Económica.

Weiler, Hans H., ed. 1980. *Educational Planning and Social Change: Report on an IIEP Seminar*, Paris: UNESCO-IIEP.

———. 1983. "Legitimation, Expertise and Participation: Strategies of Compensatory Legitimation in Educational Policy." *Comparative Education Review* 27:259–277.

West, Cornel. 1992. "The Postmodern Crisis of the Black Intellectuals." Pp. 689–705 in *Cultural Studies*, eds. Lawrence Grossberg, Cary Nelson, and Paula Treichler. New York and London: Routledge.

———. 1988. "Marxist Theory and the Specificity of Afro-American Oppression." Pp. 17–29 in *Marxism and the Interpretation of Culture*, eds. Larry Grossberg and Cary Nelson. Urbana and Chicago: University of Illinois Press.

Wetherell, Margaret, and Jonathan Potter. 1992. *Mapping the Language of Racism: Discourse and the Legitimation of Exploitation*. New York: Columbia University Press.

Wexler, Philip. 1987. *Social Analysis of Education: After the New Sociology*. London and New York: Routledge & Kegan Paul.

———. 1983. *Critical Social Psychology*. Boston: Routledge & Kegan Paul.

———. 1981. "Body and Soul: Sources of Social Change and Strategies of Education." *British Journal of Sociology of Education* 2:247–163.

Whitty, Geoff. 1985. *Sociology and School Knowledge: Curriculum Theory, Research and Politics*. London: Methuen.

Wilensky, Harold. 1976. *The New Corporatism: Centralization and the Welfare State.* Beverly Hills: Sage.

———. 1975. *The Welfare State and Equality.* Berkeley and Los Angeles: University of California Press.

Willis, Paul. 1981. *Learning to Labor: How Working Class Kids Get Working Class Jobs.* New York: Columbia University Press.

Wirt, F., and M. W. Kirst. 1982. *Schools in Conflicts: The Politics of Education.* Berkeley: McCutchan.

Wolf, Eric R. 1982. *Europe and the People Without History.* Berkeley, Los Angeles, and London: University of California Press.

Wolpe, Harold. 1986. "Class Concepts, Class Struggle and Racism." Pp. 110–130 in *Theories of Race and Ethnic Relations,* eds. John Rex and David Mason. Cambridge: Cambridge University Press.

Wood, Ellen Meiksins. 1986. *The Retreat from Class: A New 'True' Socialism.* London: Verso.

World Bank. 1989. *World Development Report.* Washington, D.C.: Oxford University Press and The World Bank.

Wright, Erik Olin. 1987. "Review Essay?" *Contemporary Sociology* 16.

———. 1985. *Classes.* London: Verso.

———. 1978. *Class, Crisis, and the State.* London: New Left Books.

Yarnit, Martin. 1980a. "150 Hours: Italy's Experiment in Mass Working-Class Education." Pp. 192–218 in *Adult Education for Change,* ed. Jane L. Thompson. London: Hutchinson.

———. 1980b. "Second Change to Learn, Liverpool: Class and Adult Education." Pp. 174–191 in *Adult Education for Change,* ed. Jane L. Thompson. London: Hutchinson.

Young, Michael F. D., ed. 1971. *Knowledge and Control: New Directions for the Sociology of Education.* London: Collier-Macmillan.

Young, Robert E. 1992. *Critical Theory and Classroom Talk.* Clevedon, Philadelphia, and Adelaide: Multilingual Matters Ltd.

———. 1989. *A Critical Theory of Education: Habermas and Our Children's Future.* New York and London: Harvester Wheatsheaf.

Youngman, Frank. 1986. *Adult Education and Socialist Pedagogy.* London: Croom Helm.

INDEX

Abercrombie, Nicholas, and John
  Urry, 454 n.4
Action (theory of), 51, 106, 241
Action research, participatory, 241,
  243, 244, 247, 274, 302
Adamson, Walter, 253, 261, 264–
  268, 270, 276
Adaptation (theory of), 85
Adorno, Theodor, 221, 223–224,
  227–229, 234, 237, 238, 240, 246,
  280
Africa, 380, 387, 423
Agency (and autonomy, and
  structure), 21, 32, 96, 99, 101,
  108, 132, 285–286, 304, 333, 335,
  372, 427, 430
Alexander, Jeffrey, 37, 41, 56, 79–81,
  89–93, 99, 101, 450 n.7
Alexander, Jeffrey, and Paul, Colomy,
  79
Alexander, Jeffrey, and Steven
  Seidman, 412
Alienation, 127, 245, 409
Altbach, Philips, 5
Althusser, Louis, 18, 118–119, 126–
  127, 129, 141, 143–152, 155,
  162, 177–180, 211–212, 225,
  230, 235, 262, 278, 287, 296, 299,
  341, 371–372, 450 n.8
Althusser, Louis, and Étienne,
  Balibar, 144–145
Alvater, Elmar, 349–351, 357–359,
  460 n.6
American social thought, 44, 56
American sociology, 42, 44, 48
Americanism, 260
Anarchism, 228
  Christian, 228, 260

Annales School, 48
Anthropology
  Structuralist, 118–119
Apple, Michael W., 5, 18, 124, 169,
  287, 309–337, 378, 383, 341–
  342, 355–357, 375–376, 379,
  382–383, 427, 447 n.2, 448 n.4,
  455 n.7, 458 n.2, 462 n.2
Apple, Michael W., and Lois Weis,
  379
Archer, Margaret, 16, 41, 43, 99,
  101–113, 342, 450 n.7
Archer, Margaret, and Michalina,
  Vaughan, 349
Argentina, 452 n.1, 453 n.5, 456 n.5
Aricó, José, 270–271, 456 n.5,
  456 n.6
Arnove, Robert, 242, 273, 275
Aronowitz, Stanley, 330, 341, 374,
  377, 418, 420, 428, 448 n.4
Aronowitz, Stanley, and Henry
  Giroux, 187, 218, 232, 375, 447
  n.7, 453 n.1, 455 n.2, 455 n.7,
  455 n.8, 458 n.2, 463 n.22
Atkinson, Paul, 191–200
Attewell, Paul, 163
Australia, 66, 218, 243
Authoritarianism, 289, 292, 334,
  359, 417
Authoritarian personality, 222
Authority, 280, 293, 395, 416
  and conformism, 260
  and education, family,
    domination, learning process,
    221
  and spontaneism, 258
  critique of, 247
  principle of, 261

Authority (*continued*)
  rational and irrational forms of,
    222
  rational, 247
Autonomy
  of school, 240
  rational, 247
  university, 224
Avalos, Beatrice, 456 n.7

Bachelard, Gaston, 143
Bailey, Kenneth, 80–83
Balibar, Étienne, 141, 152
Ballantine, Jeanne, 76
Barel, Yves, 7–8, 43
Baron, Steve, et al., 72
Barrett, Michelé, 376
Barrow, Robin, 459 n.1
Barthes, Roland, 420
Barton, Len, and Stephen Walker,
  463 n.23
Base-superstructure, 10–11, 143–
  146, 250–251, 257, 371
  and correspondence principle,
    129–130, 342
Bates, Richard, 76, 346–347
Baudelot, Christian, and Roger
  Establet, 151–156, 212, 349,
  450 n.6
Baudrillard, Jean, 424
Bauman, Zygmunt, 103
Bell, Daniel, 66, 463 n.1
Bendix, Reinhard, 56
Bennett, Kathleen, and Margaret D.
  LeCompte, 335, 391–392
Bennett, Tony, 335
Benton, Ted, 142, 146
Berger, Peter, and Thomas Luckmann,
  32–33, 296–297
Bernstein, Basil, 18, 48, 50, 71–72,
  190–201, 295, 298–299, 341,
  449 n.1
Berman, Russell, 417
Bertalanffy, Ludwig von, 81. *See*
  general systems theory
Bhaskar, Roy, 32, 452 n.4

Birbaum, Norman, 329
Blackledge, David, and Barry Hunt,
  191, 448 n.3
Blau, Peter, 56
Bolshevism, 54
Boron, Atilio, 349
Boudelot, Christian, and Roger
  Establet, 349
Boudon, Raymond, 70, 76, 122
Boudon, Raymond, and Fraçois
  Bourricaud, 42, 122
Bourdieu, Pierre, 4–5, 18, 48, 50, 73,
  97–98, 111, 112, 202–203, 225,
  230, 246, 273, 287, 295, 298–299,
  341–342, 373, 462 n.19, 464 n.5
Bourdieu, Pierre, and Jean Claude
  Passeron, 126–130, 141, 153, 155,
  175–191, 196, 200–203, 209,
  211–212, 349
Bourdieu, Pierre, and Loïc Wacquant,
  453 n.2
Bourgeoisie, 242, 254, 403
  "bourgeois" and "proletarian,"
    262
  bourgeois culture, 224
  bourgeois law, 255
  bourgeois morality, 220
  bourgeois' sociological theories, 48
  bourgeoisies' values, 253
Bowen, James, 159
Bowles, Samuel, and Henry Levin, 69
Bowles, Samuel, and Herbert Gintis,
  123, 154, 162–173, 212, 230–
  232, 235, 270, 329, 341, 348–
  349, 398, 415, 459 n.5, 462 n.20
Bowles, Samuel, Herbert Gintis, and
  P. Meyer, 70
Brandão, Carlos Rodrigues, 271, 274,
  457 n.9, 457 n.10
Brazil, 271–272, 276, 387
Bratlinger, Patrick, 376
Broady, Donald, 347
Brown, David, 424
Bulhan, Hussein Abdilahi, 380
Bureaucracy, 13
  Bureaucratic-Authoritarianism,
    359, 358, 366

Bureaucratization, 14, 67, 240, 246–247, 342, 417
  corporate bureaucracies, 231, 236
  Law of motion of, 236
  Postindustrial, 226
Buckley, Walter, 100–101, 108–109
Buildung, 222, 229
Burrell, Gibson, and Gareth Morgan, 26, 293, 449 n.3, 449 n.5
Butler, Judith, 424–425, 430
Buxton, William, 43

Calhoun, Craig, 461 n.9
Callinicos, Alex, 142
Canada, 66, 73, 218, 243, 354, 416
Capitalism, 6, 20, 299, 326–327, 236, 245–247, 397, 409–410, 416
  advanced capitalism crisis, 238
  advanced capitalism, 329, 332–335, 342, 361, 410
  capital accumulation, 233, 349–351
  capital technology advanced, 263, 278
  capital, 11, 13, 121, 257
  capitalist contradictions, 16, 397
  capitalist production, 121–125, 145, 349–355
  capitalist schooling, 348–353
  capitalist society, 234
  capitalist state, 223, 231, 341–371
  disorganized capitalism, 426
  late capitalism, 420, 427
  laws of motion of (and logic of), 235, 236
Cardoso, Fernando Henrique, 350
Carnoy, Martin, 5, 61, 169, 329, 336, 359, 372
Carnoy, Martin, and Henry Levin, 5, 169, 329, 336, 348–357, 459 n.3
Carnoy, Martin, and Joel Samoff, 359
Carnoy, Martin, and Carlos Alberto Torres, 354, 360, 456 n.7

Carr, Wilfred, and Stephen Kemmis, 449 n.2, 455 n.7, 455 n.9
Castles, Stephen, and Wiebke Wüstenberg, 12, 288, 301–302
Causality, 127, 144, 243
Cerroni, Umberto, 452 n.5
Cherryholmes, Cleo, 132–138, 452 n.6
Childs, John, 417
Chile, 157, 161–162, 242, 271–272, 452 n.1
China, 231, 360, 423
Citizenship, 88, 254, 327, 330, 337
Civil society, 327, 330, 334, 349
Class, 266, 272, 296, 304, 325–326, 332, 348, 371, 400, 407, 418
  and cultural reproduction, 37, 176–190, 342, 377
  and education, 264, 269, 271–272, 277, 280
  and gender, 396, 418, 431
  and liberal arts, 262
  and race, 418, 431
  and schooling, 280
  class conflict, 349
  class consciousness, 348, 415
  class interest, 235
  class relations, 237, 357–349
  class struggle, 46, 251, 267, 357
  class-bureaucratic reproduction model, 37, 97, 230, 341–342
  common sense of, 262
  German working, 220, 222–223
  middle-class, 200–201, 393
  popular classes, 351
  reductionism, 372, 374, 403
  ruling class (dominant), 14, 92, 253, 257, 353, 358
  structure, 357
  subordinated (lower), 275
  working class, 236, 249, 251, 260, 261, 352–357, 359
Clegg, Stewart, 343–344, 369–373
Clegg, Stewart, and David Dunkerley, 351, 370
Club of Rome, 85

Coercion, 250, 251, 253–255, 280
  and spontaneity, 259
  monopoly of, 236
Cognitive rationality, 60
Cohen, Gerard Allan, 137, 450 n.8,
  454 n.4
Cold War, 43
Cole, Mike, 450 n.8
Coleman, et al. (Coleman Report),
  69, 75
Colombia, 242
Collier, David, 359
Collins, Randall, 77, 175, 201–206,
  342, 356, 454 n.3
Colonialism (colonial state), 384,
  430–431
  colonization, 240
  internal colonialism, 91
Common sense, 256, 257, 262, 266–
  267, 272–273, 419
Commoner, Barry, 93
Commodification, 421
  of knowledge, 230, 239
Complexity reduction, 91
Communism, 11, 257. See Marxism
  and polytechnical education, 12,
    161–162
  Communist education, 159–161
  Communist Party, 71
  Italian communist party, 249, 263
Comte, Auguste, 12, 42
Communication, 223
  constraints on, 241
  theory of distorted, 245
Competence
  communicative competence, 245
  technical, 249, 252, 275, 277–
    278, 280
Communicative action, 236, 246
Conflation, 102, 103
Conflict, 97
  conflict theory, 42–43, 58, 76,
    87, 90, 106, 109, 175–213,
    351–373
  credentialism, 201–211
  social closure theory, 201–211,
    454 n.3
  structural conflict theories, 10,

  21, 30, 130–131, 351, 459
    n.3
Conformism, 255, 260
Connell, Robert W., 5, 210, 328,
  390, 394–400
Consensus, 49, 94, 253, 255
  consensus theory, 42
Construct validity, 133–134
Consciousness, 24, 232, 255, 256,
  257, 261, 266, 268, 270, 273, 275,
  332, 419
  citizens, 254
  class, race, and gender, 430
  conscientization, 419
  consumer, 231
  counter-hegemonic, 250
  critical pedagogy of
    consciousness, 234
  critical, 238–240
  false consciousness, 46, 129,
    246, 418
  of students, 233
  of the German working class,
    220–221
  political, 249, 263–264
Conservatism, 221
Contradiction, 47
Cooper, David, 463 n.22
Correspondence theories, 16, 130–
  131, 162–173, 218, 235, 270,
  278, 328–329, 342. See also
  Bowles and Gintis
  correspondence and
    contradiction, 394, 408
  correspondence model of
    schooling, 264
  correspondence principle, 3, 231,
    237, 348–349, 371
  critique of, 168–172, 397
  economic correspondence, 145,
    236
Conviviality, 229
Corporatism (corporativism)
  corporatist state, 357
Cosby, Christina, 431
Coser, Lewis, 118
Crisis theory, 238, 342–347
  crisis of motivation, 238–239

crisis of production, 237
economic crisis, 238
political crisis, 238
Critical theory, 15, 18, 21, 91, 113,
219, 222, 223, 247, 249, 285,
328–329, 333–334, 336, 342–
343, 347, 371–372, 382, 461 n.8,
403, 417, 419, 428
and classroom talk, 245
and organizational theories, 228
Frankfurt School, 18, 42, 150,
218, 328–329, 333, 342,
371–374, 424
Frankfurt School and educational
theory, 219, 225, 227–230,
233–234, 237, 241, 246, 270,
280–281, 332
of ecology, 228
of education, 232, 241
of the welfare state, 233
Cuba, 231, 360
Cultural Studies, 286, 304, 332–333
British, 376–371
Culture, 99, 286, 299, 303–304,
325, 335, 409, 416, 418, 420, 426
class, 223
codes, 195–200
cultural, 250, 262, 268, 273,
281, 336
cultural elaboration, 103, 107–
108
cultural integration, 49, 103
cultural politics, 428–434
cultural production, 363
cultural reproduction, 3, 20,
124, 335, 342–395
cultural revolution, 226
culture industries, 223–224
hegemonic, 254, 352–356
high culture, 270, 422, 434
mass culture, 223, 229, 240, 414
mediating role, 124
modern, 259
morphogenic culture theory, 101,
342
popular, 274–275, 277–280,
327, 334–335, 355, 375, 377,
422, 427–428

postmodern, 405, 408, 414, 418
theory of, 108
working class, 260, 262, 265,
267, 268, 328, 336, 355
See also Hegemony, Ideology,
Postmodernism, Reproduction,
State
Cultural capital, 246, 269–270, 277,
453 n.1
Curriculum, 296, 426, 428
hidden, 230, 237, 265, 267–270,
390–391, 408, 416, 419–420
regulation, 240
research, 241, 303
school, 260, 264, 294
theory of, 247, 331
Curtis, Brue, 349, 359
Cybernetics, 41, 84, 100, 109

Dahrendorf, Ralf, 29, 42
David, M. E., 346
Davis, Kingsley, 56
de Ipola, Emilio, 128, 129
de Saussure, Ferdinand, 119
Deconstruction, 413, 424–425, 429–
430
Deficit theories, 191–201
Deleuze, Gilles, 420
Della Volpe, Galvano, 119
Demaine, Jack, 298, 448 n.2
Demerath, N. J., and Richard
Peterson, 29, 42, 44
Democracy, 92, 327, 329–330, 331–
332, 334, 349, 415–416, 424
and development, 356
and education, 163, 349, 418
and German education, 223
democratic participation, 240,
334
democratization, 224, 275, 329–
330, 334
in Latin America, 274
liberal, 15, 326, 336, 241
radical, 279, 330, 425
struggle for, 275
theory of, 232, 326
Democratic Party (US), 68, 72

Denmark, 100, 105
Dependency, 361, 460 n.7
　dependent development, 356
　dependent state, 460 n.7
Department of Education (US), 69
De-personalization, 240
Derrida, Jacques, 132, 138, 420, 424,
　463 n.4
De-schooling, 225, 226, 232, 301
　de-institutionalization and, 226
De-mystification of the theory of
　schooling, 226
Determinism, 109
Deutsch, Karl, 74
Development/underdevelopment, 334,
　342, 351, 356, 408–412, 427
Dewey, John, 136, 160, 289–291,
　329, 417
Discourse (theories of), 118, 277,
　280
Discipline, 260, 262, 264, 265, 279–
　280
Dittmar, Norbert, 198, 199
Differentiation, 52, 57, 61, 86, 96,
　99, 392–393, 402
　theory of, 79–80, 89, 93, 95–97,
　101
Dingwall, R., and P. Lewis, 65
Domination, 106–107, 222, 234,
　247, 251, 255, 257, 280, 325–326,
　333
　and production in capitalist
　　society, 234
　critique of, 247
　dominance, 232
　forms of domination, 373–374
　pact of domination, 459 n.1
　structure of, 344
　system of, mode of, 77, 344
　theory of, 106
Dore, Ronald, 65
Dos Santos, Theotonio, 453 n.1
Durkheim, Emile, 10, 12–13, 18, 20,
　32–33, 41–43, 45, 48–51, 54,
　126, 131, 176, 178, 181, 183–184,
　191, 196, 198, 295, 449 n.5
Dussell, Enrique, 462 n.14

Ecological World Systems Theory,
　85–88
Economic, 238
　crisis, 238
　production, 237
Education, 20, 34, 36, 235, 252,
　265–267, 271, 303, 325, 328,
　333–334, 383, 411, 416
　Adult education, 264, 265, 266
　and Critical Theory, 355
　and economy, 164–167, 342
　and legitimation crisis, 238
　and the state, 341–370
　Anglo American educational
　　research, 219
　banking, 269–270
　classical versus technological, 259
　compensatory education, 198–
　　199, 388
　conservative (schooling), 261,
　　165
　critical, 234
　development, 351
　educational action research, 241
　educational change, 49, 105,
　　108, 353
　educational content, 275
　educational expansion, 88
　educational reform, 67, 224,
　　233, 353
　educational research, 15, 51, 273
　educational systems, 12, 220,
　　239, (post war) 224, 254, 268,
　　329, 390
　equality/equity, 408–409
　formal education, 67, 239
　functions of, 55, 73, 77
　German educational system, 221,
　　223, 233
　Gramsci and political, 259, 263–
　　264
　Marxist theories of, 120, 245,
　　347
　mass education, 87
　minority, 378, 463 n.24
　modern school system, 246–247
　modernism, 372–403, 408

non-formal, 46, 242, 273
political, 261
politics and education, 332, 342, 351, 408, 416–417
popular, 263, 270–279
primary, 95
progressivism, 289, 291–292, 330, 418
proletarian, 220
race, class, and gender, 70, 372–405, 417, 426, 453 n.1
reproduction, 111, 341–343
socialist, 453 n.7
sociology of, 3, 34, 106, 286, 294, 295, 298, 303
sociology of, 50, 76, 91, 106, 111, 200, 347
special education, 388
state and education, 104
technological, vocational, 97, 411
theories of, 47, 51, 187, 246, 328, 371, 383
universal (schooling), 240, 327, 334–336, 390, 410, 412, 418
women's education, 384–391
Edwards, Richard, 330
Eisenstadt, S. N., 101, 412
Elster, Jon, 120
Emancipation, 24, 30, 241, 243, 417–418
Empiricism, 424–425
Engels, Frederick, 10, 12, 30
Enlightenment, 12, 222, 267, 277, 292, 408–410, 423, 426, 428, 430
critique of, 240
dialectics of, 223, 229, 233
Postmodern critiques of, 233
Entropy (social entropy), 81, 83
Entwistle, Harold, 253, 260–261, 264–270, 276, 456 n.2
Enzensberg, Magnus, 455 n.2
Epistemology, 19, 241, 243, 331, 431
and politics, 243
critique of, 238, 408
Equality/inequality of opportunity, 57, 61, 70

Equilibrium, 41–42, 44, 47, 79, 81, 90, 100
Ethnicity, 91, 372–495. *See also* Race
Etzioni, Amitai, 99, 109
Europe, Continental Europe, Western Europe, 6, 71, 104–105, 329, 334, 413, 422, 430
Eastern Europe, 231
Everyday life, 409, 418, 426
Evolution (theory of), 41, 44, 68
evolutionary model, 45
Exploitation, 255, 326, 384

Fagen, Richard, 74
Fagerlind, Ingëmar, and Lawrence, Saha, 67
Faia, Michael, 83–86, 88, 450 n.2
Fals Borda, Orlando, 242, 243–244, 271
Family, 220, 221, 223
Fanon, Franz, 378, 380
Farrell, Joseph, 157–158, 161–162, 404
Fascism, 54, 249, 252, 264, 268, 272, 279–280, 297
Fay, Brian, 209
Feijoo, Carmen, 394
Feminism, 345, 392, 420–422, 424, 429
and parallelist position, 376–378
cultural reproduction, 392–393
difference, 392
dual systems, 397–399
educational reproduction, 400
inequalities, 389, 400
male-centered views, 413, 422
Marxism, 376, 461 n.21
post-modernism, 393, 422, 424
theories of, 377, 392–393, 407
See also Gender, Postmodernism
Finkel, Sara, 453 n.5
Fitzpatrick, Sheila, 159–160
Floud, and Halsey, 72
Ford, David, 413–414
Foucault, Michel, 132, 138, 197, 374, 380, 413, 418, 424

France, 73, 95, 97, 100, 105, 387
Frank, Andre Gunder, 453 n.1
Fraser, Nancy, 398–399
Freire, Paulo, 127, 137, 158, 242,
    244, 261, 268, 271–273, 276, 287,
    298, 334, 417, 419–420, 452 n.6,
    456 n.4, 457 n.8
Freud, Sigmund, 119, 148, 449 n.4
Friedrichs, Robert, 42
Friesenhahn, Günter, 221–222, 229
Fritzell, Christer, 349
Fuenzalida, Edmundo, 66
Fuller, Bruce, 410
Functionalism, 5, 13, 20, 36, 43–45,
    68, 70, 74, 79, 108, 237, 425
anthropological functionalism, 13, 44
dynamic functionalism, 83
functional analysis, 51–53
functionalization and production
    process, 221
Neo-Functionalism, 41, 79–113, 381,
    410
Structural-functionalist, 243, 381
theories of, 20, 35, 41, 76, 241

Gadotti, Moacir, 271, 274–276, 254,
    277–278, 456 n.2
Gajardo, Marcela, 271, 273–274,
    456 n.7
Gandhi, Mahatma, 422
García Galló, Gaspar, 159, 161
García Canclini, Néstor, 335
García Marquez, Gabriel, 432
Gardner, John, 93
Gender, 21, 292, 299, 330, 372–405,
    407
    and feminism, 389
    and education, 389
    and race, 388–392, 421–423
    and division of labor, 390–391
    and patriarchy, 390–393, 421, 431
    educational reproduction, 400
Geras, Norman, 461 n.6
Gerchunoff, Pablo, and Juan José
    Llach, 63
Germani, Gino, 74–75

Germany, 72, 90, 97, 105, 218, 223,
    272, 356
Gibson, Rex, 448 n.2
Giddens, Anthony, 8–10, 31, 33, 43,
    103, 118, 127, 372–382, 399, 415,
    431, 450 n.2, 461 n.8, 462 n.19,
    464 n.4
Gilroy, Paul, 421
Giroux, Henry, 18, 124, 218, 232,
    287, 325–334–335, 341, 364,
    374–375, 417–422, 452 n.6,
    462 n.11, 464 n.3
Giroux, Henry, and Roger I. Simon,
    291, 327, 334, 377, 422
Ginsburg, Mark, 396
Ginsburg, Mark, Kamat Sangeeta,
    Rahesware Raghu, and John
    Weaver, 464 n.5
Godelier, Maurice, 119, 128
Goldmann, Lucien, 126
Gomez Peña, Guillermo, 429
Goode, W., 56
Gordon, Liz, 65
Gorz, André, 123
Gould, Mark, 45, 91
Gouldner, Alvin, 43–44, 48, 56, 75,
    119, 125, 209
Grant, Carl, and Christine E. Sleeter,
    374
Gramsci, Antonio, 12, 151, 249–281,
    302–304, 329, 331, 344, 356,
    362–363, 371, 417, 434, 456 n.3,
    457 n.8, 457 n.11, 458 n.4
    Neo-Gramscian, 217, 239, 285,
        325, 333, 342, 356
    and hegemony, 352, 362
    See also Hegemony, Marxism,
        State
Greece and Rome, 261
Great Britain (England), 48, 66, 71,
    75, 94–95, 97, 100, 105, 218,
    294, 416, 422
Gusfield, J., 63

Habermas, Jürgen, 22–24, 27, 30,
    43, 56, 92, 210–211, 223, 229–

230, 233, 234, 236–238, 240,
241, 244, 245, 247, 293, 326,
342–347, 372, 409, 417, 431–
432, 449 n.2, 451 n.1, 452 n.2,
455 n.5, 458 n.2, 461 n.8,
462 n.19
Habermas, Jürgen, and Niklas
Luhman, 451 n.2
Hall, Budd, and Yurif, Kassam,
455 n.3
Hall, G. Stanley, 290
Hall, Stuart, 125, 376, 410, 459 n.4
Hannan, Michael T., 86
Haraway, Donna, 430
Harker, R. K., 65
Hartmann, Heide, 462 n.21
Harvey, David, 335
Hegel, G. W. F., 42, 257, 281
    concept of totality, 42
Hegemony, 251–254, 261, 263–265,
267, 270, 274, 277–280, 290, 303,
325, 328, 331–332, 337, 356, 362,
373
    counter-hegemony, 105, 250,
        256–258, 261, 264, 266, 272,
        329–331, 335–336
    cultural, 9, 250
    Historical bloc, 256–257, 267,
        278
    ideological and political, 255,
        373–383
    proletarian, 260, 262
    theories of, 87
    See also Gramsci, Culture,
        Ideology, State
Held, David, 209
Hennesy, Rosemary, 464 n.7
Hermeneutics of suspicion, 273
Historical materialism, 13, 43, 125–
126, 128, 218, 222, 251
Hirsch, Joachim, 342
Herbert, M., 75
Herriott, Robert, and Benjamin
Hodgkins, 67
Hooks, bell, 421
Holloway, John, and Sol Picciotto,
359, 460 n.6

Homeostasis (theory of), 51
    homeostatic model, 44, 100, 108
Honneth, Axel, and Hans Joas, 300
Horkheimer, Max, 219–223, 227–
229, 234, 270, 280
Hoselitz, B., 74–75
Howard, Dick, 329
Howell, D. A., and Roger Brown, 359
Hoy, Wayne, and Cecil G. Miskel, 76,
450 n.7
Human capital theory, 54
Huntington, Samuel, 359
Hurn, Christopher, 99
Husén, Thursten, 72
Husserl, Edmund, 424
Hutcheon, Linda, 434, 463 n.5
Huyssen, Andreas, 412, 428

Ideology, 46, 106, 129, 154, 236,
237, 238, 247, 257, 325, 330, 336,
363, 381, 383, 418
    'end-of-ideology-thesis,' 66
    and education, 383, 418, 462 n.22
    and superstructures, 128–129
    conception of, 121
    formation, 239
    ideological critique, 90
    of schooling, 151, 264
    theory of, 148–149
    See also Culture, Gramsci,
        Hegemony
Illich, Ivan, 156, 224–232, 242, 278,
280, 298, 408, 455 n.4, 455 n.5
Immanence, 259
India, 423
Individual, 246, 280
    development (Horkheimer), 219
    individualism, 243
    psychic development of the, 219
Industrialization, 255, 325, 410–411,
427, 429
    of work, 280
    'Industrial mode of production,"
        225, 227, 231
    postindustrial, 231
    post-Fordism, 325, 414, 427–428

Inkeles, Alex, 56
Inkeles, Alex, and D. H. Smith, 67
Institutional analysis, 86
Instrumental rationalization, 227, 229–230
    technical rationalization, 246
Intellectuals, 252–253, 262, 267, 271
Intentionality, political and social, 273
Interaction theory, 76
Iragaray, Luce, 424
Italy, 251

Jacques, Martin, 416
Jameson, Fredric, 335, 424, 427, 462 n.19, 464 n.5
Janowitz, Morris, 56
Jay, Martin, 452 n.3
Jelin, Elizabeth, 393–394
Jencks, Christopher, et al., 3–4, 69–70
Jensen, Arthur, 69–70
Jessop, Bob, 354
Johnson, Lyndon B., 69
Jones, Alwyn, 291

Kampol, Barry, 417, 421, 429
Karabel, Jerome, and A. H. Halsey, 4, 71
Karen, David, 461 n.7
Keane, John, 334
Keat, Russell, and John Urry, 452 n.4
Kellner, Douglas, 209, 329
Kelly, Gail P., 5, 389–390
Kelly, Gail P., and A. S. Nihlen, 62
Kemmis, Stephen, and Robin McTaggart, 455 n.9
Keynesian economic theory, 54
King, Elizabeth, 159
King, Martin Luther, 64, 93
Klafki, Wolfgang, 234, 241
Kliebard, Herbert, 290
Knowledge, 243, 261, 262, 264–267, 270, 277, 325, 347, 351, 411, 413, 416, 418–419
    "banking," 269

expert, 14, 302
construction of, 241
Habermas theory of, 241, 263
popular, 272, 273, 276
school, 261, 416
scientific versus popular, 244
social interest, 347
sociology of, 373, 404
types of, 23–24, 30, 180, 375, 404
validation of, 243
Kohr, Richard L., 402
Korsch, Karl, 126
Kosik, Karel, 119, 127
Krupskaia, Nadezhda K., 301
Kuhn, Thomas, 25

La Belle, Thomas J., 271, 273, 275, 456 n.7
Labarca, Guillermo, 63, 155, 453 n.4
Labor, 13–14, 121, 257, 280–281, 325, 371
    division of, 49, 411, 414
Labor Party (Great Britain), 72
Labriola, Antonio, 12
Labov, William, 192–193
Lacan, Jacques, 407, 420
Laclau, Ernesto, and Chantal Mouffe, 325, 330, 334–335, 374–375, 378, 454 n.4
Lankshear, Colin, 428
Landinelli, Jorge, 63
Lash, Scott, 414, 427
Latapi, Pablo, 455 n.9
Lather, Patti, 461 n.5
Latin America, 62–63, 74, 155–158, 263, 269–271, 273–276, 333–335, 341, 354–358, 366, 368, 387, 393–394, 453 n.1
Lawson, Alan, 290–291
Leichter, Howard, 345–346
Lefebvre, Henri, 126, 399
Legitimation, 106, 230, 254, 320, 328, 330, 331–333, 337, 361
    compensatory, 247
    crisis theory, 236

crisis, 238, 343
political, 236
Lendhardt, Gero, 14, 229, 245–246, 342
Lengermann, Patricia Madoo, and Jill Niebrugge-Brantley, 392–395
Leonard, Peter, 434
Lévi-Strauss, Claude, 48, 118–119, 126, 130, 180–181
Levine, Daniel U., and Robert J. Havinghurst, 381–389
Levy, Daniel, 350, 412, 461 n.7
Levy, Marion, 463 n.3
Liberalism, 14–15, 71, 89, 286, 290, 336, 407, 409, 417
Lidz, Charles, 45
Lilge, Frederic, 159, 161
Lilienfeld, Robert, 111
Lindblon. Charles, 365
Linguistics (theory of) and structuralism, 118–120, 413, 418, 424
Lipset, Seymour, 56
Lipset, Seymour, and Aldo Solari, 63
Liston, Daniel, 5, 48, 77, 99, 210, 326
Literacy, 325, 408, 411–412, 419–420
Literary criticism, 407
Livingston, David, 328
Lockwood, David, 31, 102
Logical positivism, 133–138, 425
London School of Economics, 71–73
Lorde, Audre, 422
Lukacs, George, 126, 424
Luke, Carmen, and Jennifer Gore, 461 n.5
Luhmann, Niklas, 41, 91, 98
Lunacharsky, Anatoly Vasilyevich, 159–160
Lynch, Kathleen, 462 n.18
Lyotard, Jean François, 413, 424, 427

Macedo, Donaldo, 419–420
Machlup, F., 65
Makarenko, Anton S., 159, 161, 300–301, 453 n.6

Malinowski, Bronislaw, 42, 44, 47, 85
Manacorda, Mario Alighiero, 12, 253, 258–260
Mannheim, Karl, 71, 121
Manuel, Frank, and Fritzie P. Manuel, 287
Manza, Jeff, 374
Marcuse, Herbert, 66, 123, 222, 227, 228, 238, 240, 293
Marini, Ruy Mauro, 453 n.1
Maritain, Jacques, 143
Marshall, T. H., 71
Marx, Karl, 10–13, 18, 20, 29, 42–43, 45, 47, 50, 121–122, 124–128, 142–145, 148, 162, 178–179, 181, 193, 224, 238, 245, 246, 249, 257, 262, 281, 288, 296, 327, 329, 371–344, 426, 450 n.8, 460, 462 n.16
Marxism, 4, 15, 42, 70, 125–126, 217, 242–246, 249, 250, 266, 270, 279, 286, 295, 297, 334, 371–444
cultural, 263, 303
Hegelian, 126–127, 144, 402
Marxist theories, 235
marxist political theory, 252
marxists social theory, 263
neo-Marxism, 20, 42, 91, 226, 239, 329, 333, 341, 349, 401–403, 416
orthodox, 375
phenomenological, 127
positivist, 144
revolutionary, 66, 68
scientific, 127
Soviet, 144, 227
structuralist, 34, 42–43, 52, 105, 108, 125–127, 141–173, 217, 262, 278–279, 286, 304, 375, 371
transformation (Marxian), 122–123
Western, 123–126, 128, 452 n.3
Masculinity, 390, 399–402
gender reproduction, 400
hegemonic masculinity, 400–401
subordinate femeninity, 400–401

Mass media, 91–92
Mauss, Marcel, 181
Mayhew, Leon, 92–93
Mayo, Peter, 261, 272–273
McCarthy, Cameron, and Michael W.
    Apple, 326, 375–378
McLaren, Peter, 329, 335, 327, 417–
    420, 423, 428, 448 n.4
McRobbie, Angela, 376
Mead, George Hebert, 296–297
Meier, Kenneth, Joseph Stewart Jr.,
    and Robert E. England, 388,
    463 n.23
Merton, Robert K., 43–47, 50–52,
    56, 83, 450 n.2
Metatheory, 5, 17, 19, 23–24, 34, 36
    structuralist, 119
Methodological collectivism/
    individualism, 104–105
Mexico, 242, 360, 369, 387
Meyer, John, and Michael T. Hannan,
    86, 88, 410
Meyer, John, Francisco Ramirez, and
    Richard Robinson, 87–88
Miles, Robert, 383–385
Miliband, Ralph, 459 n.1
Miller, John, 370, 461 n.8
Mioshi, Masao, and H. D.
    Hartootunian, 431
Misgeld, Dieter, 218, 241, 244,
    449 n.2
Modernism, 395, 407, 428
    critical modernism, 94, 371,
    462 n.19. See also Morrow
    and Torres
Modernization, 54, 73, 74, 90, 233,
    395–396, 408–414
    and modern science, 223, 225
    democratic, 280
    modernity, 239, 408–410, 413,
    415, 432
    theory of, 86, 411
Modes of production, 144–145
Moore, Clyde B., 56
Moore, Robert, 172
Morales-Gomez, Daniel A., and
    Carlos Alberto Torres, 464 n.1

Morphogenic processes (morphogenic
    model), 37, 106, 342
    morphogenic model of change,
    102
    morphogenic systems, 41, 79,
    99, 100, 107–109, 113
Morphostatic processes, 100
Morrow, Raymond A., 6, 176, 224,
    258, 278, 281, 335, 424, 455 n.4,
    458 n.12
Morrow, Raymond, and David
    Brown, 447 n.1, 464 n.6
Morrow, Raymond A., and Carlos
    Alberto Torres, 331, 341, 343–
    344, 348–349, 375, 377–378,
    462 n.12, 464 n.2
Mozambique, 432–433
Müller, Deflef K., Fritz Ringer, and
    Brian Simon, 97, 100
Murphy, Raymond, 176, 204–211,
    213, 342, 356, 374, 447 n.1
Muñoz Izquierdo, Carlos, 55

Nader, Ralph, 93
Namo de Mello, Giomar, 270, 276
Nation-State (nation), 387, 410, 412,
    416
    People-nation, 256–258, 277,
    349, 387
Nazism, 220
Neill, A. S., 291, 454 n.1
New Democratic Party (Canada), 73
New Left, 162–163, 290, 297, 326–
    329, 413, 416
New Right, 73, 326, 329, 416–417
New Zealand, 66
Nicaragua, 242, 275, 360
Nice, Richard, 177
Nielsen, François, and Michael T.
    Hannan, 86
Non-syncronous parallelism, 382–383,
    415. See also McCarthy and Apple
Norris, Christopher, 426, 463 n.4

Objectivism (objective consequences),
    46

O'Connor, James, 370, 461 n.8
O'Donnell, Guillermo, 356–359,
360.
See also Bureaucratic-
Authoritarianism
Offe, Claus, 43, 56, 234–236, 245,
342–344, 350–352, 357, 359–
362, 366, 368, 421, 460 n.6
Offe, Claus, and V. Ronge, 349
Old Left, 297, 327, 328
Omi, Michael, and Howard Winant,
371
Oppression, theories of, 392, 425
Organizational theory, 228
Owen, Robert, 288
Ozlack, Oscar, 366–368

Paci, Enzo, 127
Pareto, Vilfredo, 42
Parkin, Frank, 204, 454 n.3
Parsons, Talcott, 13, 17, 20, 29, 31,
36, 41–45, 48, 50–58, 66–68, 70,
74–76, 79–83, 89–92, 94, 100,
196, 450 n.8, 450 n.3, 452 n.5. *See
also* Functionalism
Parsons, Talcott, and Gerald Platt,
59–64, 201, 450 n.5
Paulston, Rolland, 448 n.3
Pedagogy, 195–197, 223, 234, 260,
287, 326, 337, 341, 428
Critical Pedagogy, 3, 233, 281,
326, 330, 332, 341, 408, 417–
421, 447
dogmatic, 265
German critical, 244–247
Gramsci's, 258–260
of the masses, 275
pedagogical reform, 50
socialist, 250
Pedagogical, 182–183
freedom, 240
Gramsci's conservativism, 275
Gramsci's theory, 270, 281
leadership, 222
political principle, 258
relationship, 253

Pescador, José Angel, and Carlos
Alberto Torres, 369
Philosophy, 22
and intellectuals, 256
of history, 222
philosophers, 269
philosophical problems, 219
political of education, 242
social, 219
Piaget, Jean, 45, 120
Pike, Shirley, 127
Pluralism, 265
authoritarian, 267
Policy
policy analysis, 36, 344–345,
367
policy formation, 341, 371,
367–368
policy-making, 345–347, 363–
364
public policy, 415, 427, 451–452
state, 341–342, 351, 357–58
Political economy, 164, 250, 270,
328–329, 336, 409, 421, 426
critique of, 224
political economic constraints on
the state, 235
Political system, 330, 350
political regime, 334, 366
Ponce, Anibal, 159
Popkewitz, Thomas, 328–329, 420,
426, 439, 448 n.4, 458 n.2
Popper, Karl, 449 n.1
Populism, 327, 329, 330, 333, 336
Postmodernism, 234, 326–328, 332–
333, 335, 403–405, 407, 412,
416, 422–434
and post-Marxism, 334, 369,
426
postmodern critiques, 233, 247,
408, 422–426
theory, 408, 414, 416
as cultural epoch or condition,
413–415, 427, 431
as cultural paradigm, 408, 415,
420, 427
and critical pedagogy, 417–421

Portantiero, Juan Carlos, 63
Porter, John, 73
Poulantzas, Nicos, 18, 127, 141, 150, 450 n.8
Power, 21, 290, 299, 325, 327, 333, 335–337
    critical theory of, 296, 343–345, 420
    discourses of, 137–138
    power relations, 21, 132, 325, 327, 333, 335–337, 343–345, 427
    structural theory of, 344, 363, 366, 373
    struggles, 104
Pragmatism, 329, 413
    American, 136, 138
    critical, 134–138
Price, R. F., 448 n.3
Production
    modes of, 58
Proletariat, 154, 266
    proletarian education, 220
    revolutionary, 222
    science of the, 244
Pronovost, Gilles, 327–328, 334
Przeworski, Adam, 137, 398
Psacharopoulos, George, 412
Public sphere, 15, 92–94, 240, 335
    democratic, 240–241

Race, 372–405, 407, 462 n.15
    alienation, 462 n.16
    and class, 383, 426
    and gender, 371–374, 393, 426, 430
    as ideology, 462
    cognitive psychology, 385–386
    discrimination, 378
    domination, 378
    ethnicity, 389, 422
    odernity, 381
    racism, 378–393
    social and cultural reproduction, 376–381
    theories of, 379, 407

Radcliffe-Brown, 42, 44
Ramirez, Francisco, and John Boli, 87
Ramirez, Francisco, and Richard Rubinson, 87
Rationality, 265, 342, 407–410, 413
    instrumental rationality, 77, 225, 285, 342
    "rational," 257
    rationalization, 239, 246–247, 253, 255, 259, 280, 414
Reagan, Ronald, 75, 329
Renaissance, 49
Reproduction, 5–6, 8, 17, 21, 32–38, 45, 98, 101, 236, 247, 255, 285–286, 287, 295, 303, 336, 341, 371–393, 410–411, 425
    and language, 190–201
    and transformation, 44
    complex, 122
    concept of, 6
    cultural, 10, 43–44, 76, 108, 124, 176–190, 251, 262, 278, 395–396
    educational, 176–201, 280, 341–342
    ideological, 237
    Marxist theory of education, 124, 147–148, 375
    "reproductivism," 270
    social reproduction, 3, 10, 21, 43, 76–77, 96–98, 120–125, 145–146, 149–150, 176–190, 347, 351, 395–396
    state hegemonic theory of social and cultural, 232, 347
    theories of, 17, 36–37, 123, 286, 303, 407, 421, 425
Relative autonomy, 217
    of the state, 236
Resistance, 218, 224, 237, 239, 247, 256, 258, 263, 278, 285, 325, 330, 332, 419–420, 423
    theories of, 341, 371, 375
    family of, 221
Reason
    instrumental versus objective, 222

Repression, 236
Research, for praxis, 243
Resistance, 77, 372
    in education, 375
Revolution, 168, 275, 356
    "cultural," 226
    industrial, 59, 68
    theories of, 48, 56, 113, 243, 356
Revolutionary
    change, 35, 250
    politics, 275
    postrevolutionary, 261–262
    project, 224
    transition, 251
Rex, John, 462 n.13
Rex, John, and David Mason, 376–
    378, 462 n.13
Reynolds, David, and Mike Sullivan,
    298
Rhoades, Gary, 95–96, 99
Ricoeur, Paul, 24, 420
Ringer, Fritz, 97, 454 n.2
Robertson, Roland, and Bryan Turner,
    89
Robinson, Phillip, 447 n.3
Roemer, John, 461 n.10
Rorty, Richard, 413
Rosenthal, Robert, and Lenore
    Jacobsen, 62
Rossi, Ino, 118
Rosseau, Jean-Jacques, 258–259, 268,
    408
Rostow, W. W., 411
Rules, 343–346, 357, 366–373
Russell, Davis, 365
Russet, Chyntia E., 44
Russia, 100, 105

Saint Simon, Henri conte de, 12
Samoff, Joel, 5
Sampson, Edward, 386
Saran, R., 346
Sardei, Bierman, et al., 367
Sarup, Madan, 447 n.2
Sayer, R. Andrew, and Richard
    Walker, 390

Scandinavia, 66, 72
Schriewer, Jürgen, and Klaus Harney,
    97–99
Scientific accumulation, 90
Schutz, Alfred, 296–298
Scott, Alan, 427
Selowsky, Marcelo, 70
Selznik, Philip, 56
Sève, Lucien, 299–300
Sharp, Rachel, 176, 295–296, 298–
    299, 302, 447 n.2
Shils, Edwards, 81
Shor, Ira, 329, 334, 419–420
Siegel, R., and Leonard B. Weinberg,
    345
Simmons, John, 365
Skocpol, Theda, 349–351, 452 n.2
Smelser, Neil, 56, 76, 94–96, 99,
    450 n.8
Smith, Michael Peters, 425–426, 428
Social change, 8, 32, 43, 47, 62, 104,
    334
Social movements, 21, 329, 334, 356,
    372, 415–416, 427
Social theory, 101
Socialism, 260, 264, 287–288, 299,
    327, 329–330, 332–334, 407
Socialization, 223, 231, 254, 335,
    347, 401
    of labor force, 236
    class specific, 221
Solari, Aldo, 63
Solomos, John, 382–384
Soviet Union, 12, 159–161, 231
    Sovietism, 260, 272, 280
Spencer, Herbert, 42
Spivak, Gayatri C., 424, 430
Spontaneism, 258–259, 268, 274,
    279–280
State, 10, 14, 229, 231, 234–237,
    246, 250, 334–336, 341–371,
    411
    and capitalism, 222–223
    and education, 347–348, 351–
        359, 370, 410
    and educational policy, 235
    and social control, 372

State (*continued*)
and social movements, 356–357, 417
as an arena, 351–366
authority, 359
autonomy, relative autonomy of, 11, 223, 348–401
capitalist, 221, 235, 358–361, 365–370
crisis of the, 54, 365, 461 n.8
democratic state, 91
derivation theory of the, 235, 342–344
dual nature, 355
functions, 359–363
hegemony, 329, 333, 341–349, 415
ideological apparatuses, 147, 359
interventionism, 348, 359, 365–367
legitimacy, 352, 359–361
modern, 247
notion of, 350–351
socialist, 368
STATEMOP theory, 359, 460 n.6
theories of the, 6–7, 112, 146, 342–368
welfare state, 54–55, 71–72, 240, 327, 337, 342, 357–363, 417, 451–452 n.2
Status
acquired roles, 56, 59
acquired, 59, 62
ascriptive roles, 57, 59
ascriptive, 56, 59, 62
Sternbach, Nancy, et al., 394–395
Stinchombe, Arthur, 69, 85
Structuralism, 3, 5, 13–14, 16, 18, 143, 151–162, 217, 279, 287, 304, 371, 426
Althusserian, 127–128, 141–173
and correspondence theory, 162–173
and neo-Weberian conflict theories, 18, 131–132, 342, 373
and socialist pedagogy, 158–162
in Latin America, 155–158
Post-structuralism, 132–138, 217–218, 263, 279, 407, 419, 424
post-structuralism, 14, 20, 304, 325, 328, 332, 370
structural conditions, 105
structural context (structural constraint), 47
structural elaboration, 101, 111
structuralist anthropology, 48, 118–119
symbolic, 118, 130
the capitalist school in France, 151–155
See also Althusser, Marxism, Postmodernism
Structural functionalism, 5, 16–17, 22, 41, 43, 47, 51, 56, 58, 61, 68, 70, 77, 99, 105
Structuration theory, 33, 127, 372
Structure, 27, 101, 102, 286, 328, 304
surface/depth structure, 118–119
Subject (theories of), 129, 426, 430
subjective dispositions, 46
Suchodolski, Bogdan, 159–160, 453 n.7
Suchodolski, Bogdan, and Mario Manaconda, 159–160
Sunkel, Osvaldo, and Edmundo, Fuenzalida, 66
Sutton, J. R., 65
Sweden, 95
Swidler, Ann, 293–294
Symbolic violence, 182–183
Systems theories, 9, 13, 16, 30–31, 41, 43, 67, 76, 81–82, 100, 101, 108–1009, 341, 372

Tamarit, Jose, 458 n.11
Tanzania, 360
Tavares de Jesus, Antonio, 253, 256, 274
Teachers, 269, 356, 429, 432
Tedesco, Juan Carlos, 458 n.11

Terán, Oscar, 159
Thatcher, Margaret, 75
Theology of Liberation, 434
Therborn, Goran, 330, 332, 344, 357–359, 363
Third World (developing countries), 73, 225, 269–270, 333, 431–434
Thompson, E. P., 204, 376
Time as a theoretical variable, 105
Torre, Juan Carlos, 63
Torres, Carlos Alberto, 21, 75, 127, 224, 242, 247, 251, 253, 256, 258, 271–273, 275, 335, 341, 343, 353, 360, 372, 411, 420, 453 n.2, 456 n.1, n.7, 457 n.8
Torres, Carlos Alberto, and Guillermo González Rivera, 447 n.1
Transformation, 21, 101, 285, 303, 330, 332, 336
    revolutionary transformation, 109
Tucker, Robert, 123, 289
Tumin, Melvin A., 56
Turner, Bryan, 90, 450 n.4
Turner, Jonathan, and Alexandra Maryanski, 44

UCLA (University of California, Los Angeles), 80
UNESCO, 74
Universalism, 59, 67, 300, 413–414, 422–423, 430
University (higher education), 49, 59, 63, 65, 73, 95
    as cognitive complex, 60, 64–65
United States of America, 48, 55, 61–62, 64–70, 75, 91, 94–95, 327–329, 333, 337, 348, 353–354, 356–357, 374, 387–388, 393, 416, 422, 429–430
Utopia, 287–288, 330–333

Vasconi, Tomás, 155–158, 212, 452 n.1

Vasconi, Tomás, and Inés Recca, 155, 157
Vietnam War, 64

Wacquant, Loïc, 25
Wallerstein, Immanuel, 86, 416
War on Poverty (Economic Opportunity Act), 62, 69
Ward, Lester Frank, 290
Weber, Max, 9–10, 13, 18, 29, 32, 50–51, 104, 107, 131–132, 136–137, 178–179, 181, 184, 193, 202, 204, 208, 227, 230, 245–246, 295, 342, 344, 373, 409, 449, 449 n.5, 452 n.5, 459 n.2, 459 n.4
    Neo-Weberianism, 42, 106–107, 111, 169, 201, 342, 373, 410
Weiler, Hans, 365, 449 n.2
West, Cornel, 388, 421–422
Wetherell, Margaret, and Jonathan Porter, 386
Wexler, Phillips, 5, 62, 132, 326–327, 335, 448 n.2
Whitty, Geoff, 296–298, 302–303, 325, 375, 455 n.7
Wilensky, Harold L., 452 n.2
Williams, Raymond, 356
Wilson, William Julius, 388
Wirt, F., and M. W. Kirst, 346
Wood, Ellen Meiksins, 461 n.6
Working class, 121, 123, 236, 249, 252, 260, 269–272, 277, 280, 327–328, 330
    common sense of the, 264
    German, 220, 222, 223
    liberal arts for the, 261
World system, 327, 336–337, 349, 417
Wright Mills, Charles, 42, 52, 56, 407
Wright, Erik Olin, 137, 141–142, 331–332, 356–357, 372, 459 n.5

Young, Michael F. D., 294–29
Young, Robert, 244–247, 449 n.2
Youngman, Frank, 448 n.3